# ARAFAT

*(Photo by Morad Abedrauf)*

'Arafat is really only happy when he is among children' – Um Jihad

# ARAFAT

## A Political Biography

## Alan Hart

*First American Edition*

INDIANA UNIVERSITY PRESS
*Bloomington and Indianapolis*

Map on page 8 by John Flower
Maps on page 9 by courtesy of David Gilmour

Manufactured in in the United States of America

**Library of Congress Cataloging-in-Publication Data**
Hart, Alan.
Arafat, a political biography.

Rev. ed. of: Arafat, terrorist or peacemaker?
3rd ed. 1988.
Bibliography: p.
Includes index.
1. Arafat, Yasir, 1929-    .  2. Palestinian Arabs—
Biography.   3. Jewish-Arab relations—1949-    .
4. Israel-Arab conflicts.   5. Munaẓẓamat al-Taḥrīr
al-Filastīnīyah.   I. Hart, Alan. Arafat,
terrorist or peacemaker?   II. Title.
DS119.7.A6785H36   1989      322.4'2'0924 [B]      88-45748
ISBN 0-253-32711-3
ISBN 0-253-20516-6 (pbk.)

1 2 3 4 5 93 92 91 90 89

*To my many Israeli and other Jewish friends
. . . in the hope that the story this book has to
tell will encourage them and their friends to
give peace a chance.*

# Contents

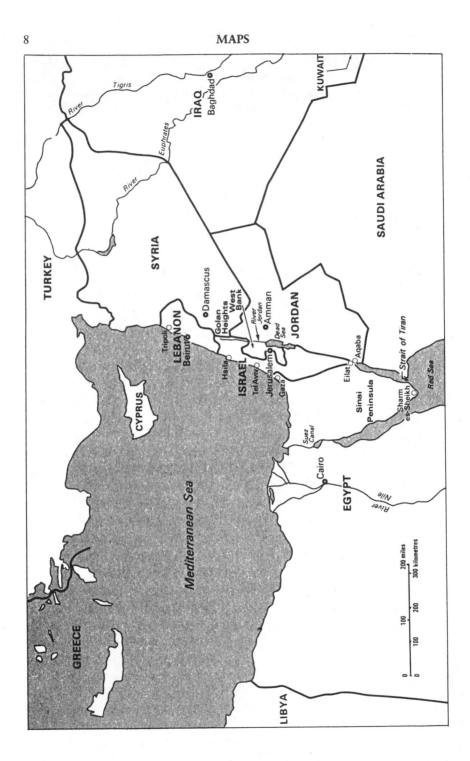

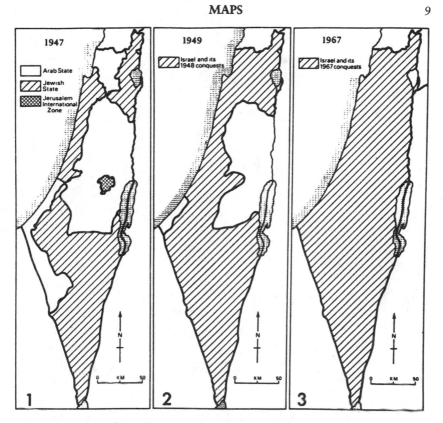

*The takeover of Arab Palestine:*
*1. The U.N. Partition Plan of 1947.*
*2. Israel after the 1948 War.*
*3. Israel after the Six-Day War of 1967.*

# Preface

For most of the past forty years, informed and rational public debate about the Arab-Israeli conflict and how to end it has been impossible. The problem, generally speaking, is that the mainstream media and the major publishing houses of North America and Western Europe have suppressed information which Israel's unquestioning supporters would regard as giving legitimacy to the existence and demands of Palestinian nationalism. In this short preface I want to explain, in summary, why this conspiracy of silence must be broken.

In the absence of a negotiated end to the Arab-Israeli conflict – on terms that will satisfy Israel's genuine security needs *and* the legitimate demands of the Palestinians for self-determination in a state of their own – the Middle East is an explosion waiting for its time to happen. The outline of what some experts see as a predictable but still preventable doomsday scenario for the region is the following.

Israel refuses to withdraw from nearly all the Arab territory it occupied in the 1967 war – a withdrawal required by the letter and the spirit of U.N. Security Council Resolution 242. On the Arab side any belief that Israel can be persuaded to exchange land for peace evaporates completely. An upheaval in the Arab world sees the overthrow of the existing Arab order (which has long been ready for a face-saving compromise with Israel) and its replacement by revolutionary regimes that will be prepared to confront the Jewish State by all means and no matter what the cost.

During a filmed interview with me for the B.B.C.'s *Panorama* programme in 1971 Golda Meir addressed the subject of what would happen if ever Israel faced certain defeat on the battlefield. What she said prompted me to ask the following supplementary question: "Are you saying, Prime Minister, that Israel would be prepared to take the region and even the whole world down with it?" Without hesitation she replied: "Yes. That's exactly what I am saying." The day after the interview was broadcast, an editorial in *The Times* of London urged its readers to accept that Mrs Meir was simply stating how any future Israeli government would respond in a doomsday situation . . . With a nuclear Masada.

The prospect of regional Armageddon is becoming a respectable subject for discussion at seminars in North America and Western Europe (and no doubt in the Arab world, Israel and the Soviet Union). Real experts seem to agree that probably no fewer than forty million Arabs would be killed if Israel went down firing its nuclear weapons. But this and the disappearance of the Jewish State might well be only the beginning of a global catastrophe. Even if the two superpowers could avoid being sucked into the last round of the conflict, the consequences of such an explosion in the Middle East could not be confined to the region. With the loss of Arab oil, trade and finance, the global economy could suffer such a shock that political and social systems everywhere would break down. In a worst-case scenario we could see what passes for democracy in the West replaced by authoritarianism as leaders struggled to maintain a semblance of order. At some point the world would need a scapegoat, and there would be another great turning against Jews everywhere.

I am trying to make a very simple point in this Preface. It is that every man, woman and child on Planet Earth has a stake in what is happening in the Middle East. At the risk of being dismissed as an alarmist, I have drawn attention to the possible consequences of an explosion in the region in order to underline the urgent need for rational debate about the way to peace – before it is too late for us all. Such a debate cannot take place until public opinion, in America in particular, is better informed about Yasser Arafat. . . who he is and what he really represents; how he has risked his credibility and his life to prepare his people for the unthinkable – compromise with Israel; and, most important of all, what he could deliver in the name of peace if only the Jewish State and its American ally would allow him to do so.

Alan Hart
December 1988

# Introduction

This book is the story of two men with the same name. One is the Yasser Arafat who is a character in Israeli mythology. The other is the Yasser Arafat who is the real life Chairman of the Palestine Liberation Organization.

According to the official Israeli view, the P.L.O. is nothing but a 'syndicate of murderers', and its leader is a man with 'bottomless hate in his heart', who would try to finish the job started by Adolf Hitler if he was given the opportunity. That is more or less the story as it has been told to the people of Israel and the world by successive Israeli governments and their apologists. The description of the P.L.O. quoted above is from the lips of the official spokesman for the Government of Israel when Menachem Begin was its Prime Minister. The description of Arafat quoted above is from the mouth of Mr Begin's successor, Yitzhak Shamir.

This book is an attempt to tell the other side of the story. And it invites three conclusions which are bound to provoke great and fierce controversy.

The first is that within the limits of what is politically possible on each side, no leader, Arab or Jew, has done more than Arafat to prepare the ground for a comprehensive settlement of the Arab-Israeli conflict.

The second is that there could have been a comprehensive settlement by 1980, and possibly sooner, if Israel had produced a leader with the skill and the courage to match that demonstrated by Arafat as he set about the task of persuading his colleagues and people to make unthinkable concessions for the sake of peace with Israel and in order to get something concrete for the Palestinians.

The third, and despite the fact that he is running out of time to prove to his own increasingly desperate people that politics and compromise can get results, is that Arafat is still the man who holds the key to peace on the Arab side. The question for the immediate future is whether the governments of the Western world – the one in Washington in particular – will be wise enough to help Arafat use that key before he is forced to throw it away.

It is my hope that the evidence which supports these three conclusions will help to promote a more informed and more honest debate about the way to peace in the Middle East – before it is too late for us all.

Because it is obvious that Arafat is still a prime target for assassination by some who claim to be his friends as well as his enemies, a question that some readers may ask is this: why did he allow me to get so close to him, close enough, that is, to learn the mystery of his past and the secrets of his organization?

The answer is quite straightforward but not easy to set down in writing. To begin with I should explain that the initiative for this book was mine and mine alone. It took me nearly two years to persuade Arafat to give me enough of his time and his trust to make the book possible. Even then I would not have succeeded without the help of his three most senior colleagues – Abu Jihad (who was assassinated by Israeli agents in 1988), Khalad Hassan and Abu Iyad. What I actually did was to convince them that an informed and honest book about Arafat was long overdue; and it was they who helped me to twist Arafat's arm.

The answer to the specific question of why Arafat allowed me to get so close to him is in two parts, and one is related to the other. The first was to do with chemistry – mine and his. In splendid and monumental contrast to his media image, the real Arafat is an incredibly warm and sensitive man. I was attracted by his many and obvious human qualities; and I was touched by the way in which these same qualities make him vulnerable. I am not suggesting that he is easily deceived. I am saying that he is easily hurt. What I think Arafat detected in me was a willingness to study him and his cause with an open mind. I think he was also impressed by the fact that I was honest with him from the beginning. I told him that some of my best friends were not only Jews but former Israeli Directors of Military Intelligence. And two former Ministers of Defence. I also told him that on the human level I had enjoyed a relationship with Golda Meir, while she was Israel's Prime Minister, that earned me the nickname of 'Golda's boyfriend'. That, I explained, was because I always sent red roses in advance of my meetings with her.

As to the second part of the answer, it is a long story. The essential facts are as follows. At the end of 1979, and before I had the idea for this book, I was involved in an unofficial but highest-level Middle East peace initiative. My mission was to open and then maintain a secret channel of communication between the Chairman of the P.L.O. on the one hand, and certain Israeli leaders on the other. On the Israeli side a key figure in what amounted to a conspiracy for peace was a leader of the Labour Party, the main opposition to Mr Begin's ruling coalition.

The idea was to use the secret channel to convey the evidence of the P.L.O.'s readiness for a political and compromise settlement to those in Israel who might be prepared to respond positively when they were in power. At the time of my initiative – which was financed by a most enlightened leader of the Jewish diaspora and a few of his friends – Israel's next election was some twelve to eighteen months away; and it was not thought that Begin would win a second term in office. When he did, my initiative was doomed. In Begin's Israel even thinking about an accommodation with the P.L.O. was treason.

Although I had previously met Yasser Arafat on a number of occasions during my reporting days for I.T.N. and then the B.B.C.'s *Panorama* programme, it was because of the peace initiative that I got to know him better and he decided to invest some trust in me.

The decision to research and write this book was taken when the peace initiative collapsed. That it had to be aborted was a tragedy because we did make some solid progress. After my second shuttle to Arafat one of the Israelis said: 'We are cooking on gas.' If Begin had not won a second term in office it is more than possible that an Israeli Labour Government would have authorized secret but direct talks with Arafat. In that event the course of history might have been changed.

I have looked upon the work that has gone into this book as a continuation of my own small contribution to the peace process.

And it is my claim that I have written the book as a good and true friend of the Palestinians and the Jews. I have a great affection for both peoples.

Generally speaking it can be said that the Jews are the intellectual elite of Western civilization. By the same token the Palestinians are, without doubt, the intellectual elite of the Arab world. Together in peace and partnership the two peoples, who come from the same melting pot, could change and develop the region for the better and, by so doing, give hope and inspiration to the whole world.

For there to be peace, Israel must concede that the Palestinians are entitled – by historical, legal and moral rights – to at least a measure of justice. At a minimum this justice must be granted in the form of a homeland for the Palestinians, on the West Bank and in Gaza. It should be noted that under this formula, and at the end of the negotiating process, the Palestinians would be recognizing Israel as the price of the return to them of less than thirty per cent of all of the land that was once theirs. By agreeing to such a formula Israel would be renouncing its commitment to the first rule of the Game of Nations, the rule which states that might is right and that justice is a concept to which the mighty need only pay lip-service. It is precisely because the leaders and governments of the strong nations have created a world without justice among nations and peoples that we late-twentieth-century human beings are on a journey into catastrophe. This is the context in which I say that Israel and the Palestinians, together in peace and partnership, could give new hope and inspiration to the world – by demonstrating that even the most intractable problems can be solved when right is allowed to prevail over might.

It was Israel's first Prime Minister, David Ben-Gurion, who said the Jews would survive 'only if they maintain their moral, spiritual and intellectual standards'. There are today an increasing number of Jews who believe that their real survival mechanism, as described by Ben-Gurion, has been placed at risk by recent Israeli governments whose actions have made a mockery of the moral principles and values of Judaism. For this reason it can also be said that Israel has much to gain on its own account, and for the sake of Jews everywhere, if it is willing to renounce its commitment to the idea that might is right.

In 1974, after the P.L.O. had been smashed in Jordan, and after it had used the terror weapon to prove it was still in business, Arafat sent the first of many signals that he was determined to persuade the liberation movement to come to terms with reality – reality being Israel's existence in more or less its pre-1967 borders. From that moment on, and to allow him to emerge as the peacemaker on his side, Arafat needed a matching political response from Israel in the form of Israel's acceptance, in principle at least, of Palestinian rights to self-determination. But each time Arafat made a political move in the direction of compromise, the Israelis replied with bullets and bombs. The more Arafat demonstrated the seriousness of his wish for a political and compromise settlement, the more determined the Israelis became to destroy the P.L.O. as a political force.

In passing it has to be said that Israel's political and military leaders have never really regarded the P.L.O. as a serious military threat. A man whose experience qualifies him to speak with unique authority on this sensitve matter is Sir Brian Urquhart. For many years he was the Under Secretary-General of the United Nations. In that capacity he was effectively the power behind four Secretary-Generals. Operating mainly behind the scenes he was the U.N.'s chief crisis manager and his speciality was the Middle East. In the diplomatic world he was known with affection as 'Mr Middle East'. It is hard to think of a man or woman who was or is a greater expert on the Arab-Israeli conflict. For a diplomat Urquhart is amazingly and refreshingly outspoken. And as far as I know he is the only non-Jew who refused to be intimidated by Menachem Begin. On one celebrated occasion when he arrived at the Prime Minister's office in Jerusalem hot-foot from a meeting with Arafat in Beirut, Urquhart was reprimanded by Begin and told that he should not speak with Arafat. Urquhart replied: 'Mr Prime Minister, I am a servant of the international community. Don't tell me who I can and cannot talk to!' Apparently Begin took the point and never raised the subject again.

On the subject of the P.L.O. as a military threat to Israel, Urquhart said this: 'The Israelis are brilliant at creating myths and then getting the rest of the world to accept them as truth. There is a great myth that the Israelis are frightened of the P.L.O. as a military force. They are not. They can handle the P.L.O. as a military outfit with both hands strapped behind their backs. What the Israelis are really frightened of is a political P.L.O.'

Since 1974 Israel's refusal to use diplomatic means to test the reality and the strength of Arafat's commitment to a political and compromise settlement has been the main obstacle to peace and, also, the main cause of the continuing slaughter that has drenched the region in blood.

From the moment in 1974 when Arafat began to set about the dangerous task of persuading the P.L.O. to face up to the reality of Israel's existence and the need for compromise, successive Israeli governments have refused even to consider the idea of a mini-state homeland for the Palestinians on the grounds that such a state would pose a military threat to Israel's security and to Western interests in the region. This particular Israeli claim – for which Henry Kissinger became a parrot – was and is without foundation.

I discovered during my own Middle East peace initiative that there are a surprising and growing number of Israeli leaders – those who have occupied the highest positions in the political, military and intelligence establishments of their country – who are prepared to say, in private, that a Palestinian mini-state would not pose an unmanageable threat to Israel's security. To make the point I shall name and quote one of them – Major-General Shlomo Gazit. And I have selected him, so to speak, because he is probably the single most informed Israeli on the subject of the Palestinian and Arab military threat to Israel.

For many years Gazit was the Head of Research in the Directorate of Military Intelligence. In that capacity, and also because he would have received relevant intelligence information from the Mossad – Israel's civilian secret service – he probably knew more than most Arab leaders about what was happening in the Arab world. For a short time he served as Military Governor of the territories occupied by Israel in 1967. After the Yom Kippur War of 1973, and against his own wishes, he was appointed Director of Military Intelligence. His brief was not only to run that agency, but to reorganize it so that there could never again be a breakdown of the kind that was partly to blame for Israel's failure to anticipate the 1973 war. The fact that it was to Gazit that Israel's political, military and intelligent establishments turned for help in their hour of need says much about the quality of the man, his abilities and his judgments. It would be foolish to dismiss his considered opinions on the grounds that they were uninformed.

During one conversation I had with Gazit he made a remark that was the inspiration for this book: 'The trouble with us Israelis is that we have become the victims of our own propaganda.' Implicit in Gazit's comment is the charge that successive Israeli governments have deceived their own people – and much of the world, too – about the true nature of the Arab and Palestinian military threat to the Jewish State. Along with some in Israel who obviously know much, much more than I do, I believe this charge can be proved by honest and objective study of all the relevant information. With the exception of a few weeks in 1948, when the embryo Jewish State was fighting for its life, Israel has never been in danger of defeat in war by any combination of Arab and Palestinian military forces.

The Six-Day War of 1967 is a good illustration of how successive Israeli governments have withheld the truth in order to promote a massively exaggerated fear of Arab military might. I was in Israel before the 1967 war and during it, and I can testify that the Israeli people were totally and sincerely convinced that they were about to be attacked by the Arabs. Their fears were justified by all the information and evidence that was available to them. The armies of the front-line Arab states – Egypt, Syria and Jordan – were mobilized; and the government-controlled radio stations of the Arab world laid down a barrage of vile propaganda about how the Jewish State was soon to be 'annihilated'. But Israel's military and political leaders knew that Egypt's President Nasser was not intending to attack and that he was playing a foolish game of bluff. In fact the Israelis helped to set the trap into which Nasser fell.

Shortly after that war, which was an unimaginable humiliation for all Arabs, and which gave Arafat the opportunity to launch Palestinian military actions against Israel with a degree of reluctant support from the defeated Arab regimes, a former Israeli Director of Military Intelligence told me that if Nasser had not given Israel the excuse to attack the Arabs, Israel would have invented a pretext for war 'within six to ten months' because its military planners had decided that the time had come to knock out vast amounts of mainly Soviet-supplied Arab armour. Months later, and more to the point, Israel's knowledge that Nasser was bluffing was confirmed in public by no less a figure than Yitzhak Rabin, who as Chief of Staff had planned Israel's brilliant victory, and who later succeeded Golda Meir as Prime Minister. In a statement to *Le Monde* in

February 1968 Rabin said, quite simply: 'We knew that Nasser did not intend to attack.'

As a consequence of the brainwashing to which Israelis have been subjected by their own governments, including the constant playing of the holocaust card, a majority of Israelis have a fear of the Arabs which is understandable given the history of the Jews, and also given past Arab and P.L.O. threats. But their fear is without real foundation, and is seen to be so when the objective facts of the conflict are examined by rational minds. The obvious conclusion, or so it seems to me, is this: only when the people of Israel have ceased to be the victims of their own propaganda will peace have a chance.

If this book helps to open some Israeli eyes my labours will have been worthwhile.

Arafat and his colleagues did not make my job easy. They did not say, 'Come, sit down, we are ready to reveal our secrets.' From the beginning the question of how much of the inside story I would get was dependent on two things – my ability to talk it out of them and the quality of my investigations. There were times when I had to be content with clues rather than a detailed account of what was really happening at a particular moment of crisis. On these occasions I had to use my own judgment in order to make two plus two equal four.

This book is divided into three main sections. The first part, 'The Man and His Cause', opens with a profile of the Chairman of the P.L.O. as he is today. It is followed by a brief account of why there is a Palestinian problem. To help the general or non-expert reader understand the true nature of Arafat's struggle, I have focused on a question that is almost never asked – which, as the Palestinians say, is strange because it is the question at the heart of the Arab-Israeli conflict: why was the State of Israel created?

The second part, 'The Underground Years', tells the story of Arafat's early life, and his confrontation with the intelligence services of the front-line Arab states as he set about creating, with others, the underground network of cells from which he hoped his own independent liberation organization would emerge. For their part the front-line Arab states did not want a resurgence of Palestinian nationalism. Despite what they said in public to the contrary, usually by implication, the Arab leaders who mattered had no intention of fighting Israel to liberate Palestine because they knew that that was a mission impossible. The other confrontation during the underground years was between Arafat and a majority of his colleagues in the collective leadership of Fatah who were opposed to his military strategy. Did Arafat really believe Palestine could be liberated by armed struggle? If not, why did he insist on military action and how did he succeed in imposing his will on others?

The third part, 'The Struggle', is the epic story of how Arafat fought not so much to liberate Palestine, but more to keep the Palestinian cause alive as first the Arab regimes, and then Israel, tried to liquidate it. In these years a major problem for Arafat was deciding when the superpowers were his enemies and when they were his friends. Here, too, is the story of the miracle of Arafat's leadership — how he persuaded a majority of his colleagues and people to make unthinkable concessions for the sake of a compromise peace with Israel and something concrete for the Palestinians.

What I set out to research and write was a biography of Arafat in which, so to speak, the human story would dominate the political drama and the action. In a sense I failed. When I started to write the book I discovered that it was quite impossible to make sense of Arafat without pausing from time to time to explain the complexities of inter-Arab and international politics with which he has had to grapple. My own view is that these necessary diversions have added substance to the whole story. And it is my hope that they will enable the general or non-expert reader to understand not only the true nature of Arafat's struggle, but why it is that his mere survival as the symbol of Palestinian hopes for at least a measure of justice has been, so far, a remarkable and astonishing achievement. On the lawn of the White House a British Prime Minister, James Callaghan, once told an American President, Jimmy Carter, that simply to survive in politics was a great achievement. From that point of view, and given the odds against him, it can be said that Yasser Arafat is the greatest survivor in modern history. If he was not a Palestinian I suspect the Jews would be the first to pay him tribute.

For readers who are not familiar with the names of P.L.O. leaders and organizations I have included a list of the principal ones at the end of the book.

If this book helps to promote a more informed and more honest debate about the way to peace in the Middle East, it will be an adequate thank-you to all of those Palestinians who gave me their time, their trust and their friendship.

Now I must express my thanks to the two people without whom this book could not have been written. The first is my bank manager who allowed me to travel, work and live on a substantial overdraft. The second is my wife, Nicole. She supported and even encouraged the decision to mortgage our home to guarantee the overdraft. She was my research assistant and librarian. She transcribed the tapes of the conversations which provided the main source material. And she typed the final manuscript. In the normal course of events I would have dedicated this book, my first, to her; but we agreed on the need for a different inscription.

Finally I want to say thank you to my editor, Jane Heller. By definition this is a most controversial book. The story is, so to speak, a minefield for a writer. Jane helped me to cross it without being blown up.

# The Man and His Cause

# 1

# The Man

'When you don't know Arafat you *can't* like him.'

The speaker was Hammadi Essid, a Tunisian-born writer and diplomat who acts as a trouble-shooter for the Arab League. His point was that people in general, and Westerners in particular, can be forgiven for having an unfavourable impression of Arafat when they are obliged to rely for their information about him on fleeting and superficial media images. What do they add up to?

Beneath his protruding, rolling eyes is a strong nose that seems too big for his smallish face. His elf-like ears are also a bit on the large side. Does he pull them? Yes. And that double-thick, almost deformed, lower lip is without a doubt the least attractive of all of Arafat's physical features. When he is angry, and the lower lip is pushed forward, his whole face is a caricature of ugliness. His general appearance is equally unfavourable. He is frequently unshaven with several days of stubble, not yet a beard, around his chin. He looks as if he needs a bath. His clothes are a mess. And his spirit is defiant. His gestures are dramatic, exaggerated and aggressive. And his tone, more often than not, is belligerent. In all, an unattractive, unimpressive and unlikeable little man. Or so it seems.

Arafat is a small man, about five foot four inches, possibly shorter; and were it not for his pot belly, now much less of a prominent feature on the Arafat landscape than it was a few years ago, he seems more or less the right weight for his height and age. He is fifty-nine.

By choice, and when time and circumstances allow, Arafat is nothing less than impeccable in his outward appearance. His various uniforms are pressed to perfection – in three Arab capitals I have bumped into one or another of his bodyguards either delivering or collecting the Chairman's clothes from a hotel laundry. His boots and shoes would pass inspection by the most demanding British or Indian sergeant major. And he takes great care of his hands and fingernails.

Underneath his chequered *kaffiyeh*, the traditional Arab headdress – 'red for the desert, black for the country and white for the town' – Arafat is completely bald except for a halo of black hair now turning to grey. Without either his *kaffiyeh* or his combat cap, the Chairman of the P.L.O. looks like a monk. And in fact Arafat's personal lifestyle could not be more simple if he was confined to a monastery.

The most striking thing about Arafat is what all Palestinians describe as his 'activities'. No matter where he is, what he is doing or who he is with, Arafat cannot be still. His eyes never stop roving. This constant searching is an essential part of his survival mechanism. His hands are nearly always busy. And when he is sitting he seems forever to be flexing and waggling his knees and beating out a coded message with his feet. 'He cannot spend one minute being still,' said Khalad Hassan, the P.L.O.'s foreign policy chief. 'He cannot.'

But it is the deep brown eyes, the eyes of a human ferret, which command the most attention and hold the greatest fascination for those who have the opportunity to observe him in close-up. Together with his nose or smell for danger, Arafat's eyes are his number-one intelligence and security system. According to Hani Hassan, Arafat's chief political adviser, Arafat never sits down until he has calculated the most difficult and, preferably, impossible line of fire for a potential assassin. 'And he is not always satisfied the first time,' said Hani. 'We can be sitting, deep in conversation . . . suddenly Arafat will stop us and ask that we change our positions. We never ask why. We don't need to. We know he has decided that he was too easy a target in the place where he was sitting.'

On matters affecting his personal safety and security Arafat insists on letting his own instinctive feelings be his only trusted counsellor. 'Sometimes,' said Hani, 'we tell him that he is not wise to trust such-and-such a person. Usually his reply is the same. "I *feel* I can trust him. It's okay."'

The proof that Arafat's instinctive feelings rarely let him down is quite simply the fact that he is still alive. And the supporting evidence was provided by Abu Iyad, with whom I discussed the details of the fifty or more attempts on Arafat's life. Abu Iyad is the *nom de guerre* of Salah Khalaf, the P.L.O.'s security and counter-intelligence executive officer. 'Tell me,' I said to him, 'why is Arafat still alive? How has he survived?'

Abu Iyad smiled. 'I will tell you the truth and a secret,' he said. 'Sixty per cent is Arafat himself – his nose or smell for danger. Thirty per cent is good luck. Ten per cent we can put down to the effectiveness of our own security agencies.'

To the eyes of a human ferret are added the instincts of the hunted animal.

In its attempts to assassinate Arafat, the Mossad has never to date used its own Israeli agents for the final act. According to Abu Iyad the Mossad prefers to 'turn' Palestinians – usually by blackmail – and work through them. The Mossad's speciality is poison.

Because a number of Arab intelligence services have played the same games with selected Palestinians, it is hardly surprising that Arafat finds it very difficult to give his trust. 'It's not easy for him,' said Hani Hassan. 'When a trusted man is killed he cries. When Arafat feels he can trust you he is so loyal in return. He is not a man who can change persons easily. When you are loyal to him it is not easy for him to sacrifice you.' Hani went on to say that with loyalty at such a premium Arafat is inclined to overlook or tolerate faults and failings in some of those who serve the cause – provided they are loyal to him.

Another main reason why Arafat has survived the many plots and attempts to kill him is his secrecy of movement. Said Abu Iyad: 'When the Chairman is travelling from A to B, by car or by plane, not even those of us who are closest to him know when he intends to make his move.'

Once during the research and interviewing for this book I had the opportunity to make a long journey with Arafat by air. He was on his way to Sana in the Yemen Arab Republic for a meeting with the P.L.O. Military Council. For the arrangements concerning the trip my link with Arafat was Khalad Hassan. It was Khalad who had finally persuaded a reluctant Arafat to allow me to travel with him. And it was Khalad who put me on standby for departure. Khalad and I met at six o'clock in the evening. 'Now you must be patient,' he said. 'The call may come in the next twelve minutes or the next twelve hours.'

It came at twenty-five minutes past midnight. Since Arafat was double my distance from the airport I guessed that he was already on his way. The obvious implication was that a delay at my end would be disastrous. For me. I need not have worried. Somebody had planned and timed my journey to the airport down to the last second. My P.L.O. car came to a stop at the V.I.P. lounge just as Arafat, covered by six bodyguards, was getting out of his — a black, armour-plated Mercedes. Not thirty metres away, engines running and ready to roll, was a medium-sized Saudi passenger jet. In less than two minutes we were all aboard and the Saudi plane was eating up the runway. I had the impression that we began to taxi before the door was fully closed.

According to one of the many, many myths about Arafat and the P.L.O., he and it are supposed to own a fleet of five, six or seven airliners. It is not so. Arafat travels by courtesy of a number of Arab governments which put aircraft at his disposal when he requests one. His two main benefactors on this account are Saudi Arabia and Algeria. When he is planning his air travel, Arafat observes two rules. He flies over certain areas only by night; and he never flies into, or out of, Beirut. Since 1982 he has not, in fact, had the possibility of using Beirut airport. But in the years when it was his most convenient departure and arrival point, he never took advantage of its facilities for fear of being hijacked or shot down by Israeli war planes. In February 1973, the Israelis did shoot down a Libyan airliner killing all 100 people on board. Arafat told me: 'I have no evidence but I would not be surprised if the Israelis thought that I or some of our other leaders were on board.'

How many times Arafat has come close to being hijacked or shot down is a matter for speculation; but what I did discover, from Arafat himself and from Abu Iyad, is that it was the practice of Israeli fighter pilots to fly close enough to allow a visual inspection of aircraft in which Arafat and other top P.L.O. leaders were thought to be travelling. Said Abu Iyad: 'I can only presume the

Israelis were never satisfied that Arafat or me was on board. Many times we were but after the shooting down of the Libyan airliner the Israelis could not afford to make another mistake. If they we.e confident they would for sure have forced us to land.'

Ironically, the closest Arafat ever came to being killed was not the consequence of one of the many attempts on his life. It was in January 1969, on the road between Amman and Baghdad, when he was indulging his passion for driving fast cars fast.

He was on his way to a meeting with the President of Iraq. Three people were in the powerful Mercedes. The official driver was asleep on the back seat; Arafat was at the wheel. Beside him was Abu Daoud, who at the time was the commander of all Palestinian militias in Jordan. It was six-thirty in the morning, the light was bad, and it was raining so hard the wipers could hardly cope. But Arafat was late, and he accelerated. Ahead of them and travelling in the same direction was a huge lorry. Arafat pulled out to overtake. A car was coming fast in the other direction and Arafat swung back behind the lorry. He touched the brakes. As the Mercedes crashed into the rear of the lorry its roof was severed from its body.

Abu Daoud, by several inches the tallest man in the P.L.O., takes up the story. 'In the split second before the impact we threw ourselves to the floor of the car. I was bleeding from my nose but I could move to free myself. Arafat was lying like a baby in the womb with his hands over his head. He did not move. He did not make a sound. I thought he was dead.'

About twenty minutes later Arafat's escort car arrived on the scene. It was a small Volkswagen loaded with bodyguards. Somehow they made room for Arafat and Abu Daoud and drove to the nearest hospital. It was more than 200 kilometres away.

Arafat's only injury was a broken hand but he was confined to a hospital bed for two days of observations. While he was in hospital the President of Iraq was among his visitors.

Most of Arafat's colleagues can tell a hair-raising tale or two about their own experiences on the road with Arafat at the wheel. Hamid Abu Sitta is one of several P.L.O. executives who will not travel with the Chairman unless he promises to drive or be driven at a safe speed. It was on the same road from Amman to Baghdad that Abu Sitta once forced Arafat to stop the car. 'I said "Look, Abu Amar, if you continue to drive at this high velocity we will not reach

Baghdad. We will both be killed. I want to go back to Amman and I will follow you in another car." By this way I obliged him to drive smoothly.' I asked Abu Sitta if Arafat had been involved in many road accidents. 'Oh yes,' he said. 'Many.'

I asked Arafat for his own explanation of why he had survived a number of road accidents in which he ought to have been killed, and the many attempts to assassinate him. He agreed that his nose or smell for danger was a very important factor. So was good luck. But there was more to it. 'I am a believer,' he said in a very matter of fact way, 'and I believe there is something unseen.'

Arafat's 'activities', his congenital inability to be still and his need always to be doing something, are the most visible manifestations of one of his several great assets – his incredible and apparently inexhaustible energy. For this he is described by friends and enemies alike as a 'phenomenon'.

As a matter of routine Arafat works between eighteen and nineteen hours a day, and that has been his way seven days a week, 365 days a year for the past twenty years and more. 'In all that time,' Arafat told me, 'I have not even thought of taking one or two days for a holiday.' On average he sleeps not more than five hours a day and often less. When circumstances allow he prefers to sleep in two shifts: between four and seven o'clock in the morning – Fatah and P.L.O. meetings usually start a nine or ten o'clock in the evening and almost never end until the approach of dawn – and between four and six o'clock in the evening. The late afternoon nap probably explains why Arafat always seems to be on his best form at midnight. In my experience that is when he is at his most thoughtful and reflective.

When I had completed the preliminary research for this book it was apparent that available information about Arafat's personal and private life could be written on the back of a postage stamp. For amusement I did write it on the back of one. My note read: 'Arafat: non-smoker, non-drinker, bachelor. Very emotional. Terrible temper.' And that was it. The mystery in which the man had wrapped himself was such that even the place of his birth – the country not the city or village – was a matter of speculation.

As I discovered from Arafat himself, the description of him as a non-smoker is not strictly accurate. 'I have never smoked a cigarette or a pipe for pleasure,' he told me, 'but I did smoke cigarettes and pipes as part of my disguises in the old days. Today I call myself a half-smoker because I am surrounded at our meetings by colleagues who do it all the time.' I understood more the point he was making when Abu Iyad later told me that he smoked 'five or six packets' of cigarettes a day.

Of all the leaders who have at one time or another dominated the Middle East stage, Israel's Golda Meir was the most celebrated non-drinker. When she asked 'What would you like to drink?' she was offering tea, coffee or water – the latter with soda if you were lucky. Arafat's personal choice of drink is even more limited than hers was. He drinks only tea and water. According to his friends Arafat drinks water only when he must, usually to help his food down; and he drinks tea only at times of his choosing. Said Khalad Hassan: 'Our Chairman is not even a social tea drinker!' But tea, or rather what he takes with it, is Arafat's one little luxury in life. He drinks it with honey. When we were alone together in his private office in Sana the only thing on his desk was a jar of honey. I got the impression that honey is to Arafat what jelly beans were to Ronald Reagan.

As other reporters and writers have discovered, Arafat is very reluctant to talk about his private life. I decided to take my main chance when we were alone in Sana with only the honey pot between us.

'Is it true that you were once engaged to be married in Kuwait?' I asked.

'It happened so.'

'You really were intending to get married?'

'It was so.'

'Were you very much in love?'

For a brief moment I thought he was going to explode and tell me in his own way to go to hell. But there was no explosion. 'You are squeezing me,' was all he said. Very quietly.

'I know,' I said, 'but these questions are important if I am to understand you as I want to.'

Arafat gazed into the distant past and then, eventually, at me. The mask was off. His eyes were moist. 'To answer your question. . . Yes, I was in love. For me the decision not to marry was very hard. Very hard.'

'Your colleagues tell me that your decision to remain a bachelor and not to have children of your own was the greatest sacrifice you have made for the cause.'

'It was so.'

'Why did you make such a great personal sacrifice?'

'I am a normal man, I would like to have a wife and children; but I did not think it was fair that any woman should be asked to share the troubles I knew I would be facing in my long struggle. It was not fair at all. This is one point. Second, I considered that I was making my sacrifice for all of my people, all of our children.'

'Tell me about the woman you were going to marry — did she understand?'

'She was very understanding, yes.'

Unexpectedly Arafat changed the mood. The sadness in his face gave way to a mischievous smile.

'You know I was once married,' he said. 'It was in 1967, after the war, when I was fighting in the West Bank. The Israelis came to the place where I was and we were surrounded. They made for me a trap. Many traps. In those days our security was not so good. What to do? How to escape? Close by me was the wife of one of my colleagues. I took her as my wife. Another of our friends had a baby. We took the baby. I carried the baby and I passed through the Israeli lines pretending to be a loving family man with his wife and child. We were so happy – holding hands and laughing. Of course I made some changes to my appearance, too. Perhaps that was one of the times when I smoked a cigarette.'

At about the same time Arafat was also flirting with the idea of marriage again. By all accounts his feelings for a woman called Nadia were such that her close friends were asking if Yasser had proposed. She replied that he had not done so and that she did not expect that he would. The relationship was greatly complicated by the fact that Nadia was already married. She was, apparently, unhappily married and living apart from her husband. But it was still a problem. Her husband died when a bag of cement fell on top of him as he was walking through a building site. Most people say it was an accident.

Arafat has always denied that his lack of a wife and a family of his own is the cause of the great inner sadness he tries so hard to disguise. But his friends and colleagues believe that his joy at being among children tells another story. The woman who probably knows Arafat best is Um Jihad, the attractive and dynamic wife of Abu Jihad, the co-founder with Arafat of the resistance movement. Um Jihad speaks for all when she says that Arafat is 'drawn to children like they are magnets'.

For the P.L.O.'s representatives around the world the first item on the agenda of any meeting with the Chairman is usually their children. Zahedi Terzi, who represents the P.L.O. at U.N. headquarters in New York, speaks for most of his colleagues on this point. 'It's almost like an inquisition. Arafat wants to know everything about my children. Where are they? What school are they attending? What class? What progress are they making? And so on. Once I came from New York to Beirut when we were in the middle of a very big crisis. Arafat as usual started with questions about my children. I said: "My God, Abu Amar, I've come here to discuss important political matters and all you want to know is how are my children doing!" Arafat replied: "No, no, you are wrong. Our children are our life. They are not less important than our politics."'

According to one of Um Jihad's stories the signs are that Arafat would have been strong on the matter of discipline with children of his own. In 1966, shortly before the first Syrian-backed attempt to kill Arafat and control Fatah, he was living with the Jihads in Damascus. Their third-floor apartment was more or less Fatah's operational headquarters at the time.

'One day,' said Um Jihad, 'our son Jihad was missing. When he did not come home we were frightened. Some of us feared that he had been kidnapped by Israeli agents. Abu Amar ran down the stairs calling for the others to follow him. They got into their cars and went searching for Jihad. It was Abu Amar who found him. He was very angry with Jihad and he told him: "Your father will not punish you – but I will. I am going to hit you." And he did.'

Some of Arafat's lifelong friends still urge him to marry. Said one who did not wish to be quoted by name: 'He needs a wife to take care of him. We know it and he knows it . . . but he says it's too late.' The odds are that Arafat will remain a bachelor. But if he can confine the struggle to politics, and survive, he might yet take a wife. Or so a few of his friends believe.

By religion Arafat is, of course, a Moslem. But he is not a zealot. One of the myths about the Chairman of the P.L.O. is that he was a member of the fanatical Moslem Brotherhood. With its origins in Egypt in the 1920s, the Moslem Brotherhood was the first modern manifestation of the kind of Islamic fundamentalism that swept the Shah of Iran from power in 1979. After the State of Israel was formed in 1948, some of those who were to become Arafat's senior colleagues did join the Brotherhood for a while. Arafat did not, though he did make use of it.

It was in Sana that I witnessed an amusing demonstration of Arafat's pragmatism on religious matters. In the Fatah base some fifteen miles or so from the capital of this still mainly mediaeval country, Arafat had planned to brief his fighters on the latest developments in his showdown with Assad. It had been Arafat's intention to address a mass gathering of his men at about midday. But shortly before he was due to speak the camp was hit by thunderbolts and torrential rain. The meeting was postponed. Some four hours later, when the weather had changed, Arafat gave the word for the troops to assemble. He was not more than a few seconds into his opening remarks when the afternoon call to prayers started. The wailing of the mullah, on tape and relayed through loudspeakers, was deafening. At first Arafat tried to compete. Then, when the mullah paused for breath, Arafat slipped in a joke about God being in agreement with him. But the competition was too much. The assembled troops could not listen to both. It was Arafat or the mullah.

Arafat whispered to a senior officer. The man hurried away. A few seconds later the mullah was cut off in mid-sentence. Arafat continued with his address.

Moslems are required to pray five times a day. For Arafat, as it is for many other busy, modern men of the faith, that obligation is an inconvenience. His approach to this problem is also pragmatic. Said Um Jihad: 'He always prays in the morning and usually he gathers the five times a day into one.'

Distant and casual observers of Arafat could also be forgiven for believing that he is a man without humour. It is not so. Arafat's ideas about what is funny are simple, almost child-like. And he does laugh. In private his favourite jokes are those which portray Libya's Colonel Qadafy as an idiot. In recent years, and when time has allowed, Arafat has also become an addict of television cartoons, *Looney Tunes* and such. Once in Tunis one of his more academically trained colleagues suggested in fun that watching cartoons meant for children was hardly a suitable thing for the Chairman of the P.L.O. to do. In response, and only half in fun, Arafat rattled off the names of six or seven of the world's most eminent psychiatrists. 'You should read them,' he said. 'They all say that watching cartoons is the best possible form of relaxation for people who live under a stress. They are right. You should try it!'

Arafat's style of leadership is refreshingly simple, essentially honest and very human. His relationship with his people is that of a fond father and a loving brother. It is on that basis that he presents himself as the leader and manages the P.L.O.'s internal affairs. It is on that basis that his style of leadership is accepted by a majority of Palestinians.

Unlike many of the kings and presidents who rule the Arab states in the style of feudal lords, Arafat does not hold court and does not like titles. He has no objection to being called Chairman Arafat, but he much prefers to be addressed by his *nom de guerre*, Abu Amar (Amar comes from the Arabic verb 'to build'). Among themselves, and despite the fact that they are all more or less his age, Arafat's colleagues usually refer to him as the 'Old Man'.

It is a self-evident truth that Arafat is loved by many of his colleagues in the leadership of Fatah and the P.L.O. I should emphasise that I am talking about Arafat the man and not Arafat the politician. It is also my impression that Arafat is loved by many other Palestinians who know him.

Nobody knew the real Arafat better than Abu Jihad, who, at the time of his assassination, was the Chairman's deputy and most likely successor. Abu Jihad said: 'The secret of Arafat is that he is living all of our emotions. Arafat is not just a political symbol. We sense and we know that he is living all of our fears, all of our dreams and all of our sufferings. When any Palestinian is suffering, Arafat is feeling the pain. When one of our fighters is killed, a small part of Arafat is killed. When one of our children dies, even from natural causes, a small part of Arafat dies. This is the real Arafat. He is not just our leader. In one person he is all of us, all of our emotions, all of our strengths, all of our weaknesses, all of our contradictions . . . Do you understand?'

A story that illustrates one of the reasons why many Palestinians are overwhelmed by what they regard as Arafat's outstanding human qualities was told to me by Zahedi Terzi.

'In the summer of 1982 my wife was in hospital here in New York. She had cancer and she was going through radium therapy. It was at the time that the Israelis had turned Beirut into hell on earth and were trying to kill Arafat and finish the P.L.O. Naturally I did not inform the leadership of my personal problem. But one of my New York colleagues did. The next thing that happens is that I get a telephone call from Arafat. He was angry because I had not told him about my personal sufferings. He said something like, "By God, don't you think you should have told me what is happening to you and your family!" I said, "Look Abu Amar, I am here, you are there—." He interrupted me. "You *must* tell me these things. I am available all of the time." I said again that my problem was a personal one and that really I did not have the right to burden him when he had so many other problems. He was no more angry but he said: "You are wrong. Your wife is our sister. You should have told me." Then he made me tell him everything. Then he wanted to know what he could do to help. Then he insisted that I keep him informed about my wife's condition. Arafat's kindness and his humanity is something unbelievable.'

A criticism of Arafat which is endorsed by all of his colleagues is that he 'wants to do everything himself'. If he was another kind of man his total involvement would be regarded as interference and would also be resented. In Arafat's case it is not so. Said Khalad Hassan: 'The problem with Arafat – perhaps I should say our problem with Arafat – is that he is a man who gives everything he has to the cause. Arafat is a normal man like the rest of us. What does this mean? He has a body, a brain, a heart and a soul; and he has energy, emotions and a great capacity to love. Arafat gives one hundred per cent of all of these things to the cause. Perhaps it is easier for him because he is a bachelor. But that is the reality. You can say that the cause is his wife and his mistress. He is devoted to this wife and this mistress from A to Z. And he is devoted in a way that makes you feel you want to follow him. In this respect none of us can compete with Arafat. We cannot catch him. I need not to be convinced that life would be easier for Arafat and the rest of us if he did not try to do everything himself. It is a problem, no doubt about it. But if you understand the man, you understand the problem.'

Recognition of Arafat's outstanding human qualities does not come only from those who are his natural political allies. Of the heavyweights, and since 1967, George Habash has been the most consistent and the most radical of Arafat's internal political opponents. Today Habash is widely recognized as the intellectual giant of the left in Palestinian politics, in much the same way as

Khalad Hassan is regarded as the giant on the right. But on the subject of Arafat the man, Habash speaks the same language as Khalad Hassan. 'In some ways Arafat is as simple as a child. He weeps and really we feel he is so passionate, so caring and so faithful. On our side we have many political differences with him as you know. We have always believed that he is a man of tactics and not strategy – and that is one of his biggest weaknesses. But as a human being how can we not love him?'

Habash also agreed with Khalad Hassan that Arafat's greatest strength is that he is a 'man of cause' and thus a leader who will never allow the P.L.O. to become the puppet of any Arab regime.

On the subject of Arafat's determination to preserve the independence of Palestinian decision-making, Khalad said this: 'In 1975 Sadat told me he feared that Arafat had sold himself to the Syrians. At this time I was very close to Sadat and I told him that he was making a fatal mistake if that was what he seriously believed. I remember also that I said the following to Sadat: "Arafat is a man who cannot by nature sell himself to anybody but himself. If he was to look into a mirror, and if he thought the image in the mirror will dominate him, he would break the mirror. This man could not be dominated by anybody."'

Putting to one side, for the moment, the matter of his celebrated and terrible temper, another attractive aspect of Arafat's human nature is his unfailing courtesy. When you are a guest in any place where Arafat happens to be, and even when he is in the tightest of corners, he is never so busy or so involved that he cannot find the time to make sure that your needs are being attended to. And if you have a problem with his staff, he will solve it. At meals Arafat is personally attentive. It is he himself who makes sure that your plate and your glass are never empty.

When he is among his own people Arafat is the last to insist on formality and protocol. But the opposite is the case when he or he and his colleagues are dealing with heads of state and the representatives of governments and international institutions. On these occasions, in public and in private, Arafat is a fanatic in his observance of protocol and diplomatic etiquette.

Late one evening in Sana I was chatting with the Chairman and some members of the P.L.O. Military Council. Most were dressed in slacks and open-necked shirts. Only Arafat, clad in his olive green field uniform, looked the part. His combat cap was on his desk by the honey pot. There was a knock on the door which was opened from the outside to reveal the head and shoulders of the Chairman's signals operator. His message was to the effect that the Saudis had made radio contact and were requesting that Arafat stand by for a conversation with King Fahd.

Arafat nodded and then went through an elaborate routine to check his appearance. He stood up and adjusted his uniform. I had the impression that he was making the creases of his trousers run in parallel. The cuffs of his jacket had to be just so. Then he put his cap on and took time to adjust it. Unconcerned that he was being observed with amusement by some of his colleagues and myself, he brought himself to attention. Still not satisfied, he proceeded with his hand to brush some imaginary hairs off his shoulders. And all this for a conversation by radio with King Fahd. To anyone but Arafat himself it would not have mattered if the Chairman of the P.L.O. had sat at the radio transmitter in his vest and pants. But to Arafat it did matter. The King of Saudi Arabia was to be accorded the respect which protocol demanded – no matter what the circumstances.

If Arafat had remained a construction and contracting engineer in Kuwait, he would today be a very rich man, 'probably a multi-millionaire' said Khalad Hassan. But apart from financing his passion for fast cars, Arafat put all of the money he made in Kuwait at the disposal of the embryo liberation movement. During the underground years, when most of his colleagues to be were not earning enough money to keep their families, Arafat paid the bills for such things as printing, publishing and foreign travel. 'In the end,' said Khalad, 'he put every penny he had into the revolution. When he was asked to give his full time to the struggle he left his business without settling his accounts with his partner, and because of that he lost a lot of money.'

The suggestion that Arafat is personally corrupt draws equal contempt from both the right and the left of the P.L.O. Khalad Hassan put it this way: 'Arafat is a totally clean man. When you work with him you cannot doubt this for one second.' George Habash was just as firm. 'In my opinion, and on the subject about which we are talking, Arafat is incorruptible.'

It was because of his total dedication to the cause and his

unsullied reputation that Arafat was asked by the majority of his colleagues to be responsible for P.L.O. finances when he became the organization's Chairman in 1969.

Though few of them are free to say in public what they know to be the truth, many Arab journalists who live and work in their own homelands are fascinated by the greed and corruption they see all around them. In private conversation one of the most informed and outspoken critics of the corruption of the Arab regimes is Egypt's Lotfi El-Khouli. He was imprisoned seven times by Nasser's regime, but he still admires Nasser. I asked El-Khouli how he compared Arafat with Nasser, and he replied:

'If we make allowances for the fact that Nasser had a home and a family, and that he enjoyed the material privileges that came from being the President, we can say that he was a clean man. And for that alone he was very rare among Arab leaders. But compared even to Nasser, Arafat is a saint. Arafat has nothing but his cause. I think that Arafat has physical, mental and moral courage of a kind that we modern Arabs have not seen before. I am quite sure the Arab world, and perhaps even your world, will come to recognize this truth in time . . . but probably not until it is too late.'

The joker in the pack of Arafat's many and obvious human qualities is his terrible temper. When he is really amused his face seems to contract. He half closes his eyes, he wrinkles his nose and his smile runs from one ear to the other. When he is angry his whole face expands like a balloon being inflated. And the warning of the storm to come is what many of his colleagues describe as the 'glitter' in his bulging eyes. According to Terzi, 'It's like the lightning before the storm.' Those whose know Arafat best detect earlier warning signs that an explosion is coming. 'You can tell from all of his activities,' said Um Jihad. 'His anger is an energy which takes control of his whole body – his hands, his legs, everything.'

From all that I heard about Arafat's temper I got the impression that a demonstration of it would be sufficient to convince a stranger that the Chairman of the P.L.O. was a ranting tyrant. He shouts, curses and shoots the air with his index finger. Said one of his colleagues: 'It's not hysteria. Arafat is never hysterical. What pours out of him when he is blowing his top is pure, naked anger. It comes from the deep like a mixture of oil and gas when the drill makes its first strike.'

On one celebrated occasion Arafat's *Chef du Cabinet* resigned in protest at the master's temper. Friends quote him as saying: 'I couldn't take any more of the shouting. I was exhausted just by having to listen. After two weeks the Chairman asked me to return. He promised me he would try not to shout so much. I knew he would try – but I also knew he would fail. I came back and here I am . . . still fed up with the shouting. In my opinion it is not so necessary.'

Perhaps because they do not spend all of their time within earshot of Arafat, most of his senior colleagues are more charitable than his senior staffers. 'In the first place,' said Khalad Hassan, 'the man is what he is. His explosive temper is another part of his human nature and that is something we can't change. He can change it and perhaps he should. But we can't. Also it is not so simple. When you are a man like Arafat who gives everything of himself to the cause you need an emotional outlet or at least a safety valve. I see very little of my own wife and children, but I do have my family, my books and my writing. Abu Jihad, Abu Iyad and the others – they have wives and children. Our families are a source of comfort to us. And when necessary we can take out our frustrations on our wives and children. That's normal. That's life. That's the way it happens. Arafat's problem is that he has denied himself a normal life for the sake of our cause. Don't underestimate the sacrifice he has made and what it is costing him as a human being.'

I asked if this meant that Arafat was unable to control his emotions. Khalad considered the question. 'I can see it may look like that to outsiders,' he said, 'but really it is not the case. To tell you the truth there are times when Arafat demonstrates that he has a greater power of self-control than all the rest of us put together. It is on these occasions that I admire him most of all.'

It is clear, however, that by no means all of Arafat's angry outbursts are spontaneous or the result of what he would regard as a provocation of the moment. According to one Fatah personality who did not wish to be quoted by name on this subject, Arafat sometimes uses his anger as a weapon to intimidate others.

I wondered if the fact of Arafat's terrible temper was a clue to a dark side of his character. I told myself that if there was a vicious and vindictive side to Arafat's character I would get some real clues of its existence by asking how he disciplines or punishes Palestinian traitors when their treachery is discovered. Over the years Israeli,

Arab, Western and Soviet intelligence agencies have recruited hundreds of Palestinians to act for them as informers and spies and, in the case of Israel's agencies, assassins. And it is no secret that Fatah and other P.L.O. organizations have been penetrated at all levels. The most successful of the Palestinian traitor-agents who were controlled by the Mossad got themselves into positions from which they could easily have killed Arafat and other top P.L.O. leaders if they had not cracked and confessed at the last minute.

According to the P.L.O.'s constitution, no Palestinian can be executed without a written order signed by the Chairman. In consultation with the P.L.O.'s legal department, the man with the executive responsibility for preparing execution orders and for submitting them to the Chairman for approval is Abu Iyad. I asked him to tell me how many such orders he had presented to Arafat for signature since 1967, the year Abu Iyad assumed responsibility for Fatah's security services.

Abu Iyad's reply was the following: 'To be exact I cannot tell you because I truly do not remember. But let me say for the record that the answer to your question is many.'

My next question was the obvious one. 'How many execution orders has Arafat actually signed?'

Abu Iyad answered without hesitation. 'Three or four.'

'Three *or* four? What does that mean?' I asked.

Abu Iyad's explanation of the 'or' was that in the period up to the end of 1983 Arafat had signed four death warrants, but only three Palestinians had been executed. The name on the outstanding death warrant is that of Abu Nidal, whose breakaway Fatah group has assassinated some thirty or more of Arafat's colleagues who advocated, or engaged in, dialogue with Jews. Abu Nidal was tried and sentenced to death in his absence. But because he enjoys the protection of the diplomatic and intelligence services of at least two Arab regimes, he has not yet presented a target for Abu Iyad's men to hit.

During the same conversation Abu Iyad volunteered the following information. 'If you want to know what I really think . . . Arafat's weak point is his refusal to execute traitors. And that's the main reason why we have these internal troubles.' This is a point of view that is shared by many of the Chairman's closest colleagues in Fatah.

To underline his own thoughts on the matter, and his frustration,

Abu Iyad told me that in bombing Beirut in 1982 one of General Sharon's main objectives was to kill Arafat. Some seventy Israeli agents, many of them Palestinians, were equipped with the very latest transmitters, each of them about the size of a packet of cigarettes. Their mission was to observe, follow and report Arafat's movements. Israeli aircraft were then given the co-ordinates for their attacks. By chance Abu Iyad's intelligence people discovered the Israeli network. After one agent confessed, twenty-seven more were captured. One of Abu Iyad's most trusted aides finished the story: 'Abu Iyad was so fed up with Arafat's opposition to the execution of traitors that he did not seek the Chairman's approval on this occasion. We had the confessions. Abu Iyad told us to take them away and shoot them. We did.'

Abu Iyad added: 'I do not complain because Arafat is a good human being. This is also one of his great strengths. I complain because he is more good than he needs to be on some occasions.'

A little lower down the leadership ladder there is a man called Hamid Abu Sitta, whom Arafat describes as 'my teacher'. Abu Sitta is an independent member of the P.L.O. Executive Committee. He lives in Amman, the capital of Jordan; and he was responsible to the Executive Committee for the day-to-day management of Palestinian political affairs in the occupied territories of the West Bank and Gaza. During my conversations with Abu Sitta I raised the subject of Arafat's reluctance to execute traitors.

Abu Sitta confirmed that he and local P.L.O. officials had made a number of requests for traitors to be executed. 'But Arafat never signs the papers,' he said. 'Always the Chairman proposes some other solution. Sometimes he asks us to confine the person. Sometimes he moves the person to a far-away place where he can make no trouble. But Arafat never gives the permission for us to make examples by execution. To tell you the truth, Arafat hates bloodshed.

'Once when I was really angry with Arafat I said, "Look, we have many Israeli agents in our ranks we must make some examples, we must execute this particular man. We have given him a fair trial and everybody knows he is a traitor." Arafat said to me the following: "It is not my way and really you should know it because I have given you the reasons many times. Also this man has sons and cousins. Three of his relatives are working with me. If we kill this man it will not serve our cause. If we kill this man his sons and their sons will become our enemies. I will not sign the paper.'"

Of the four execution orders that Arafat did sign, and leaving aside the one with Abu Nidal's name on it, two were concerned with Palestinians who supplied Israeli agents with maps and information which enabled Israeli forces to locate and hit P.L.O. bases and kill large numbers of civilians. The other was for Israel's most successful agent, a Palestinian playboy who reported on Arafat's movements with a radio transmitter disguised as a hairbrush, and who came close to killing the Chairman with poisoned rice. According to Father Ibrahim Iyad, an elderly Catholic priest in whom the Chairman has confided at moments of personal crisis, Arafat 'wept like a child' when the man who came so close to assassinating him was executed. 'To this day Arafat makes sure that the man's family is taken care of.'

It can be argued that the Palestinian people could have been spared many of the disasters which have overtaken them if Arafat had used Fatah's military strength to impose discipline on the Marxist and leftist groups within the P.L.O., and on the radical elements within his own Fatah organization. Among those who support this argument are a number of Arafat's colleagues, including Khalad Hassan, who have given the Chairman their total support in his dangerous struggle to sell the idea of compromise to his own people. But as Arafat later explains, there are good reasons why he has consistently refused to use force to settle internal P.L.O. problems.

Arafat has more than once intervened to save the lives of political opponents who would otherwise have been killed by his own supporters. One man who owes his life to Arafat is Ahmad Jabril, the leader of a very small faction within the P.L.O. which, for many years, commanded no popular support of any kind. Jabril became the focus of some international media attention in 1983 when the Syrians and the Libyans assigned to him the task of co-ordinating the rebellion against Arafat.

When Jabril joined the Palestinian underground in the early 1960s he did so as an agent for Syrian Military Intelligence, which he has faithfully served, to the detriment of the Palestinian cause, ever since. In 1966 he was the frontman for Syria's first attempt to seize control of Fatah. The plan was for Jabril to take the leadership after Arafat had been murdered. From the moment that first anti-Arafat coup failed, the Syrians determined to bend Arafat to their will; and Jabril, as he was to prove time and time again, was ever willing to do their dirty work. After 1974, and still as an agent for the Syrians, Jabril's main function was to sabotage Arafat's political moves within the P.L.O. And when he failed by political means, he organized terror attacks on Israel for the purpose of embarrassing and discrediting Arafat and those of his colleagues, the majority, who were working for a political and compromise settlement with Israel. Israel's political and military leaders were fully aware of the set-up, but it suited them to regard and project the P.L.O. as a monolithic organization. That way they could blame Arafat and justify their refusal to test by diplomatic means the reality of Arafat's ideas for compromise.

In 1976 Jabril was arrested by Fatah forces who intended to kill him. Arafat sent some of his own bodyguards to rescue him and escort him to safety in Damascus. On the second occasion Jabril was the victim of a conspiracy within his own organization. Cornered and trapped by his own associates, his life was again at stake. Again, too, Arafat sent his own bodyguards to rescue Jabril. They also gave him some money to allow him to escape from the Lebanon.

Hani Hassan was one of several Fatah executives who cited the stories of Arafat's treatment of Jabril as evidence that the Chairman of the P.L.O. is not a vindictive man. Hani added: 'In the Arab tradition a man can kill his blood brother if the brother is a traitor. This is not Arafat's way. He cannot think, even for a few seconds, to liquidate a person who has worked with him. His nature will not allow him to do it.'

'The Palestinian cause has always needed a leader who is a great actor,' Hammadi Essid commented to me, and without a doubt the Chairman of the P.L.O. is a great actor. As with his anger, he can turn on the smiles and the tears to order. And his demonstrations of this talent have led some observers who know him quite well to describe him as a 'computer'. Hammadi Essid goes much further. He said: 'Arafat has become so much of a computer that there is nothing any more genuine about his reactions. He has programmed himself to respond to any event or situation at the touch of a button.' Arafat certainly calculates his options with the speed and precision of a computer; but the machine has not taken over the man.

One of the Chairman's best live performances was at the Palestine National Council in Algiers in February 1983 when Jabril made a speech damning Arafat and his policies.

The P.N.C. is more or less the Palestinian parliament-in-exile. It is the highest Palestinian decision-making body and the P.L.O. is answerable to it. P.N.C. delegates represent Palestinian communities around the world. Arafat's objective was to persuade the P.N.C. to keep the door open to the Reagan Plan in the hope that it could be improved. At the very least he needed a final resolution which did not reject the Reagan Plan outright. Everybody knew that an outright rejection would make it difficult, and perhaps impossible, for Arafat to continue with his search for a political and compromise settlement. It was touch and go.

Jabril was working for a quite different objective. Following a script written in Damascus by his controllers in Syrian Military Intelligence, and financed to the tune of 34 million dollars by Qadafy, Jabril's aim was to split the P.N.C. and the P.L.O. Unknown at the time to all except Arafat and a handful of his closest colleagues, Jabril had a very special guest in his private villa at the conference headquarters – a senior member of Libya's Military Intelligence service who was in daily, sometimes hourly, touch with Qadafy.

Jabril's conference speech was a violent attack on Arafat and his policy of politics and compromise. Among other things, Jabril demanded a total rejection of the Reagan Plan; an end to the dialogue with King Hussein, and by implication Hussein's overthrow; and a permanent stop to all contacts with Jews.

While Jabril continued with his verbal assault, many in the large and impressive debating chamber wondered how Arafat would react. As each previous speaker had left the rostrum, Arafat had advanced half-way up the steps to meet and embrace him or her. How would Arafat handle Jabril?

Arafat uses a variety of gestures to indicate and sometimes signal the quality of his respect and admiration for others. His normal expression of welcome and respect is the traditional Arab one – a glancing kiss on the cheeks and a squeeze of the shoulders. If you are a good friend, or if he wants you to think that he accepts you as a good friend, he will take your outstretched hand and slightly twist it so that the thumbs of the handshake form a 'V' for victory sign. And if you are really a good friend whom he admires and respects, or needs, he will raise his hands and yours above his head.

The moment it was clear that Jabril had ended his speech, Arafat bounced out of his chair and darted up the steps to meet the descending Jabril. When their bodies touched Arafat flung his arms around Jabril, kissed him three times on the cheek and then spun him round to reveal that their hands were locked in the victory handshake. Then, when he sensed the audience was with him, Arafat raised his two arms and Jabril's one. The conference exploded with applause. Without saying a word the 'Old Man' had demonstrated that he was the boss. Jabril could not have been more humiliated. But he was forced to smile.

One of Arafat's great strengths is his ability and will to come out fighting after he has been knocked down and counted out. Allied to this great strength, and obviously a product of his own unfailing optimism, is Arafat's ability to lift others out of their depression and despair. As one who has given comfort and spiritual guidance to Arafat at critical moments in the past, even Father Ibrahim Iyad was consumed by doubts about the future when he arrived in Tunis a few days after the Chairman's expulsion from Syria. 'I am a Palestinian and a priest,' Father Iyad told me, 'but even I was without hope in those days when it was so clear that Assad was determined to finish us if he could. Then I spent some time with Chairman Arafat. Really it was my job to comfort him, but it was Arafat who gave me new hope. It is amazing what simply being with Arafat can do to your own morale.'

Many Palestinians can tell similar stories. Khalad Hassan, at times the most severe critic of Arafat the politician, had this to say: 'Sometimes when I am far away from Arafat and he makes what I think are stupid mistakes I get very angry. Sometimes I say to myself, "What are we doing with this man as our leader!" Then, when I am with Arafat, I wonder how it was that I had such thoughts. Arafat's secret is the effect of his personality when you are alone with him or in a small group. It's magic.'

Westerners who only know the Chairman of the P.L.O. from his media image often say that his great problem is that he lacks charisma. Although he can make effective speeches on the Palestinian stage he has not learned how to use the media to project himself and his cause. But as Khalad Hassan says, he has his own very special brand of charisma and the magic of it works through his relationships with people on an individual basis. He is at his best and his most effective behind closed doors, when he is talking with individuals or small groups in private, and when he does not have to play to dozens of different galleries. The fact is that every time Arafat opens his mouth in public he has to take account of how his remarks will be interpreted in each of twenty-two Arab capitals; in Washington, Moscow, Peking and each of the capitals of Europe – West and East; in the rival camps of the P.L.O.; and in divided Israel. That does not leave a great deal of scope for Arafat to be a convincing public speaker. His achievements behind closed doors, however, tell another story, and the best illustration of Arafat's quite remarkable powers of persuasion and leadership is the fact that he persuaded Palestinian decision-makers that they had to be prepared to make peace with Israel in return for a Palestinian mini-state, even though this meant that the Palestinians would effectively be making peace in return for less than thirty per cent of their original homeland.

Among the top P.L.O. leaders there is no disagreement about Arafat's great qualities and strengths as a human being. There is also no disagreement about what is seen within the P.L.O. as the Chairman's greatest weakness. That, in the words of all of his colleagues, is his 'individualism' – his insistence on being free to take personal initiatives when he sees a possibility of making progress. It stems not from any lusting after power for its own sake. As Hani Hassan put it: 'Arafat is a man of initiatives. It is the way he is made. He will go into any dark tunnel if he sees even the smallest light at the end of it. And when he has made up his mind to do something, it is very hard, and usually impossible, to make him change it.'

In fact, the problem of Arafat's individualism exists only because his colleagues insisted from the beginning on there being a collective leadership. The question I think future historians will have to answer is whether the Palestinian cause would have been better served if Arafat had not been to some extent the prisoner of a collective leadership.

Yasser Arafat was just about twenty-one when he committed his life to the cause, a cause which required the Palestinians to change the way the world was managed if they were ever to get even a small measure of justice; and a cause which has its roots in what happened in Palestine more than 3,000 years ago.

# 2

# The Cause

The essence of the Palestinian problem can be found in three fundamental questions. Who are the Palestinians? Where and what was their original homeland? Why, as a consequence of the coming into existence of the State of Israel in 1948, did the majority of the Palestinian people – nearly ninety per cent of them at the time – find themselves outside their homeland as unwanted refugees in the Arab countries surrounding the new Jewish State?

The answers to these questions are not hard to find in the historical facts of the matter.

The Palestinians are Arabs, the word Arab being a generic term which includes all the peoples who live in the Middle East whose mother tongue is Arabic, regardless of their religion. The majority of Arabs were converted to Islam by the followers of the Prophet Muhammad in the seventh century A.D. But the Arabs are a pre-Islamic people, originally pagan, who have lived in the Middle East, including Palestine, since what we call the dawn of human history. The Palestinians are the descendants of the Arabs who were the first and original inhabitants of the land that is today called Israel. And these ancestors of the Palestinians were in possession of that land, as its first and original owners, some 2,000 years or more before the arrival of the first of the ancient Hebrews.

Implicit in Jewish mythology, and actually stated in some Zionist propaganda, is the notion that the Arabs first came to Palestine in the seventh century, at the time when they were being converted to the Moslem faith. This is simply not true. As Cattan says: 'The

Moslem Arab conquest of Palestine did not involve any mass immigration from the Arabs of the Arabian Peninsula into Palestine or any colonization of that country. In fact, the number of invaders was very small and they were assimilated by the indigenous population. Many of the original inhabitants were converted to Islam and, as a consequence, the predominantly [Arab] Christian population became predominantly [Arab] Moslem.'[1]

When the Jews began to trickle back to Palestine in the 1880s, the descendants of those of their faith who had remained in the country since the first Jewish infiltration in about 1200 B.C. or maybe earlier numbered only some 12,000. About the same number returned over the course of many centuries. Thus by 1880 there were some 24,000 Jews in Palestine. And some of those left. The number of Palestinian Arabs at the time was close to 500,000.

The first Israelite occupation of Palestine was only an episode in the history of an Arab country which has been occupied at one time or another by most of the major powers of world history. As Cattan states: 'The Palestinians are the original and continuous inhabitants of Palestine [the land now called Israel] from time immemorial.'[2]

In 1919, America's President Wilson appointed the King-Crane Commission to investigate the Zionist claim that the first Israelite occupation of Palestine gave the Jews a right of title to the land. It said: 'The initial claim, often submitted by Zionist representatives, that they have a "right" to Palestine based on an occupation of two thousand years ago, can hardly be seriously considered.'[3] An overwhelming majority of the 24,000 Jews in residence were, in fact, strongly opposed to the creation of a Jewish State on Arab land.

A year later, during a debate on Palestine in the British House of Lords, and echoing the view of many before and since, Lord Sydenham said: 'I sympathize entirely with the wishes of the Jews to have a national home, but I say this national home must not be given if it cannot be given without entailing gross injustice upon another people. Palestine is not the original home of the Jews. It was acquired by them after conquest, and they have never occupied the whole of it, which they now openly demand. They have no more valid claim to Palestine than the descendants of the ancient Romans have to this country.'[4]

In making the point that the Palestinians are the original and rightful owners of the land that is today called Israel, I am not suggesting that the clock of history either could or should be turned back. Nor am I seeking to deny that in the name of humanity the Jews of the twentieth century have a claim to a presence in Palestine given Judaism's historical links with the land and the circumstances in which the Jews of Europe found themselves as a result of centuries of persecution which climaxed with the Nazi holocaust. My purpose is simply to give the historical record.

The founders of Zionism – originally a movement for the return of the Jews to Palestine – began to work for the support of the big powers of the day in the last years of the nineteenth century. They achieved their breakthrough in November 1917, when the British Foreign Secretary, Arthur James Balfour, wrote his famous letter to Lord Rothschild. The letter, which became known as the Balfour Declaration, announced that the British Government viewed with favour the establishment in Palestine of a 'national home' for the Jewish people, and that the British Government would use 'their best endeavours to facilitate this objective, it being clearly understood that nothing shall be done which may prejudice the civil and religious rights of the existing non-Jewish communities in Palestine'.[5]

The Balfour Declaration seemed to contain two promises – one to the Zionists, the other to the Palestinians. Down the years there has been a lively debate about them. Did the promise to the Zionists not contradict the promise to the Palestinians, and vice versa? The question is academic. At the time the declaration was made, the British had no intention of honouring the promise to the Palestinians.

The real objective of British policy was never openly stated or publicly announced; but the best clue to it – apart from what actually happened in Palestine after the Balfour Declaration, in particular Britain's early refusal to control Jewish immigration – was contained in a memorandum that Balfour wrote on 11 August 1919. He said: 'In Palestine we do not propose even to go through the form of consulting the wishes of the present inhabitants of the country. . . The four great powers are committed to Zionism. And Zionism, be it right or wrong, good or bad, is rooted in agelong traditions, in present needs, in future hopes, of far profounder import than the desires and prejudices of the 700,000 Arabs who now inhabit that ancient land.'[6]

Here, or so the Palestinians believe, is the key to understanding why the State of Israel was created. What were the unmentioned policy objectives to which Balfour was referring when he spoke of 'future hopes' which were far more important than the wishes and the rights of the Palestinians?

Part of Khalad Hassan's answer to that question was the following:

'The British and the others who thought the world was theirs to rule and exploit for their own ends did not give a damn about the Arabs or the Jews as people. What the British saw in the idea of a Jewish State – and what they were encouraged by the Zionists to see – was the opportunity to plant a European colony in the heart of the Arab world, a colony of European Jews which would serve the interests of Britain and her allies.

'At the time of the Balfour Declaration it was obvious to British and other foreign policy strategists that Arab nationalism, then in its infancy, would become a major force and factor in world affairs. It was a fair bet that the slow-burning fires of Arab nationalism would lead, in time, to Arab revolutions which, if they were successful, would produce governments which would not allow Britain and the other big powers to dominate the region for their own ends. Thus, and if there were successful Arab revolutions, Britain and the other big powers would not necessarily be able to control the economic resources and strategic assets of the Arab world. If you think about oil in the context of what I am saying you will quickly get my meaning. As you say in English, the proof of the pudding is in the eating. For many, many years you people in the West robbed the Arabs of their oil. You took what you wanted and you paid peanuts for it. You thought you were being very clever – but you were very stupid. If you had allowed the price of oil to go on rising slowly as the Arabs wanted, the global economy would not have been de-stabilized by an oil price explosion.

'What Britain and the other Europeans needed – in time the Americans also – was a mechanism to disrupt the Arab revolution. This mechanism was the Jewish State. Let me now tell you how Britain and the others believed this mechanism would work for them. And how, in fact, it did.

'The mere existence of the Jewish State and the injustice it represented would be a massive distraction to the Arab regimes. The question of how to deal with the Jewish State and the humiliation it represented to all Arabs would keep the regimes and peoples divided . . . and while the regimes were divided they could be manipulated and played off one against the other. It was the classic game of divide and rule. That was one calculation made by those who supported the creation of the Jewish State.

'Another was that the question of how to deal with the Jewish State, and the inter-Arab division provoked by that question, would make a massive call on the intellectual, political and economic resources of the Arab world. As a consequence of that the Arab states would require more time than would otherwise have been necessary to realize their development potential. The longer the Arab states remained backward and underdeveloped, the more easy it would be for foreign powers to play their divide and rule game. The inter-Arab divisions provoked by the question of how to deal with Israel would be too great for there to be any meaningful Arab unity. If Arab unity could be prevented there would be no substantial challenge to big power control of the politics and economics of the Middle East. Instead of being free to take their own decisions, the Arab regimes would find themselves becoming more and more dependent on the goodwill of the big powers. And because the big powers could control the development of the Arab world, they could also decide when they wanted it to become a market for their goods and services. . . Do you begin to see the whole picture?

'If you examine all the available evidence from an objective point of view, you will see that the plot was not just against the Palestinians – although it was we Palestinians who were required to be expendable, the plot was against the whole region, the whole Arab world. And this is why I always said that our struggle should not start in Palestine – that was only where it had to end. Our struggle should have started in the capitals of the Western world and in Moscow . . . in the capitals of those who were instrumental in creating the Jewish State to serve their own ends at the expense of the Arabs.'

In its essentials, and in many of its details, the Palestinian analysis of why the State of Israel was created is correct. Official documents and the published diaries and accounts of those who played leading roles in the drama of Palestine are littered with evidence which all points to the same conclusion.

The Palestinians attempted a full-scale revolt against the British, mainly to force Britain to stop Jewish immigration. The Palestinian rebellion, which took place in stages between 1936 and 1939, was ruthlessly suppressed. By the autumn of 1938 Britain had some 20,000 troops in the country. In effect, Britain had to reconquer Palestine. The Palestinians not only lost the fight, they also lost their leaders. Some 200-300 were detained and many were deported. Others were liquidated by British intelligence agents who used as their cover the internal struggle for power between rival wings of the Palestinian nationalist movement. By the outbreak of the Second World War the Palestinian nationalist movement had virtually ceased to exist. After the war Britain did allow some Palestinian political émigrés to return to their homeland, but it was clear that most of them were under surveillance and were not free to organize.

Before the State of Israel was proclaimed, perhaps as many as 20,000 Palestinians from the upper classes left the country with as much of their wealth and as many of their possessions as they could take. According to the authorized Israeli version of the story, there were two main reasons why the Palestinians fled. One was that they simply followed the example of their departing leaders who had no stomach for the fight. The other was that the Palestinian people were ordered to leave by their absent leaders in Damascus. Although there were occasions when absent Palestinian leaders did advise particular Palestinian communities to leave, the main reason for the Palestinian exodus was the panic and fear inspired by Jewish terrorism on a scale which the Palestinians have not yet come close to matching. Jewish terror took two forms: actual violence against the Palestinians; and a 'whispering' campaign of threats which the Jews described as 'psychological warfare'. Both were clearly designed to drive the Palestinians from their land.

The most awesome act of Jewish terror was committed at the Palestinian village of Deir Yassin. There, on 10 April 1948, some 260 or more Palestinian men, women and children were slaughtered. Some were slashed to death and one pregnant woman had her stomach cut open with a butcher's knife. That the attacking Jewish forces resorted to such savagery was partly explained by the fact that they encountered stiffer resistance than they had expected and that their homemade Sten guns were jamming and they were running out of ammunition.

This particular attack was a combined operation by the two main

Jewish terror groups: the Irgun, whose Commander-in-Chief was Menachem Begin; and the Stern Gang, one of whose leaders was Yitzhak Shamir who was eventually to succeed Begin as Prime Minister of Israel. Objectively speaking, both men were more authentic, more ruthless and more successful terrorist leaders than any Palestinian.

The official underground army of the Jewish State-in-the-making was the Haganah. One of the first of its officers to arrive on the scene at Deir Yassin after the slaughter described the work of the Irgun and the Stern Gang as 'a premeditated act which had as its intention slaughter and murder only'.[7] Another Haganah officer told the Stern Gang commander: 'You are swine.'[8]

Britain's last High Commissioner in Palestine was so outraged by what happened at Deir Yassin that he was in favour of using British forces to punish those responsible. When he was informed that no British ground forces were available – a phased British withdrawal from Palestine had been under way since February – he considered the possibility of an air strike against Irgun and Stern Gang positions. There were, however, no light bombers immediately available; and, anyway, London would not have authorized the strike. It should be added that Cunningham's anger was not simply the consequences of what had happened at Deir Yassin. In the last years of Britain's occupation of Palestine, Cunningham and many British officers and men were furious that London would not allow them to fight the Irgun and the Stern Gang with the gloves off. The British did, however, put a price on Begin's head. Underneath the Irgun leader's photograph on the 'Wanted' list was the following description: 'Height: 173 cms. Build: thin. Complexion: sallow. Hair: dark. Eyes: brown. Nose: long, hooked. Peculiarities: wears spectacles; flat-footed; bad teeth. Nationality: Polish.' It is interesting to note that many official Jewish leaders wanted Begin dead because he was too extreme. In Arafat's case, a few of his former colleagues wanted him dead because he was too moderate.

Jewish terrorists had turned against the British with a vengeance after London had announced in 1939 that it was not Britain's policy to allow Palestine to become a Jewish State. Britain's motives for this apparent turn about were mixed. One calculation was entirely cynical. Britain could not afford to have the Arabs as enemies in the coming war with Nazi Germany. Another factor was that some

British ministers were beginning to comprehend, much too late, the inevitable and disastrous consequences of the Palestine policy that had been set in motion by the Balfour Declaration of 1917.

In 1983, and quite by chance, I bumped into a very senior former British officer who was in Palestine at the time. On the condition that I did not quote him by name he told me the following: 'You will never know how angry we were at not being allowed to fight the Jewish terrorists. We were close to mutiny. It is a part of the story of Palestine that will be censored for ever and a day. But I will tell you this much. When my boys were murdered by the Irgun and the Stern Gang we used to go hunting their killers in our civilian clothes. We usually knew who the bastards were. And when we found them we knocked them off.'

On the subject of Deir Yassin and its profound implications for the Palestinians there is no better authority to quote than Menachem Begin himself. He was later to write with pride that 'This crude atrocity story had a good result.' It was that 'Arab propaganda spread a legend of terror among Arabs and Arab troups, who were seized with panic at the mention of Irgun soldiers. The legend was worth half a dozen battalions to the forces of Israel. . . Panic overwhelmed the Arabs of Eretz Israel. Kolonia village, which had previously repulsed every attack by the Haganah, was evacuated overnight and fell without further fighting. Beit-Iksa was also evacuated. . . In the rest of the country, too, the Arabs began to flee in terror, even before they clashed with Jewish forces. . . All the Jewish forces proceeded to advance through Haifa like a knife through butter. The Arabs began fleeing in panic shouting "Deir Yassin".'[9]

In retrospect it is easy for everyone, including the Palestinians themselves, to say that broadcasting the full horrific story of the slaughter at Deir Yassin was a fatal mistake. The publicity was bound to lead to much greater panic among the Palestinians and a speeding up of the exodus. So why did the Palestinians broadcast the news? The sad truth is that those who took the decision were afraid that the Arab armies were not coming to Palestine's rescue. With good reason, it was feared that Arab leaders, despite their promises and their boasts, would find some excuse to stay out of the fighting when the crunch came. After much agonizing the Palestinians responsible for what was broadcast decided to tell the full story of Deir Yassin in the hope that it would shock public opinion in the Arab world and, by so doing, force the regimes to act.

In their attempts to minimize or even dismiss the significance of Deir Yassin, some Israeli propagandists have pointed out that about one-third of the Palestinians had fled before the slaughter there. That much is true; as a general rule civilians do flee from fighting.

Deir Yassin was not the only place where Palestinians were massacred. Nasr Al-Din, Ain Al-Zeitouneh, Al-Bina, Al-Bassa and Safsaf were also places where Palestinian communities suffered at the hands of Jewish terrorists.

Another Israeli leader who was later to reveal more of the truth about the main cause of the Palestinian exodus was Yigal Allon, Deputy Prime Minister by the time of his death. In 1948 Allon was the Commander of the Palmach, the strike force of the Haganah. His account of the history of the Palmach includes the story of how he practised what he called psychological warfare in the Upper Galilee. He was anxious, he said, to 'cleanse' the area of Arabs without using his own exhausted troops. 'I gathered all the Jewish Mukhtars [local religious leaders] who had contacts with the Arabs in different villages, and asked them to whisper into the Arabs' ears that a great Jewish force had arrived in Galilee and that it was going to burn all the villages of the Huleh. They should suggest to those Arabs that they flee while there was still time.'[10]

The plan worked. The Arabs of the Upper Galilee did flee. Similar whispering campaigns were conducted in other parts of Palestine with the same effect. They were in fact a feature of Zionist military policy from the time of the U.N. Partition Resolution because the Palestinians were not only the majority in the territory assigned to the Arab state under the Partition Plan, they were also close to being the majority in the territory allotted to the Jews. As an absolute first priority the area of the Jewish State-to-be had therefore to be 'cleansed' of its Arabs.

There is also good evidence that some Palestinians were frightened out of their homes and their country by telephone and bomb threats. Such threats were a speciality of the Irgun and Stern Gang. It was the Jews who introduced the letter-bomb to the conflict.

In 1947, unwilling and perhaps by then unable to solve the problem it had done most to create by failing to control Jewish immigration to Palestine, Britain gave up trying to reconcile the conflicting but far from equal claims of the Palestinians and the Jews to the same piece of land. In short, Britain washed its hands of the problem of Palestine and asked the United Nations to deal with it.

On 29 November the U.N. General Assembly approved a plan for the partition of Palestine. It allotted fifty-seven per cent of the country to the Jews, despite the fact that they were less than one-third of the population and owned less than six per cent of the land. The U.N.'s decision had no validity in international law. I can do no better than quote Cattan:

'The legal position is quite clear in this regard. The U.N. is an organization of states which was formed for certain purposes defined in the Charter. At no time did this organization possess any sovereignty or any other right over Palestine. Accordingly, the U.N. possessed no power to decide the partition of Palestine, or to assign any part of its territory to a religious minority of alien immigrants in order that they might establish a state of their own. The U.N. could not give away what it did not possess. Neither individually, nor collectively, could the members of the U.N. alienate, reduce or impair the sovereignty of the people of Palestine, or dispose of their territory or destroy by partition the territorial integrity of their country.'[11]

The Partition Plan would not have been approved if a number of the smaller nations who were members of the U.N. had been allowed to vote freely. It was approved only because the U.S., with the tacit support of the Soviet Union, intimidated a number of small states whose votes were needed for the necessary majority. The U.S. in turn was influenced by the Jewish lobby. On this subject the U.S. Secretary of Defense, James Forrestal, was later to write: 'I thought it was a most disastrous and regrettable fact that the foreign policy of this country was determined by the contributions a particular bloc of special interests might make to party funds.'[12]

When the Palestinians and their Arab brothers rejected partition, war in Palestine was inevitable. One of the Palestinian students who threw himself into the struggle was Yasser Arafat. He was nineteen.

Eight hours before British rule in Palestine came to an end at midnight on 14 May 1948, the Jews in the country declared their independence and the State of Israel was proclaimed the following day. Under the leadership of David Ben-Gurion, the Israelis were quietly delighted that the Arabs had rejected partition and were going to fight. If partition had been implemented, the Jews, at least to start with, would have been obliged to settle for only fifty-seven per cent of Palestine. In war, and as Ben-Gurion himself said, they would take what they could get. From here on the borders of the State of Israel would be determined by force and without regard for the rights of the Palestinians or the wishes of the international community.

Though desperately short of weapons, the Palestinians escalated their own struggle against the Jews as soon as the Partition Plan was approved. The Arab regimes – with the arguable exception of Egypt's corrupt King Farouk none of them really wanted to fight – did not commit elements of their own forces until the State of Israel actually came into being. Israel's War of Independence began officially on 15 May when forces from Egypt, Jordan, Syria, Iraq and the Lebanon attacked the new Jewish State.

Until the first truce organized by the U.N. on 11 June, and despite the incompetence of the Arab fighting forces and what Arafat describes as the 'treachery' of the Arab regimes, the Israelis were in real trouble. It is possible that they would have been defeated if the Egyptians had gone straight for Tel Aviv. But the first truce, which lasted for thirty days, was the decisive turning point in Israel's favour. Under the terms of the truce the combatants were not to be supplied with ammunition or weapons. During it the Arabs received not one bullet from their Western suppliers. Israel used the truce to acquire ammunition and weapons of all kinds, mainly from Czechoslovakia. As a consequence, the Israelis were in a position to dictate the course and the outcome of the war when the fighting was resumed. After the first truce it was a one-sided contest between 60,000 well-equipped Israelis – the Israel Defence Force was born during the truce – and 21,500 poorly equipped Arab troops.

When the fighting was eventually stopped by a series of Armistice Agreements in 1949, Israel was in possession of all the land allotted to it by the Partition Plan and more than half of the land allotted to the Palestinians. The other half was claimed by Jordan and Egypt. Palestine had ceased to exist. That was one consequence of the fighting. The other was the creation of what is called the Palestinian 'refugee problem'. By mid-1949 nearly one million Palestinians were outside their own homeland in the Arab countries surrounding the new Jewish State. The Arab population of Israel was down to 139,000.

The vast majority of Palestinians did not expect to become permanent refugees. In their innocence and their ignorance most thought they would be back in their homes when the Arab armies had defeated the Jews. In Cairo, the Commander-in-Chief of the Egyptian army, Mohammed Haidar, had boasted that there would be no war with the Jews. 'It will be a parade without any risk whatsoever. The army will be in Tel Aviv in two weeks.'[13] It was said that Haidar owed his position to the fact that he was a fool who made King Farouk laugh. Egypt's Prime Minister, Mahmoud Nokrasy, did not believe Haidar. Nokrasy knew the true state of the Egyptian army. The money that should have been used to re-equip it had been spent by Farouk and his relations and friends on pleasure. Originally Nokrasy had advised Farouk to keep their country out of the war. But in the end, and to retain his job, he had gone along with the wishes of his corrupt sovereign.

The belief that the Jews would be defeated in two weeks was also proclaimed in other Arab capitals, and the Palestinian people allowed themselves to be fooled. The problem was not so much that the Palestinians were excessively naive. Their real tragedy was that they were leaderless.

In May 1948, the U.N. had appointed Count Folke Bernadotte to mediate between the Arabs and the Israelis. In Jerusalem on 16 September he had just completed his first progress report. It contained the recommendation that the U.N. should affirm 'the right of the Arab refugees to return to their homes in Jewish-controlled territory at the earliest possible date'.[14] The following day Bernadotte was murdered by Jewish terrorists. In Israel it was widely believed that Mr Shamir's Stern Gang was responsible. In December U.N. Resolution 194 did affirm the right of the Palestinians to return to their homes or be compensated.

President Truman was later to demand that Israel should give up the additional territory it had captured during the fighting and return to the borders as defined by the Partition Plan. In fact, Truman quietly applied very strong pressure on Israel for concessions on both the border and the refugee problems. The Israelis not only rejected the President's demands, in their own quiet way they also warned him that they could and would turn the American Jewish community against him if he did not drop his demands. It was the blackmail card that successive Israeli governments were to use on each and every American President in turn. Politics being what they are, Israel cannot be blamed for playing the game the way it does. The real tragedy is that successive American Presidents have always given in to the blackmail; and by so doing they have allowed the elected representatives of some three million Israelis to determine vital aspects of American foreign policy. Today the cause for alarm about the true nature of the so-called special relationship between Israel and America is the fact that Israel's arrogance and intransigence has become the major threat to U.S. and Western interests in the Middle East. Not nearly enough Americans can yet see this; but that is the reality of the present developing and deteriorating situation in the Middle East.

The essence of the Palestinian struggle since 1948, what it is that the Palestinians have really been up against, is that in 1949, when the majority of the Palestinian people were homeless and stateless as a consequence of Israel's second coming, the governments of the West and the regimes of the Arab world shared, for different reasons, the same unspoken hope. It was that the Palestinian problem would disappear.

The State of Israel came into being because Britain and the great powers of the day saw its existence as the best possible guarantee that the Arabs would remain weak and divided and unable to mount a successful challenge to big-power control and exploitation of the region's resources and strategic assets. It was for that cause that the Palestinians were required to be expendable. Their real crime is that they refused to disappear.

But there is another side to the story which needs to be emphasized.

The Zionists were not naive or stupid. They knew they were being used by Britain and the big powers. Indeed the Zionists asked to be used. And they were aware from the beginning that the day could come when Israel would be the victim and not the beneficiary of the political expediency and the opportunism that were and are the main factors which determine the foreign policies of governments the world over, in particular those which backed the creation of the Jewish State to serve their own ends. The Zionists knew that the foreign powers that had supported the creation of the State of Israel might one day decide that their best interests would be served by switching sides, in which case the Jews of Israel would become the expendable ones. Golda Meir and Moshe Dayan were just two of many Israeli leaders who told me in private that they honestly believed such a day would come.

This helps to explain why the Jewish State has become the military superpower of the Middle East. As we shall see one primary objective of successive Israeli governments was to accumulate sufficient military strength to enable the Jewish State not only to keep the Arab armies at bay, but also to frighten the Arab states into taking actions of their own to suppress and eliminate Palestinian nationalism. Israel's other primary objective was to acquire enough military and politial power to deter its friends, the U.S. in particular, from even thinking about selling the Jewish State down the proverbial river. Israel, it could be said, has planned for the day when the big powers would require it to be the sacrifical lamb on the altar of political expediency. Here also is the real reason why successive Israeli governments have deceived their own people and world public opinion about the true nature of the Arab and Palestinian military threat. For obvious reasons, sucessive Israeli governments could not afford to say in public what they knew to be the truth, that the day could come when Israel would be betrayed by friendly powers just as surely as the same friendly powers betrayed the Palestinians.

The above analysis invites the conclusion that it is not the Jews who are the real villains in the story. Israel has merely played the Game of Nations according to the rules. The real villains are those leaders who, down the years, have created a world order or system in which might is right and justice for its own sake has no place. This conclusion is shared by Yasser Arafat and every Palestinian leader to whom I have talked.

It is true that after 1948 the Arab regimes proclaimed the total liberation of Palestine to be a sacred cause and duty as well as the goal to which they said they were committed. It is true, too, that the Arab regimes would have destroyed Israel if they could have done so. But the truth is also that they knew they could not, and that is why they never had any intention of fighting Israel to liberate even a part of Palestine.

The fact that the Arab regimes knew they could not defeat Israel on the battlefield emerges with clarity from the pages which follow. For now it is enough to say that most Arab leaders knew the real fight was not with the two to three million Jews of Israel. If any part of Palestine was to be liberated, the real fight would have to be with the big powers who had created Israel to serve their own ends, and who would protect and defend the Jewish State as long as its existence was serving their overall policy objectives in the region.

Another reality which the Arab regimes had to take account of when, behind closed doors, they considered their real options, was the fact that the Soviet Union was as committed to Israel's existence as were the Western powers. It was well known that Soviet leaders had supported the creation of the Jewish State because they had calculated that its existence would provoke an Arab reaction which, over the years, Moscow could exploit for its own ends. But immediately after 1948 the fact of the Soviet Union's commitment to the Jewish State was more important than the reasons for it.

After 1948 Arab leaders drew, in private, the only possible conclusion: liberating Palestine meant confronting and, in effect, defeating the foreign powers who, by virtue of the military, economic and political levers in their hands, controlled the world. Liberating Palestine was therefore a mission impossible as long as the big powers wanted the State of Israel to survive. The essential problem for the Arab regimes, as for Israel's leaders, was that they could not tell their masses the truth. And the more impotent the regimes were made to feel by demonstrations of Israel's growing military might, the more they talked about fighting and defeating Israel. It was Arab words not Arab actions that gave credibility to Israel's propaganda claim that the country faced the prospect of annihilation.

In the context of the Palestinian struggle for at least a measure of justice, the significance of the impotence of the Arab regimes as summarized above cannot be exaggerated. It meant that the Palestinians were totally alone in their struggle. Because of their impotence the Arab regimes became, in effect, more the allies of the Western powers and Israel than reliable supporters of the Palestinian cause. It was, as we shall see, Arab regimes and not Israeli forces who made the first attempt to liquidate the Palestinian resistance movement of which Yasser Arafat became the leader.

Very many Palestinians believe that successive Arab regimes, from before 1948 to the present, have been consistent in their betrayal of the Palestinian cause. But Khalad Hassan is one who, generally speaking, refuses to condemn the regimes as traitors. And on this subject he speaks for a number of his equally perceptive colleagues in the leadership of the P.L.O. Cynics will say that Khalad Hassan and his colleagues cannot afford to condemn the regimes as traitors because they need and must work with them. But such a charge would be unfair. Khalad summed up his own feelings in the following way:

'You can say almost anything you like about the Arab regimes and it will be true. They were and are corrupt. They were and are incompetent – they do not know how to play their cards. Almost all Arab leaders are the prisoners of their intelligence services and are, as a consequence, out of touch with the feelings of their masses. Most Arab leaders rule by repression. Essentially the Arab regimes are illegitimate. And so on. But you cannot say the regimes were traitors. To be a traitor you must take a concrete decision. You must want to betray. It was never the case that the regimes wanted to betray us. They have acted in the way we know because they perceived themselves to be impotent in the face of what they and we regard as a big-power conspiracy to dominate and control the strategic assets and resources of the Middle East. If you want to know the truth, the real problem of the Arab regimes is that they have the psychology of defeat and defence. And that is the product and the consequence of the impotence they feel.'

In time and as conceived by Khalad Hassan and the others of his generation who came together to form the leadership of Fatah, one objective of the renewed Palestinian struggle was to break the Arab psychology of defeat and defence. Israel's strategy was to reinforce it. But in the 1950s Fatah's leaders-to-be were barely out of their teens. Most of them, as Khalad says, were idealistic, naive and ignorant about the true nature of the struggle that lay ahead of them. In the beginning they did not appreciate that there was such a thing as an Arab psychology of defeat and that it would prove to be the biggest obstacle in their way. They had much to learn.

# The Underground Years

# 3

# 'Touched by Treachery'

Mohammed Yasser Arafat was born in Cairo on 24 August 1929. He was the last but one of the seven children from his father's first marriage. The first-born was Inam, Yasser's eldest sister. His two other sisters were named Yosra and Khadiga. They were the third and fifth of the children. The second and the fourth were boys, Gamal and Moustapha. The last of the seven was Fathe, Yasser's younger brother.

Though the first name on his birth certificate was Mohammed, Inam said that her brother was called Yasser from the beginning. Yasser means 'easy' or, more generally speaking, 'no problem'.

Yasser's mother was a large, big-boned woman with a round but happy face. Her name was Zahwa – it means 'pride' and 'beauty'; and she was from the Abu Saud family of Jerusalem. It was one of the Holy City's most distinguished and respected families and claims a direct line to the Prophet Muhammad.

Abder Rauf Arafat, Yasser's father, was from the Qudwa family of Gaza and Khan Yunis. It was related to what Khalad Hassan described as the 'poor side' of the Husseini clan, which means that Yasser Arafat was a relative of Haj Amin Husseini who was, in the eyes of the Jews, the personification of evil on the Palestinian side. Despite the fact that he was not greatly admired by Palestine's educated elite, Haj Amin was the effective leader of the Palestinians after his appointment as Mufti of Jerusalem by the British in 1922. Britain occupied Palestine during the First World War. Against the wishes of Palestine's own Moslem notables, the British gave Haj

Amin the job of Mufti because they hoped it would make him their man. For a while he did co-operate with the British, and he did try to restrain those of his people who argued that only by violence could British and Zionist designs for Palestine be thwarted. But when violence became the chosen way of a majority of the ordinary Arab people of Palestine, Haj Amin and other leaders had the choice of leading from the front or losing their credibility. By the time of the Palestinian rebellion against the British in the second half of the 1930s, Haj Amin was the number-one enemy of Britain and the Zionists. In exile he moved to Nazi Germany where, from 1941 to 1945, he had the ear of Hitler. When that became known it was easy for Zionist propagandists to imply that the Palestinian leadership was virtually a co-instigator of the holocaust. The charge was ludicrous but inevitable in the circumstances. What is true is that Haj Amin was one of very many Arab leaders who hoped for a Nazi victory in the belief that nothing less could prevent the British from controlling the Middle East at the expense of the Arabs in general, and the Palestinians in particular.

Abder Rauf Arafat and his family took up residence in Cairo in 1927, two years before Yasser's birth. Why he moved out of Palestine remains a mystery. Some suggest that he was one of hundreds of Palestinians with strong nationalist feelings who were quietly exiled by the British. Those who believe he was exiled say this is the implication of the fact that he sold all of the land he owned in Palestine. According to Hamid Abu Sitta, Yasser Arafat once said with despair and a touch of anger: 'My father didn't leave me even two metres of Palestine.' More likely Abder Rauf Arafat simply decided that his business interests would best be served by living in Cairo. Many others did.

It was as a wholesale trader dealing mainly in foodstuffs that Abder Rauf Arafat earned his living. His most successful enterprise was a factory for making cheese which was canned and distributed throughout the Arab world.

By all accounts he was a man with great physical strength and an iron will. According to Inam he walked between fifteen and twenty miles a day – 'three miles from our home to his office and back and the rest calling on clients'. Inam also remembers her father as an excitable and passionate man who was 'always shouting'. But he seems to have been a kind man, too. Said Inam: 'I think he made quite a lot of money from his business but we never saw much of it as a family. He was always receiving calls for help from the poor people in Palestine and he never said no. He was not a man who lived for himself.' Inam added: 'It would be true to say that we were not wealthy in the material sense – but we were very rich in our minds.'

Yasser Arafat himself is unwilling to talk about his family life because, I think, he does not want to reopen old family wounds. All I could extract from him on the subject were two pieces of information. The first was his grudging confirmation that his childhood days were unhappy ones. 'It was so,' was all he would say. If Inam had not been willing to answer my questions, Arafat's early life would have remained a complete mystery.

The event which most determined the unhappy course of Arafat's early life was the death of his mother in 1933. Said Inam: 'She had trouble with her kidneys and one week after the problem started she was dead. In those days the doctors were not so advanced.'

At the time Yasser was four and his brother Fathe was eighteen months old. 'When my mother died Fathe and I were sent to live with our uncle, Salim Abu Saud, in Jerusalem.' That was the second and last piece of information given to me about those early days by Yasser Arafat himself.

The four years in which Yasser and Fathe lived in Jerusalem are a blank. The only reminder of them is a photograph taken of Yasser when he was about five. One of Arafat's colleagues said it showed an obviously miserable young boy. From Inam I learned that Uncle Salim was not wealthy, a comment which I took to mean that he was actually poor.

When Abder Rauf married his second wife, Yasser and Fathe returned to the Arafat home in Cairo, and to disaster. The stepmother was cruel to the Arafat children and the house became more or less a battlefield. The shouting and the rows, mainly between the females of the household, hurt and scarred Yasser. From that moment on and for nearly twenty years he became, to an extent, anti-women. Some fifteen years later he was to say to a fellow student at university that he had not so much as shaken the hand of a woman.

In response to the protests of the Arafat children, Abder Rauf dismissed his second wife within months of the marriage. Before long he married again and new arrangements within the Arafat household helped to limit the scope for further domestic strife. His third wife had her own quarters, and Inam was given the responsibility for bringing up her younger sisters and brothers. That is Inam's version of what happened. On the rare occasions that Yasser has discussed his family life with his closest colleagues he has always denied that he was brought up by his eldest sister. The contradiction is perhaps explained by the fact that the young Arafat resented and resisted Inam's attempts to control his life, partly because she was a woman, and partly because his own fiercely independent spirit was asserting itself. Earlier I quoted Khalad Hassan as telling President Sadat that Arafat was a man who could not be dominated by anybody. I believe that was the case from 1939 or thereabouts, when the future Chairman of the P.L.O. was ten years old.

When Yasser was nine or ten it was clear to Inam that her brother was 'not like other children either in playing or his feelings. Soon after the outbreak of the Second World War, Yasser was gathering the Arab kids of the district. He formed them into groups and made them march and drill. He carried a stick and he used to beat those who did not obey his commands. He also liked making camps in the garden of our house. And he always joined in Egyptian demonstrations. Many times I ran after him to bring him back home . . . to try to keep him out of trouble.'

From the age of ten it seems that Arafat was both a natural leader and a bully. But he also demonstrated that he had inherited his father's kindness as well as his temper. Said Inam: 'Yasser shared everything with everybody. Even the smallest piece of chocolate was shared with others. He never cared about himself. One day I brought new suits for Yasser and Fathe. Yasser made a scene and refused to wear his unless the poor kids of the area had new suits too!'

According to Inam, Yasser's energy was the subject of comment by some of the Jewish mothers in their neighbourhood. 'I remember being stopped by one of our Jewish neighbours,' said Inam. 'She said to me: "Your Yasser is so active and so clever. I think it's fish that makes boys bright. Do you feed him on fish?"'

It was after his return to Cairo from Jerusalem that Yasser, then eight years old, began to take a conscious interest in the Jews and their ways. Said Inam: 'He had been back in Cairo only a short time when he started to go to the places and the clubs where the Jews gathered. He told us that he wanted to study their mentality.'

At this point in our conversation Inam smiled and said, 'There is a funny story – but I am not sure if I should tell it to you. . . Yasser had his own special way of annoying the Jews of our neighbourhood. When the official morning prayers were over he used to go into the streets and shout at the top of his voice "God is Great! God is Great!" His only purpose was to wake the Jews who were still sleeping!'

Inam's confrontation with her brother as she struggled to play the role of mother became more acute in Yasser's teenage years. Throughout them the cause of a good deal of friction between the two was Yasser's poor record of attendance at secondary school. 'On this matter,' said Inam, 'he gave me many troubles. Our relatives used to telephone me and say "You must make Yasser go to school!" The trouble was that Yasser did go to school. Often I used to escort him myself. But he would slip away from the classroom. And often when I went to school to escort him home he was not there. The only time he seemed to be seriously interested in study was at home in the evenings with his friends. But he was acting. I used to take tea to his room, and as I approached Yasser would say, "Here comes the general!" When I entered the room Yasser and his friends would pretend to be doing their homework – but really they were discussing political and military matters.'

What was Arafat up to on the many occasions when he slipped away from school? The answer seems to be that he was getting himself a political education. According to one story that I heard he was working as a tea-boy in the Majlis, Egypt's parliament, at the age of thirteen or fourteen. When I asked Arafat if the story was true, he replied: 'It was not exactly like that but I was very close to politics as a boy. I had this opportunity partly through my relatives and partly through my own ways.'

In 1946, shortly before his seventeenth birthday, Arafat became a key figure in an operation to smuggle guns and ammunition to Palestine from Egypt.

To those exiled Palestinian leaders who had hoped that the Second World War would see the end of British influence in the Middle East and thus, also, the end of Britain's support for the

Zionist cause, the defeat of Nazi Germany and the Axis powers meant only one thing – the Palestinians would have to fight if they were not to lose part and perhaps all of their homeland. In May 1946, Haj Amin Husseini returned to Cairo to organize the second round of the struggle against the Zionist presence and British policy. It was said that the French had helped him to escape from Nazi Germany in return for a promise that he would not denounce their efforts to maintain their influence in Algeria, Morocco and Tunisia.

The Arab nationalists inside Palestine did not need Haj Amin to tell them they had to fight. They knew that. Their problem was that they did not have nearly enough weapons. The Jews on the other hand were well armed in comparison to the Palestinians. The British had allowed the development and the arming of the Haganah, the underground but official Jewish army in Palestine. And during the Second World War the British had commissioned the Jews of Palestine to make some small-arms ammunition – grenades and mines in particular. Not surprisingly a proportion of these supplies intended for British forces in the Middle East were diverted to Jewish stores. And the ability of the Jews to go on manufacturing other small arms and ammunition did not end with the war. On the other side the Palestinians were prevented by the British from organizing and arming. Abu Jihad and Khalad Hassan told me that Palestinians were hanged for being in possession of bullets and knives.

By early 1947 the Palestinians had become quite proficient at smuggling arms from Egypt to Palestine. Arafat's job was to acquire weapons – rifles were the priority – when agents brought the money to Cairo from Palestine. In the early days of the operation Arafat's main task was simply to guide those who came seeking weapons to the places where they were available in Cairo and Alexandria. Because he spoke Arabic with an Egyptian accent, Arafat also negotiated the price. The locals assumed he was an Egyptian and that greatly reduced the chance of the Palestinians being overcharged.

When the supplies in the cities began to dry up, the job of acquiring arms became a dangerous one. The next best source was the tribes of the desert. And getting through to them meant running the gauntlet of bandits and thieves who would kill for much less than the money carried by those seeking to purchase arms, or the rifles that their money did buy. It was the young Arafat who volunteered for the most dangerous of these missions. And it was Arafat's success as a gun-runner in what he himself described as 'these very difficult times' that earned the future leader of the P.L.O. his early reputation as a man of courage. Abu Adeeb is today the P.L.O.'s chief representative in Kuwait and also a close friend of the Chairman. He told me: 'When I arrived in Cairo as a student in the early 1950s, I remember meeting an old man who said that he and many others had been frightened to go where Arafat had gone to purchase guns. The same old man also predicted that Yasser Arafat would become the leader of our people.'

On his return to Cairo from one of his gun-running expeditions, Arafat paid a visit to a scrap-metal dealer. He was intending to buy a broken and battered armoured car that he had previously noticed in the dealer's yard. As Arafat stood gazing at the wreck the dealer approached him. 'Surely you are not interested in that?' he asked. 'It's no use. It's finished.'

'Oh yes, I am interested,' Arafat replied. 'I want to buy it.'

'Then you must be stupid,' said the dealer.

'In that case, you must take pity on me,' Arafat replied, 'and you should let me have it for very little money.'

The next day he returned to the dealer's yard with thirty or forty of his friends. Under Arafat's direction, and with much cursing, they pushed the armoured car to the Foreign Ministry. There it was draped with banners and became the focus of a demonstration which called on the Egyptian Government to make arms available to the Palestinians. Arafat apparently had not the smallest hope that the Egyptian authorities would respond to his request. He had planned the demonstration more as a boost to morale after the U.N. vote on the Partition Plan.

The confirmation that Palestine was to be partitioned led to an escalation of the fighting between Zionist forces and the Palestinian guerrillas whose capacity to fight had been much improved by Arafat's gun-running activities. By early 1948, and despite the fact that most Arab regimes were refusing to send them weapons, the Palestinians were not unhappy with their performance on the battlefield. But on 8 April there came news that made many Palestinians weep with despair. Abdul Khader Husseini had been killed in the battle for the control of Jerusalem. Abdul Khader was by far the greatest Palestinian fighter. Even Jewish military commanders – and later, Israeli historians and commentators – had a profound respect for his courage and his understanding of tactics and strategy. This legendary Palestinian fighter had made his name in the rebellion against the British. Then, in 1938, he was sent by Haj Amin Husseini to Nazi Germany for training. In 1941 Abdul Khader returned to Cairo where his home became the operational headquarters for the next phase of the military struggle against the Zionists. He returned to Palestine to lead the fight at the end of 1947.

One of Abdul Khader's disciples was Hamid Abu Sitta. When the news of Abdul Khader's death reached Cairo, Abu Sitta was a third-year engineering student at the University of Fuad the First. Yasser Arafat, then nearly nineteen, was in his first or preparatory year at the same university. He, too, was studying engineering. Abu Sitta called a meeting of the Palestinian students at the university. They gathered in the meeting place of the Moslem Brotherhood. When they were all assembled Abu Sitta made a short but dramatic speech. 'This is not the time for study,' he said. 'Our country is being taken away from us. What purpose will our study serve if we have no country? We must go to Palestine to fight!' During the applause and the chants of approval that followed, Abu Sitta took a box of matches from his pocket and set light to his books.

In 1983 when he was recalling that moment, Abu Sitta said this: 'The first to follow my example was Yasser Arafat. He was holding a book and some papers. He put those on the fire. He was very enthusiastic. Very passionate. Our fathers had been friends for many years and I had known Yasser since 1946. But never had I seen him so excited.'

As many books and papers were added to the flames, Abu Sitta made another statement. He told the assembled students that he was intending to move to Palestine without delay. 'But most of you are without experience of fighting,' he said. 'You must get yourselves trained and then you must follow.' Abu Sitta had received his military training at one of Abdul Khader's bases in Syria the previous year. He had also been taught how to make bombs in the kitchen of Abdul Khader's house in Cairo. On one occasion they caused an explosion and a fire in the kitchen. 'It happened,' Abu Sitta recalled with a smile, 'while Abdul Khader was teaching how to use nitric and sulphuric acid to melt bridges.'

When the book-burning ceremony was over, Arafat took Abu Sitta to one side. 'I am going to Palestine with you,' he said. 'I am ready to fight. When do we leave?'

Abu Sitta put an arm round Arafat's shoulder. 'My dear Yasser . . . you are too young and too inexperienced. We are going to fight real battles. We are not playing games. You get yourself trained, then follow me.'

Arafat pulled himself free of Abu Sitta's embrace. He was close to losing his temper. 'I know how to fight. I have completed my training. I am going with you.'

Like many other people, Abu Sitta has assumed that Arafat received his first military training from the Moslem Brotherhood and that he was, for a time, a member of that organization. It was not so. When I asked Arafat himself about his first military training, his answer was short and to the point. 'I was trained secretly by a German officer who returned to Cairo with my relatives.' I also asked Arafat if he had spent a great deal of time in the company of Haj Amin Husseini. His reply was, 'Not so much.' The man Arafat looked to as the leader was Abdul Khader Husseini. And it was probably Abdul Khader who had the greatest influence on Arafat's early thinking.

So it was, on a day in April 1948, that Abu Sitta, Yasser Arafat and a third man set off for Palestine. The third man was a Major in the Egyptian army, and probably a member of the Moslem Brotherhood.

They travelled by train from Cairo to El Qantara. But having no visas or official papers of any kind they had to avoid customs officers and the border police at the official Suez Canal crossing point. While Abu Sitta and Arafat went to ground, the Major used his influence to acquire a small boat. When night came they rowed across the canal.

Said Abu Sitta: 'Today when I think about it I have to smile. When we got into the boat, Arafat and I were without weapons. Arafat whispered to the Major: "Here we are, three men going to fight the Jews. Three men with only one weapon. We must be crazy."

'The Major laughed softly. "Don't worry," he whispered back. "I have a small surprise for you. Feel down there." There were some rifles and pistols in the bottom of the boat.'

When they had crossed the canal they made their way to Gaza.

And there they separated. The Major and Arafat went south-west to join a unit of Moslem Brotherhood fighters which was besieging the Jewish settlement of Kfar Darome. Abu Sitta went to the south-east, to Beersheba. He was of bedouin stock from that area and he had decided to fight in the part of his country he knew best.

According to Abu Sitta's memory, a Jewish force supported by some 'twenty-four tanks' – they were probably armour-plated vehicles or homemade tanks – launched an attack close to Beersheba on 10 May. After some fierce fighting, the Jews broke through the Palestinian lines. 'Then,' said Abu Sitta, 'I noticed that half of the Jewish tanks were moving away in the direction of Kfar Darome. They were going to try to break the siege there. I sent a messenger on horse to warn the Moslem Brothers and to tell them to prepare an ambush. And that's what happened. The Brothers had some artillery pieces and some mortars. As the Jewish tanks descended the slope of Kfar Darome the Brothers knocked out the first and the last and the rest were trapped. All the Jewish tanks were destroyed and the Jewish soldiers who were still alive retreated.'

On 14 May, the last day of British rule in Palestine and the eve of Israel's declaration of independence, Abu Sitta was ordered by his father to return to Cairo. 'Tomorrow,' said his father, 'the Arab armies are coming. They will do the job quickly. You must return to your studies.'

Later that day Abu Sitta started out for Cairo but he went via Kfar Darome. 'We had taken a beating at our place and I wanted a taste of victory before returning to Cairo. Arafat was pleased to see me. He thought I might have been killed. We embraced and the Brothers told me that Yasser had fired the mortar that had knocked out the first Jewish tank.'

Abu Sitta's main memory of that day was the way in which Arafat took control when the Brothers, all of them Egyptian volunteers, started to take bits and pieces of the knocked-out Jewish tanks for souvenirs. 'Arafat was very firm. He told them it was not the way for soldiers to behave on the battlefield, even if they were volunteers.'

When the two friends parted on the eve of what came to be called Israel's War of Independence, Arafat was confident that the Palestinians could defeat the Jews, provided they received the necessary arms and ammunition. The Palestinian leadership of the day, headed by Arafat's relatives, had not wanted the Arab armies to intervene. They agreed with King Abdul Aziz of Saudi Arabia that if the Arab regimes committed their own forces this would internationalize the conflict and it would then become impossible to resolve. The King's idea was that the Arab regimes should supply the Palestinians with the necessary weapons to fight their own war. It is Arafat's opinion that the Palestinians could have defeated the Jews if the regimes had taken the advice of the Saudi King.

But it was not to be. Hours after Abu Sitta and Yasser Arafat parted – Abu Sitta to return to Cairo, Arafat to continue the fight – Israel declared its independence and was attacked by elements of five Arab armies with the results we know.

When we talked about this period of his life and the making of the Palestinian tragedy, Arafat told me that in the years immediately following the war he had the opportunity to study and analyse many of the secret documents of the Arab League, which had its headquarters in Cairo. 'I was still very young but because of my family relationships I was very close to the Palestinian policy-makers, and I had the opportunity to discover the real cause of our tragedy. So many unbelievable things I discovered.' I asked Arafat what conclusion he came to as a result of his studies and his own experience on the battlefield in Palestine. He replied with one sentence. 'The truth is that we were betrayed – by the Arab regimes and, I am sorry to say it, by the British who worked so hard to create the Jewish State.'

In Arafat's view the turning point in the fighting was the first truce which came into effect, for thirty days, on 10 June. Said Arafat: 'That was the real beginning of our tragedy. Until the first truce we were controlling the whole country. It is true that the Jews had some good or strong positions but we were controlling. It was, after all, our country and we were still the overwhelming majority of the population despite the big increase in the number of illegal Jewish immigrants during and after the Second World War. The Jews had declared their state but it was not established by the time of the first truce. How within one month was the situation changed?'

Arafat gave me several answers to his own question. An obviously decisive element in the whole and very complicated equation was the fact that the Jews were allowed to use the truce to bring in fresh volunteers and an abundant supply of weapons and ammunition while, on the other hand, the mainline Arab forces and the Palestinian guerrillas received nothing from their Western suppliers.

'But that', said Arafat, 'was not the main item on the agenda of our tragedy. That was a consequence not a cause. The main item was that the Arab regimes were under the influence of Britain and some other foreign powers – but mainly Britain. And the more corrupt the regimes were, the more they were manipulated.'

I asked Arafat if he was suggesting that the regimes which then made up the Arab League – Egypt, Iraq, Lebanon, Syria, Jordan, the Yemen and Saudi Arabia – accepted the truce, and then did not fight seriously when it ended, because of pressure, including intimidation, by Britain and other foreign powers.

'That is exactly so,' Arafat replied. 'If you study what happened on the battlefield you will see the consequences of this betrayal. In some places the Arab forces could easily have captured Jewish positions if they had advanced. When our people asked the Arab commanders why they were not advancing they always said the same thing: "We have no orders." This is one point. Another is that Jews could not have captured many of our places if the Arab forces had not withdrawn without a fight. I can tell you, for example, that Haifa would not have fallen without a fight if the Arab forces had not opened the way by retreating according to their orders. It was a very dirty business. Perhaps one day we will have the time to tell the whole story. When we do I think the public opinion of the world will be shocked and disgusted. What happened to us and why is unbelievable.'

To Yasser Arafat and all Palestinians who know the whole truth, the most cynical act of betrayal was the decision of the Arab League leaders to disarm the Palestinian fighters. The decision was taken in secret, presumably by men under great and intolerable pressure from Britain and other foreign powers, long before 15 May. It was implemented the moment the Arab armies entered Palestine. Upon arrival in the places where the Palestinians were fighting or were preparing to defend themselves, the first act of the Arab commanders was to confiscate the weapons of the Palestinians. This incredible but true fact was emphasized by every P.L.O. leader to whom I talked. Abu Jihad, Khalad Hassan and Abu Iyad were three of many who witnessed the disarming of their people with their own eyes. Arafat actually was disarmed by his Arab brothers.

'I can't forget,' Arafat told me. 'When the Arab armies entered Palestine I was in the Gaza area. An Egyptian officer came to my group and demanded that we hand over our weapons. At first I could not believe what my ears were telling me. We asked why. The officer said it was an order from the Arab League. We protested but it was no good. The officer gave me a receipt for my rifle. He said I could get it back when the war was over. In that moment I knew we had been betrayed by these regimes. I was myself touched by their treachery.' There was a long pause. 'I can't forget,' he repeated.

Arafat added that the combination of Jewish terror and the disarming of the Palestinians by the Arab armies was the principal reason for the panic and the exodus of the Palestinian people and thus the creation of the 'so-called' refugee problem.

One of the many Arab League documents which confirms the extent of the conspiracy against the Palestinians was drawn to my attention by Abu Jihad. He himself was too young to fight in 1948, but he still had the receipts for the weapons that were taken from his father and his uncle. Said Abu Jihad: 'You will know that the Arab League formed its own special army of volunteers to fight in Palestine. What you may not know is that there were secret instructions from the Arab League to the commanders of that army. They were ordered not to let any group or unit be commanded by a Palestinian; and they were ordered not to let Palestinians be the majority in any group or unit.

'We can say, because it is true, that the Arab regimes of the day put on a show to pretend that they supported our cause. But really their intention was to neutralize us. Perhaps it was not their choice. They were corrupt and they were under the hand of Britain and the other big powers. But the record of what they did speaks for itself.'

When the Arab League leaders decided to accept the first truce, Abdurrahman Azzam, the Secretary-General of the League, commented privately: 'The Arab people will never forgive us for what we are about to do.'[15]

After the humiliating experience of being disarmed by his Arab brothers in Gaza, Arafat made his way to the Jerusalem sector where, he says, he fought for several months with the forces that Abdul Khader had led before his death. By the time Arafat returned to Cairo the scale of the catastrophe that had overtaken the Palestinians was clear.

By early 1949, more than three-quarters of the Palestinian people were citizens of a country which had ceased to exist. They were not merely homeless, they were stateless. They were existing, most of them, as unwanted refugees in the Arab countries surrounding the new Jewish State.

Arafat's own story is dramatic proof of how totally broken in spirit the Palestinians were. He told me: 'My relatives suggested that I should continue my studies in America. I was in such total despair that I agreed to go. I made an application for a visa and I started to plan my travel to America. For several months I was waiting only to hear that I had been granted a visa.'

# 4

# The Student Leader

The cause of the despair that led Arafat to make an application for an American visa, and which would have seen him on his way to the U.S.A. if his application had been processed and approved more quickly, was not only the fact of the catastrophe. It was his discovery that the official Palestinian leadership, still under the control of his relative, Haj Amin Husseini, had no serious plans to engage in a struggle with the new Jewish State.

Arafat made this discovery during a meeting with Haj Amin which took place in Lebanon, probably towards the end of 1949. Inam recalled that her brother had to save his pocket money to finance the trip. 'He saved more money by eating less,' she added.

According to Inam, Arafat's objective in meeting with Haj Amin was to find out if there were funds available to buy weapons and generally to support a new military struggle. I do not know exactly what Haj Amin said to the twenty-year-old Arafat, but it was probably the same as he said to Khalad Hassan when he asked for help.

In Damascus, and unknown to Arafat, Khalad Hassan was trying to form a guerrilla organization to strike at Israel. Said Khalad: 'In those days, and because we were so young and so naive, we were under the impression that if only we could make the Arabs fight, really fight, Israel would be defeated. So immediately after the catastrophe we were dominated by one idea – we had to push the Arabs to another war. We thought that if we Palestinians attacked Israel on her borders, Israel would retaliate and this would force the

Arab regimes to fight. At this time we did not begin to understand that the reverse was actually the case . . . that the Arab regimes had the psychology of defeat and defence . . . and that the more they were hit by Israel the more that psychology was reinforced. The only people who knew that were Israel's military and political leaders – but they told their people and the world the opposite of what they knew to be the truth.'

Within a month of his decision to form a guerrilla organization, Khalad Hassan had the support of more than 100 fighters who had proved their courage in 1948. They called themselves the Palestine Cultural Club. Khalad explained: 'When we were in our own country and dominated by the British we were not allowed to form political or para-military organizations. The Jews, of course, were allowed to organize themselves. They had the Haganah, their underground but official army; they had the Jewish Agency, which was more or less their government-in-waiting; and they had a host of political and labour organizations. All allowed by the British. We Palestinians had to organize ourselves under the cover of societies and clubs – clubs for scouts, clubs for sports, clubs for cultural activities and so on. And when we were outside our country we found that the same rules applied to us Palestinians – only this time it was the Arab regimes who did not want us to organize ourselves.'

The Palestine Cultural Club had a number of meetings to discuss tactics and strategy. 'But we found we were not able to do anything,' Khalad said. 'We had no weapons and no money. We did not even have money to buy food. We were starving. In the winter we had no water because everything was frozen. We used to wash with ice because we did not have the means to heat the ice to melt it.' Khalad was on the point of giving up in despair when Haj Amin arrived in Damascus.

'In the past,' Khalad said, 'our two families had not agreed on many things. But some friends arranged for me to meet with Haj Amin. He welcomed me very warmly. I told him what I had done. He slapped me on the back and said, "Very good." Then I told him we needed money. "Please," I said, "can you give us some money so that we can organize ourselves properly and buy some weapons?" He didn't give me an answer . . . and that was that. I returned to my fighters and told them we had to cancel everything. And that's how the first of my own attempts to organize a guerrilla group ended.'

Arafat said his own period of dark despair lasted for a few

months. 'Then, while I was waiting for my American visa, I began to analyse the whole situation. I saw a new way forward and I said to myself, "No, I will not leave."'

The year was 1950. Arafat was just twenty-one, and he had resumed his study for an engineering degree at the University of Fuad the First. His thinking was simple and logical. Palestine had been lost because of the incompetence and corruption of the regimes of the old and still existing Arab order. It was because they were so corrupt and so weak that the regimes had been easily manipulated and controlled by the big powers – Britain especially. The situation could only be changed by a revolution which would overthrow the regimes of the old order. It was, or so Arafat imagined, the new regimes of the future, led by a revolutionary Egypt, who would fight and defeat Israel. Logic therefore dictated that Arafat should give his total support to the forces of Egyptian nationalism.

By 1950 Arafat was already demonstrating that he had few equals as a political operator. He was extremely well connected to Gamal Abdel Nasser's Free Officers' Movement which was plotting a coup to overthrow King Farouk, the most corrupt of all Arab leaders. Arafat was now to make good use of the contacts he had so shrewdly cultivated while he was still a teenager and when he should have been at school.

Four of Nasser's closest colleagues with whom Arafat was in regular contact are worth mentioning by name. One was Abdel Hakim Amer who had fought in Palestine in 1948 and who was to become Commander-in-Chief of Egypt's armed forces in 1953. Amer was also a member of Nasser's Revolutionary Command Council (R.C.C.). Another was Kemal Hussein, an artillery officer, a former member of the Moslem Brotherhood, a member of the R.C.C. and, after 1954, a Government minister. Amer and Kemal Hussein were, in fact, the two men who, with Nasser, drew up the plan for the coup. Amer had also worked with Nasser on setting up the Free Officers' Movement. A third contact was Khaled Mohieddin, who was also a member of the R.C.C. In 1954 Mohieddin was exiled for opposing Nasser during a struggle for power, but he was rehabilitated two years later. Another of Arafat's top contacts was the man who eventually succeeded Nasser as President, Anwar Sadat. He, too, was a member of the R.C.C. who had contacts with the Moslem Brotherhood.

Arafat did not meet Nasser himself in the early 1950s. Perhaps if they had met Arafat would have discovered that Nasser had no intention of fighting Israel to liberate even a part of Palestine. Nasser knew that defeating Israel meant defeating its Western sponsors, which he was in no position to do. Arafat did not make this discovery until after he had committed the Palestinians to a military struggle which put him on a collision course with Nasser.

After the humiliating defeat of the Arab armies in 1948 and 1949, the anger which motivated Nasser as he planned his coup was not directed at Israel but at the corrupt Arab rulers, his own King in particular, who had sent soldiers to die in battle with defective and inadequate equipment, and without co-ordinated planning; and who had acted out of weakness as agents and puppets of foreign powers.

In 1950, when Arafat was casting off his own dark despair, Nasser's Free Officers' Movement was not the only nationalist force working for the overthrow of Farouk's regime. The Moslem Brotherhood had the same objective. Although Arafat was never a member of that organization, he did have lines open to its top leadership. He took full advantage of the support the Brotherhood were prepared to offer when it suited him to do so. 'You have to remember,' Arafat told me, 'the Brothers fought alongside us as volunteers in Palestine.'

It is also possible that Arafat was hedging his bets. At the time there was a question about how much influence the Moslem Brotherhood was likely to have in any new Egyptian regime. Some of Nasser's top colleagues were at least former members of the Brotherhood. And some were secret sympathizers.

From the end of the war with Israel until Nasser and his Free Officers staged their coup in July 1952, it was, in fact, the Moslem Brotherhood that dictated the course of events in Egypt. And it was a consequence of its pressures and activities that Arafat had his second experience of combat, this time in action against the British.

In 1936, a few months after Farouk had succeeded his father, King Fuad, the British had obliged Egypt to sign a new Treaty of Alliance. It gave Britain the right to station troops in the Suez Canal Zone for twenty years with an option to renew the alliance at the end of that period. In the view of Egypt's nationalists the Treaty was a humiliating sell-out to the British. But the nationalists were divided and therefore impotent. In the vacuum created by that impotence, the Moslem Brotherhood turned from being a purely religious organization to a political one and led the opposition to the British presence. In 1950, when the Brotherhood was again making the running, King Farouk decided to make use of the nationalists. His only interest was his own survival. When an election brought the veteran Mustapha Nahas back to power as Prime Minister, Farouk instructed him to give the nationalists, including the Brotherhood, more or less a free hand.

The result was a campaign of sabotage and harassment of British troops in the Canal Zone. Arafat played a leading role in what he described as 'this struggle against the British occupation'. It was while he was making hit-and-run attacks on British positions that he had the idea to establish a military training base at his university.

Abu Adeeb was a fellow student at the time. 'I don't know how Arafat did it,' he told me, 'but he persuaded the Egyptian authorities to let him set up a military training camp in the compound of our university. He even talked the Egyptians into letting him have the appropriate facilities. And Arafat became our senior military instructor.'

Arafat told the Egyptian authorities that his aim was to train any student who volunteered for a mission against the British. But Arafat's real intention was to use the facilities to train the elite of a new generation of Palestinian fighters. Arafat got away with it until 1954. In that year the Egyptian authorities closed down the camp and banned all para-military activities at the university. 'We lost our military facilities,' said Abu Adeeb, 'but that wasn't the end. Arafat became our P.T. instructor and under his tuition we all became very fit! In fact we carried on our training as before but without weapons.'

Inam Arafat recalled the new spring in her brother's step that was apparent when he emerged from his period of despair. 'At the front of our apartment we had quite a large gate which was always kept shut. I suppose it was about one and a half metres high. Every morning Yasser used to wait for the sound of the approaching train which would take him into the centre of Cairo. He never looked at his watch. He always waited for the sound of the train. We lived close to the station and he had calculated to the second the time it would take him to get from our apartment to the station. As soon as he heard the train coming he would run from the apartment and jump over the gate. He never once opened the gate. He always put his hand on the top of it and vaulted over.'

It was early in 1951, while he was training Egyptian and Palestinian students for hit-and-run missions against the British, that Arafat made the acquaintance of Salah Khalaf who, as Abu Iyad, was to become the executive responsible for the P.L.O.'s security and counter-intelligence agencies.

On the day of their first meeting the young Khalaf had turned up merely to observe Arafat in action. Unknown to Arafat at the time, Khalaf was actually investigating him for the Moslem Brotherhood, of which Khalaf was an enthusiastic member. Arafat had let it be known that he intended to run for the Presidency of the Union of Palestinian Students. To win the forthcoming election Arafat needed the support of those of his fellow students who were members of the Brotherhood. And this in turn had created a problem for its leaders. They had reservations about Yasser Arafat, partly because he had himself refused to join the Brotherhood, and partly because of his relationship with some of Nasser's most influential colleagues. At least some leaders of the Brotherhood suspected Arafat of being an agent for the military men who were soon to seize power. But as later events were to prove, nothing could have been further from the truth. In the very fluid and potentially explosive political situation then existing in Egypt, Arafat was simply doing his best to preserve his independence when circumstances obliged him to be on good terms with all and any who would support the Palestinian cause. His real problems began when the Moslem Brotherhood turned against Nasser.

The best evidence that Arafat was aware of the dangers of being seen to be dependent on the Moslem Brotherhood is the way in which he threw himself into a campaign to win votes on his own account. He called at the home or lodging house of just about every Palestinian student in Cairo. And he gave particular attention to those who were newly arrived from Palestine. The latter usually received a visit from Arafat before they had unpacked their bags.

Said Abu Adeeb: 'I was one of about fifty students who went from Gaza to Cairo to have their higher education. Every five or six students used to rent and share one apartment. I remember how surprised we were when Arafat called on us. He introduced himself and then said, "I am here to serve you. What can I do to help?" And he did the same with each group that came to Cairo.'

What does Abu Iyad remember about that first encounter with Arafat? 'From a purely Palestinian point of view I did not like his Egyptian accent. I did not like it at all. That is the first thing I remember. But I was impressed by his obvious leadership qualities as I watched him training the students. He was very dynamic. Very tough. Very passionate. And I liked the way he used to talk to the students. I remember him saying: "If you walk like this and do like this you will make the ground tremble under your feet, and you will cause an explosion like a volcano."'

From the moment in 1948 when he came to the conclusion that the Palestinians had been betrayed by the weakness and corruption of the Arab regimes, Arafat vowed that he would do everything in his power to preserve the independence of Palestinian decision-making. At the time, the Palestinians were without institutions to make decisions. But the principle that guided Arafat then still applies: if the Palestinians rely on others to make decisions for them, they will never recover any of their lost land and rights.

So it is not difficult to imagine that Arafat's fiercely independent spirit was troubled by the prospect of having to rely on the support of the Moslem Brotherhood in the election for the Presidency of the Union of Palestinian Students. There was a danger that the Brotherhood would demand a price once the election was won. It could be that the Brotherhood would seek to bend Arafat to its will and ways. And that, in the long term, could only be bad for the Palestinian cause. Related to that was another and more immediate danger. If the Brotherhood were to turn against Nasser, Arafat could find himself in confrontation with the man who was preparing to present himself as the champion and new saviour of the Arab world. In his search for a position in which he could influence events, Arafat was playing a very dangerous game. That he did not have a choice was probably no great comfort to him when the true and terrible cost of his relationship with the Brotherhood later became apparent.

The election for the Presidency of the Union of Palestinian Students was held in 1952. Each of the candidates submitted a list. On Arafat's there were eight names in addition to his own. According to Abu Adeeb there was strong competition for the Presidency. 'But the nine persons on Arafat's list won the biggest number of votes and Arafat himself got as many votes as the eight others put together.' The second name on Arafat's list was Salah Khalaf. He became Arafat's assistant. And being an influential member of the Moslem Brotherhood he was frequently in prison for short periods.

How much, if at all, Arafat was actually indebted to the Moslem Brotherhood in general and Salah Khalaf in particular is debatable. In the light of subsequent events Arafat did not appear to consider that he owed the Brotherhood any favours for its support at the election, but he seems to have considered himself bound to Salah Khalaf by a debt of honour for his personal support and his influence on those Palestinians who were members of the Brotherhood at the time, and those who were opposed to Arafat's leadership on the grounds that he was a relative of Haj Amin Husseini. By 1952 Haj Amin was without credit in the eyes of the new generation of Palestinian radicals. That Arafat considered himself bound by loyalty to Salah Khalaf is perhaps one of several reasons why in later years the Chairman of the P.L.O. refused to confront his old friend and colleague on those occasions when they found themselves on opposite sides of internal debates about policy and strategy.

As President of the Union of Palestinian Students Arafat quickly demonstrated that he possessed all the talents of leadership and that he would dominate any organization of which he was a member if he was given half a chance to do so. Said Abu Adeeb: 'Of course we had an Executive Committee. But the truth is that Arafat did ninety per cent of the work.'

If Arafat had been less than remarkably successful at solving the problems of his fellow students, it is likely that some of his colleagues would have openly resented and perhaps challenged his autocratic style of leadership. But it was difficult for any of them to be at odds with a young man who proved he could deliver the goods.

According to Abu Adeeb and other Palestinians who were students in Cairo at the time, the biggest problem facing most of them – mainly on account of their status as refugees – was money. Many did not have the necessary funds for their tuition fees and their board and lodging expenses. 'Because they were unable to pay their tuition fees in advance,' said Abu Adeeb, 'many were prevented from starting their courses on time.' Within one month

Arafat solved that problem by persuading the Arab League to pay the tuition fees of all Palestinian students. 'It was a very big victory for Arafat,' Abu Adeeb added.

On that and many other occasions Arafat's colleagues were amazed at the apparent ease with which their leader bulldozed his way through the bureaucracy of the Arab League and the officialdom of the Egyptian Government. Said Abu Adeeb: 'As well as being a brilliant negotiator, Arafat had ways known only to himself of contacting the highest people. He frequently talked with ministers, prime ministers and even presidents and kings. And nothing would stop him from doing that.'

Arafat's election to the Presidency of the Union of Palestinian Students took place shortly after Nasser's coup. Mainly because they themselves were young and unknown, Nasser and his colleagues chose General Mohammed Neguib to be their figurehead. As soon as the General was installed as Egypt's President, Arafat pulled some strings to get himself and a delegation of Palestinian students an invitation to visit him. Neguib had served as a brigade commander in Palestine and, as subsequent events were to show, he had a certain sympathy with the Moslem Brotherhood – to which he was to turn for support during his struggle for power with Nasser.

At the meeting Arafat presented Neguib with a petition. It was dedicated to the memory of the Palestinians and the Egyptians who had fought and died in Palestine. And its message to the new President, whom everybody knew to be a figurehead, was, 'Do not forget the Palestinians.' But the most unusual thing about the petition was that it was written in blood.

Abu Adeeb confirmed that it was as early as 1952 or 1953 that Arafat first began to talk about his ideas for an independent Palestine liberation movement. The response of his student colleagues was mixed, according to Abu Adeeb: 'We were all of us impressed by Arafat's achievements as a student leader. The student union that existed before his election victory was useless. It was in a state of frozen inactivity. Arafat changed all that. We also admired his dedication and his obvious leadership qualities. But if you want to know the truth I can say that not all of us took Arafat so seriously when he talked about an independent Palestine liberation movement. I do not mean to say that any of us were opposed to the idea. The point is that some of us did not think it would be possible for the Palestinians to shape their own destiny. And we thought in this way because the conspiracy against us, by the Arab regimes and the big powers, was so great.'

While Arafat was admired by virtually all of his student colleagues for his achievements on their behalf, he was not universally respected as a man. In the years before his election to the Presidency of the Union of Palestinian Students, Arafat was not, apparently, averse to settling arguments with his fists. After his election there remained for some the problem of his violent temper.

Although he did not tell me the story himself, Abu Adeeb was one of those who quietly but strongly disapproved of Arafat's explosive temper and his love of confrontation in debate. When, nearly ten years later, Abu Adeeb was asked if he would consider becoming a member of Fatah's first Executive Committee, he apparently said: 'In principle I am ready – but not if Yasser Arafat is to be our leader.' Abu Adeeb was, in fact, one of very many who decided to accommodate Arafat's temper and to accept it as a small price to pay for his many qualities and strengths.

In Arafat's opinion his most significant achievement during his days as a student leader in Cairo was his success in persuading the Egyptian authorities to let him launch and distribute a student magazine. It was called *The Voice of Palestine*. Said Abu Adeeb: 'The fact that we had our magazine meant that Arafat had performed another miracle. We knew the Egyptian authorities did not really want us Palestinians to have an effective voice of our own . . . and yet the magazine was exactly that. To this day I don't know how Arafat persuaded the Egyptian authorities to give him the necessary permissions.'

It was Arafat himself, with a conspirator's chuckle, who explained to me the real significance of *The Voice of Palestine*. 'To Palestinians it was so clear and obvious that our magazine was not for the student union. It was much more serious than that. In later years, and when we were better organized, we addressed ourselves to our Palestinian masses. But in *The Voice of Palestine* I was really speaking to those of our Palestinian brothers who could be organizers of secret cells in other countries. The magazine was distributed in many places – in Gaza, Jordan, Syria, Iraq, the Lebanon and so on. It was, in fact, our first underground way of making contact with those who could organize.' I suggested to Arafat that the magazine was actually his first recruiting sergeant in the Palestinian diaspora. 'Yes,' he said with a twinkle, 'it was so.'

Of those Palestinians who sensed that the magazine was more than it appeared to be at first glance, none — apart from Arafat himself — were to have more influence on the course of future events in the region than one of its young readers in Gaza. His name was Khalil Wazir. He was to become Abu Jihad, and with Arafat he was more or less the co-founder of Fatah. Arafat and Wazir formed the first Fatah cell. Between them they organized and set up the underground network of cells from which Fatah emerged. And in the teeth of strong opposition from a majority of their colleagues, they were the two leading advocates of Palestinian military action. Fatah as a functioning organization with a Central Committee was the product of the labours of many, however, including some who are no longer associated with it, some who are dead and some who became members of the collective leadership with Arafat and Abu Jihad.

Arafat first met Wazir shortly after the latter was gaoled by the Egyptians in Gaza during the early summer of 1954. Within a few months, and partly as a consequence of his connection with Wazir, Arafat himself was imprisoned by the Egyptians in Cairo. If a camel had not gone lame when its foot struck a metal box that young Wazir had buried in the sand, it is possible that the two men would not have met when they did.

The son of a small shopkeeper, Khalil Ibrahim Wazir was born in Ramleh on 10 October 1935; he was not yet thirteen at the time of the climax to the struggle for control of Palestine. Ramleh was some ten miles to the south-west of Tel Aviv and Jaffa and very close to Lod. The story of how Wazir and his family were forcibly ejected from their homeland is a very dramatic one.

'I remember as if it was yesterday the day the Zionist forces attacked Jaffa,' Abu Jihad told me. 'The Arabs of the city sent some cars and trucks to us in Ramleh. "Help for Jaffa," they cried. "Help for Jaffa." I remember the men and women of Ramleh getting into the cars and trucks. One man had a very old pistol and a few knives and sticks. In this time we were helping each other. We knew the Jews would come for Ramleh and Lod if they captured Jaffa. And that is exactly what happened. In one night they surrounded Ramleh and Lod and they were able to do it easily because the Jordanians withdrew without a fight. We were surrounded and alone.

'Our people could not fight – they had nothing to fight with. The Mayor and a delegation from the Municipality visited the Jewish commanders. The Mayor said to them: "Okay, you can enter the city but you must not harm the people or take prisoners, and you must allow the people to stay in their homes and live their normal lives." The Jews said "No." They wanted us to leave our homes – to leave our city.

'When we decided not to leave, the Jews put Ramleh and Lod under their artillery fire. I can't forget what happened. The top of our house was hit and we lived in the bottom. Then another shell exploded in the street and our door was destroyed by the blast. The shells were falling in every part of Ramleh and the Mayor told all of the people to take shelter in the mosques and the churches. We lived in a Christian part of the city and we went to the Roman Catholic Church. On the way some of our neighbours were killed by the shells.

'We lived in the church for two days before the Jews entered the city. Men, women and children sleeping side by side. There was not the space to put a foot between the bodies. We had to put our legs on the bodies of others. When the Jews came I went to the fifth floor. I looked through the shutters and with my own eyes I saw Jewish soldiers shoot and kill some women and children who were still in the street. I can't forget. Then I watched as the Jewish soldiers entered our houses, kicking and breaking the doors and shooting. Sometimes they pulled people into the street and killed them.

'In the church people were crying. They were saying, "Deir Yassin, Deir Yassin." We were sure we were going to be massacred. The priest made a white flag and when the Jewish soldiers entered the street of the church he went out to meet them. The priest and the soldiers entered the church. They said to all of the people, "Hold up your hands." Everyone held up his hands. Then the Jews began to separate us. They said they wanted all of the youths and the men from fourteen to forty-five. And they took them away to prison and detention camps. Those of us who were left were the kids, the women and the very old men.

'The next day the Jews allowed us to return to our homes and I can't forget what happened. In the night the Jewish soldiers came not less than ten times to our house. They pushed their way in and made a mess of everything. They said they were searching for weapons but really it was part of their policy to make us feel insecure and frightened. It was their tactic to make us run away from our homes and our country. My grandmother in that time was very old and very sick, and each time the Jews came into our house that night they pulled the covers from her bed. When the Jews realized we were not going to leave our homes they became more and more angry.

'Two days later the Jews made an announcement over their loudspeakers. They ordered us to leave our homes and assemble at certain points on the road. They said they were arranging for some buses to take us to Ramallah. We lived for three days on the roadside. At night they fired over our heads. On the second day, when the buses had still not arrived, they ordered the old men to walk to Ramallah. I was left with three of my brothers – one was still a baby – my three sisters, my mother, my grandmother and my aunt.

'On the third day the buses arrived. We had some bags with us. In one there was some bread and cheese and also a new pair of pyjamas of which I was very proud. When the Jews told us we could not take our bags on the buses, I made an attempt to get the bread and the cheese and my new pyjamas. With the innocent voice of a very young boy I spoke to one of the drivers. In Hebrew I said, "Mister, mister, I want to get some food," and I pointed to one of our bags. He said, "Okay, okay." When I put my hand into the bag there was some angry shouting in Hebrew. In that instant my mother pulled me to her chest – she had seen that a Jewish soldier was taking aim at me. He fired several shots. I would have been hit and probably killed if my mother had not seen what was happening. The bullets just missed me and entered the leg of one of our neighbours. He was from the family of Al-Marsala. Today he lives in Amman. If you go to see him he will tell you the bullets in his leg are the sacrifice he made for the life of Khalil Wazir!'

Eventually the women and children of Ramleh were put aboard the buses and sent on their way to Ramallah. But their ordeal was far from over. The worst was still to come.

'When we were more than ten miles short of Ramallah the Jews stopped the buses and told us to get out and walk the rest of the way.

They pointed and said, "Ramallah is over there, you must pass through those hills and valleys." So we started to walk. We had to move slowly. Some of the women were very old and sick and they had to stop every few minutes to catch their breath and rest. Some of the other women who were more able to walk became exhausted from carrying their children.

'On the second night the Jews shelled us with their artillery and mortar bombs. At first we took cover behind some rocks, then, when the shelling continued, everybody started to cry and panic . . . and we were running, running, running all the way to Ramallah. I can't forget what happened. Some mothers abandoned their children – they were just too exhausted to carry them further. Even my aunt told my mother to leave some children behind. My mother was carrying three children. My aunt said to her: "You can't run while you are carrying three children. You will be killed. You must leave two children behind and we will send help when we get to Ramallah." My mother refused. She said to me: "Khalil you are only twelve and you are not very strong – do you think you can carry one of your sisters and run?" I said "Yes" and I did. Some children were left behind because there was nobody to carry them. Some were left because their mothers were killed. Till now I cannot forget.

'There were no Arab forces in the area – no regulars, no volunteers, no Arab forces of any kind. The Jews knew who we were and where we were. It was a deliberate and calculated attack with only one objective. They were making sure that we arrived in Ramallah in an obvious state of panic and distress. They were hoping that our condition and the stories we would tell would cause others to be frightened and flee from their homes. It was all part of a very clever and a very successful Zionist strategy to force us to leave our homeland in fear.'

From Ramallah, and in the bigger panic that followed, Khalil Wazir and some fifty of the women and children from Ramleh managed to find places in a truck bound for Hebron. From there they crossed into Gaza. Under the U.N. Partition Plan, Gaza was to have been a part of the Palestinian Arab state. The Egyptians held on to it during the fighting and it became effectively a part of Egypt when the armistice agreements were signed in 1949. In the same way the other portions of Palestine that had been allotted to the

Arabs, and which were not conquered by the Israelis, became part of Jordan.

At the end of his story Abu Jihad smiled sadly and then said this. 'I know you are finding it hard to believe, but that is what happened. And if you care to do some research in Israel you will find the evidence to confirm that what I have said is the truth. In their books and their newspapers some Israelis are beginning to admit what they did. Just a few months ago some Israeli newspapers were very critical of Mr Rabin when he told how he and others had pushed the Palestinians from Ramleh and Lod in 1948.'

I discussed the events described above with Abu Jihad's mother. When I met her in Damascus, Abu Jihad was many miles away, under siege in Tripoli. She had not, in fact, seen her son since I had talked with him. Her story confirmed point by point all that Abu Jihad had said. Very many of the 940,000 Palestinians who fled could, if asked, tell similar stories.

By 1949 there were nearly a quarter of a million refugees in the Gaza Strip. For most of them it was to become 'a vast concentration camp'. General Burns, the Chief of Staff of the U.N.'s Truce Supervision Organization from 1954 to 1956, described the Gaza Strip in his book, *Between Arab and Israeli*:

'The Strip is about forty kilometres long, and averages eight and a quarter kilometres in width; thus it contains about 330 square kilometres. Only two-thirds of this area is more or less arable; the rest is sand-dunes spreading inland from the coast for varying distances. There are about 310,000 Arabs resident in the Strip, 210,000 of them refugees from the southern parts of Palestine now occupied by Israel. Thus there are 1,500 persons to the square kilometre of arable soil – about 3,900 to the square mile. There is water enough from deep wells for usual domestic needs, and some irrigation. The available fertile soil is intensively cultivated, with crops of wheat, barley, and millet; tomatoes, onions, and okra; oranges, plums, grapes and melons. But, of course, it is impossible for the food thus produced to feed more than a fraction of the population. The 210,000 refugees are fed by the United Nations Relief and Works Agency. The standard ration provides 1600 calories a day, mostly carbohydrates. By Western standards 1600 calories is a reducing diet. The cost of maintaining the refugees is about $27.00 per capita per annum.

'They live in little huts of mud and concrete blocks, corrugated-iron roofs, regimented row after row. Fairly adequate medical service is provided, probably better than they enjoyed before they were expelled from their native villages. It is especially good in the maternity and child-care clinics, with the result that the infant death-rate is low. Children swarm everywhere. There are primary schools for nearly all of them – little girls in cotton dresses.with fine black and white stripes, little boys in khaki shirts and shorts. There are secondary schools for a good proportion of the adolescents; and a great number of youths can always be seen, around examination times, strolling along the roads memorizing their lessons: where else could they concentrate to study? And what will all these youths and girls do when they have finished their secondary school training? There is no employment for them in the Strip, and very few can leave it to work elsewhere.

'Besides the 210,000 refugees there are about 30,000 inhabitants who can earn a living from farming or the small trades and merchandising of the area; the balance of the 310,000, not refugees by U.N.R.W.A. definition, are poverty-stricken, and are supported by a dole from the Egyptian Government. One does not see people starving or dying of disease in the streets; nevertheless the Gaza Strip resembles a vast concentration camp, shut off by the sea, the border between Palestine and the Sinai near Rafah, which the Egyptians will not permit them to cross, and the Armistice Demarcation Line which they cross in peril of being shot by Israelis or imprisoned by the Egyptians. They can look to the east and see wide fields, once Arab land, cultivated extensively by a few Israelis, with a chain of *kibbutzim* guarding the heights or the areas beyond. It is not surprising that they look with hatred on those who have dispossessed them.'[16]

In Gaza the Wazir children, their mother, grandmother and some aunts lived for a few months with an uncle. Then, when it was obvious that the Palestinians would not be returning to their homes in the near future, the Wazirs moved into rented accommodation of their own. Said Abu Jihad: 'It was very poor accommodation, actually one room measuring some two by five metres in which fourteen of us lived. It was made of very poor stones and it had some temporary roof. I can't describe to you the winters. One time the sink was taken away by the wind. Another time my mother was injured when the roof was blown away and the stones which had been keeping it in place fell on top of her. She was bleeding very badly from her face.'

Khalil Wazir's first priority was education. He was desperate to continue it. For eight months or so, and because of the crush of refugees in the Gaza Strip, he found no place in any of the schools. During that period he helped his mother to earn a little money by selling bits and pieces. 'Sweets and some novelties, mainly for children.' Then he got the chance to attend one of the schools opened by the U.N.'s Relief and Works Agency.

Because he was six years younger than Arafat and had not had Arafat's first-hand experience of the Arab betrayal, it was a year or two before Khalil Wazir began to understand what had happened to the Palestinians and why. He learned mainly by listening to those who had fought in 1948 and earlier. By the time of his sixteenth birthday Wazir was thinking along much the same lines as Arafat. 'After the catastrophe, and while we were waiting for the day when we could return to our country, we were confident that the Arab regimes which had betrayed us would be replaced by new leaders who would make the Arab armies strong and who would really fight.' There had already been four military coups in Syria.

'Then came Nasser and Neguib,' said Abu Jihad. 'In Gaza and everywhere the Palestinians were very happy. Very excited. We were sure the changes in Egypt and elsewhere in the Arab world would be the way of our return to our homeland. We looked upon Nasser as the new Saladin.'

At this historical moment in their stories Abu Jihad, Arafat, Khalad Hassan, and many others all made and emphasized the same point. During the political upheaval that followed the Arab military defeat of 1948, the Palestinian intellectuals of two generations – the old and the new – were not sitting on their hands. In every Arab country where they had taken what they hoped would be only a temporary refuge, the Palestinian intellectuals threw themselves into politics. They became socialists, conservatives and revolutionaries; they became Moslem Brothers and Ba'athists; they even became communists; they became, in short, whatever it was necessary to be to play an influential role in the politics of Arab change. And their objective was to persuade the emerging Arab regimes that the return of the Palestinians to their homeland should be the number-one priority of all Arabs. To say that Arafat and his colleagues were and are supreme opportunists is to state the obvious. But opportunism is the name of the only game they can play. According to legend Arafat once said that being the Chairman of the P.L.O. was like being the only male visitor to a brothel on a bad night for business. The obvious implication of his remark, which was directed at his fellow Arab leaders, was that the Chairman of the P.L.O. had to screw or be screwed.

Abu Jihad continued: 'So Nasser came to power. And we waited patiently. We waited and nothing changed. In those days, and because of our youth, we were without experience and we were politically naive. As a consequence we didn't know why Nasser and the other new Arab leaders were doing nothing to help us return to our homeland. We didn't know that they also were frightened of Israel and the big powers which supported her. We knew only that nothing was happening and we began again to have our despair.'

What Khalil Wazir witnessed in Gaza helped to convince him that the real intention of the new regime in Cairo was to tighten its controls on the Palestinians to prevent them taking any actions of their own. 'If you want to know the truth,' Abu Jihad said, 'the refugee camps in Gaza were prisons. And it was the same situation in the camps in Jordan, in Syria, in Iraq and in the Lebanon. Our people in the camps were totally isolated. They were not allowed any freedom of movement. They were not allowed to speak or write any word about our problem. They were not allowed to organize. They were not allowed to demonstrate. And those of us who did try to organize were treated as spies. I could tell you hundreds of stories about how all the Arab intelligence services intimidated and tortured our people in order to have their agents among us.'

Of all the Egyptian measures against the Palestinians in Gaza, one in particular added a great deal of fuel to the flames of Wazir's anger: 'It was the habit of many Palestinian refugees, at the weekends especially, to slip secretly over the border to look at their homes and their farms and their land in Israel. Usually they only looked from a distance – you can imagine what a sad experience it was for them. In those areas where the Jews were not settled the Palestinians sometimes went into their homes to see if everything was okay. And sometimes at night they used to bring fruit and vegetables from their gardens. I remember one man who returned with the motor from the pump of his well. This was the habit of the Palestinian refugees in Gaza and also in Jordan. But when the Israelis started to punish Egypt and Jordan for the activities of some few Palestinian fighters, the Egyptian authorities – and also the Jordanians – said that crossing the border into Israel for any reason was a serious crime. So it happened that hundreds of Palestinian refugees who crossed the border just to look at their homes and their land were gaoled for five, seven and ten years by the Egyptian and Jordanian authorities.'

The fighters mentioned by Abu Jihad were a very small number of Palestinians who fought in 1948 and who had managed to retain a weapon. 'The Arabs did not succeed in disarming every single Palestinian,' Abu Jihad observed. The efforts of these few fighters who were conducting what amounted to a private and often individual war of their own were pathetic, but as was to be the case time and time again in the future, the most puny Palestinian military effort gave Israel's leaders what they wanted – the excuse to mount massive reprisal attacks against the front-line Arab states in which the Palestinians happened to be.

From the very beginning the main objective of the reprisal attacks – which were always out of all proportion to the provocation – was to convey a simple message of Israel's military superiority to the leaders of the front-line Arab states. The first serious warning of this kind was delivered to Arab leaders by a young Israeli officer on 14 October 1953. His name was Ariel Sharon. On that day he and his special force, Unit 101, attacked the Jordanian village of Qibya. The attack was a reprisal for the murder of an Israeli woman and her two children. They were killed by a grenade thrown or planted by a Palestinian. In reply Sharon and his men dynamited dozens of Arab houses and buildings and slaughtered sixty-six men, women and children. Most of their bodies were riddled with bullets but there was evidence that some of those killed had been forced to stay in their homes while they were blown up around them. At Qibya the kill ratio was twenty-two to one – twenty-two Arabs killed by the Jews for every Jew killed by the Arabs. In later years, and according to my own rough estimates, the kill ratio was probably more than 100 to one in Israel's favour.

With their reprisal strategy and policy, and while they were telling their own people and the world that Israel was the threatened party in danger of annihilation, Israel's leaders succeeded more often than not in reinforcing what Khalad Hassan described as the psychology of defeat and defence of the Arab regimes. The proof of it is that Arab leaders did take fright and also took measures to contain and control the Palestinians, as described by Abu Jihad.

Events were also to prove that the Israelis were much better than the Palestinians at reading the minds of Arab leaders. While Israel's leaders knew that their reprisal attacks were intimidating the Arab leaders, the Palestinian leaders to be, Abu Jihad and Arafat in particular, were planning their strategy in the totally mistaken belief that they could force the Arab leaders to initiate a war of destiny with Israel. This was the idea that was forming itself in Wazir's head as he observed what was happening in Gaza.

Wazir's specific idea, one already fixed in Arafat's mind, was that the Palestinians could, so to speak, turn the tables on the Israelis by provoking bigger and bigger Israeli reprisal attacks. The more the Israelis could be provoked into attacking the Arab states, the more the Arab regimes would have to arm themselves; and the point would come when the Arab leaders would have to go to war if only for the sake of their honour. And then Israel, surely, would be defeated. That was the theory. To put it into practice the Palestinians needed to create commando organizations which could mount a sustained and co-ordinated campaign of sabotage in Israel – to provoke bigger and bigger Israeli reprisals.

Convinced that this was the way forward, Khalil Wazir, in 1953 and at the age of eighteen, decided to take a lead by forming his own commando organization in Gaza. 'I was trained in secret,' he said. He did not tell me how he was trained, or who trained him; but it seems clear from what he and Arafat told me about those early days that he was trained for the leadership of a commando organization by a Major in the Egyptian army, who was a secret member of the Moslem Brotherhood, and who was in good contact with Arafat in Cairo. He may well have been the same Major who accompanied Arafat and Hammad Abu Sitta from Cairo to Gaza in 1948. Arafat told me that he did not meet Wazir in person until 1954. Abu Jihad told me his first meeting with Arafat was in 1955. When I challenged Arafat about this discrepancy he was emphatic. 'No, no, no,' he said. 'Abu Jihad is wrong. It was definitely 1954.' Either Abu Jihad's memory let him down on this occasion or he was putting up a smokescreen. Perhaps he is still sensitive about his own early connections with the Moslem Brotherhood. It also seems likely that the name of Khalil Wazir was on a secret training list in Arafat's possession in 1953 – from the moment Wazir indicated that he was ready to organize a commando group.

As soon as his own training was completed, Wazir began to recruit volunteers for his group. 'The first problem was to make sure they were innocent,' Abu Jihad said.

'You mean that they were not spies or agents for Egypt's various intelligence services,' I commented.

'Yes,' Abu Jihad replied, 'that is what I meant.'

Because the Palestinians were not allowed by the Egyptian authorities to participate in any kind of para-military activities, Wazir's training programmes had to be planned with great care. 'In Gaza under the Egyptians I had to use the same tricks that my father's generation had used under the British in Palestine. I had to pretend that I was organizing a sports club. To get my boys fit I used to run them from Gaza to Deir El-Balah, a distance of some ten to fifteen miles. We left before it was light in the morning and we did not return until it was dark in the evening. Our really secret training with mines and explosives took place in the jungles close to Gaza.' Abu Jihad's jungles were mostly dense clusters of palm trees. 'When we were well prepared we began our secret operations. We were planting mines on the roads and tracks used by Israeli patrol vehicles.'

For the last few months of 1953 and the first few weeks of 1954, Wazir had an adequate supply of mines and explosives. The Major and his associates were stealing them from Egyptian army stores. But early in 1954, and as the result of a gathering crisis between Nasser and the Moslem Brotherhood, this supply line dried up. Nasser, then Minister of Internal Affairs, was locked into a power struggle with the man who was supposed to be his puppet – President Neguib. The Moslem Brotherhood was demanding a much bigger say in government. Partly for the sake of his own survival, Neguib was pushing the demand of the Brotherhood. Using a small incident as a pretext, Nasser disbanded the Brotherhood and imprisoned many of its leaders.

The Major, the key link in the chain that supplied Wazir with mines, was somehow a casualty of this first round of Nasser's showdown with the Brotherhood and Neguib – which Nasser came close to losing. It is possible that the Major was discovered to be a member of the Brotherhood and was arrested. Another possibility is that he was transferred to an Egyptian army unit far from Gaza. A third possibility is that the Major simply decided to keep a very low profile. In any event Wazir was once more in a state of some despair. He had put together a reasonably effective group of saboteurs but now he had no mines.

Not a young man to be stuck for the want of an idea, Wazir decided to experiment by making a mine of his own. He needed a heavy metal casing of some description which meant that he also required the services of a blacksmith. Who to trust? Because it was much too dangerous to rely on a local man for such a job, Wazir travelled to Rafah at the southern end of the Gaza Strip. There he found a blacksmith to make a metal case to his design. In due course Wazir packed his metal box with dynamite and fitted a detonating device. Wazir then planted his box in the sand at a point on the border which, he had calculated, was due for a visit by an Israeli patrol in the next few days or so. Perhaps he had a contingency plan to draw the Israelis to the spot.

And then along came Abdel – I do not know what his real name was – riding on his camel. As one of its feet struck the metal box, the beast let out a cry of pain. The camel went lame and Abdel cursed. When he had extracted the offending metal box from the sand he took it to the police in Gaza. They passed it to their Egyptian Military Intelligence colleagues, and two of them were instructed to trace the blacksmith who had made the box.

The two intelligence agents inquired in Gaza. They were under instructions to visit every blacksmith in the Strip if necessary. They were slow but very methodical. Eventually they found themselves in Rafah and confronted the blacksmith who had made the metal box. The poor man truly did not know the name of his customer. But as the two intelligence agents were deciding what to do next, the blacksmith's son spoke. 'I know who it was,' he said. 'I was at school with him. His name is Wazir. Khalil Wazir.'

Within a matter of hours Wazir was arrested and imprisoned. The Egyptians shaved his head and told him to prepare for a long stay. Wazir pleaded to be allowed to take his examinations in two weeks' time. His gaolers laughed and told him they could guarantee that he would not be returning to his studies.

When word of Wazir's arrest reached Arafat in Cairo he was agitated but not altogether surprised. With caution he lobbied his top-level contacts for help to get Wazir released. He was evidently successful. A month after his arrest, Wazir was set free. Some weeks later, when Wazir had done his best to persuade Egyptian Military Intelligence agents to lose interest in him, Arafat went secretly to Gaza to meet him.

I do not know in detail what Arafat and Wazir discussed during what was probably their first meeting, but subsequent events suggest they agreed a strategy to provoke Israel into making bigger and more frequent reprisal attacks on the front-line Arab states. When future historians come to write their conclusions, they will probably say the biggest mistake of Israel's leaders was in the 1950s when they allowed two young Palestinians, Yasser Arafat and Khalil Wazir, to dictate the course of events in the region. If Israel had not been committed to a policy of maximum force in the shape of massive reprisal attacks, it is likely that Arafat and Wazir would have totally failed to advance their cause. At the time the alternative was for Israel to recognize the truth – that Nasser and the other Arab leaders who mattered were not interested in military confrontation with Israel.

The main point of agreement between Arafat and Wazir was the need for Wazir's commando group to be more effective. This was dictated by two considerations. The first was to do with the consequence of Nasser's moves against the Moslem Brotherhood which, until recently, and in one way or another, had been the main supplier of the mines and the explosives on which Wazir's operations depended. With this source drying up, or even dried up, mines and explosives would be difficult to acquire. This fact alone was sufficient to dictate a more judicious selection of targets in Israel. But if the object of the exercise was to guarantee that Israel would be provoked into making bigger and more frequent reprisal attacks, Wazir would have to hit targets more vital to the Jewish State than military patrol vehicles. In the new strategy worked out by Arafat and Wazir, an obvious priority was the water sources which were the lifeblood of Israel's new settlements. The decision to sabotage these was to have consequences which even Arafat and Wazir could not have imagined at the time.

In Cairo, meanwhile, events were moving to a climax of their own. To put pressure on Neguib to stand down from the Presidency, Nasser had appointed himself Prime Minister – for the second time – in April. The following month, to tempt London into negotiations, he had called off the commando attacks on British forces in the Suez Canal Zone. That was when Arafat lost his military training camp and facilities at the University of Fuad the First. Then, in October, Nasser approved a new Anglo-Egyptian Treaty. Nasser got what he wanted – all British troops were to be withdrawn from Egypt by 18 June 1956. And the British got what they said they wanted. For seven years the Canal Zone bases were to be shared by British and Egyptian civilian technicians and, in private, Nasser indicated that he did not much care if the British technicians were military personnel – provided they were in civilian clothes and behaved like civilians. But the biggest of Nasser's concessions was his agreement to Britain's demand that British troops could return to Egypt to help repel aggression if, during the seven years, Egypt or any other Arab country and Turkey was attacked by an outside power – excluding Israel. It was Nasser's hope that his conciliatory attitude would convince the West that he wanted Egypt to be its friend and ally. At the time Nasser was also hoping that the West in general, and America in particular, would become his arms supplier. In private he had frequently assured London and Washington that he was not interested in a military confrontation with Israel.

Predictably, the Moslem Brotherhood regarded Nasser's new agreement with Britain as a sell-out to the imperial powers. On 26 October, a Moslem Brother tried to assassinate Nasser. Among the hundreds who were arrested and charged with being members of the Brotherhood and with complicity in the plot to kill Nasser was Yasser Arafat. Some of his chickens were coming home to roost. He was not himself a member of the organization, but he did use it; and in Gaza he had used it to promote an interest – confrontation with Israel – that was contrary to Nasser's wish and policy.

It was the first but by no means the last time Arafat was to be imprisoned and tortured by his Arab brothers. 'They kept me in prison for several weeks,' Arafat told me. 'I said I was not a member of the Moslem Brotherhood and I was not. Some of those who tortured me knew I was speaking the truth – but they wanted something else. They wanted me to give them all the information I had about the Moslem Brothers – names, places where I made contact with them, and so on. But they did not succeed in breaking me.'

The day came when he turned the tables on his torturers. 'I said to them, "Look, if you really want the truth, if you really want proof that I am not a member of the Moslem Brotherhood, then go and ask Abdel Hakim Amer, go and ask Kemal Hussein."' By the time he had finished talking Arafat had named virtually all of Nasser's closest colleagues as friends and contacts who would vouch for him.

'In the end,' said Arafat, 'it was Kemal Hussein himself who came to the gaol to release me.' The same Kemal Hussein who had helped Nasser to plan his coup.

What Arafat did not know as he savoured his first few moments of freedom was that some very senior members of Egypt's intelligence community were vowing to get even with him. They were angry and bitter that they had not been allowed to break him, to kill him if necessary, and they felt cheated. Their continuing insistence that Arafat was a member of the Moslem Brotherhood and, later, their ridiculous assertion that he would one day attempt to assassinate Nasser, were an indirect but major cause of the Arab humiliation in the war of 1967 and the fact that there was a war at all.

By the time Arafat was released a number of the leaders of the Moslem Brotherhood had been hanged and Nasser was the President of Egypt. Events were soon to force Nasser down roads he did not wish to travel – to confrontation with Israel and reliance on the Soviet Union for his arms supplies. The men who did most to influence those events were Khalil Wazir and Yasser Arafat – with not a little help from Israel.

# 5

# No Go With Nasser

The Arafat-Wazir strategy of provoking Israel to make bigger and more frequent reprisal attacks produced quicker and better results, initially, than either of the two men had expected.

On the night of 28 February 1955, Israel launched a two-pronged attack on the Gaza Strip. The attacks turned a regional conflict into a potential global confrontation by bringing in the Soviet Union – not so much, in reality, on the side of the Arabs, but as the supplier of arms to Egypt and later Syria. The Gaza Raid, as it became known, was, in fact, one of several occasions on which Israel's leaders inadvertently gave Arafat a helping hand. In the late 1960s Moshe Dayan told me that the Arab-Israeli conflict could be resolved if only it was taken out of the arena of East-West politics, if the Arabs and the Israelis were free to strike their own bargains. At the time it was a fair point; but it was Israel's Gaza Raid that forced Nasser to turn to the Soviets for weapons.

Israel's stated objective for the attack was to teach Nasser a lesson, and thus to force him to prevent saboteurs entering the Jewish State from the Gaza Strip. But the Israelis were demanding the impossible. Before the attack on Gaza, Nasser and the Egyptian authorities were doing at least as much as could reasonably have been expected of them to stop the movement of Palestinians across the unmarked sand border. Up to ten-year prison sentences for refugees who did cross just to look at their lost land and homes were surely evidence of that. If the necessary allowances are made for the geography of the Gaza Strip, the fact that Nasser was not master in

his own house until the end of 1954, and the circumstances of the
time, it has to be said that short of building a Berlin-type wall with
watchtowers right round the Gaza Strip, Nasser and the Egyptian
authorities were taking all possible and practical steps to prevent
the movement into Israel of Palestinian saboteurs. And after the
Moslem Brotherhood had been smashed, Arafat and Wazir had to
operate without its secret collusion.

According to Abu Jihad, the main cause of Israel's Gaza Raid was
the sabotaging of a huge Israeli water storage and pumping facility
near Faluja. 'We used a lot of T.N.T. and the explosion made a big
flood. The next day I went myself to see some of the results. The
flood waters came to Beit Hanun which was about fifteen miles
from Faluja, then they passed into the Mediterranean. I saw seeds
and plants from Jewish settlements being swept along by the flood
waters. We were very happy.' Arafat and Wazir had previously
agreed that the water storage and pumping facility was a priority
target.

On the night of 28 February, the Israeli reprisal attack was led by
two platoons of paratroopers. They stormed and destroyed the
Egyptian army's headquarters building in Gaza itself. Abu Jihad
said that one of the main functions of the Egyptian garrison was to
protect the city's well. The fighting was fierce. On the Arab side
fourteen Egyptian and Palestinian soldiers lost their lives – the latter
were full-time and regular soldiers in the Egyptian army; and three
Arab civilians including a small boy were also killed. On the Israeli
side the casualties were eight killed and nine wounded. But there
was more killing to be done that night.

When the garrison at Gaza was overrun, a signal calling for
reinforcements was sent to Rafah. In answer to it an Egyptian
lieutenant and thirty-five soldiers, mostly Palestinians, scrambled
into a truck and set off for the city of Gaza at top speed. The second
Israeli attack group was expecting the truckload of reinforcements
and had prepared an ambush, which suggests that it was probably
an Israeli paratrooper, speaking in Arabic, who sent the call for
reinforcements.

The ambush was simple and effective. The Israelis stretched a
wire across the road. Attached to it were cans of petrol which, as the
truck hit the wire, were pulled against its sides. They exploded and
within seconds the truck was in flames. The Israelis then attacked it

with machine-guns and grenades. Only two or three of those inside the burning truck managed to jump clear to make a fight of it. Twenty-two of the reinforcements were killed. The other thirteen were wounded, most of them seriously.

Nasser was totally humiliated. He had visited the Gaza garrison shortly before the Israeli attack and he had told his men they could relax. He told them specifically that he was not intending to allow the Armistice Line to become a battlefront, and that he did not believe the Israelis would attack. He obviously thought he had the Palestinians under control. In the event, some of those killed in the attack on the Gaza garrison were shot in their beds.

The Palestinian demonstrations that followed, brilliantly exploited by Wazir and Arafat, were the second and main cause of the humiliation Nasser was made to feel. Said Abu Jihad: 'After the Israeli attack I gathered the students and we dipped our handkerchiefs in the blood of those who had been killed – they were mostly Palestinians. And when the morning light came we began to make our demonstrations. We had two slogans which were our message to Nasser. "If you want to save us, train us. If you want to save us, arm us." It was the biggest demonstration I had seen in Gaza in my life. All of the people joined in. Then, because of the feeling of the people, we had clashes with the Egyptian authorities. We burned their offices. It was a very great shock for Nasser. But we had more activities planned.'

While Arafat, in Cairo, waited for his cue, Wazir despatched representatives from Gaza to a number of Arab countries, including Jordan, Syria and the Lebanon, to tell the story of the Israeli attack and the Egyptian army's defeat. Up to this point Arab newspapers had been banned from giving space to the Palestinian point of view. But Arafat and Wazir had correctly calculated that Arab newspapers would be unable to resist first-hand accounts of the most serious clash between Israel and Egypt since the Armistice Agreements of 1949. Said Abu Jihad: 'For the first time since our tragedy, our voice, the voice of the Palestinian people, was heard everywhere in the Arab world. And the story we had to tell made a big scandal for Nasser. He was humiliated.'

On cue, and still as the leader of the Union of Palestinian Students, Arafat staged a demonstration at the Arab League headquarters in Cairo. He demanded that Nasser receive him and a student delegation to consider the situation in Gaza. Anxious to placate the Palestinians, Nasser quickly agreed to the meeting. During it, and according to Arafat's memory, 'Nasser said not less than forty times that he was greatly shocked, and that he had learned many things for the first time – including how much the Palestinian people were suffering.' To buy time while he considered his options, Nasser agreed to let Arafat and his delegation visit Gaza to study the situation and make a report.

'Arafat came officially to Gaza for three days,' said Abu Jihad. 'We stayed together for the whole time and he made a very big impression on our people, not just the students but all of the people. We felt and we knew that he was living our emotions.'

On his return to Cairo, Arafat submitted a report to Nasser. It said the main problem was that Egypt and the other Arab regimes had left the Palestinians without arms to defend themselves. It would seem that Arafat was trying to persuade Nasser to let him, Wazir and others set up some kind of official Palestinian defence force which Arafat hoped eventually to turn into a commando or strike force – with Nasser's blessing.

Nasser was not only shocked and humiliated, he was also trapped. Arafat's request that he arm the Palestinians added greatly to the burden of his agony about what to do.

On the one hand the President of Egypt had to demonstrate to his soldiers, his general public and the Arab world that he would not take Israel's attacks lying down. He had also to find a way to cool and appease the Palestinians. The problem was that Nasser could not afford to have his own men directly engaged in even minor clashes with the Israelis. The simple truth was that Egypt's armed forces were no match for Israel. They were weak, ill-equipped and still badly organized. And morale could not have been lower. That was the case for using the Palestinians to retaliate against the Israelis. On the other hand Nasser could not afford to set up Arafat and Wazir as leaders of an independent Palestinian military organization.

Nasser's answer was an unhappy and unfortunate compromise. He decided that some Palestinians should be trained and armed and then let loose against Israel. But he insisted that the training, the arming and the selection of targets should be controlled by Egyptian army intelligence officers who would not officially exist. In short, there was to be no role for Arafat and Wazir or any other aspiring Palestinian leader. Nasser wanted the best of both worlds. By unleashing the Palestinians against Israel he hoped to win respect in Egypt and the Arab world. But because he would also be claiming that Egyptian forces were not involved, he hoped to be able to persuade the West to restrain Israel.

Arafat and Wazir were not fooled. They knew that Nasser was using the Palestinians for his own ends, and that he would call off the attacks by his Palestinian commandos, or *fedayeen*, when it suited him. Arafat and Wazir were naturally disappointed because Nasser had denied them a role and, more important, the opportunity to create a military organization of their own with Egyptian blessing. But they had the compensation of knowing that their activities had brought about the Israeli reprisal attack which had forced Nasser's hand. To this point their strategy was working well.

Abu Jihad told me that his secret organization ceased to function when Nasser decided to use the Palestinians. He did not say that Nasser told Arafat and himself to stand aside, but that is the obvious implication. Abu Jihad also said that Nasser's man in Gaza was a Major Mustapha Hafez. It was his job to recruit and train Palestinian volunteers for hit-and-run missions in Israel. And according to Abu Jihad the Israelis were the Major's best recruiting sergeant. 'Soon after Major Hafez arrived to take charge, the Israelis shelled and bombed Gaza city and Deir El-Balah. A few weeks later the Israelis bombed Gaza again and many civilians were injured. The hospitals were full of the wounded. Major Hafez took some of his volunteers on a tour of the hospitals and then he told them: "Now you know why you must be prepared to sacrifice your lives."'

Though he was playing with fire, Nasser was aware that even if the West did have the will and the wish to restrain Israel, the *fedayeen* attacks that he was preparing to sponsor would lead to massive reprisal attacks against Egypt eventually. So it was that he became engaged in a desperate race against time to acquire the necessary weapons and equipment to strengthen his armed forces.

An examination of the record – including Nasser's own conversations with visiting foreign leaders, diplomats and senior U.N. officials – supports only one possible conclusion. It is that

Egypt's scramble to buy arms and weapons was for defensive purposes, and specifically to deter Israeli attacks. In 1955, after the Gaza Raid, Nasser's main intention was to make the price of attacking Egypt so high that Israel would not be able to afford it. In 1965, writing about 1955, Moshe Dayan said: 'When an Israeli force operated inside Arab territory without the local army's being able seriously to challenge them, the Arab military failure was openly demonstrated to their own people.'[17] Dayan was right. That was precisely what Israel's Gaza Raid on 28 February had demonstrated. And that, in turn, is why Nasser went shopping for arms.

The record is also very clear on a related matter. Nasser and the overwhelming majority of his fellow officers wanted the West, and America in particular, to be their arms suppliers. There can be no doubt that Nasser would have called off the *fedayeen* raids against Israel if the West had even hinted that it was prepared seriously to consider his requests.

When the West refused to supply Nasser he had no choice. He did what the Zionists before him had done – he turned to Czechoslovakia and thus the Soviet Union for his weapons. In September 1955, Nasser announced a huge arms deal with Czechoslovakia. From here on the Soviet Union was directly involved. Moscow was now in a position to do the same as the Western powers – to exploit the Arabs and the Arab-Israeli conflict for its own ends. And from that day to this, most Arabs who are politically conscious, and even many who are not, have been sick in their hearts. Arafat speaks for them all when he says: 'Your Western leaders were very blind and very stupid. The Soviet Union would not have been able to put one little finger in the Middle East if the West had not forced Nasser to turn to Moscow for help. It is true that a few Arabs, mainly a few Christian Arabs, say they are Marxists. But we Moslem people cannot be communists. To be a communist is against our religion. We are also anti-communism because of our traditions, our culture and our way of thinking. Those in the West who say we Arabs are allies of the communists are either very ignorant people or they are fools and criminals.'

Israel's official and public reaction to Nasser's arms deal with Czechoslovakia was predictable. The line was that Nasser had just one objective – to destroy the State of Israel. And the arms deal was the proof. Later Dayan was to write: 'The decisive intimation to Israel of an approaching Egyptian attack was the arms deal concluded between Czechoslovakia and Egypt. . .'[18]

After studying all available and relevant information, and on the basis of my private conversations over the years with many Israelis who ought to know the facts, I am convinced that most if not all of Israel's leaders of the day knew that what they were saying about Nasser's intentions added up to a propaganda lie. But from their own point of view there was a good reason why they had to tell it and promote it.

Israel's way of dealing with the Arabs was based on one simple idea and strategy. It was that the Arab regimes would only come round to accepting the Jewish State on its own terms – which included the suppression of the Palestinian people and the denial of their rights and identity – when they had been gunned and bombed into submission. For such a policy to be implemented with success, Israel needed to be, obviously, the strongest military power in the region. Unless it was, it could not dictate its terms for a settlement. Thus the real fear of Israel's leaders as far as the Arab regimes were concerned was not so much that they would one day be strong and efficient enough to defeat Israel on the battlefield, but that the day could come – unless Israel maintained her military supremacy – when the Arabs would acquire enough military strength to deter the reprisal attacks which were Israel's principal means of teaching the Arabs the necessary lessons. If that day came Israel would have to negotiate its continued existence. In those circumstances the Israelis would have to come to terms with the Palestinians; and that, in turn, would raise profound and valid questions about the legitimacy of the Zionist enterprise and the existence of the Jewish State.

Nasser's arms deal was no more than a potential threat to Israel's ability to impose her will on the Arabs by force. The reason why Israel worked so hard to promote the idea that what it actually faced was the threat of annihilation was to convince the West that it should supply the Jewish State with whatever weapons it asked for. An indication that Western leaders knew the Israelis were exaggerating and even lying about the nature of the threat they faced was President Eisenhower's refusal to supply Israel with fifty fighter aircraft and tanks and other heavy equipment. Israel had told the Americans it required them to balance the hardware that Nasser was shortly to receive.

There was one item on Nasser's shopping list that was cause for genuine alarm in Israel, however. He had asked for, and had been told that he would receive, Ilyushin jet bombers. These would be able to bomb Israeli cities from a height at which they could not be intercepted by Israel's Meteor jet fighters. It was also true that the Meteors would be outclassed as fighters by the MiG 15s which Nasser was also to receive. But the overall military balance was still in Israel's favour – as every Western expert knew. Even in terms of manpower the Israelis were ahead. The total manpower strength of the Arab League armies was 205,000, of which 100,000 were Egyptians. Israel could mobilize 250,000 men and women in forty-eight hours. All that the Israelis could claim with truth was that Nasser's Ilyushins and MiG 15s could pose a problem for them. But even this was solved within a few months when Israel persuaded France to supply it with Mystere Mark IV fighters. From then on Israel was, in reality, the military superpower of the region.

If those who were preparing to lead the Palestinians, Yasser Arafat and Khalil Wazir in particular, had appreciated this fact, events would certainly have taken a different course.

In July 1956, Arafat completed his studies at the University of Fuad the First. He emerged from it as a qualified civil engineer. When I asked him why he had chosen to be a civil engineer, he said: 'I was advanced in mathematics. My speciality was figures and calculations. Engineering was also the most useful subject for me to study. It would not prevent me from continuing with my military march – it would even help me.'

At the end of his university life, Arafat naturally ceased to be the President of the Union of Palestinian Students, which he had used as cover for his political activities. Without delay he invented a new cover. He created and became the Chairman of the Union of Palestinian Graduates. 'In this way,' said Arafat, 'I was able to develop official links and contacts with Palestinian graduates in every Arab country and even in Europe.' The future Chairman of the P.L.O. had also to earn a living. As soon as he left university he got a job as an engineer with one of Egypt's biggest construction companies.

In his last year at university, and because Nasser had insisted that his own intelligence people would organize and co-ordinate the *fedayeen* attacks on Israel from Gaza, Arafat had been more of a spectator than an instigator of the events which were pushing Israel and Egypt to war. But he was soon to be in action again.

Left to go their own way, Israel's leaders would probably have escalated their reprisal attacks against Egypt to the point of war – albeit a limited war. They were anxious to teach Nasser a lesson he would never forget to persuade him to call off the *fedayeen* attacks which were hurting Israel; and they were eager for an early opportunity to destroy as many as possible of the new Soviet weapons which were now arriving in Egypt. But Israel's leaders were given the opportunity to fight a major war when the British and French Governments invited them to join a conspiracy to destroy Nasser.

On 26 July, Nasser nationalized the Suez Canal through which the oil imports on which Britain was almost entirely dependent at the time passed. Nasser's grand gesture of defiance was inspired mainly by America's decision, announced a few days previously, to withdraw its support for the financing of the project which Nasser considered to be the key to Egypt's development – the building of the Aswan High Dam. He was also bitter because of what he regarded as a Western manoeuvre to sabotage the prospects for Arab unity. In believing there was such a manoeuvre Nasser was probably more right than wrong. The Baghdad Pact, signed in 1955 by Turkey, Iraq, Britain, Pakistan and Iran, and with the U.S. participating in its committees, was not just an alliance to keep communism at bay in the Middle East. It was also a backdoor way of allowing Britain and the U.S. to influence events in the region through important allies who would do more or less what they were told to do by the big powers.

When Nasser nationalized the Suez Canal, the British Prime Minister of the day, Anthony Eden, decided that the Egyptian leader had to be removed. The problem for Eden and his Government was finding the pretext for an invasion of Egypt. Nasser had not stopped the flow of oil through the canal and he had made it clear that he did not intend to do so. A pretext was invented during secret discussions between Britain, France and Israel. The basic plot was for the Israelis to attack Egypt on 29 October. The next day the British and French Governments would issue twelve-hour ultimatums, which would require Egyptian and Israeli forces to stop fighting and withdraw their troops from the immediate vicinity of the Suez Canal. Anglo-French forces would then be stationed on the canal to keep the Egyptians and the Israelis apart and to safeguard shipping. The assumption of the British and the French, and the hope of the Israelis, was that Nasser would be totally humilated and toppled. (Thirty years later it was revealed, officially, that British agents were licensed to kill Nasser.)

When Egypt rejected the ultimatums, the British and the French launched attacks on Egyptian airfields and other military targets. This was followed by paratroop and commando landings in the Canal Zone. When the fighting started, Arafat immediately volunteered for service in the Egyptian army. As a second lieutenant he led the first Egyptian bomb-disposal squad into Port Said. When I asked Arafat about his experience he laughed. 'You know,' he said, 'working with bombs on the ground is simple and more safe. For dealing with bombs and mines on the ground there are rules. If you follow the rules you can survive. But when the bombs come from the air survival is a matter of chance – there are no rules.' Arafat seemed to have enjoyed his part in the war.

When the fighting was stopped at midnight on 6 November, mainly by U.S. pressure, it was Britain and France who were humiliated. On the significance of what had happened Khalad Hassan offered this thought: 'The Americans were not really doing the Arabs much of a favour by stopping Britain and France. Of course that is what the Americans wanted the Arabs to think. But really the U.S. was playing a clever game. The Americans were pleased that Britain had been humiliated and they believed they could now replace Britain as the major Western influence in the region – which is exactly what happened. Many things were changed by the war of 1956.'

Nasser was now a hero. He was the undisputed leader of Egypt and, generally speaking, the Arab world. He was hailed as the new saviour by the Arab masses, including the Palestinians. But as the Palestinians were soon to discover, Nasser was not about to change his view that no part of Palestine could be liberated by force of arms. The speed of Israel's advance in the war just ended had only served to reinforce Nasser's belief that the Jewish State would not be beaten on the battlefield in any future he could see.

During the fighting the Israelis had captured the whole of the Sinai Peninsula including the Gaza Strip, and they had also taken over Sharm El-Sheikh and the island of Tiran at the entrance to the

Gulf of Aqaba. For Israel it was, in fact, a stunning military victory. On 15 November, after the arrival of the first contingents of the United Nations Emergency Force (U.N.E.F.), British, French and Israeli forces started to withdraw. For the Israelis the sticking points were Sharm El-Sheikh and Gaza. There the Israelis intended to remain in occupation until Egypt made peace with the Jewish State. And so began a battle of wills between Israel and America. President Eisenhower was determined to make the Israelis give back every inch of Egyptian territory they had conquered, but it took him several months to do it.

While the Israelis remained in occupation of Gaza, Arafat and Wazir were kept busy there. Wazir had moved to Cairo in September to continue his studies. And it was from Cairo, in consultation with Arafat, that he directed actions against the Israelis. Said Abu Jihad: 'When the Israelis occupied Gaza, I reactivated my underground organization. They needed some arms and ammunition but in this time the circumstances were favourable to us. My commandos carried out some operations against the Israelis. It was good for them to have the experience of occupation. But mostly I was directing operations to liquidate spies and those who were co-operating with the Israelis.'

One of Wazir's secret agents in Gaza was a very young and very beautiful woman. Her name was Intissar – it means 'victory'. She was just fifteen. She was Wazir's cousin and she was to become the keeper of many secrets for Wazir and Arafat; but at this time in Gaza she had a secret of her own – she was in love with her cousin Khalil. Under the cover of her love affair, and then later her marriage to Wazir, she was also to become Fatah's secret weapon.

When the Israelis occupied Gaza in 1956, Intissar was already an experienced courier. From the age of thirteen she had been the bearer of many of Wazir's secret messages. During the Israeli occupation her job was to pass on Wazir's instructions and distribute propaganda leaflets calling on the Palestinians to resist the occupation. 'Sometimes,' she told me, 'I used to carry weapons from place to place. I remember one time when I was carrying some grenades in a basket of oranges. My mother discovered them. She was very frightened. She said that if the Israelis caught me with the grenades I would be killed. I said to her: "Mother, most of these Israeli soldiers are young boys. I am a young woman. I know how to deal with them. Please, do not worry!"'

Intissar's most vivid memory of the Israeli occupation of Gaza is the precautions that were taken by many Palestinian families, her own included, to prevent their daughters being raped by the Israeli soldiers. 'We all knew that Israeli soldiers were coming to the houses at night to take the girls and have sex with them. But we became very anxious and frightened after an incident when one Israeli soldier killed the husband of the woman he wanted to take. Then he killed the woman. If you quote me I don't think the Israelis will try to say that I am telling lies because everybody knows about that incident.

'After those killings we organized ourselves to defend the girls. The families agreed that they would cry out to warn others if Israeli soldiers came to their houses. We were frequently woken up by these cries. In some places where the entrance to several houses was a narrow street, the families used to build barricades with iron. They used to put them up in the night and take them down in the morning. My father had his own special plan. Although I was fifteen and my sister was one year older, my father made us sleep in the same room with him and our mother. And my father had a ladder which he put against the bedroom wall. It went to the roof. If the Israelis came my father's idea was that my sister and me should go up the ladder and escape to a neighbour's house. And from there we were to run away if it was necessary. My father was so anxious that he told us every night what we should do.'

When the war was over Arafat was asked if he wanted to stay in the Egyptian army. He was told that his skill as a bomb-disposal expert was highly valued and he was offered a promotion. 'They wanted me to train others,' Arafat said. 'I told them I had another job. I knew that if I stayed in the army I would have to follow rules and regulations and I would not be free to organize.'

Arafat's organizing had already taken him to student conferences in Prague and Stuttgart. Although he did not know it at the time, the network of Palestinian student organizations he helped to create in West Germany was to prove to be his best insurance policy for the future. But it was in Cairo, at the end of 1956 and the beginning of 1957, that Arafat and some of those who are today his most senior colleagues began to ask a fundamental question: where should they go from here? Fatah has its origins in the debates of that period.

Because he had a living to earn, Arafat was back at work as an engineer. But his life and his love were politics. 'I was excited,' he told me, 'because our Palestinian student organizations were taking root everywhere – throughout the Arab world and in Europe. But what was the purpose of our organizing?'

The talking in Cairo was dominated by Arafat and Wazir. Both men had no doubts at all about the way forward. But a demand for independent Palestinian military action, which they both favoured, would not have won majority support at the time. When Fatah's leaders did eventually confront the question, the division provoked by it very nearly destroyed their organization.

'Our first decision – you can say it was only a decision in principle,' said Abu Jihad, 'was that we had to organize and arm ourselves.'

The second decision in principle was that the Palestinians should not be members of any Arab political party or movement – including the Moslem Brotherhood. Abu Iyad, then Salah Khalaf, was a leading participant in the Cairo debates. 'It was very clear that Arafat and Wazir hated political parties,' he told me. 'Wazir said they were a "joke". Arafat said, and he was right, that Palestinian families were being divided because fathers and sons and brothers were members of different parties, one supporting this regime, one supporting another regime and so on.' But there was more to it than that. Arafat and Wazir were convinced that an independent Palestinian movement, even a political one, would not be allowed to survive in the jungle of Arab politics unless the Palestinians could demonstrate that they were not intending to interfere in the internal affairs of the Arab nations.

Although the Cairo debates did not define objectives, the idea that there had to be an independent Palestinian movement of some kind was firmly planted. The task to which Arafat and Wazir were now to commit themselves was organizing it. In every country and place where there was a Palestinian community, and using the student organizations as a cover for their activities, they planned to create underground political cells and unite existing ones. They had to be underground because no Arab regime wanted to see the emergence of an independent Palestinian movement.

In March 1957, the Israelis ended their occupation of the Gaza Strip after President Eisenhower had threatened to support sanctions against Israel if they did not withdraw. When the situation in Gaza was more or less back to normal, Wazir left Cairo to take a teaching job in Saudi Arabia. He needed the money but he was much more attracted by the opportunity to organize an underground network there. At about the same time Khalaf returned to Gaza where he was to spend several years teaching in the schools of the refugee camps.

Arafat himself had planned to make Cairo his headquarters. The place he called home, his family and his job were there. And with Nasser now the undisputed leader of much of the Arab world, Cairo was obviously going to be the powerhouse of the promised Arab revolution. It was there that many of the important decisions about future Arab policy and strategy would be made. Arafat intended to travel as much as his job and his employers would allow, but Cairo was the place for his base. Or so Arafat thought. But it was not to be. He was shortly to learn that his presence in Egypt was not wanted.

If Arafat had known all of the reasons why the Israelis ended their occupation of Gaza, he would probably have left Egypt in disgust before he was more or less obliged to go. He was aware that President Eisenhower had read the riot act to Israel's leaders, but he did not know that they had driven a very hard bargain. Through the offices of the U.N., and in order to give Eisenhower what he needed to get tough with the Israelis, Nasser had been required to make two secret promises. One was that he would not instigate any Egyptian military action against Israel for a period of ten years – unless he was provoked. The other was that he would prevent the Palestinians launching attacks on Israel from Egyptian soil and the Gaza Strip.

Soon after the Israelis withdrew from Gaza, Arafat said his nose detected 'a different smell' in Cairo. He also sensed a coolness in some of Nasser's colleagues whom he had previously regarded as friends and collaborators. But the first real sign that he was in trouble with his enemies in Egypt's intelligence community came when he returned from a 'secret' visit to Iraq. 'It was not really a secret visit as such,' Arafat told me. 'The real problem was that I was supposed to tell the Egyptian authorities where I was going and who I was going to see. I did not do so for obvious reasons.'

The 'obvious reasons' were that at the time of his visit to Baghdad, Iraq was Nasser's enemy. It would not be unfair to describe its ruler, King Feisal, and its Prime Minister, Nuri es-Said, as British puppets. Nasser had long believed that they were allowing themselves to be promoted by the British as the alternative to his leadership of the Arab world.

In fact the purpose of Arafat's visit was not what Egypt's intelligence people assumed it to be. Arafat did not go to Iraq to speak with Feisal and his Prime Minister. He went to talk with the men who were planning to kill them – Brigadier Karim Kassem and Colonel Salem Aref.

'When I returned to Cairo they began to squeeze me,' Arafat said. 'My employers told me that I should not have gone to Iraq. I told them it was none of their business because I had taken unpaid leave that was due to me. Then I learned that it was some Egyptian intelligence officers who were squeezing me through my employers. I decided that it was time for me to leave Egypt. Day by day it was becoming more clear that I would not be free to organize if I stayed in Cairo.'

When he left Egypt Arafat's destination was Kuwait. But that was not his first choice. 'I had a job waiting for me in Saudi Arabia but the official paperwork was delayed. While I was waiting I had the offer of another job, this one in Kuwait. I decided to take it.' The obvious implication is that he thought it was too dangerous to wait in Cairo for the paperwork that would allow him to enter Saudi Arabia. It actually arrived very soon after he landed in Kuwait.

Before the confrontation with Nasser, Arafat was to find himself at odds with the intellectual elite of his generation. And the setting for that drama was Kuwait.

# 6

# A Candle in the Darkness

Within weeks of his arrival in Kuwait, Arafat was again setting the pace he wanted others to follow. In September or October he formed what can be called the first of Fatah's underground and secret cells. It had five members – Yasser Arafat, Khalil Wazir and three others.

Wazir had survived only three months in Saudi Arabia. Without elaboration he told me there were 'many reasons' why he left that country. The Saudis were probably deeply suspicious of his underground activities and asked him to leave. Wazir went directly to Cairo where he intended to discuss his next move with Arafat. On arrival there Wazir was shocked and disturbed by his discovery that Arafat had been obliged to seek refuge in Kuwait. It was not a good sign. By mutual and secret agreement the two of them were supposed to be organizing a network of underground cells from which their independent organization was shortly to emerge, or so they hoped, yet here they were being driven from one Arab country after another.

Khalad Hassan said, 'If Kuwait's rulers had not allowed us the freedom to organize, there may not have been a Palestinian regeneration.'

Wazir left Cairo for Kuwait without delay. But he moved with extreme caution. He planned for the possibility that he would be tailed by Egyptian intelligence agents who were anxious to add to their dossier on Arafat and his activities. On his arrival in Kuwait, which remained a British Protectorate until June 1961, Wazir went to great lengths to avoid attracting the attention and interest of British security agents. As a consequence of the precautions he took it was nearly one month before he decided he was 'clean enough' to risk a rendezvous with Arafat.

When they met in August or September, it was apparently difficult for Wazir to decide which of the two of them was the most frustrated. Um Jihad was later to tell me that her husband was, in fact, even more emotional than Arafat; but that unlike Arafat he fought hard to 'keep his feelings inside of him'. She added: 'But this self-control is very dangerous for him. Sometimes he just collapses at home and I think he is having a heart attack. He is not. It is the price he pays for keeping his emotions to himself.

The cause of the frustration was not simply the difficulties of trying to organize an underground movement in the hostile environment of the Arab world. Their real fear was that time was against them. Said Abu Jihad: 'We believed, Arafat and me, that it was only by military actions that we could fix the Palestinian identity. That was our slogan. What did we mean? We were convinced that our first task was to prove to the Arab regimes and the world that we Palestinians still existed and that our problem could not be swept under the carpet. I agree with you that we were young and naive about many things in those days . . . but we knew that guns spoke louder than words in the world of the big powers. You can say we decided that we had to speak the same language as those who wanted us to disappear.'

When Arafat and Wazir talked in Kuwait in August or September 1957 they knew there were powerful arguments against the quick military action they wanted. They knew there was a strong case for taking time to build their organization and to raise money to equip it and then more time to train their fighters. But it was the time factor that worried them most. The more time passed without some military action to prove that some Palestinians had not given up the struggle, the more likely it was that the Palestinian spirit would be completely broken.

Abu Jihad continued: 'We decided, Arafat and me, that it was the moment for the talking to stop and the action to start. We did not believe the Palestinians could afford the luxury of discussions about the philosophy of how to liberate. I can say we were guided by two points. We did not need to be convinced that we Palestinians had to depend on ourselves. We had waited so long for the Arabs to help us regain our country and they had failed us. That was the first point. The second was that we were inspired by the revolutions that were taking place in the world. The revolution in Algeria was burning like a strong flame of hope in front of us. When the Algerians started their revolution in 1954, they were only some few hundred Arabs against 20,000 French troops and well-armed settlers with much combat experience. The revolution in Algeria was to us the proof that a people can organize themselves and build their military power during the fighting.'

Such was the thinking of Wazir and Arafat when they formed the first of Fatah's underground and secret cells. The other three members of it were Adel Karim who is today an Inspector of Mathematics in Kuwait; Youseff Amira, who today owns a supermarket in Kuwait; and a man named Shedid.

'At the time we were not concerned about a name for the organization we were creating,' said Abu Jihad. 'Later there was much discussion about what we should call it, and at one point we had a list of twenty names. But in the beginning, and even after we had chosen the name of Al-Fatah, there was a great need for total secrecy. We had to protect ourselves from the intelligence services of the Arab regimes. We knew they would try to put their agents inside us. So in the beginning we were an organization without a name.'

As conceived by Arafat and Wazir, the first Fatah cell was to be the nucleus of a rapidly expanding network of similar cells throughout the Arab world and beyond. Each new cell was to be responsible for raising money to buy weapons. And within a short time the leaders of the cells would come together to form the leadership of the new organization. That was the theory. Arafat and Wazir began to feel that the day when they could launch military actions against Israel was drawing near. But their optimism was not justified. It was to be seven long years before Fatah emerged from the underground.

Part of the reason seems to be that Arafat and Wazir had a massive credibility problem. To the majority of activists and intellectuals in the Palestinian diaspora as a whole, the proposition that the Palestinians could liberate their homeland through armed struggle by themselves was ludicrous. In fact Arafat and Wazir were not nearly so ambitious as they had to pretend to be in order to promote their ideas. As Abu Jihad said, their essential idea was that military action was necessary to fix the Palestinian identity. Beyond that their actual intention was to keep the pot boiling and to provoke a war between the Arabs and Israel which, they believed, the Arabs were bound to win. And that was the end point of their thinking in 1957 and for the next decade – until the Arabs lost the war that had to be won if the strategy was to be justified. Arafat and Wazir could not afford to say they saw independent Palestinian military action as a means to an end and not an end in itself, and that their real strategy was to push the Arabs into a war which the regimes did not want. So most of the Palestinian activists concluded that Arafat and Wazir seriously believed that the Palestinians could liberate their homeland entirely by their own efforts. Hence the credibility problem.

But there was another and related reason why Arafat and Wazir were to find themselves representing a minority point of view during Fatah's underground years. An easy majority of Palestinians – the masses and many who were to become leaders – were content to leave the task of liberating Palestine to Nasser and the revolutionary Arab regimes. Like Arafat and Wazir, most Palestinians were by now aware that they had lost their homeland because of the impotence and the corruption of the Arab regimes of the old order. Most Palestinians understood that it was because the regimes of the old order were so corrupt that they had become the puppets of the British and the other big powers who had brought the Jewish State into being for their own ends. When Nasser came to power, and particularly after his victory over the British and the French in 1956, most Palestinians simply assumed that everything would change, and that liberating Palestine would be a priority of the pan-Arab revolution Nasser was claiming to lead.

Of all of those who were to become P.L.O. leaders, and whose actions were to force Western public opinion to spare a thought or two for the plight of the Palestinians, none at the time was more supportive of the idea that the Palestinians should put their trust in the new Arab regimes, and in Nasser in particular, than Dr George Habash.

The future leader of the Popular Front for the Liberation of Palestine (P.F.L.P.) – the organization which pioneered the hijacking of international airliners – was born in Lydda (Lod) in

1926. He was the son of a Greek Orthodox grain merchant. At the American University in Beirut where he studied medicine, Habash was regarded by all as an outstanding and brilliant student. In 19.‾3 and with others – including Wadi Haddad, who was to become the mastermind of the P.F.L.P.'s terror operations – Habash formed the Arab Nationalist Movement (A.N.M.). It was an alliance of Arab radicals who firmly believed that Nasser would succeed in changing and uniting the Arab world. The A.N.M. pledged itself to support Nasser's efforts. At the time, in fact from 1953 until 1967, Habash was convinced that Nasser held the key to the liberation of Palestine through Arab unity, and that he would use it.

I asked Habash why, in the late 1950s and the early 1960s, he was opposed to the underground ideas about the need for an independent Palestinian liberation organization or movement. He replied: 'If you are saying that I was against the Palestinians taking their own role in the liberation of their country, our country, then that is not the case. What I opposed was the point of view which said that only the Palestinians were concerned with facing Zionism and liberating their homeland. I believed the problem of liberation was so complicated that we had to work with the revolutionary Arab regimes and the Arab masses. We had to have a co-ordinated strategy. I used to say to our colleagues in Fatah that they were wrong to believe that Algeria was a model for us to follow or copy. What was happening in Algeria was a simple or classic colonial struggle. Our situation was not the same. It was so much more complicated because of the vested interests of the big powers. It wasn't just a question of the Palestinians against the Israelis, or even the Arabs against the Israelis. We had to consider the American involvement, the Soviet involvement and so on. And that is why I insisted in those days on co-ordination with Nasser and the revolutionary Arab regimes. We can say they did not live up to our expectations and this, as you know, made us change our thinking.'

In the late 1950s and the early 1960s there is no doubt that the views expressed by Habash were shared by an easy majority of Palestinians.

Less than twenty-four hours after Arafat and Wazir had formed their first underground and secret cell, they were shaken by some bad news from a totally unexpected quarter. Shedid, the fifth member of the cell, announced that he would not be attending any further meetings. He was quitting. After a sleepless night he said to Wazir: 'My circumstances are such that I cannot continue with you.' In other words, as Abu Jihad told me: 'He decided he could not support us in the way we intended to go.'

Shedid's decision did not please Arafat and Wazir. It also made them realize how difficult it was going to be to win support for their concept of an independent Palestine liberation organization which, if they had their way, would launch military actions against Israel with the minimum possible delay. And there was more bad news to come. In the discussions that followed, Arafat and Wazir learned that their other two partners in the cell, Karim and Amira, shared many of Shedid's doubts. Seven years later Karim and Amira were to follow Shedid into the political wilderness. They chose to leave Fatah at the moment when they would have caused it to split if they had pushed their opposition to the line favoured by Arafat and Wazir. But in 1957 they were content to have their reservations noted.

Within a matter of days, and perhaps to demonstrate to Karim and Amira that they were pragmatists and not romantics, Arafat and Wazir had revised their expectations and were ready with a new strategy for assaulting what they saw as the main obstacle in their way. In their view the main obstacle was the ignorance of those Palestinians – in fact the vast majority – who believed, in good faith, that they could depend on Nasser and the revolutionary Arab regimes of the new order to liberate their homeland. Arafat and Wazir were convinced, and they were right, that the ignorance existed and persisted merely because the Arab regimes had banned all discussion of the Palestinian problem. What was therefore needed was an underground Palestinian publication, a newspaper or at least a regular magazine of substance, that would seek to convince its readers that the Arab regimes did not intend to fight to liberate Palestine and that the Palestinians had to rely on themselves by supporting the independent liberation movement that Arafat and Wazir were struggling to create.

Said Abu Jihad: 'Our opinion was that our people were living in darkness. The magazine we intended to publish was to be a candle in the darkness.'

That was the theory, but there was much work to be done before they could light the candle. With help from Karim and Amira,

Arafat and Wazir had to find a publisher whom they could trust with their lives. They had also to organize an underground distribution network. They knew they could count on the various student organizations, but they had also to penetrate the refugee camps which were tightly controlled by the intelligence services of the Arab regimes. And above all, they had somehow to raise the money to pay for the venture. That year, 1958, was mainly spent in preparation.

The magazine was to be called *Our Palestine: The Call to Life.* It was Arafat himself who provided most if not all of the money to make it possible. 'I was financing it because, let me say, my circumstances were convenient,' he said. Of the remaining four members of the first Fatah cell Arafat was, in fact, the only one who had the opportunity to make money. Kuwait was about to experience a sensational development explosion. There were fortunes to be made. From the moment of his arrival Arafat had set himself up as a construction and contracting engineer, working first for the P.W.D. (Public Works Department). In the period from 1957 to 1964 he did make a great deal of money; and as Khalad Hassan has said, there is no doubt that the future leader of the P.L.O. could have become a millionaire several times over if he had stayed in Kuwait as a businessman. 'But I was not interested in the money for myself,' Arafat said. 'I knew I would have to finance our activities until we had established our organization.'

It was shortly before the publication of the first edition of *Our Palestine* in 1959 that Arafat, Wazir and their associates chose the name Al-Fatah. Said Abu Jihad: 'It came about in this way. We said we were a movement – not a group, not a front and not an organization. But a movement for what? A movement for national liberation. Therefore we fixed our name. We were the movement for the national liberation of Palestine – *Harakat Al-Tahrir Al-Watani Al-Filastini*.' Fatah came from reversing the initial letters.

Abu Jihad punctuated his story with chuckles and laughter. 'Many of the editorials were written under the signature of Fatah. Sometimes it was the name in full. Sometimes it was F.T.H. And everybody was asking the same question. "Who is this Mr Fatah?" they were saying!'

Arafat himself put the first monthly edition of the magazine to bed. When the articles were prepared he travelled to Beirut. It was there that they had found a backstreet publisher whom they felt they could trust. With the first edition there were no problems. They had more than enough material. 'But it was not always so,' Arafat said. 'On many occasions we did not have enough articles and pictures to fill the thirty or more pages. When that happened I or Abu Jihad, or both of us, would sit in the printing shop writing more words to fill the space. And when we were short of ideas we called on our friends in Beirut to help us.'

The content of *Our Palestine* was crude propaganda. When it spoke about the future it was totally uncompromising. *Right* was defined as 'everything that hastens the disappearance of Israel'. *Good* was 'that which leads to the collapse of the usurper state'. And *peace* was 'vengeance against the butchers of Deir Yassin and the criminals of Qibya'. But making policy was not the name of the game. *Our Palestine* had only two real objectives. The first was to convince as many Palestinians as possible that they were deluded if they believed that Nasser and the other Arab leaders were serious about liberating Palestine by military or any other means. The second was to persuade as many Palestinians as possible that the only alternative was for the Palestinians themselves to play the leading role in the liberation struggle.

On how to deal with Israel, Arafat, Wazir and others who wrote the copy for *Our Palestine* did not pull their punches. But most of the anger and the contempt in the columns of the magazine was directed at the Arab regimes of the new order 'which have stopped the Palestinians' mouths, tied their hands, deprived them of their freedom of action in what is left of their own country and resisted the idea of their regroupment'.

To the Arab regimes of the front-line states, *Our Palestine* was deeply subversive literature. And according to Arafat and Wazir, the intelligence services of Egypt and Syria were ordered to take all necessary measures to prevent the distribution of the magazine. Said Abu Jihad: 'As a consequence of the activities of many Arab intelligence services we had a feast of problems. In Egypt and Syria *Our Palestine* was banned. In Jordan it was sometimes banned. In the Lebanon and the Gulf States it was okay. We were also sending the magazine to Palestinians in Europe and America.'

As well as being a leading contributor to the magazine, and also its chief photographer, Wazir was in charge of the underground distribution network. And one of his personal responsibilities was beating the ban in Syria. 'I remembered one occasion when I entered Syria from the Lebanon by car in the normal way. I had 200 copies of the magazine to distribute in Damascus. At the customs post they searched the car and found the magazines. "What is this?" they said. I was very friendly and I put on a big act. "You don't know what this is?" I said in astonishment. "You ought to be ashamed. This is *Our Palestine*. You keep it, and if you like it I will make sure you always get one for free when I pass." When I was no more in the sight of the customs post I drove very fast to Damascus!'

Many Palestinians, particularly those in the refugee camps which were under constant surveillance by the Arab intelligence services, discovered that reading *Our Palestine* was a dangerous occupation. 'There was a man called Sarraj who was a military governor in Syria,' said Abu Jihad. 'I will not forget him. He was in charge of the spies inside the camps in his area. When refugees who were caught with *Our Palestine* were brought to him, he had his own special way of torturing them. He would put his boot on their throats and he pressed down harder and harder as he asked his questions. In Syria, Egypt and other Arab countries, many Palestinians were tortured for reading our magazine. And always they were asked the same questions: "What is the name of the organization to which you belong?" and "What are the names of the people you know in the organization?"' Most had no information to give.

To Arafat and Wazir the fact that Palestinians were being tortured just for reading *Our Palestine* had its positive side. It was proof that the Arab regimes and their intelligence services were convinced that an underground and independent Palestinian organization was already in existence. In reality it was not, but if that was what the Arab regimes and their intelligence services believed, it was a safe bet that many Palestinians had drawn or were drawing the same conclusion. Said Arafat: 'It was this appearance of power – a power, in fact that we did not have at the time – that enabled us to form more cells and build the wide base for our organization.'

'Yah,' smiled Abu Jihad, 'that is the way it was. Without the appearance of power which *Our Palestine* gave us, it is possible that we might have been finished.'

As Fatah's recruiting sergeant, *Our Palestine* was a success. And it was Wazir, in consultation with Arafat and others who had formed cells, who co-ordinated the recruiting drive. His cover for that assignment was his duties as the editorial executive responsible for the 'Letters to the Editor' section of the magazine.

'Now I will tell you the secret of how we organized ourselves,' said Abu Jihad. 'In every edition of the magazine we gave an address for those people who wanted to write letters to the editor. In time we began to receive correspondence from Palestinians all over the Arab world. Many were writing not as individuals but as the leaders of local groups – political groups – which they themselves had organized under the cover of clubs and societies. Of course they took some care about what they said in writing, but they all found their own ways to hint what their real purpose was. They would say, for example, "We are smelling something good in your magazine." It was their way of telling us that they knew we were organizing and that they were interested in joining us. And then they would say, "We have an important matter that we would like to discuss with you. Please send somebody to contact us at such and such an address."

'Directly we would send one of our people to make contact. Of course we had to take many precautions. At the first meeting with each new person or group there was suspicion on both sides. We had to be certain that they were not agents for an Arab intelligence service. And they also had to be convinced that we were not the agent or puppet of some Arab regime. Then, when we were confident, we would whisper into their ears: "Yes, you are right. We are a big underground organization with many people. We have a political and military programme for liberation. We are ready for you to co-operate with us. You must form a cell and collect money and prepare for the day when we become one movement." And so it was that we developed the streams that became the river.'

It should be remembered that Arafat was still working as a construction and contracting engineer, and that Wazir was still earning his living as a teacher. But when time allowed they travelled, separately and to different destinations, to make personal contact with those who were organizing the new cells. Arafat paid the air fares and the other expenses.

There were forty monthly editions of *Our Palestine*. By the time of the last one, the proof that the magazine had served its purpose was evident – the stage was set for Fatah to come officially, but still secretly, into being. But it was with the publication of the first edition early in 1959 that Arafat and Wazir had passed the point of no return. From then on they were committed to the idea of armed struggle against Israel, which came to mean that they were also committed to a bloody showdown with Nasser's Egypt and the other front-line Arab states. The showdown was inevitable given that the Arab regimes had no intention of fighting Israel to liberate Palestine. Forty months after the launch of their magazine the implications of the stand that Arafat and Wazir had taken were obvious to both men. If they were now to fail to get the necessary support for independent military action, they would be finished as leaders. They were to come much closer to failure than either of them had imagined in their darkest moments.

In the early 1960s, before Arafat and Wazir were to find themselves in confrontation with a majority of their colleagues on the question of military action, there were three developments which helped to swing the pendulum of Palestinian opinion in the direction of support for those who were saying that the Palestinians could not rely on the Arab regimes.

The first, in September 1961, was the collapse of the union between Egypt and Syria. The two countries had decided to unite in 1958. To some Palestinian intellectuals who had committed themselves to Nasser and his view that Arab unity was the prerequisite for the liberation of Palestine, the split between Egypt and Syria was an ominous sign. If these two important countries could not maintain their union, what price the greater and wider Arab unity that was the key to liberating Palestine? Many of the Palestinians who were content to rely on Nasser did not understand his real strategy. When Nasser talked about Arab unity being the prerequisite for the liberation of Palestine, he meant that it was only when the Arabs were united that they would have the necessary political and economic leverage to bargain successfully with the West and the U.S. in particular. In short, it was only when the Arabs were united that they could persuade the U.S. to oblige Israel to come to some arrangement with the Palestinians. The Arab unity Nasser sought was not for the purpose of a military confrontation with Israel. It was this that many Palestinians did not understand in the late 1950s.

The second development was a dramatic statement by Nasser. In Gaza, early in 1962, he announced that he and Arab leaders had no plan for the liberation of Palestine. Though it was not a matter of public knowledge at the time, Nasser was responding to secret signals from the Kennedy Administration in Washington. As all American Presidents do for a few weeks every four years, Kennedy was listening to the Middle East experts in the State Department. And they were telling him, as they and their predecessors had been telling every American President since 1948, that American support for Israel's refusal to give the Palestinians something would have disastrous consequences for U.S. interests in the Arab world in the long term. Kennedy was not only listening to this advice, he was acting on it. And he decided to push for a comprehensive settlement of the Arab-Israeli conflict. Kennedy knew that the Arab regimes that mattered would make peace with Israel, provided Israel was willing to reach some accommodation with the Palestinians. As a first step Kennedy was privately pressing Israel to allow at least some Palestinian refugees to return to their homes. And this, of course, was in tune with all of the relevant U.N. resolutions of the time. In their usual way, Israel's leaders refused to co-operate. Kennedy's first response was a tough one. He told the Israelis: no compromise, no missiles. At the time Israel was awaiting delivery of some Hawk missiles.

While this particular battle of wills was going on, Nasser received word from Washington that he could help Kennedy and himself by making a public statement in which the Egyptian leader would indicate that he had no intention of fighting Israel. Kennedy himself did not need to be convinced that Nasser was not interested in war with Israel. The statement he wanted Nasser to make was for public relations purposes. Such was the background to Nasser's famous speech. The fact that he delivered it in Gaza was almost as significant as the speech itself. By saying what he said there, Nasser was trying to tell Kennedy, and Israel, that he was also prepared to deal with any outbreak of Palestinian militarism if Egypt, America and Israel could do a deal which would satisfy the minimum demands of the Palestinians. In the end, and like every American President before and after him, Kennedy backed down in the face of Israeli and Jewish blackmail. At the time the President was reluctantly supporting the efforts of his brother Robert, the

Attorney-General, to smash 'organized crime' – a euphemism for the Mafia. In the circumstances, the President did not need a crystal ball to tell him that he was making too many powerful enemies, including some who would be prepared to have him killed. With the Mafia gunning for him, Kennedy needed the support of the Jews.

The third development was the defeat of the French by Algeria's liberation movement, the Front de la Libération Nationale – the F.L.N. as it was known to the world. After more than seven years of struggle, the French lost the will to fight on. And in July 1962, the F.L.N.'s leader, Ben Bella, proclaimed Algeria's independence.

As events were to prove, Arafat and Wazir were badly mistaken in their view that they could apply the lessons of Algeria's experience of armed struggle to the situation in Palestine. But they were right in their belief that a good relationship with an independent and revolutionary Algeria would enable them to promote their own cause on the world stage. Arafat was ready and waiting to seize the opportunity.

'I started my contacts with the Algerian revolutionaries in the early 1950s,' Arafat told me. 'I was, in fact, in very good dialogue with them before they began their long struggle in 1954. I stayed in touch and they promised they would help us when they had achieved their independence. I never doubted for one moment that they would win and that their victory would be very important for us.'

On 3 July, Yasser Arafat, the construction and contracting engineer from Kuwait, was among the V.I.P.s from all over the world who were gathered in Algeria to celebrate the nation's independence from French rule. At the first possible opportunity, and with great tact and charm, Arafat reminded his hosts of their promise. 'My dear brother Yasser, we made that promise and we will honour it,' said President Ben Bella. 'In the coming days we will sit together and discuss how we can help your revolution.'[19]

It was a good start but Arafat was in a hurry. He had come to Algiers with a specific request for help, and he had vowed to his colleagues in Kuwait that he would not return without a favourable response from Ben Bella. What Arafat wanted was permission in principle for Fatah to open its first official office in Algiers. It would not bear the name of Fatah. It would be called the Bureau de la Palestine. But it would be Fatah in all but name.

Fatah's need for an official and above ground or public presence somewhere did not have to be spelled out to the Algerians. They were aware that Arafat and his colleagues were as good as prisoners in the Arab heartland. Officially they were not allowed to speak or write about their cause. Officially they were not permitted to organize. And they were denied the opportunity to meet and talk openly with politicians, diplomats and journalists from outside the Arab world. An office in Algiers would end Fatah's isolation and enable its leaders to be in touch with the world, in particular with Third World and revolutionary leaders, including the Chinese, who would be frequent visitors to Algeria.

In time Arafat would ask his Algerian friends for support of a different kind — facilities for training Fatah fighters and then arms and ammunition. But on this visit to Algiers he had decided to cross one bridge at a time. His caution was dictated by the knowledge that his request for help had placed Ben Bella in a difficult position. On the one hand the Algerian leader had good reasons for supporting the Palestinians. He believed in their cause and helping them would underline his own revolutionary credentials. On the other hand there would be problems with Nasser. The Egyptian leader was bound to oppose any move that would improve the prospects for the emergence of an independent Palestine liberation movement.

Arafat got what he wanted. In principle Ben Bella agreed to his request. Arafat was pleased, even excited. He had made a very dramatic breakthrough. But there was a nagging worry. How would Nasser respond when he learned that the Palestinians were going to be allowed to open a window on the world in Algiers? It was natural and obvious that he would regard the Bureau de la Palestine as a major threat to his policy of containing and controlling the Palestinians. In his own mind Arafat had already decided that Khalil Wazir would be the man to open the bureau in Algiers and organize its activities. If Nasser created problems for them, Wazir was the man who would solve them. On the journey back to Kuwait there was another reason why Arafat was thinking about his most trusted colleague.

At more or less the same time as Arafat was making the Algerian connection, Wazir was getting married in Gaza. His bride was the lovely Intissar, his childhood sweetheart. When he left Gaza for Cairo in 1956 they did not see each other again for three years.

Then, in the summer of 1959, Intissar was asked if she wanted to meet one of the 'very big leaders' of the underground movement.

'I said, "Yes, of course", and I was taken the next day to a secret meeting place,' Intissar told me. 'There were quite a few people there. Most of them were talking in small groups. It was like a cocktail party without drinks. Some of the people I knew, and some I didn't. Then I saw Khalil. We were pleased to be with each other again and we talked. After some time I whispered to him: "Who is this very big leader I am supposed to be meeting?"

'Khalil was serious and he began to search the faces. I followed his eyes. Then he said to me: "Don't you see him?"

'I said, "No, tell me."

'Then he smiled. "It's me, Khalil Wazir, that you have come to meet!"

'When we were alone he asked me a question. "Are you ready to continue with our secret work?"

'I answered him: "Yes, of course. You know me and what I have done for you in the past, when I was a kid. I have not changed, nothing has changed."

'He was happy but he became very serious. He said: "Intissar, we are no more playing games. We shall soon begin our long struggle. It will be very dangerous. The Arab regimes will try to liquidate us. Many of us will be tortured and killed. When we start the whole world will be against us."

'I said, "Yes, I know."

'Then he took my hands in his. He was very gentle. "Intissar, I want you to do two things for me if you are ready. I want you to take care of my secret work. I want you to type my secret papers and keep them safe. That is the first thing."

'I said, "I am ready. What is the second?"

'He said: "I want you to be my wife."

'I didn't need to think. "I am ready for that, too," I said. And I kissed him.'

While Wazir continued to earn his living as a teacher it was only during school holidays that he was free to travel to make contact with the underground cells that were being formed in Palestinian communities throughout the Arab world. From the summer of 1959 Intissar travelled with him. In public she was his adoring fiancée. In reality she was his assistant and the keeper of all of his secrets. By the time of their marriage she knew as much as Wazir about the underground network – names, people and codes. If Wazir had been arrested or killed she could have continued his work.

The couple had intended to be married in the summer of 1960. They changed their plans because of pressure from Arafat and a number of Wazir's other colleagues. At the time, and with the main exception of Arafat himself, most of those who were emerging as Fatah leaders were already married. The plea for Wazir to delay his marriage was made on the grounds that the responsibility and the pleasure of married life would claim too much of his valuable time. In short, the cause would suffer. With good humour Wazir decided his colleagues had a point. By 1962 Intissar was probably fed up with the gossip that she was more Wazir's mistress than his intended wife.

After their marriage in Gaza, Khalil and Intissar set off for a trip around the Arab world. 'We did the grand tour,' she told me with a laugh, 'but it was not what I would call a honeymoon. We went from one secret meeting to another. Meetings in the morning. Meetings in the afternoon. Meetings in the night. We did most of our sleeping in cars and planes.'

The working honeymoon came to an end on 8 September 1962. On that morning Arafat drove the short distance from his office to Kuwait airport. Wazir had signalled that he was arriving with his 'secret weapon'.

Recalling her first meeting with Arafat, Intissar said: 'He received me at the airport as if I was a visiting head of state. After we had embraced he carried our bags to the car. Then he escorted us to our cousin's home.'

I asked Intissar about her very first impressions of the future Chairman of the P.L.O. With obvious affection for the man, she replied: 'He was very courteous. Very friendly. Very kind. Very warm. That's what I remember most – his warmth.'

It may well have been Arafat's reflections about the love and the happiness his two friends shared that caused him to consider the prospect of marriage. It was about this time that he fell in love and became engaged. Later, after he had made his sacrifice, Arafat more or less adopted the Wazir/Jihad family as his own. To Khalil and Intissar he was as close as the most loving brother. To their children he was a second father. It was this special relationship with the Jihads that helped Arafat to fill the emptiness of his own personal life.

As 1962 was drawing to its close, Arafat and Wazir had reason to be satisfied. On the debit side it was undeniably true that many Palestinians, probably a majority, were still content to place their faith in Nasser and the so-called revolutionary Arab regimes. Nasser's statement that he had no plan to liberate Palestine was taken to mean that he had no immediate plan. So Arafat and Wazir could not claim that they had turned the tide. But *Our Palestine* had generated light and heat. And as a consequence there were, by the end of 1962, a growing number of influential Palestinians who were convinced that the Arab regimes could not be relied upon. This fact alone was reason enough for Arafat and Wazir to be satisfied with the results of their efforts since 1959. They had also created an underground network of cells. And it was in good shape. The body of Fatah was, so to speak, waiting for life to be breathed into it.

In Kuwait the first item on the agenda for 1963 was the discussions that would lead to the formation of Fatah's first Central Committee. What was about to begin was not so much a struggle for power, but a battle of wills about policy. Arafat was soon to find himself in confrontation with colleagues who were not frightened to say they disagreed with him.

# 7

# The Question of Leadership

Until 1963 the effective leaders of the underground network that was Fatah in all but name and muscle were the original four – Arafat, Wazir, Karim and Amira. Arafat, because of his experience and his personality, was the directing head of the four. In 1963 it was Arafat's hope that the institutional leadership of the organization he and Wazir had done so much to promote would be formed around himself, and that he would be not merely the first among equals but the undisputed leader. It was not to be.

When Fatah's first Central Committee was formed in February, Arafat was effectively demoted. He was reduced, so to speak, to being one of ten in a collective leadership; and on what for him was the most urgent matter of the moment – the need to launch military actions against Israel to fix the Palestinian identity – he was in the minority.

Thus began a battle of wills between Arafat and a majority of his colleagues and friends in the collective leadership. It was a battle over matters of principle, however, and not a struggle for power in the normal sense. At issue was the question of which form of leadership was best suited to the needs of the Palestinians in their coming struggle. This battle of wills was to dominate the internal politics of first Fatah and then the P.L.O. It did not begin to be resolved until 1983, when Arafat, no longer willing to accept the constraints of collective leadership, decided to throw caution to the winds and force a showdown with President Assad. To Arafat, the Syrian leader was the evil genius who was using his influence in

Fatah and the P.L.O. to frustrate and sabotage each and every Palestinian move in the direction of a political and compromise settlement with Israel.

From the beginning, and although he has never so much as hinted at his true feelings in public because he is totally loyal to his colleagues, Arafat was, I think, opposed to the concept of a collective leadership. He saw it as a recipe for disaster. In the situation as it was it seemed obvious to Arafat that individuals in a collective leadership would find themselves, often for the best of reasons, in alliance with a range of vested and conflicting political interests. On one level, and because the Palestinians had to be opportunists to survive, some leaders would allow themselves to be influenced by Egypt, others by Syria, others by Jordan, others by Saudi Arabia, others by Iraq and so forth. On another level, some would be more influenced by the U.S. and others by the Soviets.

In Arafat's opinion the problem, or rather the potential problem, was in two parts. The first was that a collective leadership would be open to manipulation by Arab and foreign governments and their agencies. The second and much bigger problem was that a leadership which could be manipulated by outside and conflicting vested interests would be unable to take hard decisions at moments of crisis or maximum opportunity. In short, and in Arafat's opinion, collective leadership would paralyse the decision-making process.

Apart from the evidence of events, the only real clues to the strength of Arafat's feelings about the weakness of the collective leadership system came in off-the-record conversations with two of his most senior and trusted colleagues. Both men were, and are, totally committed to the idea of collective leadership. But in another context they told me there had been a number of occasions when, behind closed doors, Arafat had pleaded to be given full decision-making powers. On each occasion the essence of Arafat's argument was that he could make progress if he was free to take decisions in the name of the leadership. And on each occasion the inference was that he could have made progress in the past if he had been empowered to make decisions instead of having to do a balancing act that resulted in no decision being made, or a decision that was not an adequate response to the opportunity of the moment.

In as much as the battle of wills over the question of leadership and then of strategy was a contest between particular individuals and personalities, it can be said that the main confrontation in the early days was between Arafat on one side, and Khalad Hassan on the other. It was Khalad who spoke most eloquently for the majority of Central Committee members who insisted on a collective leadership. And it was Khalad who led the opposition to Arafat's plan for 'premature' military action.

This confrontation came close to dividing and destroying Fatah before military operations were launched, and later caused Arafat to suspect that Khalad Hassan would one day seek to replace him as leader, a suspicion the two men can now discuss frankly with each other. 'On at least three occasions,' Khalad said to me, 'I told Arafat that if he really believed I wanted his job, I was ready to resign from my position to prove that he is wrong.'

Khalad Hassan was born in Haifa in 1928. His obsession with democracy and open debate, and therefore his loathing of dictatorship and what he calls the 'coup mentality' of Arab and other Third World leaders, is the product of his upbringing and his own experience as a boy in Palestine.

'The first to bear the family name Al-Hassan was a judge,' Khalad said. 'Long after him the family divided into two branches. One owned land and was in the property business. It was very rich. Our branch of the family was in the clergy culture and my father administered the Islamic law. He was also responsible for cultural and political matters and I can say that he was very respected and very distinguished. We were not rich but we were all right until my father died.

'For hundreds of years our family was responsible for the Cave of Saint George which was holy to the people of the three religions – Christians, Jews and Moslems. On Fridays, Saturdays and Sundays our house was the gathering place for the highly educated people of the three religions. Over the three days they used to come in their hundreds to discuss religious and political matters. Because they were so many they brought their own food, but our home became a sort of guest house and we used to provide all the other facilities. So this is the atmosphere in which I was brought up. Then, when I was six, my father became blind. As the eldest son I had to be responsible for serving the guests. It was also my duty to be at my father's side and guide him from place to place. Although I was very young I used to listen to all of the debates and I suppose you can say it was this that put the political germ inside me.'

When Khalad was thirteen his father died, and as the eldest son he had to assume responsibility for the family – his mother, who was young enough to be his sister, his four brothers and one sister, and the maid. 'So I had to study and work,' said Khalad. 'Because of my responsibilities and my age I was not involved one hundred per cent in the political and military struggle as many of my older relatives were. But I did join the Haifa branch of the Islamic Scout Movement. As I told you, the British did not allow us Palestinians to organize ourselves, so we had to meet and train under the cover of clubs and societies.'

The story of Khalad's contribution to the armed struggle of 1947-8 is not without its funny side. 'It was an open secret that when British army units came to the end of their tour of duty or were moved as part of a redeployment programme, some British soldiers and officers were prepared to sell their weapons to the highest bidder. So there was a competition between the Jews and the Palestinians to buy these weapons. To take advantage of this opportunity I got myself a job in the office of the Communications Section of the British army. My special task was to find out when various battalions were about to move. Then it was my responsibility to buy weapons from the men and officers who were prepared to sell. Unfortunately I was not so successful. Working in the same office as me, and playing the same game, was a very beautiful Jewish woman. Actually she was a Rothschild. And because she was rich and beautiful she had the upper hand most of the time.' Khalad told the story with good humour. 'Perhaps we will meet again one day,' he said.

On a day in April 1948, Khalad returned from work to find that his family had fled. Haifa was occupied by Jewish forces. The previous week had seen the massacre at Deir Yassin. Said Khalad: 'You know the Jews always say that unless you are a Jew you cannot begin to comprehend how they felt after the Nazi holocaust. I am sure that is true. But we Palestinians have a saying which is also true. Unless you are a Palestinian you cannot begin to comprehend how we felt after the massacre at Deir Yassin. Because of what happened there we really did believe we would all be killed when the Jewish forces entered our cities and towns. My mother left a message for me saying she had decided that it was better to save the lives of five than to lose six.'

The British army staff car in which Khalad was riding was

stopped by a Haganah patrol near his home. 'Its leader, Chaim, was from a Jewish family who had been friends of my family. As boys, Chaim and I had many fights. Now he wanted to take me prisoner. He said he wanted to interrogate me. I feared I would be killed. The British officer refused to hand me over. Chaim said to me, "O.K. this time, but we'll meet again." He said it in a way which meant, "I'll get you when the British are no longer here to protect you!"'

For several days after the Jews took control of Haifa, Khalad did not know whether to stay or leave. While he was undecided he telephoned some Jewish friends. 'They said they would help me if I went to them. I couldn't bear that. I said: "No, I am leaving." Then one of them said: "Look, not all Jews are the same. We are not Zionists. We are not the people who want to harm you or take your land. When your people come back they should know who were their enemies and who are their friends." I cannot say these Jewish people wanted to protect me for entirely the wrong reasons. But I had no doubts that they were very frightened about the future. They believed we Palestinians would be returning to our homes and they were looking upon the protection they were offering me as an insurance policy for their own future. Then there was nothing else to talk about. I said "Goodbye" and put the phone down.'

After the first truce ended Khalad's British friends told him there was no more hope. The Jews would win. Palestine was finished. Khalad decided to emigrate to Kenya. He was to travel there, or so he thought, in the *Empress of Australia*. She was anchored off Haifa and was taking on 1,000 British troops and a few hundred Egyptians who had been serving the British as cooks and bottlewashers. From Egypt's Honorary Consul in Haifa Khalad obtained a visa for Kenya.

'When it was time to go I was taken to the seashore in a British military vehicle. There I was to wait for a small boat that would carry me to the *Empress of Australia*. As I was waiting, some Israeli soldiers arrived. They were going to arrest me. Two British military policemen placed themselves between me and the Israelis. The Israelis began to shout and demanded that the British stand aside. "This is Israel," they said, "we are now the military authority."

'While they were quarrelling the small boat arrived. I jumped in and that is how I left my homeland. I have to say "thank you" to those British military policemen.'

Khalad's journey aboard the *Empress of Australia* ended abruptly at Port Said. He did not have a health certificate and he was placed in quarantine by the Egyptian health authorities. 'The British Administrative Officer tried to help me. He pointed out that I was in transit. Like bureaucrats everywhere the Egyptians didn't want to know. If I had had some money to bribe them it would have been different. Unfortunately I was penniless.'

A few weeks later Khalad was transfered to a temporary refugee camp in the burning sands of the Sinai Desert. 'We were about 16,000 people living in tents. It was not a refugee camp in anything but name. It was an Egyptian prison for Palestinians who happened to be refugees.'

During the year that he stayed in the camp Khalad kept himself busy with a variety of jobs. He organized a school and did much of the teaching himself. He volunteered for work in the camp clinic. He set up a committee to run the camp and make the best use of its limited facilities. And he appointed himself the camp's Escape Officer.

'My first priority was to organize the escape of the young men who were fit and ready to carry on the fight against Israel. But some I had to help for reasons of compassion. There was, for example, a man from Haifa who lost his baby daughter. She was born in the camp and she died because her mother did not have enough milk. Then the poor man's wife died. I arranged for him to escape to Cairo. Later, and by chance, he was in a position to help me. It was in his house that I had my first bath for a year!'

I asked Khalad how he arranged the escapes. 'I used the only thing I had to bribe the Egyptian guards to turn their backs – food. God knows our food was poor enough, but it was better than that on which the Egyptian army was supposed to survive. By the time I arranged my own escape I had lost about a third of my normal weight.'

Khalad made his own escape shortly after the Egyptian authorities announced that the inhabitants of the Sinai camp were to be transferred to Gaza. 'I couldn't go there,' he said. 'I needed to be with my family or to go to some place where I would be free.'

For the next few months Khalad was virtually a fugitive on the run from Arab intelligence agents. 'In Cairo and then in Jordan I discovered there was no place for Palestinians who wanted work and the freedom to organize for their cause.'

The only good news was a tip that his family was somewhere in Sidon in southern Lebanon. After a battle to get the necessary visas to allow him to pass through Syria and into Lebanon, Khalad found himself in Beirut. From there, and using the last of the money he had borrowed from a relative in Damascus, he took a taxi to Sidon. 'I was going to a city I didn't know. I had nothing to go on – no names of contacts, no addresses. Where would I stop? Who would know about my family? How would I go about asking after them? What happened next was so incredible that I would not have believed it if it had not happened to me.

'Suddenly, and for no good reason that I was aware of, I told the taxi driver to stop and let me out. I paid him the last of my money. And then, coming from a building opposite the very spot where the taxi had stopped, I saw one of my cousins. At first he didn't recognize me and I called to him. We kissed and cried and then I said: "Where is my mother? Where is my mother?"

'My cousin was astonished. "You really don't know where your mother is?" Then he looked at me in a strange way. "She is here, in this very place where you have stopped! I thought you knew."

'My reunion with the family was naturally very emotional. But it was also very dramatic. My mother had apparently offered a reward of a gold necklace to the first person to bring her news that I was alive. Each day for the past eighteen months she had spent some time alone in her room – crying her heart out because she felt guilty for having abandoned me. She believed that I was dead and she was blaming herself. At first nobody was anxious to go upstairs and tell my mother to come. My brothers, my sister and the others were afraid my mother would be so shocked by my appearance she might have a heart attack. My stomach had shrunk, I had lost so much weight and my hair was half-way down my back.'

A beautiful, sixteen-year-old girl called Nahla had opened the door to Khalad and his cousin. 'In that moment,' Khalad recalled, 'I knew that she would one day become my wife.' In time Nahla did marry Khalad. She also received the gold necklace that had been offered as the reward for news that Khalad was still alive. Her younger sister was the one who eventually went upstairs to call Khalad's mother, and she received another present.

'When my mother saw me she swayed and I thought she was going to collapse. She cried and then she became very angry at the circumstances which had reduced us to such a terrible existence. She was ashamed that she could not feed us properly – she thought I was dying of starvation. And she was ashamed of the conditions in which we were living. The room in which I slept was also the kitchen and the toilet. It was so small that when I slept I had to put my legs into the toilet.

'In the coming days I discovered how much my mother had changed. She was only twenty-eight when my father died. She was no more the sweet, innocent woman. She was tough and ready to be the head of the family.

'When we were sitting alone she said to me: 'Khalad, I must tell you how bad our situation is. Apart from the bread, the food we receive each month from the Red Cross is not enough to sustain us. For three weeks out of four we have to live on bread and onions." She also told me she had exhausted the money she had saved from my wages in Palestine. Then she spoke about the gold. In our tradition the husbands give their wives presents in gold. It is our way of providing our wives and families with security for the future.

'She said to me: "Khalad, I have some gold things given to me by your father, but I must tell you what his instructions were. Before he died he said the gold was to be used for two purposes only – to pay for the education of his sons and to provide for the requirements of our guests. If we need food and clothes we must work for them. Those were his instructions."

'I asked my mother what we were going to do.

'She said: "Khalad, I have come to a decision and I hope you will agree with it. I have four sons. Numbers one, two and three are very bright. They are always at the top of their classes. Number four is not so bright academically. I have decided that son number four must finish his studies and work. Do you agree?"

'When I told my mother that I did agree she said there was still a problem to be solved. "In the Lebanon it is the law that Palestinians do not have the right to work," she said. "You must do everything in your power to find a job for your youngest brother."'

The youngest of the Hassan brothers was eventually found work as a car-painter. 'Officially he was not employed,' Khalad said, 'he was just helping out, and he was paid secretly. The money he earned did improve our situation – but not a lot. So I decided I had to leave the Lebanon. We couldn't go on living as we were. We all had to

work and I wanted to continue my studies. It was also in my mind
that I should form a commando organization to strike at Israel.'

Khalad decided to try his luck in Syria. And it was there, in 1950
and again in 1951, that he made unsuccessful attempts to form a
commando organization. As already mentioned, the first attempt
was abandoned when Haj Amin Husseini was unable to provide the
necessary funds.

After that failure Khalad's fortunes took a turn for the better.
Attached to the Arab Institute in Damascus he began to earn good
money as a freelance teacher of English and mathematics. 'I charged
by the hour and most of my clients were wealthy,' he said.

In Syria, as in Egypt at the time, the Moslem Brotherhood was the
only organized group that was serious about continuing the struggle
with Israel. And it was in collaboration with the Syrian branch of
the Brotherhood that Khalad tried again to organize a Palestinian
strike force. On this occasion he received some help from his
brother Ali, who was also working in the Syrian capital.

'By chance Ali and I came to learn that the head of the
Brotherhood in Damascus, Mustafa Sebai, was badly in need of
somebody to teach him English. I should tell you that he was also
the Deputy President of the Syrian Parliament. Ali got the job as his
English teacher, then he fixed for me to organize Sebai's office
work. I was not myself a member of the Brotherhood. In fact, and to
tell you the truth, they refused to let me become a member because I
would not offer prayers five times a day at the proper times. I cannot
pray because I have to do it. I pray when I want to do it – and that
has been my way since childhood.' It is obvious that Khalad's heresy
did not harm his relationship with the Brotherhood.

Syria's Minister of Defence was Maruf Dawalidi. He was a secret
member of the Brotherhood. Through his contact with Sebai and
Dawalidi, Khalad struck a bargain that he hoped would lead to the
formation of a Palestinian commando group. At the time, the
Palestinians in Damascus who were eager to resume the fight with
Israel were organized as a scout troop. Part of the deal with Sebai
and Dawalidi was that Khalad's men would all become members of
the Brotherhood. In return Sebai and Dawalidi would arrange for
the scouts to be trained and armed in the mountains. 'In this way I
was using the Brotherhood as a cover,' Khalad said. 'And because
we were protected by Sebai the Syrian Government would not know

what was happening. It was a good plan and I could see the day when we would start our military actions on the borders. Then, just as we were ready to begin our secret training, there was another coup in Damascus. And that finished everything.'

The November coup was Syria's fourth in two years. After it Khalad was once more a fugitive. He was arrested and gaoled, but released when he convinced the new masters of Syria's Military Intelligence that he was not a member of the Moslem Brotherhood.

By the summer of 1952 Khalad was again without work. 'The Jews had driven us out of our homeland. The Arabs did not want us in theirs. In that moment I believed that we were living through an experience which was unique in human history. In that time we were a people without land, without homes, without jobs, without food, without dignity and, worst of all, without hope. When you are deprived of your dignity you become more animal than human – but your existence still has some meaning. When you are without hope you have nothing, and you are nothing. And that is how the Zionists, the Arab regimes and the big powers wanted it to be. They wanted to close the file on the Palestinians.'

Adding to Khalad's despair was the fact that he was once again responsible for his family. Shortly after his own move to Damascus from Sidon, he had asked his mother, his remaining brothers and his sister to join him. He had been unable to bear the thought of his youngest brother working when he should have been continuing with his studies. 'They all came but now my mother's gold was finished. The only good thing was that my youngest brother graduated before the rest of us – not bad for the one who was supposed to be the least bright! But now the gold was finished. We were educated but once more hungry.

'When we were discussing what to do next my mother suggested that I should get married. I reminded her of what she had told me in Sidon when I said that I would one day marry Nahla. She had said then: "Khalad, you must not think such thoughts. You have no work and no prospects. You are penniless. You cannot even think of marrying until you can offer Nahla a secure future."

'I said, "Mother, nothing has changed. I am once again without work. I still have no prospects. And I am still without a penny."

'In those days, and because of her own experiences, my mother had an answer for everything. "That's not your business," she said, "that's God's business. Maybe when you marry God will give you more luck."'

When a cable arrived from a Palestinian businessman offering Khalad a job in Kuwait, he did not have the money to send a reply. A friend gave him the money. When the air ticket arrived from Kuwait, Khalad did not have the money for a taxi to the airport. The same friend paid for the taxi and accompanied him to the airport.

Khalad's new life as a businessman in Kuwait began with great promise. The business was importing. Shortly after his arrival, Khalad accompanied his employer on a long foreign trip. Partly because of Khalad's negotiating skills, the trip was very productive. They returned from it with the contacts to establish many new agencies in Kuwait. Said Khalad: 'The business was expanding rapidly – but I was not receiving the rewards for my labours. I was working from eight in the morning until midnight. After a few months I was in debt to the equivalent of nine months' salary. So I came up with an answer to my financial problem. I suggested to my employer that we should reorganize the company. My idea was that we should have a board of directors, and that the directors should take a certain percentage of the profits.' Naturally Khalad suggested that he should be a director. 'My employer rejected the plan. I said, "Okay. Thank you. Goodbye."'

Having reached for the top of the ladder, Khalad found himself at the bottom again. At twenty-four, and qualified in many ways for better things, he became a typist in the service of Kuwait's Development Board. 'At the time Kuwait was still a British Protectorate. In less than one year I became the Assistant General-Secretary of the Development Board. Later I was the Assistant General-Secretary of the Planning Board. Then it was decided that I should become the General-Secretary of the Municipal Council Board. It was effectively the government.'

If it could be said that one man above all others was responsible for the development of Kuwait, that one man was Khalad Hassan. 'The British tried to stop me from having any real influence and power. They passed the word that I was a communist and a subversive. What they said about me was bullshit, and fortunately enough responsible and decent Kuwaitis knew it was.'

Before Arafat arrived in Kuwait, Khalad and others tried and failed to set up a political party on their own. In fact the party did come into being, but it was divided and destroyed from within because the founding fathers could not agree on how it was to be led and who was to make the decisions. Of great significance for the future was the fact that the personality who wanted to be the party's leader was of the same way of thinking as Arafat. Said Khalad: 'He was willing to consult with us, but he wanted the final decisions to be his own. We rejected this and I quit the party. After that, and until I met with Arafat, Abu Jihad, and some others who are no longer in the movement, it was a very hard time for me – politically speaking.' The 'others' were Karim and Amira.

In 1960, after his first meeting with the four leaders of what was to be Fatah, Khalad began to write for *Our Palestine*. That Arafat and Khalad Hassan did not meet for nearly three years when they were living in the same few square miles of Kuwait is puzzling. It is, of course, possible that the underground operation Arafat and Wazir were running was so secret that Khalad did not know of their activities. But it is also possible – because of what each may have heard about the other on the grapevine – that the two men were not anxious to meet. They may have felt the differences between them were likely to be too great for there to be a meeting of minds. Khalad confirmed that it was Karim and Wazir, not Arafat, who took the initiative to involve him and his associates in the discussions about the formation of Fatah's first Central Committee.

I asked Khalad why he had insisted on a collective leadership when Fatah's first Central Committee was formed. 'In the first place you have to take my background and my upbringing into account,' he said. 'As I have told you, I was born into the tradition of open debate and that was my experience from childhood. So you can say I was for the democratic way from the beginning. But that is only a part. I was also anti the coup mentality. I had learned that coups only lead to more coups and to the bleeding of society.

'If you want a case study of what I am talking about, look at Syria. After Israel was born, and up to 1970, there were ten military coups in that country. The present regime has stayed in power till now by suppressing its own people. This is the reaction of dictatorship. This is the coup mentality. And this is the sickness of the Arab world. It was not a road that I wanted my people to go down.'

The collective leadership was also, among other things, a device to prevent any Palestinian leader emerging as a dictator. And it was a device to contain Yasser Arafat in particular. With his reputation as a bully and a man who was prepared to shout and scream, wild eyes protruding, to get his own way, he was perceived by many who were to become his closest colleagues as a potential dictator who, given the opportunity, would build himself a military power base to impose his will by force. This was confirmed by the man whose actions and support for Arafat's way were to keep the military option alive – Hani Hassan, Khalad's brother. In fact, and as time was to prove to all of his closest colleagues, it was not in Arafat's nature to be the dictator many feared he could become. But in 1963 there was a good deal of superficial evidence to the contrary.

The first decision taken by Fatah's Central Committee was that Wazir should go to Algiers as soon as possible to open the Bureau de la Palestine. Despite the fact that President Ben Bella had assured Arafat there would be no unmanageable problems, it is evident that most of Wazir's colleagues in the collective leadership thought there would be difficulties to overcome. For that reason, and also because Fatah had no funds, Wazir was instructed to send his wife back to her parents in Gaza. To avoid unnecessary expense she was to stay there until Wazir had actually opened the office. Since they had been married for only six months, Khalil and Intissar were not excited by the order to part. But the Central Committee had spoken and that was that.

The second decision was concerned with what Khalad described to me as 'the preservation order for Fatah's virginity'. It stated that those wishing to join Fatah should first withdraw from any other political party or group to which they belonged – including the Moslem Brotherhood. 'By this time the Central Committee needed no convincing that all Arab parties were the puppets of the regimes,' Khalad said.

The virginity rule was thought to be essential for three main reasons. The first was the need to convince the Palestinians themselves that Fatah was a truly independent organization. 'I have to say that in the beginning we were very idealistic and very naive about this,' Khalad volunteered. 'In 1963 we really did believe that we could be truly independent in our decision-making. It was not until later that we discovered we couldn't be completely independent in any way until we had a state of our own.' The second reason for the virginity rule was the need to reduce the scope for mischief by the intelligence services of the regimes. It was taken for granted that they would all try to penetrate Fatah. The third was the need to convince individual Arab regimes that Fatah was not the tool of any other Arab regime.

When the debate about strategy started, Central Committee members found themselves locked into what Khalad described as 'continuous, heavy and punishing discussions'. He added: 'It was often the case that we would go straight from our work to a meeting. The meeting would last through the night and we would return to our work from the meeting. Sleeping between the hours from dawn to the time we had to start work again was a luxury.'

The Central Committee did not define what it meant by liberation. While the articles in *Our Palestine* had not left much to the imagination, it was a propaganda magazine, not a policy document. In the West it is often said that the Palestinians could have avoided many of the disasters they have suffered since the 1960s if those who became Fatah and P.L.O. leaders had started out with a clear and realistic vision of what they could reasonably expect to deliver for their people. But this begs many questions and it ignores what Fatah's real purpose was.

The majority of those who formed Fatah's first Central Committee did not see themselves as the founders of a Western-style political party. As Khalad pointed out to me, it was never their intention to say to their people, 'We have decided what is best for you, this is our objective, here is our policy, now vote for us.' In 1963 the objectives of the majority of Fatah's leaders, who supported Khalad Hassan's way of thinking, were, in essence, to prevent the Palestinian problem being swept under the carpet, and then to develop democratic institutions, including a Palestinian parliament-in-exile, which would allow the Palestinian people as a whole to determine the final outcome of the struggle. This was the democratic way forward, and there was anyway no alternative. In 1963, and for many years after, if any Palestinian leadership had advocated even *de facto* recognition of the Jewish State it would have been disowned by an overwhelming majority of the Palestinian people. If individual leaders had done so they would have been assassinated.

After 1959, and mainly because of the debate provoked by *Our Palestine*, a small but growing number of influential Palestinians began to see that the way to achieve these objectives lay in combining the best from the two existing ways of thinking. They agreed with Arafat and Wazir that Nasser and the Arab regimes could not be relied upon, and that there should be an independent Palestine liberation organization or movement to persuade the Arabs to do their duty. But they also agreed with those who said the Palestinians had to co-ordinate their strategy with Nasser and the Arab regimes, because it was obvious, at the end of the day, that the Palestinians could not get back even a part of their homeland without the support of the Arab governments and peoples; independent Palestinian military action would clearly be an obstacle to such co-ordination. Those who believed in this third way were the majority on Fatah's first Central Committee. And their leader was Khalad Hassan.

From my detailed conversations with Khalad it is clear that even he and the majority of Central Committee members accepted that the Arab regimes would not agree to participate in a serious liberation struggle unless they were compelled to do so. So the essential difference between Arafat and Khalad Hassan on the matter of strategy and tactics was about how to oblige the regimes to become involved.

'The first thing we did,' Khalad told me, 'was to examine Nasser's declared strategy. As you know his slogan was that Arab unity was the key to the liberation of Palestine. Later we came to know that even if he had succeeded in uniting the Arabs, he did not intend to confront Israel by force. In his view as we came to know it, unity would give the Arab regimes the necessary political and economic bargaining power to force America to use its influence on Israel – but that is another story. In principle we agreed with Nasser that Arab unity was the key to liberating Palestine. But we believed the unity Nasser was seeking would not come. Nasser was talking about the unity of Arab regimes, and it was obvious to us that the regimes were too divided to be united.

'Our conclusion was that unity had to come from the bottom up – from the people. So we asked ourselves a question. What was the issue or cause that no Arab could be against? Answer: the liberation of Palestine. For all Arab people liberating Palestine was a matter of honour and dignity. It was even a sacred duty. So we reversed Nasser's slogan. We said that liberating Palestine was the key to Arab unity. And that gave us our strategy.

'Through open debate, and using all the propaganda methods at our disposal, we intended to provoke and capture the imagination of the Palestinian and Arab masses. We thought we could create a new atmosphere in which no Arab leader would dare to ignore the subject of liberating Palestine in his public speeches. Whatever they might think in private, we knew that Arab leaders could not speak against the liberation of Palestine in public. So that gave us our chance. Then, when the Arab leaders were coming under pressure for action from their own masses, we would engage them in dialogue. We would ask them to join us in planning a co-ordinated strategy for the actual liberation of our homeland. We intended to ask for their support not simply because they had a duty to help the Palestinians, but also because they had a responsibility to prevent Zionism from dominating the whole Arab world in one way or another. If the leaders agreed to work with us there would be hope for all Arabs, including the Palestinians. If they turned us down we would lead a confrontation between the Palestinian and Arab masses and the regimes. And the aim of this confrontation would be to provoke a real Arab revolution that would end with the coming to power of regimes which would have the will to fight Israel.

'This was my thinking. I looked upon Fatah as the engine that would pull the Arab train towards the liberation of Palestine. Unfortunately I discovered that the train was mostly rotten.'

Khalad appeared to be saying that he had been totally opposed to Palestinian military action until such time there were Arab regimes in power that had the will to fight Israel. 'That was my view at the time,' he confirmed.

Wazir and Arafat were 'very frustrated' by the opposition to their plan for quick military action. The evidence of subsequent events indicates they were so frustrated that they at least considered the possibility of leaving the Central Committee and forming their own breakaway group. But that was an option of last resort. By hinting that they might be prepared to take such a dramatic step, they guaranteed there would be no early vote on overall strategy and policy. That done, their intention was to find ways to strengthen their own case and put pressure on their colleagues.

In what seems to have been the first move in a campaign to do just that, Arafat and Wazir summoned Hani Hassan, Khalad's brother, from Germany. In those days there was no Palestinian more eager than he to start the fight with Israel. For the first time, and not the last, Hani was about to find himself on Arafat's side and against his brother.

By 1963 Hani was what Arafat had been – the most powerful Palestinian student leader of his generation. Until the previous year his power base had been far from the battlefield. He was the President of the Union of Palestinian Students – and also many affiliated workers' unions – in Europe. In West Germany alone there were 3,000 Palestinian students and 65,000 Palestinian workers. In 1962 Hani consolidated his hold on Palestinian student power when the General Union of Palestinian Students elected him as its President at a congress in Gaza. From that moment on Hani was in a position to influence and dominate Palestinian student politics everywhere. He had also formed his own underground commando group in Germany. It was not armed but it was being trained in secret.

Said Hani: 'To tell you the truth my first meeting with Arafat was nearly a disaster. We had a big fight. He asked me to commit the students and my own commando organization to him and Wazir. I said I would but I told him there was a price. And the price was that Jordan had to be a part of the battlefield. The theory of my own organization in Germany was that we had to liberate Jordan. Arafat said: "No, no, no, no." He was prepared to make any other concession to get our support but he was not willing to consider, even for one second, the idea of fighting Hussein.

'Then I met with Wazir and it was he who really convinced me. He said: "Look, you have a good organization and you are ready to fight, but you do not have the means to fight alone and you cannot fight alone. You must be part of a big military organization which is well equipped. We are that big organization. Join us."'

At this point Hani laughed. 'Now I will tell you a secret. Because he was so anxious to have my support, Wazir gave me much false information about Fatah's military strength. He said they already had a big secret army and many weapons. He even told me they had some helicopters. I should also say that Wazir and Arafat did not tell me they were having big problems in the Central Committee and that the majority was opposing the military way.'

Unaware at the time that he had been the victim of a confidence trick, Hani returned to Germany to crusade for military action. 'I called a conference of my own organization and we decided to join Fatah on the understanding that it was ready to begin the armed struggle. Of course we didn't know we were taking sides w.th Arafat and Wazir against the others.'

Wazir changed his appearance and his identity. He became Alal Ben Amar, and under that name he travelled to Algiers to set up the Bureau de la Palestine and open Fatah's window on the world. He ran straight into trouble. Behind the scenes Nasser was pressing Ben Bella to deny the Palestinians any freedom of action. At the time the Egyptian leader was working on his own strategy for controlling the Palestinians while appearing to be giving them some freedom. The Algerian President was having second thoughts. He wanted to honour his promise to Arafat, but he was not anxious to make an enemy of Nasser. The result of his dilemma was six months of uncertainty for Wazir.

As instructed, Intissar was waiting patiently in Gaza for word that she should join her husband in Algiers. She said: 'It was a very difficult six months for Khalil. He slept in many different hotels and he was very anxious. He did open the office but many times the Algerians would not let him enter it.'

While Wazir was engaged in a war of nerves with the Algerian authorities, Intissar was experiencing a little local problem of her own. The cause of it was Wazir's change of name.

'One day I was meeting with some of my lady friends at my father's house in Gaza. It was just a social gathering. At the time the meeting was arranged I didn't know my friends were worried about what they thought had happened to me. One of the ladies produced a letter from her son who was in Algiers. In it the son told of how he had visited the Bureau de la Palestine and met Khalil.' The lady read from the letter that Khalil had insisted that his name was Alal Ben Amar and had denied that he had a wife in Gaza.

Intissar smiled as she continued with her story. 'So you can imagine what my friends were thinking because of this letter. They thought my husband had left me for another woman! I said to my friend, "Your son must have met somebody who looks like my husband. Khalil is in Beirut and I will be joining him soon."

'Later that day my father talked to me. He was very troubled. He said: "Oh my daughter, what has happened? Why are you not with your husband? Are you angry with him?" Because I was sworn to secrecy I could not tell even my father the truth. I told him not to worry.' Intissar's father died a few weeks later. He went to his grave believing that his daughter had been abandoned by her husband.

After six frustrating months in Algiers, Wazir was informed that the Bureau de la Palestine was to be closed down. He was furious but cool. In reply to the bearers of the message he had a dramatic announcement of his own to make: 'I am sitting here because President Ben Bella gave us his word. If I am now to be thrown into the street, the President must come here and do it himself!'

It was a desperate, all-or-nothing confrontation; but it was also one from which Wazir and Fatah emerged as the winners. Ben Bella gave the order for the Bureau de la Palestine to be given the same status and privileges as any other diplomatic mission in his capital. 'It was an historic moment,' said Abu Jihad. 'We had turned the first page in the story of our struggle for recognition as a people who were being denied their rights.'

Intissar left Gaza to join her husband in Algiers. By day she worked as a teacher. By night she was Wazir's secretary and special assistant – as well as being a mother to his children. On the subject of her contribution to the success of the Bureau de la Palestine, Khalad Hassan said this: 'Not many people knew it, but we could not have kept the bureau going without her. Without the money she earned as a teacher we could not have paid the expenses of running the office. In those days, and for some years to come, we were flat broke as an organization.' By this time Arafat was making enough money to have picked up the bills for the expenses of the Bureau in Algiers; but it is not difficult to imagine why Khalad and others did not want Fatah to rely on Arafat's charity.

Until the opening of the Bureau de la Palestine, Fatah's main problem was that the very idea of creating an independent Palestine liberation organization lacked credibility. 'From the moment the Algerians gave us their official blessing we had the possibility to solve this problem,' said Abu Jihad. 'The fact that we were seen to have Algeria as our friend gave us a revolutionary credibility that was worth more than gold and guns at the time.'

Of all the freedoms Wazir now enjoyed to promote the Palestinian cause, none was more valuable than the opportunity to mix and talk with the resident foreign diplomats and, even more important, the delegations which accompanied various foreign leaders to Algiers. Wazir made the Chinese his top priority. And early in 1964 his persistence was rewarded with an invitation to visit China.

On 20 March, Wazir and Arafat met in Iraq and flew from there to Peking. Said Abu Jihad: 'For this mission I was the leader because the invitation was addressed to me in my capacity as the Director of the Bureau de la Palestine.' The fact that the two men chose to rendezvous in Baghdad suggests that the Central Committee was not informed about the China visit in advance. It is possible that Arafat and Wazir were hoping the Chinese would agree to supply them with the weapons to begin the struggle, and that a surprise announcement to that effect would help them to turn the tables on Khalad Hassan and his most enthusiastic supporters on the Central Committee.

When they were asked to explain their military strategy Arafat and Wazir told the Chinese what they thought the Chinese wanted to hear — namely that they were committed to the liberation of Palestine through revolutionary armed struggle and guerrilla warfare.

In reply, and to the astonishment of their Palestinian visitors, the Chinese told Arafat and Wazir they did not believe that Palestine could be liberated by guerrilla warfare. The conditions in Palestine and the circumstances in which the Palestinians found themselves were simply not favourable. 'They told us that liberating Palestine by guerrilla warfare was a mission impossible,' Abu Jihad said. Arafat's version of what the Chinese said was even more to the point. 'They were very frank. They told us: "What you are proposing is unbelievable. You can't do it. You have no bases in the territory to be liberated and no prospect of creating them. From where will you start? There are no conditions for guerrilla warfare." I said to them, "Okay, that is what you think. But still we will start."' Was he disappointed? Surely what the Chinese had said was bad for his morale? 'No, no,' Arafat said. 'What they said only made me more determined, more stubborn.'

If their visit had ended after that first and unusually blunt exchange of views, Arafat and Wazir would have left China with nothing at all to show for their efforts. The Chinese were not about to supply weapons to a lost cause. But the talks were resumed and Arafat explained how it was that the Arab regimes and the Western

powers would succeed in sweeping the Palestinian problem under
the carpet if the Palestinians did not soon resort to military action to
prove that they still existed and were determined to insist on their
rights. The Chinese apparently warmed to the idea that it was only
by fighting that the Palestinians could fix their identity. They may
also have concluded that Arafat and Wazir were not so naive as they
had at first appeared to be.

'In the end the Chinese gave us a promise,' Abu Jihad said. 'They
told us they would supply us with some arms – but only after we had
started our struggle by our own efforts. I suppose they didn't want
to commit themselves until we had proved that we were serious and
could survive an expected Arab attempt to liquidate us.' The
Chinese could afford to adopt a leisurely attitude because the
Soviets at this time were pro-Nasser and strongly opposed to
independent Palestinian military action, so the Palestinians could
not turn to the Soviets.

Arafat returned to Kuwait. Wazir introduced himself and Fatah
to North Vietnam and North Korea. On his return to the Middle
East he launched a propaganda campaign against the Arab regimes
and those of his Central Committee colleagues who were opposed
to military action. As Alal Ben Amar, Director of the Bureau de la
Palestine, he appeared on television in Kuwait, gave press
conferences in Baghdad, Damascus and Beirut and made a speech or
two in Cairo. 'I had to choose my words with care,' he said, 'but in
each place I managed to contrast the support we had been promised
by revolutionary Asia with the lack of support from those closer to
home. Everybody realized that I was criticizing the Arab regimes
without doing so directly.'

By all accounts Arafat and Wazir did capture some new debating
ground when they discussed the significance of China's promise
with their Central Committee colleagues. But in April 1964, the two
men were very much aware that they were still in the minority camp.
If they had pushed then for a vote on the military strategy they
favoured, they would have lost.

In a few weeks, however, Arafat and Wazir got what they wanted
– a majority vote in favour of military action. They had Nasser to
thank for this. He took a decision which effectively cut the ground
from under Khalad Hassan's feet and caused him to lose his grip on
the Central Committee. Arafat, master of tactics, took full

advantage of the new situation and threatened to split Fatah if he did not get his way.

# 8

# The Decision to Fight

The event that cut the ground from under Khalad Hassan's feet, and which then created the opportunity for Arafat by degrees to impose his will and way on Fatah's Central Committee, was the founding of the Palestine Liberation Organization under the leadership of Ahmad Shuqairi. Nasser was the chief architect of the original P.L.O. He intended it to be his puppet. But its real godfather was the American State Department which, at the time, was under the direction of Dean Rusk.

Nasser was haunted by one great fear. It was that the Palestinians, left to their own devices, would drag him into a war with Israel, a war he knew he could not win. As Nasser himself was later to tell Arafat and other Fatah leaders: 'My desk was littered with intelligence reports which kept me more or less informed of your underground activities.'[20] In 1964 Nasser was extremely worried by what Palestinian guerrillas could do on their own account to provoke a war between the Arabs and Israel. But he was even more frightened by the prospect of an alliance between those Palestinians who were preparing to fight and his rivals and enemies in Syria. A way had to be found to neutralize the threat posed by the Palestinian underground. Solution: the establishment of a Palestinian institution which would give the Palestinian people a forum for self-expression, the appearance of power and a degree of independence, but which would in reality be controlled by Nasser.

Nasser was not alone in his fear. All Arab leaders, particularly those of the front-line states, were terrified of the likely consequences of allowing the Palestinians a free hand to provoke Israel. And to the extent that they were all frightened, they all connived at Nasser's scheme to create a puppet P.L.O.

The Americans have never officially admitted that their influence was a factor in Nasser's decision to create a Palestinian entity which could be controlled by those Arab regimes who were prepared, in private, to face the fact that they would need all the American help they could get if they were ever to have a chance of obliging Israel to compromise. But according to various Fatah leaders, American influence, amounting to pressure, on Nasser was very great. The following was told to me by Hani Hassan and confirmed by his brother and by Arafat:

'From the many conversations that I and my Fatah colleagues had with Nasser after we made our peace with him, it is very clear that he was heavily influenced by what the Americans were saying to him in the early 1960s. I am not suggesting there was a deal as such between Nasser and Dean Rusk, but I am saying there was a very good understanding between them – even a meeting of minds about why the Palestinians had to be controlled and prevented from taking genuine political and military initiatives of their own.

'The Americans told Nasser that if he really wanted peace with Israel he would have to accept there was not so much that could be done for the Palestinians – because Israel's existence was a fact of life. And there was nothing the Americans would or could do to change that fact. The rights and wrongs of the matter were no longer relevant. The Americans said they were prepared to put some pressure on Israel, but the most they thought they could persuade the Israelis to accept was an agreement that some Palestinians could return to their homes. The rest, the majority, would have to be content with cash compensation and a new life in an Arab country.

'Now we come to the real point. The Americans already knew that Nasser, King Hussein, the authorities in the Lebanon and many other Arab regimes were prepared to accept the Zionist *fait accompli*, and make peace with the Jewish State – provided they could get something for the Palestinians . . . a bare minimum that would allow the Arab leaders to say they had not surrendered and that they had done their best for the Palestinians. For the Arab leaders it was a matter of face. They needed American help to put pressure on Israel to save their faces. And really what the Americans were now telling Nasser was the price he had to pay for their help. The price was, of course, action by Nasser and the other regimes to prevent the resurgence of Palestinian nationalism. By implication the Americans told Nasser that if he was unable or unwilling to control the Palestinians, there would be no peace between the Arabs and Israel, and if there was no peace the Americans would be unable and unwilling to prevent an aggressive and probably expansionist Israel from imposing its will on the Arabs by force.

'When we in Fatah came to know and respect Nasser – unfortunately that was not until 1968, when it was too late – he told us these things very frankly. You should know that Arafat came to look upon Nasser as a father. I can remember one occasion, in 1969 I think it was, when Nasser told Arafat everything that was in his heart. He said it had once been his hope that he could use his influence with the Americans to negotiate Israel back to the borders of the 1947 Partition Plan. But in 1969 Nasser said the following: "I tell you frankly that is impossible. The Israelis have learned to perfection how to blackmail the Americans, and it is now the Israelis who are making American foreign policy for the Middle East. One day when you and I are gone the Americans will pay for their stupidity. But that day is far away."

'I also remember a particular conversation that I had with Shuqairi. He said to me: "Look, my son, you are still a young man, but you must be smart. If you want to do something for our people you must use this P.L.O. It is true the Arabs have created it because Dean Rusk asked them to do so. But it is all we have."'

It is not impossible that the visit to China by Arafat and Wazir was the cause of renewed pressure on Nasser from Rusk and his people at the State Department. During his time as Secretary of State, Rusk was obsessed by the need to contain China. With the Americans about to escalate the war in Vietnam, the prospect of the Chinese getting a toehold in the Middle East could not have been good for Rusk's peace of mind.

The decision in principle to create the P.L.O. was taken at the first ever Arab summit meeting. It was held in Cairo in January 1964. The main item on the agenda of the thirteen Arab heads of state who responded to Nasser's invitation was what to do about Israel's intention to divert water from the Sea of Galilee to the Negev Desert. No Arab needed to be told what the consequences of that would be. The diverted water would give life to new Israeli settlements and they in turn would make the Jewish State stronger. Not surprisingly Israel's announcement of its intention to go ahead provoked great anger throughout the Arab world. How to defuse it was Nasser's problem of the moment. And it was a problem because he had previously declared that he would regard Israeli work on the water diversion project as a cause for war. It was an empty and stupid boast, but at the time he made it Nasser considered that he had only one alternative – to throw up his hands in despair and admit that the Arabs were militarily and politically impotent in the face of Israel's strength and aggressive attitudes. Now Nasser had to find a way to climb down. He decided that the least humiliating way was to make his climbdown in good company. And that was the main reason for the first Arab summit.

Three proposals emerged from the summit. The first concerned the Arab response to Israel's intention to proceed with the water diversion project. The Arab leaders proposed to divert the water of the northern tributaries of the River Jordan in order to reduce the quantity of water Israel could divert. A far cry from Nasser's war threat. The second proposal was for the setting up of a United Arab (Military) Command (U.A.C.). Naturally Arab propagandists were free to promote this as evidence that their mighty leaders were preparing for an eventual war of destiny with Israel. In fact the Arab leaders were looking upon the proposed U.A.C. as a means of improving their defences against Israeli attacks. But even as that it came to be regarded by most Arab people as a good joke in bad taste. The third proposal was for the establishment of a Palestinian organization which would allow the Palestinian people 'to play their role in the liberation of their country and their self-determination'.[21] The P.L.O. was given its birth certificate.

Four months after the summit, East Jerusalem was the venue for the first meeting of the Palestinian National Congress. It was attended by 422 Palestinians who were, it was said, 'elected' by groups and communities throughout the diaspora. Among them were a number of Fatah members, including Khalad Hassan from the Central Committee, who presented themselves as independents. Many of the other delegates were members of various Arab political parties and movements.

As a passionate and uncompromising advocate of the democratic way, Khalad was 'horrified' by what he witnessed. The delegates had not been assembled for any sort of real discussion about strategy, policy and objectives. Their presence was required for the rubber-stamping of the programme and the documents that Shuqairi had drawn up. The two most important documents were the Palestinian National Charter and the basic constitution of the P.L.O. They were approved, the P.L.O. was declared to be in existence, and Shuqairi was elected its Chairman. A proposal that the organization should have its headquarters in Cairo was also approved. The original P.L.O. was everything Khalad had sworn that Fatah would not be – an 'elected' dictatorship and a tool of the Arab regimes. As such, and despite the fact that the regimes had promised it would not be short of money, there was little this P.L.O. could do to advance the cause of the Palestinians.

But this was not how the original P.L.O. was viewed by many ordinary and less sophisticated Palestinians at the time. Their imagination was caught by the fact that the P.L.O. was to have its own military wing which was to be known as the Palestinian Liberation Army, or P.L.A. According to Shuqairi's plan, which Nasser and the other Arab leaders had approved with varying degrees of enthusiasm – in Hussein's case there was a total lack of enthusiasm – P.L.A. regiments were to be raised in each of the front-line Arab states and further afield if possible. But the regimes had insisted on a control mechanism. All P.L.A. units were to be under the supervision of the governments of the countries in which they were stationed.

To Arafat and Wazir in particular, but also to the rest of their colleagues on Fatah's Central Committee, the implications were obvious. Until the regimes could be forced to fight, the P.L.A. would have no military significance whatsoever. It would be what it was intended by the regimes to be – the puppet army of a puppet P.L.O.

Ahmad Shuqairi was qualified on many counts to be the Puppet-in-Chief, but there was one reason above all others why he was willing to play Nasser's game. Shuqairi was a political mercenary. Though a nationalist, he sold himself to the highest bidder. In the 1950s, and for a fee, he represented Syria at the U.N. After that, and presumably for an even bigger fee, he represented Saudi Arabia. In the latter post he also earned Saudi Arabia's increasing displeasure for the way in which he went far beyond his brief when criticizing and abusing the West. The crunch came when Shuqairi refused to submit to the U.N. Saudi Arabia's complaints of Egyptian aggression in the Yemen. At the time Nasser was engaged in a war to drive the British out of the Federation of South Arabia, including Aden, and King Feisal was trying to stop him. Feisal sacked Shuqairi and Nasser thanked him by securing his appointment as Palestine's representative to the Arab League. That was his ticket to the Chairmanship of the P.L.O., again thanks to Nasser's sponsorship.

For Nasser's purpose Shuqairi had one big asset and one great talent. His big asset was his reputation among many Palestinians as a true and even fanatical nationalist. He had created this impression in the 1930s and 1940s. His great talent was his way with words. Shuqairi was a demagogue. To describe the orator in him as a sort of cross between Adolf Hitler and the Reverend Ian Paisley would not be inaccurate. According to the Israelis it was Shuqairi who first coined the phrase about 'driving the Jews into the sea'. Whatever the truth of that, the first Chairman of the P.L.O. did address the most dire threats to the people of Israel. It was this combination of the asset and the talent that made Shuqairi a perfect puppet.

As 1964 approached, and as he was later to tell some of Fatah's leaders, Nasser had faced an appalling dilemma. Unless the front-line Arab leaders were prepared to see their countries slowly destroyed as the price of maintaining the fiction that they were one day going to liberate Palestine, their best hope was for negotiations with Israel at which their main responsibility would be to get the best possible settlement terms for the Palestinians. Objectively speaking, it can be said that Israel could have had peace with the Arabs before the 1967 war if Israel's leaders had been prepared to give the Palestinians enough to save the honour of the Arab regimes.

For more than a decade Nasser had tried to live with the dilemma by resorting to deliberate and finely calculated ambiguity in his public speeches on Palestine. From what he occasionally said by implication, and provided they were willing to stretch their imaginations, Palestinians could conclude that Nasser was indeed hinting that he would one day fight to liberate their homeland. But it was really a case of their wishful thinking being confirmed by his ambiguity. At the same time, and knowing that Israel's leaders would make propaganda capital from his ambiguity, Nasser had used every available secret and private channel to assure Western leaders and their emissaries that nothing he was obliged to say in public should be taken to mean that he had changed his mind and that he now believed Palestine could be liberated by war or armed struggle.

To work, Nasser's strategy of winning time for negotiations that would give the Palestinians something had needed two things from Israel's leaders: an understanding of his dilemma, and a willingness on their part to do something positive for the Palestinians. Undoubtedly many of Israel's military and political leaders did appreciate Nasser's dilemma, but their strategy was to convince their people and the Western world that the Palestinians no longer existed. In 1971, in an interview with me for the B.B.C.'s *Panorama* programme, Golda Meir, then Prime Minister, actually said 'The Palestinians do not exist'.

In late 1963 Nasser realized that his ambiguity was working against him on both fronts. It was causing a growing number of Palestinians to lose or at least question their faith in him. And it was giving some credibility to Israel's propaganda claim that he was plotting the destruction of the Jewish State. That Israel was winning the propaganda war was worrying enough for Nasser. But as he was later to tell Fatah leaders, the alarm bells began to ring when he considered what Israel's leaders would do when they convinced the West that the Jewish State was in danger of annihilation. Then, or so Nasser believed, Israel's leaders would launch a major war in the sure knowledge that they could inflict a humiliating defeat on Egypt. In Nasser's view war was entirely logical given that Israel's aim was to use its superior military strength to force the Arabs to make peace on Israeli terms.

Nasser was reading Israel's leaders very well. His secret promise to the U.N. and the U.S. that he would refrain from aggressive action against Israel for ten years was due to expire in 1967, and the Israelis were in fact in the process of deciding that they would strike in 1967 or 1968. If the war they had in mind forced the Arabs to make peace on Israel's terms, well and good. If it did not, the Arab regimes would require another ten years or so to rebuild their broken armies. And in that time Israel could work against the Arabs on the political front.

As 1964 approached Nasser had to find a way to go on threatening Israel by implication in order to keep his credibility with the Palestinians, while at the same time distancing Egypt from the threat. And this is where Shuqairi came into the picture. Nasser could rely on him to make the necessary threats. Since the Palestinians knew Shuqairi to be an extreme nationalist and Nasser's man they – or a majority of them – would conclude that he represented Nasser's thinking. The Israelis would obviously draw the same conclusion, but Nasser could disown Shuqairi or, if necessary, have him eliminated at a time of his choosing. In that way Nasser hoped to neutralize the Palestinian underground and deny the Israelis what they would present as justification for another war. But he knew he was playing with fire.

That Shuqairi realized he was a puppet in Nasser's scheme of things is illustrated by what he told Khalad Hassan when the two men met to explore the possibility of a deal between the P.L.O. and Fatah. 'He said to me: "You do know that I was brought in to screw you!"' I asked Khalad if he was paraphrasing Shuqairi's comment. 'No,' Khalad replied, 'those are exactly the words he used.'

Khalad was one of several members of Fatah's Central Committee who was authorized to explore the possibility of reaching an accommodation with Shuqairi – before and after the P.L.O. came into being. Another was Wazir. He told me: 'When Shuqairi confessed that the regimes would not allow the P.L.O. any freedom, I said that we were ready to be his secret wing. Our idea was that we could prevent the regimes from robbing the P.L.O. of its independence.' Wazir and the Hassan brothers were convinced that Shuqairi did want a deal with Fatah. 'Many times we thought we had an agreement with him,' Khalad said, 'but he never delivered. He was not a free agent.'

A small part of the reason why Fatah tried so hard to reach an accommodation with Shuqairi was that it hoped to influence and change the P.L.O. from within. More importantly, Fatah had no choice. Nasser's calculations about the effect of the P.L.O. on the Palestinian underground proved to be extremely accurate. The coming into being of the P.L.O. was a disaster for Fatah. The underground network of cells and cadres created mainly by Arafat and Wazir collapsed. Said Khalad: 'There is no more any point in minimizing the crisis we faced. We lost most of our military cadres. They said they had taken an oath of loyalty to Palestine, not to an organization. So they left Fatah to join the P.L.A. in the mistaken belief that they would be allowed to make attacks on Israel. We managed to keep only a very few.'

Judging by subsequent events a reasonable estimate is that Fatah lost at least eighty and perhaps as much as ninety per cent of its cadres. Nasser followed up by asking the authorities in Kuwait to close Fatah's office there. Though Fatah was still an underground organization, Nasser knew from intelligence reports that the Kuwait office was its headquarters. Khalad said: 'Officially the authorities in Kuwait told us they could not allow two offices – one for the P.L.O. and one for Fatah. Officially they closed us down, but unofficially they allowed us to have a secret office.'

As he monitored the disintegration of the underground network, Arafat knew that the moment for starting military actions to fix the identity of the Palestinians would soon be lost for ever if he did not seize the initiative. In the late summer of 1964, and probably in consultation with Wazir, he decided that the time had come to force a Central Committee vote on his military strategy. He also decided that he would form his own breakaway group if the vote went against him.

Arafat was now determined that nothing and nobody would stop him launching military actions with the minimum possible delay. But it was easier said than done. He still had to find an answer to the question the Chinese had asked him. From where would he start? Since he could not operate from inside Israel he had to have a base in one of the front-line Arab states. Egypt? No chance. Jordan? No chance. The Lebanon? No chance. That left only Syria. With the Ba'ath Party well on its way to absolute power in Syria, the prospects for an accommodation with it were reasonably bright. But when the crunch came, would even a fullblooded Ba'athist regime be prepared to soak up the Israeli reprisal attacks which Fatah's military actions would provoke? That was the main question Arafat had to answer before he could confront with confidence those of his Central Committee colleagues who were opposed to his military way.

'Ba'ath' means 'resurrection' or 'renaissance'. It was the name given to the progressive nationalist party founded in Damascus in 1943 by Michel Aflik and his associates. As conceived by them, the Ba'ath Party was to be the leading advocate of a single Arab socialist nation. That was their dream of Arab unity. Under a succession of

Syrian military leaders who were to use Aflik's slogans as stepping stones to power for its own sake, the Syrian Ba'ath Party became Nasser's main rival in the contest for the leadership of the so-called revolutionary Arab world. Fatah owes its existence to that rivalry and Arafat's skill at playing one side against the other. There are today some important and influential Arabs who say that Arafat should not have exploited the divisions in the Arab world, and that because he did he has only himself to blame for the fact that he is not trusted by any Arab leader. Arafat was certainly to prove himself an opportunist without equal. But it was the Arab leaders, not Arafat, who determined that the only really effective bargaining power the Palestinians could employ was through opportunism. On the matter of trust, it also has to be said that most Arab leaders do not trust their closest colleagues further than they can see them – so Arafat is in good company.

Arafat had met Aflik and other founder members of the Ba'ath Party in the 1950s. At the time he made the contact he had looked upon it as a sort of insurance policy for the future. In the second half of 1964 his objective on several secret visits to Damascus was, in effect, to claim the insurance. He was greatly helped by the eighth Syrian coup which took place in October, and which he no doubt knew about in advance. It resulted in a purge of the remaining pro-Nasser elements in the highest levels of Syria's military establishment. The Ba'athists were in total control.

But even before the coup, events in Syria were moving in Arafat's favour. Or so it seemed. At the January Arab summit Nasser and the Syrians had engaged in a war of words. The Syrians told the assembled Arab heads of state that if they united they could defeat Israel in a relatively short time. An angry Nasser had replied by telling the Syrians they were 'out of their minds'. When Nasser then made it clear that the P.L.O. would be his puppet, the stage was set for a trial of strength between Cairo and Damascus. Shortly after the P.L.O. came into being, the Syrians made a special point of informing Arafat about their differences with Nasser. Arafat drew the obvious conclusion. He was being invited to knock on Syria's door.

Arafat's two most important contacts in Syria were the Director of Military Intelligence, Ahmed Sweidani, and the Commander of the Air Force, Hafez Assad – later to be President of Syria. These two Syrians had entirely different motives for apparently wanting to give Arafat a helping hand.

Sweidani was a militant Moslem who, in common with Nasser, did not believe the Arabs would ever defeat Israel in a conventional war. In his view the Arabs had only one military option, and that was to engage Israel in a protracted guerrilla war. Sweidani was an admirer of General Giap, who masterminded Vietnam's victory over first the French and then the Americans. Sweidani wanted all the front-line Arab states to become involved in a guerrilla war; and he wanted Syria to set the pace and take the lead. Hence his interest in seeking a marriage of convenience with Arafat and Fatah.

Assad's motivation was much more simple and much less sincere. He had set his mind on becoming the President of Syria, and he wanted the Palestinian card in his hand. Nasser had Shuqairi as his puppet, Assad would have Arafat as his – or he would destroy him.

From the beginning Arafat had no illusions about the nature of his relationship with the Syrians. They would seek to use him for their own ends. He would use them to serve his purpose. It would be an arrangement that had trouble written all over it. But in the autumn of 1964, Arafat was desperate enough to take help from wherever he could get it.

Arafat asked Sweidani for three things: the freedom to organize Fatah in Syria; permission to receive and store weapons that he was expecting from Algeria and China; and a base in which Fatah officers then under training in Algeria could train new recruits. At the time, the first twenty of Fatah's full-time officers were attending the Military Staff College in Algiers. After the formation of the P.L.O., Wazir had pulled off a coup of his own by persuading the Algerian authorities to make the places available. 'Until that time all of our training had been done on a part-time basis during the holidays,' Abu Jihad told me. 'To have places for twenty full-time officers at the College was something very dramatic for us.'

Sweidani's first response was encouraging but no more. He told Arafat he was reasonably confident that he could persuade his superiors to give Fatah the facilities it wanted; but he also said there would probably be a condition attached to any help Syria might offer. His superiors would probably insist that no actual attacks on Israel would be launched from Syrian soil. Arafat was not surprised. He had anticipated that the Syrians would want the best of both worlds. They would want the credit and the glory that would eventually come their way for giving life to the first authentic Palestine liberation movement. But they would do everything to avoid being on the receiving end of Israel's reprisals. The attacks on Israel would have to be mounted from Jordan and the Lebanon. Sweidani told Arafat he would try to give him some firm answers in December.

Arafat was now as ready as he could be for the confrontation with his Central Committee colleagues. And he was in no mood for compromise. If a majority of his colleagues did not support his plan for military action without delay, he would split Fatah and go his own way.

The Central Committee decision about whether or not Fatah would be committed to armed struggle was preceded by a debate which lasted for more than a month. In the course of it the issue which had previously divided Fatah's leaders was resolved without a vote. It was agreed that Fatah would fight.

On the question of why Khalad Hassan and other Central Committee members withdrew their opposition to the idea of military action, Khalad himself was very frank: 'You can say, because it is the truth, that we were pushed down a road we did not want to take by the coming into being of the P.L.O. Because of its existence, and the fact that it was not the genuine article that so many Palestinians were assuming it to be, we decided that the only way to keep the idea of real struggle alive was to struggle.'

Khalad and other Central Committee members who had previously opposed the idea of military action had no doubts that a day would come when their people would realize that they had been wrong to place their faith in the puppet P.L.O. But by then it would be too late and the Palestinians would have to settle for whatever the Arab regimes might manage to extract from Israel and its Western backers. A few Palestinians might eventually be allowed to return to their homes. The rest might receive some compensation. But they would be finished as a people with an identity, a culture and an existence of their own. Only by resorting to military action could Fatah demonstrate that the Palestinians could not be denied a real say in any decisions about their future.

The question that now threatened to tear Fatah apart was when should the military operations begin? Those Central Committee members who had previously opposed the idea of military action now said they would not support the actual use of force until Fatah was something more than a joke as a military outfit. It was not unimportant that Fatah had twenty senior officers under full-time training in Algeria, but that in no way made up for the fact that Fatah had lost most of its underground cadres to the P.L.O. and the P.L.A. It was not unimportant that Algeria, China and Syria had promised help, but promises were only that – promises. According to the opponents of quick military action, Fatah was simply not ready for battle. It needed time and money to recruit, train and equip the nucleus of a credible guerrilla force.

The grim reality behind these arguments is best illustrated by an account of a meeting that took place in March or April 1965, in Beirut between Arafat and the Catholic priest Father Ibrahim Iyad.

The Government of Israel had announced that it was holding the Arab states responsible for the activities of the Palestinian 'terrorists'. Frightened by the threat and the certainty of Israeli reprisal attacks, Egypt, Jordan and the Lebanon had ordered their intelligence services to seek out and destroy Fatah and liquidate its leaders. Nasser had put a price on Arafat's head. In Kuwait those members of the Central Committee who had originally opposed the idea of military action were in a panic. They were trying to make contact with Nasser to explain that Fatah was not a Syrian puppet and that he was wrong to regard it as his enemy. And Arafat himself was torn by terrible doubts. Was fighting the only way? Was there really no alternative? Did he have the right to commit the Palestinians to an armed struggle which might claim the lives of many thousands? Arafat was not afraid to ask himself these and other questions. He even had answers to them. But were they the right answers? To whom could he turn for reassurance?

It was in that troubled state of mind that Arafat, accompanied by Wazir, travelled from Kuwait to a convent in Beirut for a talk with a very special Palestinian – Father Iyad. Why Arafat chose a Catholic priest to be his spiritual adviser is a mystery. The following is Father Iyad's own account of his conversation with Arafat.

'He began by telling me the reasons why he believed the Palestinians had no alternative to fighting. His main concern was the refusal of the governments of the world to do anything for the

Palestinians. He said, and he was right, that once every year the
U.N. passed resolutions drawing attention to the injustice that had
been done to the Palestinians and affirming their rights to return to
their homes. But it was all talk. Nothing happened. I must also tell
you that Arafat was not a naive man. He said to me: "Father, I know
very well that even by fighting we cannot recover Palestine. We
must fight to tell the world that we exist. We must fight to tell the
world that there is a Palestinian people. We must fight in order to
stir the conscience of the people of the world. If we fail to persuade
the people of the world that our cause is just we shall be lost,
finished."

'He asked me if I agreed with him. I said I did with all my heart.
Then he told me what at the time was a very big secret. He said that
when Fatah started its military operations it had just seven trained
fighters – Arafat himself and six others, and that they had only five
rifles between them! He also told me they started without any
money. Apparently a friend gave Fatah a cheque for the equivalent
of something less than £1,000 – but they were told they could not
cash the cheque for two or three months because there was no
money in the account!

'When Arafat told me that story I said: "It sounds as though you
need help. Are you asking me to help?" I remember very clearly
Arafat's reply. He said: "Father, all I need from you is your
blessing." And I gave it to him.'

It was the first but not the last time that Arafat turned to Father
Iyad for moral support.

I asked Arafat if he would confirm Father Iyad's story that Fatah
had started its military operations with only seven trained men and
five rifles. It was clear that he was not altogether happy about the
question. In reply he said, 'It was not quite as Father Iyad told you.'
Perhaps he was thinking of the twenty Fatah officers being trained
in Algeria and the help promised by Algeria, China and Syria.

'And what about the money?' I asked. 'Was Father Iyad's story
about that also true in its essentials?'

Arafat laughed. 'Yes, it was exactly so,' he replied. He added:
'But really my colleagues did not need to worry so much about that.
They knew they could rely on me to cover the cheque.'

Arafat and Wazir were convinced there would be no armed
struggle if they delayed their military actions until Fatah had

recruited, trained and equipped a guerrilla army, and had raised the money to make it all possible. But that was not the main argument they used in what they had agreed would be their last attempt to persuade their Central Committee colleagues to vote for military action without further delay. Abu Jihad told me: 'Arafat and I made two main points. We said first of all that we were not a government, not an army, and we were not on our own land. Therefore we could not organize in the way our colleagues wanted. We did not have the possibility of organizing before the start of the action. Then we said our circumstances were such that we had to adopt the revolutionary way of thinking and the revolutionary strategy. And the point of it was that revolutions begin not by preparing but by starting. Therefore we said we would begin our armed struggle and build our strength through struggle.'

In support of that argument Arafat and Wazir stressed that Fatah's credibility was now at stake. They had made so much propaganda. They had raised expectations. If they did not now act they would lose the support of those in the underground network who had so far refused to join the puppet P.L.O. and the P.L.A. Said Abu Jihad: 'We also had a credibility problem in the eyes of the Chinese and others who had promised to supply us with weapons. Nobody was going to back us until we had proved that we were serious. I told my colleagues that the doors on which we were knocking would not be opened to us until we were fighting.'

Though its leaders are still not ready to talk about it openly, Fatah came very close to splitting and probably destroying itself in the days before and after the critical vote. But for the resignation of one Central Committee member, probably Youseff Amira, the vote on Arafat's demand that military action be started without further delay would have stayed at 5-5. In that event Fatah would have split. Khalad Hassan confirmed to me that the final vote was 5-4 in favour of Arafat's way.

Khalad Hassan co-ordinated the manoeuvres which resulted in Arafat's victory. Although he was a late and reluctant convert to the idea of military action, and despite the fact that he was strongly opposed to it being started before they were better organized, Khalad's head, if not his heart, told him there was no alternative to Fatah. If the Central Committee was now to split, the organization such as it was would be finished. And he very much doubted that any of them would get the opportunity to start again. If Fatah did not survive there would be no chance of creating authentic institutions which would allow the Palestinians to speak for themselves.

But Khalad's battle of wills with Arafat was far from over. It was, in fact, about to enter a new and more dramatic phase which would see Arafat refusing to obey Central Committee instructions. The cause of the confrontation to come was a difference of opinion, possibly a genuine misunderstanding, about how far the collective leadership had committed itself to armed struggle. Those Central Committee members who had opposed Arafat's demand for quick military action were under the impression that the commitment was not an open-ended one. After the vote they had argued that the decision in favour of military action ought to be reviewed once the action had started and in the light of the response of the Arab regimes. What would be the position, they had asked, if the Arab regimes decided to smash Fatah? Would Fatah then regard itself as being at war with the regimes? Or would Fatah then turn away from confrontation with them in the hope that having made its point it could come to some understanding with them about the need for a joint strategy?

In the event, military operations were launched in the name of Al-Assifa — 'The Storm' — not Fatah. According to Khalad this was a 'last-minute' decision and there were two reasons for it.

The first was that if the military operations provoked a totally hostile Arab response Fatah could claim that it was not associated with Assifa, and if that claim was accepted, Fatah would still have a political option. Abu Jihad said: 'We were too frightened of the Arab regimes to use our own name. We invented Assifa to test their reactions.' The clear implication of this ploy is that at least some members of the Central Committee did not regard the commitment to armed struggle as an open-ended one but as subject to review.

The second reason for the invention of Assifa was the need to provide Fatah with extra security cover. Said Khalad: 'We were expecting the Arab regimes to make an attempt to stop our military activities and we didn't know how long we would be free to continue them. We calculated that we could win time to establish ourselves by causing the Arab intelligence services to look for an organization that did not exist!'

The evidence that Khalad was expecting a confrontation with Arafat sooner or later is in the fact that he blocked his appointment as Fatah's first military commander. That job went to Abu Youseff. Khalad's public explanation is that since Arafat was born in Cairo and had spent most of his life there and in Kuwait he was a stranger to those areas from which it was anticipated that most of Fatah's hit-and-run attacks against Israel would be mounted. Abu Youseff on the other hand was brought up in Palestine and therefore knew the area and its people as well as he knew himself.

Perhaps that was one reason why Arafat was denied the leadership of Fatah's military wing. But there was much more to it. Mainly because they had misread his personality, Khalad and others feared that, given the opportunity, Arafat would build a military power base to impose his will by force and that he could emerge as a dictator who might also use his military power to destroy any possibility of a political and negotiated settlement. This was confirmed by Khalad's brother, Hani. With a chuckle he said: 'They did see him as a potential military dictator and that truly is the reason why they were determined to prevent him from becoming the leader.' As events were to prove, Arafat's colleagues could not have been more wrong about him.

In early December Sweidani informed Arafat that his masters in Damascus had given him the green light to collaborate with Fatah for a 'trial period'. Arafat was disappointed. All that he was really being offered was the benefit of Sweidani's advice. And in return for that the Syrians would have a big finger in Fatah's little pie. From Arafat's point of view it was a most unsatisfactory arrangement, but it was also one that he had to accept. Without Sweidani's help he had little or no chance of persuading the Syrian regime to let him have a base in which Fatah recruits could be trained, and where weapons and ammunition could be stored. And getting that base was the absolute priority.

As Arafat reflected on the lack of substance in Sweidani's report his disappointment turned to alarm. Initially he had contented himself with the idea that the Syrian regime was merely keeping its options open. But the more he thought about it, the more he realized what the Syrians were really up to. They were assuming, correctly in Arafat's view, that the regimes in Egypt, Jordan and the Lebanon would seek to destroy Fatah as soon as it showed its hand. It followed that there would come a time, in months and perhaps weeks, when Fatah would have to seek sanctuary in Syria in order to survive. In such a situation Fatah's leaders might be desperate enough to accept the conditions that Syria would present as the price of its help. And those conditions, if they were accepted, would result in Fatah becoming Syria's puppet. As Arafat saw it, and he was proved to be right, the Syrians were baiting a trap for Fatah's military leaders. If they agreed to become Syria's puppets they would survive. If they insisted on their independence they would be eliminated. Although he did not know it at the time, the Syrians had already selected the puppet leader they intended to impose on Fatah if Arafat and his colleagues refused to do as they were told. His name was Ahmad Jabril. He was to be Syria's Shuqairi and the Judas in the Palestinian pack.

Then a strange thing happened. Very soon after his last conversation with Sweidani, and while he was moving some sticks of dynamite from the Lebanon to Syria in the boot of his car, Arafat was arrested and then imprisoned by the Syrians. The man who ordered his arrest was Colonel Mohammed Orki, head of the Palestinian Department of Syrian Intelligence. Arafat was accused of being an enemy of the state and charged with importing explosives for subversive purposes!

Abu Jihad offered an explanation for the Syrians' action: 'They released Arafat after eighteen hours or so. Since he was working with Sweidani at the time, they knew, of course, that the explosives were to be transferred to Jordan. In my opinion Orki arrested Arafat to give him a shock – to remind him that he was under constant surveillance and could not make a move without the Syrian authorities knowing it.'

That is one possible explanation. Another and more sinister one, supported by subsequent events, is that Hafez Assad wanted it on the record that Arafat had been arrested and charged with subversion.

As 1964 drew to a close and Fatah prepared for military action there were four confrontations in the making. One was between Fatah and the Arab regimes in Egypt, Jordan and the Lebanon. Another was between Arafat and Khalad Hassan. Another was between Arafat and the Syrians. And another was between the Palestinians and Israel.

On the eve of Fatah's first military operation, the balance of power was broadly as follows: on the Palestinian side Fatah was not much more than an idea, and the P.L.O. was the puppet of an Arab leader who had no intention of fighting Israel to liberate Palestine; on the other side was the Jewish State. It possessed the strongest, the most efficient and the most effective army and air force in the region. It was also one year away from having its own nuclear bomb.

The struggle that was about to begin, and which has not yet ended, was indeed a fight between a David and a Goliath. But contrary to what the world believed at the time and for too long afterwards, the real Goliath was the Jewish State.

# The Struggle

# 9

# The Rebel Leader

Israel's military and political leaders could have done much to help the Arab regimes isolate and destroy Fatah in a matter of months. In retrospect there is a case for saying that it was an Israeli blunder, itself a product of the arrogance that is the hallmark of Zionist thinking, that guaranteed Fatah's survival, the resurgence of Palestinian nationalism and, finally, the regeneration of the Palestinian people as a nation without land.

Confirming what Arafat himself told me, Abu Jihad put it this way: 'This is the point in the story when we have to say thank you to Israel. If Israel's leaders had kept quiet about our first military operations, the Arab regimes and their intelligence services would have finished us very quickly. In the beginning the Arab newspapers were not allowed to publish our military communiqués. The editors and the writers were under instructions, but also they did not believe what we were saying. To them the idea that some few Palestinians were attacking Israel without the support of the Arab regimes was too crazy for words. So nobody was hearing about us. Meanwhile the Arab intelligence services were making their plans to destroy us. There is no doubt that we were in big trouble. Without publicity we could not capture the imagination of our people and then the Arab masses. Without publicity we could not have survived the Arab attempt to crush us. But Israel's Prime Minister, Levi Eshkol, made a speech in which he threatened the Arab regimes and confirmed our activities. That was the turning point. Israel saved us!'

Fatah's first military operation was scheduled for New Year's Eve 1964. On that night four Palestinian commandos were supposed to set out from the Ein el-Hilwe refugee camp in the Lebanon, cross into Israel and plant explosives at the Beit Netopha canal and pumping station. In the event they did not get anywhere near the border before they were arrested by Lebanese security agents. The four had been under surveillance for several days.

What went wrong? Abu Jihad's explanation was simply that the four talked too much. 'The Arab intelligence services had their agents in every refugee camp,' he said. 'I suppose it was very natural for these four people to tell their friends what they were going to do. And their friends told others. In those days our security was very poor.'

That was most certainly the case, but none of the four were members of Fatah. It seems that they were, in fact, on Sweidani's payroll as part-time Syrian agents. And it was Sweidani who gave Arafat their names. It may well have been that Sweidani insisted on running the first operation. The fact that Arafat agreed to it on that basis must also be seen as more evidence that Fatah's lack of competent military manpower was acute.

The arrest of the four was used by the Lebanese to cause maximum damage to the credibility of the emerging Palestine liberation group that went by the name of Assifa. Arafat, obviously, did not know that the four had been arrested and that the first military operation had failed before it started. While the four were safely under lock and key in a Beirut prison, Arafat and his associates distributed 'Military Communiqué No. 1'. On a midnight tour of the city in Arafat's blue Volkswagen they dropped copies of their communiqué into the letterboxes of all Lebanon's newspapers. Hours later the newspapers published front-page accounts of Assifa's first operation.

In the circumstances it is inconceivable that Lebanon's editors would have published Assifa's story before they had cleared it with the appropriate authorities. The Lebanese authorities must, therefore, have wanted Assifa's claim to be given as much publicity as possible. Why? The answer came two days later. After a briefing by Lebanese security officials, the same Lebanese newspapers published the details of how the four from the Ein el-Hilwe camp had been arrested. Assifa was made to look very foolish.

This must have given Sweidani cause for private satisfaction. The more Arafat was driven to the conclusion that it was impossible for him to operate from any of the other front-line Arab states, the more he would be forced to rely on Syria. And the more he had to rely on Syria, the more likely it was that he could be manoeuvred into becoming a Syrian puppet.

Arafat did not put all of his eggs in Sweidani's basket, however. Without telling Sweidani, Arafat and Abu Youseff had made preparations of their own for a second strike at the Beit Netopha canal and pumping station. On the night of 3 January 1965 a small group of genuine Fatah commandos crossed into Israel from Jordan. They reached their objective and they planted their sticks of dynamite. Their mistake was in setting the timer device, an old clock, to delay the explosion until they had crossed back into Jordan. This gave the Israelis the opportunity to locate the dynamite and stop the clock.

By first light on 4 January, the Fatah men were back on Jordanian soil. Mission accomplished – or so they thought. With the border still in sight they were ambushed by a Jordanian army patrol. The Fatah men were ordered to surrender and hand over their weapons. In the fighting that followed when they refused, one of the commandos, Ahmed Musa, was killed. It was appropriate that Fatah's first casualty – the organization's first 'martyr' – should have been shot by a brother Arab.

The shooting of Ahmed Musa was some proof that Hussein was as determined as he could be in the circumstances to prevent Fatah using Jordan as the launchpad for its attacks on Israel. Yet it was from Jordan that most of Fatah's early sabotage raids were mounted. During the first three months of 1965, Fatah carried out ten sabotage raids – seven from Jordan, three from the Gaza Strip.

But though it was at last in action, Fatah was being denied the publicity it needed to capture the imagination and thus the support of the Palestinian and Arab masses because of the total Arab ban on the reporting of Fatah – or Assifa as it was then calling itself – and its actions.

It was Levi Eshkol's threatening speech that let the Assifa cat out of the bag in which the Arab regimes were trying to keep it. On a more regular basis Fatah was also given a helping hand by Kol Yisrael (the Voice of Israel). Its Arabic news service carried reports

about the activities of the 'terrorists'. Israel's confirmation that
something was happening, and the silence in the Arab world, caused
a growing number of Palestinians and other Arabs to ask questions.
Who were these Palestinians who dared to attack Israel? Did they
have the secret support of Nasser and other Arab leaders – or were
they on their own? Even some Palestinians who had put their trust
in Nasser were beginning to express admiration for those who acted
while others talked. But who were these crazy Palestinians?

The questions had to be answered if the Arab regimes were not to
lose their grip on the situation. And they had to be answered in a
way that would discredit Arafat and his colleagues.

According to the propaganda published and broadcast by the
newspapers and radio stations under Egyptian control, Assifa was
set up and financed by Western intelligence agencies. Acting for
them, and Israel, Assifa's objective was to push the Arabs into war
before they were ready for it. Assifa was therefore seeking to bring
about the defeat of the Arabs, and all associated with the
organization were traitors. One of the most inventive pieces of anti-
Assifa propaganda was written for *Al-Anwar*, Egypt's mouthpiece
in Beirut. Its author was Shafik Al-Hout, who was later to become
the real P.L.O.'s chief in the Lebanon and one of Arafat's most
senior lieutenants. Shafik's contribution to the propaganda war was
the assertion that Assifa was an agent for CENTO, the Central
Treaty Organization for economic and military co-operation
between Britain, Iran, Pakistan and Turkey, established in 1959.
Some years later Shafik entertained Fatah's leaders with amusing
stories about how Egypt's intelligence chiefs had succeeded in
fooling themselves with such nonsense.

Jordan's idea of good propaganda was to project Assifa as
communist. This was the line suggested by the British Secret
Intelligence Service and the American Central Intelligence Agency.
At the time the S.I.S. and the C.I.A. had not resolved a dispute about
which of the two agencies would control Jordan's secret service.
Said Khalad Hassan: 'The Jordanians did not confine their
propaganda to the newspapers and the radio. I know for a fact that
they sent their reports alleging that we were communists to all of the
Gulf States. In each Arab country we were presented as the number-
one enemy of the regime – whoever that enemy was. The only thing
the regimes did not say about us was the truth – that we were a

genuine nationalist movement, struggling against impossible odds to maintain our independence. I can assure you that if we had been willing to become a tool of any intelligence agency our money problem would have ended.'

It was, in fact, Fatah's desperate lack of money that led to Arafat taking over from Abu Youseff as military commander. Khalad said to me: 'You may laugh if you wish, but that is the truth. Abu Youseff had eight children and the Central Committee simply could not pay him enough money to feed his family!' So Abu Youseff had to work for a living. When Arafat was formally asked to become Fatah's full-time military commander he wound up his construction and contracting business. As Khalad said earlier, the speed with which Arafat liquidated his business interests caused him to lose a great deal of money; but he still had enough to live on. He was also intending to use his own money to buy weapons and ammunition. But that, for the moment, was an idea he kept to himself.

Khalad and the other Central Committee members who feared that Arafat had the makings of a military dictator were not pleased, to say the least, by this latest turn of events. But with the possible exception of Wazir, there was no alternative to Arafat as Fatah's military commander. Wazir would probably have turned down the job if he had been offered it over Arafat's head.

For those who had doubts about what Arafat might do with his new power, the problem was finding a way to control his individualism. Arafat made the point that he would be on the move in the Lebanon, Syria and Jordan and that it was ridiculous in the circumstances to expect him, or any military commander, to be constantly seeking the approval of the Central Committee in Kuwait for decisions that had to be made on the battlefield and made quickly. It would take between three and five days to send a message to Kuwait and get an answer back. That was no way to run a war. It was stupid. So Arafat asked for the freedom to make operational decisions as he thought best. That was too much for the doubters on the Central Committee. As a compromise they created a small Military Committee. It was empowered to make military decisions in the name of the collective leadership, and it would give Arafat his instructions. That was the theory.

When it became obvious that Assifa could not be discredited and destroyed by propaganda means, Egypt, Jordan and the Lebanon turned to direct and brutal action. On Nasser's instructions, Field Marshal Abdel Hakim Amer, Arafat's old friend and Commander-in-Chief of the Egyptian army since 1953, issued an Order of the Day to the United Arab Command (U.A.C.). It required the armed forces of all the member states of the Arab League to regard themselves as being at war with Assifa. Said Arafat: 'We knew about the Order as soon as it was issued because Sweidani showed us a copy of it.' Said Abu Jihad: 'Hakim Amer's Order to the U.A.C. was in two parts. It required the Arab armies to prevent the Palestinians attacking Israel. And it asked the military intelligence services to collect information about Assifa.' Said Khalad Hassan: 'The regimes wanted to liquidate our movement in 1963 and 1964. The only difference was that in 1965 they had a target to hit.'

That much was true, but the regimes did not find Fatah an easy target. Its last-minute decision to launch military actions under the cover name of Assifa did succeed in fooling the Arab intelligence services for a few vital months. 'By this device we protected our organization,' Abu Jihad told me, 'but unfortunately many Palestinians paid a high price. Over a period of some months hundreds were put into prison and tortured for information about us. Some had their fingers broken. Others were made to walk on glass. And some had the soles of their feet beaten with sticks until the nerves were exposed in the bleeding flesh.'

The majority of Palestinian refugees who were tortured in the prisons of Egypt, Jordan and the Lebanon had no information to give. Assifa was as much a mystery to them as it was to their torturers.

In the early stages of what was undoubtedly a co-ordinated and ruthless offensive to destroy Assifa, the only notable success the regimes enjoyed was in Gaza. There, and at the price of breaking a few fingers and cracking a few heads, Egyptian intelligence agents did uncover three of Fatah's underground cells.

In Jordan the action to liquidate Fatah cells uncovered by that country's various intelligence agencies did not come until Israel forced Hussein's hand with reprisal attacks on Khalkilia, Jenin and Shuna. The King was not opposed to his intelligence people being as ruthless as necessary to extract information from those suspected of being members or sympathizers of Assifa. And as the shooting of Ahmed Musa proved, he had not needed Hakim Amer's directive to tell him that it was necessary to take all practical measures to prevent Palestinian saboteurs crossing into Israel from Jordan. But because the Palestinians were the majority in Jordan, the King was understandably reluctant to move in a way which could make him an enemy in their eyes. In the event, Israel left him with no choice. The message of Israeli reprisal attacks was as clear as it was crude: if he did not do what they wanted, they would use their superior military strength to destroy Jordan bit by bit. It was a cruel logic that was to take Israel all the way to Beirut in the summer of 1982. It was also a foolish logic. If Israel had secretly co-operated with the front-line Arab states, Fatah would have been destroyed before the year was out. And because Syria had no intention of promoting an independent Palestine liberation movement, the end of Fatah would have spelled the end of any hope for the resurgence of Palestinian nationalism.

From the early 1960s to the present day, Israeli propagandists and many in the West who ought to know better have portrayed Arafat and all of his colleagues in the leadership of Fatah and the P.L.O. as Marxists and puppets of the Soviet Union. Although Arafat did once try to play his negotiating cards through the Soviet Union, and although Moscow did use its influence within Fatah and the P.L.O. to sabotage the Fahd Plan (which the Americans were pretending to support) in 1981, nothing could be further from the truth. In 1965, when Fatah was fighting for its existence, the Soviet Union was firmly on the side of those who wanted the file on the Palestinians to be closed. Said Khalad Hassan: 'The Soviets were strongly advising Nasser to crush us with speed and by any means. They told him that the idea of a Palestine liberation movement belonged to "folklore". And they described us as "cowboys".' I asked Khalad how he and other Fatah leaders had learned about the Soviet attitude. He replied: 'Some years later Nasser told us what the Soviets were advising him to do at the time. And later still the Soviets themselves confirmed Nasser's story.'

Fatah's most important and best kept secret of 1965 was the identity of the individual who was effectively the Chief of Staff and Co-ordinator of Military Operations. Only two men were qualified for the job. Arafat himself and Wazir. If things had happened according to Arafat's hopes and expectations, Wazir would have moved to Beirut to take the job as soon as he found a replacement for himself to manage the Bureau de la Palestine in Algeria.

In March Wazir did take his leave of Algiers, and he travelled from there to Beirut, but not to become Fatah's Chief of Staff. Within two days of his arrival in the Lebanese capital, and after a crisis meeting with Arafat, he was on his way to Europe. Fatah had been in action for three months but the Algerians and the Chinese were very far from being convinced that it had the makings of an effective and credible guerrilla organization. So they had not yet honoured their promises to supply arms and ammunition. The conclusion reached by Arafat and Wazir was the only one possible in the circumstances. If they did not soon find a source of arms and ammunition – mines and other explosives were the priority at the time – they would have to call off their military activities and admit defeat by the end of the year at the latest.

Wazir was well briefed by Arafat on the problems he would have to solve in Western Europe. There were two main ones. The first stemmed from the fact that Fatah had no contacts with Europe's arms dealers. So Wazir would have to find his own leads to them. And while doing that he would have to take account of the second problem. It was the Mossad. According to Arafat's information, Israel's civilian secret service was enjoying more or less a free hand in the capitals of Western Europe. As Fatah was later to discover to its cost, Israel's intelligence-gathering operation was so effective that by 1967 the Mossad had files, with photographs, on every Palestinian who was active in student politics anywhere in Western Europe. In recent years Israeli commentators have speculated that it was Yitzhak Shamir who masterminded the Mossad's European operations in the 1960s.

It was expected that Wazir would be away from the front line for several months at least. Before he left Beirut there was one question that had to be answered. Who would become Chief of Staff and Co-ordinator of Military Operations? Arafat had toyed with the idea of trying to do the job himself. But if he stayed more than two or three days in any one place there was a good chance that he would be identified and arrested. He also intended to participate in as many military operations as possible.

When Arafat put the question, Wazir smiled. 'No problem,' he replied. 'The person who can do my work is already here in Beirut. My Intissar. My wife. She can be our Chief of Staff!'

At first Arafat was reluctant even to consider the idea. He did not doubt for one moment that the remarkable and beautiful Intissar could do the job. As Wazir's secret and special assistant for the past six years she had come to know all there was to know about the Palestinian underground. And it was surely the case that no agent of any Arab intelligence service would be smart enough to connect her to Fatah or Assifa unless he had concrete evidence. Moslem wives and mothers had their place, and it most definitely was not inside a liberation movement which had resorted to armed struggle against the will and wishes of the Arab regimes. What alarmed Arafat was the thought of how vulnerable Intissar would be in other ways. Since operational orders could only be passed by word of mouth, one of her many responsibilities would be to meet and brief those who were to lead sabotage missions in Israel. Inevitably some would be captured. And then it would be only a matter of time before one was broken by torture and revealed all he knew about Intissar's role and her whereabouts. And if she was captured and tortured the entire underground network would be destroyed in a matter of days.

'You do understand that she could never be taken alive,' Arafat said. He meant that if Intissar was ever on the point of being captured, she would have the choice of taking her own life or giving her bodyguard a codeword that would be his order to shoot her.

'Is she ready to make such a sacrifice?' Arafat asked.

'Yes,' Wazir replied, 'we have discussed it many times. She is ready.'

'And what about you, my dear Khalil? The love that you share with your Intissar is something out of this world. You have two sons and one day, God willing, there will be daughters. Are you ready for her to make such a sacrifice?'

It was not a question that Wazir had expected. He paused to give it thought. 'Yes,' he said finally, 'I am ready.' Later the same day the two men visited Father Ibrahim Iyad.

So it was that Intissar became Fatah's first Chief of Staff and Co-ordinator of Military Operations.

By this time Khalil was using his *nom de guerre*, Abu Jihad. Abu means 'father of'. Jihad was his eldest son. Intissar became Um Jihad, mother of Jihad. Most of their colleagues in Fatah made use of the same, simple formula to provide themselves with cover names. Arafat became Abu Amar, Khalad Hassan became Abu Sa'ed, and Salah Khalaf became Abu Iyad. With the exception of Arafat and Khalad Hassan, I shall refer to the Palestinian leaders by their cover names from here on, which is how they are best known in the West.

For six months Um Jihad's apartment in Beirut was effectively Fatah's military headquarters. 'I did everything,' she said. 'I prepared the military communiqués. I received the leaders of the groups to give them their orders for each military operation. I was the contact between one group and another. You can say that I took care of all of the needs of our fighters. I was even the one who gave them their weapons.'

I asked Um Jihad if there had been an occasion when she had worried that one of her visitors was an agent for an Arab intelligence service. 'Not really,' she replied. 'Of course our people had to identify themselves with codewords. But really I had no problems. Because of my work with Abu Jihad I knew most of them by name and face. Mostly they were the people I met on my honeymoon!'

Piece by piece the Arab intelligence services were assembling a picture of Assifa's organization and how it worked. By the late summer of 1965 Arab agents were closing in for the kill. And a day was coming when Arafat would have to make a dramatic journey to Beirut to snatch Um Jihad from danger.

In Kuwait Khalad Hassan and a majority of Fatah Central Committee members were evaluating the results of Arafat's military operations with a growing sense of alarm and panic. It was true that they were all committed to the concept of armed struggle. But it was also true that the Palestinian military effort would not contribute to the liberation of any land unless it was part of a co-ordinated Arab military strategy. In the view of Khalad and his supporters, the tragedy of the moment was that Arafat's military operations were sabotaging the prospect of any accommodation, let alone co-ordination, with the regimes in general and with Nasser in particular.

Through the summer months Khalad and others tried by various means to get to Nasser. By one route Khalad got as far as Mohamed Heikal who, as the Editor of *Al-Ahram*, was Nasser's mouthpiece. On a personal level he was also one of Nasser's best friends. By another route Khalad got as far as Fateh Hadib, the head of the Arab section of Egypt's intelligence service. 'With him I had a fight,' said Khalad, 'and he became our enemy for life.'

The results of the conversations with those who could have opened the door to Nasser were totally discouraging to Khalad and his Central Committee colleagues. 'We learned only that Nasser was being fed two lies about us,' Khalad told me. 'The first was that we were the Moslem Brotherhood in disguise and that we were intending to kill Nasser. Later Nasser told us that his intelligence people were insisting on a daily basis that Arafat was the secret leader of the Brotherhood, and that it was Arafat who would one day attempt to assassinate Nasser. The second lie was that we were a Ba'athist front and therefore agents and puppets of the Syrians. It was Heikal who told me that Nasser was fighting us because he believed we were Syrian agents.'

While apparently rejecting the idea of any accommodation with Fatah, the Egyptians had also implied that they might be willing to reconsider their position if Fatah proved it was not a Syrian front or puppet. Fatah had no intention of becoming a puppet of any regime; but the longer the confrontation between Fatah and the other front-line regimes went on, the more Fatah would be driven to relying on Syrian support, and the more it would appear that Fatah was becoming a Syrian puppet. To Khalad and his supporters – on this matter they were the majority – the conclusion that had to be drawn was obvious. If they were to have a chance of reaching an accommodation with Nasser and other Arab leaders whose support they would need if Palestine was to be liberated, Fatah would have to call off the military action. There was no other way to prove that Fatah was not a Syrian puppet and that it was not intending to become one in the future.

As Khalad and his supporters saw it, they were, in effect, being asked to decide which Arabs the Palestinians needed most. Superficially it was a choice between Egypt and Syria – the two rivals for the leadership of the Arab world. But Egypt was historically the most important Arab country and also the strongest and most powerful of the front-line Arab states. Its present ruler was indisputably the leader of the Arab world, for all his faults and failings. If Egypt was Fatah's ally there was a good chance that Fatah could, in time, win the friendship and support of most of the other Arab states that mattered. Fatah had much to lose, and precious little to gain, from being seen as a Syrian puppet.

It was also the case that Syria's motives for wanting to control Fatah were much less worthy or honourable than Nasser's. Syria wanted to replace Egypt as the leader of the Arab world, and the Syrians believed that control of Fatah would help them achieve that. Nasser was prepared to do anything to stop the Palestinians pushing him into a war with Israel, but he was not intending to abandon their cause. The essential difference between Nasser and Fatah's leaders was over what the Palestinians could realistically expect to get in any settlement and how a settlement was to be achieved.

When the decision in principle to de-escalate the military action was taken by a majority of Fatah Central Committee members, a confrontation with Arafat was inevitable. While Khalad Hassan prepared for it, Arafat was in Damascus.

There, and probably from Sweidani, Arafat learned that Um Jihad was in danger. The Arab intelligence services had apparently come to the conclusion that Assifa's operational headquarters was in Beirut. After consultations with their counterparts in Egypt and Jordan, the Lebanon's security chiefs were going for the kill.

Before the sun was up on 2 September, scores of Palestinians were to be arrested. Those already in prison were to be tortured until they broke. It was only a matter of time, perhaps a few hours, before one did break and reveal all that he knew about Assifa's organization – including Um Jihad's role and the place where she could be arrested.

Arafat took a taxi from Damascus to Beirut. The following is Um Jihad's account of what happened in the next few hours.

'It was still dark when Arafat entered my apartment. As he closed the door he put a finger to his lips to tell me not to speak. He said, "We must leave. Quickly. Quickly." I asked him what was happening. "No time for questions," he said. "I will tell you on the way."

'He was very anxious but also very calm. He said: "I will take care of the children, you must gather all of your papers and documents. Quickly. Quickly."

'Jihad and Nidal were still asleep. Arafat woke them and helped them to dress. I heard him say to them: "We have time to pack only one bag with your clothes and toys – give me what you want to take. Quickly. Quickly."

'Twenty minutes later we left the apartment. Arafat carried the boys to the taxi. He said to the driver, "Don't stop unless I say so!"

'As soon as we were on the road to Damascus I asked Arafat what was happening. "What is the matter? Has something happened to Abu Jihad?" At the time Abu Jihad was still in Europe – in West Germany. Many times I asked Arafat these and other questions but he refused to say one word until we crossed the border into Syria. Then he told me the whole story and why he was expecting me to be arrested at any moment.'

At the end of her story Um Jihad said: 'Now I must tell you something wonderful. Our comrades were tortured in unbelievable ways but they never told about me. They were burned with hot iron, they were beaten with leather straps, they were dropped into water, hot and cold, hot and cold, and they had salt put into their wounds. They suffered so much but they kept our secret. The Arab intelligence services will learn the truth about me for the first time when they read your book!'

By chance Abu Jihad returned to Beirut from Europe later the same day. He went straight to his apartment. Not surprisingly he was alarmed by the evidence that his family had left in a hurry. Said Um Jihad: 'Fortunately I left a message with the caretaker. I asked him to tell my husband that I had gone outside with my "Uncle". In those days we used to refer to Arafat as our uncle. So Abu Jihad knew where I was. In the night he telephoned me at Arafat's apartment in Damascus. I was frightened even to talk on the telephone. Then I asked him a very stupid question. "When will I see you?" I could tell from his reaction that he was surprised I should ask such a dangerous question. "Okay," he said, "maybe tomorrow, maybe the day after." I put the telephone down and went to sleep. Two hours later we heard the doorbell. It was Abu Jihad.'

That is how and why Fatah moved its operational headquarters from Beirut to Damascus.

I did not discover when or how Arafat was informed that the majority of his Central Committee colleagues were in favour of reducing military action to give them the chance to open a dialogue with Nasser. All I know is that Arafat said he would refuse to comply with any formal instruction to that effect. He told his colleagues that he was, if necessary, prepared to go his own way.

Arafat's decision to lead what can be described as the first Fatah rebellion was not taken lightly. It was not an angry and instant reaction to the news from Kuwait. The evidence is that Arafat was tortured by doubts for several days. And he did not finally make up his mind until he had talked again with Father Iyad.

'On this occasion he did not come to me at the convent,' the Father said. 'Instead he asked some friends to invite us both to dinner. When I arrived the host said to me: "You will be meeting a man who admires you very much and who wants to speak with you." After the meal Arafat and I talked alone. He told me that his colleagues on the Central Committee were asking him to give up the military way and that he was refusing to obey their instructions. He said he understood their fears that he would be pushed into becoming a Syrian puppet. But they did not understand him. "I will never, never, never become the puppet of any regime," he said. He was very quiet but also very passionate, very emotional. I asked him about the situation in Syria. Was he expecting some trouble? "Oh yes," he said, "many troubles. The regime is divided about whether to support me or not. There will be another coup soon. If certain people come to power they will try to kill me because they know I will not be their puppet."

'We also discussed the possibility of something positive emerging from further conversations with the Egyptians. I asked him what would happen if the military action was called off. He said: "Nothing will happen. None of the regimes will support us seriously until we have demonstrated by armed struggle that we are a people who cannot be ignored. If we give up now our cause will be lost."

'After that he did not speak for some moments. Then he said: "Father, I have decided that I must continue with the armed struggle. Will you give me your blessing?"

'I said: "Yes"; and I did. I told him the following: "God is love and love is justice. You will not be fighting alone." He smiled.'

As far as his colleagues in Kuwait were concerned, Arafat was now in a state of rebellion. At more or less the same time as Father Iyad had been giving Arafat his blessing, Khalad Hassan was obtaining the Central Committee's agreement to deprive Arafat and the Military Command of funds. It was the first of a number of sanctions designed to force Arafat to accept Fatah policy as determined by the majority on the Central Committee. The majority took their stand on the argument that they had approved military operations only on the understanding that the decision would be reviewed in the light of the Arab response.

For Arafat the Central Committee's decision to deprive him of funds could not have come at a worse time. He had invested the last of his personal money in Abu Jihad's mission to Europe. That had been successful; Abu Jihad did finally locate an arms dealer who was prepared to sell him arms and ammunition; but there were delivery problems still to be solved. The shipment had first to go to Algeria and from there it would be sent on as a gift from the Algerians. But the Syrians had not yet given permission for it to be received.

On 9 November, and mainly because Arafat was without the money he needed to keep his organization ticking over – most of the fighters had wives and families and they had to be fed – Fatah's military operations came to a halt. Arafat was also down to his last reserves of mines and explosives. To make matters worse, the security services in Jordan and the Lebanon were putting to good use the information they had extracted by torture from those of Arafat's men who had fallen into their hands. As a consequence of what they learned about Assifa's operations, the authorities in Jordan and the Lebanon were now much more successful in their efforts to prevent Arafat's men crossing their borders. For the next five months there were no attacks on Israel from Jordan or the Lebanon.

It was Hani Hassan, Khalad's brother, who did most to rescue Arafat from his financial troubles. He told me: 'At first Arafat did not explain the real reason for his money problems. He just said that without more money the revolution would stop. So I began to collect funds from my student organizations in Germany and elsewhere. Then I had the idea to involve the Palestinian workers in Germany. There were, as I told you, some 65,000 in Germany alone. They were in the habit of working on Sundays because they got paid double. So I made the suggestion that they should work one Sunday of every month for the organization, for Fatah, and three for themselves. They agreed and we began to collect quite a large amount of money on a regular basis.

'You can tell how important the money was to Arafat because he

sent Abu Jihad every month to collect it and to give the receipts. It
was very dangerous for Abu Jihad to be showing himself in places
where the Mossad was so well organized. It was Abu Jihad who told
me about Arafat's problems with Kuwait and how my dear brother
had persuaded the Central Committee to cut off the funds! I said to
Abu Jihad: "If you and Arafat are fighting we will stay behind you.
We had our political differences in the beginning but we are behind
the gun!"'

What one Hassan brother had taken away, another was
returning. Although he did not know it at the time, Hani was on his
way to becoming Arafat's chief crisis manager.

The real importance of the money from Palestinian students and
workers in West Germany was that it allowed Arafat to buy the time
he needed to develop a strategy for keeping the military option alive.
He had outmanoeuvred his Central Committee colleagues in
Kuwait for the time being; but he knew that Khalad Hassan would
regard what had happened as only the first round in this particular
battle of wills. The confrontation would continue. Arafat also knew
that he would be on the losing side unless he could somehow
persuade the authorities in Damascus to let him mount operations
against Israel from Syria.

Arafat's tactics were as dangerous as they were desperate. He
decided that his only real option was to play on the divisions which,
at the end of 1965, were threatening to tear the Syrian regime apart.
It was a strategy that required him to infringe, if not break, his own
cardinal rule – no interference in the internal affairs of the Arab
states. To himself at the time, and later to others, Arafat justified his
action on the grounds that he was merely playing the Syrians at their
own game. They were using him, he would use them. It was also a
strategy that was nearly to cost him his life, twice, in the months to
come, and which helped to determine that Hafez Assad would be his
prime enemy as long as he lived.

Ostensibly the ruling Syrian Ba'ath Party was divided on the
question of how best to use the Palestinians. But as Arafat knew
from his conversations with Sweidani and others, that was merely
the cover for an otherwise naked struggle for power for its own
sake. Those with the power were the President, General Amin
Hafiz, and his supporters. Those who wanted the power were the
so-called Young Turks of the Ba'ath Party – the intellectuals and the

radicals of the extreme left, and more important, the military men who represented the Alawite community. The Alawites were a mystical, secretive and predominantly Shi'a Moslem sect which accounted for no more than fourteen per cent of Syria's population. The man who believed it was his destiny to rule Syria in their name was Hafez Assad.

When Amin Hafiz came to power as a result of the 1964 coup, he was fiercely anti-Nasser and the leading advocate of the idea that the Arabs could defeat Israel on the battlefield if only they united and went to war without further delay. Hafiz was widely regarded, abroad and at home, as a pompous ass and a fool. He was both, but he was not so foolish that he refused to think about what Nasser was saying. At the third Arab summit in September 1965, Nasser had said the Arabs would be no match for Israel even if they did combine their military resources.

As 1965 was drawing to its close, Amin Hafiz was quietly convinced that Nasser was right. In that case the worst thing he could do was to back Arafat in a way that would cause Israel to hit Syria. At the end of 1965, Amin Hafiz was a worried and frightened man. He was beginning to regret that he had allowed Sweidani to talk him into giving Arafat any freedom. At the time it had seemed like a good idea. By declaring himself to be a supporter of guerrilla warfare, Amin Hafiz was able to renounce his commitment to quick and total war with Israel without losing too much face. Or so he thought.

By the end of the year the Syrian President was groping for a new Palestine policy. What emerged was a continuing commitment to armed struggle through guerrilla warfare, but it was to be a struggle that would not begin until the necessary and proper preparations had been completed. It was, in short, a policy for doing nothing. And it was this that gave the opponents of Amin Hafiz their opportunity. They could now denounce him as a traitor and present themselves, once they had seized power, as the only real and true believers in the philosophy of revolutionary armed struggle.

On the sidelines Arafat permitted himself a smile. Now was the moment for him to play his hand.

Arafat and Sweidani reviewed the situation and their options in early January. By this time Arafat was in some despair. Nearly two months had passed since his last military operation.

What they were really looking for, Arafat told Sweidani, was an argument that was good enough to persuade President Hafiz to give permission for Fatah to strike at Israel through Syria. Naturally the President would be alarmed by such a suggestion, but he could be told, by Sweidani and in the proper way, that he really had no choice if he wanted to survive as President. What Sweidani should tell him was that the best way to neutralize the opposition was to steal its clothes. His opponents were claiming that he was taking too much notice of Nasser, and that his commitment to armed struggle was not a serious one. The President would prove his critics wrong, and rob them of an excuse to move against him, by allowing Fatah to use Syria as its launchpad.

Sweidani told Arafat he thought it was an argument the President might well buy – provided he was absolutely convinced that his own man, Sweidani, had the final say about when and from where the operations were to be launched. The President would insist on that because he would be frightened by the prospect of Israeli reprisal attacks. He would want to be sure that he could stop Fatah's operations if the Israelis made the situation too hot.

It was then Arafat's turn to admit that he had no choice. In the circumstances it was the best deal he could expect to get. He gave his word that he would honour the terms of any agreement Sweidani could make with the President.

In the third week of January 1966, Hafiz approved Sweidani's plan of action. On the night of 23 January, a Fatah unit crossed into Israel to carry out the first sabotage mission from Syrian soil. Syrian control of Fatah's movements was very tight. Arafat's men had to pass through agreed Syrian army checkpoints on the Golan Heights and there was a different codeword each night. But Arafat was back in the business of proving that the Palestinians did exist. That was something to celebrate. So, too, was the fact that Sweidani had arranged for an Algerian transport plane to land in Damascus. Abu Jihad's arms and ammunition had arrived.

In Kuwait the news of Arafat's success was not well received by Fatah's Central Committee. The majority considered his action to be an intolerable and dangerous act of defiance. It was intolerable because Arafat had demonstrated a complete contempt for the idea of a collective leadership. And it was dangerous because he was, apparently, throwing himself into Syria's arms. On this point, and mainly because they were misreading his personality and his character, Arafat's colleagues were badly wrong in their judgment of him. As time was to prove, there was none among them who would fight more tenaciously than Arafat to preserve the independence of Palestinian decision-making. He was prepared, as he had just demonstrated, to be used if there was no alternative, and if the consequence of allowing himself to be used was a gain for the cause. But Arafat was not and never would be willing to allow any Arab regime or any foreign power to make decisions for the Palestinians. In time all of Arafat's colleagues, including his critics and his enemies, would come to realize that this determination was his greatest strength, and theirs, too. But that was not how it appeared in 1966.

Khalad Hassan was furious. He and his colleagues on the Central Committee had been trying for months to convince those around Nasser that Fatah was not a Syrian front or puppet, and that it was not Fatah's intention to form an alliance with Syria to enable the Syrians to challenge Nasser for the leadership of the Arab world. Who in Cairo would believe Khalad Hassan now? It was apparent that the collective leadership was not in control. In Egypt's eyes Khalad had been made to look a fool at best and a villain at worst.

If the Central Committee had taken a decision about how to deal with Arafat in the heat of the moment, it is very likely that he would have been relieved of his military command and expelled from the organization. But Khalad and his colleagues agreed among themselves to allow time for passions to cool before a decision was taken.

Quiet reflection revealed the full dimensions of the dilemma they were facing. If they did not control Arafat they were bound to fail in their attempt to establish a dialogue with Nasser and other Arab leaders. And if there was no dialogue there would be no political base for developing a joint Palestinian-Arab strategy which, at the end of the day, was absolutely necessary if one square metre of Palestine was to be liberated. That was on the one hand.

On the other there was the probability that Arafat's military actions would cause more Palestinians to rally to the cause. If that happened Nasser and the other front-line Arab leaders would take fright and might be more, not less, prepared to come to some accommodation with Fatah.

And what if Fatah did split as a consequence of Central Committee action to discipline Arafat? Who would gain from that? Khalad and his colleagues were working on the assumption that the door to Nasser might be opened if they proved Fatah was not a Syrian front. Supposing they were wrong? Could it be that Nasser's people had implied certain things simply to cause Khalad to split Fatah? The Central Committee was divided on many issues of principle, but it was still the only authentic leadership the Palestinians had. Divided it could survive. Split it might not.

Khalad told me: 'In the end we decided to discipline Arafat by suspending his membership of Fatah for a period of three months.'

It was Khalad's intention to use this time to persuade Arafat that long-term policy considerations dictated a halt to military operations. Khalad would say that he and the majority were not abandoning the idea of armed struggle. Far from it. What he and the majority wanted was a breathing space to give them the best possible chance to come to an understanding with some of the regimes. If they succeeded they would develop a joint Palestinian-Arab policy for confrontation with Israel. Then the real armed struggle would begin. At the time even Khalad was convinced that the Arab regimes lacked only the *will* to fight; and that when they did fight, Israel would be beaten on the battlefield. If they failed to carry the regimes, Fatah would lead a revolution to overthrow the existing Arab order.

The essential difference between the two men was now obvious. Khalad Hassan was a man of strategy. Arafat was a man of tactics. Whenever he saw an opportunity for movement he wanted to grab it.

It was Khalad's intention to try to convert Arafat to the majority's way of thinking by quiet and reasoned argument. But if that failed he was going to tell Arafat there was no place for his individualism in the collective leadership.

The stage was thus set for the final confrontation between the two men. Arafat would probably have lost if it had taken place. It did not because of dramatic events in Damascus, which were to see Arafat fighting for his life as he resisted a crude and heavy-handed Syrian attempt to take over Fatah.

# 10

# From Prison to Prison

At the end of the first week of May 1966, Arafat, Abu Jihad and the twenty others who made up Fatah's military establishment had their first opportunity to meet under one roof – in a Syrian prison. They were arrested after a Syrian-backed plan to assassinate Arafat had failed. The Syrian authorities were now intending to hang Arafat on a trumped-up murder charge. They were about to charge him formally with being the instigator of a murder plot of which he was, in reality, the intended victim!

If the Jihads' youngest son had not been killed when he fell from the third-floor balcony of the family apartment, and if Abu Jihad had not been released from prison to bury his son, it is very likely that Arafat would have been hanged.

Said Khalad Hassan: 'From the historical point of view we can say that our troubles with Syria began when the military men who wanted power for its own sake took over and prostituted the slogans of the Ba'ath Party. They only pretended to be Ba'athists to give themselves a sort of legitimacy before they seized power. When they were in power they saw us, correctly, as a movement that was interested in winning the support and consent of the masses. In short they knew that we were for the democratic way. And that is the historical cause of the tension between Fatah and successive Syrian regimes in particular, and between Fatah and many Arab regimes in general. Syria's military leaders never had the slightest intention of getting their power and their legitimacy from the people by democratic means. They took power by the gun and thereafter they had to maintain themselves in power by police-state methods.'

The tension Khalad described increased dramatically after the ninth Syrian coup in February 1966. For it opened the door of the powerhouse to the military men of the minority Alawite sect.

Khalad continued: 'If you are a leader with the coup mentality, and if you represent only fourteen per cent of the people of your country, it follows that you live in fear of being overthrown. The only way to counter that fear, and prevent yourself from being overthrown, is to make the majority of your people more frightened of you than you are of them. And that is what began to happen in Syria after the 1966 coup. From this point on, and by definition, Syria's military leaders had to smash or dominate any group or faction which believed in open debate. After they had closed the mouths of their own people, they turned on us. From their point of view, and because we truly wanted to follow the democratic way, we represented the only serious internal threat to them. That we also refused to allow them to possess and play the Palestinian card for their own ends was something else.'

As already mentioned, President Hafiz had hoped that his token support for guerrilla warfare would give the lie to the charge of his opponents that he was not serious about confrontation with Israel. Those who were plotting against him decided to act before he left them without any excuse to justify their grab for power.

The coup leader was a former Chief of Staff, General Salah Jadid. He was an Alawite. The new President was a former Deputy Prime Minister, Nur Ed-Din Atassi. But as the whole Arab world knew, he was only a figurehead. The real power in the land was Salah Jadid and, in the wings, another Alawite, a man who knew that he was now only one more step, one more coup away from the Presidency: Hafez Assad. As an opportunist he was the only Arab who was a match for Arafat; but he was totally ruthless in ways that Arafat could not even think of being. To that extent the struggle between the two men was a most unequal one.

Sweidani changed sides at the last minute and he was now the Chief of Staff. Presumably Salah Jadid and Hafez Assad did not want him to have his hands on the military intelligence apparatus because it was through it that they intended to take over Fatah. They were prepared to have Arafat killed if necessary, and they probably thought that Sweidani might try to help Arafat when the going got rough for the sake of old times. Sweidani eventually came to the conclusion that his new masters were the biggest of many hypocrites on the Arab stage. He made the mistake of saying so, but he managed to escape to China when he discovered that his name was on the liquidation list.

Despite much propaganda and many outward signs to the contrary, the new Syrian regime was more determined than its predecessor and at least as determined as the other front-line Arab states to avoid a conventional war with Israel. The Syrian formula for avoiding war was an apparently rock-solid commitment to the liberation of Palestine through revolutionary armed struggle — guerrilla warfare. The trick was finding the right balance. The Syrians had to sanction a sufficient amount of guerrilla activity to give credibility to their hypocritical claim that they were serious about a confrontation with Israel, but at the same time they had to make sure that the actual level of guerrilla activity was not such that it gave Israel the justification to knock the hell out of Syria. It was a very dangerous balancing act, but the Syrians thought they were clever enough to get away with it. In essence their strategy was to go one step further than Nasser in the hope of replacing him as the leader of the Arab world. Nasser had a puppet P.L.O. which was not allowed to fight. Syria would have a puppet Fatah which would be allowed to fight, but on Syria's terms.

For a few weeks it appeared that Arafat had gained much from the change of regime in Damascus. He remained free to continue with his operations against Israel from Syria, and its new leaders went to great lengths to present themselves as the true champions of the Palestinian cause. President Atassi promised that the revolution 'will encourage the Palestinian forces and assist them in all fields, to enable them to liberate their homeland'.[22]

But Arafat was on his guard. He was expecting trouble. Now that he was officially suspended from membership of Fatah and facing the prospect of expulsion, he had two reasons to resist any Syrian move to dominate Fatah. In addition to his own unshakeable determination to protect what he described as Fatah's 'virginity' at all costs, he also had to prove to his colleagues in Kuwait that they were wrong about him, that he knew what he was doing and that he could, with luck, beat the Syrians at their own game.

The Syrians intended to replace Arafat as the military leader of

Assifa with a Palestinian puppet of their choice. They wanted to bring about this change of leadership by non-violent means if possible. Their plan was to put their own man inside Assifa and then assist him to take over. Arafat was to be eliminated only if he refused to play second fiddle to Syria's puppet.

Syria's man was Ahmad Jabril. He saw himself as Shuqairi's natural successor but he had none of Shuqairi's talents, and he wanted power for its own sake. Like Arafat Jabril was an engineer. He studied for his degree at the Syrian Military Academy. There he was recruited as an agent for Syrian Military Intelligence. In 1961, Jabril formed the Palestine Liberation Front (P.L.F.). It was nothing more than an intelligence-gathering organization for his Syrian masters.

Soon after the February coup, Jabril approached Arafat with the suggestion that they should merge their two organizations. Arafat agreed without hesitation to discuss the idea. He knew that Jabril was Syria's man; but he calculated that he could more easily contain the threat of Syrian interference that Jabril represented if the P.L.F. was part of Fatah. As President Lyndon Johnson once said, it is not clever to have your enemy 'pissing on the tent from the outside' when you could have him 'inside pissing out'.

According to Khalad Hassan and Um Jihad, Fatah and Jabril did reach agreement in principle on a merger. Jabril was not satisfied, however, with Arafat's suggestion that he should have only a seat on the proposed joint Military Council. Jabril demanded nothing less than the military leadership. He justified his claim on the grounds that it was he and not Arafat who would be delivering Syria's total support for their struggle. When Arafat made it clear that he had no intention of allowing a Syrian agent to run Fatah, Jabril turned to his controllers for fresh instructions. The result of Jabril's talks with the Syrian Directorate of Military Intelligence was a decision and a plan to kill Arafat.

The murder plot was built around the idea of using an innocent third party to lure Arafat to a meeting at which he would be shot. The innocent third party was Yousef Urabi. He was a Palestinian and a captain in the Syrian army. He was set up to play the role of mediator in the dispute between Jabril and Arafat. In good faith, and believing that mediation was necessary if a confrontation was to be averted, Urabi invited Jabril and Arafat to discuss their differences at a meeting which he would chair.

Abu Jihad said: 'The truth about Urabi is the following. He was a Palestinian who was loyal to the Syrian army in which he was serving, but he was also a good friend of ours. I am the one who knows because Yousef Urabi was one of my best friends.' Um Jihad confirmed her husband's story and said that Urabi had done her 'many favours'. Khalad Hassan told me that Urabi was under consideration for election to Fatah's Military Committee.

The meeting was scheduled for 6.00 p.m. on 5 May, at a house in the Asakar district. At the last minute, but according to plan, Jabril suddenly discovered that he had a more pressing engagement elsewhere. In his place he sent the man who was to kill Arafat. He was a Syrian officer who went by the name of Adnan. Said Khalad Hassan: 'Our subsequent investigation showed that the Syrian National Guardsmen who were always on duty in the Asakar area were withdrawn just before the meeting was due to begin. They just disappeared.' Obviously the authorities did not want any official witnesses to what they knew was going to happen.

But Arafat did not show up. He also sent a representative. His name was Mohammed Hishme. And Hishme had a bodyguard. His name was Abdul Majib Zahmud. He was intructed to stay in the shadows and keep an eye on things. Hishme was under orders to discuss what had to be discussed and to say that Arafat would join them later if he could.

The man called Adnan started to shout, and at the top of his voice he accused Urabi of being a traitor. The implication was, presumably, that Urabi had somehow warned Arafat to stay away. It is possible that Adnan had assumed, or perhaps had been told, that Urabi was in on the plot. It is also possible that Adnan began to suspect that he was the one who had been trapped.

The shouting went on for several minutes. Then two shots were fired. The man called Adnan fled into the night. Urabi and Hishme were dead by the time Zahmud got to them.

Jabril had not made any allowance for the fact that his plan could go wrong. He did not wait for confirmation of Arafat's death before making his next move. Said Khalad Hassan: 'At the time he presumed Arafat to be dead, Jabril was distributing a statement. It condemned Fatah as a Saudi puppet and it accused all of us, the leaders, of being agents for the enemies of the Palestinian revolution. I can't remember the exact text because it was a rambling and incoherent propaganda statement. But it gave the impression that something very important had just happened which would change everything. In fact, and as we later came to know, Jabril was preparing the way for an announcement that Arafat was dead and that he, Jabril, was taking command of all Palestinian revolutionary forces.'

I asked Arafat why he did not attend the meeting at which he was supposed to have been assassinated. Had he been saved by his famous nose or smell for danger? He replied: 'No truly, on this occasion it was not as you say my nose. It was by chance that I was not liquidated. I did not go to that place because Abu Jihad and I were called to an important meeting with a very senior Syrian officer. He was later my witness that I was not in the place where Urabi was shot.'

Abu Jihad told me more about the meeting with the 'very senior Syrian officer'. My guess is that it was Sweidani, the Chief of Staff. Said Abu Jihad: 'The officer admitted that he and his superiors were surprised and confused by the fact that the Israelis had not attacked Syria to force the regime in Damascus to abandon its support for us – the Palestinian "terrorists". Arafat and I agreed that there was something very strange about the absence of Israeli reprisal attacks. From the early 1950s it had been Israel's policy to attack those Arab countries which, the Israelis said, were allowing Palestinian "terrorists" to cross their borders to attack the Jewish State. Many times the Israelis had made reprisal attacks on Gaza and Jordan when they really knew that Nasser and Hussein were trying to control us and prevent us from moving. Now here was Syria, openly and proudly supporting us ... and yet the Israelis were not attacking Syria! Why? What game were the Israelis playing? Anyway, some Syrians were not only surprised and confused, they were worried and frightened. They believed the Israelis were playing a trick and that it would be only a short time before Israel did launch a very big attack on Syria. So, and this was really the purpose of our meeting, they asked us to send a patrol from the Lebanon to look behind the Israeli lines to see what was happening.'

From their meeting with the senior Syrian officer Arafat and Abu Jihad went straight to their base at the Yarmuk refugee camp. There they intended to organize the patrol for the reconnaissance mission behind Israel's lines. When they arrived at the camp they were shattered by the news that Urabi and Hishme had been murdered. They grilled Zahmud about what he had seen and heard. The implications were obvious. Arafat was lucky to be still alive, but his real troubles had not yet started.

The first indication that the Syrians were intending to frame Arafat was Zahmud's arrest. The arresting officers left little room for doubting that Zahmud was to be charged with the murders. And it was clear that after a decent interval they would arrest Arafat and charge him with being the instigator of the murder plot.

Arafat told me: 'The man they arrested was completely innocent. We had satisfied ourselves about that. He saw what he saw, and he heard what he heard. But he was completely innocent. Unfortunately some people were not concerned with the truth. They arrested our man to mask the truth.'

Um Jihad had just completed the exhausting ritual of making her youngest son, Nidal, go to sleep. Nidal was not yet three years old and he had the energy of several normal children. Sometimes crawling, sometimes walking, he was here, there and everywhere. Living in a third-storey apartment, he could not be let out of sight for more than a second or two. Nearly every day Abu Jihad warned his wife: 'If you take your eyes off that child he will go to the balcony and there will be an accident.' It was only during the night hours, when Nidal was sleeping, that Um Jihad could relax in her own home. But on this night she was troubled.

At about 7.00 p.m. several Fatah fighters had stormed up the stairs and banged on Um Jihad's door. They were in a state of panic. 'Where's Abu Jihad, where's Abu Amar?' they had asked. Um Jihad said she did not know. They left in a hurry and without telling Um Jihad what they had heard – that Yousef Urabi and Mohammed Hishme had been murdered.

Said Um Jihad: 'At about eight o'clock another of our colleagues arrived. He asked me, "Are you alone?" I told him I was. I asked him what was happening. He said, "There is big trouble. The Syrians are searching over our camps and offices. I have come to protect you."

'Three hours later he said: "I cannot bear it any more. If you don't mind being alone I must try to find Abu Jihad and Abu Amar." I told him to go. To tell you the truth I was glad. He was very nervous and he was making me more nervous.

'Half an hour later Abu Ali Iyad arrived. He was a very tough man but he was loved and respected by us all. He said: "Um Jihad, I am not leaving your side until we know what is happening. The situation is very bad." He asked me to turn out the lights and he opened the doors to the balcony. We sat and we waited.'

Arafat or Abu Jihad had probably despatched Abu Ali Iyad to do whatever was necessary. If there was to be a showdown with the authorities in Damascus, Um Jihad had to be rescued. She could not in any event be taken alive. They all knew that.

Um Jihad continued: 'At four o'clock in the morning we heard the car. We watched Arafat and Abu Jihad get out. They were alone and we waited for them to climb the stairs. They were very tired and very sad. Their eyes were red and I could see they had been crying. I asked them what had happened. Abu Jihad said, "Yousef and Mohammed have been killed and the authorities are going to blame us. We are in a trap."'

They came for Arafat a few hours later. Two Syrian intelligence officers. 'They said they were taking him to prison for his own safety.' Um Jihad laughed as she told me.

'You knew they were lying,' I said.

'Of course,' she replied.

Two days later Um Jihad was in the kitchen making an early breakfast for her husband. She had left him in the lounge reading some papers. The door to the apartment opened into the lounge. The kitchen was some distance from it. 'When I entered the lounge with the coffee there was no Abu Jihad,' she said. 'I called to him. No answer. I searched the other rooms. Still no Abu Jihad. I waited about half an hour. And then I went down to the children who were playing outside the building. "Have you seen Uncle Abu Jihad?" I asked them. "Yes, he went in a car," they said. "What sort of car?" I asked. "A green car," they said.'

On the assumption that it was a military car and that Abu Jihad had been arrested, Um Jihad visited the headquarters of Syrian Military Intelligence. Did they know anything about her husband? Had he been arrested? Was he in prison? 'At every official place they gave me the same answers. Abu Jihad was not in prison, he had not been arrested and they didn't know where he was.'

For the next six days, and working mainly on her own, Um Jihad turned Damascus inside out in her search for news of Abu Jihad's whereabouts. Aware that she might herself be under surveillance, she did not try to make contact with any of Fatah's military leaders. 'In the beginning I was convinced that Abu Jihad was in prison. But I was asking myself why the Syrians were saying he was not. It didn't make sense. I began to wonder if Abu Jihad had gone on a mission. And I started to think that he had been captured or killed by the Israelis.' At the time, and because the order suspending Arafat's membership of Fatah was still in force, Abu Jihad was acting officially as the organization's Military Commander.

She continued: 'On the seventh day I decided to seek the help of the man who lived in the apartment below us. I was very friendly with his wife, and I knew that her husband was a senior official in one of the intelligence services. But I was not supposed to know that. I talked with him and he said he would make some telephone calls. Before half an hour had passed he told me that Abu Jihad was in prison, and that I could visit him if I went to the headquarters of the Military Police to get a pass.'

The prison turned out to be a military detention camp close to Damascus airport. Said Um Jihad: 'A military policeman opened the door and I had a very big shock. Inside the room were Abu Jihad, Arafat and twenty more of our comrades. With the exception of Abu Ali Iyad, all the most important military men of Fatah were inside that room! Abu Jihad hugged me and I cried. He whispered to me to keep on crying, and while he was comforting me he put a folded piece of paper into my hand. It was the text of a message he wanted me to send to the Central Committee in Kuwait.'

Um Jihad was informed by the authorities that she could visit her husband every three days. On her second visit she was given the most dangerous assignment of her life.

'Abu Jihad told me it was absolutely essential for the military operations to continue while the leadership was in prison. It was necessary, he said, for the Syrian regime to be convinced that it would not control Fatah just because it had captured the military leadership. If the military operations continued the Syrians would be frightened. Then Abu Jihad gave me his instructions. He told me to set up a secret and emergency committee to be responsible for continuing the military operations. It was to consist of three people – Abu Ali Iyad, Ahmed Attrush and me. And I was to be the Acting Military Commander. Abu Jihad said: "You tell Ali and Ahmed those are my orders and they will obey you."'

Um Jihad proved to be more than a competent commander. The number of sabotage missions launched from Syrian soil was reduced, but for the first time in months Fatah units crossed into Israel from Jordan and the Lebanon. In military terms the action did not add up to much – it never did; but it was enough to make the point that the Syrian regime could not control Fatah simply by locking up its military leadership.

There were, meanwhile, no signs that the Syrians intended to release Arafat and his colleagues. Then, six weeks after their arrest, fate intervened.

Through a senior Fatah official who was still free, Um Jihad made an appointment to meet secretly with a top Syrian leader. Said Um Jihad: 'I will tell you his name [she did] but I think you should not publish it. He was a part of the leadership but he was in sympathy with us. He wanted to tell me what was going to happen to Arafat and the others in prison.

'On the day of the meeting Abu Ali Iyad and Ahmed Attrush were in my apartment. I was going to meet the Syrian leader in the home of our comrade who fixed the appointment. I was intending to take my children, Nidal and Jihad, and stay with our comrade. I was beginning to feel not so secure in our own apartment. Ali and Ahmed asked me to leave the children with them and to return very quickly with my report of the meeting. They were very anxious. I said okay. As I was leaving the building I looked up at our apartment and I saw the door to the balcony was open. I rushed back up the stairs. Ali and Ahmed said: "What's the matter, why do you return?" I told them to close the door to the balcony because I was afraid that Nidal would fall.

'So I had the meeting. The news was very bad. The Syrian leader told me first of all that Arafat, Abu Jihad and all of them had been moved to the biggest prison in Damascus. The military investigating committee had finished its work. The civilian police had now taken over the case and that meant Arafat would be charged with a criminal and not a political offence. The Syrian told me: "They are determined to find Arafat guilty of ordering Urabi's murder and they are making it a criminal offence so they can hang him. If you want to save Arafat you must mobilize all of your friends everywhere."

'I returned to my apartment to discuss the next moves with Ali and Ahmed. I can't say we were surprised. We had suspected it was Arafat the Syrians wanted to finish. But still we were very shocked. Ahmed became wild. He said we should take the decision to explode bombs all over Syria. I told him he was crazy and that a demonstration of that kind would result in the deaths of our colleagues in gaol and the end of Fatah. He insisted that he was right. I said: "I am responsible for the decisions and you will obey my orders!"'

When Ahmed Attrush had cooled down, Um Jihad suggested they all needed time to think. The two men left.

Um Jihad continued: 'As soon as they had gone, Nidal said to me, "Mummy, Mummy, I want a drink of water." I got him a glass from the kitchen. When he had finished the drink he dropped the glass. It smashed and immediately Nidal began to pick up the pieces. He cut his hands. I took care of them and then I put him on his bed and told him to rest. I went to the kitchen for a brush and some other things to clear up the broken glass.

'At the same time I was thinking about what could be done to save Arafat's life. In the back of my mind I heard the click of a door opening and shutting. I rushed from the kitchen to the balcony – but it was too late. Nidal had fallen.

'I ran down the stairs. My baby's body was broken and bleeding. Some friends called for the doctor and the ambulance came. But he died on the way to the hospital.'

From the hospital Um Jihad went to the home of a Syrian lady friend who was well connected with the regime. 'She was entertaining some others and for half an hour I said nothing. Then she asked me why I was so quiet. I said: "My baby Nidal is dead. I want Abu Jihad to be released from prison to bury him. Please help me."'

At one o'clock the following morning Abu Jihad was released for twenty-four hours. He said: 'At first I thought it was a trick. They told me only that I was wanted at my home because there was some problem. They put me in a military car with another one following. I thought they were going to search our apartment for documents.' Abu Jihad's real fear was probably that his wife was about to be arrested.

From a neighbour Abu Jihad learned that his son was dead and that his wife was staying with friends.

Said Um Jihad: 'When Abu Jihad arrived he asked me what had happened to Jihad. I said, "It's not Jihad, it's Nidal. What happened is what you were always frightened about." We both cried but Abu Jihad was very strong. He said: "My darling, we must not let this destroy us. We are young and we will have more children."'

Abu Jihad told me: 'In the early hours of the morning I buried my son. I didn't have the money to buy a grave in a good place. I had to bury him in common ground. Um Jihad asked me where and I didn't tell her. I didn't want her to know that Nidal was not in a proper grave.'

Before the day was out Abu Jihad had talked his way to an appointment with the Minister of the Interior. That won him another twenty-four hours of freedom. Then he lobbied a number of very senior Syrian military officers with whom he had co-operated in the past and who either knew or suspected that Arafat and Fatah had not been responsible for the deaths of Urabi and Hishme. Those contacts won him yet another twenty-four hours of freedom. They also got him an appointment with the Minister of Defence – Hafez Assad.

Abu Jihad told me: 'Nobody will ever know how much effort went into arranging that meeting. When I entered Assad's office he remained seated at his desk. His eyes didn't move. They were hard and cold. His handshake was also very cold. The whole atmosphere was cold. It was like being in a refrigerator.'

Apparently the temperature did not rise during the three hours of their conversation. Said Abu Jihad: 'Point by point, detail by detail, I explained to the future President of Syria why Arafat and Fatah could not possibly have been involved in the murder of Urabi and Hishme.'

Abu Jihad's own efforts were supported and supplemented by his colleagues on the Central Committee. A number of them travelled from Kuwait to Damascus to plead for Arafat's life. Abu Jihad did not return to prison. Over a period of two or three weeks all but one of the others were released. Arafat was the last to be given his freedom. The one the Syrians refused to release was Zahmud. Abu Jihad said, 'He is still in prison – to this day.' Apart from Jabril, Zahmud is probably the only Palestinian who can identify the real killer – the Syrian agent who went by the name of Adnan.

It is not unlikely that Hafez Assad was the man who

masterminded the attempt to frame Arafat, and that he had to admit defeat when he realized that too many influential Syrians and Palestinians were aware of the truth. When I put my speculation to Arafat he said: 'It is not a question I will answer. It is for history to decide.'

I asked Arafat if he had had any doubts that the Syrians, some Syrians, were intending to see him hanged. He replied: 'That is what they were preparing for. There is no doubt about that.'

Then I asked if he had been confident all along that he would leave prison alive. He paused for perhaps as many as ten seconds before he replied. 'Yes,' he said finally, 'I was confident.'

Why had he paused for so long before answering my question?

Arafat smiled: 'I had to think about your question. So many people played a part in saving my life.'

While Arafat, Abu Jihad and the others were in prison, Colonel Mohammed Orki, the head of the Palestinian Department of Syrian Intelligence, defected to Jordan. Naturally he took his files with him. Israeli intelligence sources later claimed that Orki's defection was a big setback for Fatah and resulted in the liquidation of many Fatah cells on the West Bank. Abu Jihad denied this. He told me: 'Orki knew everything there was to know about Jabril and his stooges. But apart from the names and certain details about those of us who were arrested, he knew nothing about Fatah. We were not so concerned by what Orki did.'

Orki's defection is worthy of note only because it raises an intriguing question or two. Did he jump or was he pushed? Did Orki take leave of his Syrian masters because he wanted to – or was he ordered to defect? In other words, was his defection contrived by the regime in Damascus as another way of damaging Fatah?

When Arafat was released from prison, prudence dictated that he, too, should take his leave of Syria – at least for a while. He did so but in his own way. Disguised as a corporal in the Syrian army, and at the head of a Fatah unit of fourteen men including himself, he crossed into northern Israel.

The evidence is that the question of Arafat's leadership of Fatah's military wing was still unresolved. In the meantime he continued the military struggle in his own way. Since it was becoming more and more difficult for Fatah units to cross into Israel from the front-line Arab states, Arafat wanted to probe Israel's defences. It was necessary to find out how long Fatah units could expect to operate inside the Jewish State if they were well organized, well briefed and well supplied.

Arafat said: 'Over several days we carried out many reconnaissance missions to identify future targets. Then we made some attacks. Two I remember. One was against an observation tower. We destroyed it. Then we blew up a store full of arms and ammunition.'

Then the chase started.

Arafat continued: 'An Israeli patrol followed us for twenty-four hours. My aim was not to engage the Israelis in battle, but to find out how easy or how difficult it would be to shake them off. They were good but we were better. After twenty-four hours we lost them and we crossed into southern Lebanon.'

Then they were arrested by a Lebanese army patrol. Within hours Arafat was back in prison. This time in Beirut.

Arafat gave a false name and denied that he was the leader of the group. And for the next three weeks he was tortured close to the point of death. Yasser Arafat himself is much too modest a man to make any claim to being a hero. All he would tell me was that he was tortured in a 'very hard and tough way'. Within himself he is still obviously proud that he did not break. 'By this time in my life I was used to being tortured,' he said. 'I knew they could kill me, but I also knew they would never break me.'

Abu Jihad added this: 'Every day they beat him and kicked him. They did so many bad and cruel things to him. Perhaps one day he will tell the story himself.' I asked Abu Jihad if the torture had included the use of electricity and if they had put wires to Arafat's testicles. 'It's not for me to say,' he replied.

In the end the Lebanese did discover that Yasser Arafat, cover name Abu Amar, was the prisoner they had so nearly killed. When his torturers failed to break him, a senior Lebanese security official made contact with his counterpart in the Syrian Directorate of Military Intelligence. It was from the information the two intelligence services exchanged that Arafat was identified. Said Abu Jihad: 'That's how we discovered where Arafat was. We got the tip-off from a friend in Syrian Military Intelligence. Until then we were thinking that Arafat had been captured or killed by the Israelis.'

Arafat told me: 'When the Lebanese discovered that I was Yasser

Arafat, I was taken to meet the very top intelligence people. I met them all and we had a very good conversation for five hours. I told them many things they did not know. Many things. I told them why it was that we Palestinians had no alternative but to struggle in order to fix our identity. I also told them why it was that those Arabs who could not see that Zionism was a threat to the whole Arab world were very foolish and very stupid.'

Arafat added: 'I made some very good friends at that meeting. Later these same people, the Lebanon's intelligence chiefs, told me it was from our meeting that they began to respect our movement and me as a person.'

A free man, Arafat returned to Damascus.

What had happened was dramatic proof of the magic of Arafat's spell-binding personality, and how the magic could work when he was face to face with enemies who were prepared to give him a fair hearing.

# 11

# Playing with Fire

In Damascus Arafat and Abu Jihad reviewed the situation. They had good reason to be satisfied. Fatah had survived. The security services of Egypt, Jordan and the Lebanon had failed to destroy it. And the Syrians had failed to make it their puppet. As an organized strike force Fatah was still a small and puny outfit, its military operations were insignificant; but that was not the point. Because Fatah had survived, the idea of an independent Palestine liberation movement was alive. It was also capturing the imagination of a growing number of Palestinians — so much so, in fact, that the Palestinian tail was beginning to wag the Arab dog. Put another way, Nasser and the other front-line Arab leaders were beginning to lose control of events. The long countdown to the Six-Day War had started.

The irony is that it was Nasser's attempt to control the situation, to prevent a war, that gave Israel's military planners the opportunity to set a trap for him — with Syria's help.

By the middle of 1966, Nasser was a very worried man. He was alarmed by four developments.

The first was the coup in Damascus. Nasser was certain that Syria's new leaders would talk the most about liberating Palestine but do the least. But the fact was that the new Syrian regime was putting on a very good act, and it was convincing a growing number of Arabs — Palestinians and others — that it and not Nasser was the true champion of the Palestinian cause.

The second development was Shuqairi's changing attitude. He

was beginning to insist that Nasser and the other Arab leaders deliver on the promises they had made when they had set up the P.L.O. Of particular concern to Shuqairi was the lack of progress in the setting up of the P.L.A. Jordan and the Lebanon had refused to have any P.L.A. units on their soil. In Egypt, Syria and Iraq some units had been established, but they were very much under strength. Only ten per cent of the posts established for the P.L.A. command had been filled. And only about forty per cent of the equipment and arms had been supplied. What was happening in 1966 was therefore entirely logical. A growing number of Palestinians were realizing that Shuqairi was the puppet of the Arab regimes which, despite their words, were not intending to fight Israel. Shuqairi had to do something to counter the charge that he was a puppet. He knew that if he failed to shake off that image, he and his P.L.O. would lose out to Arafat and Fatah. In 1964 Nasser had been aware that a day might come when Shuqairi would demand more than the Arab leaders could safely deliver. But Nasser had contented himself with the thought that he could deal with Shuqairi as and when the problem arose. Unfortunately for Nasser the circumstances were now such that controlling the first Chairman of the P.L.O. was not easy. Wisely, from his own point of view, Shuqairi had established a relationship with the new regime in Damascus, and that was his insurance policy. Nasser could not afford to lose Shuqairi to the Syrians.

The third development was the changing attitude of some of those Palestinians whom Nasser had previously regarded as being among the most loyal and faithful of his supporters – those who had formed and joined the Arab Nationalist Movement in opposition to Fatah, and who had put all their trust in Nasser. Previously they had ridiculed Arafat's idea that the Palestinians should resort to military action in advance of an agreement with Nasser and other Arab leaders on a co-ordinated liberation strategy. But now even some of the A.N.M.'s leading thinkers were openly saying that the regimes – and by implication Nasser – could not be relied upon, and that the Palestinians should turn to guerrilla warfare.

The fourth development was Algeria's support for the new regime in Damascus and the revolutionary way it claimed to be representing. In June 1965, Algeria's President Ben Bella was overthrown by Colonel Houari Boumedienne. The latter was clearly a man of substance and influence. By the middle of 1966, Boumedienne was courting the Syrians and promising real support for the struggle against Israel.

When Nasser reviewed these developments and their implications his worry turned to fear. It was bad enough that his own prestige was suffering because he could no longer disguise his inability to do anything about Israel – for the Palestinians in particular, and for the sake of Arab honour in general. His dilemma was acute and appalling. On the one hand he knew the Arabs would be the losers in any military confrontation with Israel. On the other hand he could not begin the process of negotiations with Israel until its leaders gave some sign, secretly and through the Americans if necessary, that they were prepared to offer the Palestinians something at the end of the negotiating process. And on that, Israel's leaders were more intransigent than ever. The reality was that nothing could be done for the Palestinians until the Arabs were united enough to use their political and economic power to oblige the U.S. to force Israel to compromise. But Arab unity was as distant as ever. Israel's divisive influence was living up to Khalad Hassan's analysis of the origins of the conflict – that the British had perceived the Jewish State, a European colony planted in the heart of the Arab world, as a mechanism for keeping the Arabs divided.

The loss of prestige Nasser was suffering was obviously a personal blow, but it was also dramatic proof of how he was losing his ability to influence and control the overall situation on the Arab side. If he did not act, there was a real danger that the leadership of the so-called revolutionary Arab world would pass, by default, into the hands of the Syrians. And if Damascus was allowed to set the pace there could be a war with Israel. The Syrians knew they were playing with fire by allowing enough Palestinian military actions to enable the regime to pose as the true champions of the Palestinian cause and the real leaders of the revolutionary Arab world. But Damascus was seriously mistaken in its belief that it could control the fire by restraining the Palestinians whenever their activities seemed likely to provoke a massive Israeli reprisal attack. Israel would keep an account of Palestinian actions launched from and supported by Syria and, at a time of its choosing, it would use the open account as a pretext or excuse for war. As Nasser was aware, the Syrians and the Palestinians were playing into Israel's hands. He would have to find a way to influence and restrain the Syrians. But how?

In May, while Arafat and his colleagues were prisoners in Damascus, Nasser had discussed his fears with the Soviets. They had recommended that he should make a supreme effort to establish a new relationship with the Syrians – as a means of controlling them. Nasser had agreed to make the effort. In June, and probably because the Soviets leaned on them, the Syrians announced their interest in an accommodation with Nasser. In October, Cairo and Damascus exchanged ambassadors.

Then, on 4 November, Egypt signed a Defence Agreement with Syria. It stated that aggression against one of them would be regarded as an attack on both. Naturally Israeli propaganda presented it as a belligerent step and yet more proof that the Arabs were preparing to destroy Israel. In reality it was nothing of the kind. By securing a measure of control over Syrian military dispositions and policy, Nasser was hoping to prevent a war. But his gamble was as dangerous as it was desperate.

The key to understanding what really happened on the Israeli side during the long countdown to the Six-Day War is the answer to the question I raised earlier: why did Israel refrain from hitting Syria with reprisal attacks when it was the only front-line Arab state to be giving shelter, comfort and some aid to Fatah and other Palestinian action groups? During the same period, and despite the fact that it was trying to smash Fatah, Jordan was punished by Israel.

According to a most informed and widely respected Israeli writer, Ehud Yaari, that question is one of two which 'any future historian dealing with this period will have to answer'.[23]

One possible answer, which Yaari himself suggests, is that Israel refrained from attacking Syria because it was under strong U.S. pressure not to do so. That may well be part of the answer. Israel was seeking to acquire offensive weapons from the U.S. at the time, including Skyhawk combat planes with four times the bomb-carrying capacity of the Mirages the French had supplied, Paton M-48 tanks and long-range artillery. American policy to date had been to deny Israel offensive weapons. Then, early in 1965, the U.S. agreed to supply the Jewish State with the weapons it wanted. But there were conditions. One was that Israel would undertake not to initiate any pre-emptive strikes against the Arab states.

The major part of the answer, in my view, is that Israel's leaders refrained from punishing Syria on an incident-by-incident basis because, as already stated, they had decided on a policy of totting up Syria's offences to give themselves an option on a pretext for their next war. That they were determined to go to war in the second half of the 1960s is not a matter for serious dispute. Their intentions at the time are clear from what Israelis themselves have written over the years since 1967, and also from what I learned from other Israelis, including a former Israeli Director of Military Intelligence who told me that they would have 'invented a pretext for war' in the second half of 1967 or thereabouts if circumstances had not given them the opportunity before then. From the same source and others of similar quality I learned that from 1964 on, virtually all of Israel's military planners and most of its political leaders – though not Prime Minister Eshkol – were hungry for war. They wanted the opportunity to knock out a vast amount of Egyptian and other Arab armour which had been supplied by the Soviets. That was their main and specific objective. They also wanted to teach the Arabs a lesson they would never forget. If the lesson resulted in the Arab regimes being willing to make peace on Israel's terms – by acquiescing in the denial of the existence of the Palestinians as a people with rights to self-determination – that would be a bonus.

By the late summer of 1966, and because Israel had been content to simply take note of Syria's offences, it could be said that the Jewish State had established its case for attacking Syria at a time of its choosing. As Israel's leaders knew well, the governments of the West would deplore an attack on Syria, but they would not seriously dispute Israel's justification – two and more years of restraint in the face of continuing and growing Syrian support for the Palestinian sabotage missions. For those in Israel who wanted war it was a case of so far, so good. But there was a problem. It was not Syria, or Jordan or the Lebanon they wanted to attack. It was Egypt. So the question that exercised the brilliant minds of Israel's military planners was how to play their Syrian card to give Israel the pretext for war with Egypt. How, in other words, could they set a trap for Nasser?

The question was answered on 4 November, when Egypt and Syria signed their Defence Agreement. From that moment on Israel's military planners knew they could bring about the war they wanted with Egypt. All they had to do was to develop their threat to Syria to the point at which Nasser would have to make a military move – to demonstrate that his Defence Agreement with Syria was worth at least the paper it was written on. And once Nasser had been forced to make a military deployment in response to a perceived Israeli threat to Syria, the Israelis would, if necessary, invent a pretext to hit him.

In retrospect Friday, 7 April 1967, can be seen as the start of Israel's brilliant campaign of deception to trick the Arabs and the Soviets into believing that Syria and not Egypt was to be the victim of Israel's next war effort. At 9.45 on that April morning, a Syrian mortar position on the Golan Heights opened fire on a tractor that was ploughing the fields of an Israeli settlement on the narrow strip of land between the eastern shore of the Sea of Galilee (Lake Tiberias) and the border with Syria.

Israel's *de facto* borders were established by the fighting of 1948-9, which came to an end with a series of Armistice Agreements. When the Armistice Agreement between Israel and Syria was being written, it was discovered that there were places where it was impossible to draw an undisputed border line on a map. This problem arose because of the mixed ownership of land. Brian Urquhart told me: 'To solve this problem we at the U.N. – it was really that good man, Ralph Bunche – came up with what was then a revolutionary idea: the concept of the Demilitarized Zone. The U.N. was to be responsible for the D.Z.s. Everybody who owned land in them (Jew or Palestinian Arab) would be allowed to farm regardless. And no military force from either side would be permitted to enter the D.Z.s. At the time everybody thought it was a smashing idea, and that's what happened.' The U.N. rules also laid down that any disputes would be resolved by the Mixed Armistice Commission (M.A.C.).

Urquhart continued: 'The Syrians were looking down on the D.Z.s from the Golan Heights. For some time they didn't rumble what the Israelis were up to. Then it became obvious. The Syrians noticed that each time an Israeli tractor ploughed a field, it ploughed one more furrow. As a consequence the Israeli fields got bigger and the Arab fields got smaller. After a while there was a tremendous fuss in the M.A.C. But the Israelis always denied they were taking Arab land. When the M.A.C. failed to stop the Israelis, the Syrians took to firing warning shots across the bows of the Israeli tractors. The next thing we knew was that the Israelis were using armour-plated tractors. The next thing that happened was that the Syrians began to use mortars and artillery and they did hit one or two tractors. Then the Israelis began to answer back and there were full-scale artillery duels. And so it went on escalating. Today the Israelis justify their occupation of the Golan Heights by saying it was necessary to stop the fiendish Syrians from shelling the peaceful Israeli farmers. It's bullshit. Pure nonsense. It wasn't the Syrians who started it. It really wasn't. If the Israelis had not tried to push their luck as they always do, the Syrians would not have opened fire in the first place.'

Among other things Urquhart's commentary illustrates how easy it was for the Israelis to hot up the Syrian front at any time of their choosing. Once the Syrians had been provoked, the Israelis were then free to decide by how much or how little they would escalate the action.

On the morning of 7 April, Israel's military planners allowed the shooting to escalate for nearly four hours; then they ordered the Israeli Air Force into action.

The I.A.F.'s first objective was to silence the Syrian positions which were shelling Israeli settlements. Ten minutes after Israel started its air operation, three Syrian MiG 21s put in an appearance. They were shot down. Later three more MiG 21s came to the same end. Israeli Mirages were then directed to another objective. Damascus.

Three days later, under the heading 'SHOCK FOR SYRIA', an editorial in *The Jerusalem Post* very nearly gave the game away. The opening paragraph of the editorial was this:

'The significant new departure in Friday's battle against the Syrians was the fact that the Israeli planes had specific authority to pursue attackers as deeply into Syrian territory as they considered useful and that they were simultaneously sent out to "patrol" Syrian airspace as far as Damascus, in order to head off the planes before they reached Israel.'

The main purpose of Israel's actions on 7 April was to make the Syrian regime feel very vulnerable and very frightened. Said Khalad Hassan: 'I think it is not unreasonable to speculate that Syria's military leaders ordered a vast supply of underwear!'

After that it was easy for Israel's military planners to convince the Arabs and the Soviets that Israel was intending to attack and invade Syria in the not so distant future. Israel's deception strategy was based on a series of calculated leaks. On one level, high-ranking Israeli military and intelligence officers dropped hints to reporters that Israel was intending to occupy Damascus to put an end to Syrian support for Palestinian saboteurs. To give credence to these nods and winks Israel's Chief of Staff, General Rabin, went on record to say that security for Israel and any other state in the area could not be guaranteed until the Syrian regime was overthrown. On another level the Israelis sent fictitious radio messages which they knew the Soviets would intercept and pass on to Nasser. The messages told of preparations for an impending Israeli invasion of Syria.

It was then that Syria's military leaders made their secret deal with Israel. Or so I believe.

I am not at liberty to name the Palestinian and other Arab leaders who told me what they know about Syria's collusion with Israel in the countdown to the Six-Day War; they are too frightened to say in public what they know to be the truth. No Palestinian or other Arab leader volunteered information on this subject. I had to dig it out of them; and in most cases I persuaded them to talk only by using the oldest trick in the reporter's book – pretending to know more than I did. The only on-the-record comment was from Khalad Hassan. About Syria's behaviour in the weeks before the 1967 war and during it he said: 'We came to know a lot of secrets. What we learned horrified us very much. But it's too early and too dangerous for us and others to say what we know.'

From the information given to me, I am satisfied that there was a secret agreement between Syria and Israel, set down in a five-point memorandum, which was negotiated by Syrian and Israeli emissaries through the good offices of French diplomats in Spain. I did not discover what the five points were; but they can be deduced from what happened on the battlefield.

At the time the secret negotiations between Israel and Syria were taking place, the Israelis knew that King Hussein had no intention of starting a war. For their part, and through third-party contacts, the Israelis had informed Hussein that they would not make any move against Jordan if Jordan did not initiate any action against

Israel. However, the Israelis were also aware that once they started their war against Egypt, Hussein might have his hand forced by the Egyptians or the Palestinians or both. So Israel's military planners had to take account of the possibility that the Jewish State would find itself involved in a war on two fronts – the Egyptian front and the Jordanian front. Israel's military planners were not alarmed by that prospect because they were confident that their plan to destroy Egypt's air force in a matter of hours would succeed, and that when it did Egypt's ground forces would be sitting ducks.

The real problem for Israel's military planners was keeping the Syrians out of the war – at least to start with. If they had no choice, the Israelis were prepared to fight on three fronts at once, and still without fear of defeat; but they wanted a quick war. And they wanted a quick war for one simple reason. Within hours of the outbreak of fighting it would be obvious to the governments of the world that Israel had started it. That meant there would be quick and enormous diplomatic pressure on Israel to stop it. In short, Israel might have a matter of days, perhaps only two or three, in which to smash Egypt's forces and, if all went well, to destroy Nasser himself. Israel's military planners believed that Nasser would be finished by the humiliation they intended to make him suffer. But everything would depend on the speed of the Israeli advance through the Sinai Desert. If the Israelis had to fight on three fronts at the same time they would be slowed down; and if they were then required to accept a U.N. call for a ceasefire after two or perhaps three days of fighting, they might not complete their intended destruction of Egyptian armour. In that event Israel would or could be denied the total and sensational victory it was seeking in order to reinforce what Khalad Hassan described as the Arab 'psychology of defeat'.

What Israel therefore required from the secret negotiations with the Syrians was an agreement that Syria's ground forces would not initiate any offensive action against Israel if and when the Jewish State found itself at war with Egypt, and possibly Jordan. The Israelis understood that Syria's military leaders would have to put on some sort of show to disguise the fact that they were betraying their Arab brothers to save their own skins; but the Syrians could limit their involvement in the war to shelling Israel's northern settlements from fixed artillery positions. To Israel's military planners that was an acceptable price for keeping Syria's ground forces out of the war, and freeing more of Israel's own to concentrate their effort on the Egyptian front and against the Jordanians if necessary. Israel's military planners also knew it would not be a high price. The settlements might take a bit of a pounding, but the settlers themselves would be safe in their bunkers.

Syria's military leaders gave an undertaking that their ground forces would not be redeployed from their defensive positions and would not initiate any action against Israel. In return the Israelis agreed that they would not initiate any ground action against Syria – although subsequent events suggest that the only categorical assurance the Israelis gave is that they would not attack Damascus. It may well be that the Syrians thought they had a secret agreement which committed Israel to refrain from ground action on any part of Syria's soil, including the Golan Heights; but the fact is that Israel never makes an agreement without an escape clause or an ambiguity which can be argued about for decades. In the summer of 1967 the Syrians still had that lesson to learn.

By the middle of May, Nasser was convinced that Israel was intending to invade Syria. The last piece of evidence was Israel's decision to exclude its armoured formations from the Independence Day parade in Jerusalem on 15 May. The implication was that they were not on display because they were being readied for war. They were – but for war with Egypt, not Syria as Nasser thought. Israel's deception plan worked well.

Nasser now knew that if he was to retain what was left of his prestige as the leader of the so-called revolutionary Arab world, he would have to make a military move to give at least the impression that Egypt would not stand idly by if Israel did attack Syria.

That Nasser's prestige had fallen to its lowest point ever was beyond doubt. After the events of 7 April, Syria's President Atassi had begged Cairo for a practical gesture of military support. Nasser had done nothing. And that, probably, was the main reason why the Syrian regime decided to guarantee its survival by making a secret deal with Israel.

The Jordanians were also doing their best to make Nasser the laughing stock of the Arab world. The previous November, barely a week after the signing of Egypt's Defence Agreement with Syria, Israel had hit Jordan with a reprisal attack. After three Israeli

soldiers were killed by a Fatah mine, a large Israeli force had
attacked the village of Sammu on the slopes of Mount Hebron. It
blew up 125 houses and destroyed a newly restored police station.
When Jordanian army units were despatched to engage the Israelis,
they took a quick and bad beating. One way and another this was a
devastating blow to Hussein's prestige. In the face of his inability to
protect them, the Palestinians demanded that he arm them. The
Arab anger generated by Israel's attack also made it much more
difficult for Hussein to contain Fatah. The flames of the fire that
Arafat had lit were spreading. After the Israeli attack on Sammu,
Hussein's men began to ridicule Nasser for his inertia and his
inability to prevent the Israelis doing what they liked in the region
by force. In the months that followed, Jordan was frequently to
accuse Nasser of hiding behind U.N.E.F.'s skirts.

The United Nations Emergency Force (U.N.E.F.) was created in
the aftermath of the 1956 war. Troops of the U.N. force would act
as a buffer between Egypt and Israel at potential flashpoints such as
Gaza, the Negev border and Sharm es-Sheikh, an outpost on the
southern tip of the Sinai Peninsula. Israel refused to have U.N.E.F.
troops on its soil on the grounds that their presence would infringe
Israel's sovereignty; but Nasser allowed his arm to be twisted by the
U.N.'s first and last great Secretary-General, Dag Hammarskjöld. It
was, however, agreed that U.N.E.F. forces would withdraw from
Egypt if ever they were asked to do so by the Government in Cairo.
Nasser insisted on this not because he saw a time coming when he
would ask U.N.E.F. to leave, but because it was the only way of
establishing the fact that his acceptance of U.N. troops did not
imply that he was also accepting limits to Egypt's sovereign rights.
In time Nasser came to look upon U.N.E.F. as his protector. He was
not intending, ever, to initiate a war against Israel; and he reasoned
that Israel, however much it might want to attack Egypt, would not
dare to sweep aside U.N. forces in order to do so. To this extent
Jordan's charge that Nasser was hiding behind U.N.E.F.'s skirts
was not without some substance. But Hussein's men were
unspeakably foolish to taunt Nasser given the circumstances. They
probably did so because they wanted to see him humbled and
perhaps even destroyed by the Israelis. At the time Hussein and
those close to him were convinced that Nasser had authorized a
campaign of subversion in Jordan.

From Israel's point of view the most important U.N.E.F. presence was at Sharm es-Sheikh, which controls the entrance to the Strait of Tiran, beyond which is the Gulf of Aqaba and, at its end, the southern Israeli port of Eilat and the Jordanian port of Aqaba. In 1953 Nasser had taken full advantage of Egypt's ownership of Sharm es-Sheikh to impose a blockade on the port of Eilat. In the 1956 war the Israelis had captured Sharm es-Sheikh and vowed they would not withdraw. Never again was Nasser or any Egyptian leader to have the opportunity to close the Strait of Tiran to Israeli ships. Under strong pressure from the U.S. the Israelis did eventually withdraw – but on the condition that U.N.E.F. and not Egyptian troops would occupy Sharm es-Sheikh; and on the twofold understanding that the U.S. and the international community would cause the Strait of Tiran to be opened if Egypt ever closed it, and that if the international community failed to keep the Strait of Tiran open, Israel would have a valid reason for going to war against Egypt.

On 15 May, knowing that he had to make a military move to retain what was left of his credibility, Nasser declared a state of alert in Egypt. At the same time he ordered two divisions to cross into Sinai and take up 'defensive positions' along Israel's frontier. The next day Egypt requested a limited withdrawal of U.N.E.F.'s peace-keeping forces. The formal letter of request made it clear that Egypt did not want U.N.E.F. to withdraw from highly sensitive areas such as Gaza and, above all, Sharm es-Sheikh. What Nasser really wanted was the best of both worlds: a token withdrawal of U.N. personnel from observation posts along the frontier to silence those Arabs who were accusing him of hiding behind U.N.E.F.; and the Emergency Force to remain in place at Sharm es-Sheikh and other sensitive spots to avoid provoking Israel more than was absolutely necessary. From the record of Nasser's conversations at the time and after with visiting diplomats and others, it is clear that he was hoping the escalation would end there, and that the gathering crisis could be resolved by political means. It is also clear that Nasser had no strategy of any kind and that he was merely reacting to events.

Later the same day Nasser learned that he could not have the best of both worlds. U Thant, the U.N.'s Secretary-General, ruled that Nasser would have to make an all-or-nothing request. U.N.E.F. could be all in or all out. It was not for Nasser to play games with the

U.N. U Thant chose to act by the rule book to protect himself; and that meant he had to ignore the fact that Nasser was not simply trying to save his face, he was also attempting to avert a war.

Nasser knew that if he asked for U.N.E.F.'s total withdrawal, Egyptian troops would have to reoccupy the potential flashpoints, including Sharm es-Sheikh. And if he did not then reimpose the blockade on the Gulf of Aqaba – Israeli ships had enjoyed free passage through the Strait of Tiran since the 1956 war – he would be as good as finished as the leader of the so-called revolutionary Arab world. His Arab brothers would denounce him as a coward and a traitor. At best he would lose whatever prestige he had left and his influence to restrain the hotheads on the Arab side. But if he did reimpose the blockade, he would be inviting an Israeli attack. The alternative was to back down, cancel his request for a limited U.N.E.F. withdrawal and be seen to be hiding behind U.N.E.F.'s skirts. That also would cause him to be humiliated and to lose his restraining influence. Nasser was trapped. At the Defence Ministry in Tel Aviv, Israel's military planners were congratulating themselves.

For the best part of two days Nasser thought about his options. Then, on 18 May, he ordered Egypt's formal request for the withdrawal of all U.N.E.F. forces to be transmitted to U.N. headquarters in New York. But he was still reluctant to take the final step of reoccupying Sharm es-Sheikh and imposing a blockade on the Gulf of Aqaba. For three more days he took no action. In the end he convinced himself that even if Israel did resort to force, the war would not be a long or a decisive one. Like Israel's military planners, Nasser was sure the U.N. would insist on a ceasefire in a matter of days. So in Nasser's mind it all came down to one question: could Egypt's defence forces withstand an Israeli attack for a few days, probably a week at the most, without losing too much ground and too much face? It was the right question. But Nasser came up with the wrong answer. As events were to prove, he badly underestimated Israel's strike capacity. He also had no idea of how totally his own High Command had failed to reorganize and retrain Egypt's armed forces. It was one thing to possess a lot of Soviet military hardware. It was quite another to know how to use it.

The truth is also that Nasser was not convinced that war was inevitable. Since none of the big powers wanted a war in the Middle East, he continued to believe that the governments which exercised the most power at the U.N. would cause his blockade of the Gulf of Aqaba to be lifted by diplomatic means. In short, he was prepared to make all the necessary concessions after he had put on a show of force, and he was relying on the international community to get him off the hook. His mistake here was to assume that Israel's leaders would be prepared to give the diplomatic process a chance.

In the critical three days when Nasser was tortured by doubts about what to do for the best, Jordan was pouring fuel on the flames by ridiculing the Egyptian President for failing to take the final step. Hussein was allowing those under his influence to be reckless and stupid.

On 21 May, Egyptian troops reoccupied Sharm es-Sheikh. From U.N. Headquarters in New York Urquhart sent Nasser a message. 'I told him he was a bloody fool. I said that if he went ahead with the blockade the Israelis would smash him. I said to him, "Don't do it!" ' The next day Cairo announced that the Gulf of Aqaba was closed to Israeli ships. U Thant meanwhile had arrived in Cairo. But it was too late. U Thant had been too slow; he had dallied in New York when he ought to have been in Cairo and Tel Aviv. From the moment Nasser announced the closure of the Strait of Tiran to Israeli ships, war was inevitable – because Israel's military planners and the hawks in the political establishment wanted it.

There were some doves on the Israeli side. Their leader was the Prime Minister, the much maligned Levi Eshkol. He knew, as all of his colleagues did, that the Arabs were not intending to attack Israel. He had also been impressed by the advice President de Gaulle had given Israel's Foreign Minister, Aba Eban, some months previously. De Gaulle had said: 'Don't make war. If you do you will create a Palestinian nationalism and you will never be able to get rid of it.'[24]

For a week or so those in Israel who were hungry for war allowed Eshkol and Eban to go through the motions of pretending that the leadership was seriously interested in a diplomatic solution to the crisis. The pause was useful for the warmongers because it gave them time to convince public opinion in Israel and the Western world that the Jewish State was about to be annihilated. It was a monstrous lie but it was believed. And it was the Arabs who gave the

Israeli lie its credibility by threatening the Jewish State with destruction. In the name of the P.L.O., Shuqairi did his bit by announcing that Israel would soon be 'completely annihilated'. The ordinary people of Israel could not be blamed for taking the Arab rhetoric at its face value. There was no way they could have known that their leaders were deceiving them.

The timing of the war was determined by a piece of news that left Israel's warmongers in a state of frenzy. On 2 June, and in good faith, the American State Department informed Israel that it had established with Egypt the basis for negotiations which could lead to the ending of the blockade of the Gulf of Aqaba by diplomatic means. On the day that he publicly declared his intention to close the Strait of Tiran to Israeli shipping, Nasser had privately informed the U.N. and the U.S., and so Israel, that he was not serious about the blockade, that it was a gesture he had to make in order to control events on his side. The American message also said that Nasser's emissary, Zacharia Mohieddin, would be arriving in Washington for talks on Wednesday, 7 June. In short, the Americans were telling the Government of Israel that there would be no need for war if the Israelis were prepared to give the diplomatic process a little more time.

At 7.45 a.m. on Monday, 5 June, and after Levi Eshkol had been told by the military that he would be removed from office by one means or another if he continued to favour a political solution to the crisis with Egypt, Israel went to war. The world mistakenly believed that Israel was fighting for its survival.

On the same morning Abu Jihad was in Frankfurt. He had just arrived from Belgium. He was on an arms-buying mission. At about 11.00 a.m. he was located by breathless and excited colleagues. 'Come quickly,' they said, 'the war has started!'

In fact the Arabs had already lost the war. In two hours and fifty minutes the Israelis had broken the back of Egypt's air force. But Abu Jihad was not aware of this sensational development as he prepared to leave Frankfurt.

He told me: 'Directly I went to the airport to search for a plane to Damascus. No plane. I flew from Frankfurt to Zurich, from there to Geneva and from Geneva to Ankara. I arrived at about 5.00 p.m. and I met the Syrian Minister of the Interior who had been attending a conference in Geneva. Together we travelled to Damascus in a

special car provided by the Syrian Embassy. We arrived in
Damascus at ten o'clock the following morning, and I went straight
to our headquarters in the Yarmuk refugee camp for a meeting with
Arafat.' At this time Abu Jihad was still officially Fatah's Acting
Military Commander.

The next day, 7 June, Arafat and Abu Jihad went to war – in
Arafat's tiny Volkswagen car. They stuffed it full of rocket-
propelled grenades (R.P.G.s) and headed for the Golan Heights. So
far as they knew from information available in Damascus, Syria's
valiant fighting forces were locked in a struggle of destiny with the
Jewish State. According to Damascus Radio the Syrian army had
overrun a number of Israeli border settlements and was advancing
on Safad and Nazareth.

Arafat and Abu Jihad intended to reconnoitre the Syrian front
line and then direct their fighters, as they arrived, to positions from
which they could make a contribution to the Syrian war effort. But
as the two Fatah leaders drove on, they realized that there was no
Syrian war effort to support. On this, the third day of the war, the
appalling truth was that Syria's ground forces were not in action.
Nor had they been. They had not moved from their pre-war
defensive positions. To all intents and purposes Syria was not at
war. It was true that some Syrian artillery batteries were shelling
Israel's northern settlements, but that action was clearly no more
than a token gesture. From the overall situation on the Syrian front
it was possible to draw only one of two conclusions. Either the
Syrians were frightened and had never intended to fight unless they
were attacked – in which case, why were the Syrians inviting an
eventual attack by shelling Israel's northern settlements? Or the
Syrians had made some sort of secret deal with Israel – in which case
the shelling of Israel's northern settlements from fixed artillery
positions was merely the cover for Syria's betrayal of the Arab
cause.

On the night of 7 June, after a defeated Jordan had accepted a
ceasefire, Arafat and Abu Jihad were waiting for their fighters to
arrive at the Syrian front line. Said Abu Jihad: 'Then we had
tragedy. The bus carrying our commandos had a crash with a Syrian
tank in the darkness. Not less than fifteen of our men were killed or
seriously injured.' It could easily have been an accident, but it is not
impossible that the Fatah bus was rammed by a Syrian tank. Fatah

was acting alone, it was not co-ordinating with Syria's High Command; and there is every reason to believe that Syria's military leaders did not want Fatah to fight.

On 8 June, the day a defeated Egypt accepted a ceasefire, Arafat and Abu Jihad were joined by more Fatah volunteers. Some made their way from Damascus. Others crossed into Syria from Jordan. 'It was really incredible,' Abu Jihad told me. 'On the road from the Golan to Damascus the Syrians were leaving their positions and withdrawing before the Israelis attacked. So we put some of our commandos into the positions the Syrians were leaving. We also sent small groups with mortars to attack the Israelis behind their lines.'

Arafat told me: 'At this time it was for us a matter of honour. We felt we had to demonstrate that some Arabs were prepared to fight.'

On 9 June, the Israelis began their attack on the Golan Heights. The Syrians quickly accepted a ceasefire. The Israelis announced that they, too, accepted the ceasefire – but they went on fighting. They were determined to take the Golan Heights.

Israel's military planners may have intended to double-cross the Syrians all along, knowing that they could not accuse Israel of breaking a secret agreement. It is also possible that the Israelis were so astonished and so overwhelmed by the scale of their victory over Egypt and Jordan that they simply could not resist the temptation to take everything they wanted. A third possibility is that Syria's military leaders secretly agreed to let the Golan Heights be captured in return for Israel's absolute assurance that Damascus would not be attacked.

In favour of the third possibility is one very pertinent fact. By any objective test the Golan was an impregnable military fortress. Even allowing for the fact that Israeli officers led their men through a hail of machine-gun fire to take a number of Syrian positions, there is no way the Golan could have fallen to any attacking force in twenty-seven hours if Syria's military leaders had been determined to defend it.

The only consolation for Arafat and Abu Jihad was that their commandos performed well enough to delay Israel's main attack on the Golan Heights. Or so they believe. Said Abu Jihad: 'Moshe Dayan later admitted that Israel delayed its advance because their forces were being attacked from behind. It was our boys who caused the Israelis to delay.'

By the end of the sixth day, Israeli forces were in occupation of Arab land that in area was four times the size of Israel before the war. They had captured all of the Sinai Peninsula including the Gaza Strip; the Golan Heights; and the West Bank of the Jordan including East Jerusalem. The loss of the West Bank and Gaza meant that all of the territory that had been allotted to the Palestinian Arab state by the 1947 U.N. Partition Plan was now under Israeli control.

The irony was that those who planned Israel's war effort had not intended to take the West Bank. On the morning of 5 June, shortly after the first Israeli air strike on Egyptian Air Force bases, Prime Minister Eshkol had sent a message to Hussein reminding him of the tacit agreement the Israelis thought they had with him. It was sent via the commander of the U.N. peace-keeping force. It said: 'We shall not initiate any action whatsoever against Jordan. However, should Jordan open hostilities, we shall react with all our might and [Hussein] will have to bear the full responsibility for the consequences.'[25]

Although Hussein had signed a defence agreement with Nasser on the eve of the war – circumstances had left him with no choice – he was still absolutely determined that Jordan would not initiate any action against Israel. The decision to do so was made for him, over his head, by the Egyptians. There were two battalions of Egyptian commandos in Jordan. Those and other non-Jordanian Arab units were under the on-the-spot command of a member of the Egyptian General Staff, General Abdel Moneim Riad. At 9.00 a.m. General Riad was ordered by his Cairo headquarters to open the Jordan front. Cairo told General Riad a pack of lies. It said that seventy-five per cent of Israel's aircraft had been destroyed and that Egyptian ground forces had taken the offensive. The obvious implication was that the Arabs would soon have the Israelis on the run. The truth was, of course, that the Egyptians were taking a beating. Cairo wanted action on the Jordan front to relieve the pressure on Egypt.

General Riad ordered the forces under his command to open fire, and Hussein was committed to a war he did not want and which he knew would be disastrous for the Arabs. The Jordanians gave a good account of themselves. They lost their half of Jerusalem after a hand-to-hand and house-by-house struggle. But on the rest of the West Bank they did not have a chance without air cover.

In many ways the catastrophe of 1967 was, for the Palestinians, even bigger than the catastrophe of 1948. In 1948 they had lost their homes and their land, but they had lived since then in the hope and belief that Israel could be defeated on the battlefield. In equipment and manpower the Arab regimes had all that was necessary to defeat Israel – or so the Palestinians had assumed; all that was missing was the Arab will to fight. But the truth was now apparent. Despite their rhetoric, the Arab regimes had never intended to fight. This, for the Palestinians, was the bitter lesson of 1967. The regimes of the so-called new Arab order were no different from those of the old order.

What was Arafat's reaction to the scale of the Arab defeat? 'I was turned completely upside down,' he told me.

Fatah's strategy of creating an atmosphere of confrontation in which the Arab regimes would be forced to fight had backfired in the most spectacular way possible.

# 12

# The 'Popular War of Liberation'

Two days after the war ended, Fatah's leaders and other top officials assembled in Damascus for the organization's first congress. Said Abu Jihad: 'We were in despair. Many of us could not discuss what had happened without weeping. I myself was crying. Because of the way in which the Arab armies had been broken, some of our colleagues were saying that everything was finished. Some were talking about giving up the struggle and making new lives outside the Arab world.'

Before the congress opened, a number of Fatah's Central Committee members went to lunch in the Abu Kamal restaurant. As they entered they saw George Habash seated at a table next to the one they had reserved for themselves. Arafat and Habash had not met before. Said Khalad Hassan: 'When we began to speak with Habash he cried. He said, "Everything is lost." Arafat said to him: "George, you are wrong. This is not the end. It's the beginning. We are going to resume our military actions."' At the time they were brave words; and as Arafat was shortly to discover, they did not reflect the thinking of a majority of his colleagues.

At the top of the formal agenda for Fatah's first congress was the question of policy. As Khalad put it: 'Were we going to resume our military actions or not, and if so, when? The related question, which was not on the formal agenda, was concerned with Arafat's position. Officially Abu Jihad was still Acting Military Commander. Officially Arafat's suspension from membership of Fatah had expired. But from the moment of Arafat's arrest in

Damascus in May 1966, events had moved too quickly for the Central Committee to resolve the problem of what to do about him. In the second half of June 1967, Khalad and the majority were determined to block Arafat's re-appointment as Military Commander.

They were still afraid that he would emerge as a dictator. Though they could not afford to say so in public, they knew the war had proved that Israel could not be beaten on the battlefield. It followed that the Palestinian cause would have to be advanced by military *and* political means. A liberation struggle that relied exclusively on military action was doomed to failure. And there was the old fear that Arafat might use his military power to obstruct and sabotage any political initiatives that his Central Committee colleagues, the majority, might take.

Those attending Fatah's first congress were also deeply divided on the question of what form the military action, if any, should take. Some were totally opposed to its resumption on the grounds that it would result in more suffering for the Palestinians under Israeli occupation, without any gain for the cause. To others, the minority at the time, the fact that there were now nearly one million Palestinians under Israeli occupation suggested that conditions were right for a popular war of liberation. Those who entertained this idea believed they could now apply Mao Tse-tung's thoughts about revolutionary armed struggle. The one million Palestinians under Israeli occupation would be the revolutionary sea in which Mao's fish – in this case Palestinian guerrillas – would swim. On the West Bank and in Gaza the oppressed Palestinian masses would give aid and shelter to their fighters in the short term, and in the long term they would rise up against the Israelis. That was the theory. Its main attraction was that Fatah would no longer have to rely on Syria or any other front-line Arab state for its bases.

But even those who were excited by the possibility of a popular war of liberation were aware that it would be many months, and perhaps even a year or two, before such a struggle could be launched. If it was to have a chance of succeeding, the Palestinian masses in the newly-occupied territories would have to be organized and educated in the revolutionary way. So even those who were in favour of revolutionary armed struggle were against quick action. They wanted time to prepare the ground and the people.

Arafat's position was very simple, very clear and very consistent with the fact that he was a man of tactics and not strategy. He was in favour of an immediate resumption of military activity. 'I could not afford to weep with the others,' he told me. 'I considered that we now had a duty to the Arab nation as well as the Palestinian nation. It was not the Arab people who had failed, it was the Arab regimes. In my opinion we had to demonstrate that it was possible to deal with Israel's arrogance of power. I knew that if we did not act quickly the whole Arab nation, Arabs everywhere, would be infected by the psychology of defeat. And that, of course, was exactly what the Israelis wanted.'

Until Hani Hassan's arrival in Damascus from West Germany, Arafat was alone in this view. According to Hani, even Abu Jihad was in agreement with those who were arguing for time to organize the next round of the military struggle in a proper and disciplined way.

Said Hani: 'As soon as I arrived in Damascus, my brother, Abu Iyad and some of the others who were opposing Arafat came to see me. They tried in a very hard way to influence me not to support Arafat.' As previously noted, the source of Hani's power was the global network of Palestinian student unions. None were more firmly committed to the idea of armed struggle than the unions of Western Europe. And the most aggressive was Hani's own organization in West Germany. If Khalad and the others had won Hani to their side, Arafat might have been finished as a leader.

Hani continued: 'My brother and the others were astonished by what I told them. I said first of all that those of us in Europe were so totally committed to armed struggle that we were not interested in calculating how much blood there would be. And I said that if Arafat was for resuming the fight without delay, we would be with him. Then I told my brother and the others some secrets of my own.

'I told them that when the war had started on 5 June, we had taken a certain decision in Europe. We told our students they could not remain members of Fatah unless they were prepared to go to Palestine to fight. Then I said this: "Right now 450 students and workers are being trained in Algeria. They have left their studies and their jobs. We sent them to various ports in Italy, and from there they travelled to Algiers. Now they have been joined by fifty students from Cairo. At the end of July they will finish their training. Then they are coming to the West Bank and Gaza to fight!"'

After a pause for effect, Hani had asked a question: 'How can I now tell them we are against Arafat because he wants to continue the military struggle?' No answer was called for, and none was offered. Hani had made his point. The Hassan brothers agreed to disagree.

Hani's stand effectively ended Arafat's isolation; but it did not tip the balance of opinion in his favour. After several days of impassioned and at times acrimonious debate which saw Hani accusing Abu Iyad of wanting to take Arafat's place, Fatah's congress was adjourned to allow tempers to cool. Up to this point Arafat was convinced that he had lost his battle, and that the Central Committee would reject his call for a resumption of military action.

Arafat used the adjournment to visit Jordan. He asked Hani to go with him and they travelled in Arafat's Volkswagen. Hani told me: 'His morale was very low. When we had been travelling for only a few minutes, he said, "What shall I do?" And before I could answer he made a comment that worried me very much. He said: "At least history will say that I tried." I was then very hard with Arafat. "Why are you talking like that?" I said. "You have no need to say such a thing. My students are coming from Algiers and we shall fight with you."

'My own idea was really a very simple one. Most of the students who were completing their elementary military training in Algiers were from the West Bank. The plan was for them to return to their homes and to appear to be living normal lives. Because they would be covered and protected by their families and friends, I assumed it would not be so easy for Israeli security agents to track them down . . . but I was wrong.'

In Jordan, and from a source close to King Hussein, Arafat received some information which enabled him to turn the tables on his opponents when he returned to Damascus for the second session of Fatah's first congress. He learned that the Government of Israel, probably under pressure from the U.S., was considering a very dramatic peace initiative. According to the story Arafat heard, there was a strong possibility that Israel would be prepared to withdraw from all the Arab territory it had captured in the June war in return for full and formal peace treaties with Egypt, Jordan, Syria and the Lebanon. If the information was accurate, the implications for the Palestinians were, as Khalad Hassan said, 'horrific'.

The information, and the threat it was seen to represent, caused many of those attending Fatah's congress to have second thoughts about their opposition to Arafat and his call for a resumption of military action.

'We decided to put ourselves into Israel's shoes,' Khalad Hassan told me. 'For the sake of discussion we imagined that we were the Government of Israel, and we asked ourselves what we would do. We came quickly to the conclusion that if we were Israelis, we would make a dramatic peace initiative. We would declare publicly, to the Arab regimes and the world, that we were prepared to withdraw from every inch of Arab land we had captured in the Six-Day War, in return for peace treaties with Egypt, Jordan, Syria and the Lebanon.

'Still putting ourselves in Israel's shoes, we calculated that one of two things would then happen. Either the Arab states would make peace with us, in which case the future of the Jewish State inside its pre-1967 borders would be guaranteed for all time, and the Palestinian cause would be finished. If there was peace none of the front-line Arab states would allow the Palestinians to continue their struggle by any means. Or the Arab states would refuse to make peace with us, in which case Israel would still be the winner. In this case the world would say, "These bloody silly Arabs no longer deserve any support or sympathy." Israel would then be regarded as the only party which wanted peace, and it would then be able to do no wrong in the eyes of the world – even if it continued to occupy the Arab land captured in 1967.

'When we put ourselves into Israel's shoes, the mistake we Fatah people made was to assume that Israel's leaders would be clever and wise and would do what was best from Israel's point of view. So we became dominated, I can even say obsessed, by the idea that Israel might withdraw from the West Bank. At the time this was really a horrifying idea to us in Fatah. And that's why we began to think that we should resume our military activities. If the Israelis withdrew from the West Bank for peace, they would continue to enjoy the support of world opinion and we Palestinians would not be allowed to fight. We would have nowhere to fight. So we had to begin our confrontation with Israel before there was any Israeli withdrawal. To keep the possibility of struggle alive, and also to keep the Arabs on our side, we needed a situation in which we could say that we were not defeated, that we had raised the banner of struggle and that it was as a result of our actions that the Israelis had been forced to withdraw!'

Arafat's information about the possibility of an Israeli withdrawal in exchange for peace with the front-line Arab states was substantially correct. There was, however, one essential difference between Israel's position as it was reported to Arafat and the reality. The difference was Israel's insistence that it be allowed to keep troops along the Jordan River. And that was the problem for the Arabs. No self-respecting Arab leader could agree to a peace which gave Israel the right to station its troops on Arab soil. It was Israel's insistence on that condition that proved to be the fatal mistake.

For the record I asked all of Fatah's leaders if they had believed at the time that the front-line Arab states would have made peace with Israel if Israel had been willing to withdraw from every inch of Arab land captured in 1967. They all said 'Yes'. And Arafat was the most emphatic. My conversation with him on this point was as follows.

'Looking back, Abu Amar, do you think it can be said that the Israelis made a very big mistake by not withdrawing?'

'In my opinion this was Israel's big chance. They should have withdrawn. When they did not do so they made their fatal mistake.'

'Do you think all of the front-line Arab states would have sat down and made peace with Israel as the price for getting their land back?'

'There is absolutely no doubt about it. All of the regimes would have made peace on those terms if they had been offered it.'

'Including Nasser?' I asked.

'Yes, including Nasser. The regimes and the Arab peoples had so much to gain from peace. What do you think the Arab peoples would have done when their leaders told them it was no longer necessary to spend money on weapons, and that the money that had been spent on preparing for war could now be used to develop their countries to bring prosperity to all? Do you think the Arab peoples would have rejected that? They would have demonstrated their joy in the streets and their leaders would have been heroes.'

'If what you say is correct, and I believe it is, the Israelis could, in effect, have had a peace which would have killed Fatah and the Palestine liberation movement by political means – if they, the Israelis, had been sensible.'

'There is absolutely no doubt about that,' Arafat concluded. 'We would have been finished and our cause would have been lost. But Israel's leaders were very stupid. What they have done and are doing is the consequence of their arrogance of power. And this arrogance of power is spoiling everything for the Jews. In the end it will destroy Judaism. They are doing it themselves.'

On 23 June, fearing that Israel would be wise and sensible enough to make the necessary moves for peace, Fatah's Central Committee and other top officials attending the congress in Damascus approved a plan for the resumption of military action. Because those who could not reconcile themselves to Arafat and the idea of a return to military action resigned, the vote was unanimous. Arafat's position as Military Commander was confirmed, and military operations were scheduled to begin in the last week of August. Shortly before then Arafat was to establish his operational headquarters on the occupied West Bank.

If the decision had been left to Arafat, he would have travelled to the West Bank the same day and planted a mine or two in the path of an Israeli patrol vehicle the same evening. And in doing so he would have been acting in accordance with his own first law of struggle which was, broadly speaking, to take advantage of the opportunity of the day and the moment, and to leave the opportunities of tomorrow to be taken as they came.

There was, however, a good reason for the delay. On 23 June Fatah was in no shape to launch and sustain a campaign of sabotage and subversion. Its own reserves of trained military manpower were all but exhausted. Those who were called commandos could be counted on the fingers of Arafat's two hands. When the decision to resume military operations was taken, it was made on the assumption that Hani's student force would not be in place and ready for action until late August. In the meantime, and to supplement the number of fighters who would be arriving from Western Europe via Algiers, Arafat and Abu Jihad were instructed to organize a crash recruitment and training programme.

Said Abu Jihad: 'We sent our recruiting officers to all of the cities and the towns of the West Bank and Gaza. Their job was to search for volunteers and to make arrangements for them to come for training at our camps in Syria. In those two months we received perhaps 500 volunteers and I must tell you that there was a very special feeling in the occupied territories which helped us very much. When our Palestinian youths were seeing the Israeli soldiers for the first time they were very surprised. They were saying to each other, "Are these really the supermen who have broken the Arab armies? How can it be? They are small . . . mostly young boys. . . They do not take care of their appearance and they are not so well disciplined." The point I am making is that our Palestinian youths did not see the Israeli soldiers as supermen and they did not understand how the Arab armies had been defeated by them. So there was an important psychological factor at work for us. Our youths were saying, "It's not necessary to run away from these Israelis. . . We can face them. . . We can confront them." And that's why we had so many volunteers.'

On arrival at Fatah's training camps, each volunteer was investigated by a security committee. 'We had to make sure they were not Israeli agents,' Abu Jihad said. In fact the Israelis were still in the process of consolidating their hold on the newly-occupied territories, and they were not yet in the business of turning Palestinians into traitors.

Abu Jihad continued: 'In three weeks we trained them how to use not less than twenty-four different weapons – rifles, pistols, R.P.G.s, mortars, mines, explosives and hand grenades. We also trained them in tactics – how to organize patrols, how to make an ambush; and we trained them under fire with live ammunition. All these things and more happened in the day. The nights were devoted to political lectures and debates. I must say we were very democratic. Many different points of view were discussed. Sometimes Arafat gave the lectures. Sometimes Khalad Hassan. Sometimes others. All the leaders played their part. Then, at the end of each three-week training period, we were sending our people back to their towns and cities in small groups. "From where are you?" "These five are from Jericho." "Okay, here are your weapons – go." "These are from Jerusalem." "Okay, here are your weapons – go." "Hebron – go." "Nablus – go." "Gaza – go." And so on.'

As Abu Jihad's account makes clear, Fatah was not suffering

from a shortage of weapons. Khalad Hassan explained: 'We equipped ourselves very nicely with the weapons and the ammunition the Syrians had abandoned on the battlefield! On the first day of our congress we sent people to gather them up. When the Syrians came to know what we were doing we made a bargain with them. We agreed to give the heavy weapons to the Syrian army and to keep the small arms for ourselves.'

At the last minute the Syrians asked Fatah to drop its plan for a return to military action; and their demand was backed by a threat which Abu Jihad did not believe to be an empty one. If Fatah insisted on going ahead with its plan to confront Israel by military means, the regime in Damascus would confront and destroy Fatah.

Arafat had fixed 28 August as the day for the resumption of military action. By that date Hani's 500 student fighters had arrived from Algiers and had been dispersed to their home-town areas on the West Bank and in Gaza. Most of them had entered Jordan disguised as Iraqi troops. (Iraqi forces were stationed in Jordan to bolster Hussein's defences.) And the 500 or so volunteers who had completed crash training courses at Fatah camps in Syria were also in place and ready for action. Arafat himself had moved to the West Bank in the middle of August. Though he was not intending to sleep in the same place for more than two consecutive nights, he had established his headquarters in the maze of streets that made up the kasbah of old Nablus.

On 27 August, the Syrians issued their stop order and ultimatum. Said Abu Jihad: 'Directly I sent a letter to Arafat asking him to postpone the start of our offensive. I told him the Syrians were putting some obstacles in our way. Unfortunately it was too late to stop some of our actions we had planned for 28 August, and our people did make some explosions in Gaza, Tel Aviv and one or two other places. But after that Arafat did succeed in stopping the action. You will appreciate that we could not use telephones or telegrams. We had to send our operational orders by messenger.' By the summer of 1967 it was common knowledge that the Israelis had found ways to bug the telephone communications between one front-line Arab state and another. In the June war the Israelis had monitored telephone conversations between Nasser and Hussein.

Abu Jihad continued: 'Within a few days I managed to get an appointment with Hafez Assad, the Defence Minister. I was very frank with him. I said it was our Palestinian people who were under the Israeli occupation, and the whole world recognized that people under military occupation had the right to resist. I also told him that our operations would be launched from inside the occupied territories. We were not making our attacks from Syria, so no blame could be attached to him. Assad thought for some minutes and then he said: "Okay. You are right. You continue with your activities inside the occupied territories and I will speak to those who are putting obstacles in your way."'

What the Syrians were up to on this occasion remains a matter for speculation. But there are some clues. On 28 August, Arab leaders were scheduled to meet for a summit in Khartoum. Through U.S. and U.N. channels they had been informed of Israel's ideas for a permanent peace — an Israeli withdrawal from the territory it had captured in the June war in return for formal peace treaties with the front-line Arab states, and on condition that Israel could station troops along the Jordan River. At the Khartoum summit Arab leaders were to give their formal and final response to Israel's offer. The outcome of the summit was not in doubt. The Arabs would reject the idea of negotiations with Israel on the terms then under offer.

The Syrians had decided to stay away from the summit. Their decision to boycott what they knew would be a rejectionist summit was entirely at odds with their pre-war public position as the only true champions of the Palestinian and Arab cause and, by obvious implication, the only Arab country that would not rest until Israel had been destroyed. Yet the Syrians now appeared to be prepared to do anything to keep the door to negotiations with Israel open for as long as there was a possibility that Israel would withdraw from territory occupied in the June war. In the months following the war Syria's leaders seemed to have only one objective — to get back the Golan Heights before the Arab world learned they had been lost as the result of Syria's secret collusion with Israel. And that meant the regime in Damascus had to do everything possible to convince Israel that Syria was not an enemy state. One way to demonstrate that was to stay away from the Khartoum summit. Another was to put obstacles in Fatah's way. If the Syrians could tell their Israeli friends that they had prevented Fatah from trying to provoke an uprising on the West Bank and in Gaza this, surely, would help to persuade

Israel that it had nothing to fear from returning the Golan Heights to their rightful owners.

In the light of the above, why did Abu Jihad have such an apparently easy time when he met with Assad? The answer, I believe, is that Abu Jihad confronted Assad with an irrefutable argument. The world did understand that the Palestinians had a right to resist Israeli occupation. And if the Syrians were now to deny the Palestinians that right Damascus might have to answer some very embarrassing questions about its motives, questions which might not end until Syria's collusion with Israel had been exposed. Assad was sharp enough to make the right choice between two evils.

What Fatah and other Palestinian propaganda described as the 'popular war of liberation' began in the first week of September, after Abu Jihad had persuaded Assad to remove the obstacles Syria had put in Fatah's way. But it was all over by the end of the year.

By the end of December, most of Fatah's cells and networks in the occupied territories had been uncovered and destroyed by Israel's security services. Hundreds of Fatah commandos had been killed. More than 1,000 had been captured. And Arafat's own luck had just about run out. It seems that he would have been caught if Abu Jihad had not sent a snatch-squad to rescue him. And, most depressing of all from Fatah's point of view, a majority of Palestinians living under Israeli occupation were glad to see the back of those who had claimed to be their liberators.

What went wrong for Arafat and Fatah?

How one answers that question depends on what one thinks Fatah's real objectives were. To date most Western commentators and writers have been content to take Fatah's propaganda at its face value. On that basis the question they asked was the following: why did Fatah fail to provoke a popular uprising in the occupied territories? The answer given was, more or less, that Arafat and his colleagues in the leadership had little or no idea of what they were doing. In particular it was said that Arafat and his colleagues had no strategy that was appropriate to the situation. They had failed to understand that it would take some years to promote a popular war of liberation and that the actual struggle or fighting would have to be preceded by detailed political, psychological and organizational planning. Arafat, it was said, wanted results too quickly.

Such a verdict would be justified if Fatah's real objective had been the same as its publicly proclaimed goal – if, in other words, Fatah was seeking to promote a popular war of liberation which would end with an uprising and the expulsion of Israeli forces from the West Bank and Gaza. But that was not the case. As Khalad Hassan said, Fatah's leaders voted for a resumption of military activity because they believed it was necessary to deny Israel the opportunity to make an unforced withdrawal from the West Bank for the sake of peace with Jordan – a peace which, in effect, would have enabled Israel and Jordan (probably in concert with the other Arab states) to control and extinguish the slow-burning fire of Palestinian nationalism. Arafat's own objective was less specific. He wanted to fight on simply to keep the idea of struggle alive.

Fatah's decision to continue the struggle from inside the occupied territories was not part of a well planned or long-term liberation strategy. It was a tactical move in response to what was perceived to be the threat of the moment. If there had been no prospect of, or serious talk about, an Israeli withdrawal, Fatah's leaders would not have supported Arafat's call for a resumption of military action.

The more appropriate question is why did Arafat fail to generate enough popular support to keep him and Fatah in business on the West Bank and in Gaza?

The first part of the answer is that a majority of the Palestinians living under Israeli occupation simply did not believe there was anything to be gained from continuing the struggle by military means alone. The majority, the West Bankers in particular, were of the opinion that there had to be a political and negotiated settlement with Israel – a settlement which would lead to the Arabs recognizing Israel in more or less its pre-1967 borders in return for an Israeli withdrawal to those borders and the establishment of some kind of Palestinian entity on the West Bank and in Gaza. I do not suppose there was a single Palestinian who contemplated such a prospect with any enthusiasm, for it meant that they were abandoning their hopes of ever returning to their land and their homes in Israel. But they did not have much choice. If the Arab armies could be so easily smashed by the Israelis, the Palestinians had no chance of advancing their cause by military means. If Fatah had had an attainable political programme at the time, it is possible that the Palestinians in the occupied territories would have given more support to Arafat and his fighters. But in 1967 Fatah was very far from having any political programme.

The second part of the answer is that what Arafat probably regarded as the negative and even defeatist attitude of the Palestinians in the occupied territories was reinforced by the efficient but ruthless way in which the Israelis set about destroying Fatah's organization while, at the same time, deterring those who were living under occupation from supporting Arafat and his fighters. A glance at the tactics employed by Israel's military and other security services to isolate and then smash Fatah is enough to make the point.

There were: curfews, cordons and house-to-house searches; restrictions on travel and movement; long prison sentences for Fatah activists and sympathizers; detention without trial; deportations; neighbourhood or collective punishment, including the closure of schools, shops and offices, and the blowing up of houses belonging to those who gave, or were suspected of giving, shelter to Fatah activists. In December 1969, Moshe Dayan claimed that a total of 516 houses had been destroyed. Two months previously a special report in *The Times* of London had said the real figure was 7,000.

Nor was it only those Palestinians who were found guilty or were strongly suspected of being involved in sabotage operations who were punished. It was Israel's policy to punish any form of disobedience to Israeli orders and commands.

Israeli accounts of how Fatah's organization in the occupied territories was smashed play down Israel's ruthlessness and exaggerate Fatah's shortcomings. According to the authorized Israeli version of what happened, Fatah's security was non-existent and Fatah commandos, once captured, were ready and willing to betray their colleagues. There is no doubt that Fatah's security was very poor in those days – Arafat and Abu Jihad are the first to say so. But that was not the main reason why Israel's various intelligence agencies captured more than 1,000 Fatah commandos in little more than three months.

Part of the truth is that the Mossad had files on Hani Hassan's student fighters from Western Europe. Said Hani: 'The student organizations to which we belonged in Europe were naturally very democratic. And we were pleased about that. We wanted to be democratic. But it meant that we had to conduct our political affairs in the open. So when we stood for election to the student organizations our names were reported in newspapers and magazines. And our meetings were, of course, open. And that gave the Mossad agents in Europe the opportunity to keep us in their sights and to make files on us. By the time my students moved from Europe to Algiers, the Mossad had files with photographs of most of us. And when suddenly we were no more in our places in Europe, the Mossad very quickly realized where we were and what we were doing.

'When they were making their files on us, Mossad agents also received a great deal of co-operation from the authorities in Europe, particularly from the authorities in West Germany. Many years later I had the opportunity to see what the Mossad had on us. It happened after Khomeini's revolution in Iran. Until the revolution the Israeli Embassy in Tehran was a very important spy centre. After the revolution I entered the Israeli Embassy and there I found a book containing the names of many of our fighters and personalities. The names were listed in alphabetical order. They were followed by four or five lines of description – how dangerous we were and so on – and by most names there was a photograph. In my own case it was a copy of the photograph I had given to my university in Munich in 1959. And that's how the Mossad got its photographs of most of us who were active in student politics in Europe. I still have the book I found in the Israeli Embassy and it is the proof of how much the authorities in Europe were co-operating with the Mossad. Germany was, of course, a special case. The Germans were naturally feeling very guilty and they were ready to provide any facility for the Mossad. I should also say the Israelis were very guilty of practising moral blackmail on the Germans. Once I was going to meet with Willy Brandt when I was the President of the P.S.U. and he was the Mayor of West Berlin. In the end he decided he could not meet with me because he did not want to give the Israelis the opportunity to condemn him as being a "Nazi" and "anti-Jew". I know from my own experience that many Germans are sick and tired of the moral blackmail which they feel the Israelis practise on them.

'So as a result of the Mossad's work in Europe, the Israeli military authorities had a dossier on each of us at the time we were ready to begin our military activities. They knew our names and addresses and they had photographs of us. And I must say the Israeli intelligence people were very thorough. We came to know that there were two photographs with each of our files. One was a copy of the original picture – that is to say the photograph of how we looked when we entered the universities and colleges in Europe. The other was the same picture but with a drawing of a *kaffiyeh* on the head. By wearing the *kaffiyeh* you can easily transform your appearance. The Israelis were obviously expecting us to do that. Once the Israelis had all this information about us it was not so difficult for them to track us down when the action started.' After a pause Hani added: 'Nearly ninety per cent of my student fighters were killed or captured.'

The Israelis also forced some Fatah prisoners to identify and so betray their colleagues. According to Hani and others who were involved in the West Bank and Gaza campaign in the last four months of 1967, the Israelis sometimes employed 'Gestapo tactics'. Some Fatah prisoners were taken to their village and home-town areas. There, with their faces covered by hoods with eye-slits, they were made to identify their friends and associates who were members of Fatah. Those who were reluctant to do what the Israelis wanted were threatened with death or harm to their families – their womenfolk in particular – if they did not co-operate.

If the results were all that mattered, Israel's security chiefs had good reason to congratulate themselves on the efficiency of their counter-insurgency operation. One thing they failed to do was to capture or kill Arafat himself. And that was not for the want of trying.

How many times he was nearly captured is a matter Arafat prefers to keep to himself. His reluctance to talk in any detail about his escapes in the occupied territories is probably due to the fact that there may well come a time in the future when he has to go underground again. Arafat himself told me about only two of his escapes. The first was the time when he slipped through an Israeli cordon on the arm of the wife of one of his colleagues, carrying the baby of another. The other occurred in East Jerusalem. Said Arafat: 'I was intending to pass the night in one of our safe houses there. I arrived at the place disguised as an old man. In the entrance I stopped for some few seconds. Then I said, "No, no, I don't like it." And I left immediately. Less than thirty minutes later Israeli soldiers

surrounded the area and they entered the place where I would have
been staying. You can say that was one of many occasions when I
was saved by what you call my nose for danger!'

From what Abu Jihad and others said my guess is that Arafat had
at least a dozen lucky escapes in those four months. On one
occasion he passed through an Israeli roadblock in a U.N. vehicle
driven by a friend. That was one of several moments when the
Israelis had him in the bag and did not know it. Another was when
he was travelling in a bus disguised as a shepherd. Israeli police
stopped and searched the vehicle and its passengers but they were
not interested in the shepherd.

Good luck certainly played a part in helping Arafat to evade
capture. But so also did his own security precautions. He was a
master of disguise and he travelled or moved about under a number
of different names. He was at various times Abu Amar, Abu
Mohammed, the Doctor, Dr Husseini and Abdul Rauf.

Arafat's West Bank days came to an end when Abu Jihad in
Damascus was convinced that at least one of Arafat's inner circle
was an Israeli informer. Abu Jihad placed the evidence before a
number of his Central Committee colleagues, including Khalad
Hassan, and they decided to send a snatch-squad to pull Arafat out.
It seems that Arafat was left with no choice. He was, in fact, ordered
to leave. It also seems that he made his move only minutes before the
Israelis surrounded the house in Ramallah where he was staying.
According to Ehud Yaari's account: 'The Israeli security forces
encircled the villa and broke into it. They found a warm bed and
boiling tea but Arafat was not there.'[26] Beaten by the Israelis and
effectively rejected by the Palestinians living under Israeli
occupation, he was on his way to Damascus.

Seven years later Arafat was the leader of those who were
cautiously advocating and trying to sell the idea of a political and
compromise settlement with Israel – a settlement which a majority
of Palestinians in the occupied territories would have accepted in
the second half of 1967. This fact prompts a question that needs to
be answered here. In the months and years following the Arab
defeat of June 1967, was Arafat wrong to have insisted that the
struggle be continued by military means when it was clear that a
majority of Palestinians in the occupied territories were ready for
compromise?

In my judgment Arafat was not wrong, for the reasons he gave me himself: 'From the very beginning I was saying that it was only by fighting that we Palestinians could fix our identity. So far as I was concerned there was no point in discussing a solution to our problem until we had demonstrated that it was a problem which would not go away. After the Six-Day War the Arab governments and the big powers were still of the opinion that the so-called Arab-Israeli conflict could be settled by ignoring the wishes and the *rights* of the Palestinian people. We had to prove they were wrong.'

That Arafat was right was obvious to any informed and objective observer when, on 22 November, the international community accepted U.N. Resolution 242 as the basis for a just and lasting peace to the Arab-Israeli conflict.

Since 242 is a short resolution, and also because it is not possible to discuss what happened after 1967 without frequent reference to it, I quote the text in full:

The Security Council,
Expressing its continuing concern with the grave situation in the Middle East,
Emphasizing the inadmissibility of the acquisition of territory by war and the need to work for a just and lasting peace in which every State in the area can live in security,
Emphasizing further that all Member States in their acceptance of the Charter of the United Nations have undertaken a commitment to act in accordance with Article 2 of the Charter
1. Affirms that the fulfilment of Charter principles requires the establishment of a just and lasting peace in the Middle East which should include the application of both the following principles:
    (1) Withdrawal of Israeli forces from territories occupied in the recent conflict;
    (2) Termination of all claims or states of belligerency and respect for and acknowledgement of the sovereignty, territorial integrity and political independence of every State in the area and their right to live in peace within secure and recognized boundaries free from threats or acts of force;
2. Affirms further the necessity
    (a) For guaranteeing freedom of navigation through international waterways in the area;
    (b) For achieving a just settlement of the refugee problem;
    (c) For guaranteeing the territorial inviolability and political

independence of every State in the area, through measures including the establishment of demilitarized zones;

3. Requests the Secretary-General to designate a Special Representative to proceed to the Middle East to establish and maintain contacts with the States concerned in order to promote agreement and assist efforts to achieve a peaceful and accepted settlement in accordance with the provisions and principles of this resolution;

4. Requests the Secretary-General to report to the Security Council on the progress of the efforts of the Special Representative as soon as possible.[27]

The above is what the governments of the world, most notably the big powers, proudly proclaimed to be the formula for a just and lasting peace in the Middle East. Resolution 242 was a victory for political expediency. It was also the product of the international community's surrender to Israel's will and arrogance. And if it was a formula for anything, it was one that gave Israel and the Arab states the opportunity to bury the real Palestine problem once and for all — and to do that with the support and grateful thanks of those who ruled the world. Resolution 242 was a recipe for disaster for everyone involved. How men and women of intellect and knowledge could have seen it as anything else is beyond my understanding. Those who promoted 242 as a formula for peace were either ignorant of certain essential facts about the Palestine problem, or they were knowingly inviting Israel and the Arab states to bury it.

Resolution 242 as it stood was not and could not be the basis for a just and lasting peace because it ignored the problem at the heart of the conflict. The question 242 addressed was how to prevent Israel and the front-line Arab states from having another war. The West's main concern about another war was not the death and destruction it would cause, but the oil supply and price crisis it would provoke which would play havoc with the global economy. The question that ought to have been asked and answered was one concerning the rights of the Palestinians and how they were to be satisfied. By presenting the Palestine problem as a 'refugee problem' and all that was implied by those two words, 242 implicitly denied that the Paletinians had a claim or right to self-determination. For that reason it can be said that 242 was one-sided. It was in favour of Israel and against the rights of Palestinians. By implication it also cancelled an earlier U.N. resolution which called for the Palestinians to be allowed to return to their homes in Israel.

In practice this infamous resolution had two main effects. It gave a degree of international legitimacy to Israel's refusal to come to terms with the real Palestine problem – except with bullets and bombs. And it confirmed Arafat's diagnosis that the international community, the big powers in particular, did not give a damn about the Palestinians and their demand for justice.

The irony was that at the end of 1967 Arafat was in no position to challenge Israel's arrogance and the indifference of the international community because he had failed to generate popular support for the idea of armed struggle in the occupied territories. To say that the Palestine cause was more dead than alive at this time would be a considerable understatement. By all that was logical, Arafat and what he represented ought to have been finished. He probably would have been if Israel had not given him the opportunity to make a new start.

# 13

# A Taste of Victory

At the beginning of 1968 Arafat had his sights set on one objective — keeping the *idea* of struggle alive.

Though the Arab leaders who met at Khartoum had rejected negotiations and peace with Israel, Arafat knew there was a world of difference between their publicly stated positions and their private ones. The Arab leaders who mattered would make peace with Israel as soon as they obtained a deal which they could present to their peoples as being something less than a total surrender. They were counting on the U.S. to force Israel to make the minimum necessary concessions. Arab leaders were, in fact, working on the assumption that American decision-makers would be wise enough to understand that they needed the moderate Arabs at least as much as they needed Israel if long-term U.S. and other Western interests in the region were to be secured. Arafat also knew that King Hussein was not waiting for the Americans. He had already established his own secret channel of communication with Israel.

Arafat was deeply pessimistic about his chances of keeping the idea of struggle alive. Back in Damascus after his escape from the West Bank, he had his expectations confirmed. There was no way the Syrian regime was going to allow Fatah the freedom to make attacks on Israel from Syrian soil. That left Fatah with little choice. It would have to make use of the Lebanon or Jordan or both. Without too much discussion Fatah's leaders quickly decided that the Lebanon should be used only as a launchpad of last resort.

Lebanon's status as a non-combatant was accepted throughout

the Arab world. Since 1948 the Lebanese had devoted their money and energies to developing their country. As a consequence Beirut had become the Geneva of the Middle East; and on the surface the whole of this beautiful land was close to being a paradise on earth. It was also the playground for wealthy but frustrated Arabs, and many Europeans, too. So the Lebanon had no defence force to speak of. If Fatah made a habit of launching attacks on Israel from the Lebanon, the Lebanese would be utterly defenceless against Israel's inevitable reprisal attacks. And that would mean, in time, that the Lebanese, Christians and Moslems, would turn against the Palestinians — the refugees in their midst and those who were fighting for Palestinian rights. That was not a situation Arafat and his colleagues wanted to provoke. As Khalad Hassan said: 'We knew the Lebanon couldn't take it.'

Another reason why Arafat and his colleagues were not anxious to involve the Lebanon was to do with the fact that the Lebanon was heading for civil war. The population balance was changing. The day was coming when the Moslems would be the majority. If the Christian minority did not then agree to share more of its power, a civil war would be inevitable. To Arafat and his colleagues the implications were profound. If they involved the Lebanon in their struggle, they might be responsible for triggering the civil war. In any event they would get the blame for whatever did happen. Said Khalad: 'It was so clear to us all that we Palestinians had everything to lose and nothing to gain from adding to the deep-rooted problems which we knew were threatening the Lebanon's very existence. In Fatah we were also convinced that Israel would take advantage of any trouble in the Lebanon to grab more Arab land.'

In the middle of January 1968, Arafat and his colleagues decided that Jordan would have to be the launchpad for hit-and-run attacks against Israel. But to minimize the risk of an early and serious confrontation with Hussein's regime it was agreed that Fatah would not attempt to create fixed bases. The commando units were to be small and mobile. Said Abu Jihad: 'Our plan was to use a cave here, a house there and so on.' At the time, Arafat probably had no more than 300 to 400 fighters (or *fedayeen* as they were called) at his disposal. The border area of southern Lebanon was to be used only when Fatah was being squeezed in Jordan by Hussein, the Israelis, or both.

First Arafat and his men had to get access to Jordan. Said Khalad Hassan: 'We made our infiltration disguised as Iraqi soldiers. We entered in Iraqi vehicles. We wore Iraqi uniforms. And we carried Iraqi identity papers. Once inside we became Fatah again – but we kept our Iraqi uniforms and identity papers ready to wear and to use if we were in danger of being captured!'

Hussein meanwhile was under great and mounting pressure from Israel to deny Fatah and other Palestine liberation groups sanctuary in what remained of his kingdom. He had been left in no doubt that the Israelis were holding him responsible for any border violations, and that Israel was ready and willing to punish Jordan if he failed to control the Palestinians. As he later told me himself, Hussein was 'sickened' by Israel's arrogance and its refusal to make any allowance for the precariousness of his own position. There were already signs that many Palestinians in Jordan's armed forces, some of them senior officers, were in a mood to rebel. The problem at the time was not so much that they were in sympathy with Arafat and his way. The real cause of their disaffection was simply the fact they were treated as second-class citizens in the armed forces of a country to which they were totally loyal, despite the fact that they were Palestinians.

'The truth is that we were hated by our fellow Jordanian officers. And because fear was the basis of their hatred, they denied us promotion and generally treated us with total contempt because we were, they said, "traitors" or "potential traitors". We were at the time 100 per cent loyal to His Majesty and we intended to remain so; but we were also reaching the limits of what we were prepared to take in the way of abuse and contempt from those Jordanians who were running the armed forces in the King's name.' Those are the words of a very senior former Palestinian officer who served in Jordan's air force. He is today one of Arafat's most trusted lieutenants. He asked not to be named because his wife and family still live in Jordan.

From the beginning of 1968 Hussein was walking a tightrope, and he was desperate enough to do anything to avoid provoking the arrogant and aggressive Israelis. He knew there were fanatics in Israel who believed that all of Jordan should be incorporated into the Jewish State, and he did not want to give them their chance. So in February, and to signal to the Israelis that he would try his best to contain Fatah and other Palestinian action groups, Hussein announced that he was taking 'firm and forceful' steps to deal with the *fedayeen*, and that Jordan would regard the despatch of Palestinian sabotage groups from its soil as an 'unparalleled crime'.

The King's announcement was not quite a declaration of war, but it did mark the start of a Jordanian offensive against Fatah units wherever they could be found. Arafat and Abu Jihad were worried but not unduly alarmed by this latest turn of the screw. They had been expecting it and they knew they had two things going for them. The first was that Jordan's armed forces were in no shape for a serious confrontation. It would be some time before they were re-organized and re-equipped following the beating they had taken in the Six-Day War. The second was that Fatah could count on its sympathizers within Jordan's armed forces for certain kinds of help.

An example of the help Fatah did, in fact, receive from this quarter was given to me by Abu Jihad. 'Soon after the King's announcement a Palestinian officer in the Jordan army informed us that one of our temporary or mobile camps was to be attacked in the night. When darkness came we withdrew from our place and surrounded the area. Later in the night the Jordanian unit that was supposed to attack us walked into our trap. We said: "Why are you here? What do you want?" The Jordanian officer in command said, "We thought you were Israelis. You are *fedayeen*. It's okay. We are friends." And they left us.

'In February and early March we had a number of clashes with the Jordanian army and the border police, but it was clear to us that they didn't really want to fight. The highest officers, the King's uncle in particular, would have killed us on sight. But many of the ordinary Jordanian soldiers who faced us were not then of the same way of thinking. At the time they were not against us. They just didn't want any trouble.'

Although it was not Arafat's intention to establish fixed bases, a lesson he had learned from his disastrous West Bank campaign, by the end of February Fatah was in fact firmly established in its first fixed base on the East Bank. It was a refugee camp with a name that was shortly to appear in headlines around the world. The story of how Fatah came to be there was told to me by Abu Jihad.

'Before the event I am going to tell you about, this particular refugee camp was like many others in Jordan – a useful transit stop

for our fighters, a place where they could rest among friends
between missions. At the end of February a special force of
Jordanian soldiers entered the camp. They had a list of names and
they arrested some of our fighters who happened to be there
relaxing. Immediately some of the refugees began to organize a
demonstration. They ran to every place calling on the people to
come. Some went to the mosque and shouted from the loudspeaker
there. Within a very short time the Jordanian soldiers were
surrounded. The people were shouting, "Release our fighters,
release our fighters."'

The previous November a number of children from this
particular refugee camp had been killed by Israeli mortar and
fragmentation bombs in what Western military attachés who later
visited the scene described as a reprisal attack, which had hit its
intended target with 'scientific accuracy'. The mortars had fallen in
the main street and had hit the police post, the ration centre and the
girls' school. The attack had started just as the girls were leaving
their school building. As a consequence of that attack the people of
the camp had ceased to believe that Jordan's armed forces either
could or would protect them; and they had come to look upon the
*fedayeen* as their only defenders.

Abu Jihad continued: 'The people of the camp were very angry
and very emotional but they were not violent. They just went on
making their demonstration by shouting slogans. When the
Jordanian commander saw there was nothing he could do, he
released our fighters. Then he led his men out of the camp. What
happened next was completely spontaneous. The people declared
their camp to be a "liberated area"; and without any orders from
Arafat or me some of our fighters started to bring their heavy
weapons to the camp. They were no longer afraid to display them.
The people of the camp said "Come and defend us," and the fighters
responded.'

Later Arafat visited the refugee camp. He was moved to tears by
the spirit of resistance he found there. The name of the place was
Karameh. It means 'dignity'. He decided to make his headquarters
there.

I asked Arafat if some sixth sense had told him that a moment of
destiny was approaching. He seemed to be amazed by my question.
'That is exactly what I was feeling,' he said.

On 18 March, several Israeli children were wounded when their schoolbus hit a Fatah mine. A doctor travelling with them was killed. According to the Israeli scorecard, it was the thirty-seventh act of sabotage and murder carried out by Palestinian terrorists based in Jordan. In all, six Israelis had been killed and forty-four wounded.

That Israel would launch a big reprisal attack was taken for granted. Said Abu Jihad: 'Many Palestinians passed by Karameh to tell us what they were seeing with their own eyes – Israeli troops and armour massing in Jericho and on the road from Jerusalem. In their newspapers and on their radio the Israelis were also declaring that there would soon be an attack on terrorist bases in Jordan. We asked ourselves why the Israelis were making their intentions so obvious. From the military point of view what they were doing was surely not good security.

'Very quickly we realized what Israel's strategy was. In the first place the Israelis were sending a message to Jordan. By showing their hand so openly the Israelis were saying to Hussein and his forces the following: "We mean business. We intend to smash Fatah. If you get in our way we'll smash you, too." By this tactic the Israelis were hoping to persuade Jordan to stay out of the fight.

'With us the Israelis were playing a much more clever game – or so they thought. They knew the rules of guerrilla warfare as well as we did. Rule number one is that a guerrilla force does not stand and fight a regular army. So the Israelis were thinking that we would follow the rules. And if we did withdraw just before they attacked, they would not have the opportunity to kill or capture us so easily and in such great numbers. In short they were challenging us to break the rules of guerrilla warfare and to stand and fight. With all the world publicity that was focused on the situation at the time, because of the Israeli build-up, they calculated that we could not afford to be seen as cowards who ran away. So they believed there was a good chance that we would stand and fight for the sake of our credibility. And that meant that they could finish us. They believed we were rabbits and that we were no match for the mighty and all-powerful Israeli war machine. As a matter of fact, Moshe Dayan told reporters in Israel that the fighting, when it started, would be all over in a very few hours. He promised to parade captured terrorist leaders in Jerusalem.'

Fatah did decide to stand and fight.

Said Arafat: 'While the Israelis were making their preparations, Abu Iyad and I went to talk with the commander of the Iraqi forces in Jordan. He told us it was obvious that the Israelis were preparing a very big invasion force and that Karameh was to be the main target of their attack. I said we knew that. Then he advised us to follow the rules of guerrilla warfare and withdraw to the mountains. He said: "You cannot face them. It is impossible. Withdraw and let their ploy be in vain." And he offered to help us make our withdrawal.' The Jordanians later gave Arafat the same advice.

Arafat continued: 'I thanked the Iraqi commander for his advice and then I said the following: "After the Arab defeat of 1967, there must be some group to give an example to the Arab nation. There must be some group who can prove that there are people in our Arab nation who are ready to fight and to die. So I am sorry. We will not withdraw. We will fight and we will die.'

On the evening of 20 March, Arafat addressed his fighters. 'We were some 297 persons to be exact,' he told me. 'Many were young boys. Really some of them were children still.'

It was one of the child fighters who asked if they could defeat the Israelis. Said Arafat: 'I tried to laugh but really I wanted to cry. I answered: "No, my brave one, we cannot defeat them. We are less than 300 and they will be many thousands who are equipped with the latest American tanks and other weapons. We cannot defeat them but we can teach them a lesson."'

By all accounts Arafat made the speech of his life. But it was not the speech of a commanding general or a politician. 'He was speaking from his heart and as the head of the Palestinian family,' said Abu Jihad. And that is when Arafat can move mountains.

On the evening of 20 March, Arafat was asking his fighters to die for their cause. He told them: 'The Arab nation is watching us. We must shoulder our responsibility like men, with courage and dignity. We must plant the notion of steadfastness in this nation. We must shatter the myth of the invincible army.'

Shortly before midnight Abu Jihad left Karameh. He told me, 'It was decided that I should go to Damascus to collect some anti-tank weapons and some R.P.G.s.'

How was the morale of the defenders of Karameh on that night?

'Really it was unbelievable,' Arafat told me. 'They were speaking as though we were the invincible army and that it was the Israelis who were the small and insignificant group.'

And what were Arafat's own thoughts on that night? Was his decision to stand and fight really just another tactic, a response to the opportunity and the needs of the moment? Or did he believe he and Fatah could somehow survive the coming battle?

I put these questions to Arafat. His reply was the following. 'Really I was not making any calculation of the kind you suggest. My only objective was to teach the Israelis a lesson and to give the Arab nation an example. To tell you the truth, I was not expecting that any of us would be alive after the battle of Karameh.'

There, I believe, is part of the real reason why Abu Jihad left Karameh. I think Arafat believed he would die fighting at Karameh. And my guess is that he begged Abu Jihad to absent himself from the battlefield in order that he should survive to take over the military leadership.

At five o'clock on the morning of 21 March, while Abu Jihad was asleep in Damascus, the Israelis struck. They crossed the River Jordan at various points along a fifty-mile front. But the main ground force headed straight for Karameh. Israeli helicopters had meanwhile landed paratroopers at Karameh's back door. They were advancing from the rear. Israel's battle plan was now clear. Karameh was to be surrounded. Fatah's end was near. For once Arafat and the Israelis were thinking the same thoughts.

One of the first Israeli paratroopers to set foot in Karameh later described it as looking like a ghost town. 'On loudspeakers we called on the inhabitants to come out with raised hands to the square in front of the mosque, but we seemed to be talking to the walls.'[28] At this point it is very likely that the Israelis were confused and not a little anxious. According to their latest intelligence information, Fatah and its military leadership were bottled up in Karameh. Had Israel's famed intelligence services got it wrong? Had Fatah slipped away in the night?

To his own battle plan Arafat had given a lot of thought. The Israelis were not to be engaged until they were inside Karameh. And the key to it all was hitting Israel's armour. If Fatah could take out some of their tanks, the Israelis would have a psychological problem or two. Arafat had a theory, which time has proved to be more right than wrong, that on a man-for-man basis the Israelis were no better than any other well-motivated fighter once they were denied, or could not take advantage of, their superior military hardware – their tanks and fighter aircraft in particular.

And then it happened. Said Arafat: 'Our fighters, our children, they came up from their secret places and they threw themselves at the Israeli tanks. Some climbed onto the tanks and put grenades inside them. Others had sticks of dynamite strapped to their bodies.'

The impact of what happened next was to change the course of history. The Israelis leapt from the tanks which had been hit and ran for cover and their lives.

That was, of course, only the beginning of the battle of Karameh. The Israelis recovered from their shock and slowly they began to make their overwhelming superiority of numbers and fire power count. Then, at about eleven o'clock, when a third of Arafat's fighters were dead, the Jordanians joined the battle.

Under the cover of Jordanian artillery fire, Arafat and his fighters withdrew to new positions around a temporary field H.Q. which Abu Jihad had established on his return from Damascus via Amman. On hand were fresh supplies of ammunition – including the R.P.G.s and anti-tank weapons Arafat had asked for – as well as water, food and blankets, and reinforcements.

Abu Jihad said: 'We started to receive our fighters from Karameh at about two o'clock in the afternoon. When Arafat arrived with Abu Iyad and Abu Lutuf we made plans to continue the fighting. We sent small groups to hit the Israelis behind their lines.'

Late in the day the Israelis decided to cut their losses and withdraw. Their casualties were twenty-eight killed and ninety wounded. The other evidence that the Israelis had been given a bloody nose was the eighteen tanks they were obliged to abandon on the battlefield. According to Arafat and Abu Jihad, Fatah's losses were ninety-three killed and 'many' wounded. Um Jihad told me they were at the time afraid to announce the number of their dead. Jordan's losses were put at 128 killed and wounded.

Many Palestinians believe that the Jordanian involvement was completely spontaneous and came about because Jordanian officers with a grandstand view of the battle let their hearts rule their heads when they saw what was happening. According to this theory, which I think Abu Jihad wanted me to accept, the Jordanians were motivated by their admiration for Arafat and his fighters, and their own sense of shame that the Palestinians were fighting alone. My guess is that Abu Jihad talked the Jordanians into laying down an artillery barrage to give Arafat and his men the opportunity to withdraw, and that the battle simply developed a new momentum of its own once the Jordanians did open fire.

In any event, Arafat and his fighters would very likely have been killed or captured if the Jordanians had not intervened. But such a conclusion in no way diminishes Fatah's triumph. In the context of the whole story of the Palestinian struggle, no battle was more important than the one that took place at Karameh. If Arafat had been defeated there the Palestinian cause would have been lost. That is certainly Arafat's judgment.

Instead, the *fedayeen* became the heroes of the Arab world. Overnight Palestinians everywhere hailed Fatah's 'victory' at Karameh as the 'resurrection' of the Palestinian people. And Arabs everywhere were deeply impressed. They were also relieved and thankful. Karameh did not take away the burden of shame that all Arabs had carried since 1948, and to which a great weight was added in 1967; but Karameh did make the burden lighter and more easy to bear.

Fatah was set to make a comeback. And it was Israel that had given it the opportunity to do so.

Israel's Karameh operation was not a total failure, however. What the Israelis did at Karameh was to establish a new and outrageous norm for their behaviour. From this point on Western governments and media institutions simply accepted, often without regret, that invading other countries was Israel's way.

# 14

# The Dawn of Reality

The Arafat who rose from what should have been his grave was
much more powerful than the pre-Karameh man. For one thing his
hold on Fatah was much more secure. Said Hani Hassan: 'After
Karameh we continued to say that we were a collective leadership.
And in many important ways we were. But after Karameh it was
accepted by all of the founding fathers, the historical leaders as we
call them, that nothing could stop Arafat from becoming the
dominating personality.'

'You mean that after Karameh nobody could challenge Arafat for
the leadership and expect to win,' I said.

He smiled. 'Yes,' he replied, 'that is what I really mean.'

Khalad bowed gracefully to the inevitability of Arafat's swift rise
to power as the first among equals in the collective leadership. He
did so partly because it was inevitable; and partly because he was
beginning to realize that his hatred of the 'coup mentality' and his
dedication to democracy had caused him to misread Arafat's
character and personality. Arafat's decision to fight and die at
Karameh was dramatic proof that Arafat was a man of cause. If he
had been the power-hungry dictator of Khalad's private fears, he
would not have prepared himself for martyrdom. Khalad was the
first of the majority of Fatah's leaders who had opposed Arafat to
perceive that he was, in fact, a remarkable human being who just
might have what it was going to take to inspire the Palestinians to
pursue the struggle – alone if necessary and no matter what the cost.

The first transfer of real political power to Arafat came after a conversation between Khalad Hassan and Abu Iyad. The conversation took place in Khalad's house in Kuwait after the Central Committee had decided it was time to appoint an official spokesman. 'You have to remember that we were still a secret organization,' Khalad said. 'Our faces and our real names were not known.'

The choice was between Arafat and Abu Jihad. The final decision was left to Khalad and Abu Iyad, the two men who had done most to block Arafat's way after the Six-Day War. Khalad told me he did not express a personal preference for one or the other. Later the same day Abu Iyad issued a statement that the leader known as Abu Amar was Yasser Arafat, and that he was to be Fatah's official spokesman.

Arafat learned of his appointment from a radio news bulletin. He did not tell me about his feelings but I imagine he was relieved that the confrontation with Khalad and the majority of his colleagues on the Central Committee was over.

If the job had gone to Abu Jihad, as it easily could have done, he and not Arafat would probably be the Chairman of the P.L.O. today.

The first fruits of Fatah's triumph at Karameh were ready for picking before the celebrations were over. Said Abu Jihad: 'The day after the battle, and for the next three days from seven o'clock in the morning until nine o'clock in the evening, I sat under a tree in Salt. I had only my notebooks and some pencils. My job was to take the names and addresses of the thousands of volunteers who came to join Fatah. In those three days we received close to 5,000.' Over the course of the next eighteen months or so, a further 25,000 volunteers joined Fatah to fight.

The rush of recruits was too much for Fatah's fledgling and still rather amateur counter-intelligence service. Said Abu Iyad: 'After Karameh the Israelis dumped hundreds of agents and spies on us — Palestinians they recruited on the West Bank and in Gaza mainly by intimidation and blackmail. They used our men, our women and even our children. The youngest one I interviewed was eleven years old. Undoubtedly some of the agents and spies who were among us did give vital information which enabled Israel's air force to make very accurate attacks on our bases. But we also came to know that many of our people were being forced to act as traitors.'

I asked Abu Iyad how he came to know. He replied: 'Very simple. They came and told us. They said, for example, that they had been taken to such-and-such a place and taught how to use invisible inks for preparing their secret messages. But as a result of Israel's game we also had our opportunity. We told some of our people to continue to spy for the Israelis, but only to give the information we prepared. So we created many double-agents. In this way we were able to feed the Israelis wrong information. And some of the information we received back from our double-agents helped us to anticipate Israel's moves. We also opened a reform and rehabilitation school to deal with the problem of the Israeli agents and spies. It was for those who had been brainwashed by the Israelis. At the school we washed their brains again and it was a kind of intellectual fight.'

An early warning of how easy it was for Israel's various intelligence agencies to reach out and touch Fatah's leaders came soon after Karameh when a letter-bomb found its way to Abu Jihad's desk. It was addressed to him and Abu Sabri, another Fatah Central Committee member. Said Um Jihad: 'Abu Sabri was on the point of opening it when Abu Jihad shouted, "No, no, stop! Give it to me." He made just a small opening and he saw enough to know it was a bomb. He was on his way to a meeting with the other leaders, so he gave an order for the bomb to be left under a tree. They defused it after the meeting.'

More evidence of how support for Fatah was growing in the Palestinian diaspora was given to me by Abu Jihad. 'Within a day or two of the battle of Karameh many cars and trucks began to arrive at our new headquarters in Salt. They were bringing us presents of blankets, clothes and food from Palestinian communities across the Arab world. From these gifts we had enough food to feed our fighters, including the new recruits, for three months.'

It was from these spontaneous expressions of non-violent support for the Palestine resistance movement that a whole range of ancillary services was developed as the Palestinian diaspora became involved in the struggle. There was a development explosion as Palestinian schools, Palestinian clinics, Palestinian hospitals and Palestinian orphanages were established. With these came a Palestinian bureaucracy. There was also a revival of Palestinian culture. The regeneration of the Palestinian people was under way.

A key factor in the process was the dramatic change in Fatah's standing and relationship with Egypt and Jordan. Until the Arab defeat of 1967 the regimes in those two countries were more or less at war with Fatah. For reasons of their own they were as anxious as Israel and the big powers to prevent a resurgence of Palestinian nationalism. Every attempt that Khalad Hassan and other Fatah leaders had made to establish a dialogue with Nasser was blocked by Egypt's intelligence chiefs. The Arab defeat of 1967 gave Fatah the opportunity to try again.

This time the circumstances were more favourable because many of Nasser's political colleagues realized that a defeated Egypt needed Fatah. Khalad explained: 'Immediately after the war I met with Mahmoud Riad, the Foreign Minister. I told him it was a tragedy that we had been prevented from getting to Nasser before the war; and I said it was imperative that we did now meet him to discuss a joint strategy. So I asked Riad to persuade Nasser to meet our leadership. Riad said he would do his best and he was also very, very frank about his own feelings. He begged us to make some military operations in the newly-occupied territories. Such action was necessary, he said, to distract the attention of the Egyptian and other Arab masses. If we didn't focus their attention on the idea of continuing struggle, the masses would turn against their regimes.'

Riad failed to persuade Nasser to meet any of Fatah's leaders. Because his intelligence chiefs were still telling him lies, Nasser continued to be convinced that Fatah was his enemy and that Arafat intended to kill him.

The man who caused the door to Nasser to be opened was Lotfik El-Khouli. He told me: 'At the time I was the editor of a magazine which was the organ of all the socialist forces in the Arab world, and I had just been released from prison. In those days I was in and out of prison like a yo-yo because the people around Nasser didn't like what I was writing.

'I went to see Heikal and I begged him to persuade Nasser to meet Fatah's leaders. Heikal raised the question of the intelligence reports. I said, "These are nonsense." And I told him I had known several of Fatah's leaders since the days when the Bureau de la Palestine was opened in Algiers. I also said that I believed Egypt would lose very much if there was no co-operation with Fatah. I agreed with Heikal that there were big political differences between Nasser and Fatah; but I said I was confident they could be resolved by discussion.

'To cut a long story short, Heikal agreed to ask Nasser to meet Fatah. When Nasser had listened to Heikal he said, "But what you are saying is the opposite of what our intelligence people are telling me." Heikal then made a suggestion. He said to Nasser: "If I meet with some of Fatah's leaders, and if I am convinced that our intelligence reports are wrong, will you then meet with Arafat?" After some thought Nasser replied, "Yes, I will."'

As a result of Heikal's efforts a meeting between Nasser and a four-man Fatah delegation headed by Arafat was scheduled for November 1967. Arafat was to be accompanied by Abu Iyad, Abu Lutuf, who was to become the P.L.O.'s official Foreign Minister, and Abu Hol, who was soon to be responsible for intelligence.

Arafat arrived from the occupied West Bank still wearing his pistol. Nasser's security people demanded that he part with it for the duration of the talks. Arafat refused. It may well be that Nasser's security people were only doing their job and no more. But given how hard Egypt's intelligence chiefs had worked since early 1965 to prevent a Nasser-Fatah meeting, it is not unreasonable to speculate that some in Egypt's intelligence services were intending to provoke an incident which would allow them to cancel the meeting. When Arafat refused to surrender his weapon, Nasser was consulted about what should happen next. He was also advised that under no circumstances should he agree to receive an armed Arafat. Nasser sent word that Arafat was his guest and should be allowed to keep his gun.

Minutes later, Nasser's first words to Arafat were about the pistol. He said: 'My intelligence people are telling me that you insist on bringing your gun because you intend to kill me. At this very moment that is what they are saying.'

Arafat the great actor was more than equal to the challenge of the moment. Very slowly he unbuckled his gun-belt. Then, with both hands, he offered Nasser the belt and the pistol. 'Mr President,' he said, 'your intelligence people are wrong. I offer you my freedom fighter's gun as proof of that fact.'

For the first time Nasser smiled. He replied: 'No. You keep it. You need it, and more.'

Said Lotfik El-Khouli: 'I talked with Arafat and his colleagues straight after the meeting. They told me that when Nasser used the word "more", they knew he was going to support Fatah.'

According to El-Khouli and others, Nasser was 'fascinated' by Arafat. He was also furious with his intelligence chiefs.

After the meeting with Arafat, and when he was alone with his private thoughts, Nasser asked himself a question that was to haunt him until he died. As he later posed it in private conversations with those of Fatah's leaders who became his friends, the question was this: why had his intelligence chiefs lied to him about Arafat and Fatah? Obviously their main intention was to prevent a Nasser-Fatah dialogue. But why?

To Nasser and Fatah's leaders the implication was that at least some of Nasser's top intelligence people were secretly collaborating with, or at least being manipulated by, the C.I.A., and through it the Israeli intelligence agencies, and that their overall game plan was to create a situation which would bring about Nasser's downfall and the cancellation of the Palestine liberation movement. In the countdown to the Six-Day War some of Israel's leaders had left no room for doubts that their main objective was to inflict on Egypt a defeat so humiliating that Nasser would have no choice but to resign. Since Fatah's escalation of the conflict gave them their opportunity, the co-operation between Nasser and Fatah that might have resulted had they met in 1965 or 1966 was clearly not in Israel's interests. The record of what actually happened tells us that Nasser did announce his resignation on 9 June 1967, and that he withdrew it the following day. Informed Israeli sources suggested that an attempted coup had failed.

It is entirely possible that the governments of Israel and the U.S. did not give the plot official sanction. The attitude of both may have been 'Do it, but don't tell us.' Having opposed the British and French attempt to get rid of Nasser with Israel's help in 1956, the U.S. could not afford to be seen to be playing the same game a decade later. And in 1967 the U.S. State Department was convinced that the crisis could be resolved without a war, if Israel was prepared to give diplomacy a little more time. This fact suggests the State Department would not have known, even unofficially, what the C.I.A. were doing.

From Arafat himself I extracted only one on-the-record comment on the subject. He said, 'The Israelis were only part of a very big conspiracy.' Other Fatah leaders suggested that the C.I.A. gave Hussein and the Syrians the tip that the real business of 1967 was to get rid of Nasser. Among other things this could explain why Jordan's propagandists projected Nasser as a coward who was hiding behind U.N.E.F.'s skirts.

Even while he was meeting with Arafat in November 1967, Nasser took steps to make sure that Fatah's leaders would never again find his door to them closed. He told Arafat that Fatah could rely on Heikal if the official channels were blocked. And in Fatah's presence, Heikal was instructed to that effect.

Though it had all the appearances of a political marriage of convenience, Nasser's relationship with Arafat was rooted in a genuine affection which each man had for the other. As Hani Hassan has said, Arafat came to look upon Nasser as a 'father'. But it was not until Karameh that the relationship between Nasser and Arafat, and between Egypt and Fatah, really blossomed. After the battle Arafat was surprised and delighted by a request from Nasser. It asked Fatah to receive a delegation of Egyptian army officers who wanted to study what had happened at Karameh on the battlefield. The delegation came and went; and its visit was followed by an invitation to Arafat and others who had taken part in the battle to lecture at Egyptian military academies.

Said Arafat: 'I myself gave some lectures in Egypt, and I made some arrangements for many of our fighters to talk about their experience and to tell how it was possible to face the Israeli aggression. These were very proud moments for us.'

It was, however, in Jordan that Fatah's immediate gains from Karameh were most apparent. The situation there was transformed overnight. Fatah's presence in Jordan was accepted by the regime as a regrettable fact of life; and the *fedayeen* began to enjoy a freedom of movement that was entirely new to them.

Abu Jihad explained: 'Karameh opened the door for us to be free in Amman. And with this new freedom we opened many more doors. As you know, we didn't have passports because we were officially citizens of nowhere. But after Karameh, and because of the popular support for the *fedayeen*, we were free to travel using only our Fatah identification papers. So without passports we were going from Jordan to Iraq, from Jordan to Syria and the Lebanon, from Jordan to Egypt, from Jordan to Kuwait and Saudi Arabia, from Jordan to Algeria and Tunisia and so on. We were above the ground and free to move. And that meant we were free to organize. It was for us a major breakthrough.'

After Karameh, and because of the extent of popular support for the *fedayeen*, the fact that Fatah did have to be tolerated as a necessary evil, at least for the time being, was accepted even by those around Hussein who were well known for their anti-Palestinian feelings and their willingness to dance to the C.I.A.'s tune. (There has never been a pro-Western Arab leader without a C.I.A. functionary among his ministers and top advisers.)

With no safe ground left on which to manoeuvre, Hussein decided to let events take their course. And while he waited to see what would happen, he entertained two hopes. The first was that he could come to some understanding with Arafat about the scale and conduct of Fatah's military activities. It was now inevitable that Arafat would want to use his new strengths and his new freedom of movement to hit Israel harder. From Jordan. And it followed that Israel would escalate its reprisal attacks. Hussein knew he was powerless to stop these developments. But if he could reach an understanding with Arafat there was at least the chance that they could between them stop events from slipping totally out of control.

Hussein's second hope was that he and Nasser could somehow persuade the U.S. to use its leverage to oblige Israel to withdraw from the Arab territory it had occupied in the Six-Day War. As Hussein saw it at the time, persuading the U.S. to do the right thing ought not to be impossible because the U.S., along with the rest of the international community, was committed to Resolution 242, and it called for Israel to withdraw.

There was a problem in the fact that 242 was open to interpretation. The original draft had called for the withdrawal of Israeli armed forces from *all* territory occupied in the recent conflict. But the Israelis had said they would not accept 242 as a formula for peace if the word 'all' appeared in the final text. Since an earlier point in the resolution emphasized 'the inadmissibility of the acquisition of territory by war', those responsible for drafting 242 in the name of the international community ought to have told the Israelis that the word 'all' was staying in the final text. But they did not do so. Israel was thus able to claim, with apparent justification, that it was not required to withdraw from all occupied territory and that the extent of any Israeli withdrawal was open to negotiation. Israel could sabotage any peace move simply by saying, 'We don't agree to withdraw from here.'

All that Hussein, Nasser and the other Arab leaders had going for them was the willingness of the governments of the world to acknowledge that the spirit of 242 called for a more or less total Israeli withdrawal in return for peace. Hussein was hoping that he and Nasser could persuade the U.S. to oblige Israel to honour the spirit of 242, in which event, as Arafat was soon to learn from Nasser, Jordan and Egypt would make peace with Israel. The only difference between Hussein and Nasser was over what, if anything, could be done for the Palestinians.

Hussein was still quietly confident that the peace that Resolution 242 seemed to offer would give him and the other front-line Arab states the opportunity to extinguish the fire of Palestinian nationalism. The King was sure an easy majority of West Bank Palestinians would be happy to see the end of Israel's occupation, and would therefore welcome the peace which made it possible. In addition Hussein could promise constitutional changes which would give his Palestinian subjects a greater say in the running of their own affairs. A measure of autonomy, perhaps. But under the Jordanian flag, of course. The *fedayeen* might wish to fight on, but if they did, Hussein and the other front-line Arab leaders would be required by their peace treaty obligations to disarm and if necessary destroy them.

Nasser for his part did not dispute the fact that formal peace treaties with Israel would require the front-line Arab leaders to use whatever force was necessary to crush those Palestinians who would still insist on the right to continue their armed struggle. For the sake of peace with Israel, Nasser himself was prepared to use all necessary measures to liquidate Palestinian militarism. But if it came to a final showdown with the *fedayeen*, Nasser did not believe the regimes would win an easy or quick victory – as Hussein seemed to be assuming. The way the Palestinians had fought at Karameh was surely proof of that. In the end, of course, the regimes would triumph, and they would therefore be in a position to guarantee the peace with Israel. But for how long and at what price?

By now Nasser had taken his own measure of Yasser Arafat and he did not need to be convinced that the Fatah leader was, indeed, a man of destiny, and that he and his colleagues in the Fatah leadership would not be stopped until they had obtained at least a measure of justice for their people. The more Nasser thought about it, the more he was convinced that peace on the basis of Resolution 242 would not allow the fire of Palestinian nationalism to be contained. If Arafat and his colleagues and others like them were to be driven underground again, they would make an alliance with every dissident and disaffected element, with every radical and revolutionary group, and with the Moslem Brotherhood and fundamentalists of every kind. That was what Nasser would do in Fatah's place. The Palestinians twice betrayed would be the engine of a real revolution. The Arab regimes who had made their peace with the Jewish State would be swept aside and the Arab world would enter a new Dark Age of chaos and anarchy. That, Nasser feared, was the price the Arabs would eventually pay for a peace that totally ignored the Palestinian claim for justice.

If the peace that came with the implementation of 242 was not to lead to an eventual upheaval in the Arab world, the leaders of the Palestine liberation movement would need to be convinced that the Arab regimes were not washing their hands of the Palestine problem. That meant that even as they were making their peace with Israel the Arab regimes would have to pledge their support for the Palestine liberation struggle. And they could do so only if its leaders were willing to abandon the idea of armed struggle and to continue their fight by political means.

That being the case, there was only one thing Nasser could do. He had to make the effort to persuade Palestinian leaders that they, too, had to face certain realities. And here Nasser was helped by the refusal of the governments of the Western world to give meaning to 242 by requiring the Israelis to make the necessary withdrawal for peace. The delay in implementing the resolution gave Nasser the time to work on the Palestinians in stages. Stage one would see him persuading Palestinian leaders to develop a political programme. Stage two would see him trying to persuade them to put away their guns and to continue their struggle by political means.

After the Six-Day War Nasser had decided that Shuqairi's days as Chairman of the P.L.O. were numbered. His wild rhetoric about annihilating the Jewish State had once served Nasser's purpose.

Now it was nothing but a huge and damaging embarrassment to the Arab cause. After his November meeting with Arafat and his colleagues, Nasser had decided that Fatah should take over the P.L.O. – provided its leaders, Arafat in particular, showed themselves to be practical men who were prepared to come to terms with reality – under Nasser's guidance.

It was at the November meeting that Nasser made his opening move with the suggestion that Fatah's leaders should sit down and work out a political programme which would define the objective of their struggle. In principle this was not an idea that Arafat and his colleagues were enthusiastic about since they did not look upon themselves as leaders in the normal sense of the word. As the 'true democrats' of Khalad Hassan's vision, they saw themselves as the engine of the regeneration and the builders of the democratic institutions which would allow the Palestinian people as a whole to determine policy and to set the final objective of their struggle.

Nasser was not at all impressed by this way of thinking. It was, he told his new Palestinian friends, a sign that they were 'idealists', 'romantics', and 'dreamers'. It was their right to dream, but they had to live in the real world. And if they were truly to serve the interests of their people they had to be practical and draw a distinction between what was desirable and what was attainable. Politics, as the British had said, was the art of the possible. By all accounts Nasser did not offer his own ideas about how realistic Fatah's leaders should be; he knew he could not make decisions for them.

The evidence of how much Arafat and his colleagues allowed themselves to be persuaded by Nasser's arguments was soon available. A few days later a number of Fatah leaders met at Lotfik El-Khouli's house in Cairo. El-Khouli said: 'Among those who came for the discussion were Arafat himself, Abu Iyad and Khalad Hassan. The idea for the meeting was Nasser's – no doubt about that. And so far as I know it was the first time that any of Fatah's leaders addressed themselves to the question of a political programme and what should be in it. I came to know that Nasser's intelligence people bugged the whole discussion. That caused trouble for me because I was very critical of Nasser's refusal to let Egypt be governed in the democratic way. But it was not harmful to Fatah. The transcript showed that Arafat and the others were taking Nasser's advice very seriously.'

Fatah's full response to Nasser's challenge was delivered in Paris on New Year's Day, 1968, in the form of an official statement outlining the organization's ideas for the setting up of a Democratic State of Palestine. The concept was a formula for dismantling the Jewish State by politics; but it was not what the Israelis claimed it to be – an invitation for them to commit suicide. The Democratic State of Fatah's vision was to be one in which Jews and Palestinian Arabs would live as equals and without discrimination. Arabic and Hebrew would be the official languages of the non-sectarian State; and a Jew could be elected President.

Arafat himself put it this way: 'What we in Fatah were telling the world even in those days was so clear, so obvious. We were saying "No" to the Jewish State, but we were saying "Yes" to the Jewish people in Palestine. To them we were saying, "You are welcome to live in our land but on one condition – you must be prepared to live among us as friends and as equals, not as dominators." I myself have always said that there is one and only one guarantee for the safety and security of the Jewish people in Palestine, and that is the *friendship* of the Arabs among whom they live. It is so clear, so obvious.'

Because it required the disappearance of the Jewish State, the Fatah formula for a non-violent solution to the Palestine problem drew only contempt and ridicule from the Israelis. And the international community took its cue from them. Fatah's idea was dismissed out of hand as being not worthy of any serious consideration or study, which was a tragedy for all those involved; there was much that was extremely positive in Fatah's thinking. But also raised was the question of who spoke for the Palestine liberation movement – because Fatah's proposal was also rejected by the P.L.O., of which Fatah was not a member in 1968, and by virtually every other Palestinian action group or front, on the grounds that it was an unthinkable concession. Some of Fatah's critics were willing to accept only those Jews who were living in Palestine up to the moment of Israel's declaration of independence in 1948. Others wanted to put the clock back to 1917, and to accept only those Jews who were in residence on the eve of the Balfour Declaration.

In July, four months after Karameh, the fourth P.N.C. meeting was held in Cairo. It approved seven new articles for inclusion in the Charter. Article 6 stated: 'Jews who were living permanently in

Palestine until the beginning of the Zionist invasion will be considered Palestinians.'[29] So Fatah's concept of the Democratic State was officially rejected by the highest Palestinian decision-making body. But this official rejection of Fatah's vision did not reflect or represent the reality of what was happening in Palestinian politics, not least the fact that Fatah was the only liberation organization with substantial and genuine support among the Palestinian masses. It was therefore more truly representative of the Palestinian people and potentially more powerful than all the delegates from the other organizations put together.

Another fundamental truth about what was really happening in Palestinian politics was explained to me by Khalad Hassan: 'There were two to three million Israelis in Palestine. From the practical point of view it was stupid in 1968 to talk about kicking them out or throwing them into the sea. Those in the other Palestinian organizations who said they were opposed to Fatah's concept of the Democratic State knew in their heads that we were right, and that they also would have to accept the reality we had already faced – the fact that *all* the Jews of Israel would be in our Democratic State.'

At this point, and to make a point, Khalad told me an interesting story: 'One of Fatah's critics at the time was a Palestinian writer who was a very good friend of mine. I asked him why he could not bring himself to write about Fatah's concept of the Democratic State. He said to me the following: "Khalad, I know in my head that you and Arafat are right. In our heads we all know that we have no choice. In our heads we all know that we have got to live with the three million Jews who are in Palestine . . . but the problem is not in our heads – it is in our hearts. And my heart will not let my hand write the words you speak."

'The only real difference between Fatah and most of our Palestinian critics in the other organizations was that we in Fatah were prepared to acknowledge certain realities in public – our critics were not. So we knew that they knew certain realities did have to be faced. And that is why we were confident our concept of the Democratic State would prevail if ever it was put to the test of negotiations.'

Events proved Khalad to be right. When Fatah took control of the P.L.O. in 1969, its concept of the Democratic State did prevail. It was not official policy. That was defined by Article 6. But it was the policy that Fatah was ready, willing and able to deliver, given the opportunity to do so by Israel and the international community.

From the moment Fatah's leaders put up their Democratic State idea for discussion, the international community ought to have seriously questioned Israel's assertion that Arafat and his colleagues were committed to the annihilation of the Jewish people in the Jewish State. But the Western world, as ever, showed that it preferred to believe Fatah's intention was what Israel alleged it to be rather than what Fatah's leaders stated it to be.

With no prospect of any Western political support for their cause, despite the fact that they were beginning to face realities on the ground, Fatah's leaders decided to knock again on Moscow's door. Up to this point the Soviets had shown no interest in the Palestine liberation movement. As we have seen, they in fact urged Nasser to liquidate it; and they had assumed he would succeed. After Karameh, Fatah's leaders were hoping the Soviets would take them more seriously, but Moscow was still not interested in the Palestinian cause and would not receive Arafat or a Fatah delegation.

Said Hani Hassan: 'The Soviets knew that Fatah came from the right. So they had a problem. They could not support us and the local communist parties in the Arab world. We were not communists and the Soviets knew it. That is one point. Another, and this is still today the case, is that Fatah was much too independent for the Soviets. They knew that most of us with influence in Fatah would never compromise our independence by allowing ourselves to dance to Moscow's tune. So they knew they could not exploit most of us for their own purposes. In the circumstances it would have been surprising if the Soviets had seen Fatah as a natural or useful ally.'

On the subject of why Fatah's leaders were so anxious to establish a relationship with the Soviet Union in the summer of 1968, Khalad Hassan said the following: 'To get the support of the international community for our cause it was our wish and our policy to have relations with every country – in the West and the East. But because we were ourselves beginning to be educated about the reality of international politics, we realized that we couldn't expect to advance our cause without the support of at least one of the two superpowers. We had knocked on the door of the U.S. and its Western allies and we had received no answer, so we wanted to try with the Soviets. We had no choice. We also knew that we could not expect to open any doors in Eastern Europe until Moscow gave its allies the green light.'

Nasser was pleased by the speed with which Fatah had responded to his suggestion that it should define the objective of the liberation struggle in order to get itself, with his backing, a share of the political action. And he was the first to appreciate that Fatah's leaders had taken a huge step down the road to reality by acknowledging that the physical presence of three million Jews in Palestine was a fact of life that had to be lived with. He now had to persuade Arafat that there was nothing to be gained, and perhaps much to be lost, by continuing with the fiction that liberation – even as it was now defined by Fatah – could be achieved through armed struggle. Before Karameh, the task of persuading Arafat to accept such a proposition would have been daunting enough, as Khalad Hassan and others knew from experience. After Karameh, Nasser assumed it was going to be much more difficult. Evidence of growing support for the military way had been reflected in the decisions of the fourth P.N.C. As well as officially rejecting Fatah's concept of the Democratic State, P.N.C. delegates had approved an amendment to the Charter, which was embodied in Article 9. It stated the following: 'Armed struggle is the only way to liberate Palestine. Thus it is the overall strategy, not merely a tactical phase. The Palestine Arab people assert their absolute determination and firm resolution to continue their armed struggle and to work for an armed popular revolution for the liberation of their country and their return to it. They also assert their right to normal life in Palestine and to exercise their right to self-determination and sovereignty over it.'

And there was more. Article 21 stated: 'The Arab Palestinian people, expressing themselves by the armed Palestinian revolution, reject all solutions which are substitutes for the total liberation of Palestine.' Article 28 declared: 'The Palestinian Arab people assert the genuineness and independence of their national revolution and reject all forms of intervention, trusteeship and subordination.'[30]

Nasser did not need to be told that Article 28 was aimed at his developing relationship with Arafat. Nasser was convinced that the P.L.O. without Fatah was setting a course for disaster and he was now determined to execute all the necessary manoeuvres to make certain that Fatah did join the P.L.O. and dominate it in the name of realism. But first he had to persuade Arafat to abandon the idea of armed struggle.

Nasser knew he had to handle Arafat with great care. The Fatah leader would reject any interference in his organization's internal affairs and any encroachment on the independence of Palestinian decision-making. Nasser also knew that if Arafat was to have a remote chance of persuading even his own supporters in the rank and file of the *fedayeen* movement that more could be achieved by politics than fighting, the arguments Arafat would need to employ behind closed doors would carry conviction only if they were the product of his own learning experience. Nasser had discovered Arafat's real secret. It was that he could sell more or less anything to his people – provided he really believed in what he was selling.

In that difficult summer of 1968, when the Israelis were escalating the conflict by using their fighter aircraft as flying artillery to hit *fedayeen* bases in Jordan, Nasser had to find a way of completing Arafat's education by exposing him to the facts of international political life, but leaving him free to draw his own conclusions.

Nasser was about to visit Moscow. He decided to take Arafat with him. But the Egyptian leader could not seek the permission of his Soviet hosts since they were bound to say they had no interest in meeting Arafat. So he arranged for Arafat to travel under the name of Muhsin Amin on an Egyptian passport, as an official member of the Egyptian delegation. Only when they were safely in Moscow would Nasser spring his little surprise on his Soviet hosts. Arafat had no objection to the scheme. He was pleased enough to have the opportunity to start a relationship with Soviet leaders.

In the event the visit did not live up to Arafat's hopes. But it did more than fulfil Nasser's expectations. He had known exactly what the Soviets would tell Arafat. They would say, for openers, that the Soviet Union was committed to the existence of the State of Israel inside its borders as they were on the eve of the Six-Day War. And before Arafat had time to recover from the impact of that bombshell, the Soviets would also tell him they had not the slightest intention of supporting or encouraging Palestinian militarism.

And that, as Arafat himself confirmed to me, was exactly what he was told in Moscow. But not apparently by Soviet leaders.

Chairman Brezhnev, Foreign Minister Kosygin and President Podgorny did not agree to receive Arafat. He told me: 'At the time they were not interested to open a dialogue with me. They were dealing with the situation through Nasser and on the basis of 242. I said that 242 didn't give the Palestinians anything, but the Soviets were all the time stressing their support for a negotiated and peaceful settlement on the basis of 242.'

It was through conversations with members of the Kremlin's Afro-Asian Solidarity Committee that Arafat was informed of the Soviet Union's official position and attitude.

Three weeks later Khalad Hassan and Abu Jihad went to Moscow for follow-up talks with the Afro-Asian Solidarity Committee. According to both men the discussion was 'very tough'. Said Abu Jihad: 'The Soviets were very suspicious about us. They wanted to know everything about our organization. In particular they wanted to know the details of our relationship with China and why and how the Chinese were supplying us with weapons.' It was at this point that Abu Jihad either lost or came close to losing his temper with his Soviet hosts. 'I was angry and I was very direct. I said: "We have knocked on your door not once, but twice. In fact, we have knocked on your door ten times in recent years – and never once have you answered. How can you not understand why we turned to the Chinese for our weapons!"'

Like Arafat before them, Abu Jihad and Khalad Hassan left Moscow with the clear impression that the Palestinians would not receive Soviet support for their cause until they were ready to accept Israel's existence inside the borders as they were on the eve of the Six-Day War.

So in 1968, the Soviets were taking what could effectively be described as a pro-Israel and anti-Palestinian stand. I asked Khalad Hassan how disappointed he and his colleagues in the Fatah leadership were at the time. He replied: 'Emotionally I can say that we were very disappointed and very depressed. But we were also beginning to understand international politics. At one point in our conversation with the Soviets I said the following: "Please let me summarize what I think you are telling us. You are saying there is no way you are going to be drawn into a confrontation with the Americans for the sake of us Palestinians in particular and us Arabs in general." The Soviets were very frank. They replied to the effect that I was understanding them perfectly.

'About our relationship with the Soviet Union as it developed over the years I must tell you something important. The Soviets were always very frank and very honest with us in Fatah. They never, never, never encouraged our armed struggle. And they always, always, always said that Israel should remain and that we Arabs and we Palestinians had to make a political settlement with the Jewish State. We came to respect Soviet leaders for the frank way in which they dealt with us. And we were completely honest with them. They once told me they would rather deal with Fatah's rightists who said they were not communists than with the "adventurer leftists" of our liberation movement.'

Arafat's visit to Moscow was, in effect, the end stop on a journey into reality that had started the previous November when he had travelled to Cairo for his meeting with Nasser. It was time to take stock. Given that both superpowers were committed to Israel's existence and to peace between the Arab states and Israel on the basis of 242, as were Egypt, Jordan, the Lebanon, and probably Syria, too, it was clear that Fatah and the Palestine liberation movement as a whole would be called upon to make a choice between two evils as the peace process gathered momentum.

The first was to work with the Arab regimes who were prepared to make peace with Israel. This option would require the liberation movement to abandon the idea of armed struggle and to continue its fight by political means should Nasser and the other Arab leaders succeed, or at least make headway, in obtaining a measure of justice for the Palestinians. This option required the Palestinian leaders to place an enormous and, at the time, totally unjustifiable faith in the goodwill and competence of the Arab leaders and regimes whose support they needed. It also required the Palestinians, leaders and people, to accept the Arab interpretation of political reality.

The alternative was to oppose a negotiated settlement between the Arab states and Israel on the basis of 242, and to confront those Arab regimes who were in favour of, and working behind the scenes for, just such a settlement. This would require the Palestine liberation movement to set itself up as the vanguard of the first real Arab revolution. The first objective of this revolution would be to overthrow those regimes that were contemplating or who made peace with Israel on the basis of 242. The second and much longer-term objective of the real revolution would be to create a new, radical and united Arab society. It would be led by democratic regimes which, in turn, would be prepared to marshal all their resources – military, economic and political – for a final showdown with Israel and those of its big power allies that supported the Jewish State at the expense of the Arabs. Those who favoured this option argued that basically all that was needed for it to succeed was the Arab will for confrontation and Arab unity to make it possible; the military, economic and political means already existed.

The Israelis would no doubt argue that the Palestinians had a third option – that they should recognize Israel and its right to exist. The trouble with that proposition is that if the Palestinians were to recognize Israel before Israel recognized Palestinian rights to self-determination, the Palestinians would be renouncing their claim to the land that was once theirs; and they would be legitimizing Israel's possession of it. That is the position according to international law. And that is why the Palestinians have not and cannot recognize Israel until Israel recognizes Palestinian rights to self-determination.

As the end of 1968 approached, Arafat and his senior colleagues in Fatah's leadership were secretly reconciled to the idea of putting their trust in Nasser and taking the first option.

Arafat was greatly influenced by his affection for Nasser and his respect for his judgment about what it was possible for the Arabs and the Palestinians to achieve, given that the world was dominated and controlled by foreign powers with a vested interest in Israel's existence regardless of the price the Palestinians and the Arabs were required to pay for it. Arafat's own conclusions were more or less the same as Nasser's. When I was talking with Arafat about the nature of his personal relationship with Nasser, I asked him if it was true that he regarded the Egyptian President as a father. In a voice which told of his affection for Nasser, Arafat replied: 'Oh yes. Oh yes. It was so. And I can say he was dealing with our cause as a Godfather.'

Arafat had not, in fact, changed his mind on the matter of armed struggle and what could be achieved by it. As Father Iyad's evidence makes clear, Arafat had never seriously believed that the Palestinians alone could liberate their country by armed struggle. Though he could not say so in public, he had always looked upon the military way as the means of fixing the Palestinian identity to prevent the Arab regimes, and also the international community, from washing their hands of the Palestine problem. In the beginning Nasser had opposed the idea of an independent Palestine liberation movement and had tried to liquidate it. Now he was ready to back it. And if the price of Nasser's support was a continuation of the struggle by political means – in the event of peace or the prospect of peace between the Arab states and Israel – then so be it. Nasser was a pragmatist and so was Arafat.

Arafat's calculation of the likely cost of taking the second option was another reason for rejecting it. Quite apart from the fact that his own first rule was 'no interference in the internal affairs of the Arab states', a confrontation between the Palestinians and the regimes of the existing Arab order was guaranteed to bring more death, more suffering and more misery to the Palestinian people. Arafat was not prepared to expose his people to more suffering than was absolutely necessary, especially when there was an alternative. From all that I have learned about Yasser Arafat, I am convinced that Hammad Abu Sitta was telling me nothing less than the truth when he said 'Arafat hates bloodshed'. Arafat was by no stretch of the imagination a revolutionary or even a radical leader. The second option was not one that his conservative and middle-class values would allow him to take – except, possibly, as a policy of last resort.

When Arafat and his Fatah colleagues decided that the Palestinian cause would not be well served by a confrontation with the Arab regimes to prevent them making peace with Israel on the basis of 242 – assuming the Israelis wanted peace on that basis – the stage was set for a battle of wills between the head and the heart of the Palestine liberation movement. It was to give its powerful enemies the opportunity to strike in the hope of cancelling for ever the Palestinian factor in the Middle East equation.

# 15

## Conspiracy Everywhere and Catastrophe in Jordan

On 15 September 1970, representatives of the High Command of Jordan's armed forces, each of them fiercely anti-Palestinian, had an audience with King Hussein. The meeting was at the request of the generals. They told the King that unless he gave the order to smash the *fedayeen*, they would confine him to his quarters and do the job without his blessing. Hussein himself later confirmed to me the substance of this story.

According to the way it was reported in the West, the two-part civil war in Jordan was fought to determine who ruled Jordan – Hussein or Arafat. In fact, as the crisis in Jordan was developing, Hussein and Arafat were actually on the same side. Both men were doing all they could to avoid an all-out confrontation, which was being provoked by their own extremists. And both men were aware that American and Israeli agents had their irons in the fire and were doing their bit to guarantee that a crisis within the ranks of the liberation movement became a catastrophe for the Palestinian people.

If it has to be reduced to personalities, the real question at the heart of the confrontation that led to civil war was who ruled the Palestine liberation movement – Yasser Arafat or George Habash? But it was not that simple. Nor was it really a question of personalities.

The division in the liberation movement was about policy. Arafat headed those in the leadership who believed the movement had to work with the front-line Arab regimes even though they were ready to make peace with Israel. Habash was the leader of those who favoured the revolutionary way, and who believed that the revolution had to begin in Jordan – by provoking a confrontation to bring down Hussein. The confrontation that led to civil war was not between a monolithic and homogeneous Palestine liberation movement and the regime in Jordan. It was between a wing of the movement – in terms of numbers a small minority of Palestinian activists – and the regime. The truth is that Arafat lost control of events on his own side soon after he became the Chairman of the P.L.O. And the question that has to be asked is how much was his handling of the division and the crisis within the P.L.O. to blame for a civil war which neither he nor Hussein wanted? Should Arafat have made use of Fatah's vastly superior military strength to suppress the activities of those Palestinian radicals and leftists, a minority in terms of *fedayeen* numbers, who were provoking the confrontation with Hussein's regime?

When Habash recalled his first meeting with Arafat in the Abu Kamal restaurant in Damascus immediately after the Six-Day War, he said, 'From the first conversation it was obvious that Arafat and me would have very different ideas about how to conduct our liberation struggle in the new situation as it existed after the Arab defeat.'

At the end of 1967, Habash and others who believed they could apply the teachings of Marx and Lenin to the struggle formed the Popular Front for the Liberation of Palestine. The P.F.L.P. was a merger of two small guerrilla groups which had been sponsored by Habash's Arab Nationalist Movement and Ahmad Jabril's P.L.F., which was a front for Syrian Military Intelligence. In due course the P.F.L.P. split – twice. On instructions from Damascus, Jabril broke away from the P.F.L.P. to form the P.F.L.P.-G.C. – General Command; and Nawef Hawatmeh and his supporters broke with Habash to form the Popular Democratic Front (P.D.F.). But Habash's P.F.L.P. continued to be Fatah's main rival and the leading champion of the revolutionary way.

It was not until December 1968 that the P.F.L.P. demonstrated how different from Fatah it was going to be in so far as the conduct of the armed struggle was concerned. Fatah's policy was to confine the violence to the land of Palestine. Arafat and his colleagues in the Fatah leadership knew that if they struck at Zionist interests outside Palestine, they would make enemies of foreign governments and alienate the international public opinion they had to win if they were to advance their cause. The P.F.L.P. did not agree. At the end of December, two of its gunmen opened fire on an Israeli passenger plane at Athens airport. It was the start of a P.F.L.P. terror campaign against Jewish interests inside and outside the Middle East, and which was to see the P.F.L.P. emerge as a hijack specialist. The organization's terror chief was Dr Wadi Haddad. Frequently he set a pace which was too hot for Habash. When eventually Haddad died in Eastern Europe after being poisoned by a foreign intelligence agent in Algiers, Habash was not overtaken with grief. In his oration at Haddad's funeral in Damascus, Habash was critical of his old comrade. To some Palestinians, including Fatah's leaders, this was the proof of what they had long suspected – that Haddad had forced the P.F.L.P. to extremes which Habash had known to be harmful to the Palestinian cause but which he had been powerless to stop.

In reply to the first Athens incident, the Israelis blew up *thirteen* Arab airliners which were parked at Beirut airport. Even the spokesman for the U.S. Administration was instructed to describe Israel's reprisal as 'an act of arrogance and disproportionate'. Quite apart from the fact that it totally failed to discourage further attacks on Israel's civilian planes, mainly because Haddad felt he had been challenged by the opposition to show what he could do, Israel's reprisal gave the P.F.L.P. what it most wanted at the time – publicity and, in the eyes of some Palestinians and other Arabs, a certain revolutionary credibility.

To some extent Haddad and the men of violence in the P.F.L.P. were intent on revenge. But there was method in their madness, or so they thought. Unlike Fatah, the P.F.L.P. was not a popular organization in the sense that it had roots in the masses. It was, essentially, a small group of embittered intellectuals who discovered Marxism and Leninism in the way drowning men find floating wreckage to cling to. But they knew that selling Marxism to the Palestinian masses would be no easy job, since communism and Arabism are not natural allies. So their first aim was to capture the imagination of the Palestinian masses by attacks on Jewish interests, and then to educate and brainwash. In this way, generally speaking, the P.F.L.P. thought it could compete with Fatah for popular support and eventually build a mass organization of its own.

But what was really driving Habash, the P.F.L.P. and other radical individuals and groups who said they favoured the revolutionary way was a fear that they were being outmanoeuvred by Arafat, and that if Fatah was allowed to dominate the liberation movement it would end up making so many compromises, in the name of facing up to reality, that the Palestinians would get nothing. The main objective was, in fact, to frustrate and sabotage the developing partnership between Arafat's Fatah and those Arab states, Egypt and Jordan in particular, which were working for peace with Israel.

For obvious reasons the P.F.L.P. and other leftist and radical groups were alarmed in February 1969 when Fatah joined and, with Nasser's help, took effective control of the P.L.O. It happened at the fifth P.N.C. meeting in Cairo. Out of a total of 105 seats, 57 were allotted to the guerrilla organizations; and 33 of the 57 were given to Fatah. As a consequence Fatah was in a position to secure Arafat's election to the post of Chairman.

From one point of view it could be said that the leftist and radical groups had nothing to fear because Fatah's freedom of action was now determined by the objectives and policies laid down in the Charter which was, in theory, the Bible of the liberation movement. The Charter, as we have seen, committed all who were members of the P.L.O. to total liberation by armed struggle, and this could not be amended except (in the Charter's own words) 'by a majority of two-thirds of the total membership of the National Council of the Palestine liberation organization at a special session convened for that purpose'.[31] Because those likely to oppose Fatah's way were over-represented in the P.N.C. of the time, it was unlikely that there would be a two-thirds majority for amending the Charter in the foreseeable future. Arafat's hands were therefore tied. That, at least, was the theory. But in practice, and because Fatah was the biggest, the strongest and by far the most popular of the various liberation organizations and fronts, there was nothing to stop Arafat and his colleagues from pursuing policies which were not in accord with the

Charter. And as time was to show, although Fatah's leaders never said so in public they did not, in fact, feel bound by the exact words of the Charter when its provisions were not, in their view, serving the best interests of their people.

A few weeks after the fifth P.N.C. there came dramatic news which confirmed the P.F.L.P.'s worst fears about the direction P.L.O. policy would take with Fatah at the helm and Arafat the Chairman. The bearer of the news was Khalad Hassan. He was one of four Fatah leaders who had been elected to the P.L.O.'s fifteen-man Executive Committee. He was now the head of the Political Department and was thus responsible for, among other matters, foreign policy. In April Khalad returned to Jordan with news that he had scored his first (and, in historical terms, his greatest and most important) diplomatic triumph. Against all expectations he had persuaded King Feisal of Saudi Arabia to support Fatah and through Fatah the Palestinian cause and claim for justice. The significance of Saudi Arabia's support for Fatah cannot be exaggerated. As time proved, with Saudi Arabia on its side Fatah was indestructible – as long as it was pursuing policies the Saudis could endorse.

When they were arranging Fatah's takeover of the P.L.O., Arafat and his colleagues had asked the Egyptian President about the possibility of Egypt providing some financial support for the liberation movement. In his conversations with me, Khalad Hassan was very frank about Fatah's money troubles at the time. He said: 'We were broke. We had some weapons and ammunition because the Chinese had been supplying us on a regular basis and for free since 1964. As a matter of fact we offered to pay the Chinese but they always insisted we should accept their help as a gift. But when we took over the P.L.O. we had no money to pay living expenses and administration costs. To tell you the truth we did not have enough money to feed ourselves.'

Nasser was in no position to help them with funds. He suggested they should turn to the Saudis for support on that front. When Khalad Hassan set off for Saudi Arabia, travelling by car and camel and intending to enter the country unofficially, he vowed that he would succeed where his colleagues had failed. Previously Abu Iyad, Abu Jihad and even Arafat himself had knocked on Saudi Arabia's door. But all they had discovered was that it would not be opened to them until the King gave the word. And that he was not intending to do. Khalad knew that he had somehow to get to Feisal; and that was the purpose of his mission.

Why was Feisal so unwilling to receive Fatah's leaders? Why was he not even prepared to listen to their plea for help? Feisal was violently opposed to communism. There was no man alive, including the hardliners who walked the corridors of power in Washington, who was more fiercely anti-communist than this particular Saudi monarch. Certain Western intelligence agencies – the C.I.A. and Britain's S.I.S. in particular – had convinced the Saudi regime that Fatah's leaders were communists. Said Khalad: 'It was all a dirty lie to discredit us. Feisal was an exceptionally wise and shrewd man, and as a rule he could see through every Western attempt to deceive him. But on this matter, and because of his own strong views, he was ready to believe what he was told about us without so many questions.'

Another cause of what Khalad described with a smile as the 'misunderstanding' between Fatah and Feisal was Shuqairi's behaviour and attitudes before and after he became the first Chairman of the P.L.O. The Saudis had never forgiven Shuqairi for becoming Nasser's man in the days when he was supposed to be working for them at the U.N. When Shuqairi, as the Chairman of Nasser's puppet P.L.O., had called for the overthrow of all the reactionary Arab regimes, the possibility of a relationship between the Saudis and the Palestine liberation movement had ceased. But now that Shuqairi was out of the way, and the P.L.O. was under new management, Khalad was hoping to be able to make a fresh start in Saudi Arabia.

The only thing Khalad had going for him when he arrived in Saudi Arabia was a good friend with a useful name – Fahd Al-Marak. This Saudi gentleman was a diplomat. Said Khalad: 'Fahd Al-Marak fought in Palestine in 1948, and all his life he considered it was his duty to help the Palestinians. From the beginning he supported us with money.' Apparently Fahd Al-Marak was also one of the very few in the Saudi kingdom who was prepared to help the Palestinians without first obtaining a nod of approval from Feisal.

Khalad continued: 'My friend took me to the Al-Yammamah Hotel in Riyadh. As you know, visitors are not allowed to have a room unless they are sponsored by the Government, a company or a

Saudi citizen. The receptionist asked Fahd Al-Marak who was sponsoring me. My friend replied with one word, "Fahd", which was, of course, his own name, and that of the Crown Prince [now King] and Minister of the Interior. As we had hoped, the receptionist assumed that I was a guest of the Royal Family! My friend had chosen this particular hotel because it was one where many of Crown Prince Fahd's guests did stay.

'So believing that I was a guest of the Royal Family, they gave me a luxurious suite. For the next eighteen days nothing happened. I made many telephone calls to various personalities and always I was given the same answer – "Nobody is here." Then I received a cable from Arafat wanting to know what was happening. He was wondering if I had got lost in the desert!'

It was Arafat's cable that gave Khalad his first bright idea. Without more ado the head of the P.L.O.'s Political Department sat down and wrote a letter to the Chairman. In it he said he had not yet met the King, on account of the fact that His Majesty was much too busy, but that a meeting was expected soon. After paying warm but sincere tribute to Feisal, Khalad concluded his letter by saying he was sure 'that a man like Feisal will never put me down'. As it happened Khalad had no intention of sending the letter. He left it open on the desk in his suite and went for a walk, knowing it would be read and that its contents would be passed to the appropriate authorities while he was out. 'But my little ploy didn't work,' Khalad said. Still nothing happened.

A day or two later, and by chance, Khalad learned that Feisal's personal physician was a Palestinian who had been the Hassan family doctor in Haifa. Khalad and Fahd Al-Marak invited him to dinner. He came and Khalad told him about his mission and how desperate he was to get an audience with Feisal. Khalad said: 'I was advised to tell the physician everything because it was known that he would report my every word to the King. He did, but still no response from His Majesty. After that I tried to meet with some of the Princes of the Royal Family, but I was told in a very blunt way that unless I met with the King there was nobody who could help me.'

I interrupted the flow of Khalad's story to ask him if he was by this time beginning to feel that he had failed. 'No,' he replied, 'I was still looking upon my mission as a challenge. But you can't believe how frustrated I was . . . twenty-four hours a day in my hotel room for more than twenty days with no radio, no papers, nothing to read and nobody to talk to. It was horrible.'

Khalad was now desperate enough to take a risk. He had learned that the King held a weekly 'non-protocol' audience for leaders of the tribes. Said Khalad: 'With the people from the tribes it was quite impossible to practise protocol – the leaders just arrived without checking and waited for their turn to meet His Majesty.'

On the appointed day of the week, and dressed as a tribesman, Khalad joined 200 genuine sons of the desert who were assembling for the audience. He watched carefully as each in turn approached the King. Some gave him a petition and said only a few words. Others were more talkative. As each man took his leave, the King whispered instructions to an aide.

Suddenly it was the turn of the impostor to face the King. 'I said: "Hello, Your Majesty. I am Khalad Hassan of Fatah. I am staying in the Al-Yammamah Hotel and I am here to meet with you. And I am not leaving Riyadh until I do meet you. Thank you very much." Then I ran away!'

A very anxious Fahd Al-Marak was waiting for Khalad. The thought that he might not see his friend again had apparently crossed his mind while he waited. 'Fahd asked me if I had met the King. I said, "Yes." He said, "Did you shake hands with him?" I said, "Yes." Fahd asked: "Did he say anything against you?" I said, "No, he was just looking at me and smiling."'

As fast as they could the two conspirators then spread the word that Khalad had been received by the King. Though not at all justified by the facts, the implication was that Khalad had also received Feisal's nod of approval. Later the same day, and thanks to Fahd Al-Marak's efforts, Khalad was invited to dinner at the home of Feisal's brother-in-law.

Khalad continued: 'At sunset the King's brother-in-law and his guests went to pray. I joined them and they were very surprised. They said, "You are a man with Western ways and you pray?" I said, "Why not?" Then they were astonished. They said, "Do you mean you are not a communist?" I laughed and told them I was most definitely not a communist and never could be.'

Before the evening ended the brother-in-law's brother disappeared for a few minutes. Khalad said: 'He returned with a

Kalishnikov rifle and a revolver and he asked me if I would accept them as a present. I said, "Do you want to see me in gaol? If I carry those weapons to the hotel I will be arrested." The brother smiled. He said: "Okay, I will bring them to you at the airport when you leave." I thanked him but said even that was not possible because I would be arrested and gaoled by the Jordanians if I arrived in Amman with weapons. The brother was astonished. "Is that true?" he asked me. I said, "Certainly." He was even more astonished. He said, "Do you mean to tell me you are fighting the Zionists and you are not allowed to have weapons?" I told him that was the case and part of the reason why I was in Saudi Arabia. And then he said the following. "I promise you these two guns will go with the first shipment of weapons from Saudi Arabia to Amman."'

During the afternoon of Khalad's twenty-third day in Saudi Arabia, the telephone in his hotel suite rang for the first time. The voice on the other end of the line informed Khalad that his appointment with the King was fixed for eight o'clock that evening.

The bad news came at five minutes to eight when Khalad was told by the Head of Protocol that he had been allotted only fifteen minutes with the King because there were many other appointments. Khalad told me: 'To the Head of Protocol I said: "All right, thank you." To myself I said: "This is ridiculous! What can I achieve in fifteen minutes? Answer – nothing." I was very depressed, and then, as I was about to enter the King's room, something wonderful happened. I looked back and I saw the guards were raising their hands in a form of prayer, wishing God to give me success with His Majesty. It was too much for me and I cried. And I was still trying to hide my tears when I shook hands with Feisal.'

By the time of this historic meeting the fact that Feisal and not Nasser was the effective leader of the Arab world was widely acknowledged in one way or another. Only Fatah's political opponents in the Palestine liberation movement and a relatively small number of other Arab leftists and radicals denied this reality. Nasser was still the leader above all others who had a special place in the hearts of most Arabs. Without really understanding how Israel and the West had conspired to deny Nasser the opportunity to advance the cause of Arab nationalism, most ordinary Arab people seemed instinctively to know that he was a far better leader than circumstances had allowed him to be. So Nasser could still command the affection of the Arab masses. But it was the man Khalad Hassan was now preparing to engage who had the power – the economic and political leverage that came from oil.

In the few seconds that he permitted himself to reflect on these and similar thoughts, Khalad regained his composure. And with it came the realization of what was at stake. If Feisal could not be persuaded to support the Palestinian cause as it was represented by Fatah, the days when moderate and pragmatic men like himself and his colleagues could influence events on the Palestinian side would be numbered.

Khalad continued: 'We started to talk and the King left his desk to sit by me on the couch. With so much on my mind, and so much to say, I was very anxious because Feisal was limiting our conversation to generalities and the time was racing away. Ten minutes passed. Then fifteen. After twenty minutes had gone the Head of Protocol came in to remind the King of his next appointment. Then the prayers of the guards were answered. Without taking his eyes off me, Feisal made a small and hardly noticeable gesture with the fingers of one hand. It was the sign that he didn't want any more appointments. I was so relieved.'

Four hours later the two men were still talking; but Khalad had no cause for celebration. He said: 'After four hours I couldn't see anything in his face or his eyes to tell me that I had convinced him. I was beginning to think I had failed. And still I had not made a specific request for help.'

As all with first-hand experience of Feisal know – including myself – talking with him at length was a testing and frustrating experience. Feisal never, or almost never, said what he meant in a direct way. He preferred to speak, as it were, in parables. Once after a long interview with him I dared to ask why he spoke in such a way. The King permitted himself a thin, enigmatic smile. And through an interpreter he said the following: 'If I say the wrong thing, or if I say the right thing in the wrong way, the Middle East will go up in flames!'

Soon after midnight Khalad decided that he had to take the initiative. 'I gathered all my courage and I said the following to Feisal: "Your Majesty, it seems to me that you don't want to be the ruler and the saviour of the Middle East." He replied: "Who said I want to be that? It is enough for me to be the servant of God in

Mecca." I said: "Your Majesty, I didn't mean yourself to be the ruler of the Middle East, or to dominate the region, I am talking about your faith and ideology." The King replied, "What has this got to do with the reason why you are in Saudi Arabia?" And this was my opportunity to speak as frankly as the circumstances would allow.

'I said the following: "Your Majesty we Palestinians are going to fight for our rights by one way or another. And that means we are going to accept support from wherever it comes. Until now only the leftists are supporting us. [As Feisal knew, Khalad was referring mainly to the Chinese.] This is not what we in Fatah want. We do not want to be committed to any foreign ideology, to any government or any leader. We want to be truly independent, but we can be that only if we can take support from many sources. You can help us to be independent. If you do not we shall be obliged to go on with only those who are supporting us now."

'The King remained silent, and still I couldn't tell what he was thinking. I decided to summarize my case in a way that I knew would appeal to him. I said: "Your Majesty, let us suppose that you are in the desert on your camel with plenty of water. I am walking towards you and I am dying of thirst. If I ask for water will you give me some and let me ride with you on your camel?" The King replied, "Yes, of course, that is our tradition." I said: "Now let us suppose that we have travelled some distance together, that I ask for more water, and that you tell me I can have more only if I am prepared to do something for you. Can I refuse what you ask, even if I don't want to do it?" The King said, "Maybe." I said: "With respect, Your Majesty, I cannot say no to whatever you ask because you will abandon me and I will die. So I have no choice." The King said, "That is logical." I continued: "Now let us suppose that when you are making your demand on me another man with a camel and plenty of water arrives on the scene. Would you agree that if I don't want to do what you ask me I now have a choice because I can take water from the other man?" The King said, "Yes." Finally I said: "Your Majesty, that is our position. If we have to take help from only one source we will be trapped. It is only when we have many willing to support us that we can be independent."'

Khalad was exhausted. But that no longer mattered. There was nothing more that he could say to influence Feisal. In the silence that

followed, Khalad watched as the third man in the room moved
closer to his King. The third man was Rashad Faraon, one of Feisal's
most trusted counsellors.

According to Khalad's memory the last few minutes of the
conversation went as follows:

*Feisal:* 'Rashad, give Khalad what he wants.'
*Khalad:* 'No, Your Majesty. First of all I want something from you
  – then from Rashad.'
*Feisal:* 'What do you want from me?'
*Khalad:* 'I want you to impose a liberation tax amounting to five per
  cent on the salaries of all Palestinians working in Saudi
  Arabia.'
*Feisal:* 'Agreed. What else?'
*Khalad:* 'We need some nominal financial support from you
  personally.'
*Feisal:* 'All right. What else?'
*Khalad:* 'We need also a nominal financial support from the
  Government.'
*Feisal:* 'Is twelve million dollars a year enough?'
*Khalad:* 'It is more than enough.'
*Feisal:* 'What else?'
*Khalad:* 'We need arms and ammunition.'
*Feisal:* 'All right. Rashad, you will make the necessary arrangements.
  See that Khalad gets whatever he wants from what we can
  spare.'

Later that day Khalad met with a senior Saudi army officer. For
once the remarkable Palestinian was out of his depth. 'I said to the
officer: "Look, I am not a military man, I don't understand
weapons. But we are *fedayeen* and you know the type of arms and
ammunition we need. Will you, please, make me a list showing
what is available and from where the items can be collected?" The
officer said, "Certainly." He made the list and I gave it to Rashad.
The next day it was agreed.'

Khalad returned to Amman. 'Two weeks later,' he said, 'twenty-
eight big Saudi army trucks arrived with arms and ammunition. The
Saudis distributed them to our bases all over Jordan. The
Kalishnikov and the pistol they had wanted me to have in Riyadh
were presented to me personally.'

The next time Khalad met Feisal was at a meeting of Islamic Foreign Ministers. 'As a mark of respect I was the last one to say goodbye to the King. I said to him, "Your Majesty, thank you for what you have done." He put his hands on my shoulders and said: "Look Khalad, what I did is not for you personally. It was for the cause you represent. So don't overestimate yourself." He paused, then he added, "But I have to tell you something. People have the sign of success on their forehead. You are one of those."'

Feisal lived for six more years. During that time no man had a greater affinity with him than Khalad Hassan. He made no deals and no bargains with the Saudis. As Khalad said, 'That is not the way the Saudis work.' But the unspoken agreement between Khalad and Feisal and then between Khalad and Feisal's successors was that as long as a Fatah-dominated P.L.O. advocated policies which the Saudis could support without wrecking their special relationship with the U.S., Saudi Arabia would do everything in its power to advance the Palestinian cause by political means, and would stand by the P.L.O. no matter who tried to destroy it.

The new Chairman of the P.L.O. used Feisal's gift of arms and ammunition to escalate the military confrontation with Israel, which he was committed to doing until and unless there was progress towards an acceptable compromise with the Jewish State. As logged by the Israelis (whose statistics were much more reliable than the fantastic claims of the *fedayeen*) there were 97 terrorist infiltrations and incidents in 1967; 916 in 1968; and 2,432 in 1969. In the same period Israel's casualties, killed and wounded, were 38, 273 and 243.

On a scale of ten it could be said that Arafat escalated the conflict to point three. The Israelis replied by escalating it to point eight. (Point ten was Israel's invasion of the Lebanon and siege of Beirut in the summer of 1982.) Until about the time Arafat became the Chairman of the P.L.O., the Israelis had been content to respond to *fedayeen* actions either on a one-for-one basis or, more often than not, by launching an attack as a reprisal for a number of *fedayeen* actions. Either way the Israelis were responding. In early 1969 that policy was abandoned. To counter Arafat's escalation, the Israelis adopted a new policy of 'Active Self-Defence'. What it meant in practice was that the Israelis were no longer content to respond. From here on they were taking the war to the *fedayeen* wherever they were.

As well as blasting *fedayeen* bases in Jordan – mainly from the air – the Israelis also struck at some of Jordan's vital installations. In June, for example, Israeli commandos sabotaged the East Ghor canal, a fifteen-million dollar showpiece of American aid to Jordan and its farmers. In August, as soon as the canal was repaired, the Israelis blew it up again, leaving fruits and vegetables rotting on 500 square miles of Jordan's best agricultural land. These acts of Israeli terror had one purpose – to force Hussein to control and smash the *fedayeen*.

As the confrontation between the *fedayeen* and Israel escalated on one front, it spread to another. Early in 1969, Arafat sent 500 of his guerrillas into southern Lebanon with orders to prepare for hit-and-run attacks from there. For reasons I have stated, Fatah's leaders were reluctant to involve the Lebanon in the fighting; but in 1969 they considered they had no choice. As Abu Jihad explained: 'With Israel hitting us so hard in Jordan we had to be flexible. We had to move as the circumstances dictated. When the Israelis were making it too hot for us in Jordan, we had to launch some operations from across the Lebanon border.' After the Palestinian tail had wagged the Arab dog with such disastrous consequences in 1967, Nasser was never again to allow the *fedayeen* to mount attacks on Israel from Egyptian soil.

On the scale of ten, Arafat escalated the confrontation along Israel's border with the Lebanon to point two or thereabouts. With artillery barrages, air strikes and occasional mini-invasions which were called search-and-destroy operations, the Israelis escalated it to point six. As in Jordan, Israel was using its vastly superior military power to do more than hit the *fedayeen*. It was also seeking by military means to persuade the civilian population of southern Lebanon to refrain from giving shelter to the *fedayeen*. Israel's other objective was to persuade the Government in Beirut to act.

Israel's decision to take the war to the *fedayeen* in southern Lebanon led to frequent and increasingly serious clashes between Arafat's fighters and the Lebanese army. Behind the scenes, and as he told Arafat and other Fatah leaders at the time, Nasser was begging the Government in Beirut to show restraint and to give him more time. According to Fatah leaders, Nasser told the Lebanese that he and Hussein were doing their utmost to persuade the U.S. to force Israel to make the necessary withdrawals for peace on the basis of 242. Nasser also told the Lebanese he was confident that

Arafat and his Fatah colleagues would not obstruct such a peace
and would agree to continue their struggle by political means in the
event of peace.

Some Americans were beginning to listen to Hussein and Nasser
and other Arab leaders. So the Egyptian President was not
exaggerating when he told the Lebanese there was a chance that
their restraint might be rewarded.

From early 1969, Nasser and Hussein had been performing a sort
of double-act to put pressure on the Americans to bring about an
Israeli withdrawal to the borders as they were on the eve of the Six-
Day War. Nasser was doing the shooting and Hussein the talking.

In March, Nasser had opened fire across the Suez Canal to launch
what came to be called his War of Attrition. It went on for sixteen
months and was essentially a static war limited to exchanges of
artillery and tank fire. Naturally Israel's leaders presented Nasser's
action as yet more proof that he was the enemy of peace. But the
truth, as Israel's leaders knew, was quite the opposite. By hotting up
the Suez Canal front, Nasser was sending two messages. The first
was to the Israelis, warning them that he could still hurt them and
would continue to do so until they realized that they also needed
peace. The second message was to the Americans. To them Nasser
was conveying the desperation of the Arabs and warning the U.S.
Administration that unless it used its influence on Israel to make
peace the drift to war would continue.

In April, Hussein went to Washington to convey the same
message to the Americans but in the normal diplomatic way. As he
later confirmed to me himself, the King emphasized that he and
Nasser and most of the other Arab leaders who mattered were more
than ready to make peace with Israel, but that he and other Arab
leaders who wanted peace could do nothing in public until Israel
was at least committed to a withdrawal to the borders of 4 June
1967.

Immediately after Hussein left Richard Nixon, the President said:
'We've got to help the King. We cannot let American Jews make
policy.'[32] Unfortunately five more years were to pass before Nixon
realized just how much it really was in America's interest that Israel
and the Jewish lobby be prevented from dictating American foreign
policy in the Middle East, but by then it was too late – Nixon was
embroiled in Watergate.

In 1969 the man who was supposed to be in charge of U.S. policy for the Middle East was William Rogers, the Secretary of State. He was trying his best to devise a peace plan which Nasser, Hussein and other Arab leaders would accept, one that would give substance and meaning to 242. Unfortunately his position, his authority and his ideas were being undermined by Nixon's National Security Adviser, Henry Kissinger.

At the time Kissinger was opposed to any initiative which required the Israelis to give up occupied territory in return for guarantees of peace. Since it was obvious to anybody who could take a rational view of the situation that there could be no peace without at least an Israeli commitment to withdraw, it has to be said that Kissinger was opposed to peace itself at the time. Kissinger's view was that an Israeli withdrawal, or even an Israeli willingness to talk about withdrawal, would be a victory for the Arab (mainly Palestinian) radicals and leftists, whose terrorist attacks would then be seen to be justified. It would also be a victory for the Soviets who had re-armed Egypt and Syria. Quite apart from the fact that Kissinger chose to ignore the Soviet Union's commitment to Israel's existence inside the borders as they were on 4 June 1967, he seemed unable to grasp that it was the *absence* of an Israeli commitment to withdrawal that was creating the conditions for the growth of Arab and Moslem extremism of all kinds. Speaking for Arafat and all of his Fatah colleagues on this subject, Khalad Hassan said the following:

'The first thing we have to say is that Kissinger did not begin to understand what was happening in the Middle East. But much more important was the fact that he didn't want to understand. To Kissinger the Arab states and Israel were mere pawns on the global chessboard. To Kissinger the only players who mattered were those in Washington and Moscow. Beyond that Kissinger was obsessed by two ideas. The first was that he, Henry Kissinger, was the most brilliant man in the West. I suspect he went to sleep telling himself that if the Americans were truly wise they would one day make him President. In any event, he had a very unhealthy lust for personal power. His second obsession was the idea that the Soviets were behind all the problems in the world including the troubles in the Middle East. I do not myself think that Kissinger ever seriously believed this nonsense. I think the truth is that he promoted it because he had no choice. He was both the ambassador and the prisoner of America's military-industrial complex. The men who control it were his real backers and he had to say what they wanted to retain their support. If you want me to speak very frankly I will add this: I believe Henry Kissinger is a political prostitute, and deep down I would not be surprised if he hates himself for doing what he's done in the Middle East and elsewhere. Later on I will prove to you that he is also a terrible liar.'

On 9 December Secretary of State Rogers outlined his plan. It required Egypt to make peace with Israel in return for Israel's withdrawal from the Sinai Desert. Beyond that the Rogers Plan called for negotiations between Jordan and Israel to bring about an eventual Israeli withdrawal from the occupied West Bank in return for peace with Jordan, and to settle the future of Jerusalem and the 'Palestinian refugee problem'.

Because Rogers and most of his staffers at the State Department had long been convinced that Nasser was sincere in his privately expressed wish for peace with Israel, the gist of the American plan had been conveyed to Cairo a month previously. Nasser told Washington that while he welcomed the evidence that the U.S. was at last coming to grips with the real obstacle to peace between the front-line Arab states and Israel – Israel's occupation of the Arab territory captured in the Six-Day War – he could not make a separate peace with the Jewish State. In other words, and as he also told the Americans and later Fatah's leaders, Nasser wanted an American plan for a comprehensive peace – total peace for total withdrawal. Hussein was disappointed because the Rogers Plan had not made Israel's withdrawal from the West Bank a condition for peace with Jordan; but he was satisfied with Nasser's personal assurance that Egypt would not go down the road to peace alone.

Israel's response was swift and predictable. Golda Meir called an emergency meeting of her Cabinet and the Rogers Plan was rejected. The only beneficiaries of Israel's rejection of the first Rogers Plan were those in the Palestine liberation movement who favoured the revolutionary way – the P.F.L.P. and the other leftist and radical groups. They were now set to make great political and propaganda capital at the expense of the Fatah realists.

Though Arafat and his colleagues in Fatah's leadership had not said openly that it was their policy to work with the regimes who wanted peace with Israel, and that they were prepared to continue their struggle by political means alone in the event of peace between the front-line Arab states and Israel, it was obvious to those who favoured the revolutionary way that this was, indeed, Fatah's policy, and that it did not intend to be bound by the Charter. Israel's rejection of the first Rogers Plan meant that the leftists and the radicals were able to point an accusing finger at Arafat and his Fatah colleagues and to cause some embarrassing questions to be asked. They argued that all that the Arab regimes had managed to persuade the Americans to do was to produce a plan which paid lip-service to the 'Palestinian refugee problem' but ignored the Palestinian claim for justice. The Israelis had rejected it; the Americans, as always, had surrendered to Israel, and there was nothing the Arab regimes would or could do about it because they were the puppets of the West. Armed struggle and revolution was the only way to liberation.

Within days of Israel's rejection of the Rogers Plan, it was obvious to Fatah's leaders that the argument of those who favoured the revolutionary way was reaching the hearts of the *fedayeen*. Even many Fatah loyalists were beginning to say that the leftists and the radicals had a point. Was there now not a good case for starting the revolution in Jordan by overthrowing Hussein?

The evidence of how much Fatah's leaders were worried by the charge that they had sold out to the regimes which wanted peace with Israel was evident at the Arab summit in Rabat shortly after Israel's rejection of the Rogers Plan. The highlight of the meeting was a clash between Khalad Hassan and Nasser.

Khalad told me: 'Reading from an official statement, I said I did not believe there was any point in Nasser and other Arab leaders even trying to make peace with Israel. I said it was clear the Israelis were rejecting everything and preferred territory to peace. And I suggested to Nasser that he should abandon his search for a political settlement and unite the Arabs for war. Nasser was furious. He threw away his papers and left the chamber – but not before he told me I was a "dreamer" and that unity was something that would never exist in the Arab world.' In fact, Nasser said much more before he stormed out. He asked a series of pointed questions about who was going to do the fighting. And his own unspoken but implied answers were to the effect that in the event of another war,

his Arab colleagues would again make excuses or secret deals with
Israel to stay out of the fighting. By obvious implication Nasser said
that many of his Arab colleagues were gutless, loud-mouthed
hypocrites. According to Fatah leaders it was at the same summit
that Algeria's President Boumedienne told Nasser he was so
'disgusted' by Syria's hypocrisy that he was withdrawing his
opposition to Egypt's attempt to reach a political settlement with
Israel.

Khalad added: 'After the summit we came to know about the
special reason why Nasser was so angry. The Americans had
informed him that they were trying to improve the Rogers Plan.
They had taken Nasser's point that he could not make a separate
peace with Israel, and they were intending to come up with a
comprehensive formula which Nasser and Hussein could accept. In
other words, the Americans had told Nasser that the second Rogers
Plan would call for an Israeli withdrawal from Egyptian territory
and the West Bank. There was, however, a problem for the
Americans. In the coming months they would have a terrible time
persuading the Israelis to accept the second Rogers Plan. And the
Americans had asked Nasser to help them by doing his best to make
sure the Rabat summit did not take any radical or rejectionist
decisions. Through Heikal, I myself saw letters from the U.S. State
Department to two American ambassadors in the region. They were
asked to do everything to persuade Arab leaders to prevent Arab
radicalism from expressing itself at the Rabat summit and if
possible to postpone it.'

I think it is probable that Khalad provoked Nasser by
arrangement, so to speak, with his Fatah colleagues, to give Fatah
the opportunity to demonstrate to its own supporters that it had not
sold its soul to the regimes which wanted peace with Israel. And
Khalad had to be the one to do it because it was at him, and what he
represented as Fatah's leading rightist, that the radicals of the
liberation movement were directing most of their verbal fire. The
P.F.L.P. had earlier tried to wreck Fatah's relationship with Saudi
Arabia by sabotaging a Saudi oil pipeline in the Lebanon.

For a short time it seemed that the explosion of anger at Rabat
had damaged Fatah's relationship with Nasser. But the rift was
healed early in 1970. Fatah's leaders explained to Nasser why they
had been obliged to demonstrate that they were not his puppets. In

return Nasser told them all there was to know about the on-going peace process. Khalad said, 'Nasser was very frank, very honest. He said the following: "The Americans have told me I can have Sinai back any time I like. But I don't care about that. The problem is the West Bank and Gaza, and I will not make peace with the Israelis until they are out of there." To prove to us that he was sincere, Nasser then told us something we didn't know and which surprised us very much. He said that as far back as the Khartoum summit in 1967, he had authorized Hussein to do anything with the Americans in order to get the Israelis out of the West Bank.'

From what Khalad told me it is clear that Nasser was blaming himself for the loss of the West Bank; it was, after all, Egypt's generals who had forced Jordan into the Six-Day War after they had lied to Nasser, and then to Hussein, about what was happening on the battlefield.

There was an unspoken understanding between Nasser and Fatah in early 1970 that if the P.L.O. did not seek to sabotage the Arab attempt to make peace with Israel on the basis of 242, and if in the event of peace the P.L.O. agreed to continue its struggle by political means, then Nasser would make every effort to persuade Hussein to allow the Palestinians to exercise their right to self-determination on the West Bank. And naturally they could have Gaza, too. When I asked Khalad if he could confirm that this was, in fact, the understanding, he replied: 'Yes, you are right. But I have to say for the record that even we in Fatah were not yet thinking in terms of a West Bank and Gaza state as the price of our recognition of Israel.'

By agreeing to work with Nasser, Fatah's leaders were also committing themselves to co-operate with Hussein, since Nasser and Hussein were partners in the peace process. It was, therefore, quite impossible for Arafat and his Fatah colleagues to be, so to speak, pro-Nasser and anti-Hussein. It was not, and could not be, Fatah's policy to confront the regime in Jordan and to overthrow the King.

But even as Fatah's leaders were telling Nasser that they were prepared to co-operate with Hussein, it was clear that the P.F.L.P.'s call for the King's overthrow was supported, in principle, and on the emotional level, by a majority of the *fedayeen* – including now a majority of Fatah loyalists. And adding to Arafat's obvious

difficulties in managing this situation was a widespread feeling that
Hussein could be overthrown if only the Chairman would give the
word.

The first Fatah personality to draw my attention to this state of
affairs was a man who (in 1970) was destined to occupy a top place
on Israel's list of most wanted Palestinian terrorists. His name, or
rather his *nom de guerre*, is Abu Daoud. In this book, and as he put
it himself, he is 'speaking frankly for the first time in public'. When
some in Fatah turned to terror after the P.L.O. had been crushed
and driven out of Jordan, Israeli and Jordanian intelligence sources
asserted that Abu Daoud was one of the masterminds of what was
called the Black September Organization. In fact, Abu Daoud was
not a Black September terrorist. While the terror operations were
taking place, he was actually organizing a plot to overthrow
Hussein – which ended when he was betrayed and imprisoned in
Jordan.

In 1970, Abu Daoud was the commander of all Palestinian
militias in Jordan, which meant he was in the best possible position
to know what the rank and file of the *fedayeen* were really thinking.

'But first let me tell you what my own feelings were at the time,'
Abu Daoud said. 'I was of the opinion that we not only could but
should knock off Hussein. Next I must tell you very frankly that this
was the feeling not only of the leftists and the so-called radicals in
the other guerrilla organizations, it was also the feeling and the wish
of the majority of us in Fatah – the fighters and the young officers.
Among ourselves – I am talking now about Fatah's young officers –
we discussed the question of overthrowing Hussein very seriously
and very frequently. We also discussed our views with Arafat, and I
told him on more than one occasion that I thought we were making
a terrible mistake by not moving against Hussein. This, I think, is
some proof that we were a democratic organization. Anyway,
Arafat always said, "No." He told us that making war against
Hussein or any Arab regime was not the way to liberation.'

I asked Abu Daoud why he and others had been so confident that
Hussein could have been overthrown.

'It is a long and complicated story. And because of the situation as
it is today there are many – including, I am sure, Arafat and Hussein
– who would prefer the truth not to come out. But I do not myself
believe there is any longer a point in hiding it.

'The essential fact is this: from the time of Karameh in 1968 until June 1970, we in Fatah were enjoying the support of about fifty per cent of Jordan's armed forces. After June 1970, and partly because of the foolish and criminal activities of the leftists in our movement, we began to lose that support. We can speak about these foolish and criminal activities later. So after June 1970, we lost our chance. But until then, and from the time of Karameh, we in Fatah, plus those in Jordan's armed forces who supported us, could have changed the regime in Amman.'

After a pause Abu Daoud continued: 'I don't think it would be wise for me to give you names, but this much I can also tell you. On several occasions between 1968 and 1970, Jordanian army officers approached Fatah to ask if we would make a coup with them. Once a very pro-Hussein officer tried to make a deal with Habash and the P.F.L.P., but this was a trap. When the anti-regime officers approached Fatah they were very serious. But always Arafat and our leaders said, "No." To understand this you must know something of the real history of Jordan. In part it is a history of failed coups. After so many failures those who wanted to change the regime and the system in Amman were frightened to act alone. And that is why they wanted to co-operate with us.'

According to Abu Daoud the period of maximum opportunity for Fatah and its friends in Jordan's armed forces was February to June of 1970. As he explained, this was the period when Palestinian and Jordanian attitudes were hardening because of the severity of Israel's attacks and, following its rejection of the Rogers Plan, the first real evidence that Israel was on the West Bank to stay. The Israelis were going ahead with a scheme to requisition Arab land in Hebron and settle Jewish families on it. To many in Jordan's armed forces this was a strange time for Hussein and Nasser to be begging the Americans to help him make peace with an arrogant, aggressive and totally uncompromising Israel.

Given that an easy majority of Fatah loyalists were in favour of engaging Hussein's regime in a fight to the finish, why was it that the leadership's policy of no confrontation prevailed? I put this question to Abu Daoud. He replied: 'The answer is not so complicated. Unlike the P.F.L.P. and the other leftist and radical groups, we in Fatah had some discipline. This is one point. Another is that we were a democratic organization. From the beginning we agreed we would not discuss our internal divisions in public, but at our secret meetings we were free to say what we liked. Even the least experienced of our fighters were free to criticize the leadership and to tell Arafat he was wrong. So after all the discussions we were ready to accept the decisions of our Central Committee. Then there was a third and very important point. In Fatah many of us knew that if we turned to the gun to solve our internal problems, we would be giving our enemies the opportunity to destroy us.'

So in Fatah, the biggest and the most powerful of the organizations which made up the P.L.O., a very difficult situation was under control.

In the final countdown to civil war in Jordan, the more Arafat and his colleagues in the Fatah leadership demonstrated their determination to co-operate with Hussein – even though he was pushing for peace with Israel on the basis of 242 – the more the leftist and radical elements in the P.L.O. were seeking to provoke a confrontation with the King's armed forces. Early June saw serious fighting between the *fedayeen* and Jordan's armed forces. As on previous occasions, the shooting was started by the P.F.L.P. and the Nawef Hawatmeh's Popular Democratic Front. As on previous occasions, too, Arafat and Hussein worked as one to defuse the crisis. Nearly three weeks later, when Habash was still blocking an agreement which Arafat had negotiated with Hussein to prevent further fighting, the Chairman of the P.L.O. denounced his P.F.L.P. colleague in public. 'Our masses can no longer tolerate an extremist demagogue who does nothing to change the status quo,' he thundered. Though Arafat did not name the P.F.L.P. leader, it was obvious to all that Habash was the 'extremist demagogue' he had in mind. For Arafat to attack a P.L.O. colleague in public was something of a sensation. It was a measure of the Chairman's growing frustration and despair.

In terms of numbers and as we have seen, those on the Palestinian side who were actually doing the provoking were the minority of those actively engaged in the liberation struggle. But it was this minority that dictated the course of events, and it was helped by Jordanian, Israeli and American *agents provocateurs* to sabotage Arafat's policy of co-operation with Hussein. As early as November 1968, Hussein had said that it was more than possible that Israeli agents had provoked shooting incidents in Amman 'to create confusion and thus prepare an opportunity for Israel to strike'.

By the time of the June fighting the various *fedayeen* organizations were in occupation of enough of Jordan for the area under the P.L.O.'s control to be called a state within a state. And from June the supporters of certain *fedayeen* organizations were behaving in an appalling and unforgivable way in what, when all is said, was a host country. In the towns and cities where the *fedayeen* and not the Government of Jordan were the authority, including parts of Amman, the leftists and the radicals did their best to promote anarchy and chaos. They set up roadblocks, hijacked vehicles and extorted money from local businessmen and traders. Supporters of Hawatmeh's P.D.F. took to broadcasting their Marxist propaganda from minarets and raping the local women. These were some of the 'foolish and criminal activities' to which Abu Daoud was referring. Fatah's fighters and supporters were not models of acceptable behaviour either. Fatah also had its hooligan elements, *fedayeen* cowboys who swaggered around, heavily armed, as though they owned the place and could do what they liked. But generally speaking the *fedayeen* who served under Fatah's banner were not an undisciplined rabble.

Not surprisingly the P.D.F.'s behaviour and activities caused the liberation movement as a whole to lose the support and then the sympathy of those Jordanians, including many Palestinians, who had previously admired the *fedayeen*. Instead of winning friends in the only front-line Arab state in which it had a reasonably secure base, the P.L.O. was making enemies. But there were other forces at work, directed by equally foolish and ruthless men who were determined to discredit the P.L.O. and wreck Arafat's policy of co-operation with Hussein.

After the June fighting, one particular *fedayeen*, or so-called *fedayeen*, organization began to make a quiet name for itself. Known as the Victory Battalions, its specialities were hijacking cars – usually those belonging to high Government officials and senior army officers; kidnapping army officers; and generally harassing the families of those in the military and political establishments. It was soon obvious that whoever was directing the operations of the Victory Battalions had inside information about the movements of senior military personnel. When it was later discovered that this so-called *fedayeen* organization was a creature of Jordan's High Command, nobody was really surprised.

Those who directed the Victory Battalions had two objectives.

One was to cause those officers known or suspected of being hostile to the regime and in sympathy with Fatah to change their feelings. Abu Daoud said, 'Those around the King who wanted to crush us were working day and night to tip the balance of power against us.' The other and more general objective was to discredit the *fedayeen*. Like the extremists around Arafat in the P.L.O., the extremists around Hussein were pushing the country to civil war.

In June the governments of the West expressed their outrage at a reported attempt on Hussein's life. According to Abu Iyad there was no attempt. He told me: 'It is true that shots were fired at Hussein's car – but the King was not in it. And the shots were not fired by Palestinians. They were fired by Jordanian army officers posing as *fedayeen* whose superiors then rushed to the King and told him that there had been an attempt to kill him, and what good luck it was that he was not riding in the car at the time!

'Those who had the idea to make the phoney assassination attempt were of the opinion that Hussein was not tough enough and not anti-Palestinian enough. They were pushing him to hate the Palestinians as much as they themselves did.'

Abu Iyad was well placed to know what was happening. Apart from the fact that he was the executive responsible for the P.L.O.'s various intelligence agencies, he was also, before the civil war, on excellent terms with Hussein. Until the civil war Abu Iyad was, in fact, the most pro-Hussein member of Fatah's leadership. He attended all or nearly all of Arafat's meetings with the King; and when there was business to be done with Hussein when Arafat could not be in attendance, it was Abu Iyad who represented his Chairman.

Hussein himself had no knowledge of who was behind the Victory Battalions until it was too late. He was in no way involved in the plot to discredit the *fedayeen*. And he was at least as anxious as Arafat to avoid a civil war. Sometimes Hussein was infuriated by Arafat's apparent unwillingness to use force to curb his own extremists; but when Hussein was honest with himself, and when he compared his own situation to Arafat's, he had to feel some sympathy for the P.L.O. Chairman. Hussein was, after all, the King. He had a country and all the institutions of the state were at his command – in theory. But still he, the King, could not control his own extremists. So how much more difficult was it for Arafat? That thought was frequently in Hussein's mind, and he discussed it more than once with Abu Iyad.

According to Abu Iyad, other Fatah leaders and my own detailed research in Jordan, Israel and Western Europe, Israeli agents were responsible for some of the incidents which caused the *fedayeen* to be hated in Jordan and which helped to set the stage for the civil war. In most cases Israel's agents were Palestinians who had been turned by blackmail of one kind or another, and who then joined a *fedayeen* organization.

Abu Iyad explained: 'On a few occasions in the past the Israelis have used sophisticated and dangerous drugs to programme the minds of their Palestinian traitor-agents. Later, and if you like, I will give you the details of one such incident. It was actually a Mossad attempt on my life. But generally speaking the Israelis relied on three simple but effective methods of blackmail to turn Palestinians into traitors. I should also tell you that the Mossad recruited or turned most of its Palestinian agents in Western Europe.

'The first method was money. Mossad agents had dossiers on most and probably all Palestinians who were studying and working in Europe. And the Mossad kept a special watch on those Palestinians who were obviously living beyond their means and were spending on gambling, women and so on. I think I don't have to tell you how these stories ended. Actually the Palestinian traitor-agent who came closest to killing Arafat was something of a small-time playboy who had his gambling debts paid by the Mossad.

'Another favourite Mossad trick was threatening Palestinians in Europe that they would not have their work permits or their travel documents renewed unless they co-operated with the Israelis. This was a blackmail technique the Mossad used a lot in West Germany because its agents were able to play on the German guilt complex. And by doing this they succeeded in getting from the German authorities all the necesary official information about the Palestinians . . . details about when their work permits were due for renewal and so on.

'The Mossad's third way was threatening Palestinians in Europe that their families on the West Bank and in Gaza would suffer if they didn't co-operate with the Israelis. When the Mossad agents made their approaches they usually had photographs and sometimes film of the subject's family. And from the information the Mossad agents revealed, it was clear that they knew everything there was to know about the families – names, habits, problems, weak points and so on. Sometimes the threat was that the family would lose its means of earning a living. Sometimes it was a threat of physical violence and death. But often the implication was that the women in the family would be raped. The Mossad agents knew how crazy we Arabs can become when the honour of our women is threatened.'

When Abu Iyad had finished telling me these things, there was a thin smile of contentment on his fat, round face. I asked him to explain that. 'I was thinking about how brave and loyal our Palestinian people are when you take everything into account,' he said.

He went on: 'Over the years, and by using the blackmail and terror tactics I have described, the Mossad prepared many Palestinians to make attempts on the lives of our top leaders – Arafat and me in particular. But always their attempts failed. Do you know why? At the very last minute, no Palestinian was prepared to kill any one of us. At the last minute, when they could, in fact, have killed us, the Israeli traitor-agents always said, "No, I can't do it." And then they confessed.'

To illustrate his point Abu Iyad told me the dramatic story of one of the first of many Mossad attempts on his own life. 'I was working one day in my office in Amman. The telephone went. It was one of my most trusted secretaries calling from another room. She said to me, "Abu Iyad, I have a very big personal problem. Please, can I come and discuss it with you." I said, "For you, my dear, anything. Come now if you want." She arrived and very soon after the tea came. Before we started to talk about her problem the telephone went again. I turned away from her to answer it. When I put the telephone down I could see she was very tense. Very frightened. While I was studying her face I picked up my glass of tea. It was actually touching my lips and I was about to take the first drink. Suddenly she jumped up and knocked the glass away from my lips and out of my hand. "No, Abu Iyad!" she shouted. "Don't drink! The tea is poisoned! *I have poisoned your tea!*" She had tipped the poison into my tea from a secret compartment in the ring she was wearing, a ring she was given by her Mossad controller. The poor kid put her arms around my neck and cried her heart out. She confessed the whole thing. The Israelis had discovered she worked for me and they had said her family would suffer if she didn't do what they wanted.'

If Hussein could not somehow be obliged to do Israel's dirty work and confront the P.L.O., Israel's leaders knew they would sooner or later be forced to make a choice between reducing the kingdom to rubble, or occupying what was left of it. That was the logic of Israel's military policy. But there were obvious problems. From Israel's point of view the first option would have been too expensive in terms of lost prestige and international support – even Israel's best Western friends and allies would not have been able to support and condone such Israeli ruthlessness; and the second option would have been too dangerous because of the risk of the Israelis being sucked into a Vietnam-type situation and trap. Hussein had to be forced to smash the P.L.O. for them.

When Israel's intelligence chiefs set their Palestinian traitor-agents to work in Jordan, all the evidence suggests that they were not being mere opportunists and that they were proceeding according to a carefully prepared plan. The evidence, or so Arafat and his colleagues believe, is in the answer to the question: why really did Israel decide to use its air force against the *fedayeen* in early 1969?

By the summer of that year Israel's leaders were beginning to admit what every military expert knows – that guerrilla activities and infiltrations cannot be stopped with air strikes. When pressed to explain the real reasons for their use of air power, Israel's leaders said it was 'to give us a respite', 'to keep the enemy off balance', 'to keep the initiative' and 'to achieve longer-term aims'.

What were those unspecified 'longer-term aims'? With the benefit of hindsight, Arafat and his colleagues are sure of the answer. As Arafat put it: 'The Israelis were using their air power not to fight us, but to drive us into the towns and the cities where we could be more easily hit when Hussein was forced, by one means or another, to attack us.'

By July 1970, Israel's military planners were going quietly up the proverbial wall. For more than a year they had been hitting Jordan very hard – and in the process they had tried the patience of Israel's Western friends to near its limits – and their agents in Jordan were continuing to do all that was possible to provoke a confrontation between the *fedayeen* and the King's armed forces; but Israel's longer-term strategy was not working. The June fighting between the *fedayeen* and the King's men had not, as the Israelis had hoped, led to an all-out confrontation. And contrary to Israel's expectations, Hussein was still refusing even to contemplate a final showdown with the P.L.O. From Israel's point of view it was bad enough that the King was working with Arafat to prevent an explosion. Worse still was the fact that Hussein had let it be known that he would rather abdicate than do Israel's dirty work. In fact Hussein did decide to abdicate, but he was persuaded by Nasser to change his mind. From his conversations with Fatah's leaders and with Nasser, the King knew there was no danger of Jordan being taken over by Arafat's P.L.O. He was aware that the leftist and radical elements in the liberation movement had an infinite capacity to cause trouble, but he also knew they did not pose any military threat to his regime without Fatah's support. In so far as there was a real threat to his throne, it came not from the Palestinians, but from the King's so-called friends in the Military High Command who, like the Israelis, were angry that he would not give the order for an all-out and final offensive against the P.L.O.

The Israelis were desperate, and in July they asked their American friends to help them twist Hussein's arm. It may be that the Israelis simply asked for help and were given it without question. It could also be that the Israelis effectively blackmailed the Americans into blackmailing Hussein. Since Henry Kissinger was at the time talking about expelling the Soviets from Egypt and the Middle East, and since Kissinger and the Israelis maintained that Arafat and his colleagues were Soviet puppets, it is not difficult to see why there was a meeting of minds. In any event, the Americans decided to help Israel. It was probably Kissinger who masterminded the operation to fix Hussein; and it is even more likely that the fixing was done through Kissinger's famous back channels. Kissinger was later to boast that he put together what amounted to his own intelligence service – the 'back channels' – and that he used it whenever he did not want the institutions of government to know what he was doing. That Kissinger put himself above the due political process and above the law of his own and other lands is beyond doubt.

The story of how certain Americans blackmailed Hussein into moving against the P.L.O. was told to me by Abu Daoud as it was told to him, in the most extraordinary circumstances, by the King himself.

The meeting at which Hussein revealed all to Abu Daoud took place in a prison cell in Amman. The date was 18 September 1973. With Egypt's President Sadat preparing to launch his war for peace, Hussein had taken two decisions. The first was that he was not going to fight. The second was to declare an amnesty for political prisoners. Abu Daoud was among the prisoners to be released. The following is Abu Daoud's account of the King's story.

'The King came in person to unlock the door to my cell. Considering I was in prison because I had organized a plot to overthrow him, you may think that is very strange. But that's how it happened. Hussein is a man of great humility. He is also a good human being. I think perhaps he was sorry because I had been so badly tortured.' It may also have been that Jordan's intelligence chiefs refused to obey the King's order to release Abu Daoud.

'Before I tell you what he said to me,' Abu Daoud continued, 'there is some background information you must know. At the time the King was very dependent on American money. Each year they gave him the cash to pay the expenses of his court and the salaries of his army. It was supposed to be a secret but in the Arab world it was well known. The Americans paid this money to the King twice a year – in January and July. Now to what the King said.

'He told me the main reason why he moved against us in 1970 was because the Americans threatened to remove him from power if he did not do what they wanted. And according to what the King said, it happened in this way. In July he received no money at all – in other words, the normal payment for the second six months was delayed. In early August he received payment for only one month and not six months as usual. Immediately the King spoke to the American Ambassador on the telephone. He asked the American, "Why do you pay only one month?" The Ambassador replied with just one sentence. He said: "Your Majesty, you should know the United States only backs the winning horse." The King told me he was very angry, but he said nothing and put the telephone down. He realized, of course, that the Americans were telling him they regarded what was happening in Jordan as a race between two horses – the King and Arafat.

'Now the way I have told you the story so far makes it sound as though the King moved against us because of the money. But that was not the point. As Hussein told me, the money was only a symbol or code for the real American threat. What they were actually saying to him was, "If you are not prepared to move against Arafat and the P.L.O., then we Americans don't need you and we won't pay you. In other words, Your Majesty, if you don't do what we want, we'll put one of your generals in your place!" Of course, the Americans did not make the threat in these terms. But that is the message they intended the King to get when they cut off his funds. And the King got the message. That is the story as Hussein told it to me himself in the course of our conversation in my cell.'

As a man of honour, Hussein's instinctive reaction would have been to abdicate rather than give in to such an appalling threat. But he knew only too well that if he did abdicate any of his generals the Americans might put in his place would not stop until there was no more Palestinian blood to flow.

In Arafat's opinion Hussein would still not have allowed himself to be forced into taking the offensive against the P.L.O. if he had not believed that he had Nasser's support for such action. And in Arafat's view – more implied than clearly stated – the biggest of many crimes committed by the leftists and the radicals within the P.L.O. was a particular demonstration they made which humiliated Nasser and caused him, in his anger, to send Hussein a message which the King wrongly interpreted as backing from Cairo to move against the *fedayeen* at a time of his choosing.

The occasion for the demonstration was Nasser's acceptance of the second Rogers Plan on 23 July 1970. A few days later Hussein, and then the Israelis, accepted it too. The second Rogers Plan conceded the principle that the Israelis ought to withdraw from the West Bank as well as Egyptian territory, and it required Israel, Egypt and Jordan to accept the services of a U.N. mediator, Gunnar Jarring. Part of the package was a call for a ceasefire, which Nasser and Israel also accepted, thus bringing to an end the War of Attrition on the Suez Canal front. As it turned out, the Jarring Mission, and with it the Rogers Plan, was doomed – mainly because the Israelis were not intending to withdraw from the West Bank. But at the time of its unveiling the second Rogers Plan did represent a ray of hope to Nasser and Hussein.

Said Khalad Hassan: 'I agree with Arafat. Our real troubles in Jordan started because of the way we Palestinians rejected the second Rogers Plan. Though when I say we Palestinians I really mean the leftists. Nasser gave us advance warning of the Rogers Plan, and he said this: "I am going to accept it. You are free to reject it – that is your right. But whatever you decide, *do not criticize me.*"'

The P.L.O. officially rejected the second Rogers Plan, and Chairman Arafat went through the motions, in public, of saying that the liberation movement would continue its armed struggle. If he had said less in public, Arafat and his Fatah colleagues would have lost their credibility with the rank and file in their own organization. But unofficially and in reality, Fatah's unspoken understanding with Nasser, and by extension Hussein, was still holding. If the Rogers Plan and the Jarring Mission led to peace between the front-line Arab states and Israel, Fatah would agree to continue the struggle by political means alone.

Knowing this to be the real position of the Fatah leadership, the leftist and radical fronts within the P.L.O. decided to stage an anti-Nasser demonstration. Arafat said, 'I begged Habash and the other leftists not to make such a demonstration. I was completely against it. When they refused my request, I said to them, "At least let us go and talk with Nasser before making any demonstrations." And they refused me again.'

So the leftists took to the streets in Amman with slogans and banners condemning Nasser as the 'traitor' and an 'agent of American imperialism'. And the demonstration was led by a donkey with a picture of Nasser on its face.

Arafat told me: 'It was very rude. Very offensive. Very stupid. It was also our fatal mistake. Nasser was our protector. Since 1967 he had been saying to Hussein, "Do anything you like to make peace with Israel and get back the West Bank. I will support any move and any action you take for that purpose – but I will not support any attempt to liquidate the *fedayeen* movement." When I told you Nasser was dealing with us as a Godfather, that is what I meant.' After a pause, and in a voice which betrayed his contempt for the leftists, Arafat said, 'If they were trying to make trouble between me and Nasser they succeeded.'

According to Khalad Hassan, Arafat himself then made a mistake which added insult to Nasser's injury. 'At a meeting of the P.L.O.

Executive Committee we decided to send delegations to various
Arab countries,' Khalad said. 'Really Arafat had to be in two places
at once – Cairo and Baghdad.'

In the event of a Jordanian offensive against the P.L.O., Arafat
was counting on the 17,000 Iraqi troops in Jordan coming to his
aid. Iraq's leaders had given the P.L.O. a promise to that effect. So it
was important for Arafat to maintain the best possible relations
with the regime in Baghdad.

Khalad continued: 'The problem was that relations between
Cairo and Baghdad were horrible at the time. As a compromise I
suggested that I should head a delegation to Baghdad, and that
Arafat should lead the main delegation in Cairo. It was so obvious
that Nasser would be even more angry if Arafat went to Baghdad
first. I begged, really begged, Arafat to go to Cairo first. That was
what we agreed. I set off for Iraq. On the way we had a crash and my
two bodyguards were killed. Anyway, I arrived in Baghdad and two
hours later I was astonished to see Arafat there. I said to him
something like, "My God, Abu Amar, you are crazy! We cannot
afford to antagonize Nasser more." He said, "Yes, I know that. But
I am also the Chairman and it is my responsibility to keep our
organizations together. The majority insisted that I come here
first."'

When Arafat finally arrived in Cairo from Baghdad, Nasser
refused to meet him. 'But twenty-four hours later our good friend
Heikal again caused Nasser's door to be opened,' Khalad said. 'And
Fatah's relationship with Nasser was once more on a good basis.' It
was so, as Arafat is fond of saying; but the damage had already been
done. In his anger and humiliation Nasser had told Hussein he
would not object if the King thought it was time the *fedayeen* were
taught a lesson.

Said Arafat: 'I came to know later that Nasser had only meant to
tell Hussein to teach us a little lesson, to twist our tail.
Unfortunately Hussein interpreted Nasser's remark as the green
light to move against us. And this was the price we paid for the way
in which the leftists humiliated Nasser.' On the day Nasser died he
told Arafat he blamed himself for not making his message to
Hussein clear.

In early August, Hussein began to redeploy his forces. Tanks and
other armoured vehicles were being switched from the border with

Israel to locations around Amman and some other cities. When the pattern of what was happening became clear to Fatah's field officers they requested a meeting with Arafat.

Said Abu Daoud: 'We told Arafat we thought it was necessary for us to take action to prevent the tanks from reaching Amman and the other cities. We said the Jordanians would not be able to mount an offensive against us if we could confine their main forces to the border areas. Arafat was very firm. He said, "These are Arab tanks. We cannot attack them. We will defend ourselves if the time comes but the way to liberation is not by fighting our Arab brothers."' Clearly, Arafat was not intending to take any offensive action against the regime in Jordan. But certain Palestinians did take the initiative, and in the most dramatic way possible.

At their last meeting in Cairo, Nasser had warned Arafat that further provocations to Hussein's army had to be prevented at all costs. Said Arafat, 'When I returned to Amman I told everybody what Nasser had said. And once more I begged the leftists to stop their provocations. I told them very frankly they were creating a disaster for our people. But once more they refused me . . . and you know what happened.'

On 6 September, Habash's P.F.L.P. mounted what can only be called a spectacular and sensational hijack operation. On the first day P.F.L.P. terrorists hijacked four international airliners. One, a Pan-Am jumbo jet, was blown up at Beirut airport after its passengers had disembarked. Two others – one belonging to T.W.A., the other to Swiss Air – were eventually forced to land at Dawson's Field, a strip of desert in Jordan, where more P.F.L.P. terrorists were waiting. The attempt to hijack an El-Al plane in the air was foiled by Israeli security agents on board. They killed one of the terrorists and captured another. Her name was Leila Khaled. The El-Al plane landed safely in London. Israel demanded Leila Khaled's extradition. The P.F.L.P. demanded her release. And the P.F.L.P. backed its demand by hijacking a British B.O.A.C. airliner. It, too, was forced to land at Dawson's Field. By now a total of three very expensive planes and about 600 hostages were in the P.F.L.P.'s hands.

The hijackings led to clashes between the *fedayeen* and Hussein's forces. With the lives of the hostages at stake, Arafat and Hussein – two very desperate men who had each lost control of their own extremists – agreed a ceasefire. But the P.F.L.P. and the P.D.F. rejected the agreement.

Co-operating fully with the International Red Cross, Arafat's first priority was to secure the release of the hostages. He demanded a meeting of the Central Committee of the Palestine Resistance (C.C.P.R.). This was the only committee on which all the military groups were represented, including those who were not members of the P.L.O. For once Arafat decided that he would not even try to get a unanimous decision. He said he wanted and would accept a majority vote on the release of the hostages. In the drama of the time, the P.F.L.P. were suddenly heroes in the eyes of the *fedayeen*. Some Fatah fighters had switched their allegiance and joined the P.F.L.P. out of admiration for the hijackers and those who had planned the operation. So, as ever, Arafat was swimming against the tide of popular and emotional opinion.

Some say Arafat told the C.C.P.R. he would resign the Chairmanship of the P.L.O. if the vote went against him. In any event, he got the majority he wanted and the release of the hostages was ordered. The P.F.L.P. responded by releasing all but sixty of the hostages and by blowing up the three airliners before they took their leave of Dawson's Field, using the sixty remaining hostages as their shield and guarantee of safety.

After the release of most of the hostages and the destruction of the airliners, the P.F.L.P. was suspended from the C.C.P.R., and it was warned that a strong stand would be taken against the P.F.L.P. for any future action which 'harmed the revolution'. Then to many observers Arafat seemed to be backtracking when he said he would not allow the P.F.L.P. to become 'isolated and vulnerable'. In fact this was Arafat's way of asking for just a little understanding from the international community for his political problems with Habash and his extremist colleagues.

The monster hijack was the last straw for Jordan's High Command. But still Hussein refused to give the order for an all-out offensive against the P.L.O. He was worried about the fate of the sixty remaining hostages (they were eventually released unharmed); and he was even more troubled by what might happen to his country if the Syrians decided to intervene on the side of the *fedayeen*. About the Iraqis the King did not have to worry, however. As he knew by now, Iraq's Defence Minister had taken a huge bribe to keep his forces out of any fighting! One of the sources of this information was a high-ranking Jordanian Air Force officer, a Palestinian who is today one of Arafat's top advisers. He said: 'I was at the Mufrak air base when the Iraqi Defence Minister arrived. He was personally carrying two large but light and obviously empty suitcases. His visit was unscheduled and completely secret. Officially the visit didn't take place. He was having a whispered conversation with a very senior Jordanian officer and then he saw me. He was very surprised and he looked very embarrassed and, if I may say, very guilty. But he said nothing to me. Two hours later the minister left. He was carrying his own suitcases again but it was obvious they were now quite heavy. From what I saw with my own eyes, and from what I heard later, my guess is that the two suitcases were full of American dollars! I can't prove it but that is what I think. It is also what they think in every defence ministry in the Arab world. Nasser's contempt for many of his Arab colleagues was absolutely justified.'

Hani Hassan added a postscript to the bribe story and the first round of the civil war. He said: 'In my opinion Arafat was counting on the Iraqis, not the Syrians. He was so confident the Iraqis would fight with us if the Jordanians attacked that I don't believe he had even considered the possibility that Hussein could crush him! I also think the way the Iraqis deceived him completed his education about Arab politics.'

Hussein was still in a state of indecision when his generals called on him to deliver their ultimatum. I think it is not unreasonable to assume that when they took their decision to force the King's hand, Kissinger's 'back channel' influence was decisive.

The Syrians put on a token show of support for the *fedayeen* when the Jordanians launched their offensive. They made a ground advance without air cover across the border into Jordan; but they turned for home as soon as Damascus was informed that the Israelis, with Nixon's approval, would engage them.

Nixon and Kissinger appeared to be obsessed with the idea that the Soviets were behind an Arafat plot to take over Jordan. Said Khalad Hassan: 'You know what was between us and the Soviets at the time – nothing. The only thing the Soviets did as the crisis approached was to send a stream of urgent messages, mainly through Nasser, asking us all to cool it and to avoid a confrontation in Jordan at all costs. On this occasion, and on many more in the future, it was the Soviets who were behaving like statesmen and the Americans who were acting in a dangerous and reckless way. That is the judgment of Fatah's leading rightist – me. And it is also the truth. As for the charge that we were attempting to take over Jordan – that was bullshit as I think you will agree now that you have heard our story.'

At the start of the year Arafat had warned that 1970 would be 'the year of international conspiracy' against his people and their cause. How right he was. It was also a dangerous year for Arafat personally. It had opened with two attempts on his life.

According to Abu Iyad both were the work of one of Israel's two main intelligence agencies, either the Mossad or the Directorate of Military Intelligence. When the Israelis decided to put some real effort into trying to assassinate Arafat – that decision seems to have been taken late in 1969 – they knew they had to overcome Arafat's secrecy of movement if they were to be successful. By 1969 the Israelis had a number of Palestinian agents around Arafat, but they never had the possibility of knowing when Arafat would move. Said Abu Iyad: 'The Israelis solved this problem by getting one of their agents to fix a bugging or homing device to Arafat's Volvo car. The idea, obviously, was that Israeli fighter planes would lock on to its signal. Rockets would be fired and bang – no more Arafat.'

I asked Arafat how the device was discovered. He laughed and said, 'The first time an Israeli war plane followed me I thought it was bad luck or a coincidence. Maybe. Then I realized they had some means of knowing my movements. Remember I am an engineer. I knew what to look for and I found the device.'

Abu Iyad added, 'After that Arafat changed his bodyguards. We never discovered the identity of the Israeli agent on this occasion, but the Chairman was taking no chances.'

For their second attempt the Israelis took the risk of exposing one of their deep-cover agents inside Iraqi Military Intelligence. This agent sent Arafat a letter-bomb. Said Abu Iyad: 'Actually it was made to look like a package of documents. It was sent from Iraqi Military Intelligence headquarters in Baghdad to the Chief of Iraqi Military Intelligence in Jordan. It was completely official and was addressed in the proper and normal way to Arafat personally – for his attention only. As was normal, the Chief of Iraqi Military

Intelligence in Jordan sent the package to Arafat by special messenger and without delay. This was a routine procedure. You should not forget that we had been infiltrating into Jordan through the Iraqis since 1968. Well, the package arrived when Arafat, myself and others in the leadership were having a meeting. Arafat let the package stay on his desk for some time while we talked. He gave no indication that he was suspicious of the package. Suddenly he stopped our conversation and said quietly, "Take it away. It's a bomb. I can smell it."'

How did the story end? Said Abu Iyad: 'When we opened the package in the proper way there was a very big explosion. If it had been opened in the room where we were most of us would have been killed.'

When the civil war started on 17 September, Hussein's generals vowed they would succeed where the Israelis, and before them the Syrians, had failed. They assigned a special force to the task of locating and killing the Chairman of the P.L.O. Arafat was not to be taken alive.

Abu Iyad said: 'The Jordanian special force did discover the house where Arafat was staying. You must remember there was a curfew. Movement was difficult to impossible. They surrounded the house and attacked from all sides. It was destroyed. At the time I was under arrest. They caught me while I was moving from one house to another during a short truce to allow people to get water and foodstuffs. They told me Arafat was dead. Unfortunately I believed them and they obliged me to make a broadcast saying that and calling on my people to stop fighting. Perhaps they did believe Arafat was dead. Perhaps they tricked me. But Arafat was still alive. He had slipped out of the house minutes before it was surrounded.'

Having failed to kill Arafat, Hussein's generals refused to guarantee him a safe passage to Cairo to attend the emergency Arab summit that Nasser had convened to halt the fighting. At the time the King was effectively without power. The generals had taken over in all but name. They refused to implement a truce which Hussein had accepted in answer to the call of the Cairo summit. To make their point the generals ordered the shelling of the place where Sudan's President Numeiri was staying. He was in Jordan as the representative of the Arab leaders attending the summit. His job was to arrange the truce and to guarantee Arafat's safety. He failed.

It was at this point that Nasser told Hussein he would order Egyptian troops to impose a ceasefire if the King could not control his generals. The man who did outwit Hussein's generals was Sheikh Saa'd Abdullah Assalim. Today he is the Crown Prince of Kuwait. At the time he was that country's Minister of Defence and he was sent by the Cairo summit to succeed where Numeiri had failed. Khalad Hassan said: 'When he arrived in Amman the Jordanians followed him. They were hoping he would lead them to Arafat and then, when they had located the Chairman, they were going to kill him – Arafat. Sheikh Saa'd stripped down to his underwear and gave Arafat his top robes. Arafat then travelled to Amman airport disguised as Sheikh Saa'd and in a Jordanian armoured personnel carrier!'

When I was conducting my own peace initiative a decade later, I had occasion to ask Arafat if he felt he could trust Hussein with his life. After only a brief pause for thought, he replied, 'Hussein, yes . . . but not some of those around him.'

On 27 September 1970, the first phase of the civil war in Jordan came to an end when Arafat and Hussein shook hands in Cairo. Nasser did not believe that the truce he had forced Jordan's generals to accept would solve any problems. But he was hoping it would buy the time that he and Hussein needed to make something of the Rogers Plan. On that score Nasser and Hussein were aware that much would depend on the struggle for power that was taking place in Washington. If Rogers continued to have some influence on U.S. policy for the Middle East, there was a chance that the American Administration would cause Israel to make the necessary withdrawals for peace. But if Kissinger's influence continued to grow and if, God forbid, Kissinger won his fight to become Secretary of State, then there would be no hope. Kissinger was against any peace that would leave the Soviets with even the smallest vestige of influence in the Middle East.

For his part Arafat had the consolation of knowing that he had been right to put his trust in Nasser. Although the Egyptian leader had in a sense been partly to blame for what had happened – by sending an angry and ambiguous message to Hussein – he had honoured his promise to do everything in his power to prevent the liberation movement being liquidated once the Jordanians had launched their offensive. Arafat now knew that within the limits of what was possible on the Arab side, the Palestinian cause was safe in

Nasser's hands – provided the Palestinians were free to make their own decisions about what they would and would not accept by way of a settlement to their claim for justice. So it is not difficult to imagine how completely shattered Arafat was when, twenty-four hours later, he learned that Nasser had died of a massive heart attack.

Said Khalad Hassan: 'We were in Damascus when the news of Nasser's death came through. Arafat, myself and the Syrian President were sitting in the Algerian Embassy. In words I cannot begin to tell you how empty and how lonely we felt. Arafat and the President wept. They cried and cried and cried. It was finally Arafat who spoke for us all – and I am sure most Arabs – when he said, "We have lost everything."'

That Arafat and his colleagues in Fatah's leadership did realize the Palestinians had lost their protector was one of two main reasons why they worked so hard to make the truce work.

Said Khalad Hassan: 'In the past, and as you know, I had had many differences with Arafat. On some important matters we continued to have differences. And no doubt in the future we will disagree again. But this much you must also know. . . In the period after Nasser's death I was proud that we had such a man as Arafat for our leader. In their hearts if not their minds the majority in our liberation movement were bitter and wanted revenge. Up to 3,000 of our people had been killed – most of them were civilians – and many more were wounded. So our people were talking openly about the need for revenge. But not Arafat. At all of our meetings he spoke only of the need for reconciliation with Hussein's regime. This Arafat was not a politician. Politicians only say what the people want to hear. This Arafat was a statesman. He was giving the lead in one direction when the majority wanted to go in another. And he was very honest with the leftists. To them he said, "You refused my ideas. Here are the results. You are responsible for what has happened." And he warned them that our movement would be "committing suicide" if they provoked another confrontation with Jordan's army.'

From November the extremists on both sides – in the P.L.O. and the Jordanian army – did their best to provoke another confrontation. But according to Abu Iyad it was the Jordanians who did most of the provoking. He said: 'They did it in a clever way. Instead of trying to enter the refugee camps in and around Amman, they hired houses close to the camps and fired from them.' In January 1971 there was a serious outbreak of fighting between the *fedayeen* and Hussein's forces. And Habash renewed his call for Hussein's overthrow. After that, and on his own initiative, Abu Iyad negotiated an agreement with Hussein which Abu Iyad was hoping would deny the Jordanians the excuse to make a second and final offensive against the P.L.O. The agreement committed the P.L.O. to withdraw all of its heavy weapons from Amman and confine them to the area around Jerash and Ajlun. If Hussein's generals had been seriously interested in making an accommodation with the P.L.O., Abu Iyad's agreement could have been the basis for it. In the event, all that Abu Iyad's agreement did was to postpone the final showdown and to make it easier for the Jordanians when they went for the kill. This led Abu Iyad to conclude that he had been deceived by the King.

The second main reason why Fatah's leaders were anxious, even desperate, to co-operate with Hussein was that they knew they had no alternative. If Fatah was to lose its base in Jordan, where else could it put down roots?

In theory Syria was as ready as ever to give the liberation movement, including Fatah, a home. But Syria was totally opposed to the idea of an independent Palestine liberation movement. Because Arafat and most of his Fatah colleagues were not willing to become Syria's puppets, Syria was not and could not be an alternative to Jordan. In fact, the possibility of an accommodation between a Fatah-dominated P.L.O. and Syria had ceased to exist in November 1970 when Arafat's old adversary, Hafez Assad, came to power in a bloodless coup.

Assad was the only Arab leader who was as cunning and ruthless as the Israelis and Kissinger. He was also an expert at playing both ends against the middle. A man who relied on the Soviets for his defence and who was still able to do secret political business with the Americans and the Israelis had to be, so to speak, one hell of a good poker player.

Over the years to come Assad and Arafat were to pretend they were on the same side. In reality they were not. There was no trust between them. If Assad had been prepared to allow the Palestinians to make their own decisions, within the framework of what was possible on the Arab side, the Syrian President could have had more or less the same relationship with Arafat as Nasser had had. Such a relationship might have changed the course of history. Assad plus Arafat plus Saudi Arabia's wealth and political power would have been more than a match for the Israelis. If they had been willing to work as one, Assad, Arafat and the oil-producing Gulf States could have succeeded in forcing the Americans, by one means or another, to oblige Israel to make the necessary withdrawals for peace. But it was not to be, mainly because Assad wanted to play the Palestinian card for his own ends.

Since Syria was not an alternative to Jordan as a P.L.O. base, that left only the Lebanon as a place where the *fedayeen* could regroup and at least defend themselves if they were pushed out of Jordan. But that was not an option Fatah's leaders wanted to take up.

Said Khalad Hassan: 'As I have told you, we in Fatah always knew that it would be a very big mistake for the liberation movement to entrench itself in the Lebanon. But it wasn't simply a question of us knowing that the Lebanon could not take the Israeli attacks that would result from our presence, or that the Israeli attacks would succeed one day in turning the Lebanese against us even if we behaved like angels. There was much more to it.

'You see, we in Fatah had studied Zionist political literature in its original Hebrew, and we were completely aware of Israel's long-term strategy regarding the Lebanon. At all costs the Israelis were committed to maintaining a Christian-dominated regime in the Lebanon. If you don't want to take my word for this you should read, for example, the published conversations between Moshe Sharett and Ben-Gurion. Now, by the late 1960s the Israelis had a real problem – because of the demographic change that was taking place in the Lebanon. The population explosion was such that the Moslems were on their way to becoming the majority, and it was obvious that a day was coming when the Moslem majority would insist on having most of the political power – according to their numbers and the democratic principle. Now what were the Israelis to do? The only way they could guarantee to keep a Christian minority in power in the Lebanon was to intervene by force. But the Israelis needed a pretext to involve themselves in such a way. And it was clear to us in Fatah that if we moved into the Lebanon, we could give the Israelis exactly the pretext they needed to do what they liked there by force. To sum up, we in Fatah were perfectly aware that by entrenching ourselves in the Lebanon we would be playing right into Israel's hands with disastrous and predictable consequences for ourselves, the Lebanese and the whole Arab world. Now do you see why we in Fatah were so anxious to reach an accommodation with Hussein?'

For all of that, because they did not have an alternative, it was to the Lebanon that the *fedayeen* fled when Hussein's generals went for the kill on 13 July 1971. The offensive was directed with great enthusiasm by Jordan's Prime Minister of the day, Wasfi Tal, a former chauffeur and a former part-time agent for Britain's S.I.S. Wasfi Tal is a name to remember. His days were numbered.

The Jordanians used everything they had – tanks, planes, artillery. It was a vicious, merciless onslaught to drive the *fedayeen* out of Jordan completely. Syria's President Assad assisted the Jordanians by closing his borders to *fedayeen* reinforcements.

One indication of what happened on the battlefield is the fact that one hundred or more of Arafat's fighters surrendered to Israeli forces rather than be captured alive by Hussein's men. On condition that I did not name him, a Fatah loyalist who came close to surrendering to the Israelis told me the following story:

'We were six altogether and we had seen with our own eyes how the Jordanians were torturing our people before they killed them. We ran in the direction of the border with Israel. As we made our approach to the Jordan River we raised our Kalishnikovs with both hands above our heads to indicate to the Israelis that we wanted to surrender. I didn't see the Israelis but I heard them. In Arabic they were calling to us in friendly voices. "Hello, *fedayeen*. Come, *fedayeen*. Put down your weapons and you will be safe. You are welcome." I was just standing there, thinking. And then something very strange happened. I wanted to move forward. I had decided to surrender. But my legs would not advance my body. My brain said, "Put down your gun. Save your life. Move forward." But my heart said, "Stop. You can't do it." And my heart won. Then I started to run away from the Israelis. I was crying and I was ashamed of myself. And my comrades were running with me. I suppose the Israelis could have killed us. But they didn't fire a shot. Perhaps they felt sorry for us. Who knows?'

Another story about how really terrified many Palestinians were was told to me by a man who is today a senior Fatah engineer. He said: 'As you know, many Palestinians who had become citizens of Jordan and who were serving in the King's army defected to us during and after the September fighting. The regime then passed a law saying that any officer who joined the P.L.O. and was caught would be hanged. As a consequence of that many officers brought their families with them when they joined us. A number of these officers and their families were based at the Gaza camp in the forest of Jerash in northern Jordan, where I was. On 13 July, when we were surrounded by the Jordanians, but just before the fighting started, I heard four pistol shots from close by and then a man crying. I rushed to see what had happened. One of these officers was kneeling on the ground. By him were the bodies of his wife and three children. He had just killed them. He was my friend and I said to him, "Why do you do this thing?" He was still crying and he said, "I could not leave them to be killed by the Jordanians. I know what will happen when they come. If I am finished in the fight they will still kill my wife and children because they are mine. I couldn't let that happen." Then my friend asked for God's forgiveness and he killed himself. A few minutes later there were more pistol shots. And more. Two other officers killed their families and then themselves. This is what I saw with my own eyes. Later, I heard that a number of other officers did the same thing.'

On 19 July, Wasfi Tal announced there were no more *fedayeen* bases in Jordan. In six days it was all over. Hussein's generals had finished what they had started in September 1970 – Black September as it came to be called by the Palestinians.

Hani Hassan said: 'One month after Black September Hussein summoned all the P.L.O. leaders to meet with him. And he made to us a very dramatic statement. He said, "There is no more a reason for us to be fighting. The Americans have promised me I can have the West Bank back."'

To some of the P.L.O. leaders present, Hussein's statement was an indication that perhaps the Americans were serious about trying to implement the second Rogers Plan.

Hani continued: 'The implication was obvious to us all. The Americans had told the King they intended to put enough pressure on the Israelis to force them to withdraw. We were completely stunned and there was a great silence. Even Arafat did not speak. Finally it was me who broke the silence on our side. I said: "Your

Majesty, you are right. If you get back the West Bank you will be our hero, we will salute you and there will be no need for us to fight – if you get the West Bank back. In the meantime we will want to see what happens."

'The problem for Hussein was in Washington. He had just been there. At the time he was speaking to us, Rogers had still some influence on America's policy for the Middle East. And it was Rogers or his people in the State Department who made the promise to Hussein. But by the early summer of 1971, Rogers had lost his battle and Kissinger was the dominating influence. And Kissinger was not interested in a comprehensive peace. At that time he was not interested in peace at all. Kissinger's only objective was to get the Soviets out of the Middle East and out of Egypt in particular. Kissinger had studied all the files and information on Nasser's successor, Anwar Sadat, and he had come to certain conclusions. These conclusions were that Sadat was a vain man – Kissinger actually called him a "clown" in private – who could be dominated by Kissinger if he, Kissinger, was prepared to flatter him enough. In short, Kissinger decided to put the real Middle East problem on ice, to kill the Rogers Plan and to work with Sadat – in the first place to get the Soviets out of Egypt. When that was done Kissinger believed he would himself have great influence and prestige and would then be in a position to talk Sadat into making a separate peace with Israel. Kissinger knew, of course, that with Egypt neutralized, the other Arabs would never be able to fight. He also knew that when Egypt was neutralized, the Israelis would be free to do what they liked in the Middle East – for themselves and for America. And in that situation it would not be necessary for an American Administration to put pressure on Israel to withdraw from the West Bank. Once Egypt was neutralized Israel would be the superpower of the Middle East and those other Arab states who wanted peace, Jordan in particular, would have to make it on Israeli and American terms.

'Now Hussein knew what was happening in Washington and he was very depressed. And he came to certain conclusions of his own. The first was that the Rogers Plan and the idea of a comprehensive settlement was dead – because Kissinger had effectively killed it. The second was that Kissinger didn't give a damn about the West Bank, and that no American Administration of which he was a part would ever put pressure on Israel to withdraw from it. Hussein then came to a decision. In effect he said to himself the following: "Because of the Kissinger approach and policy it is now every Arab leader for himself. That being so I might as well take the necessary action to completely secure what is left of my country. There is no more any point in fighting with my own generals to avoid a final showdown with the P.L.O." And in that frame of mind the King said to Wasfi Tal and his generals, "Okay, do it!"'

I asked Hani if it was also the case that Hussein decided to finish the P.L.O. in Jordan because he wanted to prove to Kissinger that he was master in his own house and could make peace with Israel on terms which ought to be acceptable to the U.S.

Hani replied, 'That is possible, but I am sure the explanation I gave you is the main reason why the King acted in July.'

In reality there are few, if any, men who enjoy a more honest relationship with King Hussein than Hani Hassan and his brother Khalad. It was not always the case but it is so today. For that reason alone, Hani's analysis of why the King decided to expel the P.L.O. from Jordan in July 1971 is most probably correct.

It invites the conclusion that it was Henry Kissinger who was, in one way or another, mostly to blame for wrecking the Rogers Plan and all the effort and hope for peace that Nasser and Hussein had invested in it, with Fatah's understanding. It must also be said that Israel's leaders were blind not to see that peace was there for the taking after Hussein had expelled the P.L.O. from Jordan, if they had wanted it. I personally believe that Golda Meir really did want peace, but I also think she was the outstanding example of those in Israel who had become the victims of their own propaganda.

There was, however, a ray of hope on a distant horizon. The C.I.A., or at least a part of it, was totally opposed to Kissinger's approach and the policies that would inevitably flow from it if ever Kissinger became the U.S. Secretary of State – which he did in July 1973. Up to the level of Deputy Director, and perhaps higher, the wise men in the C.I.A. knew that Kissinger's approach spelled disaster not only for the Arabs but, in the long term, for America's own best interests in the region. My guess is that one of the great untold stories of the second half of the twentieth century is the running fight between the C.I.A. and Kissinger, as American intelligence agents struggled to prevent an American Secretary of State from destroying the prospects for peace in the Middle East.

There remains the question of Arafat's responsibility for the suicidal confrontation with Hussein's regime – a confrontation Arafat did not seek and which he tried by diplomacy to avert. Was there more he could or should have done to prevent a minority of leftists and radicals from dictating the course of events on the Palestinian side?

The majority view among Fatah's top leaders was and still is that Fatah should have used as much force as necessary to isolate and control the leftists and radical groups to prevent them provoking a confrontation with Hussein. To illustrate how keen Arafat's colleagues were to use force, Abu Daoud told me the following story.

'On one of the many occasions when we were having a problem with Habash and the P.F.L.P., Arafat was away in Cairo. In his absence the leadership gave me an order to use force to isolate the P.F.L.P. – and I refused to act on this order. I said to the leadership: "As you know I am personally opposed to our policy. I believe we should be confronting Hussein in the proper way. But on this matter I am in agreement with Arafat. We cannot use the guns to settle our internal problems and contradictions."'

In the past, the two Hassan brothers had been on opposite sides in many arguments and debates about Arafat and his ideas. But on this question they were as one. Very candidly Hani said: 'I think we lost Jordan because Arafat refused to discipline the leftists. I think we were right to debate with the leftists and the radicals without putting any pressure on them, but when we had decided our line, which was to co-operate with Hussein, we should have disciplined and punished those who did not follow it and who broke the many ceasefire agreements we made with the King.'

Khalad said: 'I think we made a very big mistake by not using our superior military force to deal with the leftists and the so-called radicals. As a matter of fact we had two opportunities to contain them. The first was before the confrontation of Black September. We could have done it at any time in 1969 and before August 1970. The second was after the fighting of September. That is when we really should have acted. The leftists were finished and we in Fatah brought them back to life again for the sake of national unity. But in my opinion those were only our second and third mistakes. The first and the biggest was allowing the leftists to be a part of the P.L.O. in the first place. When we took over the P.L.O. in 1969, most of the leadership, especially me, wanted to exclude the leftists. They had no popular base. They represented only themselves. If the composition of the P.L.O. had been decided on true democratic principles, according to popular support for each of the various groups, the leftists would not have got a single seat. But Arafat insisted on all the organizations being included – for the sake of national unity. And Abu Iyad supported him. I said we already had national unity – the unity of the Palestinian people. We had lost our land and our homes and we wanted them back. You didn't have to convince the people to be nationalists, they were nationalists by definition. But you did have to convince them to be Marxists and so on. I said that if we allowed the so-called Marxists to impose an irrelevant ideology on our struggle, it would cause confusion and lead, in fact, to disunity among the people. But Arafat said all organizations had to be included.'

Khalad added a sort of philosophical footnote. 'If we want to put our mistakes in Jordan into their true perspective, and if we want to be fair to everybody, including the leftists, we have to say it's not only human beings who have to grow up and who must pass through childhood and adolescence before they are reasonably mature and a little bit wise. Political parties and even liberation movements have to go through the same growing up and learning process. And on their way they make mistakes due to inexperience, too. So you have to take account of how inexperienced we were in those days. In 1968, when we first started to infiltrate into Jordan, Fatah as a political organization was less than five years old. And for two of those five years we were an underground organization. You can't conduct a real political debate when you are underground. And the P.F.L.P. and other leftist groups were not much more than twelve months old. So we were very inexperienced and we did have so much to learn. In Fatah, and thanks largely to Nasser, we did learn very quickly that we had to come to terms with reality. Don't forget it was as early as January 1968 that we in Fatah conceded the principle that all Israelis who were prepared to live among us as equals were welcome in our Democratic State. So early in our political life this was a very big step forward, a very big concession to reality if you like; but the world gave us no credit for this dramatic proof that we in Fatah were practical men who were adjusting to reality as we became more experienced. And I will tell you something else. It is not easy to be wise all the time when you are permanently angry because of the injustice that has been done to you. Every day we Palestinians have to face our humiliation. I look in the mirror and I know what I see. There is Khalad Hassan. I shave his face, I clean his teeth and so on. I am real. I am me. But the Israelis tell me I don't exist. Really they know I do and they prove they know by dropping bombs on me. But they have to say I don't exist in order to deny me my rights. What kind of madness is this? Can I really be wise all the time when I am required to be part of such madness? I am telling you these things not to excuse or justify our mistakes in Jordan and elsewhere, but to explain them.'

Part of the reason Arafat did not use force to control and contain the leftists had its roots in what happened in Palestine in the years from 1936 to 1939, when the Palestinians revolted against the British occupying forces who were holding the ring while the Jews established their European colony in the heart of the Arab world.

Arafat said: 'During the revolt our Palestinian leadership was divided and the rival groups fought each other.'

The main split was between the uncompromising nationalists who were led by Arafat's relative, Haj Amin Husseini, and those who supported the Nashasshibis and the idea of working with the Jordanians for the sake of an eventual compromise with the British and the Jews.

Arafat continued: 'Because of this internal fighting many of our leaders were assassinated. Now, when the history of those times came to be written, the British and the Israelis put their own cover on the story. They said what had happened was proof of the difference between the civilized Jews and the uncivilized Arabs. While the Jews were creating a homeland the stupid Arabs of Palestine were killing each other. That is what has been written in Western books – you can read them. As always there was a grain of truth in what the Israelis and their Western allies said – but it was only a single grain and a very small one. Essentially the story as it has been told by the Israelis and their supporters is a propaganda lie. The truth is that when our leaders turned to the gun to solve their internal problems, our enemies took advantage of the situation and launched a campaign of assassination to destroy our leadership. Many of the killings were done by British agents. As a young man and a student leader in Cairo I had the opportunity to study these matters. I was horrified. And I made a vow that my generation would never repeat the mistakes of the past.

'In Jordan, when we were having big problems with the leftists, my colleagues in Fatah came to me and said: "Look, Abu Amar, our situation is critical. We must follow the Algerian way and we must be prepared to liquidate those in our movement who are harming our cause." Really I understood what they were saying. But I was very firm. I said to them: "Look, we cannot compare ourselves with the Algerians. We cannot compare ourselves with any liberation movement. Our situation is unique because we are not in our own land. And because we are not in our own land our enemies are all around us and inside us. If we begin seriously to fight with each other our enemies will take the opportunity to destroy us as they did in the 1930s."'

At about the same time as Fatah's leaders were wanting Arafat to sanction the use of force, Hani Hassan was acting as an extra pair of eyes and ears for the Chairman. He told me: 'I came to know that some of the leftists and even some of our Fatah colleagues were playing games with the Syrians. They were plotting against Arafat. I came to know these things because I followed them to their hotels and I had my own secret ways of knowing what they had discussed. One day I made my report to Arafat and I said to him: "Abu Amar, you must take action. These leftists and some of our colleagues will destroy our movement and they may even try to kill you. Please, Abu Amar, you *must* act! You must liquidate them!" Arafat said, "No." I was astonished and I said to him, "You are crazy!" I will never forget his reaction. He smiled very sadly and put both of his hands on my shoulders. Then he said: "Hani, you are a young man and you have much to learn. You are right to be against these leftists and those of our colleagues who are plotting against me. Truly I am more against them than you are. But we have to finish them by political means." And then he told me the story of 1936 and 1939.'

Was Arafat right or wrong? When really pressed in argument, as they were by me, even many of those who were Arafat's critics are prepared to concede that it is an open question. And indeed it is. If Arafat had sanctioned the use of force, and if the leftists and the radicals had meekly surrendered to Fatah's will without firing a shot, then perhaps the course of history would have been changed. But if they had resisted a Fatah attempt to control them Arafat's nightmare would undoubtedly have become a reality. Hit-men representing the intelligence services of the Arab regimes and Israel would have moved swiftly to take advantage of the situation and the Palestinian leadership would probably have been wiped out. The Arab regimes and Israel could then have told the world that the Palestinians had destroyed themselves. And the world in its innocence would no doubt have believed that to be the truth.

But as Arafat himself said to me, 'Who knows?' I had put to him the suggestion that his critics also had a good case when they said it would have been possible for Fatah to advance the cause more quickly by political means if the leftists had been controlled by force: 'Maybe they are right,' he replied. 'Who knows?'

There was another important reason why Arafat refused to allow guns to be used to settle internal disputes about policy. He said: 'If we had used the guns to solve such problems we would have made a nonsense of our democracy and our masses would have lost confidence in us. They would have said, "You want to impose your views by force. You are no different from the other Arab regimes. You want power for its own sake. We are not prepared to struggle and to die for that." You see, democracy is not just a political slogan. It is a way of life. In a democracy the people must be free to say what they think and what they want – which is why I insisted that all of the liberation fronts and groups should be included in the P.L.O. And I have always believed that this freedom was essential to our struggle. My own slogan is that *only free men will fight*. Now let me tell you what I mean.

'From the beginning I knew that our struggle would be a very long one and that it would have to continue for many years, perhaps even beyond the lifetime of my generation. I also knew that we would be the defenders and the Israelis would be the attackers once we had demonstrated that the Palestinian problem could not be swept under the carpet. And this is where my slogan is important. Do you think my people would have continued this struggle for so long, and would have suffered so much pain and misery, if the only reason for continuing was the fact that I was dictating to them at gunpoint? Of course not. Our resistance continues because it is the will of our people freely expressed. To tell you the truth it is not by our guns that we have survived against such impossible odds. If it was a question of guns and military technology we would have been finished many years ago. Israel is the superpower of the region and we are resisting it with the equivalent of bows and arrows. We have survived because of our democracy. We have survived because our democracy gives our people the freedom to say "Yes" or "No" to the idea of resistance and struggle. And on this matter of democracy and how it strengthens the will to resist we are giving all the Arab peoples and regimes a lesson. Even Nasser didn't understand that only free men will fight. As a leader you can have the latest and best military equipment in the world, but if the people have not the will to fight or to defend themselves, you have nothing. And people who are not free have not the will to resist beyond a certain point unless they are fanatics. If you are an ordinary Arab and you live in a dictatorship under a regime which you know doesn't care what happens to you, why should you give your life for such a regime? This was the lesson the Arab regimes ought to have learned after the 1967 war. So I repeat, we have survived because of our democracy. It is our lifeline and in Jordan and later I was not willing to cut it or even to risk cutting it.'

Once Arafat had ruled that force would not be used to contain the Palestinian opposition to Fatah's policy of co-operation with the Arab regimes who were ready for a just peace, there was only one way for the groups which made up the P.L.O. to resolve their fundamental differences – by talk.

Arafat is a consensus politician. In the period from 1969 to 1971, and throughout the years that followed, the Chairman's commitment to the seemingly impossible task of creating a consensus within the P.L.O. was much criticized by many of his Fatah colleagues on the grounds that it was 'paralysing the decision-making process'. From the perspective of 1984, two conclusions are in order. The first is that Arafat's commitment to consensus-making delayed by some years the day when the Palestinian leadership was free to commit itself in public to the kind of compromise that Fatah's leaders, especially Arafat himself, knew to be necessary if the Palestinians were ever to achieve even a measure of justice. The second is that Arafat's approach was justified and vindicated by time and events. As we shall see, it was by talking behind closed doors and not with guns that Arafat obliged the leftists and the radicals to come to terms with reality. He never lost sight of a fundamental truth which his more impatient Fatah colleagues were not always prepared to face. As Arafat himself put it to me: 'You can't *impose* compromise. If you do it will be discredited the next day, the next month or the next year. In our situation compromise will work only if it comes through discussion and debate and by agreement.'

I asked Arafat to suppose that we could turn the clock back to 1968 or thereabouts. 'If we could do that,' I said, 'would you handle the crisis in Jordan in a different way?'

He replied: 'No. I wouldn't deal with that situation in any other way.'

The events in Jordan were the first test of the quality of Arafat's leadership of the P.L.O. In my judgment he emerged from it with much to his credit. The debate about his refusal to sanction the use of force against the leftists is really an academic one anyway. Even if he had used force and it had worked, the showdown in Jordan would have been delayed but not averted. The Israelis and Kissinger were determined that the Palestine liberation movement would be liquidated. Five years later, when the P.L.O. had recovered from its setback in Jordan and was beginning to win important political victories, it was the same team – Israel plus Kissinger – that went into action again. As Arafat said, 'So far as my people are concerned, the only difference between the civil war in Jordan and the civil war in the Lebanon is that it was the Lebanese Christian militias and the Syrians and not Hussein who were required to do the dirty work for Israel and Kissinger's America.'

# 16

# The Terror Weapon

The truth about the Black September (Terror) Organization can be summed up as follows. It was a part of Fatah. The entire leadership, including Arafat, debated the playing of the terror card. But the decision to use terror was not taken by the leadership. With the exception of Abu Iyad who, at the time, was widely regarded as Arafat's number two, all of Fatah's top leaders were opposed to the use of the terror weapon. The decision to resort to it was taken by embittered individuals within the ranks of Fatah's fighters. As one of them put it to me: 'You can say the Black September Organization was the soul of the commandos who were ready to sacrifice themselves to keep the resistance movement alive.' Abu Iyad himself says he believes the movement would have been finished if the terror weapon had not been used. In any event, it can be said that Fatah's leaders lost control of their organization.

I asked Khalad Hassan if he would object to such a conclusion. He said: 'No, it's fair, but it's not entirely the truth. If leaders are wise they know there are times when they cannot control events, and that if they try to do so the attempt will backfire on them. The tragedy was so big. So many people were killed. So many lost fathers, husbands, brothers and cousins. Naturally there was great bitterness and anger on our side. Adding to it was the widespread belief – which was, in fact, the truth – that the Americans, certain Americans, had been largely responsible for pushing Hussein to do Israel's dirty work. Our fighters also knew that the Iraqis had betrayed us, that the Syrians had closed their border to make it easier for Hussein, and that some other Arab regimes were secretly pleased by what had happened to the P.L.O. In Jordan and Syria and elsewhere in the Arab world the government-controlled newspapers were declaring with obvious pleasure that the P.L.O. was finished. In the circumstances as they were, an explosion of anger and despair was inevitable.'

What would have happened if Arafat and the majority of his colleagues in Fatah's leadership had condemned the use of terror from the outset, and if they had then tried to stop it being used? I put that question to Khalad. He replied: 'We would have lost our credibility as leaders; nobody in the rank and file of our movement would have listened to us; and the terror operations would still have taken place. And some of us would have been assassinated. Probably I would have been the number-one target because it was known within our movement that Khalad Hassan was the most outspoken critic of the use of the terror weapon. In the leadership our problem was to find a way to associate ourselves with the grassroots decision to play the terror card, in order to give ourselves the necessary credibility to act, when we judged the time to be right, to control and eventually shut down the terror machine. That was Arafat's intention and objective from the beginning. Most of us in the leadership supported him one hundred per cent. I myself supported him one thousand per cent.'

If Arafat's strategy for controlling and then shutting down the terror machine had been allowed to work, the Munich operation in September 1972 would have been Black September's last. In the event, and because the Israelis insisted on a shoot-out at Munich airport, that operation ended in disaster and marked only the beginning of a vicious and dangerous escalation of the conflict, which was to take the Middle East and very nearly the world to war in October 1973.

The story of the Black September Organization and Arafat's struggle to put it out of business begins in Cairo. There, on 28 November 1971, Wasfi Tal was assassinated as he was entering the Sheraton Hotel for a meeting of the Arab League's Joint Defence Council. At the time of Hussein's final offensive against the P.L.O. and until his death, Wasfi Tal was serving as both Jordan's Prime Minister and Minister of Defence.

According to Black September's claim at the time, Wasfi Tal was its first victim. And according to history his murder marked the official opening of its international terror campaign. But Black September's claim was incorrect. It is certainly true that Wasfi Tal was hit by shots fired at him from outside the hotel by one of three Black September terrorists. But as the Egyptian coroner revealed before he was instructed to keep his mouth shut in public, the bullet that actually killed Wasfi Tal was not fired by the Palestinians. According to witnesses, including two Arab leaders, Wasfi Tal got out of his car, was hit immediately by a bullet fired from inside the hotel, grabbed for his own gun, ran to the hotel for cover and then collapsed as more bullets from outside the hotel hit him. And as the coroner revealed, Wasfi Tal was dying from the first bullet when the Black September gunmen opened fire.

So who really killed Wasfi Tal? According to new evidence that can now be disclosed with the help of Khalad Hassan, the most plausible answer is that he was assassinated by a Jordanian secret service agent whose controllers were part of a plot involving President Sadat and, probably, one or some of Kissinger's back-channel associates to prevent Arafat and his Fatah colleagues from advancing their cause by political means after their military defeat in Jordan.

The most sensational of Khalad's revelations concerns the motive for the killing. He told me: 'At the moment of his death, Wasfi Tal was twenty-five minutes away from signing an historic agreement with the P.L.O. And the man who was to have signed for the P.L.O., in the presence of the Arab League's Defence Ministers, was me.' The actual agreement had been concluded the previous day in secret talks between Wasfi Tal and Khalad Hassan. Wasfi Tal, the most powerful man in Jordan at the time, was acting alone; he had committed himself, as Prime Minister and Minister of Defence, to an agreement he knew would be opposed by many around the King.

As the fatal shot was fired at Wasfi Tal, Khalad was on his way to the Sheraton Hotel in a car. He said: 'As soon as I got out of the car a man whom I would like to meet again – to thank him – came up to me and said, "Please, Khalad, don't enter the hotel by the front. Go through the back door." I said, "Why?" He said, "Please, just do what I suggest." Then, as I was going to the back entrance, I saw a journalist friend of mine. As soon as he recognized me he started to

call out, "Khalad, come here quickly, I'm in trouble, help me!"
When we were close he said, "I'm not in trouble but I must speak to
you in my car." I still had twenty minutes before my meeting with
Wasfi and the other Defence Ministers so I said, "Okay." As soon as
we got into his car he started the engine and we drove away. I said,
"In God's name what is happening?" He replied: "Khalad, trust me,
we will talk inside my house." We entered his house and I said,
"Okay, now tell me why you've hijacked me! What's wrong?" He
replied, "Are you a fool? Wasfi Tal has just been assassinated. If you
had set foot in the Sheraton you would have been killed!" Possibly
these two people saved my life – but we lost the agreement with
Wasfi.'

The obvious implication is that Wasfi Tal was assassinated to
prevent the agreement he was about to sign from being
implemented. According to what Khalad told me – and he gave me a
long and detailed account of the negotiations – the main point of the
agreement was that the P.L.O. would return to Jordan as a political
organization. And the essence of the bargain that was struck
between the two men was that in return for a P.L.O. commitment to
pursue the liberation struggle by political means alone, Jordan
would recognize the P.L.O. as the only legitimate representative of
the Palestinian people. This recognition was, in fact, contained in
Article 3 of the agreement.

That a majority of P.L.O. leaders were prepared to abandon
armed struggle as the way to liberation, even at the cost of splitting
the P.L.O. – the P.F.L.P., the P.D.F. and a small Iraqi-sponsored
group had said they would undermine the agreement – was
dramatic evidence of how desperate the majority of leaders were to
avoid being forced to make a last military stand in the Lebanon.
After the P.L.O.'s expulsion from Jordan, despite his belief in
consensus politics, Arafat was apparently prepared to pay any price
for a return ticket. When I put this observation to Khalad, he
nodded gravely. 'Yes,' he said, 'you are right. And in view of what
has happened in the Lebanon in recent years, I cannot emphasize
too much that we in Fatah were not naive. For the reasons I have
explained to you before, we knew the Lebanon was a trap for us. We
knew that if we were forced to entrench ourselves in the Lebanon,
the Israelis would turn it into a killing ground and that we would
have to continue with our military struggle simply to defend

ourselves and our people. And that was the importance of my agreement with Wasfi Tal. It was not only giving us the opportunity to continue our struggle by political means in the most favourable environment, it was saving us from being pushed into the Lebanon trap. As it happened, and because of Wasfi Tal's assassination, we were pushed into the trap. And once we were caught it was inevitable that the Israelis would not stop until they had destroyed us – or at least until they had gone to the outer limits of what it was possible for them to do to destroy us.'

I asked Khalad if he thought that many of the disasters which have happened since 1971 could have been avoided if Wasfi Tal had lived. He replied: 'In theory, yes; in reality, no. In theory there's a strong case for saying the Lebanon would have been spared its agony – but I am not so sure even about that. If Wasfi had lived, and if we had made our agreement with him work, the Israelis and Kissinger would have found ways to de-stabilize Jordan in order to liquidate us there. So perhaps we would have ended up in the Lebanon anyway. My agreement with Wasfi would have given us all an opportunity to end the violence, but there is no reason to believe that Israel's leaders had any intention of ending it until the Palestine liberation movement had been destroyed. If I am to be realistic I suppose I have to say the only real gain for us from my agreement with Wasfi would have been in the field of public relations. Our new realism would have been welcomed by objective and open-minded people in the West, and we would have won more understanding and support for our cause. But even that might have been counter-productive. As you must now be aware, honest study of the real history of our struggle shows one thing above all others: the more we Palestinians have shown ourselves to be ready to face up to reality and to solve our problems by political means, the more the Israelis have escalated their military actions – because they are not willing to meet us on the political battlefield. On that we are at least their equals and they know it.'

The man who was ultimately responsible for Wasfi Tal's lone decision to come to terms with the P.L.O. was Saudi Arabia's King Feisal. Said Khalad: 'It was on a train journey from Alexandria to Cairo that I convinced Feisal to be the mediator between us and the Jordanians. There were four of us in the special compartment – Sadat, Feisal, Arafat and me. The fact that Feisal agreed to be the mediator was very important for us. In our Arab tradition the party which causes the mediation to fail becomes the enemy of the mediator. So frankly speaking, that put Hussein and his people at a disadvantage to start with!'

Wasfi Tal did not involve himself until the last minute, when the negotiations were on the point of breaking down.

Khalad continued: 'After our conversation on the train, Feisal was completely aware of what was at stake for us Palestinians, for the Arabs generally and for the world.' On the train, Khalad and Arafat told Feisal that if he did not help them to secure a political base, they would lose control to the leftists and the radicals in the P.L.O. – including those in Fatah who were now turning to terror. As Khalad put it: 'We were pleading with Feisal to give us the opportunity to direct the anger and bitterness on our side away from violence and into support for positive political action. We didn't need to tell Feisal that if we lost control there would be an escalation of violence which would give the Israelis the opportunity to cause havoc in the Lebanon and elsewhere, and which would lead in time to the collapse and defeat of Arab moderation and, eventually, the downfall of the pro-Western Arab regimes. That's what was at stake – and still is. And Feisal knew it. He also knew that Kissinger was a fool, and that it was Kissinger's approach which was pushing the region and the world to disaster by cutting the ground from under the feet of those of us in Fatah who were trying desperately to give the lead in a positive and political way.'

Throughout the official negotiations, the Jordanians stuck to their position – 'No' to the P.L.O. and, by implication, 'No' to Feisal. I asked Khalad if he knew what Hussein's own position was at the time. He said: 'If I have to answer that question I would say Hussein himself didn't know what to do. But for sure some of those around him, generals and civilians, were one hundred per cent against any agreement with us.'

With only a few days to go before the meeting of the Arab ministers in Cairo, there was still no agreement. Khalad continued: 'Feisal was getting more and more angry. When his patience was exhausted he sent Hussein a very tough letter asking him to say "Yes" or "No" by a certain time. Don't ask me what Feisal was planning to do if Hussein's answer was not the one he wanted. I really have no idea. It was a matter between the two Kings. All I can tell you is that Amman was subjected to enormous pressure by Saudi Arabia.'

At that point, and without consulting Hussein, Wasfi Tal decided to make himself responsible for Jordan's decision about the P.L.O. He flew to Cairo to attend the meeting of Arab League Defence Ministers. As soon as he arrived in the Egyptian capital he was subjected to great pressure from all of them. But it was the ministers from Saudi Arabia and Kuwait who applied the greatest pressure. As a result of it Wasfi Tal began his secret talks with Khalad Hassan.

Apart from the Black September Organization and certain people in Jordan's military, political and intelligence establishments, President Sadat had a very good reason for not wanting Wasfi Tal's agreement to be implemented. To Sadat the unacceptable part of it was Article 3 – Jordan's recognition of the P.L.O. as the only legitimate representative of the Palestinian people. By November 1971, Sadat was enjoying back-channel communication with Kissinger, and he knew enough about Kissinger's approach and thinking to be certain that a deal with Kissinger's America was possible. If Sadat would expel the Soviets from Egypt, Kissinger would reward him with the return of the Sinai in exchange for a separate peace with Israel. But Sadat by choice did not want a separate peace. He wanted any settlement to be comprehensive to the extent that Jordan would be included. And Jordan was the problem. If Hussein was free to represent the Palestinians, it was possible, Sadat thought, that Kissinger would be able to persuade Israel to withdraw from the Sinai and the West Bank – or at least enough of the latter to keep Hussein happy. But if Hussein was prevented from representing the Palestinians because of Article 3 in Wasfi's agreement the Israelis would not negotiate about the West Bank. And that would leave Sadat with a choice of either going it alone, which was very dangerous, and did eventually cost him his life, or insisting on a say for the P.L.O., which would mean that the Israelis and Kissinger would not be interested in any deal. In short, if Wasfi Tal's agreement was implemented, Sadat would have to settle for a dangerous separate peace or nothing. If Egypt got nothing at all from the so-called peace process, Sadat would be in serious danger on his home front. The country was on the boil. The living standards of the masses were appalling and falling. Without the money and other development resources that would come with peace, there was a big and growing risk of an internal explosion. Egypt needed peace, and to make peace Sadat wanted Jordan with him, and that would be impossible if Wasfi Tal's agreement was implemented. It was a vicious circle.

For Kissinger and those of his associates who had put so much effort into forcing Hussein to crush the P.L.O., its return to Jordan would have been an obvious and major setback – at a time when Kissinger was beginning to make the right people believe that he should be Secretary of State. In addition, a political P.L.O. would start to win friends in the Western world and that, in turn, would make it more and more difficult for the U.S. to support Israel's continuing insistence on using military means to solve a political problem. There was also the question of Sadat's reaction. When Sadat was told that Israel would not enter into negotiations with Jordan if it was not free to represent the Palestinians, would Sadat then have the courage to go for a separate peace? If the answer to that was no, Kissinger's whole strategy for the Middle East might be doomed to failure. There was also the danger that Jordan would set a precedent. Once one Arab state had recognized the P.L.O. as the only legitimate representative of the Palestinians, would not others do the same? If they did, and for as long as Israel refused to deal with the P.L.O., the U.S. would have a credibility problem with the Arabs, and that would help the Soviets. From several points of view it is not difficult to understand why Kissinger and his associates would have regarded Wasfi Tal's agreement with the P.L.O. as a source of potential and very real problems.

So who killed Wasfi Tal? Who pulled the trigger of the revolver from which the fatal shot was fired, and who authorized the assassination? When I put these questions to Khalad the first part of his answer was the following. 'If you are asking me to identify the actual killer, I will not. I do know who it was and so, I may say, do two Arab leaders who were at the Sheraton and saw what happened with their own eyes. They were Arab Foreign Ministers. I also know that Wasfi's widow was eventually informed of the whole truth. All that I am prepared to say is that the actual assassin was a Jordanian element.'

I let the silence run and then I said, 'I suppose the obvious answer

is that Wasfi Tal was shot by a Jordanian assigned to protect him.'
Khalad did not respond at first. Then he said, 'I trust the record of
our conversation as it will be set down in your book will quote *you*
as saying that and not me.'

Sadat's role in the murder plot was a subject to which I returned
on a number of occasions in the course of my many conversations
with Khalad, knowing that as with all of Fatah's leaders revelations
came in bits and pieces, and as the result of patience and persistence
on my part.

According to Khalad's account, which I later discovered to be the
truth as it is generally accepted in the Arab world, Sadat's personal
contribution was in the form of an instruction that Wasfi Tal was
not to be given any Egyptian security cover. When Sadat was asked
about this at the time his story was to the effect that Wasfi Tal was
hated by many in Egypt, that he feared there would be an
assassination attempt, and that he did not want to take the
responsibility for Wasfi's life. On these grounds Sadat apparently
suggested that the Jordanians should protect their own man.

Khalad said: 'It is true that Wasfi was not well liked by many in
Egypt, to say the least. But the rest of Sadat's story was a
fabrication. If he had really been worried about an attempt on
Wasfi's life – I mean an attempt that he didn't know about in
advance – it was his responsibility and duty as the President to give
an order doubling and trebling the number of Egyptian security
agents assigned to protect Wasfi. If Wasfi had been given even the
normal and minimum Egyptian security protection I do not believe
he could have been killed in the way he was.' Shortly after Wasfi
Tal's death, Jordan's Chief of Staff said, 'A man like this should
have been better protected.'

To Khalad I then said, 'So what do we conclude – that certain
persons unknown in Jordan conspired with President Sadat and
others in Egypt to kill Wasfi Tal in order to prevent the
implementation of his agreement with you?'

Khalad replied, 'We do.'

'And what about the involvement of certain persons unknown in
America?' I asked.

Khalad said: 'On such a serious matter I don't think it is right for
me to speculate about things I cannot prove. There are certain
conclusions to be drawn but I would prefer to keep them to myself.'

One last question remained. 'If Wasfi Tal had lived, would he have succeeded in making the agreement work?'

Khalad's answer to this was very revealing, and astonishing in its implication. He said: 'First you must know that Wasfi was a very tough, very ruthless but very honest man. Second you should not forget that he was *the* strong man in Jordan at the time. Third you should remember that he had reorganized Jordan's armed forces. That is for background. Now I will tell you of something he said to me in our last secret talk on the day before he was killed. These were, in fact, almost his last words to me. He said: "Supposing the King does not accept this agreement. . . Will you support me in anything I may do?" I said, "Yes, anything."'

The clear implication is that Wasfi Tal was prepared to oblige King Hussein to go into exile if he opposed the agreement with the P.L.O. If that had actually happened, and if Arafat and his colleagues had proved themselves to be politically effective, it is very likely that Israel would have come under great pressure from international opinion to withdraw from the occupied West Bank, because it would have been clear that the Palestine problem was very close to a solution within the limits of what was possible given Israel's military strength.

As Khalad Hassan said earlier, it is very likely that the Israelis and Kissinger would have worked together to de-stabilize a new regime in Jordan – one headed, perhaps, by President Wasfi Tal – in order to create the pretext for Israel to finish the P.L.O. by military means. But maybe the Israelis and Kissinger would not have had things all their own way. In the light of subsequent events, in particular the fact that the Deputy Director of the C.I.A. was the linkman in a secret dialogue between Nixon and the P.L.O., it is possible that the new situation which would have been created if Wasfi Tal had lived could have seen Kissinger and the anti-Kissinger faction of the C.I.A. engaged in a dramatic showdown of their own. As Arafat said in another context, who knows?

Wasfi Tal's assassination effectively sabotaged the efforts of P.L.O. leaders who were trying to direct the anger and despair of all those engaged in the liberation struggle away from violence and into support for positive political action. And as Arafat and Khalad Hassan had predicted to Feisal on the train from Alexandria to Cairo, the leadership then began to lose control of events to the men of violence – the Black Septemberists of Fatah and extremists in the other guerrilla groups, principally the P.F.L.P. For the latter the use of the terror weapon was not a new experience. For those in Fatah it was.

Among those in the rank and file of Fatah's fighters who helped to bring the Black September Organization into being from the bottom up was a young man whose *nom de guerre* is Ben Bella. At the time of our conversation he was a special assistant to Abu Iyad. When I was discussing the coming into being of the organization with Ben Bella, he said: 'I will tell you a secret. After Wasfi Tal's death we had hundreds of applications from people wanting to join the Black September Organization. Many, of course, were from our brothers in Fatah; some were from our comrades in the other organizations; and some were from civilians in the diaspora who had not previously belonged to any *fedayeen* group. They were all saying the same thing: "At last you have found the way to make our voice heard in the world." '

I asked Ben Bella about Arafat's attitude to the Black Septemberists. He said: 'At the time Arafat could not afford to speak against us in public because he knew that what we were doing had the support of the majority in the rank and file of our movement. Our way was the popular way. But in our private meetings he took every opportunity to tell us we were wrong. I remember an occasion when he said to some of us, "You are crazy to take our fight to Europe." I was very angry and I said, "Abu Amar, maybe you are right, maybe we are crazy – but tell me this: is it not also crazy for us to sit here in the Lebanon, just waiting to be hit every day by Israeli fighter planes, and knowing that we will lose some ten or more fighters every day without advancing our cause – is that not crazy, too?" '

It has often been said by reporters and writers who made some effort to understand the Palestinian side of the story that Black September was 'more a state of mind than an organization as such'. In fact it was both. It was an organization within an organization; it had a command structure of its own; and it enjoyed the freedom of Fatah's communication and intelligence-gathering facilities. Its leaders were Abu Youseff, Kamal Adwan and Abu Hassan Salameh. Those who were serving in Israel's various intelligence agencies at the time soon came to know this. In the weeks following

Wasfi Tal's assassination, the Mossad penetrated Black September. Mossad agents, Palestinians who had been turned by blackmail and threats in Western Europe, were among the hundreds who applied to join the organization. And the day was coming when the Israelis would demonstrate, in the most violent and dramatic way possible, that they knew all there was to know about Black September's leaders – who they were and where they could be located and killed.

About his Fatah colleagues who turned to terror, Khalad Hassan had this to say: 'From the beginning, and as you know, I was opposed to the playing of the terror card. But I have to tell you something else. Those of our Fatah colleagues who did turn to terror were not mindless criminals. They were fiercely dedicated nationalists who were doing their duty as they saw it. I have to say they were wrong, and did so at the time, but I have also to understand them. In their view, and in this they were right, the world was saying to us Palestinians, "We don't give a damn about you, and we won't care at least until you are a threat to our interests." In reply those in Fatah who turned to terror were saying, "Okay, world. We'll play the game by your rules. We'll make you care!" That doesn't justify what they did, but it does explain their thinking and their actions. Perhaps one day Third World action groups will turn to terror to make you Westerners care about the poverty that is killing many millions every year. When that day comes you'll call those who act terrorists, but you'll have only yourselves to blame for what they do – because you didn't care enough until you were made to care.'

Abu Hassan Salameh was the director and co-ordinator of Black September operations in Europe. His first headline-making operation was the hijacking of a Sabena airliner in early May 1972. Four of his terrorists caused the plane to land at Israel's Lod Airport. There they threatened to blow it up, killing themselves, the ninety passengers and the crew of ten, if Israel did not release 106 Palestinian prisoners. After waiting for nearly twenty-four hours, Israeli commandos dressed as white-overalled airport technicians stormed the plane. It was all over in two minutes. Two of the four hijackers were killed and one of six wounded passengers died later.

At the end of May, Lod Airport was again the setting for a terror operation. On this occasion the action was planned by the P.F.L.P. but was actually carried out by three members of the Japanese terrorist group known as the Red Army. The P.F.L.P.'s terror chief, Wadi Haddad, had taken for granted the fact that no Palestinian would be able to do the job he had in mind. The three kamikazis arrived on an Air France flight from Paris and Rome. Being Japanese they did not come under suspicion and they passed into the customs hall to await the arrival of their luggage. As soon as their cases arrived they opened them, whipped out submachine guns and grenades and opened fire on the crowd. The final casualty figures were twenty-five killed and seventy-eight wounded. Two of the terrorists committed suicide. The third was overpowered before he could take his own life. When the P.F.L.P. claimed responsibility for the attack, it described the operation as its 'Deir Yassin'. It was also clear that it had wanted to show the Black September Organization that whatever it could do, the P.F.L.P. could do better.

Arafat and those of his colleagues in the leadership who were opposed to the use of the terror weapon were horrified by the slaughter at Lod Airport – the violence of the attack and the loss of life, the harm that had been done to the Palestinian cause in the eyes of the world, and the prospect of an escalating terror campaign which would be fuelled by the rivalry between the two organizations.

It was at about this point that Arafat and all of his colleagues in Fatah's top leadership decided that they had, so to speak, to join the terrorists in order to beat them. What was about to be performed was an act of crisis management of a most unusual kind. But it was crisis management nonetheless. I asked Khalad Hassan if that was a fair way to put it. He said: 'Very frankly, yes. We had to associate ourselves with what was happening in order to give ourselves the credibility to take control of the situation and then turn off what you would call the terror tap. And it is for this act of crisis management that Arafat, myself and others in the leadership who were against the use of the terror weapon are called terrorists.'

As the executive in charge of Fatah and P.L.O. security and intelligence services, Abu Iyad assumed the responsibility for planning and organizing one Black September operation which he and others hoped would enjoy the support of the collective leadership. And if the strategy worked, that operation would be Black September's last.

The objective of the operation – the taking of a number of Israeli hostages to secure the release of 200 P.L.O. prisoners in Israel – was agreed without too much debate. It was Abu Iyad's announcement of where the hostages were to be seized that shocked a number of his colleagues. The hostages were to be Israeli athletes and they were to be taken in Munich, at the Olympic Games, thus guaranteeing a live worldwide television audience for the drama. Some of Fatah's leaders argued that the idea of disrupting the Olympic Games was outrageous. Sport, they said, was a religion in the West and the East, and to interfere with it would be a mistake. From the public relations point of view the P.L.O. would lose more than it gained. Other leaders argued that Fatah should stick to one of its original principles and confine the action to Palestine. So why not seize the hostages in Israel? And if that was not dramatic enough from the public relations point of view, why not change the objective as well as the venue and take American hostages in Israel? Abu Iyad won the argument. Could he have done so without Arafat's support? I think not.

Though Abu Iyad did have the executive responsibility for organizing the Munich operation, work on preparing and then implementing the detailed plan was done by many. In Munich, according to Hani Hassan, Palestinian students and workers played a 'very critical part' in the operation. 'As a consequence hundreds of them were expelled from Germany when it was over,' he said. From other Fatah leaders I learned that the operation would not have been possible without the support and facilities provided by one Arab Government. Presumably the facilities included help with the transmission of messages and the movement of weapons and men.

At about five o'clock in the morning on 5 September, one of eight Black September terrorists tossed a piece of paper out of the first-floor window of the Israeli quarters in the Olympic Village. It announced that the organization was holding nine Israeli hostages who would be shot if Israel did not release 200 P.L.O. prisoners.

The German Government informed the Israeli Government of the situation. Israel's reply was uncompromising. Israel rejected the ultimatum and any idea of negotiations with the terrorists to free the hostages. And Israel demanded an immediate counter-attack. In fact, the Israeli Government delayed its reply until its security agents had landed in Munich from Tel Aviv. Their brief, the Israelis said, was to 'advise' the German police.

It was, so to speak, Germany's show; but there is no doubt that the Israelis called the shots. The Germans allowed this to happen partly because it was Israeli lives which were at stake; partly because the Germans were prepared to acknowledge that the Israelis were the experts; and partly because the Israelis applied pressure amounting to intimidation on the Germans – pressure for a shoot-out, that is. From my own conversations with some who were in authority in Germany at the time, I am completely satisfied that Chancellor Willy Brandt favoured a non-violent end to the affair. He wanted to exchange the lives of the Israeli hostages for the lives of the Black September terrorists. In this event, Black September would have been able to claim that its action had resulted in worldwide publicity for the Palestinian cause, but it still would have failed, and would have been seen to have failed, to achieve its objective – the release of 200 Palestinian prisoners in Israel.

A little more than fourteen hours after Israeli security agents effectively took charge on the ground in Munich, the nine hostages and five of the eight terrorists were dead.

At about 10.00 p.m. the terrorists and their hostages had been taken in two helicopters to Fürstenfeldbruck military airport. There, some 150 metres or so from the landing zone, a Boeing 727 was waiting with its lights on to fly them to Cairo. Though they suspected a trap, the terrorists had been told that Egypt had agreed to hold the hostages until the Israeli Government released the P.L.O. prisoners.

When the helicopters landed, five marksmen, an unknown but substantial number of police armed with submachine guns, plus 600 men of the Frontier Guards, were in position. There was also ample floodlighting at the throw of a switch.

The two helicopter pilots stepped down from their machines and were followed and covered by two terrorists. Two more terrorists, one from each helicopter, walked the 150 metres or so to inspect the waiting Boeing. They discovered there was no crew on board. As these two were walking back to the helicopters, the marksmen opened fire. The two terrorists started to run, one was hit and took cover under a helicopter. The two who had been covering the pilots were dead or dying. From inside one of the helicopters another terrorist returned the fire and one marksman was killed.

At 10.50 p.m. the police called on the terrorists to surrender. The call was repeated in Arabic by an Israeli security agent. For the next two hours and fifteen minutes nothing happened. Then, while the nine hostages and six of the terrorists were still in the two helicopters, the police opened fire. One terrorist jumped down from one of the helicopters and threw a grenade into it. Another fired shots into the second helicopter. And that is how what Abu Iyad described to me as 'a tragedy for the Israelis and us' ended.

In the two hours and fifteen minutes while nothing was happening at the Fürstenfeldbruck military airport, Golda Meir and her senior ministers were agonizing about what to do. To avoid giving the impression in Israel that there was a crisis, the Cabinet was not convened. Instead, senior ministers called on Golda at her official residence in Jerusalem. The evidence that some and perhaps a majority of Israeli ministers wanted to give the highest priority to saving the lives of the hostages was the fact that Moshe Dayan made one of his many threats to resign. Rumours that Dayan was at least considering resignation were rife in Jerusalem and Tel Aviv. Hours after the hostages were killed, but before Israel and the world was informed that they were dead, *The Jerusalem Post* carried a headline which said, 'Despite Rumours Dayan Stays'.

Dayan's willingness to risk sacrificing the lives of the Israeli hostages was brutal and callous. But in the event it did serve the wider Israeli interest and cause. Quite apart from the fact that it denied Arafat the victory he needed to restore *fedayeen* faith in his leadership, Dayan's tough stand at Munich undermined further the low and poor morale of all those Palestinians who were involved in the liberation struggle. And as a result of that, Arafat was now to find himself struggling for his own survival as leader.

After the failure of Fatah's Munich operation, Arafat was so desperate that he had to buy time by pretending to be in favour of a plot to overthrow Hussein. And when the pretending had to stop the man with the responsibility for organizing the plot, Abu Daoud, was betrayed to the Jordanians. What follows is a very dramatic illustration of the dangerous games Arafat has had to play in order simply to survive and fight another day for moderation and compromise.

Israel's response to Fatah's Munich operation was a massive attack on *fedayeen* positions and Palestinian locations in the Lebanon. It was a combination of devastating air strikes and a land invasion in which Israeli ground forces ransacked Palestinian properties and destroyed whole villages. Between 300 to 500 Palestinians were killed. As always happened when the Israelis used their jet fighters as flying artillery, most of the dead were civilians, mainly women and children, and it was entirely consistent with Israel's policy of taking thirty to forty and sometimes many more Palestinian lives for each Jew killed as a result of Palestinian actions.

But this attack, just three days after Munich, was only the beginning of a new escalation of Israel's war against the P.L.O. in the Lebanon. One result of the regularity and intensity of Israel's attacks was that the *fedayeen* were finding it more and more difficult to mount guerrilla actions. The other result was increasing pressure on Arafat from the Lebanese authorities for agreements on the setting up of prohibited zones – areas of the Lebanon that would be off limits to the *fedayeen*. To prevent a serious confrontation with the Lebanese army, Arafat agreed to do more or less everything the authorities in Beirut asked of him. But as some Fatah field commanders saw it, Arafat was making too many concessions to the Lebanese at a time when the *fedayeen* were running out of territory in which they could be reasonably secure. The result, in the autumn, was a rebellion by some Fatah officers against Arafat's co-operation with the Lebanese authorities. A potentially serious crisis was defused by the intervention and mediation of the Algerian Ambassador. The main rebel leader, Abu Yusef Al-Kayed, was exiled to Algeria.

Throughout 1972, and to compensate for the curtailment of his freedom to launch attacks on Israel from the Lebanon, Arafat concentrated more of his fighters in Syria's border regions, and it was from Syrian territory that most of the *fedayeen* attacks were mounted. In October and November, the Israelis responded with massive air and artillery attacks on *fedayeen* areas and infiltration routes in Syria. At the same time the Israelis admitted they were not confining their attacks to *fedayeen* targets. They were hitting villages 'just to make examples' – in other words, to persuade local Palestinian and Syrian communities that it was not worth their while to give aid and comfort to the guerrillas. After that the regime in Damascus took action to deny the *fedayeen* access to Israel through Syrian territory.

Abu Daoud summed up the feelings of the rank and file in the *fedayeen* movement as the end of 1972 approached as follows: 'It wasn't only Arafat and our top leaders who knew that we had no security and no future in the Lebanon and Syria. We all knew it, and we were telling ourselves that unless we could take Jordan our liberation movement was finished.'

If Fatah had been united Arafat might have been able to disassociate himself (and Fatah) from the renewed call for Hussein's overthrow and then the plot actually to get rid of him. But Fatah was divided. The truth about what had happened and was still happening inside Fatah was told to me by Hani Hassan.

He said: 'After our expulsion from Jordan a leftist current developed inside Fatah. For the first time in the history of our organization there were those among us who so much wanted the Soviets to be on our side that they were prepared to some extent to let the Soviets use them. I must also tell you and, please, do not misunderstand me, that none of our Fatah leftists were communists or pro-Soviet in any way. They became self-styled leftists and radicals purely to make themselves attractive to the Soviets. And I have to say their thinking was very logical. They said: "It is the Americans who are really behind this attempt to liquidate our liberation movement and our cause. If we are to survive, we must therefore have the other superpower behind us in a practical way."

'Then our Fatah leftists made a tactical alliance with the other leftist organizations – the P.F.L.P., the P.D.F. and so on. And Arafat saw this as a very big threat. To avoid a split in Fatah, and also to keep control of the P.L.O., he then made his own tactical alliance with the whole of the left. Myself, Khalad and the rightists in Fatah were very much opposed to this Arafat tactic. We said: "Yes, it is true that we must have the support and the backing of the Soviets – but not in a way that will compromise our independence."

'Arafat said he agreed that nothing was more important than preserving the independence of Palestinian decision-making. But he also said we had a need to play tactical games. His strategy as he explained it to us was very clever for the time. What he was saying, in effect, was this: "There will come a day when we will have to have the support of the Soviets if we are to advance our cause by political means. However, there is a problem. Yasser Arafat, the Hassan brothers, Abu Jihad and most of the top Fatah leaders are much too independent for the Soviets. And that means Moscow will not support Fatah unless it feels it has its own men on the inside." That also is a reason why Arafat was willing to make an accommodation with the leftist alliance.'

It was early in 1971 that the Soviets had made their first move to get a hand on the P.L.O. Hani said: 'A man from the Soviet Embassy in Amman made contact with us. He asked for a meeting with Arafat. Since we had tried and failed to establish a good relationship with the Soviets, I told him, "Okay," and I took him to the mountains to meet Abu Amar. To tell you very frankly I was astonished by what this Soviet man said to Arafat. He said to the Chairman, "Now I think you will understand the lesson that without the co-operation of a superpower you cannot do anything." He was meaning, of course, that it was the Americans who had been responsible for what happened to us in Jordan in September – which was true – and that we needed the Soviets if we were to protect ourselves against the Americans. By obvious implication he was also saying the Soviets would help us – but on their terms.'

It was as a result of that mountain-top meeting that Arafat was invited to make his first official visit to Moscow. But even then the Soviets held back the formal invitation until the P.L.O. had been expelled from Jordan. They were obviously assuming, or at least hoping, that Arafat would be desperate enough to become, more or less, a Soviet puppet. But the Soviets were in for a surprise. Yasser Arafat was not willing to trade the independence of Palestinian decision-making for Soviet support. To make the point he gave his Soviet hosts a little lecture about how he looked upon Fatah and the P.L.O. as his virgin. So the Soviets were disappointed with Arafat, and that was why Fatah's leftists were given a warm welcome when they turned to Moscow for help.

Of Fatah's top leaders, the one who decided to play at being a radical and a leftist for the sake of gaining some practical Soviet support was Abu Iyad. That was another reason why Arafat felt obliged to make an accommodation with the leftist alliance within the P.L.O.

When the leftists in Fatah added their voice to the renewed call for a strategy to overthrow Hussein's regime, Arafat and the Fatah rightists would have been in no position to exercise any control over events if Arafat had not associated himself with the plot. The demand for a strategy to overthrow the regime in Jordan had, in fact, been irresistible since March. In that month Hussein had announced his plan for a United Arab Kingdom. It was a proposal to give the Palestinians in residence on the West Bank full local autonomy, under Jordanian control, when the Israelis had withdrawn. (In essence the Reagan Plan of 1982 was almost a carbon copy of the Hussein Plan of 1972.) Even those like Khalad Hassan, the moderates or the realists as they prefer to be called, were under no illusions about Hussein's intentions. 'It was a plan to put the P.L.O. out of business,' Khalad said.

That certainly was one of Hussein's objectives; and he was no doubt motivated in part by his discovery that he could have been removed from power by his own Prime Minister if Wasfi Tal's agreement with the P.L.O. had been implemented. But there was another reason why he was anxious to win the support of the West Bank Palestinians for his peace efforts. Under pressure from its own hardliners and extremists, Israel's Labour Government was pushing ahead with ever more ambitious schemes to settle Jews in the occupied territories. In the Gaza Strip, General Sharon had just evicted 1,500 bedouin families from 33,000 acres of their land. Their houses were bulldozed, their water wells were filled with sand and their trees were damaged. Under pressure the Israeli Government announced that it would resettle twenty per cent of the bedouin families. The rest? Well, they could find somewhere else to live. When moderate Israelis themselves protested against this theft of Arab land, they were met with a blast from Y Ben-Poret, an Israeli journalist who was widely regarded as a mouthpiece for the Ministry of Defence. It was, he wrote, 'Time to rip away the veil of hypocrisy.' And he asked his readers to remember that in the present as in the past, 'there is no Zionism, no settlement of land, no Jewish State without the removal of Arabs, without confiscation!'[33] Hussein got the message. Unless the Israeli colonization of the occupied territories could be stopped by peace, there would be nothing left for the Arabs to negotiate about.

I asked Arafat if Hussein's announcement of his United Arab Kingdom plan was another of those moments in history when the Israelis could have had the peace they said they wanted. He replied: 'No doubt. No doubt. If the Israelis had had any sense they would have said to Hussein the following. "Your Majesty, we like your plan. Tomorrow we will withdraw from the West Bank. The next day you will come to Jerusalem to sign a peace with us." Hussein would have replied: "I am ready, but we can do better. Tomorrow you withdraw from the West Bank and the Sinai Desert and Gaza. The next day President Sadat and I will come together to Jerusalem to make peace with you!"'

The Israelis could not have withdrawn so quickly, but taking the point Arafat was making I said, 'Do you really believe Hussein and Sadat would have responded in the way you say?'

Arafat replied: 'Certainly. On my life. For an Israeli withdrawal they would have made peace and the P.L.O. would have been finished. Absolutely finished. Sometimes I think we are lucky to have the Israelis for our enemies. They have saved us many times!'

Abu Iyad was given the executive responsibility for organizing the plot to bring down Hussein but Abu Daoud was in charge of the operation on the ground in Jordan. He explained: 'I was the logical man for the conspiracy because of my experience as the commander of all the *fedayeen* militias before we were expelled from Jordan.'

For Abu Iyad himself it was the opportunity to make good a promise and a threat he had made in public, and then to Hussein's face, in the month before the P.L.O.'s expulsion from Jordan. Abu Iyad, it will be remembered, was the one who had committed Fatah and the P.L.O. to withdraw its heavy weapons from Amman and other cities in order to avoid a final and suicidal confrontation with the Jordanian army. In the middle of June 1971, Abu Iyad had begun to suspect that the Jordanians did not intend to honour the agreement he had made in good faith. There were signs that the King's men were preparing for a final offensive. On 15 June, at a *fedayeen* base in Jerash, Abu Iyad made a public speech in which he issued a warning and a threat to Wasfi Tal and Hussein. Jordanian intelligence agents made their reports and Abu Iyad was summoned to a meeting with Hussein and Wasfi Tal.

Recalling the moment, Abu Iyad said: 'The King had the intelligence reports of my speech in his hands. He said: "Abu Iyad, we have been friends and we have worked together to defuse many problems . . . What is this? Are these reports true?" I looked directly at the King and I told him the following: "Your Majesty, there is no need for you to rely on your spies. I will repeat to your face what I

said in Jerash. If any harm comes to my people in Jordan, I will chase
those responsible to the ends of the earth and I will kill them!'"

At the eleventh session of the P.N.C. in Cairo early in January
1973, the P.L.O. was formally committed to a policy of
overthrowing Hussein. The vote was a great triumph for the leftist
alliance, and a great defeat for the rightists and the realists who were
still the overwhelming majority of Fatah's top leaders. But generals
without troops are useless in battle. The vote was also dramatic
confirmation of the direction in which the tide of popular opinion
inside the liberation movement had been running, with gathering
force, since the P.L.O.'s expulsion from Jordan.

Arafat had probably known for many months that a P.N.C. vote
in favour of such a foolish policy was inevitable; and that may have
been one reason, perhaps the main reason, why he decided to
associate himself with the plot to overthrow Hussein at an early
stage. If he had opposed the popular will, it is possible that he would
himself have been overthrown by reasonably democratic means at
the eleventh P.N.C. At the very least he might have found himself in
a position in which he had no choice but to resign. That was, in fact,
precisely what happened to Khalad Hassan at the eleventh P.N.C.!
And the truth was that Khalad had voiced not only his own views,
but those to which the real Arafat was committed.

The highlight of the P.N.C. meeting was a dramatic and highly
charged confrontation between Khalad and Abu Iyad. Khalad said:
'Really I don't want to talk about it in detail because today we are
good friends again. There's no need to open those old wounds. In
our passions of the moment we both said things we later regretted.
My departing political message was very straightforward. I told my
leftist colleagues they had learned nothing from our past mistakes –
which were really their mistakes; and I said they were setting our
movement on a course which would bring nothing but disaster for
our people.' Khalad told me that he resigned his seat on the P.L.O.
Executive Committee after his showdown with Abu Iyad. I imagine
he would not have been re-elected at that P.N.C. anyway.

As the P.N.C. was committing itself to Hussein's overthrow, Abu
Daoud was putting the finishing touches to his plan for the actual
attempt to bring down the regime in Jordan. He had, in fact, been
working on it for six months. Until the day he was betrayed and
then arrested by Jordan intelligence agents, Abu Daoud was, he

said, 'ninety-nine per cent certain' that Arafat was not playing games and that he was seriously involved in the conspiracy. The one per cent doubt was due to Abu Daoud's knowledge that 'Arafat bets on everything and likes to have all the strings running through his hands to give himself as many options as possible.'

In support of his view at the time that Arafat was seriously backing the plot, Abu Daoud told me: 'Normally I reported to Abu Iyad. But on several occasions I discussed my plans and needs with Abu Iyad and Arafat. On one occasion I asked Arafat for help to get some good men. On another I asked him for help with weapons. Truly he was putting on a good show of convincing me!'

The following is Abu Daoud's own account of his betrayal and arrest.

'On this particular occasion I was in Jordan disguised as a bedouin in traditional robes and I was travelling with a Saudi passport. I spent three days in Amman talking with my essential people, and then I went to see a man called Jaber. It was not an important meeting. Apparently he could help us with places to hide our vehicles. The only reason why I went to see this man was because Abu Iyad asked me to.

'I met the man Jaber and as soon as I looked into his eyes I saw a traitor. It was just an instinctive feeling from deep inside me. I took him to a room where we could be alone and I said to him the following, "I want you to know that if any man betrays me he will die. Be careful." And then he left me.

'In the evening Jaber came to see me and he invited me to his house. I went. It was outside Amman. On my return to the city I found an ambush waiting for me outside the Ministry of the Interior. The police asked for my passport and said, "Okay, we'll go to the police station." But I knew they were taking me to the intelligence centre. As soon as I entered there I found waiting for me the top five men in the Jordanian intelligence service. I gave them a big smile, and the Chief of Intelligence asked me, "Why do you smile?" I said, "Because you make such a good reception for me!" It was obvious they were very well prepared for me and that I had been betrayed.'

Who betrayed Abu Daoud and why?

Those, I think, are the easy questions. Abu Iyad betrayed Abu Daoud to the man Jaber, who was clearly a Jordanian agent, for the purpose of aborting the plot to overthrow Hussein. That, today, is Abu Daoud's own conclusion.

But why did Abu Iyad decide that the plot had to be aborted? The answer, I suspect, is simply that Arafat told Abu Iyad that Abu Daoud's operation had to be shut down somehow. But that begs further questions. Why did Arafat want the operation to be shut down? What was so compelling about his reasoning that caused Abu Iyad to act in the way he did? Why was it necessary for Abu Daoud to be betrayed? Why could he not have been stopped in some other way?

The answer to each of these questions is related to the fact that Arafat was in possession of highly-secret information. The secret was that President Sadat said he was preparing to lead the Arabs into a war of destiny with Israel. And the word was out that the Palestinians should do nothing to provoke Israeli attacks on any of the front-line states, excluding the Lebanon, while the Arab armies were making their preparations.

Although Arafat had never intended to give Abu Daoud's plan an operational sanction, the P.L.O. Chairman knew he was not by any means in total control of events. So there was a possibility that the plan could be activated without his knowledge once Abu Daoud was ready. If that happened, and if Jordan was de-stabilized, the scope for disaster was limitless. On a worst-case scenario it could lead to direct Israeli involvement in what was left of the kingdom. In that event the armed forces of Egypt and Syria would have to be placed on the alert, and be prepared for any eventuality. That would set back, and perhaps destroy, the prospects for an Arab war based on the idea of an Arab surprise attack. Abu Iyad's problem was mainly that he could not disclose the reason why the plot had to be aborted.

Abu Daoud was arrested on 8 February 1973. He was tortured – I felt the pain as he described to me his experience – and sentenced to death. On two occasions he was prepared for execution.

On the first day of March, the Black September Organization mounted another of its hostage-taking operations. This time the action took place in Sudan. Eight Black September terrorists entered the Saudi Embassy in Khartoum where a diplomatic reception was being held for the American *chargé d'affaires*, Curtis Moore. A number of hostages were taken including Moore himself, his

Ambassador Cleo Noel, the Belgian *chargé d'affaires* Guy Eid, the Saudi Ambassador, and the Jordanian *chargé d'affaires*. Black September then made its demand. In exchange for the lives of the hostages it wanted the release of Abu Daoud and sixteen of his fellow conspirators who were also under sentence of death. Two deadlines came and went. Moore, Noel and Eid were then taken to the Embassy basement and machine-gunned to death.

Black September and the P.L.O. were condemned and reviled around the world. And the stage was set for the Israelis to mount their most spectacular counter-terror operation. A week previously, and probably believing that Black September or P.L.O. leaders were on board, the Israelis had shot down a Libyan airliner that had strayed over the Sinai. Between 40 and 100 passengers and crew were killed. But the world had forgotten that and much else. After the Khartoum killings the Israelis could do no wrong.

Israel's counter-terror organization went by the name of the Institute for Special Tasks – in Hebrew, *Ha Mossad L'Tafkidim Meyuhadim*. It was set up after the P.F.L.P.'s attack at Lod Airport at the end of May 1972 after a very honest and open debate in Israel about whether or not Israelis should resort to the methods of the terrorists in order to beat them. The Government decided that the ends justified the means. So Israel officially began to use the terror weapon, and, as ever, the Israelis were more efficient than their Palestinian enemies.

The Institute's main task was assassinating P.L.O. leaders, particularly those known to have been involved in the planning and the execution of Black September operations. Most of the assassinations were quick and quiet jobs. Usually the P.L.O. targets were shot at point-blank range with silenced guns. Occasionally a bomb would explode under a hotel bed. A number of assassinations took place in Western Europe. And more often than not the governments of Western Europe turned a blind eye to what was happening. The question of when was a terrorist a terrorist was much too complicated.

The Institute's biggest, most daring and most successful operation was carried out with the help of Israeli commandos, some of them disguised as *fedayeen*, in the heart of Beirut on the night of 10 April 1973. The targets were Black September's leaders and, if possible, Arafat.

Of special interest to the Israelis were two apartments on Verdan Street. One of them was the home of Kamal Nasser, the P.L.O.'s official spokesman, and Kamal Adwan, one of Black September's top three leaders. Also known to the Israelis was the fact that Abu Iyad slept in a bed in Kamal Nasser's apartment four to five nights a week. The other apartment was the home of Abu Youseff, another Black September leader.

Abu Iyad told me that he personally was expecting an Israeli attack, and that a week before it came he had warned his three friends to arrange for a strong security guard. He also told me they all said, 'It can't happen here.'

On that day, 10 April, four men went to lunch at the Ali Samakara restaurant – Abu Iyad, Abu Youseff, Kamal Adwan and Kamal Nasser. Said Abu Iyad: 'After lunch we went home and I slept on my bed in Kamal Nasser's place.'

At six o'clock in the evening the four went off to a meeting of the P.L.O. Central Committee. To the surprise of all it ended at 8.30 p.m. The four decided to have an early night in. They returned to the two apartments on Verdan Street.

Said Abu Iyad: 'Abu Youseff went to his place and the rest of us were in Kamal Nasser's apartment. After a short time, and because we were the best of friends, Kamal Nasser asked me to leave. He said: "Abu Iyad, I have got to do some writing this night. If you stay I cannot. Please do me a favour and go some place to entertain yourself." So I left the apartment.'

About thirty minutes past midnight, Abu Iyad heard shots coming from the Fahkani district where Arafat had his headquarters and where the P.L.O. Chairman actually was at the time. Abu Iyad said, 'Then, and for the next half an hour, I was not very concerned. I thought it was probably some minor clash between two of our organizations. Then one of our people found me and said, "The Jews are coming."'

The Israeli move on Arafat's Fahkani headquarters was held up by *fedayeen* resistance. That gave Arafat himself time to escape. He took refuge in the Christian (or enemy) half of the city.

Today it is Abu Iyad's opinion that the Israeli attack on Arafat's headquarters was a diversion. He said: 'They wanted Arafat, but only if they could take him without too much trouble. I am sure the main targets were Kamal Adwan, Abu Youseff and myself.'

In Verdan Street the two apartments were covered by one armed guard. He never heard the shot that killed him. As he lay dead, the Israelis fixed mines with magnets to the doors. When they exploded, the Israeli hit-teams stormed the apartments, firing with submachine guns as they went.

Said Abu Iyad: 'To give you some idea of the intensity of the Israeli fire power, they put 200 bullets into the bed where they assumed I was sleeping! I know because I counted them myself. I think they were very disappointed to find me not at home!'

Nobody who was in the two apartments could have survived the Israeli attack. And nobody did. To those Palestinians who came to know the details, the most sickening aspect of the Israeli attack was the way in which Kamal Nasser was killed. Abu Iyad said: 'It was a ritual killing. Because Kamal was our spokesman they finished him off by spraying bullets around his mouth. And before they left the Israelis laid out his body as though he was hanging on a cross.'

The following month the Lebanese army moved against the P.L.O. Was it an attempt to smash the P.L.O.? 'No, not yet,' said Hani Hassan who, at the time, was enjoying a good relationship with the Lebanon's President Suleiman Franjieh. 'At this time the Lebanese Christians wanted to confine us to the refugee camps to prevent us making an alliance with the Patriotic Front forces – the Moslems and the Druzes. It was never our intention to take sides in the civil war that was obviously coming to the Lebanon. And we faced a very big dilemma. In the end we decided to reject the idea that we should confine ourselves to the camps. We feared that we would be crushed by the Christians and the Israelis if we allowed ourselves to be confined and neutralized in such a way. So that's why there was a confrontation between us and the Lebanese army in May.'

The fighting was stopped when those Arab leaders who were preparing for war with Israel asked for it to be stopped. They were worried that what was happening in the Lebanon could lead to complications which might harm their preparations for war.

It was, in fact, the Yom Kippur War which saved the P.L.O. from probable extinction, and which gave Arafat the opportunity to continue the struggle by political means.

# 17

# The Olive Branch

On the eve of the 1973 or Yom Kippur War, it was difficult to see that Arafat's Palestine liberation movement had any future.

As an organization capable of initiating serious military action against Israel it was finished. The terror machine had also been shut down, although there were continuing acts of terrorism by lunatic fringe groups. After Munich Arafat had begun to make progress in his effort to persuade those in Fatah who had turned to terror that its use was counter-productive and was seriously eroding support for the Palestinian cause. And after the Khartoum killings Arafat had Abu Iyad on his side of the argument. It also has to be said that the Israelis strengthened Arafat's hand when they wiped out the two Black September leaders in Beirut. So in the run-up to the Yom Kippur War, the Chairman's military strategy was entirely a defensive one. As the Israelis stepped up their war against the Palestinians in the Lebanon, the *fedayeen* under Arafat's command had only one objective – survival.

That was not how Israel's leaders presented the situation to their own people and the world. They pointed to the fact that in July 1972 Arafat had returned from Moscow with a promise that the Soviets were about to start sending arms and ammunition to the P.L.O. direct – for the first time in the history of the conflict. The actual arrival of the first Soviet shipment was then said by Israel's leaders to be the proof that the P.L.O. were preparing for a new offensive, and that the Soviet Union was now openly on the side of those who were seeking to bring about the destruction of the Jewish

State and people. In truth, Arafat was trying to improve his defensive capabilities at a time when, despite what they were saying in public, Israel's leaders thought they probably needed only a few more weeks, months at the most, to finish the P.L.O. by military means.

A valuable insight into what was happening on the P.L.O. side was given to me by Shafik Al-Hout and confirmed by Arafat himself. Shafik was the P.L.O's chief representative in Beirut and the Lebanon. He said: 'As a result of what happened in Beirut on 10 April 1973, the entire population of the city went on strike. The Lebanese people weren't protesting because three of our Palestinian leaders had been killed. They were protesting because the Israelis had been allowed to enter the capital, with no obstacles in their way, and had then been able to do what they liked for a few hours. So the people of Beirut were saying to President Franjieh, "What the hell are you going to do to stop the Israelis coming again? We must be defended!" When it was our turn to meet with the President, we asked the same question, "How are you going to protect our Palestinian people in the refugee camps and their other places?"

'Franjieh was very frank with us. He said: "Look, in the first place you Palestinians are not here by invitation. In the second place there is nothing I can do to protect you." We were stunned. Then the President said: "If you decide to protect your people by your own means I cannot say no to that – but don't count on me." That's what he actually said to us. "Don't count on me. Protect yourselves." And that's why Arafat went to Moscow to persuade the Soviets to sell us some weapons. What happened after that was sadly inevitable. The more we improved the means of defending our people against Israel's attacks and also those of Israel's Christian allies in the Lebanon, the more the Israelis and their allies escalated their attacks on us.'

This escalation did not end until the summer of 1982, when the Israelis invaded the Lebanon and went all the way to Beirut to finish the P.L.O. once and for all by the most brutal military means. And it was this which exposed the limits of how far the Soviets were prepared to go to enable the Palestinians to defend themselves.

Said Hani Hassan: 'I will tell you a very big secret. Perhaps it should remain a secret, but I think it is important for you to know the truth. When we were about to face the Israelis in 1982, and when our dear Arab brothers had refused to let us have anti-tank weapons to help us slow the expected Israeli advance, we sent Abu Walid on a very special and top-secret mission to Moscow. He took a guaranteed cheque for one hundred million dollars. We wanted to buy some Soviet rockets which would allow us to hit cities in Israel. It was our intention to say to the Israelis, "Look, we've got these rockets in place. They are for defensive purposes only but we will fire them if you come to Beirut." The Soviets didn't allow Abu Walid to finish making his case before they told him "No." '

The P.L.O.'s situation in 1972 was not, however, the same as it was in 1982. If it had failed to survive by military means in the period between its expulsion from Jordan and the Yom Kippur War, the P.L.O. would have lost everything. But the Yom Kippur War was a turning point in the P.L.O.'s fortunes. It gave Arafat the freedom he had long been seeking to continue the struggle by political means.

About the war itself, Arafat and his colleagues have many valid questions which still cry out for answers. From their knowledge of what was really happening on the Arab side, they are convinced that the Yom Kippur War had Kissinger's blessing, if not his encouragement. According to this theory, Kissinger's objective (he was to become Secretary of State two weeks before the war) was to teach the intransigent Israelis a lesson that would give him the opportunity, and the leverage, to impose his will on the peacemaking process, mainly for the purpose of obliging Israel to give back to Egypt enough territory, in stages, to tempt Sadat into making a separate peace with the Jewish State.

As Kissinger well knew, the danger of a full-scale Arab-Israeli conflict, plus the threat it posed to Western interests, would be removed once Egypt was seriously involved in the peace process. If Egypt could be neutralized in this way, the U.S. would not then have to worry about putting pressure on Israel to withdraw from the West Bank and the Golan Heights. However much the Palestinians and other Arabs might object to Israel's continuing occupation of these Arab lands, they could not make war without Egypt. And what this meant, in turn, was that Jordan, Syria and the Lebanon would have the choice of either making peace on Israeli and American terms – terms which by definition required the Arab states to deny the Palestinian claim to justice – or living with no peace, and all that that implied – including attacks by the Israelis whenever they wanted to make a point. This was the essence of Kissinger's strategy; and on the eve of the Yom Kippur War it could be said that Israel's intransigence was the obstacle in the way of its implementation.

It is today a matter of record that Kissinger was involved in a number of highly secret discussions with Sadat's emissaries and, through his own back channels, with Sadat himself. It is also a matter of record that the Nixon Administration was united in its anger at what was rightly regarded as Israel's intransigence as far as Egypt was concerned. To a Kissinger memorandum, Nixon added the following note: 'The time has come to quit pandering to Israel's intransigent position. Our actions over the past have led them to think we will stand by them regardless of how unreasonable they are.'[34] Despite Kissinger's assertions that the U.S. and its intelligence agencies had no idea that the Egyptians and the Syrians were going to attack Israel on 6 October, it is also a matter of Arab record that Kissinger was sending Sadat secret messages to the effect that a little heating up of the military situation would be appreciated in Washington.

It was Golda Meir who first introduced me to the idea that Kissinger was in favour of Sadat's war effort. Her revelations came during the course of my last private conversation with her. It took place just a few weeks before her death from cancer in November 1979. The setting for our final talk was the lounge of her very modest home in the suburbs of Tel Aviv. Golda's own best friend and special assistant throughout most of her life in politics was a witty and wonderful woman named Lou Kiddar. Three years before Golda's death I had made Lou promise that she would call me when Golda's end was near. Lou remembered and kept her promise.

There was a third party in the room during my last conversation with Golda. He was there at my invitation. He wanted to meet Golda and I was, so to speak, doing him a favour. In return, and though I did not make a point of saying so at the time, he was also performing a service for me – he was my witness.

My conversation with Golda lasted for more than four hours. During the course of it we smoked two packets of cigarettes – each. Nearly one hour was devoted to Golda's blow-by-blow account of the Yom Kippur War and why the Israelis were taken by surprise.

At an early point in her account of the fighting, Golda told me how she had excused herself from a kitchen Cabinet meeting, in the same room where we were sitting, when Dayan had suggested that Israel should 'surrender' its front-line positions along the Suez Canal to prevent a further loss of Israeli life. Golda told me: 'I said to my colleagues, "*Surrender*, what is this word surrender? It has no meaning in Hebrew!" Then I went to the lavatory to vomit.'

Golda also told me how she was constantly on the telephone to Nixon 'begging' him to begin the airlift of fighter planes and tanks to replace those Israel had lost in the opening hours of the war. At the end of her graphic account of these telephone talks, I asked her whether she suspected that Kissinger was blocking her requests. She replied, 'I'm sure that is exactly what was happening. And that's one of the reasons why I insisted on going to Washington myself.'

When I asked Golda how much, if at all, she had ever trusted Kissinger, she gave me two answers. The first was a silent one. She raised her right hand to her eye level, and then she formed a circle by closing her thumb and index finger together. But it was not a complete zero. Her thumb and index finger did not quite touch. Then she said, 'I'll tell you a story. When Kissinger was in Israel my Cabinet colleagues used to call him Henry and slap him on the back. He responded by slapping them on the back and calling them by their first names. I never allowed that sort of relationship to develop. I always insisted that he called me Mrs Meir or Madame Prime Minister. And I always called him either Mr Secretary of State, or Dr Kissinger.' Golda laughed. 'I always told my colleagues that it was a mistake to be on first name terms with such a man.'

When Golda had finished her long and detailed account of the Yom Kippur War, I suggested to her that the only conclusion to be drawn was that Henry Kissinger in effect made use of Sadat to set up the Israelis for a limited war, to teach them a lesson, in order for him to begin a peace initiative on his own terms. Beyond that, the obvious implication of what Golda had told me was that Kissinger was responsible, in one way or another, for withholding the vital American intelligence information that would have enabled Israeli intelligence to draw the right conclusions.

Without a pause for reflection Golda replied: 'That is what I believe. That is what we believe. But we cannot ever say so . . . what I mean is that we cannot even say so to ourselves.'

For their part, and because they were enjoying an excellent relationship with King Feisal, certain Fatah leaders, Khalad Hassan in particular, were very well informed about what was really happening on the Arab side during the long countdown to the Yom Kippur War. And according to their insights, the story begins in July 1972, when Sadat kicked the Soviets out of Egypt.

At the time the official American line was that the U.S. had been taken by surprise. But if Sadat is to be believed, certain Americans not only knew what he intended to do about the Soviets, but had promised to reward him when he had done it.

Khalad Hassan said: 'Of all the Arab leaders, none were more pleased by Sadat's action than Feisal. The Saudis had been urging him to remove the Soviets for some time, in order to give the Americans the incentive to become seriously involved in the peacemaking process. But Feisal was extremely angry because Sadat had not apparently made any sort of bargain with the Americans. In other words, Sadat had done the Americans a mighty favour and had asked for nothing in return. So Feisal asked me to put some questions to Sadat.

'I met with Sadat and quoting Feisal I said the following: "Why did you kick out the Soviets for nothing? The Americans will never do anything for you without a price. And the Israelis will never give you anything without something very big in return and in advance. So why do you do everything without a price?"

'This was Sadat's reply. "You tell Feisal he doesn't know about everything that is happening. And you also tell Feisal that I have some very specific commitments from the Americans about what they will do to help us now that I have expelled the Soviets." '

It may well be that Sadat was exaggerating and that he had not, in fact, received any specific American commitment. But in the circumstances, there can be little doubt that certain Americans had given Sadat good reason to believe that he would be rewarded if he ejected the Soviets. In this context it should be remembered that Kissinger, through his back channels, had been exchanging messages with Sadat for more than a year.

In the weeks following his decision to expel the Soviets, Sadat discovered that his American friends either would not or could not deliver on their promises, actual or implied, and that the U.S. was not willing to put the Israelis under the sort of pressure that was necessary to oblige them to withdraw from the occupied territories in accordance with Resolution 242. Sadat then started to mend his fences with Moscow. By November he was again buying arms from the Soviet Union. Sadat also went to Saudi Arabia for talks with Feisal.

Khalad continued: 'Sadat told Feisal he had come to the conclusion that the Americans were not serious, and that the deadlock in the Middle East could only be broken by another war. Sadat then said he intended to lead the Arabs in a war of destiny which would push the Israelis back to the 1967 borders. As Feisal himself told me, he then said, "Brother Sadat, are *you* serious?"

'Sadat insisted that he was and he asked for three things from Feisal to make a long war possible: enough wheat to feed his people; a guarantee of spare parts for his industry and his military machine; and a guaranteed supply of oil. At the time Egypt was still importing oil. In addition, Sadat also said he needed a guarantee that Feisal would use the oil weapon against the Americans and other Western nations who helped to sustain Israel's war effort.

'Feisal told Sadat he would give him all the help for which he had asked, and more, but on one condition. Feisal said: "The condition is that you will fight for a long time and that you won't ask for a ceasefire after a few days. You must fight for not less than three months." Sadat said he accepted Feisal's condition.

'On the basis of Sadat's word, Feisal then began to take the whole war effort very seriously. I don't think it is for me to reveal the details of Feisal's strategy, but I can tell you the war Sadat promised to fight was to have involved the whole Moslem world. Because of the arrangements Feisal made to support Sadat, Moslem troops were going to come from as far away as Pakistan – as and when they were needed.

'Unfortunately, and as Feisal and all of us discovered when it was too late, Sadat had deceived Feisal. He never had any intention of fighting the big war he talked about. He was playing games with Feisal in order to strengthen his own hand in the game he was playing with Kissinger.'

According to the Palestinian version of the conspiracy theory – which I later discovered to be the private view of other Arab leaders – Sadat was pretending to be committed to leading a major war effort in order to drive a hard bargain with Kissinger, and he needed

Feisal's backing to give his bargaining position credibility. Syria agreed to play the war game by Sadat's rules. Jordan refused. Abu Daoud said: 'When Hussein released me from prison he told me the Egyptians and the Syrians were going to fight a war for peace. He also said he had no intention of involving Jordan.'

There is ample evidence to suggest that Kissinger was having nightmares about the Arabs using their oil weapon. In April 1973, Feisal sent his Oil Minister, Sheikh Yamani, to Washington. Yamani's brief was to tell Kissinger and others that Feisal would not increase oil production as required by the West if the U.S. did not take genuine steps to bring about an Israeli withdrawal from the occupied territories. According to well informed reports at the time, Kissinger suggested to Yamani that he should not breath a word about what Feisal had said to anybody else. According to Yamani, Kissinger's line was that it would not do the Arabs any good if they were seen to be making threats. Yamani said he believed Kissinger did not want public disclosure of what Feisal had said because it would make public opinion think too deeply about the price the U.S. and other Western nations might have to pay for America's continuing refusal to oblige Israel to withdraw from the occupied territories.

Given that the Israelis were adamantly refusing to make even the token withdrawal from Sinai that was necessary to give Sadat the opportunity to negotiate, it is easy to see that Kissinger himself was facing an appalling dilemma. He could throw up his hands in despair and admit, at least to himself, that Israel had got him beaten before he started, which meant he would take office as Secretary of State without a policy for the Middle East, knowing that continued Israeli intransigence was bound to provoke Feisal and other Arab leaders into using their oil weapon sooner or later – with catastrophic but predictable consequences for the global economy. Or he could make use of Sadat's war to teach his Israeli friends a lesson, and for the main purpose of creating the opening which would allow him to push Israel into negotiations with Sadat.

In his book, *Autumn of Fury: The Assassination of Sadat*, Heikal tells how the Egyptian President was receiving secret messages from Kissinger via a number of different channels, including the C.I.A. The messages were to the effect that the Americans would welcome some military action by Sadat. Heikal also quotes Saudi Arabia's

C.I.A. liaison man as telling him that the Americans had even said
they might be prepared to do a little heating up themselves, given
that the Israelis were 'showing signs of increasing obstinacy'. Heikal
then adds this revealing sentence: 'As late as 23 September, when
David Rockefeller met Sadat at Bourg El-Arab, he passed on the
same message – a little heating up would be in order.'[35] The date
itself is of some significance. It was the day after Kissinger was
sworn in as American's Secretary of State, and fourteen days before
Egypt and the Syrians launched their surprise attack on Israel.

In his own book, *Years of Upheaval*, Kissinger says that the U.S.
was as much surprised as Israel by the Arab attack. He admits that
everybody on the American side, including himself, was in
possession of all the information which invited the conclusion that
Egypt and Syria were intending to attack, but that every American
expert and analyst totally failed to interpret the information
correctly. The real problem, according to Kissinger, was that he and
others failed to cause the right questions to be asked. He says first of
all that he and others were complacent about their own
assumptions. Their main assumption was that Sadat would not
launch an attack because he had nothing to gain from military
adventures. That is simply not true. And nobody knew better than
Kissinger what Sadat stood to gain. Kissinger's other explanation is
as astonishing as it is revealing. He says that America's failure to
interpret correctly the information which told of the coming Arab
attack was, and is, 'inexplicable'.[36]

The moment of truth about Sadat and his real war aims came on
the second day of the conflict. Among those present in the Egyptian
War Room was one of the P.L.O.'s senior military advisers, who
was there as an observer, representing Arafat. He told me this:

'By the beginning of the second day of the war the Egyptian
crossing of the Suez Canal had been completed. Egyptian forces
had, in fact, established a firm line five miles inside what was
previously Israeli-occupied territory. At the beginning of this
second day I said to myself, "This is really it. In two or three days
we're going to be in Tel Aviv! Sadat is actually going to achieve what
Nasser said was impossible!" Really, for a short time that's what I
was telling myself. Then I began to see that nothing was happening.
The Egyptian army was at a standstill. Very slowly I walked around
the War Room, and one by one I looked into the faces of the

Egyptians who were directing the war. I knew them all as former colleagues. Finally I asked the questions which they knew had been passing through my mind. "What is happening?" I said. "Why have you stopped? Why are you not continuing the advance when the gate to Tel Aviv is open?" They were very embarrassed. Poor chaps. I was angry in my quiet way, but really I felt very sorry for them. At first nobody answered me. They looked at the ground. They looked at the ceiling. Everywhere but at me. So I said again, "Why?" Then I got the answer. "No orders. We are not advancing because we have no orders. There is no plan and there will be no advance."

'In that moment I knew what had happened. We all knew. As far as Sadat was concerned the war was over. He had made a deal with the Americans in order to turn himself into an instant hero, and he was waiting now for Kissinger to oblige the Israelis to negotiate. It was a moment of profound significance ... not only for us Palestinians but for the whole Arab world. For the first time in my life I was ashamed to be an Arab. I left the War Room and I cried my heart out.'

On the same day, thousands of miles away in Washington, Kissinger was confident enough to assure his Washington Special Action Group (W.S.A.G.) colleagues that Egyptians forces would not advance beyond the line they were establishing five miles into what was previously Israeli-occupied Sinai. The W.S.A.G. was a crisis management committee chaired by Kissinger and which included, among others, the Deputy Secretaries of State and Defense, the Director of the C.I.A., and the Chairman of the Joint Chiefs of Staff. In his book Kissinger notes that some of his W.S.A.G. colleagues were worried that Sadat would continue to advance. Kissinger says he told them his judgment was that Sadat would just sit there, on the other side of the canal, and that he did not believe Sadat would make any further advances.[37] Given that the whole world was under the mistaken impression that Egyptian and Syrian forces were closing in for the kill, and that Israel really was fighting for its life this time, it is inconceivable that Kissinger would have been foolish enough to put his reputation on the line with such a prediction if he had not had advance information about the limits of Sadat's war aims.

When Sadat launched his attack, Kissinger also knew that crossing the canal would not pose too many problems for the

Egyptians because the Israeli defenders were too thin on the ground. I discovered this truth for myself as early as 1970, when I toured Israel's front-line positions. At the time I was surprised that Israel's defence of the canal was in the hands of so few; and I was amused by the games the Israelis were playing to make the Egyptians think that a much bigger Israeli defence force was on hand. When I returned to Tel Aviv I said to Golda Meir, 'Prime Minister, I've just discovered one of your state secrets.'

She said, 'Which one of many?'

I said, 'Well, I've just returned from a visit to your positions along the Suez Canal, and I went from one end of the line to the other.'

'And what conclusions did you arrive at?' Golda asked.

'Very simple,' I replied. 'You're so thin on the ground, Sadat can take the canal any time he wants it.'

For a moment or two Golda froze in genuine horror. Then she relaxed. 'I was under the impression we had a policy of not allowing foreign journalists to visit more than one front-line position at a time,' she said. Then she smiled. Finally she said: 'I regret to say you are right. But for God's sake don't tell the Egyptians!'

In his book, Kissinger cheerfully admits that once the fighting started he was expecting a repeat of the Six-Day War but in half the time.[38] It is this fact that gives the final clue to what Kissinger was actually thinking and what his real strategy was as he conspired with Sadat. The Egyptians would cross the canal. Sadat would become a hero throughout the Arab world overnight. The humiliation of all previous Arab defeats in battle would be washed away. Sadat would at last be free to negotiate as a winner. The Israelis? Well, they would be shocked. But within a matter of days, probably two or three at the most, they would be knocking the hell out of the Egyptians and the Syrians. Then, when Kissinger decided that honours were even, he would require the Israelis to accept a U.N. call for a ceasefire. Then the long negotiations for a phased Israeli withdrawal from the Sinai would begin, with Kissinger the peacemaker in the driving seat.

Unfortunately for the newly-appointed American Secretary of State, it all went badly wrong. Kissinger lost his ability to control events and did not regain it until after President Nixon had put the world on a nuclear alert. Terrifying but true.

There were two main reasons why the war escalated to the point at which an American President applied the first pressure to the nuclear button.

The first was that Israel lost much more equipment than anybody had thought possible – dozens of aircraft and up to 500 tanks in the first day or so of the war. The Arab attack had really hurt Israel – or so it seemed. But the truth was even more sensational. When the Israelis were mobilizing their reserves for the counter-attack, many and probably most of those 500 tanks were found to be in an unfit state for action. The Israelis eventually admitted this to Kissinger in secret, but what they told him was probably much less than the whole story of their self-inflicted disaster.

What the Israelis were really suffering from was not so much a surprise Arab attack – which was, anyway, very limited in its objective – but the consequences of a monumental dereliction of duty by Moshe Dayan, their Defence Minister. Dayan hated paperwork and the administrative part of his job. And the truth was that he had not dealt with the routine administrative work adequately, nor had he caused others, including his Chief of Staff, to see to it. As a result, Israel's war machine was not ready for action when the first real crisis came. In truth Sadat exposed a problem which the Israelis were then able to deal with when Nixon decided to resupply Israel, and when thanks to Sadat's agreement with Kissinger the Egyptian forces would not advance more than five miles from the canal. The Israelis ought to have been grateful to Sadat for causing them to identify a problem of their own making.

The most immediate consequence of the situation was that the Israelis required much longer than Kissinger's estimated two or three days to respond to the Arab attack.

The other part of the reason for Israel's delay in getting its counter-attack going was simply the fact that Israel's leaders were temporarily paralysed by the psychological impact of what was happening. Despite what they had been telling their people and the world for so many years, they had never seriously believed the Arabs would dare to attack all-powerful Israel. This arrogant and complacent way of thinking was also one of the reasons why Dayan had not bothered to keep the Israeli war machine in good order. He had truly believed it would not be needed except when the Israelis wanted to teach their Arab neighbours a lesson, this despite the fact that he was one of those who did much to promote the propaganda lie that Israel was in constant danger of annihilation by the Arabs.

The second main reason for the escalation was to do with the fact that Golda Meir lost control of some of her generals when the tide of war turned and the Israelis were on their way to another magnificent military victory. The particular general who caused her the most problems was Ariel Sharon.

On 16 October, one of Sharon's special task forces crossed the canal in the central sector and began to operate behind Egyptian lines. As it soon became clear, Sharon's target was the Egyptian Third Army. He was intending to trap it and then smash it. And it was the prospect of that happening which caused the alarm bells to ring in Washington and in Moscow.

For Kissinger the destruction of the Egyptian Third Army would have wrecked everything. Though he had lost control of events, he could still use the war to his advantage, to get negotiations going, if Sadat emerged from the war with something left of his early October reputation as a winner. If the Egyptian Third Army was destroyed, a totally humiliated Sadat would be unable even to think about negotiations with Israel. And all of Kissinger's efforts would have been for nothing.

The Soviets had their problems, too. They also could not afford to sit and watch as Sharon destroyed the Egyptian Third Army. What little real credibility the Soviets enjoyed in the region would be destroyed if they allowed Sadat to be humiliated.

Kissinger sent messages to Golda Meir begging her to restrain Sharon. She tried and failed. Sharon continued with the preparations for his offensive. On 20 October, Kissinger was so desperate that he went to Moscow. Then, on 25 October, it was announced that American forces around the world had been placed on a Red (Nuclear) Alert.

There were two theories about why that happened. One is that the world really was on the brink of a nuclear holocaust. According to this theory, the Soviets were intending to intervene directly to stop Sharon destroying the now trapped Egyptian Third Army, and Kissinger persuaded Nixon to order the nuclear alert to warn Moscow that there were no limits beyond which the Americans would not go to keep the Soviets out. The other theory is that the Soviet threat and the American response were the outcome of a deal Kissinger made with the Soviets.

In my last conversation with Golda, I asked her which of those two theories she accepted. She said, 'If you had asked me that question at the time, I'm not sure what answer I would have given you. Today I am inclined to the second view.'

I asked: 'Does that mean you think Kissinger and the Soviets were playing games to frighten you?'

Golda said, 'Yes.'

I asked, 'Did they succeed?'

She said, 'Yes.'

What happened next was told to me by Golda herself in the following way: 'I climbed into a helicopter. I flew to Egypt – imagine that, Golda Meir in *Egypt* – and there I confronted Sharon. I said to him: "I am your Prime Minister, and I order you not to move against the Third Army." '

And that, more or less, is how the Yom Kippur War ended. Golda got some Egyptian sand in her shoes. The trapped Egyptian Third Army was saved, and with it Sadat's face. A ceasefire agreement was signed and, in the end, Kissinger got his way. As he had always intended, the Yom Kippur War did create a new situation in the Middle East, which enabled the American Secretary of State to impose his will on the so-called peace process. In the coming months, and by means of his much publicized shuttle diplomacy, he was to persuade Israel and Egypt, and then Israel and Syria, to sign what were called Disengagement Agreements. Sadat got a little of the Sinai back, enough to persuade him that it was worth his while to go on working with the Americans, even when doing so required him to betray the Palestinians and the wider Arab cause. In the end it was his willingness to sell his soul for peanuts – actually to a peanut farmer called Jimmy Carter – that cost him his life.

What the Yom Kippur War did above all else was to set the stage for an epic but ludicrously unequal struggle between two men. The struggle was about which of the two of them would most influence the course of events in the Middle East. One man was Henry Kissinger. The other was Yasser Arafat. To be faithful to the record of events I have to add that in the beginning it was a struggle between Kissinger on the one side, and between Arafat and Feisal on the other. But Feisal was assassinated.

This struggle was, so to speak, the background theme to much of what happened between 1974 and 1977, when President Jimmy

Carter and his Secretary of State, Cyrus Vance, restored some sanity and decency to American policy in the Middle East. The essential difference among many between Kissinger and Vance was that Vance was interested in real peace. And as a good human being himself, Vance understood Arafat better than any American before or since (it was Vance who wrote a 'Dear Arafat' letter to the Chairman when the Americans needed the P.L.O.'s help to free the hostages in Iran).

Kissinger's objective was not to bring peace to the Middle East. His aim was to arrange matters so there could not be another war between the Arab states and Israel. War had to be prevented simply because it posed a threat to American and Western interests in the region. Beyond that, Kissinger the global strategist was not much concerned about the fate of the Arabs or even his fellow Jews in Israel.

Within the context outlined above, and as previously noted, Kissinger's first objective was to neutralize Egypt by giving Sadat the opportunity he so desperately wanted to start negotiations with Israel, and to force Israel to entertain the idea of negotiations with Sadat. Once Sadat could be involved in the so-called peace process, and once he was convinced he had something to gain from it, there would be no turning back. Egypt would be out of the business of war, and without Egypt the other Arab states could not fight Israel even if they wanted to. In that event the Arab states would have to make peace on Israeli and American terms. Kissinger's conclusion was that the Arab states could have peace if Israel became more interested in peace than territory, but Israel's condition would be that the Arab states abandoned the P.L.O. And that suited the American Secretary of State.

Arafat's response to the challenge and threat of Kissinger's strategy was swift, bold and courageous. Four months after the Yom Kippur War ended, the Central Council of the P.L.O. issued what was described as a 'Working Paper'. It called for Arab and international recognition of the right of the Palestinians 'to establish a national authority on any lands that can be wrested from Zionist occupation'.[39] The implications were profound but not well understood at the time. The phrase 'national authority' was the agreed P.L.O. code for 'mini-state'.

The P.L.O.'s Working Paper of February 1974 was a clear signal to Israel and the world that Arafat and a majority of his colleagues in the leadership were committed to working for not merely a political settlement, but one which would require the Palestinians to accept the loss, perhaps for all time, of seventy per cent of their original homeland in exchange for a mini-state of their own on the West Bank and in Gaza. Arafat and most of his senior colleagues in the leadership knew this was the nature of the compromise they had to make, but they also knew they needed time to sell it to the rank and file of the liberation movement. If in 1974 Arafat and his colleagues had openly admitted the true extent of the compromise they were prepared to make, it and they would have been repudiated and rejected by an easy majority of the Palestinians who were actually engaged in the liberation struggle.

Arafat told me: 'Our tragedy at the time was that the world refused to understand there were two aspects, two sides, to the question of what was possible. First there was the question of what it was possible for the Palestinians to achieve in practical terms – given the fact that the two superpowers were committed to Israel's existence, and the fact that Israel was the military superpower of the region. But there was also the question of what it was possible for the Palestinian leadership to persuade its people to accept. When a people is claiming the return of 100 per cent of its land, it's not so easy for leadership to say, "No, you can take only thirty per cent." '

After a pause Arafat added: 'You say to me, and you are right, that our public position on the compromise we were prepared to make was ambiguous for many years while we were educating our people about the need for compromise. But I must also tell you that our real position was always known to the governments of the world, including the governments of Israel. How? From 1974, even from the end of 1973, certain of our people were officially authorized to maintain secret contacts with Israelis and with important people in the West. Their responsibility was to say in secret what at the time we could not say in public. You know who these people were. You can talk with them . . . ' I did, as I shall shortly recount.

It was, in fact, to be five long years before Arafat received an official P.N.C. mandate to negotiate on the basis of the mini-state compromise, which was endorsed in principle in 1977. If he had been put to the test of actual negotiations by Israel between 1974 and 1979 it is possible that Arafat could not have delivered peace on the basis of the mini-state formula without splitting the P.L.O. But after the 1979 P.N.C. meeting there was no danger of a split on the issue of compromise. If Israel's Prime Minister of the day, Menachem Begin, and Arafat had met in 1979 for negotiations, Arafat could have said with confidence that he was in a position to deliver.

When I first met with Arafat at the start of my own peace initiative in the second half of 1979, he was still jubilant because of what he had achieved at the end of his five-year struggle to sell compromise. Though it was a private conversation, I hope he will not mind me quoting from it. He said: 'We have turned our people around. No more this silly talk about driving the Jews into the sea. Today my people are prepared to live with the Jews as neighbours in a mini-state of their own. It is a miracle! How far we have travelled in five years.'

Arafat was of course helped by the lively Hassan brothers, the cool Abu Jihad, the Machiavellian Abu Iyad and others of his senior Fatah colleagues. Abu Iyad's role was an interesting one. By agreement with Arafat he was all things to all men. When, for example, the Arafat players needed to pluck an extremist chord in order to placate the radicals in the P.F.L.P. and elsewhere, it was Abu Iyad who plucked it – but usually as part of a double act with Arafat. To outsiders, including myself at the time, it sometimes seemed that Abu Iyad was opposing Arafat. But it was all part of the game that Fatah leaders played to outmanoeuvre and outwit those who were opposed to the mini-state compromise.

When we talked in the second half of 1979, Arafat told me that over the course of the critical five years, 1974 to 1979, he lobbied each and every individual member of the P.N.C. At the time there were 300. One by one, and when circumstances allowed, he summoned them to Beirut from all over the world for a private and personal conversation behind closed doors. For nearly two of those years the P.L.O. was caught up in the first round of the civil war in the Lebanon in which, unknown to reporters, Arafat was playing the role of mediator and fighting for his own survival. For much of the rest of that period Arafat was organizing the P.L.O.'s defences as the Israelis escalated their attacks on the Lebanon. And still he found the time to receive and lobby every individual member of the

P.N.C. 'I kept a record of the time I devoted to those conversations,' Arafat told me. 'It was a total of 550 hours over the five-year period.' He also kept a record of those who said 'Yes' and those who said 'No' when he asked them to cast their vote, at the appropriate time, in favour of the mini-state compromise. As he came to the end of his story, Arafat extracted a small notebook from his hip pocket. It was obviously the last of many in which he had chronicled his conversations with P.N.C. members. 'It's all here,' Arafat said with triumph. 'Let me tell you the figures . . . 296 votes in favour of the mini-state formula, only four against. Imagine that. This was the miracle.'

I tried to get Arafat to tell me who the four objectors were. He refused.

I said, 'One of them has got to be George Habash.'

After a pause, and still with a huge smile on his face, Arafat said, 'Yes, one of them has got to be George.'

I said, 'He may be only one P.N.C. vote but the P.F.L.P. can make a lot of trouble for you.'

Arafat was amused by my assertion. 'You think so?' he said.

'Well, put it this way,' I replied, 'in the past he has caused you no end of trouble. Perhaps, for example, you wouldn't have been crushed and expelled from Jordan if Habash——'

Arafat cut me off and the smile had disappeared from his face. 'That is the past,' he said, and then he paused. 'I am talking about today and the future.' Pause. 'Don't you worry about George. He's a dreamer, an idealist, but he's okay.'

I said, 'You mean he's no problem.'

'That's what I mean,' Arafat replied.

In fact, Habash and his P.F.L.P. did accept the mini-state formula at the 1979 P.N.C. And Habash himself told me that once the mini-state was established he would be prepared to work for the creation of a Democratic State of Palestine by political means, provided the Israelis were willing to engage in dialogue. He said: 'If we can settle our complete problem with the Jews now living in Palestine by peaceful means – very good. Only a criminal would reject that. I am not a criminal. I just don't believe the Zionists want to live with us as equals.'

I do not know how Arafat argued his case with each of the 300 P.N.C. delegates, but I think I can guess what his winning point may have been in many if not all of those one-to-one conversations. Before I took my leave of Arafat to fly to Cyprus and from there to Israel, I told him there was something I had to know which we had not yet discussed. I said: 'When I have conveyed the substance of our talk to my Israeli friends, they will ask me three questions. The first will be "Is he serious?" Their starting point will be that you are not, and that you're only saying you want peace because you haven't got a military option. Their second question will be "Can he deliver?" Their third question will be "Why, really, is he willing to make such a compromise?" It is this last question that I am not yet in a position to answer. I think much could depend on what your answer is.'

Arafat leaned back in his chair. He raised a hand to his shoulder and then let it fall slowly down his body. It came to rest on the pistol of his holster. 'I will tell you,' he said. His voice was quiet and flat and he was clearly struggling to keep his emotions under control. 'This military uniform disgusts me. I want the killing to stop. In my eyes I try to smile. In my heart I am crying.'

Before the Yom Kippur War even Khalad Hassan, Fatah's leading realist, would have opposed the mini-state concept and compromise. He said: 'That we Palestinians should make such a concession to Israel was not even in the outer reaches of my thinking. Never!' So why was it that in a few weeks, and because of the Yom Kippur War, Arafat and a majority of his colleagues in the leadership went for the mini-state compromise, knowing they faced the prospect of being labelled as traitors for advocating such a policy?

Said Arafat: 'Really it was not so complicated. When we made our study of the new situation which existed after the war, we understood that Kissinger would not relax his pressure on the Israelis until he had forced them to make a token withdrawal from the Sinai – not much, just to return some few grains of Sinai sand, but enough to make Sadat commit himself and Egypt to the negotiating process. This was, as you know, Kissinger's purpose when he negotiated the Egyptian-Israeli Disengagement Agreement which was signed in January 1974. And we realized, of course, that once Sadat was committed to the negotiating process, the Arab states, all of them, would make peace with Israel as soon as the Israelis were willing to withdraw from the occupied territories. That is the first point. The second is that we also knew the Arab states would make peace without us if we did not express our demands in a realistic way ... I mean if we did not produce a political programme which the Arab regimes could support.

'So the situation was very critical for the P.L.O. I can say it was a matter of survival. Why? What would have been the peace the Arab states would have made without the P.L.O. if Israel had been wise enough to withdraw? The peace of 242. And what does 242 offer the Palestinians? Some compensation for the refugees and perhaps, I say only perhaps, the return of some few refugees to their homes in Palestine. But what else? Nothing. We would have been finished. The chance for us Palestinians to be a nation again, even on some small part of our homeland, would have passed. Finished. No more a Palestinian people. End of story.'

Undoubtedly it was their fear that the P.L.O. could be abandoned by the Arab states which caused Arafat and his Fatah colleagues to devise a political programme based on the maximum concession the Palestinians could make. But there was, as Hani Hassan told me, another pressure on the leadership. He said: 'Our Palestinian people on the occupied West Bank and in Gaza were desperate, and many of them were demanding a political programme which would give the Israelis every possible incentive to withdraw in exchange for peace. So Arafat had to tell them, "I hear you." '

If Arafat had been free to spell out in public the full and true extent of the compromise for which he and his Fatah colleagues were campaigning inside the P.L.O. from the end of 1973, Israeli and other Jewish propagandists would have had a difficult time. As it was, and throughout the period from 1974 to 1979, they faced virtually no opposition as they set about the task of convincing a mainly indifferent and largely uninformed Western world that there was no such thing as a 'moderate' Arafat. He was what he had always been. A terrorist. And in the 1970s, as in the 1960s, the key to Israel's propaganda effort was the assertion that the P.L.O. was a monolithic organization. With such an approach Israeli and other Jewish propagandists were able to damn Arafat, Fatah and the whole Palestine liberation movement on the strength of isolated terrorist actions by minority P.L.O. groups and factions which were opposed to compromise and whose leaders were, therefore, Arafat's political enemies.

In these years Arafat had almost no room for manoeuvre. He had
a choice of either showing his real hand in public, which would have
led to splits and fighting within the P.L.O. and thus to the creation
of an atmosphere and a situation in which he could not have sold
compromise, or keeping quiet and getting on with the job of
creating the consensus for compromise by discussion and debate
behind closed doors. To me Arafat said, 'Do you call that a choice?'
He chose the latter even though it meant he could not discipline and
punish the wreckers for fear of upsetting the delicate political
balance within the P.L.O. And as a consequence he knowingly set
himself up for character assassination by the Israeli propaganda
machine. So Israel won the propaganda war without a fight, and
Western public opinion was, on the whole, easily convinced that
Yasser Arafat was a terrorist when he was, in fact, doing more than
the Israelis, the Americans and most Arabs put together to find a
formula for a real and just peace.

But as Arafat has said, governments in the West and Israel were
not uninformed about what was really happening behind the scenes
in the P.L.O. In secret, Arafat's emissaries were telling the Israelis,
the Americans and the Europeans what the Chairman could not say
in public about the full and true implications of his commitment to a
negotiated settlement based on the mini-state formula.

Early in 1974, audiences were applauding a new star on the
London diplomatic stage. His name was Said Hammami. As a child
he had been evicted from his home in Jaffa. He remembered the
Jews giving his family half an hour to pack its bags. The rest of his
childhood was spent in refugee camps. At Damascus University he
graduated in English Literature and Philosophy. The love of his
private life, apart from his wife and two children, was English
poetry. He was very much at home in London. The fine mind was
also an open one. Hammami could, and frequently did, consider the
Arab-Israeli conflict from both sides. To all who knew him,
Hammami's voice was that of sweet reason. He was by any
standard a man worthy of respect and admiration. For all that,
because he was a Palestinian his presence in the diplomatic
community was not officially recognized. He was a citizen of nowhere
and a known associate and friend of the terrorist leader Yasser
Arafat. Because of his work for the P.L.O. in general and Arafat in
particular, he was targeted for assassination by the Mossad.

Hammami's official job, unofficially, was to represent the P.L.O. in London. His general brief was to explain to anybody who would listen that Arafat and the mainstream leaders of the P.L.O. were committed to, and working for, a mini-state solution to the Palestinian problem and thus, by definition, a political settlement which would see the P.L.O. recognizing Israel at the end of the negotiating process.

But there was much more to Hammami's work. He had been charged by Arafat with the responsibility for opening and maintaining a secret channel of communication to Israel. As Khalad Hassan confirmed to me, part of Hammami's secret brief was to tell any Israelis who were prepared to listen what Arafat and his colleagues could not say in public. And the first message that Hammami had for Israel was of such profound significance that it ought to have changed the course of history, and would have done so if the Israeli Government of the day, or any since, had been even remotely interested in making peace on the basis of an overall settlement which included a measure of justice for the Palestinians.

The message came down to this: from that moment at the end of 1973 when they were committed to the mini-state formula, and making allowance for the fact that they still had much work to do to sell the compromise it represented to their supporters, Arafat and his colleagues had, in fact, given implied but obvious *de facto* recognition to the State of Israel, inside the borders as they were on the eve of the 1967 war. This acceptance of Israel was implicit in the fact that the Palestinian mini-state on the West Bank and in Gaza was to be Israel's *neighbour*. As Arafat confirmed to me, the best he and his Fatah colleagues could do in advance of an actual peace agreement, one based on the P.L.O. mini-state formula, was to give the Jewish State this implied but obvious *de facto* recognition; formal or *de jure* recognition would follow naturally at the end of the negotiating process. This was the essence of the message that Hammami had to pass on to Israel.

For some years past, successive governments in America and Western Europe have insisted, and do still today insist, that the P.L.O. cannot become a party to negotiations until it recognizes the existence of the State of Israel. In other words, recognition of Israel is the price the Palestinians must pay for the privilege of being allowed to take part in negotiations about their own future. On the face of it this demand seemed reasonable to many people – in fact to the vast majority of people in the Western world. If the P.L.O. really was prepared to give formal and *de jure* recognition to Israel at the end of the negotiating process, why could it not do so at the beginning?

The problem of recognizing Israel is, as Khalad Hassan put it, 'the very devil of a problem', and the demand that the P.L.O. should recognize the Jewish State at the start of the negotiating process was *totally unreasonable*.

According to international law (and also the will of the international community as it is represented by the General Assembly of the U.N.) the acquisition of territory by war does not give the conquering and occupying power the right to title to, or sovereignty over, the conquered and occupied territory. What this means with regard to the Arab-Israeli conflict is that Israel's occupation of Arab land beyond the borders of the U.N.'s 1947 Partition Plan is illegal according to international law and inadmissible according to U.N. resolutions. That, so to speak, is one half of the recognition problem.

The other half is that according to international law, acquisition of territory by war can be legitimized only if other parties with a claim to the territory occupied recognize the occupying power. So according to international law, the Palestinians would be waiving their rights and their claim to their land the moment they recognized Israel. This is the reason why no Palestinian leadership can recognize Israel before or until Israel recognizes the rights of the Palestinians to self-determination. As Khalad Hassan put it: 'If we recognize Israel before Israel recognizes our rights to self-determination, we will not only be waiving our claim to all of our land, we will be eliminating our right of existence!'

Arafat made the same point in his own way. He said: 'Our situation would be this: we would have survived the many attempts to destroy us in order to commit suicide. I confess we have sometimes behaved in a very foolish way – but we are not completely mad! Naturally the Israelis, some Americans and even some of our Arab brothers would like us to commit suicide in such a nice, unmessy way. But I am sorry to say we cannot oblige them!'

Arafat then asked me a question. 'Why is it,' he said, 'that the people of the Western world refuse to understand this matter which is so fundamental to our case and our struggle?' In reply I said: 'Abu Amar, the problem is not that so many people refuse to understand. The problem is that most people simply don't know these things – because nobody tells them.'

Governments, however, know these things. So why have they insisted on the P.L.O. recognizing Israel in advance of negotiations when they know that by doing so they are asking the P.L.O. to renounce the Palestinian claim to land and rights of self-determination?

In their own answer to this, the most controversial of all questions, Arafat and all of his colleagues in the P.L.O. leadership are united. Khalad Hassan was their spokesman, and the following is what he said:

'If you don't mind I will begin my answer, our P.L.O. answer, with an exaggeration in order to make a point. From the moment we Palestinians showed that we would not allow our problem to be swept under the carpet, the nations of the world, especially those with influence on Israel, had a choice of two main options. One was to screw the Palestinians and by definition the Arabs. The other was to screw the Jews of Israel.

'In reality that was not the choice. It is perhaps becoming so, because of Israel's intransigence, but it did not have to be. In reality, and once we Palestinians had showed by our resistance that we would not give up our struggle until we had obtained some justice, the choice for the Western nations, especially America, was the following: to put pressure on Israel to cause the Jewish State to make an accommodation with the Palestinians – this was possible on our side from 1974 on; or to give Israel the licence to liquidate the Palestine liberation movement by all necessary means.

'The problem was and is that Zionism *cannot* make an accommodation with us Palestinians even though we have long been ready for it. From the very beginning the Zionists said, "It's us or them." We have to admit, and we do, that we responded to the Zionists in the same way in our early days. We said, "It's them or us." And some of us – not me, or Arafat or anybody in Fatah – talked about driving the Jews into the sea. But in time we Palestinians, many of us, grew up. As I told you before, we passed from our political childhood, to adolescence and to maturity. And we saw and accepted the need for us to face the reality of Israel's existence. Then we produced our mini-state formula. Then we risked our credibility and, frankly speaking, our lives to sell it to our people. What was the result?

'The more realistic we became, and the more obviously realistic we became, the more we began to win the understanding and the support of international public opinion. That, too, had its consequence. After Kissinger, thank God, was out of office, the governments of the West, especially the one in Washington, began to feel themselves under an obligation to put put real pressure on Israel – which from time to time they did. But unfortunately for us, the Zionists had anticipated the pressures they might one day face and they had prepared their defences. I can say, because it is true, that the Zionists have resisted American pressure as successfully as we have resisted Zionism's attempt to liquidate us and our cause!

'Now I am almost ready to answer your question directly, but to give you the complete background picture I must explain that Zionism has two main defences against American pressure. The first is the power of Jewish money which allows the Jews of America, seven per cent or so of the population, to more or less decide who will become the President in the White House. Perhaps it would be more true to say that their money allows them to decide who will not become President. But however you put it, the first fact of American politics is this: unless you are very, very, very rich in your own right, or unless you can milk corporation funds, you cannot be a candidate in an American Presidential race and expect to go the distance unless you have the support of Jewish money. One day, perhaps, Senator Glenn will tell the world about the problems he faced on this account during the current Presidential race. So more often than not the Jewish lobby in America has a very big say in the making of the President. For the same reason it also has a very big say in the breaking of a President. What do I mean? Every President wants a second term in office. Unfortunately that makes him vulnerable to Jewish lobby blackmail at any moment during his first term. And the weaker the President is, I mean the more problems he's got, the more vulnerable he is.

'I suspect many of your readers will say that I am fantasizing about the influence of the Jewish lobby. Unfortunately I am not. What I have been telling you is political science fact not fiction. Most Americans who know anything about anything, know that what I've said is true. But they don't like talking about it because they know it's made a nonsense of what they call democracy. I'm a democrat and an unashamed rightist, but when I hear American Presidents lecturing the world about the quality of their democracy, I never know whether to laugh or throw up. I'm anti-communist and against coups, but I don't want American-type democracy either. One day I suppose the American people will realize how their Presidents have allowed three million Israelis and their lobby in the U.S. to run American foreign policy. And when that day comes there'll be a backlash against the Jews. And do you know who'll get the blame? We Arabs and we Palestinians in particular. We Arabs didn't kill six million Jews or persecute them. Europeans did that. But we Palestinians paid the price. I think I'm entitled to say that life has not been very fair to us!

'While I'm on the subject of the Jewish lobby at work I must tell you a depressing but funny story. Once when I was in America I was approached by a Jewish Congressman who was beginning to understand our case. He asked me to give him some information to include in his future speeches. So we sat together and we produced a list of points which he promised to make over a period of weeks. Nothing sensational. Just a point here and there to cast a doubt or two on the lies the Zionists were telling about us. Anyway, he also promised to send me copies of his speeches, newspaper cuttings and so on. The weeks passed, the months passed and I didn't hear from him. Then I found myself in America again. I said to him, "So what happened?" He was very sad and he shook his head from side to side. He said: "Khalad, even you would never believe what my people did to me. I made the first speech. And for the next seventy-two hours my phone didn't stop ringing. In the office, at home, in the morning, in the night. Myself, my colleagues, my friends, my wife, my kids – we were all going nuts. It was a deliberate campaign of harassment and some abuse. And the objective was simply to make my life intolerable because I dared to make a point in the P.L.O.'s favour. Frankly, I couldn't take any more of it. So I did what all American politicians do in the circumstances – I retracted what I'd said in the first speech and never made any of the other points we agreed. I'm sorry." I said, "Don't worry, I understand." And then his Jewish sense of humour took over. He said: "I'll tell you something, Khalad . . . If your Arab people were just five per cent as ruthless as my Jewish people, and if your Arab people were just ten per cent as efficient as my Jewish people at the job of political blackmail – well, you'd have had your mini-state a long time ago . . . And come to think of it, you'd probably have had the whole of America as your maxi-state!'

'So anyway, that is one of Zionism's two main defences against American pressure on Israel – political blackmail made possible by superb Jewish organization and money. The other main defence is Israel's incredible military strength, conventional and nuclear. Why really do you think Israel has become such a formidable military power, with 600 to 700 nuclear warheads and cruise missiles of its own? Because of the Arab military threat? That's the biggest joke of all. Apart from a few weeks in 1948, and as I think you now understand, Israel has never, never, never faced the threat or even the prospect of annihilation by the Arabs. No, I'll tell you why Israel is a military superpower.

'In one way the Zionists have always been very far-sighted. They knew from the beginning that the West might one day betray them just as it betrayed us to make way for the Jews. So the Zionists said to themselves, "Nobody is going to betray us." And the real reason why Israel is a military superpower today is because it has prepared for the time when the U.S. might exert real pressure. When or if that day comes, the Israelis will say to the Americans, "You can't make us do anything against our will. We are too powerful." What can the U.S. do then? Invade Israel to impose a settlement? Of course not. What the U.S. could do is to cut off the money that keeps Israel alive. But what would happen in Israel then? My guess is that sixty to seventy per cent of the Jews would leave Israel – assuming they were not prevented from going by the fascist military junta that would then be in control. And what happens next? The Israeli fascists would then try nuclear blackmail on the U.S. "Restore the money or we'll hit selected Arab targets with our nuclear weapons." And what if the U.S. called the Israeli bluff? It wouldn't be a bluff. Madmen like Sharon will carry out their threat. And my guess is that Sharon would threaten to take out the Gulf oil fields with his first nuclear strike. Now I am ready to answer your question about why the Americans and others have insisted and are insisting that we commit suicide by recognizing Israel before Israel recognizes our rights to self-determination.'

Though I did not tell Khalad at the time, I was in possession of evidence which supported his fears. On a day in 1980, I was sitting in the outer office of one of Begin's senior ministers. I was waiting for him to return from a meeting. When he arrived he threw me his usual big smile of greeting, put his arm on my shoulder and propelled me to his inner sanctum. I made for the chair opposite his desk on which there was not so much as a single sheet of paper. The Minister sat back, put his feet on the desk and was lost to me. He was *very* worried about something. There was a crisis of some sort but it was clearly not an emergency which demanded action by him. I knew the Minister quite well and I had a great deal of respect for him. Eventually I said: 'You've obviously got a problem. I hope it's not personal. Do you want me to make another appointment?'

For perhaps another full minute he said nothing. He was still far away. And I had the impression he was really frightened for probably the first time in several years. Finally he spoke. 'I've just heard a terrible story. And it happens to be true. I know. I've checked it.'

'Oh?' I said.

The Minister said: 'It concerns our famous General Sharon. Do you know what that lunatic has just done . . . He's sworn a secret oath. He's taken a vow that if this or any future Government of Israel attempts to withdraw from the West Bank, he'll set up headquarters there and fight to the death to prevent a withdrawal.'

I said, 'Do you think he's serious?'

The Minister looked hard at me. 'Do you?'

I said, 'Yes.'

'So do I,' the Minister replied. 'He's mad enough to nuke the whole Arab world provided he can find a way to protect this little country from the fall-out!'

Khalad continued: 'The answer to your question is that we are required to commit suicide by recognizing Israel before Israel recognizes our rights to self-determination because the U.S. and therefore the Europeans are frightened of Israel. Once upon a time the question the Americans and the Europeans used to ask themselves was, "Who do we need most to help us dominate the region and protect our interests there?" But when we Palestinians demonstrated by our resistance that our problem could not be swept under the carpet, and once it was clear that the Arab states were supporting our realistic political programme, the question changed. Then the U.S. and the Europeans knew they had to do something to help us, to help themselves, but the question they asked themselves was, "Who are we most afraid of – the Arabs or the arrogant, bullying, neo-fascist state that Israel is on its way to becoming? Who can make life most difficult for us – the Zionists or the Arabs?"

'When the question was posed in that way, it was not such an easy one to answer for the truth was that the West could not afford to have either the Zionists or the Arabs as enemies. So the question became, "Yes, but who can we least afford to have as our enemy?" For the reasons I have stated, the Americans decided, for themselves and the Europeans, that they were, on balance, more frightened of Israel and the influence of the Zionists than they were of the Arabs. Of course the Americans and the Europeans – I am talking of governments – could not afford to admit that they were frightened of Israel and that they were, as a consequence, allowing Israel to dictate what their foreign policies would be. So with Israel's help they came up with this clever way of putting the blame on us. In effect what the Americans said was: "Of course we are ready to put the necessary pressure on Israel, but we can't reasonably be expected to do that until the P.L.O. recognizes Israel." So we took and are taking the blame for America's refusal, out of fear, to do what is necessary to oblige Israel to make an accommodation with us. But really we have not been to blame since 1974.

'That was such an important year. In the leadership we were committed to an accommodation with Israel, and as leaders we were already working to convince our people that there did have to be an accommodation with those who had taken our land and our homes. It is true that we could not afford to declare our real hand in public, but in politics, especially the politics of peace and war and life and death, the moves that matter never take place in the open. So there was nothing unusual about the fact that we were using secret channels to tell the world about our real position. In that context it is impossible to exaggerate the importance of Said Hammami's work. If the Israeli Government of Yitzhak Rabin had responded to the signals we were sending through Hammami, we could have had a just peace in a very few years. What were we hoping for from Israel? I'll tell you.

'In 1974 we were hoping the Israelis would say the following, or something like it. "We hear you, and we are interested. We don't necessarily believe what we are hearing and we are not convinced you can deliver the unthinkable compromise you are talking about. But we are encouraged. Let's keep in touch and, who knows, we might one day find ourselves talking about an accommodation with you." Unfortunately Rabin's Government was not remotely interested. And in Kissinger the Rabin Government had a friend who was as committed as any Israeli to the destruction of the P.L.O. As a matter of fact, Kissinger was the architect of the attempt to liquidate us in the Lebanon after we had outmanoeuvred him in our own dealings with Nixon, and after we went on to score two big political triumphs – the first in October 1974, when the Arab summit at Rabat recognized the P.L.O. as the only legitimate representative of the Palestinian people; the second in November 1974, when Arafat made his dramatic appearance at the U.N. in New York.'

Hammami's message got through to Rabin's Government on a regular basis over a period of more than four years. Hammami's contact in Israel was Uri Avnery, a former Member of Parliament, the editor of a weekly magazine, and the country's most celebrated 'dove'. The Palestinian and the Israeli made their first contact with each other after Hammami, at the end of 1973, had published two articles in *The Times* of London. In one of them he called for mutual recognition between the P.L.O. and Israel. Avnery has confirmed that he did on a number of occasions speak with Rabin himself. Apart from passing on messages, Avnery also set up the Israel Council for Israeli-Palestinian Peace.

At the time of the Hammami-Avnery dialogue it was assumed by most commentators that Hammami was to some extent a loner, and that he was setting a pace he wanted a reluctant P.L.O leadership to follow. That was not at all the case. Hammami was Arafat's ambassador.

In January 1978, a man who was assumed to be an Arab, and who gave his name as Adel on the telephone, was shown into the P.L.O.'s basement office in London. Hammami stood up to shake his visitor's hand. 'Adel' shot and killed Hammami.

Said Hammami was not the first P.L.O. representative in Europe to be assassinated. But he was the first of a number of special Arafat envoys, some twenty or more, to be murdered in the period from

January 1978 to December 1983. All those who died had one of two achievements to their credit. Some, like Hammami himself and Issam Sartawi, had succeeded both in establishing good contacts with certain Israelis who were highly critical of what they rightly regarded as the folly of Israeli Government policy, and in capturing the understanding and even the support of certain non-Israeli Jews who had previously been pillars of the Zionist establishment. The other Arafat envoys who were murdered were those who had succeeded in establishing excellent relations with certain European governments and institutions such as the E.E.C. Commission. Most if not all of those who were eliminated had one thing in common: they were generators of support for the P.L.O. in places where successive Israeli governments had previously enjoyed a complete and unchallenged freedom of influence.

The identity of the leader of the organization responsible for the assassinations has never been a secret. His cover-name is Abu Nidal. His real name is Sabri Khalil Banna. Until the moment in 1973 when Arafat and his colleagues in the leadership committed themselves to an accommodation with Israel, Abu Nidal was a Fatah loyalist. But at that point he broke with Fatah and set up his own organization in Iraq. And from there he became a fanatical opponent of the leadership's policy of compromise with Israel.

Abu Iyad said: 'At the time there were many in Fatah who shared his views but they were against a split in the movement. So Abu Nidal was in despair and he turned to assassination.' In fact, Abu Nidal vowed to kill any Fatah official who had contact with Israel. Abu Iyad continued: 'He put the names of some fifty Fatah leaders on his hit-list. They were not the very top leaders. They were those who were close to the top leaders and who were doing special work for them – for Arafat in particular.'

Abu Iyad disclosed that it was as early as 1975 that Fatah tried Abu Nidal *in absentia* and sentenced him to death. After Hammami's assassination, the P.L.O.'s Political Department made a request in Arafat's name for Abu Nidal's extradition. The regime in Baghdad refused even to consider it. After the next assassination, the murder in June of the P.L.O.'s representative in Kuwait, Fatah made another request, this time in public, for Abu Nidal's extradition. Again the Iraqi regime refused to consider it. At that point Abu Iyad ordered his own hit-men into action. They made

two attempts to kill Abu Nidal in Baghdad. And both failed. Said
Abu Iyad: 'On both occasions the Iraqi authorities stopped us.' In
July and August newspapers around the world reported a shoot-out
between Fatah and Abu Nidal's group. The action took place in
Paris, Beirut, Istanbul and Karachi. I asked Abu Iyad what all that
was about. He smiled. 'You can say it was a kind of rehearsal,' he
said. 'We were drawing them out. We had to establish who they
were and where they were. During the course of the next year, and
without any publicity, we quietly liquidated a number of them,
mainly in Europe.'

I asked Abu Iyad why Fatah had failed to date to kill Abu Nidal
himself. He said: 'Abu Nidal is not a person, he is a state. When
he was in Baghdad he lived inside a very secure area where many
of Iraq's leaders also live. When he travelled, which was not often,
he enjoyed Iraqi diplomatic cover. And he enjoys the same protection when he is working with the Syrians and the Libyans. But
I promise he'll die as soon as he presents a target we can hit!'

Fatah's leaders, including Arafat himself, are convinced that the
Mossad had a hand in Abu Nidal's operations and, more to the
point, that the Mossad was the agency which actually selected some
and perhaps many of Abu Nidal's targets.

Said Abu Iyad: 'You will appreciate that we are still at war with
Abu Nidal and the Mossad, so there is much in the way of detailed
intelligence information I cannot reveal to you. However, I will tell
you enough to make you think. We know when, where and how
Mossad agents, two or three to start with, penetrated Abu Nidal's
organization. It happened in Morocco where, as you know, there is
a happy, thriving community of Jews – including many who could
pass themselves off as Arabs and fool anybody. And I mean
anybody.

'To tell you the truth it was quite by chance that the Mossad
succeeded in penetrating Abu Nidal's organization. The Israeli
intelligence people had what you might call a lucky break. At the
time the actual operation to make the penetration was being
organized by the Moroccan intelligence service and the C.I.A. And
there is quite a story to that. . .

'So the C.I.A. and the Moroccan intelligence service were co-
operating on this mission to make the penetration of Abu Nidal's
organization. Why the co-operation? Two main reasons. One, there

is a very good relationship between the two agencies. Two, Abu Nidal recruits most of his people from North Africa.

'But as you know, the C.I.A., or at least a part of the C.I.A., has a very special relationship with the Mossad. They exchange information on a regular and even round-the-clock basis. So the Mossad came to learn what the C.I.A. was doing . . . and that was the Mossad's opportunity to put its own agents inside Abu Nidal's organization. In time, and with the co-operation of the Moroccan intelligence service, we discovered that definitely two and possibly three of the first agents to penetrate Abu Nidal's organization were working for the Mossad.

'I can tell that one of the agents who made the penetration for the Mossad got very close to Nidal himself. Very close. You can ask me – is that really so easy? The answer is yes, and I'll tell you why. It is to do with the character and personality of Abu Nidal himself. You must know two things about him. First he is a very simple man, I mean he is not so well educated. Second, and more important, he is a very unstable man. He has a split mind and a sick mind. One minute he is up and one minute he is down. One minute shouting and the next minute calm. Now, it is a fact, and I know any intelligence expert will confirm it, that when an organization is run by such a personality, penetration is very easy. Let me put it another way. If Abu Nidal was a different kind of personality, if he was all the time balanced and calm, he would be more thoughtful and cautious . . . Then the Mossad would not have had such an easy job.'

I asked Abu Iyad to tell me what he thought was the main function of Mossad's agents inside Abu Nidal's organization. He said: 'I am sure they had several functions, but the main one was, how shall I put it, to help choose the targets which Abu Nidal's organization was going to hit. Target selection.'

I said, 'Do you think Mossad agents sometimes did the killing?'

Abu Iyad replied: 'In most cases we know who the actual assassins were . . . But this information is still, let me say, classified.'

Finally I asked: 'Who really killed Said Hammami? We all know he was assassinated by the Abu Nidal organization, but was he targeted by Mossad agents on the inside? Is it possible even that the man Adel was himself a Mossad agent?'

Abu Iyad replied: 'On this matter you must draw your own conclusion – but I will give you one more piece of information

which is not any more a secret. It was even reported in the British
newspapers and it is true. A long time before he was assassinated,
Said was warned by your British Special Branch that he was one of a
number of P.L.O. people on the Mossad's hit-list. The Special
Branch people told Said the information had been passed to them by
the C.I.A. According to what Said told us at the time, and we
believed him – why not? – the Special Branch also said the British
authorities had warned the Israeli Embassy that all known Mossad
agents in Britain would be kicked out if the Israelis started any
shooting.'

One conclusion from this, which I put to Abu Iyad, was that Israel
stood to lose too much politically if its Mossad agents assassinated
Hammami and others like him, and that was why the Mossad
penetrated and used Abu Nidal's organization.

For a moment I thought Abu Iyad was going to say no more on
the subject. Then he became very angry. With great bitterness he
said: 'If you want to know what I really think – I'll tell you. If the
Abu Nidal organization did not exist the Israelis would have
invented it. That's the way the Mossad works.'

In nine months, two of the world's three most powerful and
influential leaders were destroyed. On 9 August 1974, President
Richard Nixon resigned in disgrace, broken by the Watergate affair.
On 25 March 1975, King Feisal was assassinated. In the period
between these two events, Yasser Arafat won two enormous
political victories. At the Rabat summit in October 1974, Arab
leaders and therefore their governments recognized the P.L.O. as
the only legitimate representative of the Palestinian people. What
that meant, among other things, was that King Hussein was no
longer free to negotiate for the Palestinians. This was a shattering
blow to Kissinger and Israel's Government. Then, in November
1974, Arab recognition of the P.L.O. was effectively endorsed by
the international community when Arafat made his dramatic
appearance at the U.N. General Assembly in New York. Neither of
these two victories would have been possible without Feisal's
support for the P.L.O.

President Nixon was among the very first people in the world to
be fully and honestly briefed about the reality of Arafat's
commitment, from the end of 1973, to peace with Israel – a
commitment which, as soon as it was made, implied *de facto*

recognition of Israel's existence. Nixon well knew that any Israeli government even remotely interested in peace would buy Arafat's mini-state formula. He also knew that if an Israeli government agreed to negotiate on it, the Arab-Israeli conflict would be ended as soon as Arafat and his colleagues in the leadership had persuaded enough of their supporters in the rank and file of the liberation movement to accept the need for the compromise.

It was Nixon himself who sent General Vernon A. Walters to the Middle East in March 1974 for a secret rendezvous with two P.L.O. leaders. At the time Walters was the Deputy Director of the C.I.A. But it was clearly understood by Nixon and the P.L.O. that Walters was participating as the President's special representative.

The two P.L.O. representatives were Fatah's leading rightist, Khalad Hassan, and, for political balance, a prominent Fatah leftist, Majed Abu Sharar. Khalad Hassan was there in his capacity as the Chairman of the P.N.C.'s Foreign Relations Committee and also as Arafat's personal representative. Majed Abu Sharar was at the time responsible for Fatah's information department. (In October 1981 he was killed when a bomb exploded underneath his bed in a Rome hotel room. It was assumed that Mossad agents were responsible.) At the time of the secret meeting the P.L.O. did not apparently know that Walters was associated with the C.I.A.

Said Khalad: 'First of all we told General Walters about the background to our thinking on the need for a political settlement. But the main business was to brief him fully and in detail about the reality of our commitment to peace with Israel. We were also very honest about our internal problems. We said we were leaders who were leading from the front, and that we had many obstacles to overcome before we could expect to convince our people of the need to make peace with those who would still be occupying seventy per cent of our homeland when the peace was made.

'For us, as far as I can remember, General Walters had three main questions. The first was about what he called "technology". He said, more or less, "We Americans are the technology carriers in the region. What technology will you use?" He was obviously referring to arms, machinery and so on. The real purpose of his questions under this heading was to find out if we were going to be Soviet puppets. I explained to him why it was that most of what he had heard about our relations and involvement with the Soviets was bullshit. And I said very frankly that it was not our intention to be the puppet of any foreign power. But I also drew his attention to a number of facts. One was that Fatah was of and on the right. Another was that our leadership was the only one in the Arab world which believed in and was practising democracy. And then I said to him: "Yes, you are right. We have some so-called Marxists, some so-called radicals and some so-called leftists in our ranks . . . but do you know why some Palestinians and some Arabs are looking to Moscow?" And I told him it was because the U.S. had left them with no choice. I said that was the folly of the Kissinger strategy in particular, and the folly of American and Israeli policy since 1948 in general. I also told him very frankly that we found it difficult to take the U.S. seriously in some ways. American Presidents and officials were always talking about the need to stop the commies blah blah blah. What we wanted to see, I said, was the coming of the day when the Americans would realize that it was their policies and their attitudes in many parts of the world which were making so-called communists out of peoples who were crying out to be the friends of America — if only the Americans would not insist on dominating their lives. So I said to him, "You Americans want to stop the advance of communism but you are actually promoting it." Which is, of course, the story of what is happening in Latin America today because of Reagan's policy there. So you see we gave a good account of ourselves on this bullshit question about the P.L.O. being a communist puppet.

'The General's second question was about how a Palestinian mini-state would perform and project itself in the Arab arena. He said: "Are you going to speak the Palestinian language or the Pan-Arab language?" We said we were Palestinians and Arabs and that we believed in Arab unity and would work for it. But we also said our voice would be our own, and that just as we were not willing to be the puppet of the East or the West, so also were we not willing to be dominated by any Arab regime. And we told him frankly that we saw certain problems ahead for us in the Arab arena.'

Once when I was chatting with Arafat I ventured the suggestion that one of the main reasons why the Arab regimes had never really wanted there to be a Palestinian state was because it would be a model of democracy which the undemocratic and mainly illegitimate regimes would regard as a dangerous threat. Arafat became very serious. He said: 'It is so. You are right. And I tell you frankly it is a matter which worries me very much. In our mini-state our democracy will be a model which many Arab peoples will want to copy. Then perhaps they will demand the democracy that we Palestinians are enjoying. And how will the regimes react to that? There is no doubt the regimes are frightened of our democracy. Perhaps that is the number-one cause of many of our problems in the Arab world.'

Khalad continued: 'The General's third question was about Jordan. He simply said, "What about Amman?" What he meant was, "Okay, let's suppose you have your mini-state . . . What about Hussein? Will it be your policy to overthrow him in due course?" And we told him all the reasons why this was another bullshit question. We also suggested that if he wanted to know what had really happened in Jordan and why, he should look into the dark corners of certain official American intelligence agencies, and that if he didn't find the evidence there he should look into or up or along some of Kissinger's back channels. In direct answer to his question we explained why it had never been our policy to overthrow Hussein and why it never could be.'

How did this most secret of secret meetings end? Khalad told me: 'General Walters said three things. The first was that he was impressed by what we had said. The second was that he believed President Nixon would be impressed. But it was his third point which made us so happy because it convinced us that he was totally sincere and serious. It was not only what he said, but the way he said it. He told us: "If what you say is so, and if I am right to be impressed, then we Americans have lost a lot of time."

'We had a firm agreement to meet again as soon as possible after General Walters had briefed Nixon. We also agreed that a third meeting might be necessary.'

What happened next? Khalad said: 'The first message I got from General Walters said there could be a delay of one month before he could tell us when we would meet again. The second message said there would be no more talks and that the dialogue was over. Finished. I was informed in the most clear way, and I may say with regret, that General Walters had been forced by Kissinger to cut the contact.'

Now to a most interesting clash of evidence. In his own book

Kissinger devotes less than two dismissive lines to a meeting between General Walters and the P.L.O. in March 1974. Kissinger also says the March meeting was the second that Walters had with the P.L.O. According to Kissinger the first meeting took place in Rabat on 3 November 1973. On that occasion, and still according to Kissinger, the P.L.O. person told Walters that the Palestinians could not be confined to a mini-state on the West Bank and in Gaza; and that Hussein would have to be overthrown in order for the Palestinians to have Jordan as part of a bigger homeland. In addition Kissinger says that the P.L.O. person refused to say under what, if any, conditions the P.L.O. would recognize Israel; talked of the possibility of returning Israel to the borders of the 1947 Partition Plan; and refused to make any concrete proposals.[40]

The point at issue is not whether there was or was not a meeting between Walters and a P.L.O. person on 3 November, or even whether a P.L.O. person did or did not say what Kissinger says and implied he did. The point at issue is that Kissinger links the first meeting he describes to the second one in March which he does not describe by saying that it failed to advance matters beyond the point of the first one.

Like most P.L.O. leaders, Khalad Hassan has read Kissinger's book several times. With it open in front of us, I asked Khalad to explain the enormous difference between his story and Kissinger's. Khalad gave me a small, sad smile and then said: 'Alan, I've told you many times before, and no doubt I'll have to tell you many times in the future, this man Kissinger is a big liar.'

If Khalad Hassan is right, the conclusion must be that Kissinger sabotaged what was effectively a Nixon-P.L.O. dialogue, a dialogue which Nixon authorized as part of his own effort to explore the possibility of a comprehensive settlement, and one which promised much for all who were interested in ending the Arab-Israeli conflict on the basis of a total Israeli withdrawal from territory occupied in 1967 in return for a total peace, and a measure of justice for the Palestinians.

In their different ways Arafat and the two Hassan brothers told me, quite specifically, that they were convinced that the Government of Israel and the Jewish lobby in America had made use of the Watergate affair to break Nixon before he forced Israel to make the necessary withdrawals for peace.

Even if there was such a conspiracy, it could never be proved. But there is one question that has to be asked. Is there any hard evidence that Nixon was seriously committed to a comprehensive peace and, if necessary, a confrontation with Israel in order to bring it about? The answer is yes – quite a lot of evidence.

In June 1974, about two months after Kissinger had sabotaged the Nixon-P.L.O. dialogue, Nixon went to the Middle East. He visited Egypt, Saudi Arabia, Syria, Israel and Jordan. From Kissinger's own account of Nixon's visit to Israel, and also from Israeli newspaper reports, it is clear that the President was very frank, even blunt and tough, with the country's leaders.

On 17 June, and right across its front page, *The Jerusalem Post* carried a headline which said, 'Nixon Urges "Statesmanship for Peace" by Israel'. The reporters were Asher Wallfish and David Landau. The opening three paragraphs of their story were the following:

'U.S. President Richard Nixon last night called upon the leaders of Israel to choose the "right way" of statesmanship and recognize that "continuous war is not a solution for Israel's survival".

'Mr Nixon was replying to a toast by Professor Ephraim Katzir at a state banquet given in his honour by the Israeli President at the Knesset's Chagall Hall.

'The alternative was politically easier, said Mr Nixon – adhering to the *status quo* and resisting initiatives. But initiatives might lead to negotiation.'

According to the same report, Nixon also said, 'Peace takes courage just as war does.'

In *Years of Upheaval* Kissinger says Nixon was even more emphatic in his private conversations with Israel's leaders. According to Kissinger, Nixon told them that continuous war was not only a wrong policy, it was also 'not right'. And Kissinger quotes Nixon as saying the following: ' . . . some might say in this country and many of our very good friends in the Jewish community in the United States say it now: let's go back to the old days. Just give us the arms and we can lick all of our enemies and all of the rest. I don't think that's a policy. I don't think that is viable for the future . . . time will run out!'[41]

As far back as October 1973, Kissinger had warned the Government of Israel that Nixon might be preparing to cut off arms supplies as a form of pressure. During my last conversation with Golda Meir she told me something Kissinger had said to her when he visited Israel as the Yom Kippur War was ending, and as American weapons were pouring into the country: 'Very quietly Kissinger said to me, "Mrs Meir, do you mind if I give you some advice . . . Now that this airlift is under way, you must use the opportunity to take everything possible from Nixon – every tank, every plane, every bomb – because the day may come when he will not any more be willing to supply you. The pressures from the Arabs are such that he can no longer resist them." '

According to Khalad Hassan, Nixon made two secret promises to Feisal. Both were contained in personal, handwritten letters from the President to the King. The first was sent shortly after Nixon returned from his Middle East tour.

Said Khalad: 'This first letter I saw and read with my own eyes. Feisal showed it to me because of one particular sentence in it which was for us. I will tell you precisely what it said, and remember this is Nixon writing to Feisal personally: "Your Majesty, trust me that I will realize justice for the Palestinians." '

According to Khalad the bigger or wider promise of the letter was that Nixon would take all necessary steps to oblige the Israelis to withdraw to the 1967 borders in accordance with the spirit of Resolution 242. There was, however, one qualification. Nixon apparently told Feisal that he could not guarantee to deliver a quick solution to the problem of Jerusalem.

The second letter was sent after Nixon's return from Moscow at the beginning of July. It seems to have been a response to a letter or message from Feisal, in which the King asked what Nixon planned actually to do if Israel and its friends in America succeeded in denying the President the political support he needed to begin to apply real pressure on Israel.

Said Khalad: 'I did not see Nixon's second message, but Feisal told me about it, and we discussed it at some length because what Nixon said was so sensational and, for him, so dangerous. He told Feisal that if he found his way blocked by Israel and the Jewish lobby, he would throw away his prepared text when he made his next State of the Nation report, and that he would tell the people of America, live on T.V. and radio, the whole truth about how Israel and its friends in America were the obstacle to peace. In other words, Nixon was preparing to expose the way in which the Government of Israel and its supporters in America controlled American foreign policy.'

Nixon's visit to Saudi Arabia had ended on what diplomats regarded as a sensational note. In his farewell speech Feisal made an explicit and therefore extraordinary and totally unprecedented reference to Nixon's Watergate problems and American domestic politics. In normal circumstances King Feisal of Saudi Arabia would have been the last man to break the convention that a leader of one country does not seek to interfere in the domestic affairs of another. But the following is what he said:

'What is very important is that our friends in the United States of America be themselves wise enough to stand behind you, to rally around you, Mr President, in your noble efforts, almost unprecedented in the history of mankind, the efforts aimed at securing peace and justice in the world . . . And anybody who stands against you, Mr President, in the United States of America or outside the United States of America, or stands against us, your friends, in this part of the world, obviously has one aim in mind, namely, that of causing the splintering of the world, the wrong polarization of the world, the bringing about of mischief, which would not be conducive to tranquillity and peace in the world.'[42]

I asked Khalad how he interpreted Feisal's remarkable statement. He said: 'It was Feisal's way of telling the Jewish lobby in America a number of things. The first was that he knew the lobby was using the Watergate affair to break Nixon. The second was that he, the King of Saudi Arabia, was prepared to support Nixon in any confrontation with the lobby. Feisal was hinting that he would if necessary be prepared to use the oil weapon in a way that could destroy the wealth which was the source of the lobby's power.'

On 24 July, the United States Supreme Court ruled by a vote of 8 to 0 that Nixon must surrender subpoenaed Watergate tapes. As Kissinger notes, that was the beginning of the end of President Richard Nixon.

Kissinger tells of a telephone call from Nixon on the evening of 6 August. Nixon told Kissinger that he had just received an Israeli request for long-term military assistance. According to Kissinger, Nixon said he would turn it down and that he was intending, with immediate effect, to cut off all military supplies to Israel until it agreed to a comprehensive peace. Nixon then asked Kissinger to prepare the papers which would be the order to cut off all military supplies to Israel. Kissinger then quotes Nixon as saying he regretted he had not taken such action earlier and that he was sure his successor would thank him.[43]

Three days later, on 9 August, Nixon resigned in order to avoid being impeached.

The above does not prove there was a conspiracy to break Nixon. But it does suggest that Arafat and his colleagues and other Arab leaders have grounds for their suspicions.

With Nixon gone, Kissinger's next move was to repeat in Jordan what he had done in Egypt. He was hoping to persuade Israel to give Jordan a little of its land back in order to lock Hussein into the negotiations and Arafat out. Kissinger's assumption, probably correct at the time, was that Arafat and the P.L.O. would be finished as soon as Hussein was negotiating for himself and the West Bank Palestinians. So at this time Kissinger's strategy was to kill the P.L.O. by politics. But the U.S. Secretary of State was in for a very nasty shock. Arafat was about to trump Kissinger's one King with two Kings of his own!

To say that what happened at the Arab summit in Rabat at the end of October was a defeat for Kissinger and a victory for Arafat would be a considerable understatement. The summit approved two main resolutions. One recognized the P.L.O. as the only legitimate representative of the Palestinian people. In the Arab world this effectively gave the P.L.O. the status of a government; the P.L.O.'s future was thus guaranteed in so far as it was possible for the Arabs to guarantee it. The second resolution required Hussein to commit himself to handing over the West Bank, when it was liberated, to the P.L.O. From a practical point of view, the immediate consequences of the Rabat summit decisions were that Hussein was no longer free to determine the future of the Palestinians of the occupied West Bank or to speak for them; and that he was no longer free even to negotiate the return of the West Bank without the P.L.O. as his negotiating partner – unless, of course, the P.L.O. gave him a mandate to negotiate on its behalf. Kissinger's strategy was in ruins.

Arafat's victory was won by two Kings – Feisal and King Hassan of Morocco. In the months preceding the summit, and even at the summit itself, Hussein was utterly opposed to the idea of the P.L.O.

being recognized as the only legitimate representative of the Palestinians. Khalad Hassan said: 'I can tell you very frankly that Hussein would have said "No" to us at Rabat if those two Kings had not used all their powers of persuasion on him.'

A diverting sideshow of the summit was the arrest by Moroccan security agents of six of Abu Iyad's men. They had been ordered by their chief to find a way of killing Hussein before he left Rabat! According to Abu Daoud, relations between Arafat and Abu Iyad were 'very bad' in the weeks following the Rabat summit. I said earlier that Abu Iyad played an important role in helping Arafat to sell the mini-state formula. That is quite true, but he did not become a believer in the need for compromise until the beginning of 1975. From then on Arafat had all of his senior Fatah colleagues with him in his struggle to sell compromise.

The question for Israel's leaders after the Rabat summit was how to deal with the P.L.O. From here on they had only two options. The first was to accept the P.L.O. as a negotiating partner at some stage in the future, when they had reason to be satisfied that Arafat could deliver the compromise they knew he was committed to and was struggling behind his own lines to sell. The second was to liquidate the P.L.O. and all it represented by military means. Israel's leaders went for the second option.

In the event, the decision to resolve the Palestinian problem by brute force was not taken until Israel's own extremists were in power. Their leaders were Menachem Begin and General Ariel Sharon. Begin became Prime Minister in 1977. But the difference between his two administrations and the last Labour coalition led by Yitzhak Rabin was more one of style than substance. Rabin and his so-called moderate Labour colleagues wanted to finish the P.L.O. and even the Palestinian people by military means, but they were wise enough to know that Israel would lose too much in terms of international sympathy and support if they did the job all at once. So Rabin's preferred policy was to destroy the P.L.O. and the Palestinian people by stages. The year 1977 was not a watershed in Israel's history. As Arafat put it, 'It was business as usual after Begin came to power. The only real difference was that Begin was honest about his intentions. Those who ruled before him were hypocrites and liars who deceived their own people first and then the world.'

I asked Arafat whether he drew a distinction between successive Israeli governments and the people of Israel.

Arafat replied with great enthusiasm: 'Yes, yes, yes. Certainly. This is why we have always said that Zionism will be defeated when the Jews of Israel reject it. You see it really is possible to be a Jew in Israel or a Jew in Palestine without being a Zionist. What is Zionism in practice? It is a policy for liquidating the Palestinian people. By definition, and in practice, a Jew ceases to be a Zionist in the real meaning of the word when he agrees to stop liquidating the Palestinian people and to live with them in peace and on equal terms. This is fundamental to our case. We will still want to liquidate Zionism as I have described it, and that will always remain our objective. In that sense you can say the destruction of Zionism is our ultimate goal . . . because when it is destroyed, when the Jews in Israel have rejected it, our two peoples can live together in real peace. That is the day our dream of a Democratic State of Palestine will come true. I think so. In the meantime, and until they are ready to share our dream, we are prepared to live by them as neighbours.'

When the news of what the Arab leaders had decided at Rabat broke, Kissinger was in Yugoslavia. He was furious – so angry that he forgot to make an allowance for the fact that he was among people who were also friends of Arafat and some of his most senior colleagues, including the Hassan brothers.

Said Hani Hassan: 'I don't want to compromise our friends in Yugoslavia, so I won't tell you exactly what Kissinger said in his anger, but I can speak about his meaning. He left our mutual friends in no doubt that he was going to punish us, and punish us in a very big way, in the Lebanon. He didn't use the word *liquidate*, but it was clear to our friends who heard what he said that he was intending to finish us, or rather cause us to be finished. Frankly speaking, I am the man who can give you the real inside story of this Kissinger conspiracy because me and Arafat were the two who worked together to try to stop the civil war. And it was my responsibility to have the secret contacts with the Lebanese authorities and even President Assad when we were all fighting each other. But we'll come to this in time. The reason for Kissinger's anger was partly the fact that he had lost Hussein as a negotiating partner. But there was much more to it. He said the Arabs had made the war and had emerged from it with just about enough honour to allow them to negotiate – and then the Palestinians were the ones who were taking the benefit!'

Khalad Hassan said: 'I can independently confirm what Hani

said. I was also told by our Yugoslavian friends that Kissinger said
at one point that he had got to find a tailor to make a new suit for the
P.L.O., and he apparently implied in the most obvious way that it
would be a suit for a funeral – ours, of course!'

What happened in New York two weeks after the Rabat summit
could only have been bad for Kissinger's blood pressure. On
Monday, 13 November, Yasser Arafat made his dramatic
appearance at the U.N. to open a General Assembly debate on 'The
Question of Palestine'. He was being honoured and treated as a
Head of State for the day. As the P.L.O. Chairman was preparing to
make his entrance to the Assembly debating chamber, the nearest
thing there is to a world parliament, Israeli Ambassador Tekoah
was preparing to leave it. As Arafat entered the chamber the
representatives of the nations of the world rose to their feet, almost
as one, and gave him a standing ovation. They did the same 101
minutes later when he left. Only the Americans remained seated.

For Arafat himself the world was not quite a perfect place on this
November day. I said to him: 'Abu Amar, in a perfect world you
would have used that opportunity to spell out your true position
without ambiguity – in other words you would have outlined the
reality of the compromise you were working for . . . is that not so?'

Again the sad smile. Then Arafat said: 'Yes, of course. With all
my heart that is what I wanted to say. But it was not politically
possible at that time for the reasons we have discussed. So I had to
send my signals in what you call my ambiguous way.' At this point
the smile disappeared and Arafat let some bitterness into his voice.
Then he said: 'But really I was not so ambiguous. Yes, my speech
required my listeners to think for themselves and to make a
connection between certain ideas . . . but I said enough for people of
goodwill, even Israelis of goodwill, to understand that I was
offering a very big compromise in the name of my Palestinian people
. . . Is that also not so?'

Given that there were limits to what he could say in public in an
unambiguous way, Arafat's speech was a masterpiece of clarity –
provided his listeners were prepared to listen and to do, as Arafat
said, just a little thinking for themselves. The cleverness of Arafat's
speech was the way it linked together two particular ideas.

He spoke first of all about the Palestinian dream – the coming
into being of the Democratic State of Palestine in place of the more

or less exclusive Jewish State. And on this he said: 'When we speak of our common hopes for the Palestine of tomorrow, we include in our perspective all Jews now living in Palestine who choose to live with us there in peace and without discrimination.'[44] That was one of the two central ideas. The other was the P.L.O.'s wish to establish a 'national authority' (still in November 1974 the code for the mini-state) on any land on the West Bank and in Gaza from which the Israelis could be persuaded to withdraw. He linked these two ideas with a question: 'Have I not the right to dream?' What he was actually saying for those with ears to hear was, as he put it to me: 'Yes, I have the right to dream. We all have the right to dream . . . but as a practical man who is prepared to face the reality of Israel's existence, I recognize and accept that dreams do not always come true . . . and that is why we talk about our national authority – that is what we are prepared to settle for, a little homeland of our own, in order to have peace with Israel, until the day when the Israelis decide of their own free will to join with us in the creation of the Democratic State of our dreams.'

Arafat ended his speech with the two sentences for which he will always be remembered. 'I have come bearing an olive branch and a freedom fighter's gun. Do not let the olive branch fall from my hand.'

On 22 November the international community, with the exception of Israel and the U.S., acknowledged that the Palestinians had rights. On that day U.N. Resolution 3236 recognized the rights of the Palestinian people to 'self-determination, national independence and sovereignty'. Arafat's victory was confirmed. It was official, so to speak. And Resolution 3237 granted the P.L.O. Observer Status at the U.N.

This surely was the moment in the history of the Arab-Israeli conflict when wisdom demanded an Israeli response by some means other than the gun. The time was right for an accommodation because both sides, the Israelis and the Palestinians, had won. Israel had won the military war. Its military superiority, and its frequent demonstrations of it, had resulted in an Arab and Palestinian willingness to face the reality of Israel's existence – making allowance only for the fact that Arafat still had some way to go before he could deliver compromise without splitting the P.L.O. And the Palestinians had won the political war by proving they existed and that their problems could not be swept under the carpet. Unfortunately Israel's leaders simply did not have it in them to respond with anything but the gun.

At the U.N. Israel's response to Arafat's speech was predictable. Ambassador Tekoah condemned the Arab states as being 'in the vanguard of a fanatical assault on the Jewish people'. And he condemned the U.N. for inviting Arafat to address the world body. The P.L.O. was nothing but a 'murder organization' and the U.N. had 'capitulated' to it. Israel, the Ambassador said, 'will not permit the establishment of P.L.O. authority in any part of Palestine. Israel will not permit the P.L.O to be forced on the Palestinian Arabs.'[45] Even as Tekoah was speaking the Palestinians on the West Bank and in Gaza, those who had previously lost faith in the liberation movement, were going wild with delight and were re-committing themselves to the P.L.O. in general and to Arafat in particular.

On the ground the Israeli Government responded by speeding up the development of its settlements in the occupied territories; and then on 1 December the President of Israel officially confirmed what everybody had unofficially known for years – that Israel possessed the potential to produce nuclear weapons.

On 19 November, just six days after Arafat's appearance at the U.N., four Israeli civilians, including two women, were killed in a P.D.F. terror attack on an apartment building in Beit Shean. The P.D.F. said it carried out its attack to demonstrate that Arafat's waving of the olive branch did not mean he had dropped his gun. The fact that the Palestinians were ready for compromise did not mean they were militarily finished and were ready to negotiate because they had no alternative. The P.D.F. was, it said, seeking to demonstrate that the Palestinians would be negotiating from strength. The logic was, I think, as sincere as it was ludicrous. But, as ever, Arafat and the whole P.L.O. was damned by the action of a misguided minority faction.

Arafat's appearance at the U.N. General Assembly had four principal stage managers, two Saudis and two Algerians. The two Saudis were Feisal and Omar Saqqaf, the King's Foreign Minister and his most trusted counsellor and friend. Saqqaf was also Khalad Hassan's best friend and mentor. The two Algerians were President Boumedienne and the sitting President of the General Assembly, Abdelaziz Bouteflika.

Arafat had not at first been enthusiastic about the idea that he himself should be the one to go to New York. Khalad Hassan told me: 'When we got the word that the way was clear, Arafat was full of doubts. He said to me. "Why don't *you* go . . . you're the Chairman of the P.N.C. Foreign Relations Committee." And he wasn't joking. He really wasn't. I said to him: "Abu Amar, you're crazy. You're our Chairman. You're our symbol. You're Mr Palestine. It's you or there's no show." '

Further evidence that Arafat was in an uncertain state of mind is the fact that some of his colleagues stole his Algerian passport, rushed it to the Egyptian Foreign Minister and asked him to call the American Embassy to arrange for an America visa to be stamped in the passport with the minimum possible delay. Said Khalad: 'I wasn't there at the time, but I believe it was very amusing. Those who stole the passport returned in fifteen minutes – with the visa. And they said to Arafat, "Now you've got to go!" '

I asked Khalad why he thought Arafat was not so enthusiastic in the beginning. He said: 'To tell you the truth I don't know. I'm sure he was weighing many factors. But you must remember one thing . . . it was 1974, and in those days Arafat was not experienced in the conduct of international affairs. To me the United Nations was a game – I had been there so many times. To Arafat it was still a mystery.'

'You mean Arafat was worried that he would be out of his depth and that he might not do such a good job as you or others?' I asked.

Khalad replied: 'Yes, I think so. But you can't blame him for that. In fact, I think you have to admire the way he was being honest with himself.'

Once the decision was made, Arafat, as usual, threw himself wholeheartedly into the drafting and re-drafting of the speech he was to make. Khalad said: 'It was a real committee job. Drafts, drafts and more drafts. When we thought we'd got it about right, we asked one of our most celebrated poets to put the finishing touch to it.'

Obviously one major consideration in Arafat's mind was the question of his personal safety. I asked Abu Iyad if he as the executive responsible for Fatah and P.L.O. security had been worried that Arafat might not leave New York alive. He said: 'As a matter of fact – no, not at the time. It was my opinion that America could not afford to allow Arafat to be assassinated on American territory; and they had asked us to help by keeping the visit as short as possible. I've got a theory that in Western countries you must leave yourself to the protection of the local security agencies and put all the responsibility on their shoulders. Your safety then becomes a political matter and not a security issue. And that in my opinion is the best protection.' Abu Iyad has a relationship with the Soviet K.G.B., and it is reasonable to assume that he would have sought its opinion before giving his own to Arafat.

All who accompanied Arafat on his journey to New York were full of unqualified praise for the professional and courteous way in which the various U.S. security agencies looked after them and their Chairman. And it was certainly not an easy job. Tens of thousands of Americans, by no means all of them Jews, were assembled for a rejection and protest demonstration at the Hammarskjold Plaza in the shadow of the U.N. headquarters building. The banners told their own story: 'P.L.O. is Murder International'; 'U.N. Becomes a Forum of Terrorism'. A trade union leader called for an embargo of 'poisoned Arab oil'. Most of the speeches were extreme in the extreme. The message of many was simply one of hate. Even Senator Henry Jackson, the champion of Soviet Jewry, told the mob that the U.N. decision to recognize the P.L.O. 'threatens the already pale prospect of peace'. Meanwhile the Jewish Defense League was promising that Arafat would not leave New York alive. The promise was made at a press conference by the J.D.L.'s director of operations. He had a pistol on the table in front of him. The scene and the threat made the T.V. news bulletins. It was quite a reception for a man who was more seriously committed to peace than all of Israel's leaders put together.

On the Saturday before Arafat's arrival the U.N. headquarters building and complex had been hermetically sealed off from the outside world. The Chairman of the P.L.O. was landed by helicopter in its compound at 4.00 a.m. on Monday. From there he went to a suite in the main U.N. building. He did not leave it until noon when it was time for him to make his speech. After it, there was a lunch and reception at the U.N. In the late afternoon Arafat and his party were transferred to the Wardorf Towers Hotel. Zahedi Terzi, the man who was about to become the P.L.O.'s Observer-Ambassador at the U.N., takes up the story:

'Apparently this hotel was one of the best places for security. They had mounted police around the place. They had snipers on the building. They had snipers in the building. They had machine-guns on the floor. They had police dogs on our particular floor. And we could not move from one room to another among ourselves without showing our special identity buttons.

'That night we all went to bed believing we were guaranteed a good long sleep and a relaxing new day. We knew the plan. It was, in fact, quite well known. Arafat was to have breakfast with Mrs Marcos of the Philippines and lunch with President Franjieh of the Lebanon. I fell asleep quickly. At midnight there was a knock on my door. One of Arafat's aides said, "Get ready. We're leaving."

'This time we travelled to the airport in cars. I expected a very fast convoy. In fact they wanted us to leave one car at a time and with different intervals of time between each departure. There was no panic but I felt there was trouble around – I mean trouble coming. Arafat's car was the last to arrive – two hours after the rest of us. Then we took off for Cuba. It was the special plane belonging to Algeria's President Boumedienne. Some of us speculated about the possibility of our plane being hit by a missile. I can tell you we were worried. But we made it.'

So why the change of plan at midnight?

I asked Abu Iyad to tell me if Arafat changed his departure plan simply because he was taking his usual precautions or because there was a plot against him. He replied: 'I think it was both. Even I don't know. The surprise to me was not that he moved when he did, but the direction he went in when he did move. I think that is the clue. Everybody thought he would return to Africa or to the West – but he went to the South . . . because it was near, because it was secure.'

There is not enough evidence to support any firm conclusion. My own guess is that Arafat probably thought that he would be attacked in the air.

On 25 March 1975, King Feisal, the man who had done most to bring about the P.L.O.'s political victories, was murdered. The assassination happened in the throne room when Feisal was receiving a delegation from Kuwait, and at the moment when the King and his visitors were surrounded by a small army of cameramen. Into their midst came Feisal Ibn Musa'ed. He was one of the King's many nephews. He approached Feisal, took out a gun and shot the King dead. The assassin was arrested immediately, condemned to death on 2 April, and decapitated in the public square in Riyadh on 18 June.

The first official announcement of Feisal's death said Feisal Ibn Musa'ed was 'deranged'. But many people knew this was not true; and five days later the Ministry of Information announced that the theory had been discarded by the authorities.

One of many who knew the assassin was not insane was Abu Daoud. He said: 'For some years I was a teacher in Saudi Arabia and Feisal Ibn Musa'ed was one of my pupils. I can tell you he was quite sane. This was the fact and it was well known to very many people because Feisal Ibn Musa'ed was something of a celebrity.'

Is there an explanation for why the Saudi authorities put out a cover story for five days and then refused to say anything further about the assassination in public?

Said Khalad Hassan: 'When they made the first announcement the Saudi authorities strongly suspected, and later proved to their own satisfaction, what the truth was. But if they had given a hint of what they suspected on the day Feisal was murdered, they would have lit a fire of Moslem and Arab anger which would have spread from one end of the Moslem and Arab world to the other in a matter of hours. You people in the West are fortunate that the Arab leaders, the Saudis in particular, are more responsible in many cases than your own leaders.'

What did the Saudis believe the truth to be? 'I can tell you,' Khalad said. 'It's no more a matter of what they suspect. It's what they know . . . but they cannot talk about it in public. Ibn Musa'ed was the King's nephew and the killer – but he was only a tool and a weapon in the hands of others. The assassination was planned and directed by American agents with the help of at least one Israeli agent – a woman.'

As it was told to me by Khalad and other P.L.O. leaders who know the Saudis well, and also by Abu Daoud, the outline of the story of how King Feisal was set up for assassination is no longer a secret to many Arab journalists and a number of Western reporters who specialize in Arab affairs.

For a period of some years before the assassination, Ibn Musa'ed was living mainly in America. Khalad said, 'He was on drugs and he was in debt – which made him a target for blackmail and manipulation.'

According to Khalad and other P.L.O. leaders who claim to know the whole inside story from the Saudis, Ibn Musa'ed was the perfect candidate for the set-up as far as his American and Israeli controllers were concerned because he had two quite separate grievances against King Feisal.

He blamed the King for the death of his own father, who was killed shortly after Feisal introduced television to Saudi Arabia and allowed women to appear on the air. Ibn Musa'ed's father was among demonstrators who occupied the first T.V. station and threatened to destroy it. Saudi police surrounded the building, shots were eventually fired and people were killed – including Ibn Musa'ed's father. Ibn Musa'ed then swore in public that he would one day revenge his father by taking the King's life.

Said Khalad: 'One of the most important facts in the whole story is that King Feisal forgave Ibn Musa'ed and more or less adopted him as his own son. And that is why the potential assassin continued to enjoy unquestioned access to the King.'

The other grievance was dynastic and is a matter of record. Ibn Musa'ed's mother belonged to the Rasheed clan which had been defeated at the beginning of the century by King Feisal's father, the founder of Saudi Arabia, and thereby lost its chance of becoming the ruling family of the kingdom.

According to Khalad, Abu Iyad and others, the raw intelligence information about Ibn Musa'ed and his background was gathered over a number of years, and as a matter of routine, by C.I.A. agents in Saudi Arabia. This is entirely logical; but it does not necessarily indicate that those who set up Ibn Musa'ed for assassinating Feisal were C.I.A. agents. There are a number of American agencies and many individuals with access to, or who can get access to, low-grade information in the C.I.A.'s files.

Khalad continued: 'So Ibn Musa'ed was vulnerable on two points . . . and those who set him up played with him in a very clever way. They deepened the feeling of revenge within him and they did it by providing him with a girlfriend who was a Mossad agent. This beautiful girl was the key to him. It was she, with the help of drugs, who pushed the ideas into him. She was with him all the time he was in America until he left for Saudi Arabia to do the killing. Then she disappeared. Completely without trace. She did not receive the last letter Ibn Musa'ed wrote to her. In it he said, "By the time you receive this I will have achieved a great victory." '

I asked Khalad if he knew of any hard evidence which proved that the girlfriend was a Mossad agent. He replied: 'How do you prove such things? What I can tell you for sure is that Saudi and other investigations easily and quickly established that she was a dedicated Zionist. You should also not forget the Saudis had more than ten weeks to interrogate the assassin. In that time they built up a picture of what had happened and they reconstructed some of the dialogues between Ibn Musa'ed and his girlfriend.'

I asked Khalad if at any time in his many conversations with Feisal he had gathered the impression that the King suspected he might one day be assassinated by his American or his American and Israeli enemies. Khalad replied: 'I *know* Feisal had that feeling. To tell you the complete truth, he once told me it was likely to happen.'

In New York, Zahedi Terzi, the P.L.O.'s Observer at the U.N., told me: 'I can tell you from my knowledge, it was the common diplomatic assumption that the Americans killed King Feisal. As soon as the news came through that is what all the private diplomatic gossip was saying. It was not unexpected.'

When the news of Feisal's assassination broke, Israel's Ambassador in Washington was apparently so overcome with delight that he 'danced a jig' in his office . . . that, at any rate, is the story as it was reported to Israel by some Israeli newspaper correspondents in Washington.

I asked Khalad to explain as he saw it the American and Israeli motive for killing Feisal. The following was his reply:

'They had two main motives – what we can call the long-term motive and the short-term motive. And in my opinion, in fact in the opinion of most if not all Arabs, the long-term motive was the most important one. The Americans and the Israelis had a very good understanding of Feisal. They knew he was the only living Arab leader who had the personality, the capability, the desire, the will, the determination and also the necessary power and influence to bring about Arab unity over a period of some years. Shortly before his death Feisal told me he thought he needed ten more years. So the truth, my dear, is this. If Feisal had lived we Arabs would have succeeded in putting our act together. In other words we would have had sufficient unity to deploy our collective economic and political strength to force America to force Israel to withdraw to the 1967 borders for the sake of peace with the Arabs and the Palestinians. To put it another way, if Feisal had lived, the day was coming when an American President would be forced to do what Nixon was stopped from doing. When Israel and the Jewish lobby finished Nixon, Feisal vowed to himself that he would continue the fight so long as he had breath in his body to do so. So from the American and Israeli point of view, Feisal had to be liquidated at some point.

'The short-term motive was really we can say in two parts. What I mean is that there were two reasons why they decided to kill him when they did. One was concerned with the immediate past. The other was concerned with the immediate future. So far as the immediate past was concerned, Feisal was the man who had done most to keep the P.L.O. alive, and to help us win our two great political victories at the Rabat summit and the U.N. So to that extent Feisal's murder was a revenge killing.'

Less than three weeks after Feisal's assassination, civil war broke out in the Lebanon. Said Khalad Hassan: 'Feisal was our protector, and Feisal had the power and influence within the Arab world to prevent Kissinger from turning the Lebanon into his private killing ground. I am not saying Feisal could have stopped the civil war from starting. I am saying that if he had lived, he would have used his influence with other Arab leaders to bring the situation under control, with our help . . . '

According to Kissinger's account of the first phase of the civil war in the Lebanon – it gets one sentence in passing in his book – what happened was very simple. The P.L.O. tried to take over the Lebanon, and President Assad of Syria wisely intervened to stop that happening. As it relates to the policy of the Chairman of the P.L.O. and the Commander-in-Chief of its military forces, Kissinger's assertion bears no resemblance to the truth. But as it relates to what some P.L.O. leaders thought they could do, in alliance with their Moslem allies, Kissinger's assertion is not too far from the truth. Some P.L.O. leaders, including Fatah's own leftists, thought they could take over the Lebanon in association with their Moslem allies. The leader of the Moslem crusade to change the political system in the Lebanon – to give the Moslems a fair say in government – was the Druze warrior chief, Kamal Jumblatt.

Khalad Hassan said: 'What was happening in the Lebanon was in one way an extension of the on-going rivalry and struggle for regional power and influence between Sadat and Assad. When I said this at the start of the civil war, many of my Arab League colleagues laughed. But the proof of the pudding was in the eating – the fighting was stopped at the end of 1976 when the Saudis helped me to persuade Sadat and Assad to shake hands.'

When the civil war started, Sadat was supporting the Christian militias. Good Moslem though he claimed to be, Sadat did not want to see a Moslem takeover in the Lebanon. He feared that such an event would encourage the growth of Moslem fundamentalism in Egypt. The fundamentalists were, of course, Sadat's enemies, and it was they who killed him in the end. Assad's interest in the Lebanon was also, contrary to what many people believed at the time, to prevent a Moslem takeover – partly because he knew the U.S. and Israel would never allow it, and partly because he knew that he would not be able to control the Moslem factions for his own ends if they did ever become the dominating power in the Lebanon. Assad was mainly interested in maintaining the *status quo* in the Lebanon. The most he had to do was to make sure the Moslems did not lose any ground. In reality, therefore, Sadat and Assad were not on opposite sides, though the Egyptian President did not trust Assad enough to take a chance on that being the case. The Soviets did their meddling mainly through the Syrians and Fatah's leftists.

Next to the Americans, the most dangerous of the interfering foreigners were the Israelis. They were in the process of setting up their Lebanese puppet army in the south under the command of the renegade Christian officer, Major Saad Haddad. Israel's main interest, apart from smashing the P.L.O., was to do everything necessary to prevent a Moslem takeover, even when the Moslems were the majority.

Officially the civil war in the Lebanon began in April. There is general though not complete agreement that the fighting was triggered by a Christian ambush on a busload of Palestinians in Beirut. But that was not the beginning of the story.

Said Hani Hassan: 'The real story begins when Kissinger made the first move of his counter-attack after our victories at Rabat and the U.N. Kissinger's people asked President Suleimann Franjieh to "do a Jordan" in the Lebanon – in other words, to crush the P.L.O. as Hussein had done. I must tell you I have records of all the dates, times and places of the meetings between the Americans and Franjieh and his people. I also know everything that was said. It was my business to know. You should also not forget that I had the confidence of Franjieh because he knew that Arafat was playing the role of mediator in the Lebanon crisis and that I was negotiating with all the parties for Arafat.

'So anyway, Kissinger's people asked Franjieh to finish the P.L.O. At first Franjieh said "No" and he was very angry. He said to the Americans: "Look, first of all we Lebanese are civilized and that is not the way we behave. Second, even if I wanted to do what you ask, I cannot. Our army is small, weak and divided on sectarian lines and I do not have the power."

'The American reply was astonishing. The man who was representing Kissinger said to Franjieh: "You must put to one side this question of being civilized, it's not relevant." As Franjieh knew, the American was really saying, "Cut out this crap about being civilized!" Then the American said: "You say you can't do it. Okay, we accept you have a point there . . . but remember that's also what Hussein said to us when we asked him to do the job in Jordan. We helped him and we can help you." What the Americans mainly meant was that Israel would arm and support the Christians.

'At first Franjieh said "No" to the Americans. But he came under very strong pressure from the hardliners in his own Maronite community – from the Phalange Party of Pierre Gemayel in particular. So in time Franjieh said "Yes" to the Americans, not completely, but he agreed to co-operate. So began the serious co-operation between the Christian militias and the Israelis. And so began the civil war.

'Now I must tell you something very important. When the fighting started, and even before that, Arafat, Khalad, myself and all the rightists – really you can say the mainstream leadership of Fatah and the P.L.O. – we decided that under no circumstances would we allow it to become a Lebanese-Palestinian conflict. We had learned the lessons of Jordan and, more important, we knew exactly what Kissinger's game was. So the truth is that from the very beginning Arafat set out to be the mediator of the conflict.

'In my opinion this is the period when Arafat became a real

statesman. Of course he had his own Palestinian reasons for wanting to put out the fire in the Lebanon as quickly as possible – and we'll come to those reasons later; but really Arafat was the only leader who was working to prevent the Lebanon from being torn apart and destroyed. Kissinger and the Israelis didn't give a shit about destroying the Lebanon. If that was the price that had to be paid for crushing the P.L.O. and keeping the Christians in power – well, that was fine by them. Really Kissinger and the Israelis were the real killers, the real murderers. As for Arafat the statesman, I think he was trying to handle the crisis in the same way that Feisal would have done if he had been alive.'

During the opening months of the fighting, when Arafat was in control of events on his own side, the mainstream Palestinian forces kept a low profile and generally did everything possible to avoid being drawn directly into the conflict on the side of the Moslems. This, to say the least, was not an easy policy for Arafat to enforce because the Moslems were the P.L.O.'s natural allies. And the leftist organizations within the P.L.O., including Fatah's own leftists, had formed a Patriotic Front alliance with Jumblatt. Then, in September, Arafat authorized Hani Hassan to undertake a secret and dramatic peace initiative.

Hani continued: 'With the support of President Franjieh I went by helicopter to one of the main bases of the Christian militias. Really it was very dangerous. I thought there was a good chance they would shoot me dead as soon as I stepped down from the helicopter. Anyway, we talked and talked. I told them we didn't want to take sides and that we wanted to make an arrangement with the Christians. I said that was what I had come to negotiate, and I produced what I called my Lebanese-Christian-Palestinian paper. Eventually we had the basis of an agreement which could be signed. So far so good. Then I produced what I called my Lebanese-Lebanese-Palestinian paper. I said it was obvious that we had to have a similar non-interference agreement with the Moslems. At first the Christians were very angry. They said, "What business is it of yours to solve the Lebanon's internal problems!" Then I became very angry and I said: "Look, there are certain facts on the ground. We Palestinians are here in the Lebanon and we have to have an accommodation with both sides." Eventually they agreed to let me continue with the mediation effort.

'So I came to Jumblatt and I said: "Look, if you are ready to sign an agreement by which the P.L.O. commits itself to non-interference in the Lebanon's internal affairs, Arafat can bring this war to an end very quickly." And I told him the Christians were ready to agree. I said if we all acted quickly we could prevent the conflict from being internationalized.

'Jumblatt rejected me. He said: "Are you foolish? Are you a traitor? Do you not know the Syrians are backing us, and that they are going to back us all the way until we have changed the system in the Lebanon and have put an end to Christian domination!"

'I laughed. I said: "My dear friend, Kamal . . . you are wrong. You don't begin to understand what is happening. The Syrians will never support the overthrow of the Christian regime in the Lebanon. Do you not know there was a secret agreement in 1973 between the authorities in Beirut, the Government of Israel and the regime in Syria? Do you not know that under the terms of that agreement the Israelis said they would allow the Syrians to move inside the Lebanon, to protect their own interests, but on condition the Syrians did not enter Christian areas and did not seriously threaten the *status quo*? Do you really not know the Syrians have this secret agreement with Israel?" Jumblatt was astonished but he refused to believe me. So I told Jumblatt he was uninformed. I said the Syrians would support him – but only to the extent of bringing about some minor changes in the Lebanese system, which would give the Moslems a more fair and bigger voice in the Government in Beirut, but not a dominating voice. Still he refused to believe me. Then came a very dramatic change; in fact, two very dramatic changes.

'In January and February, Jumblatt and ourselves had talks with the Syrians about the formation of a new Government in Beirut. It was then that Jumblatt realized that what I had been telling him about the Syrians was true. So he was very angry. He came to me and said, "I'm sorry, Hani, you are right. The Syrians have deceived me. They are only playing games, using us as a way of keeping their influence in the Lebanon. Please tell Arafat to make the peace on a Lebanese-Lebanese basis. To hell with the Syrians! Tell Arafat to do anything he likes to make the peace and I will support him!"

'Naturally, Arafat was very happy. He now had all the cards in his hand to bring the civil war to an end before it was internationalized. But unlike Jumblatt, Arafat was very wise. Arafat did not say "To hell with the Syrians!" Arafat was the first to recognize that the Syrians did and do have a very big stake in the Lebanon, so what he wanted was a compromise between the Christians and the Moslems which was acceptable to the Syrians. Why was Arafat insisting on working with the Syrians? He knew that if the Palestinians found themselves in confrontation with the Syrians, the Christians and the Israelis would make an alliance which would end with the defeat of the P.L.O. in the Lebanon. Truly, Arafat saw the catastrophe of 1982 coming and he did everything possible to try to stop it in 1976.

'So Arafat went to speak with the Syrians. In effect he said to them: "Look, as a result of our mediation efforts I can bring about an end to the civil war. But I understand and respect your interest in the Lebanon . . . can we now co-operate to make the peace?" '

Unfortunately the Syrians rejected Arafat. They did not want Yasser Arafat, Chairman of the P.L.O., to be the peacemaker in the Lebanon. They knew that if he did make the peace he would strengthen the P.L.O.'s political base in the Lebanon. In turn that would mean the P.L.O. was less and less dependent on the Syrians, and that the Syrians would have less and less freedom to interfere in the P.L.O.'s internal affairs. The Syrians were also beginning to like what they were hearing from Kissinger. He was sending signals which implied that the U.S. would find it much easier to help Syria in negotiating with Israel if the U.S. did not have to deal with the Palestinians. The messages were not yet an invitation to Syria to move against the P.L.O., but they were preparing the way for the invitation.

Hani continued: 'At the time Kissinger and his people were very worried – and with good reason from their point of view. It was taking much longer than they had hoped to build the alliance of Israeli and Christian interests which was to be the weapon for smashing the P.L.O. And what was worse from Kissinger's point of view was that Arafat was defusing the Lebanon's internal crisis. And if Arafat did succeed in making the peace, then the prospects for a strong alliance between Israel and the Christians might be destroyed – because the Christians would not need it. So Kissinger had to find a way of bringing the Syrians directly into the conflict against the P.L.O. He had a maximum and a minimum objective in mind. His maximum objective or hope was that the Syrians could be persuaded to crush the P.L.O. But if that was not possible, he believed that Syria's intervention would have two positive results. First, by controlling and dominating the overall situation in the Lebanon, the Syrians would effectively deny Arafat the opportunity to score a political victory which would allow him to consolidate his political base in the Lebanon. Second, with Arafat effectively neutralized by the Syrians, and unable to make the peace between the Christians and the Moslems, the Christians and the Israelis would have all the time they needed to put together the alliance that would allow them to crush the P.L.O. in the future . . . But first Kissinger and his people had to find a way of bringing the Syrians into the conflict against the P.L.O.

'They found their way through Jumblatt. Kissinger's people came to him and won his confidence. Then they said to him the following: "Look, we Americans have a really serious dilemma about what to do in the Lebanon. We want your help, so first let us be honest and tell you our problem. You know that we Americans regard the Lebanon as being in our sphere of influence. You know we are committed to keeping the communists out. And you know for these many years past we have been working with the Christians at the expense of the Moslems. So now to our problem. We are losing our ability to control the situation and to keep the communists out because the Christians have lost their power. So we have decided to solve the problem in a way which we don't like, but which we must accept because we have no choice. We are ready to work with you and your fellow Moslem socialists – provided you can convince us you are not communists."

'Jumblatt was very impressed by this apparent American honesty. And he said he was ready to work with them. The Americans then told him two things: one, that they were prepared to support his struggle to change the system of government in the Lebanon – to give the Moslems the dominating say in accordance with their numbers; and two, that the Americans would use their very considerable influence with Damascus to prevent the Syrians from obstructing Jumblatt's struggle.

'The Americans were, of course, lying. It was only a trick, a deception. But Jumblatt believed them! Worse still was the fact that all the leftists in the P.L.O., including our Fatah leftists, our

so-called leftists, believed that Jumblatt's agreement with the
Americans was a serious one. As a matter of fact, the Americans,
and then Jumblatt for them, were so convincing that even the local
communists believed the story!

'So what did Jumblatt then do? Believing that the Americans were
really with him, he committed himself to a renewed struggle against
the Christians, and a fight with the Syrians if they tried to intervene.
And all of our leftists joined him in making that commitment.

'What were the Americans really up to? I'll tell you. Previously
they had asked Assad to do the job for them – to move against us in
the Lebanon. But Assad had not given them the answer they
wanted. He told them that in theory and in principle there was
nothing he would like more to do than capture the P.L.O. card to
play it as his own, and to the satisfaction of the Americans in return
for their help in negotiations with Israel. But Assad was a little bit
frightened. According to his propaganda he was the champion of
the Palestinian cause, and he was not anxious to expose himself as a
hypocrite. He also did not like the idea of getting bogged down in
the Lebanon. So at first, and like Franjieh in the beginning, he was
not anxious to do what the Americans wanted. So the Americans
decided to give him a little incentive. And that's why they pretended
to be willing to work with Jumblatt. It was really what we can call
the Druze Factor at work. The Americans knew there was an
historical bad feeling between the Druze and Assad's minority
Alawite tribe. So by pretending to be working with Jumblatt and the
Druze, the Americans were sending Assad a message. They were
saying: "If you won't do the job, we'll support the Druze and you'll
finish up with a Lebanon which is totally hostile to you." It was a
classic piece of political blackmail. Assad said, "Okay, I'll do what
you want."

'Arafat and I tried to make Jumblatt and our leftist colleagues
see they were walking into a Kissinger trap, but they refused to
listen. Myself I said to Jumblatt: "Look, the American knife is
dripping with our blood! The Americans are making this war to
finish us. How can you believe what the Americans are telling
you!" '

Arafat was also very tough with Jumblatt. What did he say to
Jumblatt? This was the only question about these times that the
Chairman was happy to answer on the record. He said: 'I told

Jumblatt that he might be the expert on internal Lebanese affairs, but that he knew nothing about the Arab and superpower conspiracies against my people. I said, "I am the expert on international conspiracies against us and you should listen to me." '

When it was obvious that Syria was intending to intervene in the Lebanon, Arafat made one last desperate attempt to halt the fighting between the various Christian militias and Jumblatt's Patriotic Front alliance of radical Moslem and leftist P.L.O. forces. He was hoping that a ceasefire agreement might still be enough to keep the Syrians out. He went first to Damascus with a seven-point ceasefire agreement for Assad's approval. Said Hani: 'Assad told Arafat, "Okay, I'll give you forty-eight hours to arrange a ceasefire. After that I'm not responsible for what happens." Arafat later said to Hani: 'When I was leaving the President's office I wondered why Assad had agreed to so much without argument. I am very suspicious.'

Back in Beirut, Arafat summoned all available P.L.O. leaders and Jumblatt to an emergency meeting. Hani said: 'As soon as Arafat started to talk about a ceasefire, Jumblatt got up to leave the room. He said he had no need of a ceasefire and he was going to talk to his American friends to get them to stop any Syrian move. Arafat shouted at him: "Stop and sit down! You cannot leave. We have to make a ceasefire agreement between you and the Christians and you must give your agreement now." As a matter of fact the meeting agreed on a ceasefire, but it was only a game. Our Fatah and P.L.O. leftists had no intention of honouring it. They were committed to fighting the Syrians when they came. They were about to walk right into the trap Kissinger had set for us and there was nothing Arafat could do to change the situation. He was the leader in name only. And that's how the P.L.O. was committed to a confrontation with the Syrians.'

With the Syrian army ready to move on 31 May 1976, Arafat decided to leave the Lebanon. His intention was to lobby various Arab leaders. He wanted them to put pressure on Assad. The best Arafat could now hope for was Arab political intervention to limit the disaster he knew the Palestinians would suffer as a result of Syria's military intervention. Said Hani: 'Before he left, Arafat gave one last order. He drew a red line which he said P.L.O. forces should not cross under any circumstances. The effect of the red line was to ban P.L.O. forces from entering Christian areas. He still wanted to let the Christians know they were not in danger from P.L.O. forces. Jumblatt was furious with Arafat's decision but Arafat was right and very wise. What was his thinking? He was really protecting the south of Lebanon where we had eleven refugee camps which were now undefended because our forces were regrouping to oppose the Syrian intervention. Arafat knew that if P.L.O. forces crossed the red line he had drawn, the Israelis would invade from the south. So he was trying to protect Palestinian lives and land in the south. He was wanting to deny the Israelis an excuse for invading. But he was thinking even further ahead. He knew we could not stop the Syrians and that they would most likely disarm us in all the areas under their control when the fighting was over . . . so if we lost land in the south to the Israelis while we were fighting the Syrians, we would be completely finished even as a movement capable of defending ourselves. In my opinion it was this brilliant Arafat decision which kept us alive in the Lebanon until 1982.'

When Arafat left the Lebanon the fighting between the Syrians and the P.L.O. had not started and Damascus airport was still open to him. From there he flew to Cairo for the start of what turned out to be a journey into despair. With the possible exception of the day in 1948 when he was disarmed by the Egyptians while he was fighting to prevent a Jewish takeover of Palestine, the days and then the weeks he was away from the Lebanon were the most miserable of his life to date. The Arab leaders promised much but did nothing. The message was clear. They were all secretly pleased the Syrians were cutting the P.L.O. down to size. And the Arab leaders would do nothing until Assad had completed the job. The word which dominated official Arab commentaries about what was happening in the Lebanon as the Syrians set about imposing their will was *tahjim*. It means 'cutting down to size'. With Feisal dead, the spirit of Arab resistance was also dead. The Arab leaders, all of those who mattered, wanted peace at almost any price. Kissinger was forever telling them he could be more successful on their behalf if only there was not a P.L.O.

I asked Arafat to tell me about his real feelings in the eight weeks or so that he was out of the Lebanon and was rediscovering that when the crunch came the Palestinians were all alone. There was much he wanted to say, but not a lot he was prepared to say. 'I know what I feel in my heart but it's not wise for me to tell you,' he said. And then, as if he was talking aloud to himself and not to me, he said quietly, 'This was the greatest conspiracy of them all.' I asked him if he thought the situation would have been different if Feisal had lived. 'Oh yes,' he replied, 'no doubt about it. If Feisal had been alive we could have ended the civil war in the Lebanon by early 1976. Kissinger and the others would not have been able to play their games.'

I asked Hani if he thought the Syrian intervention was, in fact, a part of a huge conspiracy to finish the P.L.O. once and for all to give Kissinger every possible incentive to persuade Israel to withdraw to the 1967 borders for the sake of the peace that the Arab states so desperately wanted. He said: 'Very frankly I do believe that and I will tell you why. It's really very simple. We know it was the Americans who pushed the Syrians into doing the job. But we also know, do we not, the Soviets are in Damascus. I think the two superpowers were hoping we would be finished. I do not believe the Arab states wanted us to be finished, but I think they hoped we might be . . . do you understand what I am trying to say?'

The story of Arafat's return to the Lebanon is a dramatic one. Since he could not fly to Damascus because Syria was at war with the P.L.O., and since Israeli naval vessels were patrolling in Lebanon's coastal waters, the Chairman of the P.L.O. was, in fact, trapped outside. And that is why he did not return for six to eight weeks. His actual return, at considerable risk of his life, was prompted by a report that Abu Iyad had been proclaimed General Commander of all P.L.O. forces.

Was it a coup? Said Abu Daoud: 'It was not an attempt to depose Arafat. It was a reaction to the situation on the ground in the Lebanon. When you are fighting for survival your leader must be among you.'

It was aboard an Egyptian corn ship that Arafat, heavily disguised, returned to the Lebanon. Sadat made himself personally responsible for Arafat's safety. There are several different accounts of what happened during the voyage and I do not know which one of them is the true story. According to one account, the corn ship was stopped and searched by an Israeli naval patrol vessel. According to this story, the Israelis had Arafat in their hands and did not know it. Abu Iyad's version is that the corn ship was stopped and challenged by the Israelis, but the captain was smart enough to convince them that his was a totally innocent vessel – only corn, no guns. According to Arafat himself it was a decoy ship that was stopped and searched by the Israelis and not the vessel he was aboard. Khalad Hassan said: 'I don't really know what happened . . . but I heard at the time that thirty-two of our people were captured by the Israelis when they stopped and searched the decoy ship.'

I asked Arafat to tell me what would happen if he was ever in real danger of being captured alive by the Israelis. He said: 'It is very difficult for me to speak about such a matter in these times.' He meant, 'I would rather not tell you.' And then in a very matter of fact way he said: 'I will never be taken alive. In such a situation as you talk about, one of my bodyguards will shoot me dead.'

'So you do have a personal Doomsday Plan?' I asked.

He nodded.

Abu Iyad told me that most top P.L.O. leaders have the same arrangement with their bodyguards. He said: 'We have a secret word, many different words, but they all mean the same. You see, we have to consider the demoralizing effects on our masses of one of our top leaders being captured alive – Arafat in particular. To tell you the truth we never used to think about this so much . . . but we started to think seriously when the Israelis said that if they ever captured Arafat alive, they would suspend him in a net from a helicopter and fly him over our Palestinian masses on the West Bank.'

Arafat's troubles were far from over when he returned to the Lebanon. Those in the P.L.O. who had insisted on a confrontation with the Syrians were for continuing with it to the bitter end, even though the Syrian army, on the ground in massive strength, was in total control. Arafat wanted the fighting to stop and he was ignored. Said Hani Hassan: 'Arafat on his return was alone and without power. Even his bodyguards were not with him.' Arafat would probably have lost the leadership, and soon after that the P.L.O. would have been finished as anything but a Syrian puppet, if Hani and his brother Khalad had not performed some diplomatic miracles.

Hani opened a dialogue with Assad, for which he was condemned as a 'traitor' and a 'prostitute' by the Fatah leftists and all those who

were for continuing the struggle against the Syrians. But Hani's
conversations with Assad did not produce a solution. The Syrian
President was willing to come to an accommodation with the
P.L.O., but he would deal only with Arafat, and on condition that
no other Arab leaders were involved. Assad wanted Arafat to be his
puppet. Without that, there was no deal. The bargain was never
struck, and in the end it was Saudi mediation which saved Arafat
and enabled the P.L.O. to retain the freedom to make its own
decisions. For this Arafat was to thank both Hassan brothers.

Decisions taken at a mini-summit in Riyadh in October and then
confirmed by a Cairo meeting of most Arab leaders transformed the
Syrian army into an Arab Deterrent Force. What this came to mean,
in effect, was that the Syrian occupation continued for the main
purpose of controlling Palestinian forces. It is fashionable to say
that order was re-established in the Lebanon thanks to the
intervention of the Syrian army; but it should not be forgotten that
order could have been re-established some months before the Syrian
intervention if Arafat's attempt to mediate an end to the civil war
had been allowed to succeed at the time when Jumblatt was ready to
take the Chairman's advice. Clearly the Syrian intervention, when it
started, was about much more than re-establishing order.

The P.L.O. survived again, but even as he was picking up the
pieces, Arafat knew that its biggest survival test was still to come. It
was entirely predictable that the Israelis would try to succeed where
Assad and Kissinger and others had failed.

In the course of 1976 the Mossad made its most determined
attempt to kill Arafat. The Chairman of the P.L.O. was to have died
after eating pellets of poison which had been prepared to look like
grains of rice. The Palestinian traitor-agent who was to have put the
poison into Arafat's food went by the cover name of Abu Sa'ed. He
had been working inside Arafat's office for four years. In the course
of those four years he had apparently passed a great deal of useful
information to the Mossad.

Abu Iyad said: 'Abu Sa'ed was well equipped. The Mossad gave
him, for example, a very small but powerful radio which looked like
a hairbrush. As he demonstrated to us when we discovered it, he
was able to transmit and receive messages on it.'

I asked Abu Iyad how they caught Abu Sa'ed. He said: 'We didn't
catch him. He confessed. After four years of working for the

Mossad he finally got his order for the big operation. "Kill Arafat."
But when the moment came he was not able to do it. He was first
of all a Palestinian and his conscience wouldn't let him do it.'*

*I am aware that many readers will feel that I have given too much credence
to a number of the P.L.O.'s conspiracy theories – in particular the theory of a
Watergate connection. My reply is this: like it or not, most Palestinians and very
many other Arabs, both people and leaders, sincerely believe the Watergate crisis
was *used* (not created) by some of Israel's supporters to break President Nixon
and thus to prevent him from honouring secret promises to King Feisal, who was
assassinated in mysterious circumstances shortly after Nixon's resignation. The
point is not whether there was such a conspiracy – even if there was it could not
be proved. The real point is the most Palestinians and other Arabs *believe* there
was a Watergate connection. And it is what they *believe*, as well as what they
know and can prove, which shapes their thinking and their actions. At some risk
to my own credibility I was not, therefore, prepared to censor what Arafat and
others had to say about a number of highly controversial matters. If the way a
people thinks and acts was determined more by what is actually the case and less
by what is believed to be case, there could by now have been a negotiated end
to the Arab-Israeli conflict. From an objective point of view it can be said that
the existence of the Jewish State has not to date been seriuosly threatened by any
combination of Arab military force – but most Israelis *believe* the contrary to be
the case. From an objective point of view it can be said that the P.L.O. is committed to peace with Israel inside more or less its pre-1967 borders – but most
Israelis *believe* this is not so.

# 18

# Showdown in the Lebanon

When Jimmy Carter entered the White House he said that 1977, the first year of his Presidency, was 'the brightest hope for peace that I can recall'.

On one side of the Arab-Israeli conflict, and as Carter and his admirable Secretary of State, Cyrus Vance, well knew, there was rock-solid evidence to justify such optimism. From 1973, and really since 1967, the Arab states which mattered had not only been willing to make peace with Israel, they were desperate for peace. And the Arab price for a full, formal and final peace with the Jewish State was also well known: an Israeli withdrawal from the Arab land conquered in the 1967 war, and something concrete for the Palestinians – a mini-state on the West Bank and in Gaza, to be established when the Israelis had withdrawn. There was also an Arab willingness to make minor and mutual border modifications to suit Israel.

Arafat, as we have seen, was working to sell compromise to his own people. In March 1977 there was dramatic proof that he was making solid progress, and that the Palestinians were facing up to the reality of Israel's existence. At its March meeting the P.N.C. approved the mini-state formula in principle. It was an historic breakthrough and a huge personal triumph for Arafat. From that moment on, while it might have been necessary for Arafat to have contained a minority of his leftists by force, which he could and would have done, the Chairman could have delivered the compromise implicit in the P.N.C.'s acceptance of the mini-state formula, if he had been put to the test of negotiations by Israel.

Shortly after that P.N.C. meeting, Arafat sent a document of some twenty-five pages or so, which I have read, to President Carter. It set out the reality of the P.L.O.'s compromise position, and it explained in detail why a Palestinian mini-state, in a confederation with Jordan, would not and could not be a threat to Israel's security. Arafat's document was delivered into Carter's hands by Crown Prince (now King) Fahd of Saudi Arabia. Carter, like Nixon before him, was fully briefed about the reality of Arafat's position and what he could deliver in the way of compromise.

As Carter was expressing his optimism about the prospects for peace, there was only one question of importance waiting for an answer: would he have the guts to stand up to Israel and the Jewish lobby when the test came? The question was to be answered in the first few days of October.

On 1 October a joint U.S.-Soviet declaration was published which was, in effect, an outline plan for a comprehensive settlement of the Arab-Israeli conflict. It contained all the necessary ingredients for peace, and it presented them in a way which ought not to have provoked offence or alarm in the mind of any rational Arab or Jew who was seriously interested in peace. The P.L.O. was not mentioned; this was to make it easier for the Israelis to accept the declaration as a discussion document. And there was no reference to Resolution 242; this was to make it easier for the P.L.O. to give its seal of approval.

Essentially the joint U.S.-Soviet declaration required the Arab states and the Palestinians to make peace with Israel, and therefore to formally recognize Israel at the end of the negotiating process, in return for an Israeli withdrawal 'from territories occupied in the 1967 conflict'. Beyond that the two superpowers were jointly to guarantee the security of all borders in the region. Effectively, and in addition to real peace, Israel was being offered a superpower guarantee of its existence. The Israelis were required to recognize 'the legitimate rights of the Palestinian people'. The obvious implication was, of course, that at some stage in the negotiating process the Israelis would have to agree to the establishment of a Palestinian mini-state on the West Bank and in Gaza.

The idea was that 'the representatives of all of the parties involved in the conflict, including the Palestinians' would meet in Geneva to talk their way to a settlement of the Arab-Israeli conflict based on the principles set down in the joint U.S.-Soviet declaration.[46]

The Arab states and the P.L.O. welcomed and accepted the joint U.S.-Soviet declaration as a basis for negotiations leading to peace with Israel. Since acceptance of the declaration implied recognition of Israel at the end of the negotiating process, a minority of P.L.O. leaders were unhappy because the P.L.O. had not been mentioned by name, and because there was no specific commitment to the establishment of a Palestinian mini-state. But Arafat had no problem in persuading his leadership colleagues to accept the declaration as a basis for negotiations with Israel.

I asked Arafat if he had truly believed that the Americans and the Soviets had between them opened the door to peace. He said: 'Yes, yes, yes. I was very happy, very excited. It was an historic moment. For the first time the two superpowers were committed to doing something for us Palestinians. Truly I believed there would be peace with some justice for my people. I was more optimistic than at any moment in my life.'

The Israelis rejected the U.S.-Soviet declaration, and Menachem Begin sent his Foreign Minister, Moshe Dayan, to Washington to bully and blackmail President Carter into tearing up the joint U.S.-Soviet declaration and substituting for it a joint U.S.-Israeli declaration, the terms of which Dayan then proceeded, more or less, to dictate to Carter and Vance. By the terms of the U.S.-Israeli declaration – which was, in effect, the list of Israel's conditions for its attendance at any Geneva conference – the Palestinian problem was back to being a 'problem of refugees'; the Palestinians had no legitimate rights to self-determination; 242 was back on the agenda – which meant the P.L.O. could not accept it; the question of a Palestinian entity was removed from the agenda; and Israel would 'discuss', not negotiate about, the West Bank. Dayan also announced that Israel would walk out of Geneva if the question of a Palestinian state was brought up.

In the weeks before and the days after the publication of the joint U.S.-Soviet declaration, there was much debate about how the P.L.O. was to be represented in the Geneva talks. At one point after the publication of the declaration, Arafat was bending over so far backwards to be helpful that he even said the Palestinians did not have to be represented by a P.L.O. official. But the debate and the search for a formula was an irrelevance. Israel was not prepared to withdraw from the West Bank or to recognize Palestinian rights to self-determination; Israel was not prepared to give the Palestinians anything except, when really pushed, a small measure of local authority on the West Bank, under Israeli occupation.

Khalad Hassan said: 'The sad truth is that Carter surrendered to Dayan's blackmail and threats; and it was Carter's capitulation which killed the first and perhaps the last real hope for a comprehensive peace.'

One day, perhaps, an historian will be able to tell us why Carter surrendered to Dayan. The President had so much to gain from standing up to Israel. There can be little doubt that negotiations on the basis of the joint U.S.-Soviet declaration would have led to a comprehensive peace if Carter, with Soviet help, had required Israel to be reasonable. In that event, Jimmy Carter would have guaranteed himself a second term in the White House; he would also have gone down in American history as, probably, the greatest American President of all.

Soon after his surrender to Dayan and Israel, Carter wrote a sad letter to Sadat urging the Egyptian President not to overestimate the ability of an American President to bring pressure to bear on Israel. It was as if Carter was saying sorry for his failure to stand up to Dayan.

The stage was thus set for Sadat's single-handed peace initiative with Israel. Up to this moment, Arafat's relationship with Sadat had been good on both the political and personal levels. By all accounts Abu Amar was the favourite uncle of at least one of Sadat's children. But the friendship turned sour when Sadat launched his own dramatic initiative for peace. It was not, however, Sadat's go-it-alone approach that was responsible for the breakdown in their personal relationship. The cause of that – and some serious political trouble for Arafat – was the appalling way in which the Chairman of the P.L.O. was treated by Sadat when he was preparing to launch his peace initiative.

At the time, Arafat was acting as the mediator in a dispute and simmering crisis between Egypt and Libya. On 9 November, Arafat received what he described as 'an urgent message' from Sadat. It was a summons for Arafat to attend the Egyptian Parliament to hear an important statement the Egyptian President was intending to make. Sadat's speech was a call for an all-out effort to get the Geneva talks started. Then, as Arafat sat listening and nodding his approval, the Egyptian President dropped his bombshell: 'I am so determined to have peace that I am ready to go to Israel.'[47]

As soon as Sadat sat down, Arafat stormed out of the chamber. He was actually running for his car when he was grabbed by Vice-President (now President) Mubarak. Arafat shook him off, shouting, 'Don't you realize what Sadat has done to me!' Mubarak was persistent and Arafat compromised, as he ususally does. The Vice-President's house was on the way to the airport. Would Arafat not agree to stop off there for thirty minutes or so? Arafat agreed. He stayed for thirty minutes to the second. And then, still in a black rage, he was on his way to Damascus for an emergency meeting of the P.L.O.'s Central Committee. The cause of Arafat's anger was not what Sadat had said, but the fact that the Egyptian President had tried to give the impression that the Chairman of the P.L.O. was supporting his forthcoming visit to Israel. Arafat knew what would happen when he arrived at Damascus. Half of his colleagues, and perhaps more, would accuse him of being involved in a peace plot with Sadat. And they did just that.

Said Khalad Hassan: 'I felt very sorry for Arafat. They gave him hell. And really for a time it created some difficult internal problems for him.'

Arafat himself said: 'There is no doubt that Sadat tricked me and was using me. I was and still am very sure he did it to cause problems for me and, also, to cause splits and divisions among our Palestinian people. To me it was the first proof that Sadat was not being faithful to us Palestinians and to us Arabs. From then on I was convinced he was only playing games to disguise the fact that he was really working for a separate peace. If it wasn't so, if he wanted to be faithful, he could have done the same thing – yes, even the visit to Jerusalem – in another way.'

I said, 'What other way?'

Arafat replied: 'In my opinion he should have called a meeting of Arab heads of state to discuss the whole strategy with them. It should have been done in consultation. It should have been a joint or collective initiative. If Sadat had gone about it so, the whole situation would have been completely changed . . . That is what I would have done in his place.'

With some astonishment I said to Arafat: 'Are you telling me that if Sadat had asked the other Arab leaders for a mandate to visit Israel he would have been given such a mandate?'

Arafat replied: 'I think so, yes; but for the purpose of a test case. And much would have depended on how Sadat presented his ideas to the Arab heads of state and me. If I had been him I would have said to my Arab colleagues the following: "Give me the chance. I will go and I will sacrifice myself. If I succeed the success is for all of us. If I fail the failure will be for me only." If Sadat had done that he would have been a hero – win or lose. And it would have been a totally different story, with different results.'

I asked Arafat what he would have seen as the purpose of Sadat's visit to Jerusalem had he had the approval of all Arab leaders. He replied: 'Obviously the purpose would have been to challenge Israel to come to the Geneva conference to talk to everybody, including us Palestinians, about everything. To talk on the basis of the U.S.-Soviet declaration. Probably the Government of Israel would still have said "No". But if it said "No" after a Sadat visit to Jerusalem, then the whole world would have known for sure that Israel was the only obstacle to peace. You see, if Sadat had been faithful, if he had been willing to work to a co-ordinated strategy, we Arabs would have not been the loser either way.'

I asked Arafat whether he believed that Sadat did not ask for an Arab mandate to visit Jerusalem because he did not think he would get it, or because he had already committed himself in secret to a separate peace with Israel.

Arafat said: 'The second for sure. No doubt about it. You must not forget it was on Dayan's advice that Sadat dropped all references to the P.L.O. in his speech to the Israeli parliament. That's only a small point, but it is a point.'

When Sadat returned from his historic visit to Jerusalem, he invited the Arabs, the Palestinians and the Israelis to what he called a pre-Geneva summit in Cairo. The Arab states and the P.L.O. refused to attend. Only the Israelis showed up. There were a number of Middle East experts who said that the Arabs and the P.L.O. should have attended, if only to cause the Israelis to walk out – thus demonstrating again that Israel was the obstacle to peace. I put this point to Arafat.

He said: 'For the reasons I told you before, it was already too late.

The moment had passed. When Sadat did not co-ordinate his strategy with the Arab leaders as I suggested, we knew he was playing games. Another minor point. When the Israelis arrived at the Cairo meeting they saw a small Palestinian flag on the conference table with all the other Arab flags. The Israelis said they would leave if the Palestinian flag was not removed from their sight. The Egyptians said, "Okay, flag goes, you stay." What Sadat ought to have said when he was consulted about a solution to this crisis was: "Look, this is an Arab country. We can decide what little flags to put here. Your right is only to insist on your own flag. If this little Palestinian flag so upsets you – then go!"'

Arafat smiled: 'I will tell you another little story to make the point. In the days we are talking about, many Western leaders and others used to say to Crown Prince Fahd, now His Majesty King Fahd, "Yes, but what about the problem of Arafat and the P.L.O.?" Fahd used to say: "My problem is not Arafat and his problems. My problem is not even the Americans and the Israelis. My problem is that I can't stop Sadat saying 'Yes' to the Americans and the Israelis." '

Sadat signed his separate peace with Israel in March 1979. On 6 October 1981 he was assassinated by Moslem fundamentalists. I asked Arafat if he had any sympathy for Sadat when he was killed. He said: 'As an old friend, yes. I am a human being. He was my old friend. Far away from this policy, far away from this plot against my people, he was my friend.'

There are people who believe that Sadat was worthy of sympathy because Carter did not back him by putting pressure on Israel when Begin demonstrated that he was not intending to honour the Camp David accords relating to autonomy for the Palestinians of the West Bank. I asked Arafat if this was a point of view he shared. He said: 'No. Not at all. If Sadat was seriously interested in something of substance and value for the Palestinians, even just the Palestinians of the West Bank, he should have walked out of the Camp David process before he signed the separate peace. He could have said: "You see, my people, you see, my friends all over the Arab world, I have tried . . . but the Americans and the Israelis are not interested in real peace." If he had done that he would have been a hero. And then, *perhaps*, the Americans would have been forced to deal with Israel.'

In theory, the agreement Sadat signed with Israel on the basis of the Camp David accords of September 1978 provided for more than a separate peace between Egypt and Israel. On paper there was provision for the Palestinians of the West Bank and Gaza to enjoy a measure of autonomy. Unfortunately the Camp David accords were open to interpretation; and Israel's interpretation gave the Palestinians of the West Bank and Gaza nothing that could remotely be called self-government. The Israelis were to keep control of even water and land resources.

It was Arafat, his Palestinian people, and the Lebanese who were to pay the full and terrible price of Sadat's separate peace with Israel. Within one month of the signing of the separate peace, and with Egypt officially neutralized by it, Israel began a five-month blitz on the Lebanon. Some 50,000 Palestinian refugees fled northwards as their camps were bombed and strafed by Israeli jet fighters, and sometimes pounded by long-range artillery; 175,000 Lebanese fled from the south and became refugees in their own land; thousands, Palestinians and Lebanese, were killed. In Beirut Western diplomats openly admitted they were shocked and sickened by the scale of the Israeli attacks and the apparent indifference of their governments.

Arafat said: 'You do realize what was happening . . . This was the beginning of Israel's Final Solution of the Palestinian problem by military means. What happened in the summer of 1982 when Sharon came all the way to Beirut to finish us started here . . . one month after Sadat signed his separate peace. What was the Israeli strategy when they started their final offensive in April of 1979? What was the purpose of these murderous and indiscriminate attacks on our unarmed Palestinian and Lebanese civilians? I will tell you. Their purpose was not simply to terrorize and to kill, their main objective by terrorizing and killing was to turn the people of the Lebanon, Christians and Moslems, against my Palestinian people. With every bomb they dropped, and with every shell they fired, the Israelis were saying to the Lebanese: "We wouldn't have to be doing this to you, and we wouldn't have to be destroying your beautiful country, if the Palestinians were not among you . . . really you should not blame us for what is happening . . . you should blame the Palestinians . . . really you should hate the Palestinians." In such a way Begin, Sharon and the others were preparing the ground for their invasion, the Jewish Final Solution to the Palestinian problem.'

A long pause followed this. Eventually Arafat spoke again.

He said: 'You know, Alan, it is not really my way to compare the Israelis or some Israelis with the Nazis. I don't think it really serves any purpose to speak in such a way. But I have to tell you something from deep inside me. When I think over the tactics, the strategy and the firepower the Israelis have used to try to liquidate my poorly armed and mainly unarmed refugee people, a people with justice on their side, I think it is fair to say the Israelis, certain Israelis, have behaved like Nazis, are Nazis in their minds. Let us suppose for the sake of argument that you are Hitler. You give the order to liquidate a people who happen to be Jews by killing them in gas chambers. Now let us suppose that I am Begin or Sharon. I give the order to liquidate a people who happen to be Palestinians by bombing and strafing their refugee camps and by dropping cluster and fragmentation bombs among them. Am I really any different from you, any better than you, because I am liquidating a people by more conventional means, more acceptable means? What is the crime . . . is it liquidating a people or the means by which a people is liquidated? Are we really saying it's okay to liquidate a people by some means but not by others? I hope many Israelis will read your book and I hope some of them will think about their own answers to the questions I have asked.

'So we are talking about the beginning of Israel's final offensive in April of 1979. Why did it take the Israelis so long – three years – to come all the way to Beirut? I think there were two main reasons. First of all the Americans were slapping the naughty little Jewish boy on the hand from time to time and were saying, "Tut, tut, you are making it too obvious. Do you want the whole world to know what you are doing to the Palestinians? You must ease up from time to time. If you don't the world will get mad with us, and then we'll have to put some pressure on you. Now we don't want that, do we?" The second point is that the Israelis didn't intend to take three years . . . but as you know there was a ceasefire and we kept it for nearly a year. Sharon and his generals were very angry because Yasser Arafat proved he could honour a ceasefire agreement . . . so that also is what delayed them.'

Even as the Israelis were bombing and blasting the Palestinians of southern Lebanon in the summer of 1979, Arafat and other P.L.O. leaders and top officials were continuing to take important and brave initiatives for peace. One of the most significant of these initiatives – the one that attracted President Carter's personal support – started by chance in Washington.

On a Saturday in June an American official, Jim Lenard, lunched at the home of a certain Arab Ambassador in Washington. Lenard had one of the toughest and most impossible jobs in the world. He was trying to advance the so-called Palestinian autonomy talks provided for in the Camp David accords. Since the Israelis would not talk to the P.L.O., the Americans and Sadat were hoping and praying they could find some West Bank and non-P.L.O. Palestinians to be their negotiating partners. But Lenard had just returned from the West Bank and he knew that was not possible. He told the Arab Ambassador that the U.S. had to find a way to talk to the P.L.O.

Later that day the Arab Ambassador invited Hassan Rahman for a drink. He was the P.L.O.'s representative in Washington. He was told what Lenard had said, and was then asked to come up with a formula which would allow the Americans to talk with the P.L.O. Rahman said: 'If the Americans are serious, it's easy. I'll go to work.'

Rahman's formula, which he cleared with Arafat in Beirut, was a P.L.O. offer to accept 242, and thus to recognize Israel, if 242 could be stretched to include four or five vague words which recognized Palestinian rights to self-determination. In its final form, the P.L.O.'s offer was passed to Ivor Richard, Britain's Ambassador to the U.N. and the sitting President of the Security Council. Richard told me: 'In my opinion it was potentially the biggest breakthrough since 1948. Its importance was impossible to exaggerate.' Richard then passed the document to his American counterpart, Andy Young, for transmission onwards and upwards to his superiors.

When Carter saw the offer, his opinion of it was the same as Richard's. In secret the various parties were consulted. Israel rejected the formula, and so also did Sadat, Hussein and Assad.

Rahman told me: 'The Israelis rejected it for obvious reasons. Sadat rejected it because he didn't want to share his exclusive relationship with America. And Hussein and Assad rejected it because, at the time, neither of them could bear the thought of a direct relationship between the P.L.O. and the Americans. Assad still can't, of course.'

Carter did not give up; he sent a special envoy to the Middle East to sound out the Israelis on the possibility of a new U.N. resolution which would include the P.L.O.'s formula. The Israelis rejected the idea. Begin refused to deal with the P.L.O. on any terms, and he was determined that nobody in the U.S. Administration should either.

And that really was that . . . except that Begin and his ministers decided that Carter had got to be punished for daring even to think about talking to the P.L.O. As Rahman told me: 'I am sure you know that Israel draws a red line for each and every American President – a red line that he must not cross. Carter crossed it. And he had to be punished.'

Carter's punishment was a demand by Israel that he fire Andy Young. Of course the Government of Israel made no such demand. That is not how the system works. What happened, as usual, was that the Jewish lobby was instructed to kick up an almighty fuss. Young's crime was that he met with the P.L.O.'s man at the U.N., Zahedi Terzi, for fifteen minutes in the house of Kuwait's Ambassador to the U.N., Abdullah Bishara, on 26 July. But as the Israelis knew from a copy of Young's report of the meeting in their possession, Young had not been involved in any of the secret politics. He had met with Terzi and Bishara to discuss the postponement of a U.N. debate to win time for Carter while he tried to interest Israel in a new U.N. resolution.

Why did Begin and his ministers want Young's head in particular? Said Rahman: 'They knew he was Carter's best and closest friend in the Cabinet. Young's resignation would hurt the President more than anything else. It did.' Carter wept as he read Young's letter of resignation.

It was after Carter's failure to make something of this particular P.L.O. initiative that I was asked, by people in the international community who care a great deal about what is happening in the Middle East, to undertake a peace initiative of my own. As I have previously said, my brief was to set up a secret channel of communication between Arafat and certain Israeli leaders with myself as the linkman. Not all of the ministers in the Israeli Government of the day were zealots like Begin and Sharon. And most, though not all, of the opposition Labour Party leaders were men who were prepared to acknowledge, in private, that there is a Palestinian problem to be solved by political means. Since I am not free to name any of the Israeli leaders who were involved in the initiative, the story of it cannot be told. There is, however, one important fact I want to reveal. When the crunch came, Arafat was prepared to have a secret meeting and discussion with an Israeli leader – it could have been one of two as far as the Chairman of the P.L.O. was concerned – and it was the Israelis who could not deliver. They wanted to meet Arafat, but they were frightened that their careers would be finished if the secret leaked.

By 1979 Yasser Arafat had done the maximum possible on his side to prepare the ground for a compromise settlement with Israel. He had persuaded his people to make peace with the Jewish State while it retained seventy per cent of their homeland. And Arafat was free to negotiate openly on that basis after the 1979 P.N.C. gave him a mandate to do so. Arafat's credibility with his own Palestinian people depends, and has depended since 1974, on his ability to deliver something concrete through political means, to prove that compromise can get results.

In this context the high point of Arafat's credibility was 1979. From the end of 1979, and with no evidence that compromise would produce results, it was inevitable that some Palestinians would begin to lose faith in Arafat's idea that politics was the only way.

In May 1980, Fatah's Congress produced a first draft resolution calling for Israel's 'liquidation'. It was not a serious resolution. But it was a warning shot to Arafat from some Fatah leaders, the leftists in particular, expressing their frustration with politics and compromise, which were getting them nowhere. The best evidence that Arafat saw the seeds of a rebellion is the fact that he appointed Abu Jihad as his offical deputy. Up to this point Abu Iyad had been widely regarded as the unofficial number two.

At the 1981 P.N.C. it was Abu Iyad who gave voice to the doubts that many in the rank and file of the liberation movement were beginning to have. He said it was evident that politics and compromise were not enough. Clearly, he wanted to mix terror with politics. To me in 1984 Abu Iyad said: 'I think we made a mistake in 1981. I think we should have mixed what you would call terror with politics – to make the world care again.'

Was this an indication that Abu Iyad and those who shared his views in 1981 were beginning to have doubts about the wisdom of Arafat's approach and the need for compromise with Israel based on the mini-state formula? Abu Iyad said: 'No, not at all. In 1981, and still today, I am for the mini-state formula and all the compromise and facing up to reality it represents. I just don't think it will come about by politics alone.'

On 16 July 1981, and after a bruising Israeli general election campaign, Begin was given the first chance to form Israel's next government. (His own Likud Party won less seats than the main opposition Labour Party, but as the incumbent Prime Minister he was given the first opportunity to form a coalition with other groups and factions.) On the same day, 16 July, Begin ordered the biggest Israeli airstrikes on southern Lebanon to date. The following day Israel's Chief of Staff, General Eitan, ordered the bombing of the heart of Beirut. At least 134 Palestinians and Lebanese were killed. Hundreds were wounded.

The next day, knowing that his credibility would suffer a damaging blow if he continued to hold his fire, Arafat gave the order for the P.L.O. to shoot — and rockets rained down on Israel's northern settlements. Arafat claimed that 'Begin, like Hitler, is going for the Final Solution.'

According to highest-level U.N. sources, Arafat was right. Begin and Eitan had intended to go for the kill, and had not intended to stop until the P.L.O. was finished. According to the same sources, Eitan's plan was to reduce to rubble those parts of Beirut in which the P.L.O. was known to be, and then to follow up with a swift land invasion in concert with the Christian militias. The general aim was to kill Palestinians wherever they could be found. It is assumed that Begin and Eitan stopped because of the pressure of world opinion and, perhaps, a message from America's new President, Ronald Reagan.

On 26 July, Arafat agreed to a ceasefire in the Lebanon after overcoming enormous problems in persuading the Fatah leftists and many of his field commanders to accept the idea of a ceasefire.

In all probability there would not have been a ceasefire if Brian Urquhart, the U.N.'s Under Secretary-General, had not been personally responsible for bringing it into being. He first obtained Arafat's agreement. He learned about the Israeli stand when he was telephoned at three o'clock in the morning by Reagan's special Middle East envoy, Philip Habib. He said that the Israelis had three demands that had to be met before they would agree to a ceasefire.

Urquhart told me: 'I said to Phil, "Forget it. If you want the fighting stopped, I'll stop it. I have Arafat's agreement. But I'm not going to put in any fine print and spend the next ten years arguing about it with our Israeli friends." Basically what the Israelis wanted to do was to extend the ceasefire to Jordan and God knows where else. They were asking Arafat to guarantee that no Palestinian would ever fire another shot from anywhere, and that no Palestinian terrorist would ever cross into Israel from anywhere. Arafat couldn't guarantee that and the Israelis knew it. Phil said the Israelis were insisting on their demands. I said: "Look, I can guarantee Arafat will stop the shooting in the Lebanon and he means it. But if you're trying to include the entire Palestine liberation struggle – forget it. I'm not going to do it and I don't think that's what we should be talking about now. I mean, after all, who the hell invaded southern Lebanon? The Israelis. Who started this shooting match we're trying to end? The Israelis. For Christ's sake, do you want to stop the fighting or don't you?" The Israelis dropped their demands and they agreed finally to a simple ceasefire covering the Lebanon. And they didn't like it one bit. They said later the ceasefire covered other places. It didn't.'

Two hours into the ceasefire U.N. forces discovered a rocket with a crude timer device. It was to send the rocket into Israel within a matter of minutes. Urquhart said: 'Our boys simply cut the wire and hoped for the best. It was the worst thing they could have done but fortunately it was such an elementary set-up nothing happened. It was clearly designed to break the ceasefire and embarrass Arafat. When I heard about this I phoned him and said, "Now I know, now I really know what your problems are!" He said, "Are you serious?" I said, "Yes, I'm serious." And then Arafat said; "If I make an agreement with the U.N. I take it extremely seriously. I think we regard you as people who understand us. You are our friends. You can't do much to help us but we regard it as important to co-operate with you. We want the ceasefire and we'll keep it.'

It was later discovered that Palestinian agents working for the Syrians had set up the rocket. Presumably Damascus would have preferred to see the Israelis pressing on with their attack. According to Abu Iyad the Syrians had tried and failed to kill Arafat in an ambush three or four months previously.

On 5 August, Begin presented his new Government and announced that he would never deal with the P.L.O. Israel's new Minister of Defence was General Sharon.

According to a very senior U.N. official (not Urquhart on this occasion) Sharon, unlike Begin and Eitan, was very much in favour of the ceasefire – because it gave him, the in-coming Defence Minister, time to shape a much more comprehensive plan to smash . the Palestinians by military and political means. Today it is, in fact, a matter of record that Sharon did oppose the Begin-Eitan strategy of destroying the P.L.O. in the Lebanon because he realized that finishing the P.L.O. in the Lebanon would not by itself solve the Palestinian problem.

There were three elements to Sharon's plan to dispose of the Palestinian problem once and for all. The first was to be the destruction of the P.L.O. in the Lebanon. The objectives when the invasion was launched were to be the complete destruction of the P.L.O.'s military power, the complete destruction of the P.L.O.'s military and political infrastructure, and the liquidation of Arafat and as many top P.L.O. leaders as possible. The second element in Sharon's comprehensive plan was the creation of a Palestinian puppet leadership on the West Bank and in Gaza. It is a matter of record that Sharon proceeded to implement this aspect of his plan in November 1981. In that month he charged the civilian administrator of the occupied territories, Menachem Milson, with the task of creating a puppet Palestinian leadership. The third element in Sharon's comprehensive plan was the overthrow of King Hussein. At the end of the day, and if his plan had worked, Sharon was intending to say to the Palestinians that the Israelis were going to stay on the West Bank and in Gaza for ever, that Greater Israel was now a fact of history, but that the Jewish State recognized that Palestinians who objected to this must have a homeland of their own, and there it was, Jordan – take it and welcome.

While Sharon was putting the flesh on the bones of his battle plan, the political action was focused on what came to be called the Fahd Plan, the Arab peace plan that was shortly to be presented in the name of Crown Prince (now King) Fahd of Saudi Arabia.

In fact the Fahd Plan had started life as a five-point P.L.O. peace plan which was unveiled by Khalad Hassan in Western Europe in April 1977. Khalad explained: 'We realized that the peace process was getting nowhere because nobody could agree on the principles for peace. So we said O.K., let's put the principles to one side and let's work on the problems from the other end with a plan for the implimentation of withdrawal.'

The P.L.O. plan called for the Israelis to withdraw from the territories occupied in 1967 and hand them over to the U.N. In not more than one year, and in co-operation with the representatives of the Palestinian people, the U.N. would arrange for elections to be held to allow the Palestinians to determine their own future. If the majority voted for an independent state on the West Bank and in Gaza, it would be established by a U.N. resolution. After that the P.L.O. peace plan called for the legal representatives of all interested parties to sit down and discuss and resolve all outstanding problems. Khalad said: 'By all interested parties we meant the U.S., the Soviet Union, the European Common Market, the Arabs and, of course, the government of Israel. We were prepared for the discussions to take many years; and we were ready to abide by the United Nations Charter and to have all disputes settled by reference to international law.'

Unfortunately the P.L.O. failed to generate the necessary international support for its practical plan because, as ever, the American Administration and the governments of Western Europe were not willing to make Israel be reasonable. In despair Khalad, Arafat and others in the leadership went to Crown Prince Fahd for help. In turn, and also in some despair, he discovered that it was impossible to interest the Americans and the Western Europeans. Eventually Fahd came up with his own eight-point plan. The principles of it were outlined by the Crown Prince in the middle of August 1981, shortly after the second Begin government came to power in Israel and, as previously noted, just as Sharon was putting the flesh on the bones of his battle plan.

In essence the Fahd Plan was a variation on the theme of a total Israeli withdrawal from Arab territory occupied in 1967, with provision for a Palestinian mini-state, in return for a complete and final peace and thus the recognition of Israel by all Arab States and the P.L.O. at the end of the negotiating process.

On 25 November, Arab leaders were due to meet at Fez in

Morocco to approve the Fahd Plan. Point Seven recognized 'the right of all countries in the region to live in peace'. As all the principal players knew, including Israel's leaders, this was the Fahd Plan's commitment to peace with Israel at the end of the negotiating process.

The significance of what was about to happen at Fez was therefore great. If the Arab leaders and Arafat approved the Fahd Plan as a basis for negotiations with Israel and America, it followed that by approving it the Arabs would be giving implied but obvious *de facto* recognition to Israel with immediate effect and in advance of negotiations. And if that happened the U.S. would no longer have a plausible excuse for its refusal to accept the P.L.O. as a party to the negotiations and to put the necessary pressure on Israel for withdrawal once the negotiations had started.

In advance of the Fez summit Arafat had indicated that he was in favour of accepting the Fahd Plan. Hani Hassan told me: 'Arafat himself was not very happy about the Fahd Plan. However, the problem for him was not Point Seven – the implied but obvious *de facto* recognition of Israel. We had already given that with our mini-state formula. The problem for Arafat was that he was smelling some dirty international play. To tell you the truth, I was the first one to speak out against the Fahd Plan because from the beginning I sensed the play was not right. And when I did speak out I nearly lost my relationship with the Saudis, and I had a big row with Arafat. He said to me, "You can't speak to the Saudis in such a way." But really I must tell you, Arafat was in a very difficult position. He was convinced that Sharon at any moment would find an excuse to break the ceasefire and begin the final offensive against us. And Arafat knew we would not survive without the diplomatic support of the Saudis when Sharon came for us. So that is why Arafat said we could not afford to upset the Saudis.'

In circumstances which to this day have not been fully explained, the Fez summit collapsed. Allegedly the Arab leaders could not agree among themselves and were in a state of total disarray. All that was known for sure by the outside world was that the decision of Syria's President Assad to stay away was the cause of the summit collapse.

Khalad Hassan said: 'What I can tell you for a fact is that Fez was informed that Assad was not coming only twenty minutes before his expected arrival. His room, security arrangements, everything was prepared.'

Why did Assad stay away? According to Hani Hassan, the Soviets, with the help of two of Fatah's leftist leaders, talked him into sabotaging the Fez summit. The Soviets were apparently frightened that the U.S. was serious in its professed support for the Arab peace plan; and they feared they were about to be excluded from influence in the Middle East. Soviet policy for the region has been, and continues to be, very consistent. The Soviet Union will support any peace initiative if it can have a share of the credit for peacemaking – in order to retain some influence in the region. If it is not invited to share in the peacemaking, it will wreck any peace initiative.

Khalad Hassan has a different opinion about how the Fez Summit was wrecked. He believes the Americans were mainly responsible for Assad's last-minute changes of plan. Khalad said: 'The Americans wanted the summit to collapse because they could not bear the thought of there being an Arab peace plan on the table before they were ready with what came to be called the Reagan Plan.

Another possibility, a third theory, which has its supporters among P.L.O. leaders, is that Khalad and Hani Hassan are both right – that for different reasons both the Soviets and the Americans had a hand in causing the Fez summit to collapse. Those who support this view say that neither of the superpowers wanted there to be a major political initiative before Sharon had been given his chance to finish the P.L.O.

Perhaps that was the thought King Hassan of Morocco had in his mind when he announced the suspension of the Fez summit. He said, 'The subject is dangerous and the consequences are grave.'

In the middle of January 1982, Sharon himself paid a secret visit to Christian West Beirut. His purpose was to brief his Christian allies on what was expected of them when the invasion started. He took the commanders of the Israeli-backed Christian militias on a tour of the vital points which he wanted them to seize when the war began.

From the end of January, Sharon was ready to go. And wanted to go. But there was the question of the ceasefire which the whole world knew that Arafat was keeping. The Israelis continued to tell the world that the ceasefire was not confined to the Lebanon, and that Israel would be perfectly within its right to regard P.L.O. action from Jordan or anywhere as a violation of the ceasefire. But the Israelis were lying. And the lying led to a very dramatic confrontation between Urquhart and General Yehoshua Saguy, Israel's Director of Military Intelligence. The showdown took place in Begin's office. It followed Israel's capture of three Palestinian guerrillas who were infiltrating from Jordan. Sharon had wanted to use this as the pretext for his invasion.

Said Urquhart: 'I was in the process of telling the Prime Minister the incident was not a breach of the ceasefire. Saguy interrupted to say it was. I'm afraid I lost my temper. I said: "Look, General, when I am talking to the Prime Minister you will oblige me by shutting up because you are deliberately misinforming the Prime Minister, and you know damn well that what you just said is untrue. And if you want to have an argument about it I'll take you on in public, because I know and you know that what you've just said is a big, fat lie!" And Begin said: "You're absolutely right, Mr Urquhart. I believe you and I'm very sorry for what General Saguy has said. I know those people came from Jordan." '

At the end of January there was a secret meeting of Gulf Defence Ministers. There were no aides and advisers present. Only the Ministers themselves. I asked Arafat to tell me what, if anything, he knew about the purpose of the meeting. At first he did not seem anxious to say what he knew or suspected. So I said: 'Well, let me speculate and get you to comment. I think they knew Sharon was about to go for his Final Solution – I think they had known that since the wrecking of the Fez summit; and I think they were meeting to decide to take no military action to oppose Sharon and support you. And my guess would be that when the meeting was over they sent a message to Washington which said, in effect, "We are not going to make any military moves . . . " '

Arafat said: 'I am happy you understand what we were really facing in those days. There is so much to say but now is not the time . . . but I will tell you something else. After that meeting I met with a very important Arab leader. I will not tell you which one, but I will tell you what he said to me. He looked into my eyes and he said this, exactly this: "We know there is going to be an attempt to liquidate you. You will ask us for help and it will not come. Be careful."

In April Reagan announced that he was thinking about a new and more even-handed approach to the Middle East. Arafat is among those P.L.O. leaders who believe the announcement was a thank-you message to those Arab leaders who had indicated that they would not sanction force as a means of opposing Israel's expected invasion of the Lebanon. The implication of what P.L.O. leaders told me is not that there was a deal between Reagan and various Arab leaders; but that the Reagan Administration was saying, in effect: 'We are grateful that you will not obstruct an Israeli invasion of the Lebanon and we will reward you with real pressure on Israel when the P.L.O. has been destroyed.'

After a pause, Arafat said: 'In the Carter and Vance years there was no major conspiracy against us. Vance was really a good man and he tried very much to help us. Perhaps we didn't help him enough . . . I'm not sure. But when Reagan and Haig came to power they were determined to succeed where Kissinger had failed.'

At about the same time as Arafat was learning that his Arab brothers were not intending to help him – they were not even willing to supply him with anti-tank weapons to slow down the expected Israeli advance – the Chairman had a meeting with Urquhart. In the course of it he asked the U.N.'s Under Secretary-General to give a message to Israel's leaders. Arafat said: 'Please tell these stupid people in Jerusalem they will be sorry when I'm gone. I am the only one who can deliver the compromise to make the peace.'

To me in 1984 Urquhart said: 'It is tragic. Arafat was speaking nothing less than the truth. From the beginning he has been the only Palestinian leader who could talk about dealing with Israel and not be killed the next day for saying so.' That is also the opinion of all of Arafat's senior colleagues in the leadership of the P.L.O.

Throughout April and May the Israelis brazenly broke the ceasefire on a number of occasions by bombing P.L.O. positions in southern Lebanon. Their objective was quite simply to provoke Arafat into returning the fire, to give Sharon the excuse he needed to go. Just once, on 9 May, the P.L.O. did return the fire, and some rockets fell on Israel's northern settlements.

Abu Daoud said: 'At this moment Arafat was in great danger. Some of our field commanders returned the fire without an order from the Chairman. If Arafat had had his own way we still would not have fired a single shot. But he also knew that if he gave an immediate order to stop the firing, he probably would have been overthrown there and then. Really I am not exaggerating. So what did he do? He said to the field commanders: "Okay, you will fire some few rockets, but you will stop when I give the order!" In my opinion Arafat survived because of that.'

The only one who refused to obey Arafat's order to stop was the leader of the P.F.L.P.-G.C., Ahmad Jabril. Since Jabril never makes a move without an order from his masters in Syria's Directorate of Military Intelligence, it seems reasonable to suppose that President Assad approved Jabril's action. Abu Daoud said: 'Arafat told Jabril he would isolate him. This time the Chairman was very serious and Jabril stopped.'

It appears that Sharon realized he had overplayed his hand. The world knew he had been provoking Arafat. So the P.L.O.'s return of fire was not a good enough excuse to justify the invasion.

On 20 May, Sharon had a conversation in Washington with U.S. Secretary of State Haig. During the course of it, Haig gave Sharon the green light. From subsequent and obviously well informed Israeli accounts of the meeting, all that seems to be in doubt is precisely how Haig gave Sharon the signal to go. To cover his own back, Haig seems to have conveyed the message more by what he did not say in answer to Sharon's questions. Israeli accounts make it very clear that Haig's main concern was that there should be an unquestionable breach of the ceasefire by the P.L.O. if Israel was to have a chance of persuading world opinion that what it was about to do in the Lebanon was even remotely justified.

That meant Israel's Defence Minister had a real problem. And it was Arafat. In so far as he had the power to control events on his own side, the Chairman was simply not going to give Sharon the excuse he needed.

Arafat was in Saudi Arabia on the day the invasion started. His presence there meant, obviously, that his chances of restraining his frustrated P.L.O. forces from returning fire in the event of an Israeli attack were greatly reduced. It is inconceivable that Israel's intelligence agencies did not know where Arafat was.

On the night of Thursday, 3 June, there was an attempt to assassinate Israel's Ambassador to Britain, Shlomo Argov. He was shot in the neck as he was leaving the Dorchester Hotel, and he remained close to death after a two-hour brain operation at the

National Hospital for Nervous Diseases. The attack was made by Arab students in London who received their orders from Abu Nidal's headquarters in Iraq.

The following morning, while Arafat was driving at top speed from Saudi Arabia to the Lebanon, wave after wave of Israeli aircraft rocketed and strafed Palestinian quarters in Beirut. It was, the Israelis said, not the start of their invasion, but merely a retaliation for the attack on Argov in London. With no Arafat to impose restraint, P.L.O. military commanders hit back at Israel the only way they knew how. And that gave Sharon the excuse he needed.

The P.L.O. leadership is united in the belief that the Mossad, through its penetration of Abu Nidal's organization, was responsible for the order to kill Argov to give Sharon the pretext for the reprisal attack that was guaranteed to force the P.L.O.'s hand in Arafat's absence. Arafat and his colleagues are the first to admit there is no concrete evidence to support this claim.

A quick glance at the balance of forces in what Sharon intended to be a war of destiny tells its own story. Israel committed 90,000 men, 1,300 tanks, 12,000 troop and supply trucks, 1,300 armoured personnel carriers, as many helicopters and warplanes as required from a total strength of 634 combat aircraft. Israel also threw its navy into the attack. In addition it should be noted that Israel was fighting with the latest available military technology – some of it so new that the Americans had not had the time or the opportunity to evaluate it under real battlefield conditions. The Christian militias were a killing machine in their own right. And they were on Israel's side. So, too, was the Israeli puppet, Major Haddad, in the south. The fighting strength of the P.L.O., including the Lebanese who fought with it, was not more than 15,000 men and boys – with no air force, no navy and no mobile armour. And, generally speaking, little modern or sophisticated weaponry of any kind.

Israel was also taking on Syria. But the Syrian war machine was neutralized after the Israelis quickly destroyed the entire Syrian air defence system in the Lebanon and shot down ninety-two Syrian warplanes. Then the main Israeli thrust was against the P.L.O. In truth Assad did not want to fight the Israelis, he just happened to be in their way. Just as thousands of diaspora Jews volunteered to go to Israel in 1967, so thousands of diaspora Palestinians volunteered to go to the P.L.O.'s aid in 1982. Many arrived in Damascus and found their way to the battlefield blocked by the Syrians.

An American expert, Clifford A. Wright, was later to say that a fertile topic for study and analysis was the P.L.O.'s defence of Beirut. He said, 'That the Israelis were unable to dislodge the P.L.O., not for the lack of trying, is probably the most important and as yet unexplored facet of the war.'[48]

I asked Arafat to comment on Wright's observation. He said: 'Really it is very simple. Analysis is not necessary. What we proved by our steadfastness in Beirut was again the lesson of Vietnam as well as of our own struggle from the beginning . . . you cannot kill or defeat an idea, in this case the idea of a Palestinian identity, with bombs and bullets. You cannot. This is why the Israeli warmongers are so stupid. If they really want to solve the Palestinian problem by military means, they will not succeed until they have killed every last Palestinian man, woman and child.'

For sixty-seven days of the eighty-six-day war, after the Israelis had raced northwards in true blitzkrieg style, Arafat and all of the inhabitants of Moslem West Beirut were under siege. And because of television the world had its first real opportunity to study the ugly side of Zionism's face, a side which previously only the Palestinians had seen in close-up. Generally speaking the people of the world were shocked and sickened and horrified by what they saw. Their governments said they were equally shocked, but they did nothing.

For me one of the most fascinating of Arafat's revelations about these dramatic days was the fact that he personally was the main target of many of the attacks by Sharon's warplanes. 'It was sniping by jet fighter,' Arafat said with a chuckle.

As Arafat and his colleagues in the leadership were later to discover, the Israelis had a network of some seventy agents on the ground in West Beirut – Palestinians and Lebanese Moslems. Each of them was equipped with the latest and most sophisticated pocket transmitter no bigger than the size of a packet of cigarettes. The seventy agents were selected from among 1,200 potential collaborators whose names were in the files of Israel's various intelligence agencies when Sharon got down to the job of planning the Beirut assault in August 1981. The seventy who were finally selected were trained for six months in Israel. Their task was to shadow the P.L.O.'s top leaders and to report their positions as frequently as possible. And then the bombs would fall. Abu Iyad told me that probably forty of the seventy agents were assigned to cover Arafat. He was the priority target. The other priorities were Abu Iyad, George Habash and Abu Jihad – in that order.

I asked Arafat when he had first realized that he was himself the prime target for Israeli bombs. He replied: 'I had my suspicions on the second day of the war, and on the fourth day, or perhaps the fifth, I was convinced. But we didn't discover the Israeli network and the truth until nearly the end of June.'

How many times did Arafat come close to being killed? He said: 'It depends on what you mean by "close". If you mean how many times were the Israeli planes more or less on target, I can say dozens. If you mean how many times should I have been killed because of the accuracy of the Israeli attacks, I can say twelve . . . Yes, I had twelve lives from these Israeli bombs.'

What was the time lapse between Arafat's arrival at a given location and the arrival of the bomb? He said: 'Sometimes it was as long as twenty minutes or so. But usually it was ten minutes or less. Sometimes just a very few minutes.'

How did Arafat and his colleagues discover the Israeli network? 'By accident,' Abu Iyad told me. 'It happened exactly in this way. At the end of June, perhaps 27 June, one of our Palestinian girls came to me. She was very frightened but also very much in control of herself at the moment. She said, "Abu Iyad, my family is dead." I said, "I'm sorry." She said, "I want to tell you why they are dead." And then she took the small transmitter from her handbag. "You know what this is," she told me. I nodded. She said: "*I* killed my family with this. I am an Israeli agent. I reported Abu Amar's position . . . the bombs came . . . and my family is dead." '

As a result of the girl's confession, twenty-seven Israeli agents were identified and arrested by Abu Iyad's security people in forty-eight hours or so. Many of the others were identified because the first agent gave Abu Iyad the key to the whole operation. He said: 'The Israelis changed the code words once and sometimes twice a day. The agents on the ground only knew one half of the code. So each day, and sometimes twice a day, they had to go to Israeli-Christian checkpoints on the line dividing Beirut to get the other half. So naturally we had our people watching and, well . . . the rest you can guess.'

Abu Iyad gave instructions for the first twenty-seven to be taken away and shot. The others were executed one by one as they were uncovered and after they had confessed.

On 3 July, the Israelis imposed a formal blockade on the Moslem half of the city. They cut off water and electricity, and they prevented other forms of fuel, food and medical supplies from going in. After that, Sharon's strategy for finishing the P.L.O. was obvious to everybody. The blockade, so Sharon thought, would force most of the 500,000 Lebanese to flee. When they had gone only the Palestinians and a minority of Lebanese Moslems would be left. With his planes and his tanks Sharon would then reduce West Beirut to rubble. And nobody would remain alive. But the majority of Beirut's Moslems refused to be bombed, starved and terrorized into leaving their homes and their city. And from the moment they refused to go, Sharon could not win. He subsequently showed his anger by ordering Israel's air force to make some terrifying attacks on West Beirut.

There were, however, two occasions when Arafat thought the end had come. The first was in mid-July, some two weeks after the Israelis imposed the blockade.

Arafat said: 'A delegation of leaders and notables representing the whole Moslem community came to see me. They came to plead with me to give up the fighting because, they said, the P.L.O.'s position was hopeless and there was no point in causing more casualties and further destruction to the city. They said to me: "Why are you going on? The Arab regimes are not going to help you. The governments of the world are not going to help you. Has anybody promised you anything? No. If you had evidence that something was coming to help you, we would continue to support your struggle. But nothing is coming. There are no miracles . . . So please, Abu Amar, we ask you to give up the fighting now." All this they told me.

'I said to them: "My dear friends, if that is what you really want I am ready now, this moment, to give the order to stop the fighting. You have the right to ask me to stop and I will respect your wishes. But first, please, listen to what I have to say." And then I spoke to them about the lessons of Arab history. It was a long talk and I made many points. In the end I said we owed it to future generations to stand and die if necessary. I said that if we gave up our struggle now, the spirit of Arab resistance would be crushed for ever. And finally I spoke of the sickness in our existing Arab world. I said the sickness existed because each new generation had been betrayed by its fathers. And I asked them a question. I said: "Are we going to be just like all the other generations and betray our children, or are we going to be the first generation to set an example of how to be steadfast?"

'When I had finished they came close to me and their tears were flowing. They said: "Abu Amar we are ashamed of what we said. You must fight on and we will die with you." '

The second occasion when Arafat thought the end had come was on a day early in August when Israeli tanks completed their encirclement of West Beirut and seemed to be closing in for the kill.

Arafat said: 'Although I didn't tell my colleagues at the time, I was completely upside down – confused – for some hours. I couldn't understand how the Israelis had completed their encirclement in just six hours. So I went and I prayed for thirty minutes. And when I finished my prayers, I said to my colleagues, "I feel the winds of paradise are blowing . . . " According to our religion and our traditions I was saying two things. First that I was ready to fight and die as a martyr and so to enter paradise. Second that I expected to die. Then I issued my final battle order with that slogan: 'The Winds of Paradise Are Blowing'. The change in the morale of our fighters was unbelievable, incredible, I can't tell you how things changed. If the Israelis were really coming all the way into Beirut, we were ready for them.'

I said, 'You really were expecting to die?'

'Oh yes,' said Arafat. 'No doubts. No doubts at all.'

And so to Arafat's favourite story of the war. Through intermediaries, Arafat and Sharon talked to each other from time to time. Perhaps it would be more accurate to say they sent each other messages. In the first week of August or thereabouts, Arafat did not remember the exact date, Sharon had one very special message he wanted to send to the Chairman of the P.L.O.

At the time Sharon was demanding Arafat's surrender. And he had summoned Philip Habib, Reagan's special envoy, to his presence. The Israeli Minister smashed the top of a desk with his huge fist and screamed at Habib, 'Who *are* these Palestinians? They are not like Arabs . . . they don't run from the fight . . . I've thrown everything I've got at them, and still they are there! *Tell Arafat I've only got my atom bomb left!*" '

As he was required to do, Habib conveyed Sharon's message to Sa'eb Salam. A former Lebanese Prime Minister, Salam was Habib's link with Arafat. He listened with patience as Habib painted a picture of Sharon's ugly mood and then gave the message which was, in fact, to underline another demand for Arafat's surrender. When it was Salam's turn to speak he said the following: 'I have no need to consult with Arafat. I can give you his answer now. Truly this Sharon does not understand the Palestinians. They have decided to die, and if they must die, *how* they die is of no consequence to them . . . so tell this stupid Sharon to drop his atom bomb – that is Arafat's answer!'

Salam then made the short journey to Arafat to report the substance of his conversation with Habib. When he got to the punchline, 'So tell this stupid Sharon to drop his atom bomb', Arafat said nothing – he just smiled. But it was not this time the sad and weary smile of a man who had heard it all before. It was instead an open, full smile of a man who knew he had beaten Sharon. That the P.L.O. would now have to withdraw from Beirut and the Lebanon was, in one way, a small price to pay for such a victory. In another way it was a high price. Arafat's secret hope for some years past had been that he could negotiate his way out of the Lebanon and into a Palestinian mini-state. He had hoped, so to speak, to trade the P.L.O.'s presence in the Lebanon for a mini-state on the West Bank and in Gaza. That option was now gone. The future, as ever, was a question mark. But at least there was a future. That much was now guaranteed. When an Israeli Defence Minister, Sharon of all people, was obliged to admit that he could finish the P.L.O. only by dropping an atom bomb, that, surely, proved something.

# 19

## Confrontation with Assad, Partnership with Hussein

It was to be three years before it was clear that Sharon had achieved the opposite of what he intended. In the summer of 1982 his main objective was to finish the P.L.O. – to cancel it as a factor in the Middle East peace equation. What he actually did was to create the circumstances which gave the P.L.O. the chance to make an alliance with King Hussein – an alliance which gave the Chairman new political strength and which was, in effect, a guarantee that Israel's days as the obstacle to P.L.O. participation in the peace process were numbered. The price Arafat and the Palestinians had to pay for this alliance was a bloody and final showdown with Syria's President Assad. It is a story punctuated by Syrian plots to kill Arafat. In the summer of 1985, Syrian intelligence chiefs were still trying to figure out why their last attempt to assassinate Arafat failed. The intention was to shoot his plane out of the sky while he was flying from Amman to Tunis after Hussein's announcement in Washington that Jordan and the P.L.O. together were ready for negotiations with Israel under the umbrella of an international peace conference. It is possible that the Soviets were involved. Hani Hassan, himself the target of a number of Syrian assassination attempts, said, 'I won't give you the details – it's too early. It's enough to say that with the help of our Jordanian friends we discovered this latest plot to kill Arafat before it was too late.' (At the time the plot was uncovered I was supposed to be meeting with

Arafat. It was the first time the Chairman was unable to keep an appointment with me.)

To many Palestinians and a few informed observers the first hint of Arafat's determination to throw in his lot with Hussein was the P.L.O.'s response to the Reagan Plan – or perhaps I should say Arafat's handling of the P.L.O.'s response. The plan was unveiled by the President on 1 September 1982, the day after Arafat was evacuated in style and with ceremony from the ruins of West Beirut. (At an early stage in the battle for Beirut some Palestinian leaders had considered the possibility of the P.L.O. recognizing Israel by accepting U.N. Resolution 242 – to start a political process and stop the invasion. The Saudis were asked to explore the possibility of such a deal with Washington. They did. In reply, and shortly before he was sacked by Reagan, U.S. Secretary of State, Alexander Haig, sent the following message: 'I would not recommend that the P.L.O. recognizes Israel at this time. If it does Sharon will unleash the full power of Israel's military might on Beirut . . . and we will be unable to stop him.' I am not at liberty to name the P.L.O. and other sources of this information but I am satisfied the story is accurate.)

While Arafat was on his way to Tunisia and his departing fighters were being dispersed to remote parts of the Arab world, Reagan said three things: 'yes' to self-government in association with Jordan for those Palestinians already living in the occupied territories; 'no' to an independent Palestinian state; and 'yes' in principle to the idea (as required by 242) that Israel should withdraw from territory occupied in 1967 to allow the Palestinians to be self-governing. That was the essence of the Reagan Plan. Subsequent American statements implied that the P.L.O. might have something to gain from aligning with Hussein.

In Israel Begin's government rejected the plan outright. Two weeks later Sharon sent Israeli troops into the heart of Moslem West Beirut to provide the cover for an operation by Christian (Phalangist) militias to liquidate remaining P.L.O. 'terrorists'. According to Sharon's figures there were some 3,000 still at large. And according to Israeli accounts Sharon told Phalangist commanders, 'I don't want a single one of them left.'[50] While the Israelis were holding the ring, up to 1,000 Palestinians – most of them old men, women and children – were slaughtered in the Sabra and Chatilla refugee camps. When Arafat negotiated the agreement for the P.L.O.'s evacuation from Beirut, he had sought and obtained a number of assurances from the Americans. One was that the safety and wellbeing of Palestinian civilians in the refugee camps would be guaranteed. Another was that Israeli forces would not be permitted to enter West Beirut. 'These were not just understandings,' Arafat told me. 'They were part of the agreement which all parties signed.' Sharon's pretext for breaking the evacuation agreement was the assassination, on 14 September, of the Lebanon's (Christian) President-elect, Bashir Gemayel. Sharon claimed he was sending Israeli forces into West Beirut to protect the Moslems from the vengeance of the Christians. But the truth was something else. As Israeli writers have explained in detail, Sharon's move was part of an 'elaborate scheme' conceived before the assassination on 14 September.[51] Bashir was Israel's collaborator. Today it is generally accepted that a Syrian intelligence agency was responsible for his murder. Israeli writers have named the killer as Habib Shartouni and told how he received the order from his control, 'a Syrian intelligence operative in Rome'.[52] Assad's motivation was simple and obvious. He wanted his collaborator, Bashir's brother Amin, to be the President of the Lebanon. On this Assad got his way.

Although the Reagan Plan fell far short of what the P.L.O. could accept, Arafat and his colleagues in the mainstream leadership did not reject it outright. They were prepared to explore U.S. thinking for signs of flexibility. Was it possible, they wondered, that limited self-government could lead in time to full self-determination and the establishment of a Palestinian mini-state in a confederation with Jordan? When he unveiled his plan Reagan had seemed to be hinting that this was a possibility. He said, for example, 'The final status of these [occupied] lands must, of course, be reached through the give and take of negotiations.'

In February 1983, the P.N.C. met in Algiers to consider, among other things, its formal response to the Reagan Plan. By this time an Arab summit in Fez had approved the Fahd Plan. So all the Arab states and the P.L.O. had given implied but obvious *de facto* recognition to Israel inside secure borders.

Arafat's objective was to stop the P.N.C. sending a totally negative reply to Reagan. He wanted room to manoeuvre. A majority of P.N.C. delegates were prepared to see what, if anything, he could make of the Reagan Plan in co-operation with Hussein. (As far back as 1979 the P.N.C. had given Arafat a mandate to discuss with Hussein the possibility of a confederal arrangement between a future Palestinian mini-state and Jordan.) But the leftist P.L.O. groups, and many of Fatah's own leftists, wanted an outright rejection of the Reagan Plan. They pointed to the fact that it specifically ruled out the idea of a Palestinian state and they said, anyway, that Reagan was not serious. Unfortunately for Arafat there was some good evidence to support what his opponents were saying. When Reagan outlined his ideas he called for an immediate halt to the building of new Israeli settlements in the occupied territories. The Israelis responded by building more and Reagan, in the six months since he unveiled his plan, had done nothing to stop them.

To avoid splitting the P.L.O. Arafat fudged and compromised. The result was a final P.N.C. resolution which rejected the Reagan Plan as the basis for negotiations, but which left Arafat with just enough scope to work with Hussein and other Arab leaders on trying to persuade Reagan to improve his plan.

At the time many Western commentators said Arafat had made a fatal mistake. What he ought to have done, they said, was to split the P.L.O. on his own terms. And that, they said, would have given Reagan the incentive to make moderate Palestinians a better offer. Perhaps. But there was a very good reason why Arafat refused to split the P.L.O. at Algiers in 1983.

Even as they were meeting in Algiers, Arafat and his senior colleagues knew that President Assad, with the assistance of Libya's Colonel Qadafy, was preparing to promote a Fatah rebellion. To have split the P.L.O. then would have played straight into Assad's hands. Arafat's strategy was to force the Syrian President to make the first move. When he did he would expose himself once and for all as the man who wanted to possess and play the Palestinian card for his own ends. And when he was forced to show his hand in public, the rebellion he intended to promote would not win the support of the Palestinian masses because they would understand what Assad's game was.

Assad's great fear was that a partnership between Arafat and Hussein would rob him of the Palestinian card and lead to a settlement of the Palestinian problem. In that event, and from Assad's point of view, there was a danger of an overall settlement of the Arab–Israeli conflict from which only Syria would be excluded. In

short, Assad feared that he might find himself isolated with no prospect of making peace, which he desperately wanted, unless he was
prepared to pay for it by letting the Israelis keep the Golan Heights.
Thus Assad's intention was to take all necessary measures to prevent Arafat concluding an agreement with Hussein.

A senior Fatah leader said: 'When we began our contacts with
Jordan we received a message from Assad. He said that if the P.L.O.
reached an agreement to work with Hussein, he would close Syria's
borders to us, withdraw recognition from Arafat and Fatah and set
up a new P.L.O. Naturally Assad did not give us this message himself. He sent it through a certain channel, actually another Arab
president, but it was official.'

The Fatah dissidents and rebel leaders-to-be, a handful of senior
field commanders, were themselves divided. Some, like Abu Musa,
had opposed Arafat's political way since 1974. Others, like Abu
Salah, were simply frustrated to the point of despair because
Arafat's policy of politics and compromise was not producing
results. They found unity in their opposition to the Reagan Plan and
Arafat's determination to explore it. The Fatah dissidents were also
incensed by the corruption Arafat tolerated in some who were loyal
to him, and there were many in the rank and file of the liberation
movement who shared the view of the dissidents on this point. Even
the majority of Arafat's most senior colleagues wanted their leader
to deal with the corruption around him. But they also knew it was
not so easy for the Chairman to act. The problem was not simply
that he had to put a premium on loyalty for obvious reasons. It was
also the case that the corrupt elements – none of them top leaders –
enjoyed the support of certain Arab regimes the P.L.O. could not
lightly afford to offend. As always, Arafat's room for manoeuvre
was very limited.

The Syrian President and the Libyan leader had prepared for the
possibility that Arafat would persuade a majority of P.N.C. delegates assembled in Algiers to give a positive response to the Reagan
Plan. If that had happened Assad and Qadafy were intending to trigger the Fatah rebellion within a matter of days. Assad's co-
ordinator of the rebellion in-the-making was his faithful Palestinian
puppet Ahmad Jabril, the leader of the Syrian-backed P.F.L.P.–
G.C. He was chosen to be the co-ordinator of the rebellion because
Assad's intelligence chiefs did not trust the Fatah dissidents. They

wanted Arafat removed from power but they would probably not join a conspiracy to kill him. On that count only Jabril could be relied upon. Unknown to all but Arafat and his most trusted senior colleagues, Jabril had a secret and rather special guest in his apartment at the Algiers conference complex. Said Khalad: 'Jabril's special guest was a very senior member of Qadafy's military intelligence service. His job, with Jabril's help, was to monitor the proceedings and the mood of the P.N.C. and to report regularly by radio to Qadafy. Our people listened in so we knew more or less how the plot was unfolding!'

When Arafat and his colleagues refused to give Assad the pretext he needed to trigger the rebellion, the Syrian President was obliged to bide his time. Like Arafat, Assad could not afford to be seen as the one who initiated the fighting, even through his proxies.

Assad thought his second chance had arrived when, in April 1983, it seemed that Arafat and Hussein were close to an historic agreement to work together. After rejecting a draft document written by Hussein, Arafat offered his own version of a provisional agreement. The King was apparently satisfied because it gave him the greenlight to explore with the Americans all previous peace proposals including the Reagan Plan. But as Arafat was shortly to tell his colleagues, he said to Hussein, 'I am not a King. I must get this approved. Give me 48 hours'.

Behind closed doors in Kuwait, Arafat tried to persuade his leadership colleagues to approve his provisional agreement with Hussein. He said the cost of not going to the limits to make politics work would be more massacres. But the Chairman lost the argument and his agreement with Hussein.

According to Western and other commentators at the time, the usual had happened. Arafat, it was said, had once again lacked the courage and the wisdom to confront a minority of leftists and hardliners and split the P.L.O. on his own terms. In fact, as the Hassan brothers and Abu Iyad confirmed to me, Arafat's provisional agreement with Hussein was rejected by the majority in the leadership – 'leftists and rightists, realists and dreamers' – because the majority did not believe the Reagan Plan provided enough to satisfy even the minimum aspirations and demands of the Palestinian people. The truth about the Kuwait meeting was that a majority of Arafat's colleagues would have approved the agreement with Hussein if the Americans had been prepared to add to the Reagan Plan what Khalad Hassan described as an 'evolutionary element'. In other words, the majority wanted an assurance that the limited self-government on offer to some Palestinians in the Reagan Plan would lead, in time, to real self-determination and a Palestinian mini-state in a confederation with Jordan. By the time Arafat arrived in Kuwait it was clear that Reagan was not prepared to give such an assurance. If the P.L.O. had given Hussein a mandate to discuss the Reagan Plan as it was, Assad would then have had the pretext he wanted to trigger the rebellion. And because of the strength of rank and file opposition to the Reagan Plan, such a rebellion might well have generated enough popular support to bring about the downfall of Arafat and the leading moderates or realists who supported his political way. Assad would have had evidence enough – for his own purpose – to condemn them as traitors.

In front of his colleagues Arafat accepted his defeat with good grace. But in private he was furious. And it was in that moment of fury – perhaps alone, perhaps in consultation with Hani Hassan – that he decided the time had come to provoke a final confrontation with Assad, no matter what the cost. If the Chairman of the P.L.O. could not win himself the freedom to work with Hussein, the Palestinian cause would be lost. To really understand why Arafat decided that a final showdown with Assad could no longer be avoided we must take a step back to 1977.

A truth I have discovered since I completed the manuscript for the first edition of this book is that President Carter *was* prepared to confront Israel and require it to make peace on terms which Arafat could accept. Through the good offices of Crown Prince (now King) Fahd of Saudi Arabia, and acting entirely on his own initiative, Carter arrived at a secret understanding with Arafat – so secret that many of the Chairman's most trusted colleagues did not know about it at the time.

In Chapter 18 (page 432) I revealed that it was Crown Prince Fahd who delivered by hand to President Carter a secret document outlining the full and true extent of the concessions Fatah was prepared to make for peace with Israel. Carter was evidently very impressed by the Fatah document. The essence of the secret understanding with Arafat was that Carter would, at a time of his choosing, put the necessary pressure on Israel when Arafat accepted U.N.

Resolution 242. But it was not so simple. To make it possible for Arafat to accept 242 without being overthrown or assassinated, Carter was prepared to accept that Arafat would have to qualify his acceptance by saying that the implied recognition of Israel would not take effect until Israel had recognized Palestinian rights to self-determination. It was a good way around a difficult problem. But when Carter and Vance were ready to confront Israel, Arafat could not deliver his side of the bargain.

What went wrong? According to a very senior P.L.O. leader who did not wish to be named because he was anxious not to be credited with exposing what for Arafat is still a very raw nerve, Assad got wind of what was about to happen and summoned the Chairman to Damascus. The Syrian President was brief and brutal. He told Arafat he would destroy the P.L.O. if Arafat gave Carter what he wanted. The Chairman did not need to be convinced that Assad could and would carry out his threat.

Supposing Arafat had been free to give Carter what he wanted in the late spring and early summer of 1977. . . Would the President have been able to deliver his side of the bargain? Could he have fought *and won* the necessary battle with the government of Israel and its supporters in America? Subsequent events, in particular Carter's collapse on the matter of the joint U.S.–Soviet Declaration of October 1977, suggest the answer is no. But to be fair to President Carter it must also be said that his experience of Arafat's delivery problems was undoubtedly one of several reasons why he did not fight to prevent Israel sabotaging the U.S.–Soviet initiative. On reflection I think this was the unspoken thought in Arafat's mind when, talking about Vance and by implication Carter, he said, as quoted on page 450, 'Perhaps we didn't help him enough. . . I'm not sure.'

In the summer of 1977 Crown Prince Fahd was furious because Arafat could not deliver. In the spring of 1983 King Hussein was furious because Arafat could not deliver. On one occasion it was Assad alone who prevented Arafat from playing his political cards. On the other his influence was a factor. That is why Arafat concluded he had no alternative to provoking a confrontation with Assad in order to determine once and for all who was going to make Palestinian policy – Arafat in control of a more or less independent P.L.O., or a Syrian President in control of a puppet P.L.O. with

Arafat deposed or dead. The stage was thus set for an epic struggle between the two great opportunists of Arab politics, two men who had been at war with each other for the best part of twenty years.

In passing it has to be said that Hussein's anger at Arafat's inability to deliver was short-lived. Hani Hassan travelled to Amman to brief the King. Hussein was informed that he should regard his agreement with Arafat as being 'postponed not cancelled'. Hani also explained that Arafat was intending to confront Assad in order to win the P.L.O. the freedom to make its own decisions. From conversations with Hani I got the impression that His Majesty was pleased by the news but doubtful about the prospects of Arafat emerging from a confrontation with Assad as the winner.

At the time of his choosing, early May 1983, Arafat triggered the Fatah rebellion by making drastic changes in the command of Fatah forces in the Lebanon. His new appointments were Arafat loyalists who were despised by the dissidents for their alleged cowardice. Ten days later the dissidents charged that Arafat had carried out a 'military and organizational *coup d'état* in Fatah'. They were right. A week later Arafat stripped the dissident officers of their military powers. They replied by announcing that they would remain in their posts 'to correct the line of the revolution'. The rebellion was now official. The next day Arafat cut off money, food and fuel supplies to the rebels. Effectively he was saying to them, 'Support the legal leadership or go with Assad.' The Chairman went through the motions of pretending that he was still interested in an accomodation with the rebel leaders, but in reality he knew they had gone beyond the point where they could accept a face-saving formula. If they were to retain their credibility in the eyes of their own supporters, 400 or 500 men at the time, the rebel leaders would have to fight. And, more to the point, Assad would be obliged to support them or lose much of his credibility. The final showdown between the Chairman of the P.L.O. and the President of Syria had started. But it was Arafat and not Assad who was calling the shots.

To Assad's great surprise Arafat went from his headquarters in Tunisia to Syria and confronted the rebels. By being in Syria and the Lebanon, Arafat more or less contained the rebellion for a time. But that was not his main objective. As the Chairman confirmed to me, his main purpose was to say to Assad, in effect, 'So what are you going to do now?'

On 24 June, Assad responded by kicking Arafat out of Syria – having tried the previous night to kill him. By chance I left Damascus on the same plane as Arafat. When I was allowed by his bodyguards to join him, the deported Chairman of the P.L.O. was scribbling notes on a Tunis Air sick-bag. But he was in remarkably good spirits. And he was a picture of perfect happiness when a Palestinian woman came from the rear of the plane to ask Arafat to bless her baby. The mother obviously felt she was as close as she could be to a heavenly presence. With the expertise of an experienced and loving father, the bachelor Arafat took the baby in his arms and kissed it gently on both cheeks. To nobody in particular he said, 'My children . . . they are all my children.' Seconds later we were discussing Assad's latest attempt to kill him.

The previous day Arafat had been with his loyalist forces in their headquarters at Tripoli. In the late morning he was invited to Damascus for talks with Assad's brother, Rifaat. Arafat suspected that a trap was being set for him, but he still made the journey. A Soviet official was among those who told Arafat he would not be in any danger.

Arafat said: 'To tell you the truth the talks with Rifaat went very well. When we parted for the evening Rifaat said, "I'll tell my brother I think we can settle this problem between you."' Arafat believed that Rifaat was genuine and was not part of the plot.

President Assad knew that Arafat did not as a rule sleep in Damascus because he suspected, with good reason, that he might not wake up alive. So the President assumed that Arafat would travel back to Tripoli that night. In fact, Arafat went to ground in Damascus. But he did send a small convoy of cars back to Tripoli – including one that could be taken for his own armour-plated Mercedes. What happened next?

Arafat said: 'Exactly what I predicted. Assad's special forces attacked what they thought was my car with machine-guns and rocket-propelled grenades. I think we lost thirteen of our brave fighters.' One of the few survivors later told Arafat that the first of the Syrian attackers to arrive on the scene said, 'It wasn't you bastards we were after.'

While Western commentators were speculating about the downfall of Yasser Arafat, various P.L.O. delegations were engaged in protracted discussions with Assad and his ministers. The public story was that both sides were interested in finding a formula for uniting the P.L.O. on terms which could lead to a reconciliation between it and Syria. In reality Arafat knew that a reconciliation was impossible; and it soon became clear that Assad was using the discussions as the cover for an attempt to get rid of Arafat by means other than the bullet. Over a period of months, and to each in turn, Assad offered the leadership of the P.L.O. to three of Arafat's most senior colleagues! The first to receive the offer was Abu Lutuf, the P.L.O.'s official Foreign Minister. The second was Abu Iyad. The third was Khalad Hassan. In each case, and as Khalad Hassan revealed to me, the offer was the same. Assad would agree to a reconciliation if the P.L.O. dumped Arafat. There are some who believe that Abu Lutuf was half-tempted by the offer. There was also to come a time when certain Arab regimes would urge Khalad Hassan to do what Assad wanted and depose Arafat.

Arafat meanwhile was plotting his next move. It was to be the greatest gamble of his life – so far. In September, and without consulting any of his senior colleagues, he returned by boat to Tripoli. Once there he was effectively trapped. The Israelis would not let him leave alive by sea. Assad would not let him leave alive by land. Arafat was throwing down the final challenge to Assad. As the Chairman himself confirmed to me, he was saying to the Syrian leader, 'Here I am again – kill me if you can.'

Assad decided to accept the challenge. He ordered his generals to plan a final assault on Arafat's last stronghold in the Lebanon. But he was careful, of course, to maintain the fiction that he was merely supporting a legitimate Fatah rebellion.

In December, as Assad closed in for the kill, Western and other commentators were writing Arafat's obituary. This was one trap from which he could not escape. In a B.B.C. radio interview Patrick Seale, *The Observer's* Middle East specialist, confidently predicted that Arafat would be finished in a matter of hours. In the same programme even the neutral and sympathetic Peter Mansfield concluded that the P.L.O. would soon have a new Chairman who would probably be a Syrian puppet.

Then Arafat threw down his challenge to Arab leaders, the Saudis in particular. In effect, and as he told me, he was saying to them: 'You have influence with Assad. You can save me if you wish. I am asking you to chose. Who is to be the leader of the P.L.O. – me or Assad?'

One of the first Arab leaders to hear from Arafat himself was a senior and very influential member of the Saudi royal family. This personality was visiting Kuwait. Arafat asked the P.L.O.'s representative there, Awni Battash, to make arrangements for the Saudi prince to go to the P.L.O.'s office to listen to a radio message from Tripoli. When the connection was made, and with the Saudi prince standing by, Arafat asked Battash how frankly he should speak. Battash replied: 'Say what is in your heart, Abu Amar, and our friend will listen.' When the prince was on the line Arafat held his radio-telephone to the sound of the fighting. Then he said, 'Your Excellency, my refugee people are dying . . . you can stop this slaughter!'

It is, however, likely that Arafat would have been defeated and left to die fighting if all of his leadership colleagues had not used their persuasive powers to make the Saudis and other Arab leaders put pressure on Assad. With Abu Jihad at his side, Arafat's main contribution to his own survival was the inspiration he gave to his hopelessly outnumbered fighters. When Assad launched his final offensive he had counted on finishing Arafat in eight days – four days to overrun the refugee camps and four more days, if necessary, to blast Arafat out of Tripoli itself. But another heroic military stand by Arafat's fighters made a nonsense of Assad's schedule and won the time for other P.L.O. leaders to work another diplomatic miracle.

There were a number of reasons why many Arab leaders were, to say the least, reluctant to save Arafat by putting pressure on Assad to stop the fighting. One was simply the fact that all Arab leaders were, and still are, frightened of Assad. In the Arab world it is an open secret that certain of Assad's intelligence chiefs are the terror masters of the region. Down the years, and through proxy agencies, they have blackmailed Arab leaders for money or political support or both. More often than not a death threat from some Syrian-controlled terror group was enough to produce results. But these terror masters have used violence on many occasions. As creators of mayhem in the Lebanon they have matched Sharon and his associates. When the attempt on the life of the Emir of Kuwait was made on 25 May 1985, many uniformed Arabs automatically assumed the attackers (Shi'ite extremists of the underground Da'wa party) were acting as proxies for Syria.

Another reason why Arab leaders were reluctant to put pressure on Assad was to do with the fact that they had needed him, since 1975, to be a restraining influence on the mad mullahs in Iran. Yet another factor was, obviously, the traditional and historical ambivalence of Arab leaders to the whole question of liberating Palestine. As I have tried to show, there is a part of every Arab leader which wishes there was no Palestinian problem to be solved. In a friendly but frank conversation with a senior P.L.O. leader some years ago an Arab ruler said, 'To tell you the truth there are times when I wish the ground would open up and swallow you Palestinians.' Though he did not say it in so many words, he was acknowledging that the Arab regimes could and would have made peace with Israel a long time ago if there had not been a regeneration of Palestinian nationalism. Once the regeneration had taken place the inability of the Arab regimes to right the wrong that had been done to the Palestinians, brother Arabs, was exposed. In that context Yasser Arafat was a daily reminder of Arab impotence.

All this underlines why Arafat was, indeed, taking the greatest gamble of his life by quite deliberately placing himself at the mercy of Arab leaders. In the end the arguments deployed by P.L.O. leaders were good enough to persuade the Saudis and others to put pressure on Assad. In the end, and like Sharon before him, Assad was obliged to let Arafat escape.

But it was only Arafat's nose for danger, plus some secret help from Egypt's President Mubarak and possibly the Americans, which saved the Chairman and many of his 4,000 fighters from being killed at the last minute. Some Israelis were intending to do in Tripoli in 1983 what they had tried and failed to do in Beirut in 1982. There was, in short, an Israeli plan to liquidate Arafat and his fighters in Tripoli. That the government of Israel was deeply divided about the wisdom of direct military intervention does not change the fact that there was a plan for such action. When Mubarak learned about it he quietly announced, through diplomatic channels, that he would respond to any obvious show of Israeli force by tearing up Egypt's peace treaty with Israel. He also said Egypt would fight. In secret Mubarak and other Arab leaders persuaded former U.S. Secretary of State, Alexander Haig, to use his influence on Begin. My own guess is that it was the Americans who tipped the balance by persuading the Israelis they had too much to lose from preventing Arafat's escape or killing him. At the time of writing official information about this episode is classified as secret by all of the governments involved. For this reason my P.L.O. and other sources did not want to be named.

The evacuation itself was scheduled to take place between five and seven o'clock on the morning of Tuesday, 20 December. On that same morning, while it was still dark, high-flying Israeli planes dropped scores of mines into the water between the dockside at Tripoli and the waiting Greek ships. The mines were set to explode while the evacuation was taking place. On a hunch that the Israelis had 'planned something dirty', and much to the annoyance of his uncomprehending colleagues who were not trapped in Tripoli, Arafat delayed the evacuation by disputing the agreement about what his departing fighters could and could not take with them. He told me: 'The mines exploded on schedule. We would have been cut to pieces if I had not changed the departure time.'

When Arafat was sailing away from Tripoli a B.B.C. TV news reporter observed that a defeated Chairman of the P.L.O. was on a journey into 'obscurity'. There had been no call for the last rites but Arafat was finished. The same message went out to the world from correspondents around the Middle East. Experts in all the major capitals of the world were of the same opinion. Less than forty-eight hours later Arafat was again to demonstrate his genius for turning disaster into triumph. If he had wanted to teach the media a lesson for constantly underestimating him, he could not have chosen a better or more spectacular way to do it.

On 22 December the Greek ship carrying Arafat through the Suez Canal stopped at Ismailia. The Chairman of the P.L.O. stepped ashore. There to welcome him, officially, was Egypt's Prime Minister, Fuad Mohieddin. Together they were whisked by helicopter to Cairo. And there, his face wrapped in smiles, Arafat embraced President Mubarak. It was a gesture of reconciliation that sent shock waves of astonishment and anger through the Arab world and far beyond. At the time Egypt was an outcast in the Arab and Moslem world. Officially Arab governments and the P.L.O. were still bound by the resolutions of the Baghdad rejection summit of 1979. These resolutions – the Arab response to Sadat's separate peace with Israel – stated that Egypt would not be admitted back into the bosom of the Arab family until it had admitted the errors of its ways, i.e. renounced its separate peace with Israel. Arafat had neither a P.L.O. nor an Arab mandate for his visit. It was his personal diplomacy at its best.

Apart from the Egyptians themselves, the Americans were the only ones to welcome Arafat's gesture. Israel was angry and bitter. An official statement from the government of Israel said: 'Egypt's welcome for the head of the murderous P.L.O. is a severe blow to the peace process . . . The existence and activities of the P.L.O. contradicts peace . . . The ultimate disappearance of this organization is a prerequisite for the achievement of stability and peace in the region.'[53] Sharon declared in public that Israel should have used military means to prevent Arafat being rescued.

The reaction of the Fatah rebels and their Syrian sponsors was just as predictable. Arafat had proved himself to be as big a traitor as Sadat. The rebels warned Arab governments 'not to deal with Arafat from this day forth'. For the first time the Fatah rebels also received a measure of support from other leftist P.L.O. groups which opposed Arafat's policy of politics and compromise. In the name of the P.F.L.P., George Habash joined the Fatah rebels in calling for Arafat's removal as Chairman.

Most of the pro-Western Arab regimes maintained an embarrassed silence. In private they had already acknowledged their need to have an Egypt at peace with Israel back in the Arab family, but they were not willing to take the necessary steps for fear of bringing the wrath of Assad upon themselves. So the silence of the pro–Western Arab regimes was in no way a sign of grudging approval for what Arafat had done. Behind the scenes Arab leaders were disturbed and angry.

For two weeks after his dramatic reconciliation with Mubarak, Arafat was, in fact, in real trouble. As his colleagues and friends in the leadership of Fatah assembled in Tunis the issue of Arafat's future was very much a live one. Stretched to their emotional limits by the human cost of the conflict with the rebels and Assad, and exhausted by their diplomatic efforts to save the Old Man, most of Arafat's colleagues were furious because he had taken such a step without consulting them. The only one of his senior colleagues

Arafat did consult in advance of his visit to Cairo was Abu Jihad who was at his side in Tripoli. No one is more loyal to Arafat than Abu Jihad, but even his reaction when he learned what his leader intended to do was one of astonishment. He told his colleagues in Tunis that he had begged the Chairman not to meet with Mubarak until he had secured the approval of the collective leadership.

During the two critical weeks when Arafat's future seemed to be in the balance I maintained a regular contact with a number of P.L.O. leaders, including Khalad Hassan. After one particular conversation with him I thought the odds were against Arafat surviving as Chairman. Later I came to the conclusion that Arafat could and would have been deposed if any of his senior Fatah colleagues had had the ambition to take over as Chairman. Arab pressure on some of them was strong.

Arafat himself did not underestimate the anger his initiative would provoke. Even the reaction of his colleagues and friends in the leadership was exactly what he had calculated it would be. At the height of the leadership crisis he ignored a summons to return to Tunis to explain himself to his colleagues. When asked by a Palestinian friend why he was refusing to go to Tunis, Arafat replied, 'If I go now they will lynch me!' When asked by the same friend about his tactics for defusing the crisis, Arafat looked to the heavens and made a gesture with his hands. Then he said: 'I have thrown a lot of pieces into the air. When my colleagues have collected them they will be calm and ready to discuss this objectively.'

Why, really, did the Chairman of the P.L.O. go to Cairo?

It was important for Arafat that he should take the first opportunity to thank President Mubarak personally for the secret but crucial role he played in preventing the Israelis from sabotaging the evacuation and killing many of the departing P.L.O. fighters including, probably, Arafat himself. It was also Arafat's intention to give a kiss of life to Arab unity. As he told me, he was hoping that his example would encourage other Arab leaders to throw off more of their inhibitions about welcoming Egypt back into the Arab fold. Arafat is not one of the many hypocrites who pay only lip-service to the call for Arab unity. But the main reason for his visit to Cairo concerned the P.L.O.'s survival. The truth was that Arafat desperately needed a reconciliation with the leader of the only Arab country at peace with Israel in order to give himself — and therefore the

P.L.O. – some way of playing his political cards. The alternative
was not, as the B.B.C. reporter had observed, a journey into obscurity; but without a relationship with Egypt, and after all that had
recently happened, Arafat's ability to influence events from distant
Tunis would have been greatly limited. Hani Hassan put it this way:
'The visit to Cairo guaranteed that we could continue to occupy our
place at the centre of the Arab stage. Brother Khalad said: 'Without
the political cover the Mubarak visit gave him, Arafat would have
had no cards to play. He did not want to go to the Arabs and kneel
as a beggar. That is not his way.'

Arafat's escape from Tripoli and the official leadership's endorse-
ment of his personal Cairo initiative marked the end of the first
phase of the Chairman's showdown with Assad. What, so far, had
he achieved at the expense of more death and more suffering for his
refugee people in the Lebanon? He had, in fact, achieved his first
objective. He had drawn Assad into the open and forced the Syrian
President to demonstrate that there were no limits beyond which he
would not go to prevent the Palestinians from making their own
decisions. Western reporters and other foreign observers were continuing to buy the fiction that the Fatah rebels and other P.L.O. dissidents enjoyed a great deal of support among the Palestinian masses; and as a consequence of this Western public opinion (and Western governments, too) were constantly and grossly misinformed
about what was really happening as the confrontation between
Arafat and Assad entered its second phase. But after the Tripoli
campaign, which had seen Assad demonstrating that he was as willing as Sharon to kill Palestinians, the vast majority of Arafat's
people were aware of the truth – that Assad was using the cover of a
minority rebellion to cancel the authentic P.L.O. as a factor in the
Middle East peace equation. Most Palestinians now realised that
Assad was trying to succeed where Sharon had failed. When the
Fatah dissidents had first voiced their grievances about the corruption Arafat tolerated in some of those around him, they enjoyed, as
I have noted, a measure of popular support. But the moment the
rebels (and other P.L.O. dissidents) were seen to be on Assad's side
and helping him to do his dirty work, they lost all credibility and
were finished in the eyes of the vast majority of Palestinians.

In 1984 Arafat's main objective was to prove what was that he enjoyed the support of an easy majority of the Palestinian people; that his P.L.O. and not Assad's Palestinian puppets represented and spoke for the majority; and that the majority backed the Chairman's efforts to secure a political and compromise settlement with Israel – within the framework of a comprehensive peace. It has to be said that there were in the majority or loyalist camp many doubts about whether America and Israel were seriously interested in peace based on some justice for the Palestinians; but these legitimate doubts did not change the fact that the vast majority were with Arafat.

The only way Arafat could prove these things was by convening a meeting of the P.N.C. – to endorse his leadership and to give him the mandate he wanted to formulate a joint strategy with King Hussein. It was Arafat's announcement that he wanted the Palestinian parliament-in-exile to be convened that marked the beginning of the second phase of his showdown with Assad. For his part the Syrian President was determined to prevent the P.N.C. meeting as long as Arafat remained the Chairman of the P.L.O. According to Arafat and his senior colleagues, Assad was confidently predicting to all Arab leaders and the U.S. State Department that the P.L.O. would have a new Chairman by the end of November 1984. (Arab leaders did, in fact, believe that Assad's confidence was justified. In the summer of 1984, and reflecting what they were learning from official sources, a number of Arab journalists told me that Arab leaders were expecting to welcome a new Chairman of the P.L.O. before the end of the year.) The implication is surely obvious. At an early point in 1984, Assad was totally confident that his hit-men would succeed in killing Arafat if he failed to persuade Abu Lutuf or Abu Iyad or Khalad Hassan to depose the Chairman.

This second phase of the showdown between Arafat and Assad took place mainly on the diplomatic level and mostly behind closed doors. When the game started Assad believed he was holding two trump cards.

The first was his ability to use his influence to deny the seventeenth P.N.C. a venue. Because the Palestinians are without a homeland of their own they have obviously, to convene their parliament-in-exile on the sovereign soil of an Arab state. This meant (as it did every year) that until an Arab government agreed to act as host by offering its capital or some place in its country as the venue, no meeting of the P.N.C. could take place.

Through the spring and summer of 1984 Arafat's own first choice for the venue was again Algiers. But the Algerians were horribly compromised. As one of the very few Arab regimes with genuine revolutionary credentials it wanted to host the seventeenth session of the P.N.C. But its leaders were under immense pressure from Assad. Eventually he used on them an argument which sounded very plausible but which in fact lacked substance – as future events were to prove. According to my P.L.O. sources Assad's argument to the Algerians was as follows. As things stood a meeting of the P.N.C. would result in the P.L.O. being split into two more or less equal and viable parts. Such a split would have disasterous consequences for the Arabs as well as the Palestinians themselves. Surely the Algerians did not want such a responsibility on their shoulders. . . They did not and it seemed that Assad had won.

In September I was sitting with Arafat in Tunis. We were discussing the situation as friends and not as author and subject. He knew I understood perfectly well that his P.L.O. did represent and speak for the majority, but that, I said, was hardly the point, I went on: 'Because the outside world doesn't know what is really happening, the conclusion being drawn is that you can't convene a meeting of the P.N.C. because you no longer command majority support . . . and because of that what little credibility you enjoy in the West is being eroded fast.' With no visible sign of concern in his face Arafat said: 'Yes, I know. I understand what you say. It is so.' In the pause that followed he exchanged a conspirator's glance with two of his colleagues. When he faced me again I could see triumph dancing in his eyes. 'I will tell you a secret,' he said. 'His Majesty King Hussein has invited us to have our P.N.C. in Amman.'

It was a sensational development. The issuing of the invitation by the King was an act of faith and courage. It was Arafat's opinion that even as we were talking Hussein was under great pressure from Assad, and other Arab leaders, to withdraw the invitation. But there were other considerations. If Hussein withstood the pressure, Arafat was going to have to match the King's courage by selling Amman as the venue to his supporters. For emotional more than political reasons not all Arafat loyalists would find it easy to forget the past. But I left the Chairman convinced that the P.N.C. would be convened in Amman. When we parted I said, 'If you have the P.N.C. in Jordan you will not only defeat Assad, you will change the course of history because the West will finally get the message that you are a man of peace and can deliver.' Arafat smiled. 'We hope so,' he said. 'We hope so.'

According to my P.L.O. sources Assad suffered a moment of panic. He flew to Algiers to say he would withdraw his opposition to the convening of the P.N.C. there on condition that Algeria would insist on the attendance of all P.L.O. groups including, of course, Syria's puppets. On that basis Algeria confirmed its invitation to Arafat. But the Chairman was not without options. He did not have to accept conditions. He had an invitation from Iraq in his pocket as well. (Earlier, the mullahs of Iran had offered Tehran as the venue for the P.N.C. In reply to their spokesman, and as he told me himself, Arafat had said he could consider such an invitation only if Iran was prepared to agree to a ceasefire and negotiations with Iraq.)

On 12 November, and as required by the P.L.O.'s constitution, Arafat made a formal request for the seventeenth session of the P.N.C. to be convened in Amman. Assad was then obliged to play what he thought was his second trump card. If by one means or another he could prevent at least one-third of the active P.N.C. delegates from travelling to Amman, the Palestinian parliament-in-exile could not be convened. If a meeting did take place without the required quorum of two-thirds of the delegates, it would be nothing more than a gathering of Arafat loyalists without the constitutional power to make legal and binding decisions. In that event Arafat would be the loser. Assad was confident of his ability to deny Arafat the quorum he needed.

So it became a game of numbers. In theory the P.N.C. was legally assembled when two-thirds of its 564 delegates were present. But 181 of these seats or places were allocated to Palestinians living under Israeli occupation on the West Bank and in Gaza. And Israel were not about to let Palestinian delegates under its control attend the P.N.C. Because of the Israeli ban on their participation, the 181 delegates from the occupied territories were regarded as 'non-active' members of the P.N.C. That left 383 'active' delegates. And that meant Arafat needed a quorum of 255.

As late as 20 November, two days before the Palestinian parliament-in-exile was called to order, Assad was still confidently assuring Arab leaders and the west that Arafat would not have a quorum and that within a matter of days the P.L.O. would have a new Chairman. Assad's confidence was the result of three steps he had taken to guarantee that more than one-third of the active P.N.C. delegates would not show up in Amman.

Step one had required no effort. Assad simply warned the delegates from among the Fatah rebels and other dissident P.L.O. groups under his control that they would be finished if they dared to attend the Amman meeting. Step two had required some effort. Syrian authorities confiscated the passports of pro-Arafat and independent P.N.C. delegates living in Syria and the Lebanon who were still at their places of residence after 12 November. Step three had required more effort. The sitting Speaker of the P.N.C. was Khalad Fahoum. He lived in Damascus and had long been known for his pro-Syrian views. Arafat and his Fatah colleagues had previously accommodated them for reasons of political expedience. On 12 November Fahoum, in his official capacity, rejected Arafat's request for the P.N.C. to be convened in Amman. In the normal course of events it would have been Fahoum as Speaker who sent out the invitations. When Arafat invoked alternative but constitutional procedures for convening the P.N.C., Fahoum went to work for his real master – Assad. He telephoned scores of P.N.C. delegates in the Arab world and beyond. His message to each of them was the same: Arafat had no chance of getting a quorum and the P.N.C. could not be legally convened. On that basis Fahoum advised delegates not to waste time by travelling to Amman. He also made a point of saying that it was President Assad and not Yasser Arafat who was enjoying the support of Arab leaders upon whom the P.L.O. depended. The implication was obvious. Continued support for Arafat would alienate Arab leaders. Some to whom Fahoum spoke on the telephone said frankly that they were committed to Arafat and what he represented and would be going to Amman. Others declared themselves to be undecided. But many more said that having listened to Fahoum they would take his advice and stay away. On the basis of these telephone conversations and the pledges he received, Fahoum presented Assad with a list of definite absentees. To this list Assad added the names of those whose passports had been confiscated and the P.N.C. delegates from among the Fatah rebels and other P.L.O. dissidents. The total came to more than the blocking third Assad needed. He convinced himself that the P.N.C. could not be convened and that he had Arafat beaten. Said Hani Hassan: 'There was one important thing Assad didn't know. It was for security and tactical reasons that a good number of delegates told Fahoum they would not be going to Amman. Some had already obtained their air tickets. Others booked their seats as soon as they put down the phone – having told Fahoum they would not be going!' And that, it seems, was the main reason why Assad's second trump card turned out to be a joker.

A week before the P.N.C. was convened Khalad Hassan told me the official leadership was expecting 'a quorum plus ten'. In the event Arafat got a quorum plus six on the first day with more delegates arriving later. The late arrivals had faced transit problems at Arab airports where Syrian ambassadors and intelligence agents could exercise their influence.

On the figures alone it still looked as though Arafat had only just scraped home. In terms of the two-thirds majority required to convene the P.N.C., and to give legal authority to its decisions, that was the case. But the figures in no way reflected the true level of support for Arafat and the general thrust of his policies. If all of the 564 places in the Palestinian parliament-in-exile had been filled – in other words, if all P.N.C. delegates had been free to travel to Amman, not less than 500 of them, and probably more, would have endorsed Arafat's leadership. One who would have travelled to Amman to take his seat if the Israelis had been wise enough to help promote Palestinian moderation and realism was Elias Freij, the Mayor of Bethlehem. Mayor Freij was one of the first Palestinians to call publicly for an accommodation between the P.L.O. and Israel. On the eve of the seventeenth P.N.C. he told reporters: 'The vast majority of people in the occupied territories are in favour of holding the P.N.C. in Amman. It is opposed by a small and extremist minority which will always reject whatever is on the table.'[54] Mayor Freij was right. Yet still today many Western newspapers and other media institutions insist on exaggerating massively the significance of the divisions in P.L.O. ranks. From time to time the media, including the B.B.C. as I write, refers to the 'Arafat *faction*' – the clear implication being that one faction is much the same as another, i.e. that anti-Arafat factions enjoy more or less the

same support among the Palestinian masses as the Chairman and
his mainstream Fatah organization. And that is a nonsense. It is, of
course, impossible to establish a precise level of popular and real
support for those in the liberation movement who oppose – or who
*say* they oppose – Arafat's policy of politics and compromise, but an
informed guess would be that Arafat's political opponents speak for
not more than ten per cent, and probably less, of the Palestinian
people. If you ask how many Palestinians seriously believe that
Arafat's policy of politics and compromise will get results, you get a
completely different answer; but that is a completely different question. I cannot help thinking that the media's refusal over the years to
give Arafat a fair deal has been a major obstacle to understanding in
the West and thus a major obstacle to peace itself.

The seventeenth P.N.C. answered the question of who was going
to make Palestinian policy. Arafat was now free to develop a joint
approach with King Hussein – assuming the authentic P.L.O. and
Jordan could find enough common ground. To this extent it could
be said that Arafat had emerged the winner from his showdown
with Assad. The question of what Assad could and would do to
wreck a Jordan–P.L.O. initiative was for the future.

At the P.N.C. King Hussein outlined his own ideas about what
had to happen if Jordan and the P.L.O. were to work together and
have a chance of persuading the Americans to support their efforts.
The King called for an international peace conference at which all
parties would be represented. (As agreed later this included the
P.L.O. *in its own right* but as part of a joint delegation with Jordan).
That was the good news for most of his Palestinian listeners – the
delegates and those watching the procedings of the P.N.C. live on
television in the occupied territories, Jordan, Syria and beyond. The
bad news, or so it seemed at the time to even many Arafat loyalists,
was the King's insistence that U.N. Resolution 242 *had* to be the
basis of negotiations for a comprehensive settlement of the Arab–
Israeli conflict. But the King was wise enough to give the Palestinians a choice. He said: 'If you find this option convincing we are
prepared to go with you down this path and present the world with
a joint initiative for which we will marshall support. If, on the other
hand, you believe the P.L.O. is capable of going it alone, then we say
to you "God speed, you have our support. The decision is yours.
Whatever it is, we will respect it."'[55]

It was a generous and clever speech with many coded messages. For the first time in public Hussein was telling the Americans and Israel (and Assad) that it was no longer possible to exclude the P.L.O. from the peace-making process. On the assumption that Arafat could deliver the P.L.O. to work with Jordan on the terms stated, Hussein was saying, in effect, that if the P.L.O. was not allowed a place at the conference table, albeit as part of a joint delegation with Jordan, there would be no negotiations because Jordan would not participate without the P.L.O. The King was guaranteeing the P.L.O. a place at the conference table – assuming, of course, that the Americans and enough Israelis were interested in peace on terms the Arabs could accept with honour. In the thirty-eighth year of the conflict Hussein had found a way to call Israel's bluff.

For a few hours after the King had spoken it seemed that Arafat was once again in trouble, and that his task of persuading the P.N.C. to give him a mandate to work with Hussein would be difficult and perhaps impossible. The first impression of many Palestinians, delegates and others, was that the King was asking them, as the price of his support, to accept 242 and by so doing recognize Israel before Israel had recognized Palestinian rights to self-determination. In fact that first impression was wrong. But in the emotional atmosphere of the time, and given their painful memories of the past, it was not difficult to understand why many Palestinians, delegates and others, had failed to grasp precisely what Hussein was offering them and what he expected in return. Having missed the point of what Hussein was really saying, many P.N.C. delegates were talking themselves into what Khalad Hassan later described as a 'negative mood'. Arafat responded to it with a pre-emptive strike. He resigned. In the course of the next few hours scores of people, P.N.C. delegates and Palestinians not usually active in P.L.O. politics, visited Arafat in his hotel suite to beg him to change his mind. To nobody's surprise he did. And that is how he guaranteed that he would get a mandate to work with Hussein.

Most foreign observers were easily convinced that what had happened was a piece of pure 'Arafat theatre'. But there was more to it. Having talked about that performance with the star himself and most of his senior colleagues, I believe Arafat would not have taken up the burden of leadership again without an assurance that he would get his mandate to work with the King.

The climax to several weeks of discussions between P.L.O. leaders and Hussein, and between the Chairman and his leadership colleagues, came on 11 February 1985 in Amman. On that day the Chairman and the King signed an historic agreement to work together for peace. The agreement was based on the idea of 'land for peace' – a phrase which Abu Iyad had asked delegates at the seventeenth P.N.C. to ponder. As Hani Hassan explained to me in detail, the essence of the P.L.O.'s agreement with Jordan, and what the P.L.O. was saying when it signed the document, came down to this: 'For reasons the world *ought* to understand the P.L.O. cannot accept 242 and by so doing recognize Israel until Israel recognizes Palestinian rights to self-determination . . . However we are prepared to make 242 work in practise, and to negotiate on it, under the umbrella of an international peace conference, provided it is accepted that the aim of negotiations will be the following: one – an Israeli withdrawal from Arab territory occupied in 1967 as required by 242; two – the establishment on the West Bank and in Gaza of a Palestinian state in a confederation with Jordan; three – recognition by all states, including the Palestinian state in a confederation with Jordan, of Israel's existence within secure and guaranteed borders; four – agreement by all parties involved to continue talking about all outstanding problems and to resolve them by peaceful and democratic means.' The agreement demonstrated that Hussein had not been demanding that the P.L.O. suddenly reverse itself and say that accepting 242 was no longer a problem. What the King had demanded, and now obtained, was the P.L.O.'s commitment to the principle and spirit of 242 – land for peace. For all practical purposes the P.L.O. had therefore accepted 242 as the basis for negotiations in the context of *all* relevant U.N. decisions.

In summary it can be said that on 11 February 1985, Jordan and the P.L.O. together opened the door to negotiations on terms that no rational Israeli government and people could refuse. By the end of May, and with the help of other Arab leaders, Hussein had convinced President Reagan that this was, indeed, the case. The spring of 1985 had seen a procession of Arab leaders to Washington led by King Fahd. Though they all refrained from making explicit public statements because they did not want to provoke Assad's vengeance, they each carried the same message to Reagan: the West would lose everything in the Middle East if the U.S. did not help to keep Arab moderation alive by doing whatever was necessary to oblige Israel to respond positively to the Jordan–P.L.O. initiative. It was Hani Hassan who co-ordinated the Palestinian effort to secure Saudi Arabia's unequivocal support for the authentic P.L.O. after Arafat's triumph at the P.N.C. When it was clear that Arafat was again enjoying the support of the Saudis, Syrian agents placed a 40lb. bomb outside Hani's home.

Reagan's first public response to Hussein's news that Jordan and the P.L.O. together were ready for negotiations came during an impromptu news conference which he shared with the King at the White House on 29 May. When Hussein was pressed by reporters to explain why he was calling his initiative the 'last chance' for peace, it was the President – after saying they would take no more questions – who answered. He said: 'I think the conditions have never been more right than they are now to pursue peace. And who knows whether those conditions will ever come as close together as they have now. So that's why I think the term "last chance" is used. And I think we ought to keep that in mind, that perhaps it is the last chance.'[56] Later, and knowing that Hussein had been speaking for Arafat, Reagan issued a formal statement. In it he said that he hoped the King's 'courageous steps forward' would lead to direct negotiations between the parties by the end of the year. The statement added, 'We will do our part to bring this about.'[57]

# 20

# The 'Last Chance' – Going or Gone?

For some weeks it seemed that the Reagan administration was seriously committed to the idea of using the Jordan-P.L.O. agreement as the vehicle for advancing the peace process. Even Arafat declared himself to be happy with what Hussein had achieved in Washington.

On his return to Amman the King told the Chairman that Secretary of State Shultz had agreed to a three-stage plan for creating the conditions which would enable the U.S. to accept the P.L.O. as a party to negotiations, and to deal with it on that basis. Stage one was to be a meeting between Assistant Secretary of State Murphy and a joint Jordanian-Palestinian delegation. If that meeting took place, and was successful, stage two was to be a statement from Arafat. In it the Chairman of the P.L.O. would recognize Israel in its 1967 borders by accepting U.N. resolutions 242 and 338 as the basis for negotiations. In short, Arafat was going to be required to say himself, in public, what was implicit in his 11 February agreement with Hussein, *and* what he had authorized the King to say for him in Washington. If Arafat made the statement in a form acceptable to the Americans, Murphy would be instructed to meet with him in Amman. That was to be stage three. In other words, formal U.S. recognition of the P.L.O. seemed to be the prize which Hussein was now dangling in front of Arafat and his leadership colleagues.

The King also told Arafat he had made some progress in his effort to persuade Shultz that negotiations with Israel would have to be conducted under the umbrella of an international conference to which all interested parties – including the Soviet Union – should be invited. (Hussein and Arafat were insisting on an international framework for negotiations because they knew the Soviet Union would use its Syrian and Palestinian proxies to wreck any peace process from which they, the Soviets, were excluded. For his own part, Syria's President Assad feared that Hussein and Arafat could be tempted by the U.S. to make a separate peace with Israel, as Sadat had done. And that, in turn, was why Assad had done so much to try to prevent Arafat making an accommodation with Hussein, *and* why he would now stop at nothing to sabotage the partnership and discredit Arafat. Remember the name *Achille Lauro*.)

What seemed like a new sense of realism on the part of the Reagan administration in May 1985 was, in fact, consistent with its first evaluation of the significance of the Jordan-P.L.O. agreement. Back in February, just three days after Hussein and Arafat signed the agreement, a senior administration official had told reporters, among them Don Oberdorfer of *The Washington Post,* that the Jordan-P.L.O. agreement was a 'milestone' on a long road. On the understanding that he would not be identified, the same source then said the following: 'Before there has never been a Palestinian commitment to the peaceful resolution of the problem. Now there is.'

When Arafat and his leadership colleagues had digested Hussein's report on his mission to Washington, they were prepared to give Shultz the benefit of the doubt and to proceed on the assumption that he was serious about involving the P.L.O. in the peace process. But Arafat and his colleagues were not naive. They were very much aware that the Reagan administration, like all its predecessors since the days of Eisenhower, might surrender to Israel and the Zionist lobby in America when the going got rough.

For the projected meeting between Murphy and the joint Jordanian-Palestinian delegation the Americans imposed a condition which Arafat had either to accept or reject: none of the Palestinians selected to attend should be members of the P.L.O. Arafat the pragmatist accepted this condition. He had no choice. By the middle of July he had passed to the Americans, via Hussein, a list of seven names from which the Americans were required to choose and approve four. In view of what was about to happen, it is worth noting that the Americans had previously said, on the record, that once they had approved the names of the Palestinians for the talks, Israel would not be allowed to veto them.

By the end of the second week of August the Reagan administration indicated that four of the P.L.O.'s nominees were acceptable. The four were: Hanna Siniora, editor-in-chief of the respected East Jerusalem newspaper *Al Fajr* and, for many years, an advocate of dialogue with Israel; Faiz Abu Rahmeh, a lawyer and, in political terms, a lightweight from Gaza; Henry Cattan, an ageing jurist of international repute who had been living in Paris for many years (see note 1); and Nabil Sha'ath, a businessman based in Cairo and a former adviser to Arafat. Of the four only Sha'ath had presented a problem for the Americans in the context of their promise to Israel that they would not talk or meet with P.L.O. people until the P.L.O. recognized Israel's right to exist. Sha'ath was a member of the Palestinian parliament-in-exile (P.N.C.), the highest decision-making body on the Palestinian side and, as we have seen, the institution which determines the policy guidelines for the P.L.O. and its chairman. The Americans said that Sha'ath 'fell within the parametres we've set for defining a non-member' (of the P.L.O.). The Israelis and the Zionist lobby in America did not agree and said that for all practical purposes the P.L.O. and the P.N.C. were part of the same terrorist machine. The Israelis and their lobby argued that on that basis the U.S. would be breaking its word if the Murphy meeting with the joint Jordanian-Palestinian delegation as named went ahead.

For a week or so it looked as though the Reagan administration was going to break with tradition and prevent Israel making American foreign policy for the Middle East. Murphy himself was anxious to get the talks started. Strongly supported by most senior officials and advisers in the State Department he urged his boss to give him the greenlight for the meeting. Murphy told Shultz there was no chance of starting a peace process worthy of the name if they did not honour their commitment to Hussein and, by implication, Arafat.

On 7 September *The Washington Post* and other leading American newspapers carried front-page stories which fuelled speculation that Murphy was soon to meet with the joint Jordanian-Palestinian delegation. Then the proverbial excrement hit the fan. More in private than in public, Israel and its unquestioning supporters in America went to work with their usual skill and vigour. Behind their determination to have the Murphy mission cancelled was their suspicion, and perhaps their knowledge, that the meeting was intended to be only the start of a process that could end with the U.S. recognizing the P.L.O. as a party to negotiations.

The pressure on Shultz was intense. But for once the Zionists did not have things all their own way. Some of the richest and most influential Palestinians in America – all of them American citizens – made a co-ordinated effort of their own to lobby the Secretary of State. One of their number was on first-name terms with Shultz and arranged a meeting with him. Like Murphy before them, they made the case for not allowing Israel to veto Sha'ath, killing what even President Reagan had described as the 'last chance' for peace. Shultz was reminded that Sha'ath was a very gentle and sophisticated man who had been educated in America and, more to the point, who had done much to influence and support Arafat when he was risking his credibility and his life to sell the idea of compromise with Israel to the P.N.C. in the 1970s. The message to Shultz was clear. If out of fear of offending Israel and its lobby the Americans could not bring themselves to talk to a man with Sha'ath's credentials as a moderate and peacemaker, there was no hope – not now, not ever.

But Shultz was not moved. As one of those who met with him was later to tell Arafat, the Secretary of State had lost the will to stand up to Israel and its lobby. And that, more or less, was the message Murphy conveyed to emissaries from Hussein and Mubarak when they begged him to make one more attempt to persuade his boss to see the light. Murphy was, in fact, reduced to telling his friends in private that he could not 'deliver the seventh floor' (of the State Department, where Shultz had his office).

In places where diplomats and others with inside knowledge met to discuss the likely consequences of the cancellation of the Murphy mission, it was being said that Hussein, Mubarak, Arafat and other Arab leaders were not alone in their despair. According to an inside story from what was described as a Jerusalem deep-throat', Israel's Prime Minister, Shimon Peres, was also very angry in private. He was said to have told his close friends that Shultz was a 'very stupid man' who had 'blown it'. What Shultz ought to have done, Peres

was reported as saying, was to present Israel with a *fait accompli*.
In other words, Shultz ought to have sent Murphy to Amman to
meet with the joint Jordanian-Palestinian delegation and to have
held back on the publicity until the meeting had started. In that
event there would have been a crisis in Israel, of course. The unity
of the fragile coalition government Peres led would have been severely tested. The Likud half of the coalition would have denounced the American move as a sell-out. But Peres was very much
aware, or so it was said, that Israel had nothing to lose and, possibly, much to gain from a meeting between Murphy and the joint
Jordanian-Palestinian delegation. If the meeting took place, and if
Arafat then failed to follow up by making his promised statement,
Israel would no longer have a problem convincing the world that
the Chairman of the P.L.O. was incapable of delivering and was,
therefore, a man with whom Israel could not be expected to do
business. But if the Murphy meeting did take place, and if Arafat
*did* then make his promised statement, a whole new situation
would exist – one in which Peres would have the option of calling
an election to obtain a mandate to test Hussein *and* Arafat in
negotiations. In this event, Peres would have had the best possible
chance of winning an election and emerging as a real peacemaker
without provoking the civil war in Israel that even many Israelis
and other Jews fear is inevitable – because of the polarization now
taking place in Israeli society and the growing extremism of those
on the hard right who are opposed to compromise of any kind.

Helping to give credibility to the story of Peres's anger was the
known fact that he considered the Zionist lobby in America to be
his enemy. In his view, or so it had been reported by a source
beyond question, the Zionist lobby had become the 'Likud lobby'.
And it was an open secret that many hard-core activists in what
is variously called the Zionist/Jewish/Israel lobby in America had
come to regard Peres as a 'traitor' – because they believed, with
good reason in my opinion, that he would be prepared to make
peace on terms which Hussein and Arafat could accept, provided
he could find a way to do it without provoking a civil war in
Israel. (In a conversation with me in 1980 Peres said that Begin's
objective in colonizing the West Bank was to create the conditions
for civil war and, by so doing, to prevent any future government
of Israel withdrawing for peace. As I recall the conversation, Peres

said, explicitly: "Begin knows well that no future Israeli Prime Minister is going down in history as the leader who gave the Jewish army the order to shoot Jewish people.')

Against this background the point of the story about the reported private anger of Peres is that Shultz had done nobody a favour, except perhaps himself, by allowing Israel's hardliners and their allies in America to stop the Murphy mission. The Secretary of State may well have guaranteed himself a more comfortable time in office, but he had pulled the rug from under the feet of those Arab and Israeli leaders who were trying, despite their respective internal problems, to advance the peace process.

As usual, it was the Arabs who had to pick up the pieces after another failure of nerve by an American administration. And it was Hussein and Mubarak, with Arafat's encouragement, who took the lead in trying to keep the peace process alive. To the surprise of many observers they were given a helping hand – or so it seemed at the time – by Britain's Prime Minister, Margaret Thatcher.

In the middle of September Mrs Thatcher made an official visit to Egypt and Jordan. Obviously the trip was arranged long before the Murphy mission was torpedoed, but the timing of her arrival in the Middle East was perfect so far as Mubarak, Hussein, and Arafat were concerned. Close to total despair, the Egyptian President and the Jordanian monarch were prepared to beg Mrs Thatcher to take a British initiative to put pressure on the Americans. In both Cairo and Amman Mrs Thatcher was told that, as far as the Arabs could see, American policy was to erect a series of obstacles to peace. As soon as one was removed by Arab effort another was put in its place.

At a press conference in Cairo Mrs Thatcher said enough to indicate that she believed the Reagan administration had been wrong to allow Israel and certain of its American supporters to veto Murphy's meeting with the joint Jordanian-Palestinian delegation. On the subject of who should be included in the Palestinian part of the delegation Mrs Thatcher said: "It is important that those names should not include people extremely prominent in the P.L.O. but it could include people who have been associated with the P.L.O. as long as they reject terrorism.' And in Mrs Thatcher's view there were 'a number of P.L.O. members who have rejected terrorism as the way forward'. She added: 'Whether we like it or not the [Palestinian] delegation is going to be selected by the P.L.O.'

But it was on her next stop that Mrs Thatcher demonstrated she was serious about doing something to keep alive the initiative represented by the Jordan-P.L.O. agreement. At a state banquet in Amman she said that any peace settlement must take into account 'the legitimate rights of all the people and states in the area including, of course, the Palestinians'. The next day, at a farewell press conference in Aqaba on the Red Sea, the British Prime Minister dropped a political bombshell. She announced that she had invited two members of the P.L.O.'s Executive Committee to London for talks with the Foreign Secretary, Sir Geoffrey Howe. The two for London – they would be going as part of a joint Jordanian-Palestinian delegation – were to be Mohammed Milhem, a teacher by training and a former mayor of Halhoul on the Israeli-occupied West Bank; and Bishop Elia Khoury, Suffragan Archbishop of Jerusalem. 'We know Bishop Khoury and Mr Milhem to be men of peace,' Mrs Thacher said. 'They personally support a peaceful settlement on the basis of the relevant United Nations resolutions and are opposed to terrorism and violence. I know they will reaffirm their positions during their stay in London.' The history-making visit was scheduled for mid-October or thereabouts.

Explaining more about her decision Mrs Thatcher said: 'I hope that this will be seen as a fresh and constructive step to support King Hussein's initiative. That is its purpose. *I hope this will help the United States to take a similar step.*' (My italics.) As several British observers noted, this was the clearest possible hint to the Reagan administrtion that it should stop making difficulties and start making peace.

Most Israeli reactions were predictable. The scripts for them could have been written in advance by anyone with a passing knowledge of the history of the conflict. How dare the British give encouragement 'to an organization whose aim is the destruction of the State of Israel'. The Likud leader and Foreign Minister of the day, Yitzhak Shamir, was in America. He accused Britain of 'undermining the peace process'. By inviting the two P.L.O. executives the British had 'struck a heavy blow against the chances for peace and against those working for peace'. If the situation in the Middle East had not been so tragic and so dangerous, the comments of this former Jewish terrorist leader would have been funny. Not even a majority of Israelis would have described Shamir as one of those who was working for peace. (In October 1986 Shamir took over from Peres as Prime Minister under the terms of the coalition agreement – an event described by Israel's most illustrious former Foreign Minister, Aba Eban, as ushering in 'the tunnel at the end of the light'.) Of the heavyweight Israeli leaders in government only Peres chose to make a measured response. For obvious political reasons he had to condemn Mrs Thatcher's decision; but even in cabinet he did not go beyond saying that he could not understand her readiness to meet with members of an organization 'which today engages in terrorism'. Though it might have been wishful thinking on their part, some observers, myself included, wondered if the lack of agression in the Peres response was a sign that he was secretly relieved that somebody was doing something to move the peace process forward. In advance of her dramatic statement Mrs Thatcher did inform Peres of what she intended to say.

The P.L.O.'s public response to Mrs Thatcher's gesture of support was naturally one of gratitude; but in private Arafat was cautious, even worried. He knew better than anyone else that whenever the P.L.O. was on the point of making a significant political gain his enemies struck – either to prevent the P.L.O. from capturing new political ground or, once the gain had been made, to cancel it. As all western governments knew, but chose not to admit, most acts of Palestinian terrorism since 1975 had been the work of Libyan-financed, Syrian-directed, anti-Arafat factions which did not command the support of more than ten per cent of the Palestinian people at the most. On the other side of the coin, as we have seen, there was, for example, Israel's invasion of the Lebanon in 1982. That particular attempt to liquidate Arafat and many of his leadership colleagues was made because Sharon, Begin, Shamir, and other Israeli leaders of their kind were alarmed by the fact that the P.L.O.'s claim that it was ready for a political settlement was beginning to be taken seriously in the West. In the summer of 1982 the logic of the men in power in Israel was as clear as it was cruel. And it went something like this: 'If we can no longer convince the world that the P.L.O. is nothing but a gang of murderers, the day will come when even our friends will require us to negotiate with Arafat. Never! Let's kill him.' Late in 1985 Arafat's sixth sense was telling him that history was about to repeat itself.

The first warning of trouble ahead for Arafat and the P.L.O. came less than a week after Mrs Thatcher issued her invitation to Khoury and Milhem, and nearly three weeks before they were due in London. A spokesman for the Abu Nidal organization declared that both men would be assassinated if they did not announce their refusal to accept Mrs Thatcher's invitation. The threat was taken very seriously in the Arafat camp, but even more serious than the threat itself was what it implied. As Arafat and his leadership colleagues knew well, the Abu Nidal organization was being directed by a Syrian intelligence service – actually by Syrian air force intelligence. Its head was General Muhammed Al-Khouli and he was President Assad's most trusted colleague and friend. Arafat later told me that the threat from the Abu Nidal organization was part of the evidence which suggested to him that Assad was planning something 'very dirty' to discredit the mainstream P.L.O. and wreck the relationship with Jordan and what it represented. (Remember again the name *Achille Lauro*.)

Then there was the question of what Israel and its intelligence agencies would do to try to prevent the P.L.O. being taken seriously as a party to negotiations. I can now reveal that Arafat and his senior leadership colleagues were expecting Israel to attack them in Tunis.

A month before Mrs Thatcher issued her invitation to Khoury and Milhem I had lunch with Abu Iyad in Tunis. During the course of a conversation lasting several hours I raised the subject of Israel's escalating threats to take heavy military action against the P.L.O. (In view of what was about to happen readers who do not make a habit of following the complexities of Israeli politics should know something of the tensions between Peres and the then Defence Minister, Yitzhak Rabin. As the two most senior figures in the Israeli Labor Party of the day – Rabin was a former Prime Minister – the two men were theoretically on the same side. But the truth, as all of Israel knew, was that the two men detested each other. And on top of their long-standing personal differences was now the fact that Peres had become – at least in private – a pragmatist, who did not rule out the possibility of an eventual deal with the P.L.O. – if that was what was necessary to prevent the disintegration of the Jewish State. Rabin, on the other hand, was a hardliner. I do not think it is unfair to describe him as the Sharon of the Labour Party. It is also worth noting that it was Rabin who, as Chief of Staff in 1967, planned Israel's brilliant war strategy.) In the summer of 1985 Defence Minister Rabin was frequently vowing to fight terrorism by any means and in any place. As I monitored Rabin's rhetoric, I saw a pattern which suggested to me that he was preparing Israel and world opinion for a spectacular strike against Arafat. *Where* was the question.

Since about the time of Arafat's accommodation with Hussein, and the reopening of P.L.O. offices in Jordan – including one for the Chairman – there had been a marked increase in the number of attacks against Jewish settlers on the occupied West Bank. Rabin and some other Israeli leaders were telling the world that Arafat and the P.L.O. were to blame for this escalation of violence. And Rabin had warned Jordan that it should not regard itself as being immune from punishment for giving shelter, comfort, and respect to the terrorists. But the claim that Arafat and the P.L.O. were responsible for the escalating violence was, essentially, a propaganda lie. As even some Israeli reporters had said in print, there was good reason to believe that more than three-quarters of the attacks on Jewish settlers were random acts of violence by frustrated Palestinian individuals who were being driven to despair by the repression and humiliation of occupation by Israel. Over lunch I discussed the implications of these and related matters with Abu Iyad. In order to draw him out I suggested that Rabin was going to use the escalation of violence on the West Bank as a pretext for an attack on the P.L.O. in Jordan with the aim, perhaps, of killing Arafat. I asked Abu Iyad what he thought about such a scenario.

He became very serious. 'No,' he said, 'the Israelis will not attack us in Jordan.' Pause. 'They will come for us here.'

That was a possibility I had previously considered myself and rejected because I thought it was too fantastic. 'Are you being serious?' I asked. 'Surely even the Israelis, even Rabin, would not go so far?'

Abu Iyad smiled. 'Perhaps you do not know your Israeli friends as well as you think you do.' Pause. 'Yes, they will come for us in Tunis. As a matter of fact we are expecting them.'

On 1 October, ten days after Mrs Thatcher invited the two
P.L.O. executives to London, and two weeks before they were
scheduled to arrive, Rabin's jets bombed and destroyed Arafat's
headquarters in Tunis.

In the view of Arafat and all Arabs, this was an act of Israeli
state terrorism. If the Chairman had been at work in his private
office – which, when he was in Tunis, he usually was at the time
the Israelis struck – he would have been blown to pieces. In the
event he was away from his office, but forty-five of his staff, and
twenty-five Tunisian civilians were killed, and more than 100 people were injured. (One day Arafat will no doubt reveal why he
was not in his office. He was certainly not where many journalists
reported him to be when the bombs fell – jogging on the beach.
It was Arafat himself who told reporters that story. But it was,
apparently, his way of telling them to mind their own business
when they asked for a minute-by-minute account of his movements!)

After denying that his intention had been to kill Arafat or any
specific P.L.O. leader, Rabin told the Knesset's foreign affairs and
defence committee that 'the recent increase in terrorist attacks' had
left Israel with 'no choice' but to attack the P.L.O.'s headquarters.
What Rabin described as the 'last straw' was the murder five days
previously of three Israelis – two men and a woman, each of them
in their 50s – aboard a yacht in a marina at Larnaca, Cyprus.

To this day there is a question mark over the identity of the
three Israelis. Israel claimed they were 'innocent tourists' who were
slaughtered by a three-man hit-squad from Fatah's famous Force
17. This elite commando unit was formed by Abu Hassan Salameh
in the early 1970s. Its principal job was to protect Arafat, to keep
him alive. The P.L.O. denied that Force 17 was involved in the
Larnaca killings and claimed that the three Israelis were Mossad
agents who were monitoring the P.L.O.'s attempts to ship men
and weapons through the Mediterranean to the Lebanon. P.L.O.
leaders later told me their own intelligence services had identified
the woman who was killed as an Israeli agent who had set up and
triggered the car bomb which killed Abu Hassan Salameh in Beirut
in 1978.

One reason for not believing that the Larnaca killings were the
work of Force 17 was the fact that one of the killers was a twenty-

eight-year-old Englishman, Ian Davison, from Tyneside. A carpenter by training, Davison had taken himself off to join the P.L.O. after being moved to tears and anger by television pictures of the massacre of Palestinians at the Sabra and Chatilla refugee camps in Beirut. As several P.L.O. leaders later said to me in private, there was no way that a sympathetic but naive young Englishman could have been member of Arafat's bodyguard, or even a party to its deliberations. When Davison and the two Palestinian gunmen surrendered to the police one of the Palestinians shouted to reporters. 'We belong to no organization. We belong to the Palestinian people. We are the people everyone forgets and we die in thousands.' I suspect he was telling the truth. My reconstruction of what probably happened is that official P.L.O. intelligence sources did identify what they genuinely believed to be at least one Israeli agent – the woman. Word of the find leaked into the Fatah ranks. From on high – perhaps from Abu Iyad, perhaps from Arafat himself – came the order that no action which might jeopardize the London talks was to be taken. Some in Fatah's rank and file were frustrated and angered by the order. Two of them, and Davison, decided to undertake a freelance operation. By doing so they played into Rabin's hands.

On the positive side for Arafat – apart from his survival – was the fact that very few western reporters took Israel's claim that Force 17 was responsible for the Larnaca killings at face value. More to the point, very few editorial writers accepted Israel's explanation of why it had bombed Tunis. An easy consensus of opinion among informed and influential people in the western world was that Israel's hardliners had tried to blow up the peace process because there was a danger, in their eyes, that it might lead to the P.L.O. being recognized as a party to negotiations.

A subject for debate among some P.L.O. leaders was the role of Prime Minister Peres. If it was true that he was, at least, a potential peacemaker on terms the P.L.O. could accept, why had he approved the bombing of Arafat's headquarters? The same question was being asked by many diplomats and other interested parties. One answer provided to their friends in Washington by sources close to Peres was that Rabin had played a very rough game. According to the story, Rabin had threatened to join the Likud hardliners in the coalition government, to force through a

decision to bomb Arafat in Jordan, if Peres did not go along with
the plan to attack Tunis.

The complicity of the Reagan administration is still the subject
of debate. Arafat himself went public with a claim that the White
House had had advance knowledge of the Israeli attack on Tunis
and was therefore 'part of the plot to assassinate me'. What can
be said for sure is that the Reagan administration *did* know that
Israeli war planes were on their way to Tunis and could have
ordered them to turn back. It is inconceivable that the planes could
have flown 1,500 miles over the Mediterranean, and have been
refuelled somewhere – perhaps in the air, as Israel claimed – without being identified by American (and Soviet) radar and satellite
tracking stations and other devices. It is reasonable to suppose that
the Israeli planes were tracked by the Americans (and the Soviets)
for most, if not all, of their long journey. Implicitly acknowledging
this on 4 October, a statement from the American Embassy in
Tunis said: 'Even if American units had detected the combat planes
over the sea, *their final destination could not have been known
before they reached their objective.*' (My italics.) The idea that the
Americans were unable to make even an inspired guess about Rabin's objective does not deserve to be taken seriously. In this context Arafat could not be blamed for attaching some weight to
Reagan's own first reaction to the Israeli attack. The President
said he thought the Israelis had the right to attack and had 'hit
the right target'.

P.L.O. and other Arab intelligence agencies also claim to have
evidence – supplied perhaps by the Soviets from their listening devices in the heavens – of a telephone conversation between Rabin
and Robert MacFarlane who, at the time, was Reagan's National
Security Adviser. In the conversation Rabin is alleged to have
speculated about three possible target areas for the attack on Arafat: Saana, Amman, and Tunis. MacFarlane is alleged to have given
the greenlight for Tunis, by what he did not say, when it was named
as a possible target. Partly for political reasons, partly because they
do not want to compromise their sources, the Arabs are not yet
ready to say what they think they know about this sensitive matter.
(MacFarlane subsequently resigned from the Reagan administration but during 1986 he travelled secretly to Tehran, disguised as
a priest and bearing an Irish passport, to offer the ruling Ayatollahs

arms and military spare parts in exchange for the release of American hostages being held in the Lebanon – this at a time when America's official policy was no negotiations with terrorists and those who sponsored and supported them. On matters relating to the Middle East the truth is often stranger than fiction.)

Then came the hijacking by four Palestinian terrorists of the Italian cruise liner, *Achille Lauro*, and the murder on board of a sixty-nine-year-old American citizen in a wheelchair, Leon Klinghoffer. This time Israel tried to pin the blame on Arafat himself. In fact, it was as a result of Arafat's mediation, conducted for him by Hani Hassan, that the hijack was quickly ended with the loss of only one life and the surrender of the four hijackers to the authorities in Egypt. The telling of the full, incredible and horribly complicated story of the *Achille Lauro* affair would require another book. In the space available to me for this update I can report only the following.

Two months after the hijack Arafat told me his verdict was that Mohammed Abu Abbas, the leader of a minor P.L.O. faction, who had apparently planned the operation which resulted in the hijack, was a 'fool'. Arafat's word. Abbas had allowed himself, Arafat said, to be used by former Palestinian associates who were controlled and directed by Syrian intelligence officers. Their job, as we have seen, was to plan and co-ordinate terrorist operations by Arafat's Palestinian opponents to discredit the Chairman and his mainstream P.L.O. Now consider this.

As the drama of the *Achille Lauro* affair was unfolding there came a moment when Arafat thought he would be able to prove beyond a doubt that the P.L.O. had been set up by the Syrians and, possibly, the Mossad, through its penetration of Palestinian and other Arab groups opposed to him. The moment came as a result of Hani Hassan's presence in Cairo. In a hotel bedroom he forced Abbas to tell him everything he knew, including, and especially, the names of all those who had been involved in the *Achille Lauro* operation. (Abbas had only intended to use the ship as a means of getting the four guerrillas on board into Israel to mount an attack. The hijack was never a part of Abbas's own plan.) On the basis of what Hani learned, Arafat persuaded President Mubarak to send the four hijackers by air to Tunis. Arafat was intending to interrogate them when they arrived until they broke, and then to put them on trial. At the White House President Reagan said on camera that if Arafat was serious about trying the hijackers that was 'fine' so far as he, the President, was concerned. The civil Egyptian plane carrying the four hjackers and Abbas took off for Tunis. Under pressure from the U.S. the authorities in Tunisia refused it permission to land. At 34,000 feet over the Mediterranean the Egyptian plane was then intercepted by American F14 Tomcat fighters and forced to land in Sicily. There American troops were under orders to seize the four hijackers and Abbas, by force if necessary. It was only when Italian troops arrived in strength, and made it clear that they, too, had orders to shoot if necessary, that the Americans backed off and allowed the Italians to take the Palestinians into custody.

One possible explanation for why the Americans hijacked the hijackers is simply that Reagan and his people felt the need to prove their 'Rambo' credentials. But Arafat has another view. His conclusion, one which I think is worthy of serious investigation, is that persons as yet unknown did not want the Chairman of the P.L.O. to get his hands on the Palestinian terrorists, because what he might have learned from them could have enabled him to unravel the mystery of who really master-ininded the hijacking of the *Achille Lauro*.

As a direct consequence of the *Achille Lauro* affair – and the successful way it was exploited by the Israelis and Zionist lobby groups everywhere – the London meeting with the joint Jordanian-Palestinian delegation, including the two P.L.O. executives, did not take place. The British Foreign Secretary said he cancelled the meeting because he had received 'unambiguous assurances' that Khoury and Milhem would publicly reject terrorism and violence of all kinds, and this they had refused to do (see below). Naturally the Israeli propaganda machine made the most of the British story. It was the final proof of what Israel had always said – the P.L.O. was nothing but a gang of murderers and it was time for the world to understand why Israel would never negotiate with it. What few people knew was that the British story, which enabled Israel and its supporters to make a convincing case against involving P.L.O. representatives in the peace process, was very far from the truth.

In Tunis a detailed statement of the P.L.O.'s version of why the London talks had not taken place was issued by Khalad Hassan, the P.L.O.'s most articulate spokesman and, among other things, the man who negotiated the Jordan-P.L.O. agreement with Hussein. He was also the man charged by Arafat with the responsibility for managing the London crisis when it became clear that the Thatcher government wanted a way out and was going to blame the P.L.O. Unfortunately the substance of Khalad's detailed statement was not widely reported in the West, to say the least.

To start with it has to be said that the 'unambiguous assurances' Howe spoke of were given by the Jordanians and not the P.L.O. And the real story was about the circumstances in which the assurances were given.

In retrospect it can be seen that the London talks were in trouble from the moment the *Achille Lauro* was hijacked. They were doomed by the murder of Klinghoffer. (Those ultimately responsible for the hijack and his death achieved their objective.) In America – I was there at the time – news of the killing provoked a wave of hysteria which swept across the country. The media tried and convicted the P.L.O. and, by obvious implication, Arafat himself, before any of the evidence was in. In this very emotional and highly charged atmosphere the Reagan administration put pressure on Mrs Thatcher to cancel the London meeting. There was also a serious problem for her on the home front. An Israeli cabinet minister, Professor Amnon Rubenstein, flew to London uninvited. His task was to rally the various Jewish lobby groups in Britain to put yet more pressure on the Prime Minister. (While all this was going on an American citizen, who happened to be a pro-Arafat Palestinian, was blown to pieces by a bomb when he opened the door to his office in Santa Ana on the west coast of America. His name was Alex Odeh. He had a wife and young children. He was killed by a well-known Jewish terrorist group which is the American face of a monster alive and well in Israel. Despite the fact that Odeh was widely regarded as a man of peace – he often spoke publicly about the need for dialogue between the P.L.O. and Israel – his death and the manner of it were largely ignored by the American media.)

As the pressures to cancel the London meeting mounted, the word was that Mrs Thatcher and her Foreign Secretary intended to resist them. For the first time in many years a British government was not going to be intimidated by Israel and the Jewish lobby.

Or so it was said in the corridors of power. But it was what Mrs
Thatcher and Howe did next which caused the London meeting
to be cancelled and gave them the pretext, or the excuse, to blame
the P.L.O.

Mrs Thatcher and Howe drafted, or had drafted for them by
Foreign Office officials, a statement which Khoury and Milhem
would be required to endorse in London. On the issue of the
P.L.O.'s readiness to make peace with Israel the British statement
went beyond what the P.L.O. had agreed to say. But on the matter
of violence in general the British statement went far beyond what
the P.L.O. ever could say so long as Israel remained in occupation
of the land taken by force in 1967. More on this in a moment.

The British statement was transmitted to Hussein's advisers in
Amman. Part of the text was handed by the Jordanians to Khoury
as he was leaving the airport. He did not have the time to consult
with Arafat or any of his senior colleagues. A more experienced
political animal than the Bishop would probably have said to himself, 'This smells. I am not going anywhere until I have consulted.'
Milhem was in America and did not even see the British statement
until he arrived in London. Meanwhile the government in Jordan
gave the British Foreign Office 'unambiguous assurances' that
Khoury and Milhem would endorse the statement. One P.L.O.
view is that the Jordanians were hoping that Khoury and Milhem
could have their arms twisted in London and that all would be
well. Another P.L.O. view – the popular one – is that those around
Hussein who had all along opposed his agreement with Arafat
took the opportunity to ensure that the P.L.O. would be blamed
when the talks did not take place.

As soon as Milhem saw the British statement he knew he could
not endorse it as it was. The biggest problem was the wording
which committed him and Khoury, and therefore the P.L.O., to
'opposition to all forms of terrorism *and violence from whatever
sources'.* (My italics.) Implicitly the British government was demanding that the P.L.O. renounce even the right of the Palestinians
to resist an illegal Israeli occupation by armed struggle. As anyone
interested by international affairs ought to know, the right of all
people under occupation to resist by armed struggle is enshrined
in the U.N. Charter on Human Rights.

Milhem briefed Arafat by telephone. The Chairman then in-

structed Khalad Hassan to discuss possible amendments to the
British statement with Milhem. On the subject of violence the
P.L.O. was ready to offer a form of words which renounced terrorism but which drew a distinction between terrorism and 'armed
struggle', as recognized by the U.N., to be the legitimate right of
the Palestinians. The British government was not interested. It told
the Jordanians to tell the Palestinians they should accept or reject the British statement as it was.

In the end, and because of the political pressures generated by
the hijacking of the *Achille Lauro* and the murder of Leon Klinghoffer, Mrs Thatcher lacked the courage to finish what she started.
Instead of breathing new life into the peace process she gave it a
kiss of death.

For the diplomats, officials and lobby groups who were directing
Israel's anti-P.L.O. offensive in America and Western Europe the
hijacking of the *Achille Lauro* was a propaganda prize of the highest order. As Thomas L. Friedman reported in the *New York Times*
of 17 October, Israeli officials felt they had Arafat 'on the ropes'
and would soon be able to deliver a decisive blow to his prestige
and credibility – one that would 'knock him out of the peace process once and for all'.

The strong implication at the time was that Israel's famed intelligence services possessed hard evidence to support Israel's
charge that Arafat himself had approved the plan to seize the Italian
cruise liner. But it soon became clear that Israel's case against
Arafat was based on nothing more than guilt by association. At a
press conference General Ehud Barak, Director of Israeli Military
Intelligence, was asked if he did, in fact, have any evidence linking
Arafat to the hijacking of the *Achille Lauro*. His reply was no. But
he went on to say that Mr Abass's office in Tunis was 'little more
than a hundred yards from Mr Arafat's headquarters'. Barak then
said that given what Israel knew about the workings of the P.L.O.
and 'Mr Arafat's close working relationship to Mr Abbas', there
was 'a very strong probability that Arafat knew of the plan to seize
the *Achille Lauro*'.

The one valid question provoked by Barak's allegation in particular and by Israel's assertions in general can be posed in the
following way. Given that Abu Abbas *was* a member of the
P.L.O.'s Executive Committee – by virtue of the fact that he was

the leader of a small pro-Arafat faction of the P.L.O., actually a wing of the Palestine Liberation Front (P.L.F.) – why did the Chairman not have knowledge of Abbas's plan to smuggle four guerrillas aboard the *Achille Lauro* for the purpose of launching an attack when the vessel reached Israel? (The assumption behind the question is, obviously, that all military operation by groups which make up the P.L.O. are approved by the collective leadership.) I put this question to Arafat in the most blunt and direct way possible. His straightforward reply was that member organizations did not have to discuss or clear plans for military operations with the collective leadership *provided* the P.L.O.'s rules of engagement were followed. The main rule was that military operations had to be confined to legitimate targets in Israel and the territories occupied by Israel in 1967.

My own conclusion is that Arafat's conspiracy theory about the hijacking of the *Achille Lauro* is supported by the facts. I am in no doubt that Abu Abbas was what Arafat described him to be – a 'fool' who was used by former Palestinian associates who were, in turn, under the direction and control of Syrian intelligence officers. The objective of the operation was to discredit Arafat and the P.L.O. I also have to say that I would not be surprised if the Mossad, through its penetration of Syria's intelligence services, was involved. While I was in America, at the time of the hijack, a very senior senator, one of many who support Israel without question in order to guarantee the funds for their re-election, told me he was as sure as he could be, from excellent sources of his own, that Israeli agents had played a role in what he described as the '*Achille Lauro* sting'. The same opinion was held by more than a few diplomats and other government officials in capitals of the western world, but none dared to say in public what they believed in private because Israel's representatives and Zionist lobby groups were everywhere on the offensive.

Arafat and his leadership colleagues were realistic in their assessment of the damage done to their credibility by the *Achille Lauro* affair. They saw it for what it was – a political and public relations disaster for the P.L.O. The hard evidence the Chairman needed to prove that the P.L.O. had been set up was snatched from him when the Egyptian plane carrying Abu Abbas and the four terrorists to Tunis was hijacked by the Americans. (It later transpired that Colonel Oliver North was Reagan's 'Rambo' for that operation.)

In the wake of the *Achille Lauro* affair Arafat had two main and related concerns. The first was that Israel and the Reagan administration would capitalize on the P.L.O.'s loss of credibility by seeking to advance the peace process at the P.L.O.'s expense. In other words he did not want the anti-P.L.O. sentiments generated by the *Achille Lauro* affair to give the Reagan administration the excuse, and perhaps the incentive, to abandon completely the idea of involving the P.L.O. in the peace process as a partner with Jordan.

Arafat's second main concern was that an Israeli government led by Shimon Peres might go throuh the motions of offering enough in the way of territorial compromise to tempt Hussein to enter into negotiations without the P.L.O., assuming that he, the King, could arrange the wider Arab cover such a move would need.

In the days and weeks following the hijacking of the *Achille Lauro* there were a number of important political developments which suggested to Arafat that Israel, America and some of his so-called Arab friends were indeed conspiring to exclude the P.L.O. from the peace process. There were also early warning signs that it would be only a matter of time before a desperate Hussein decided to drop the P.L.O. as a negotiating partner in order to protect his own relationship with the U.S.

The first significant political development was the sabotaging by the Reagan administration of an effort to invite Arafat to celebrations marking the fortieth anniversary of the U.N. General Assembly in New York. More than eighty heads of state and government and a number of special envoys had accepted invitations to the ten-day commemoration set for the middle of October. Arafat was not originally invited but a resolution to do so was drafted after Israel's attack on his Tunis headquarters. The sponsors of the draft resolution were seven nations from the non-aligned group: India, Iraq, Kuwait, Nigeria, Senegal, and North Yemen. When the Security Council unanimously condemned Israel's attack with only an abstention on the part of the U.S., a number of U.N. representatives thought the moment was right to take advantage of the sympathy for Arafat. Thus came the idea to invite him to the anniversary celebrations. That was the public story, but there was much more to it.

As I can now reveal, Arafat wanted to attend the General Assembly celebrations in order to make his statement confirming that the P.L.O. was ready to negotiate a peaceful settlement of the Palestinian problem, within the framework of an international conference and 'on the basis of the pertinent U.N. resolutions including Security Council resolutions 242 and 338'. In other words Arafat was going to say, in the most appropriate place, what he would have said earlier if Shultz had not allowed Israel and the Zionist lobby in America to sabotage the Murphy meeting with the joint Jordanian-Palestinian delegation. Arafat knew, of course, that such a statement in such a place at such a time would make headlines around the world. There would be no way the media could ignore, play down or distort his message. Arafat's hope was that such a speech would force the Reagan administration to be serious about involving the P.L.O. in the peace process. (Though some readers may find it difficult to believe, it is a fact that in international politics *where* something is said is often as important as *what* is said.)

The resolution to invite Arafat was drafted *before* the *Achille Lauro* was hijacked, but it was not ready for presentation to the General Assembly until *after* the event. Even so, and as Elaine Sciolino reported on the front page of the *New York Times* on 15 October, the resolution 'would most likely have passed easily' if it had been put to the vote. But there was no vote. The resolution to invite Arafat was withdrawn. Why? American diplomats told other delegates that President Reagan might cancel his participation in the session if Arafat were to attend. What really happened was neatly summed up by an Arab diplomat in a comment to the *New York Times*. He said, 'The fact is the U.N. needs the United States, and we need the U.N.' As it had done in 1947 to secure the passing of the resolution to partition Palestine, the U.S. had resorted to pressure amounting to blackmail to get its way.

The stage was now set for Israel's Prime Minister to make his entry. On his way to New York Peres called for the P.L.O. to be excluded from the peace process. In his speech to the General Assembly he declared himself to be ready for direct negotiations with Jordan. To tempt Hussein to respond positively Peres said he was prepared to consider some form of international framework for the talks. (Previously Peres and the hardliners in Israel had been as one in rejecting the King's call for an international framework. At the time of his U.N. speech Peres was bargaining with the Soviets to establish the price they would pay for a decision by Israel to set aside its objections to the Soviet Union's participation. He was asking Moscow to re-establish diplomatic relations with Israel and to allow 20,000 Jews to leave the Soviet Union for Israel.) Peres also hinted that he contemplated giving back some of the land occupied by Israel in 1967.

In Israel the Peres speech provoked a storm of protest by Likud members of the coalition government and other hardliners. The hint that Peres would be prepared to trade some land for peace inspired the Finance Minister, Yitzhak Modai, to announce that he would allocate considerably more government funds to the building of new (illegal) Jewish settlements on the West Bank.

At the time of his U.N. speech Peres had only one more year to serve as Prime Minister before handing over to Shamir under the terms of the coalition agreement. The U.N. speech fuelled speculation that Peres would pull out of the coalition and fight an election on the issue of land for peace – if Hussein would respond positively.

After the Peres speech the King came under immense pressure from his American, British, and other western friends. The logic of their argument was not new, but it was given new force by the fact that Peres was running out of time and would soon be replaced by a man opposed to compromise of any kind. The Arab choice, Hussein's friends said, was either to negotiate with Israel while Peres was Prime Minister in order to get back some land with the hope, perhaps, of getting more over a period of years; or to accept that Israel's illegal occupation of the West Bank, the Gaza strip, and the Golan Heights was an unchangeable fact of history. As ever those who were pushing this logic – the political establishments of the West who had no stomach for a showdown with Israel and its lobby groups – were not concerned with what was fair and just for all parties, including and especially the Palestinians. In the politics of expediency there was as ever no place for what was legally or morally right. It no longer seemed to matter that

U.N. resolution 242 required Israel to withdraw from all of the land it conquered in 1967, subject only to agreed border modifications. Since Peres could not deliver the whole of the 242 loaf, the Arabs should be sensible and settle for a few slices.

As Arafat acknowledges, there is no evidence to suggest that Hussein took his decision to break with the P.L.O. as early as October 1985. (As we shall see later the break came in February the following year.) What Hussein did do in response to the overtures from Peres, including those made during a secret meeting between the two leaders in Paris, was to orchestrate a new game of musical chairs on the Arab side. The music started when the King made a friend of his old enemy, President Assad.

The clear implication of Jordan's accommodation with Syria was that Hussein was seeking to create an Arab consensus for negotiations with Israel which would obtain the best terms he could extract from Peres, terms which by definition would not be acceptable to the P.L.O. and the vast majority of the Palestinian people it represented. Hussein knew the Americans had informed Assad that a Peres government would be prepared to trade the Golan Heights for a signed peace with Syria. The other implication of the King's accommodation with Assad – Arafat's number one enemy – was that a day could come when Hussein and Assad together would be willing to move against the P.L.O. and those Palestinians who continued to support it – if Peres (and the Americans) made it worth their while to do so.

In due course Hussein discovered that Assad was prepared in principle to endorse the idea of negotiations with Israel, provided they were conducted under an international umbrella. But one big problem had to be solved before there could be any official or formal joint strategy for negotiations. In the same way that King Hussein needed Syrian cover for a deal with Israel, Assad needed his own back protected from Iraq's President Saddam Hussein. Assad's fear was that Saddam would denounce him as a traitor and turn on Syria – if and when he was free from his war with Iran. (King Hussein was backing Iraq in the war. Assad was supporting Iran.) With the tacit approval of the Arab states which matter most, and which were naturally anxious for an end to the Iran-Iraq war, King Hussein set about the task of trying to arrange the cover Assad needed.

The P.L.O.'s first positive move after the cancellation of the London talks and the *Achille Lauro* affair was in the form of a statement denouncing and renouncing 'all forms of terrorism'. Made by Arafat himself in Cairo on 10 November, this statement became known as the Cairo Declaration. Arafat said that violators of it would be severely punished. To reduce the scope for other parties to make propaganda at the P.L.O.'s expense by deliberately misrepresenting its position on violence, the Cairo Declaration drew a clear distinction between terrorism and legitimate armed struggle as guaranteed by the U.N. Charter to be the right of all peoples under occupation. So the Cairo Declaration made clear that it was terrorism which was being renounced. The struggle against Israeli occupation would be continued by all legitimate means in the absence of negotiations.

Israel's official reaction to the Cairo Declaration was one of scorn and abuse expressed by Shamir's Foreign Ministry. Its spokesman said, 'What Arafat is saying is that he won't kill Jews in Europe but that everybody in Israel is a target now.' In a front page headline the popular newspaper, *Yediot Aharonot*, said, 'Only a simpleton would believe Arafat.' To this simpleton and other seasoned observers these and other peevish responses betrayed a fear on the part of some Israelis that Arafat's statement would result in the P.L.O. being taken seriously again by the U.S. as a party to negotiations. Some Israeli hardliners and their lobby friends in America were worried that Peres would go to the negotiating table if secret talks then in progress produced a formula for U.S. acceptance of the P.L.O. as a party to negotiations.

On the West Bank a group of the most bigoted Jewish settlers called for preparations for a civil war that would be launched if the Peres government did try to hand back any of the land occupied by Israel in 1967. The call was made by a magazine which was the mouthpiece for the inhabitants of the settlement of Ariel. It said: 'Let everyone prepare himself mentally to stand up in Judea, Samaria and Gaza and raise his hand – and his weapon – against his brother.' An article in the same magazine signed with the pseudonym 'M. Ben Yisrael' (Son of Israel) went much further. It warned: 'At this hour of national emergency most of the means justify the ends. . . We may witness widespread underground activity, a rebellion in the army, subversion in the security services, an armed uprising in Judea, Samaria and Gaza and finally one Jew fighting another.' (The tragedy was, and is, that a Jewish civil war would not have been a prospect if successive American presidents had prohibited the building of illegal Jewish settlements in the Arab territories conquered by Israel in 1967.)

The responsibility for co-ordinating the efforts to advance the peace process fell to the U.S. Assistant Secretary of State, Richard Murphy. He was trying to narrow the gap between what Peres could deliver and what Hussein could accept. But Murphy also went on the record to say he accepted that the P.L.O.'s Cairo Declaration had been made in 'good faith' and was a positive development. Though it was not widely reported, the Murphy statement helped to convince some observers, including me at the time, that Murphy himself *was* still serious about trying to involve the P.L.O. in the peace process. (The essential difference between Murphy and all other senior members of the Reagan administration seemed to be that he was tired of pretending that there was an alternative to the P.L.O. as the representative of the Palestinian people.)

Peres's speech to the U.N., Hussein's expressions of goodwill to Peres, Arafat's Cairo Declaration and Murphy's shuttle diplomacy created an impression of progress. There was even a degree of optimism that the end of 1985 or the beginning of 1986 would see a breakthrough. The Reagan administration was reported to be willing in principle to invite all parties, including the P.L.O., to an international peace conference. At the time Arafat was receiving conflicting advice. Some who claimed to know what was happening behind the scenes told him the Reagan administration was serious about peace on terms the P.L.O. could accept. Others told the Chairman the Americans, certain Americans, were setting a trap for him.

In January, after a storm of diplomatic activity, the Reagan administration confirmed to Hussein that it was ready to convene an international conference to which the P.L.O. would be invited if it was prepared, in advance, to accept U.N. resolutions 242 and 338. The obvious implication was that the P.L.O. was being asked to play its only negotiating card – recognition of Israel inside more or less its 1967 borders – in exchange for U.S. recognition of the P.L.O. Since Arafat and his leadership colleagues had agreed to the principle of such an exchange in the early summer of 1985 in order to get the Murphy mission of that year off the ground, there seemed to be no reason why Arafat could not now make his promised statement. (Readers will recall that in May 1985 Hussein agreed, or said he had agreed, a three-stage plan with the Reagan administration to create the conditions that would enable the U.S. to recognise the P.L.O. After Murphy had met a joint Jordanian-Palestinian delegation, Arafat was to make his recognition statement on the firm understanding that Murphy would then meet him to signal U.S. recognition of the P.L.O. Readers will also recall that Arafat was not put to the test on that occasion because Secretary of State Shultz allowed Israel's hardliners and their lobby friends in America to sabotage the plan. Murphy was not allowed to meet with the joint Jordanian-Palestinian delegation.)

At the beginning of the new year, 1986, there was reason to be optimistic about the prospects for peace . . . assuming the American offer was what it seemed to be. Arafat was now to be put to the test. Would he, could he, deliver?

The P.L.O.'s first response to the American offer was in the form of three proposed statements, any one of which Arafat was prepared to make in the P.L.O.'s name. The texts of the proposed statements were presented to Hussein and his advisers. As we shall see in a moment, the text of the second of the three proposed statements was by far the most explicit. On the subject of the P.L.O.'s readiness for negotiations with Israel it gave the Americans more than they were demanding, and it went further still than Hussein had in committing the P.L.O. when he briefed the Reagan administration on the significance of the Jordan-P.L.O. accord in May 1985. It was truly what Arafat later described to me as his 'maximum possible statement' in advance of negotiations.

On 19 February, to the astonishment of those of Arafat's senior colleagues who had negotiated the Jordan-P.L.O. accord with Hussein, the King announced that he was dropping the P.L.O. as a partner in the peace process. In a speech lasting more than three hours he claimed that the P.L.O. had broken its word by refusing to accept 242 as the price of an invitation to an international conference. But Hussein's long speech was much more than a repudiation of the P.L.O. He strongly implied that Arafat and his leadership colleagues were unworthy of the Palestinian people, and he made a thinly-veiled call for the Palestinians on the occupied West Bank to find themselves a new leader. The obvious implication was that they should look to His Majesty for that leadership. (If they responded, Hussein was clearly intending to negotiate with Peres.)

As Hussein told it, the story of the breakdown was not without an element of truth. Arafat *did* change his position to the extent that he insisted on the Americans making a statement of their own when he made his. But this Arafat demand had a context which the King (and the media) did not give. The record of what really happens speaks for itself.

The following is the text of the offer made in writing to Hussein by the Reagan administration in January:

When it is clearly on the public record that the P.L.O. has accepted resolutions 242 and 338, is prepared to negotiate with Israel, and has renounced terrorism, the U.S. accepts that an invitation will be issued to the P.L.O. to attend an international conference.

The following is the text of the statement (the second of the three) that Arafat was prepared to make in response to the American offer:

On the basis of the Jordanian-P.L.O. accord of 11 February 1985, and in view of our genuine desire for peace, we are ready to negotiate within the context of an international conference with the participation of the permanent members of the Security Council, with the participation of all concerned Arab parties and *the Israeli government* (my italics), a peaceful settlement of the Palestinian problem on the basis of the pertinent United Nations resolutions, including Security Council resolutions 242 and 338. The P.L.O. declares its rejection and denunciation of terrorism which has been assured by the Cairo Declaration of November 1985.

It was after Hussein had seen and approved the text above that Arafat added his condition. The Chairman would not make the P.L.O. statement until the King had obtained from the U.S. a written assurance that it would make a statement of its own supporting the Palestinian right to self-determination. The U.S. would then be required to make its declaration simultaneously with the P.L.O.'s statement. The text of the P.L.O.'s statement, plus its demand for an American statement, was handed by one of Arafat's colleagues to a very senior State Department official in Amman. The American's first reaction was 'Who the f★★★★★★ hell does the P.L.O. think it is – a superpower?'

Arafat's decision to add a condition was prompted by the P.L.O.'s discovery that the American offer was not what it had seemed and was assumed to be. The trouble started when Arafat, in response to questions from his colleagues, asked Hussein to confirm that an American invitation to the P.L.O. to attend an international conference would amount to U.S. recognition of the P.L.O. The answer from the Americans was no. Understandably this changed much so far as the P.L.O. was concerned. Among themselves Arafat and his senior leadership colleagues then asked a number of valid questions. What, for example, would be the situation if the P.L.O. made its statement and the international conference either did not take place, because Israel refused to attend, or if the conference failed, because Israel was not prepared to give enough to satisfy the minimum demands of the Palestinians in particular and the Arabs in general? The answer was all too clear. The P.L.O. would have played its only negotiating card – recognition of Israel – for nothing in return. The P.L.O. leadership would then be finished, discredited in the eyes of most Palestinians and condemned as traitors by many.

Against the background of the whole history of the conflict it is surely not surprising that Arafat and his leadership colleagues began to feel they were being drawn into a trap. Underlining their fears, and undermining their confidence, was the knowledge that some of the Reagan administration were still committed to a policy of cancelling the P.L.O. as a factor in the Middle East peace equation. From very well informed sources the P.L.O. had learnt, for example, of a comment made by Admiral John Poindexter soon after he succeeded MacFarlane as President Reagan's National Security Adviser in November 1985. (Before the end of 1986 Poindexter had resigned – the first casualty of the 'Irangate' or 'Contragate' affair.) When asked about his strategy for the Middle East Poindexter was alleged to have said in private that his aim would be 'to divide and divide the P.L.O.', to reduce it to a level of impotence which would allow Hussein to negotiate without it.

In Poindexter's reported view such a strategy had a good chance of working because of what he called 'the new Russian factor'. This was apparently a reference to the fact that in the middle of 1985 the Soviets had informed the Americans that they were no longer interested in keeping the Middle East pot boiling because the situation in the region had become too dangerous. On the strength of this message from Moscow – which suggests that Mr Gorbachev is very, very serious about reaching a global accommodation with the U.S. – some in Reagan's National Security Council had concluded that they were now free to cut the P.L.O. down to size by any means. It no longer mattered if the radicals took over because Moscow would not give them aid or comfort. If the P.L.O. wanted to stay in business it would be on America's terms, and there was nothing Arafat or any Palestinian leader could do about that.

The real problem of the moment on the P.L.O. side was that Arafat could no longer be certain about what American policy was and who was making it. (As the world was subsequently to learn from the 'Irangate' or 'Contragate' scandal, the Reagan White House was a place of plots and intrigues with vital foreign policy decisions being taken behind the Secretary of State's back.) So in the circumstances as they were in February 1986, Arafat decided to take out an insurance policy. That explains his demand for an American statement in support of the Palestinian right to self-determination. He was, in effect, requiring the Reagan administration to prove that it was serious before he played his only negotiating card.

It has to be said that Arafat's demand for an American statement in no way reduced the significance of what he was prepared to say in his own statement. This most important point not lost on Murphy. He tried to persuade Shultz that the time had come for the U.S. to indicate that it did support the Palestinian right to self-determination in order to trigger the Arafat statement which did meet the U.S. conditions, and which would open the door to negotiations . . . provided the Reagan administration would speak with one voice and was prepared to stand up to Israel's hardliners and their lobby friends in America. The most Shultz was prepared to offer was an American statement supporting the 'legitimate rights' of the Palestinians. Murphy then sent a message to Hussein

saying there was no more he could do and that it was now up to
the P.L.O. to accept or reject America's terms.

That was the position when Arafat and his team sat down with
Hussein and his advisers for what was to be their last meeting.
From the P.L.O. side there was an explanation of why the proposed
American statement as not quite enough to solve the outstanding
problem. The Camp David accords had paid lip-service to the
'legitimate rights' of the Palestinians, but Israel's Prime Minister
of the day, Begin, and his successors, had been allowed by the U.S.
to strip the phrase of all meaning. Who, the P.L.O. asked, could
guarantee that Peres or any future Israeli (or Arab) leader would
not do the same? If the U.S. was serious, it could improve its
proposed statement by giving some definition to the phrase 'legitimate rights'. Arafat, the pragmatist, was still seeking to avoid
a breakdown. He had himself accepted that the Americans were
not going to let the term 'self-determination' pass their lips. What
he was now prepared to settle for as a compromise was a form of
words from the Americans which would indicate that legitimate
rights included 'political rights'.

But it was too late. The King's three-hour speech repudiating
the P.L.O. was already written and waiting to be delivered. It was
in fact written, translated into English and French and printed for
distribution in both languages and Arabic *before* the P.L.O. and
the Jordanians sat down for their last meeting, i.e. when there was
still, in theory, the possibility of an agreement!

One clue to what really may have happened in the days before
the breakdown in Amman is provided by a dramatic exchange
which took place during the last round of discussions. Abu Iyad
banged the table and said, 'If we accept what is on offer from the
Americans, we will be finished!' Abu Odeh, one of Hussein's Ministers and senior advisers snapped back, 'If you don't accept, *we*
will be finished!' The implication of Abu Odeh's unscripted remark, made in the King's presence, is that the Jordanians were
under great pressure from the Americans – pressure to negotiate
with Israel while Peres was still Prime Minister, and pressure to
blame the P.L.O. for the breakdown if Arafat refused to accept
242 without some form of U.S. recognition of Palestinian political
rights.

While reserving their judgement about Murphy and his role, Arafat and his senior leadership colleagues are convinced that other and more influential members of the Reagan administration did set a trap for the P.L.O. According to this conspiracy theory, the hope of those who set the trap was that the P.L.O. would play its only negotiating card in order to stay in the political game in partnership with Jordan, and would then be discredited in the eyes of its supporters when it was seen to have played the card for nothing of substance in return . . . leaving the way clear, or clearer, for Hussein to negotiate without the P.L.O.

If Arafat and his colleagues are wrong, it would have to be said that it was they who missed an historic opportunity to advance the peace process and guarantee themselves a share of the political action. But this argument assumes, does it not, that Peres was willing and courageous enough to fight an election, and take the risk of provoking a civil war, in order to get a mandate to negotiate with Jordan and the P.L.O., *and* to be able to give back enough land to satisfy them both. This argument also assumes that the Reagan administration was ready to back Peres by itself standing up to Israel's hardliners and their powerful lobby in America. But if this was the case, why did the Reagan administration make life difficult to impossible for Arafat at a critical moment by saying that an American invitation to the P.L.O. would not amount to U.S. recognition of the P.L.O.? But that is hardly the point. It is that the statement Arafat was prepared to make *did* give the Americans all and more than they were demanding, and had demanded for many years. As we have seen from the text of the statement, the P.L.O. committed itself to negotiations with parties 'including the Israeli government'. Not even Hussein had gone that far in a public statement. On balance my conclusion is that not enough parts of the Reagan administration were serious about advancing the peace process on terms the P.L.O. could accept and live with. I think that some of the key figures in an incompetent Reagan administration were playing games to divide and weaken the P.L.O. There probably never was a peace process worthy of the name.

As the Palestinians saw it, the strategy of Hussein and Assad after the breakdown in Amman was to push the P.L.O. to the fringes of Arab politics – to make it irrelevant and to give Jordan and Syria the freedom to make peace on the best terms they could get from Israel and the U.S.

Hussein's role was to create an alternative leadership to the P.L.O. – if not himself, Palestinian stooges who would betray their cause for money or power or both. To his end the King's intelligence chiefs tried to promote an anti-Arafat rebellion. When it failed – most Palestinians were amused rather than angered by this demonstration of Jordanian foolishness – Hussein kicked Arafat's people out of Jordan and closed down their offices. Among those expelled were Abu Jihad and senior Fatah officers with Jordanian passports and who were married to Jordanian nationals.

Assad's main role in the conspiracy was to put an end to the P.L.O.'s military presence in the Lebanon. That explains why the Shi'ite Amal group, Syria's closest ally in the Lebanon, launched its attacks against Palestinian refugee camps around Beirut and to the south. As a former Syrian intelligence officer said to me, Assad's thinking was not hard to follow. If the P.L.O.'s fighters could be driven from the Lebanon and confined to bases in faraway Yemen and possibly Algiers, Arafat would have no way of influencing the situation on the ground. In that event, and denied a political role, the P.L.O. would be out of business. At best Arafat would be reduced to the status of a political beggar.

# 21

# Uprising in the Occupied Territories

Denied a role in the politics of peacemaking, and unable to influence events by military means, the P.L.O. was in serious trouble. Again.

It was, in fact, another of those moments in the history of the conflict when Israel – if it had been willing to offer Jordan and Syria land for peace in accordance with the letter and the spirit of U.N. Resolution 242 – might have been able to neutralize the P.L.O. by political means. Despite the fact that all Palestinians out of nappies knew it was Hussein and not Arafat who had broken the Jordan-P.L.O. Accord, a majority of those in the occupied territories would have learned to live with their anger and would have given the King the opportunity to deliver – if he had been able to say to them, 'Follow my lead because I've got guarantees that I can negotiate a peace which will end Israel's occupation.'

To prevent the P.L.O. being cancelled as a factor in the Middle East peace equation Arafat knew he had to play the 'internal (occupied territories) card'. When the uprising in Gaza and the West Bank started on 9 December 1987, the world was led to believe that the P.L.O. was taken as much by surprise as Israel. Nothing could have been further from the truth. The explosion of anger and despair which became an uprising or popular revolt against twenty years of Israeli occupation was spontaneous, but it could not have been sustained for days, then weeks, then months without advance and detailed planning. I can now reveal that the man who planned and co-ordinated the effort which guaranteed the uprising a long life was not Abu Jihad – who was subsequently assassinated by Israeli agents – but the Chairman of the P.L.O., Yasser Arafat himself. I can also reveal that one of the secrets of Arafat's success in sustaining the revolt was his ability to talk directly to Palestinian demonstrators by satellite!

According to Hani Hassan, the Chairman started to think seriously about the need to play the internal card as far back as September 1982 – while the P.L.O. was being evacuated from Beirut after Israel's invasion of the Lebanon. (For its truly heroic stand against Israel on that occasion the P.L.O. did win – for itself and for what it represents – a lot of new respect around the world; but from all other points of view what happened in that long, hot summer of 1982 was a disaster for Arafat and his organization. The P.L.O. lost its last remaining base in the front-line Arab states. As a consequence Arafat lost his ability to influence events on the ground. At the time there were many Palestinians who feared that the P.L.O. was being isolated and pushed to the fringes of Arab politics. And that, in turn, was why most Palestinians were prepared to support Arafat's attempt to keep the P.L.O. in the political game by accommodating Hussein.)

The countdown to the uprising in the occupied territories actually started in 1983 when Arafat ordered a 'General Exercise' in and around Nablus. 'General Exercise' was the Chairman's code for a confrontation between P.L.O. supporters and the Israeli army. It was Arafat's way of testing the feelings and the mood of Palestinians throughout the occupied territories. According to Hani the response was precisely what Arafat had thought it would be. The confrontation in Nablus took place, but there was no support for the idea that it should be sustained and extended. A popular uprising was still the stuff of dreams.

Thinking back over my conversations with Arafat at the time, I can remember how depressed he was. I recall, for example, the moment when I told him I was thinking about writing a novel based on the idea of a successful uprising in the occupied territories. He gave me one of his sad, knowing smiles and said, 'It's not so easy.' He was still haunted by his failure to provoke a popular uprising on the West Bank and in Gaza in the weeks and months following Israel's capture of those territories during the 1967 war. Twenty years on he was also facing the fact that Israeli and Jordanian counter-intelligence services would stop at nothing to prevent an uprising being organized. But there was another, more profound reason for Arafat's caution and his refusal to indulge in wishful thinking. He accepted that leadership outside the occupied territories did not have the right to demand sacrifices including death from its supporters inside. He went on to say that it was for the people under occupation to decide for themselves when they had had enough.

Arafat did not however let the matter rest there. He instructed some of his most senior and trusted leadership colleagues – among them Hani Hassan – to make the most thorough and detailed study of why the 'General Exercise' in Nablus had failed to inspire even a token demonstration of widespread popular support.

'We came to a very dramatic conclusion,' Hani told me. 'We discovered that the silent majority of our people in the occupied territories had given their hearts if not their minds to the Islamic fundamentalists.'

What explained this enormous shift of popular opinion, a change of heart which suggested, among other things, that Arafat's moderate P.L.O. was in danger of becoming an irrelevance? In a word – despair. There was first of all, and obviously, the despair born of nearly twenty years of occupation and often brutal Israeli repression. But in the wake of Israel's invasion of the Lebanon and its siege of Beirut in 1982 there were 'two new factors of despair'.

The first was the realization that Arafat's policy of politics and compromise was getting the Palestinians nowhere. Though Israel still choses to deny it, Arafat's P.L.O. is committed to recognizing the Jewish State inside its 1967 borders in exchange for a Palestinian state on the West Bank and in Gaza. Sharon's blitzkrieg in the Lebanon made every Palestinian realize that the more Arafat demonstrated he was ready for peace (and on terms which people in Israel and any rational government would accept with relief), the more determined Israel became to liquidate Palestinian nationalism by military means.

The second bitter lesson for a new generation of Palestinians was that they were on their own when the crunch came. The proof (if more was needed) was the way the Arab regimes sat on their backsides and watched as Sharon tried for weeks to finish the P.L.O. On the Palestinian side in particular, and in the Arab world in general, it was never much of a secret that some Arab regimes were hoping that Sharon would succeed.

Against that backdrop it was inevitable that more and more Palestinians in the occupied territories would begin to see Islamic fundamentalism as the only force capable of changing the status quo. What surprised and shocked P.L.O. leaders was the *number* of Palestinians who had moved or who were moving in the direction of the fundamentalists. Hani said: 'We discovered that not less than *sixty percent* of our young people in the occupied territories were thinking that Islamic fundamentalism had more to offer than the P.L.O.'

In the face of that reality what was Arafat to do?

One option, in theory, was to sit back and let the various fundamentalist groups make the running, with a view to later hijacking their bandwagon if it got rolling. But Arafat's nature would not let him even consider such an option. He cannot and never will play second fiddle to anybody. Also, the possible consequences of letting the fundamentalists make the running were too awful to contemplate. There was first of all the obvious danger that the P.L.O. would become an irrelevance for a majority of Palestinians in the occupied territories. But that was not the worst-case scenario. If there was a popular uprising which did cause change, and the Islamic fundamentalists could claim most of the credit, Arafat — even if the P.L.O. did retain some of its credibility — might not be able to deliver the compromise he struggled between 1974 and 1979 to sell to his people, and which he has defended ever since.

The conclusion was obvious. If the Chairman of the P.L.O. was to stay in control of events on his own side, he had to give a new lead. So it was that Yasser Arafat threw himself into the task of constructing bridges to every politically active group in the occupied territories, especially those that made up the Islamic fundamentalist current. Arafat's primary objective was not so much to inspire or provoke a popular uprising, but to have in place an all-embracing network capable of supporting and sustaining an explosion of frustration and despair when it happened. Arafat's slogan was 'Friday the mosque, Sunday the church.' For some years past Abu Jihad had been putting into place a new underground network of Fatah cells with special attention to youth groups.

The fact that Arafat did succeed in putting together such a broad coalition without Shin Bet, Israel's counter-intelligence service, getting even a faint smell of what was happening under its nose is a considerable tribute to his own organizing skills and the ability of others (Palestinians in general, Islamic fundamentalists in particular) to keep their secrets. In retrospect it seems reasonable to suppose that Arafat's success was the main reason for the subsequent dismissal of Shin Bet's chief.

During the early discussions about the formation of an alliance of common cause, it seemed that a tactical accommodation with the groups which made up the Islamic current would not be possible. The obstacle so far as the fundamentalists were concerned was the P.L.O.'s stated position on Afghanistan. The P.L.O. was committed, in public at least, to supporting the Soviets. This, of course, was a red rag to the bull of Islamic fundamentalism. To get around this obstacle the P.L.O. had some explaining to do, and behind closed doors it had no choice but to tell the truth. The P.L.O. got itself committed to supporting the Soviets because of a statement to that effect by Farouk Kaddumi, its official spokesman on foreign affairs. Kaddumi is the only seriously pro-Soviet figure in the P.L.O.'s mainstream leadership. His statement committing the P.L.O. to support for the Soviets did not reflect the view of most of his colleagues, but they could not afford to contradict him. When you do not have one of the superpowers as your friend and ally you cannot afford to go out of your way to make an enemy of the other. When this explanation was given, the fundamentalists were pragmatic enough to appreciate the P.L.O.'s dilemma and live with it.

While Arafat was constructing the framework for the broad coalition of groups and organizations which was to manage the uprising when (and if) it came, events beyond his control were raising the political temperature in the occupied territories to where an explosion of Palestinian frustration and despair would be inevitable. Hani said it was the impact of three separate developments that fixed the Palestinians' determination to revolt – no matter what the cost to themselves in further suffering and lives lost.

The *first*, in 1984, was Israel's decision to raise the taxes paid by the Palestinians in the occupied territories and, at the same time, to further reduce the amount of water they were allowed to draw from their wells. Hani said: 'This was all part of Israel's policy to make life so unbearable that many Palestinians would leave. On this particular occasion the Israelis were putting special pressure on the Palestinian upper classes.' To this extent, Hani added, the Israelis were hoping for a repeat of 1948, when up to 30,000 Palestinian notables fled with their possessions before the main fighting started.

I asked Hani if there could be a repeat of 1948 or something like it. His reply helped to explain much of what was happening in the occupied territories. 'The Israelis will never again succeed in forcing our people to leave. For perhaps the first time, *all* of our people in the occupied territories are truly understanding their situation and their options. Quite apart from the obvious reasons why they *must* hang on to their land at all costs, they know they are not wanted as refugees or citizens in other Arab countries. They know they would not be allowed to organize for their cause in other Arab countries. They know they will never have security except in their own homeland. They realized that they have no-where else to go. And it was this realization which gave birth to the new and popular determination to resist and reject Israel's occupation.'

From this moment on, every Israeli action to crush the spirit of the Palestinians in the occupied territories was totally counter-productive.

The *second* development was the failure of Arab leaders to give the Palestine question anything like its proper priority at the emer-gency summit in Amman in November 1987. In his report to *The Guardian* at the time, David Hirst described their lack of will as 'an eloquent yardstick of the low condition to which the Arabs have sunk'. The Palestinians themselves saw the summit as further proof that Arab leaders – out of a combination of impotence and subservience to the U.S. – were continuing to water-down their commitment to the Palestinian cause.

During the preparations for the summit a very senior P.L.O. official warned Hussein that there would be an uprising in the occupied territories if Arab leaders did not give a sign that they were seriously committed to liberating at least a small part of Palestine. Apparently the King laughed. Talk of an uprising was nonsense. It really was time, he said, for the P.L.O. 'to stop dream-ing.'

The *third* development, in early December 1987, was the failure of the Reagan-Gorbachev summit in Washington even to consider what could and should be done to advance the Middle East peace process. The P.L.O. was not surprised by the Reagan Administration's lack of interest or concern, but it had been led to believe that the Soviets intended to raise the subject. (Arafat himself had not expected much, if any political support from the Soviets. A few months previously a very senior Soviet official had told him that the Kremlin had a Jewish lobby problem of its own.)

Obviously, no outside power had the will to force Israel into being serious about exchanging land for peace. If there was to be change, the Palestinians in the occupied territories would have to force the issue themselves. The odds against them were alarmingly high, but for the first time in twenty years they were united and psychologically prepared for a confrontation with the Israeli army, whatever the cost. The messages from the mosques on Fridays and the churches on Sundays had been heard. Arafat and his senior leadership colleagues were asking themselves how many small incidents it would take to provoke the Israelis into an over-reaction that would help guarantee the uprising a long life.

The first planned provocation was the stabbing death of an Israeli – a policeman according to the P.L.O. – in Gaza City's Palestine Square. That was followed by the assassination of a Shin Bet agent. But it was an act of Israeli revenge that gave Arafat's network of organizers, the P.L.O.-United Leadership for the Uprising, the chance to prove itself. Four Palestinians were killed when their vehicle was deliberately rammed by an Israeli truck. The funeral became a demonstration. The Israeli army over-reacted. Two Palestinian demonstrators were shot dead (one for throwing a petrol bomb) and dozens were injured. The rest – the stones and in reply the brutal beatings, shootings and deportations – is television history.

The most pleasing feat for Arafat and Abu Jihad was having beaten Israel's counter-intelligence service at its own game. It was six long weeks before Shin Bet even started to recover some of the ground it lost in the occupied territories. The delay was due in part to the virtual disintegration of its own network of informers. Many informers simply withdrew their services out of fear. Some just disappeared.

It was inevitable that mass arrests and other, more routine counter-intelligence work would give Shin Bet some victories in the underground war being fought; but the uprising continued, partly because the activity on the Arab side was supported by the vast majority of the 1.5 million Palestinians in the occupied territories. And, for the reason Hani gave, the support came from all social classes. On television we never saw how the Palestinians were sharing everything – water, food, fuel and provisions of all kinds – to enable communities to carry on more or less as normal in the face of Israeli curfews and restrictions of all kinds, as well as strikes by Palestinian shopkeepers.

Then there was Arafat's secret weapon.

Shin Bet's counter-attack was based on a tried and trusted strategy – first the midnight knock and mass arrests, then curfews, cutting telephone links, jamming Palestinian radio stations and closing down Palestinian presses. They assumed the uprising would run out of steam when the organizers of the demonstrations could no longer communicate with each other and, more important, when those who were inspiring the resistance in other ways could not be heard or read. Such a strategy was however predictable; and Yasser Arafat had planned to be one big step ahead of Israel's counter-intelligence service.

From a British company (Racal-Tacticom in Reading) Arafat had purchased some space-age radio equipment – a transmitter and scores of mini-receivers – which enabled him to plug into the Arab communications satellite (ArabSat) and talk directly to Palestinian demonstrators on street corners where they were confronting the Israeli army!

About the impact of Arafat's spiritual presence on the front lines Hani spoke with great excitement. 'You can't imagine it,' he said. 'The confrontations were very tough. Even when they were not being killed or seriously wounded our people took a lot of punishment. So naturally there were times when their morale was low. And that's when Arafat lifted their spirits. Somebody would produce a receiver to link the demonstrators to the Chairman. The one who spoke with Arafat directly was overcome with emotion and enthusiasm. He would proudly tell the others, "I've just talked to Abu Amar. He says we must continue." '

When the Israelis realized the effect Arafat was having on the situation by remote control they moved quickly. The Jewish lobby in London made a fuss in Parliament and the media about a named British defence contractor having sold 'military radio equipment' to the P.L.O., a 'terrorist organization', through Arafat's office. The objective of that lobby exercise was, presumably, to prevent the sale of more receivers for distribution in the occupied territories.

On 16 April Arafat was shattered by the news that Israeli agents had assassinated Abu Jihad at his home in Tunis. For this act of state terrorism the Mossad and Israel's Directorate of Military Intelligence pooled their resources. (Two weeks previously Hani had expressed to me his fear that Prime Minister Shamir and Defence Minister Rabin would give their intelligence services the licence to kill top P.L.O. leaders.) In his first public statement about the murder of his deputy, Arafat said the U.S. was implicated.

According to the family and others who knew him best, Abu Jihad's last days were the happiest of his life. He saw the uprising as proof that a new generation of Palestinians was ready to continue the struggle. To some of his colleagues Abu Jihad said, 'My work is just about done. Soon it will be time for me to pass the torch to others.' He was also pleased that Palestinians inside and outside the occupied territories were at last speaking with one clear and loud voice about who should represent them at peace talks – the P.L.O. In his last days Abu Jihad's favourite story was one which illustrated how the uprising had united all classes in the occupied territories. 'In the old days,' Abu Jihad would say, 'some middle and upper class mothers would tell their sons not to make confrontations with the Israeli military. Now if they find their sons at home these same mothers are saying to their sons, "Why are you not outside throwing stones?"''

At about 11:30 p.m. on Friday, 15 April, Abu Jihad arrived at his home in Sidi Bou Said, a suburb (to the north-east) of Tunis. Home was a modest, whitewashed villa with bright blue shutters. Though it occupies an exposed corner position at a road junction, the property is enclosed by a wall about eight feet high. (It should also be noted that the villa is inside what many local people call the 'Forbidden Zone', so called because of its security status. The Presidential Palace and the American Ambassador's residence are almost within shouting distance of the villa where Abu Jihad lived.

When a year or so previously Abu Jihad had been looking for a family home, he was directed to this particular location. Tunisian officials told him there was no other place where his security could be guaranteed.)

On this night Abu Jihad planned to leave for Baghdad. So he asked Mustapha, his armed driver, to wait for him in the car. It was parked in the road by the gate, which is the only entrance to the villa.

Abu Jihad the family man had come home to say goodbye to baby Nidal and Hanan – the youngest of his five children – and to the wife he adored. It would have been an emotional parting. As many Palestinians learned from earlier editions of this book, Abu and Um Jihad (Khalil and Intissar Wazir) were the great love story of the Palestinian regeneration. They were never really happy when they were apart. When in 1983 it had seemed that Arafat and Abu Jihad were going to die fighting in Tripoli, Um Jihad made a dangerous journey from Amman to northern Lebanon to be at her husband's side. Unable to contemplate life without her childhood sweetheart she was determined to die with him. Two years later their life changed dramatically when Um Jihad became pregnant. It happened, Abu Jihad later told me with good humour and a broad grin, when they were 'celebrating' the P.L.O.'s victory over Syria's President Assad. (When Arafat, against most expectations, succeeded in convening the P.N.C. in Amman to prevent Assad taking over the P.L.O.) When baby Nidal came into the world – he was named after their first-born who died so tragically while Abu Jihad was fighting to save Arafat's life in 1966 – Um Jihad decided that being a mother had once more to become the top priority in her life. As a consequence she was no longer so free to travel with Abu Jihad. And that made the moments of their partings even more tender.

By one o'clock Um Jihad was drifting to sleep in her husband's arms. Going round in her mind were the words of Abu Jihad's last love letter. It was in the form of a poem and it was, she later told me, the most beautiful of all of his many letters and poems. It was written as ever to inspire their love through the days they would be apart. She would read it every day until he returned. Baby Nidal had long been asleep in a cot close to the bed and not more than two inches from a window across which was drawn a ceiling-to-floor curtain. It is one of two such windows in the main bedroom. At ten minutes past one Abu Jihad got up to answer the telephone. He took the call at his desk in the bedroom. It was a call from a colleague advising him that his flight was delayed.

In what were to be the last ten minutes of his life, Abu Jihad decided to watch a video cassette of the latest confrontations in the occupied territories. While the video was running he returned to his desk. The sound was turned down low. Provoked and perhaps inspired by the images on the video monitor Abu Jihad then took up his pen to write to the local leadership of the uprising in the occupied territories. . . Outside the Israelis were closing in for the kill.

According to the Tunisian investigators' reconstruction of events, the advance party of three Mossad agents, two men and a woman, had arrived in Tunis on Tuesday, 12 April. Posing as tourists, they travelled on Lebanese passports and apparently spoke perfect Lebanese Arabic. They had, it seems, three main tasks: to provide the transport for the Israeli commandos who were to land on the beach not far from Abu Jihad's villa – for this they hired two Volkswagen mini-buses and a Peugeot estate car; to find the safest and fastest route to the villa; and to keep it, the villa, under surveillance. The Mossad did a brilliant research job on the route. The one its agents chose was for the most part secondary tracks – sand and dirt in some places – which cut across the well-lit main roads, where the Israelis could have run into problems. (P.L.O. security officials are convinced that there were more than three Mossad agents in place in Tunis and that the details of the plan to kill Abu Jihad were worked out over a period of several weeks. According to this view the three Mossad agents who arrived on Tuesday had only one main job – to provide the transport and to act as chauffeurs for the hit team.)

The hit team and its backup – thirty or so commandos, according to unofficial Israeli sources – were transported from their base near Haifa in a fast missile boat. The commandos came ashore in dinghies. The spot chosen for the landing was perfect. A fifty-metre sprint across the beach put them under the cover of tree-like shrubs, where they could re-group without the danger of being observed. The hotel which the Mossad agents were using as their base is out of sight but not more than a few hundred metres away.

My own timed run over the route the Israelis took to Abu Jihad's villa suggests that the commandos made their landing at about one o'clock. The three Mossad escorts and their vehicles were probably waiting in the shrubs when the commandos hit the beach.

Meanwhile . . . In the sky above, an Israeli Boeing 707 was pretending to be a civilian aircraft on a flight path from Sicily to Tunis. Among those on board were – according to Marie Colvin's reconstruction of events for *The Sunday Times* of 24 April – three top Israelis: the Deputy Commander-in-Chief, the Air Force Commander and the Director of Military Intelligence. The Israelis in the sky were co-ordinating the action on the ground and were ready with contingency plans for any emergency. It is reasonable to assume that they were in constant touch with Defence Minister Rabin in Tel Aviv. And it is very likely that arrangements were made for Prime Minister Shamir and other members of the inner cabinet to listen in. (That could explain why Shamir said that he first heard about Abu Jihad's assassination 'on the radio'!)

It seems that the Israeli commandos were intending to pose as Tunisian Special Forces if they were stopped or challenged by Tunisian policemen. According to Um Jihad and Hanan, the Israelis were dressed in very dark blue, almost black, combat uniforms identical in colour and style to those worn by Tunisia's Special Forces, whose duties include guarding the President.

The three vehicles carrying the Israeli commandos arrived at the target zone just before 1.20 a.m. The journey from the beach would have taken them ten minutes or less. The commandos in the two mini-vans were the back-up teams. Their job was to secure the road junctions, to watch for unexpected arrivals and to be ready for any emergency.

The first Palestinian to die was Abu Jihad's armed driver. He was shot through the heart. He had been standing outside Abu Jihad's car smoking a cigarette. The cigarette was still in his fingers when his body was found.

The hit team, eight commandos, split into two groups of four. One group entered the grounds of Abu Jihad's villa from the rear by climbing over the wall from a neighbour's garden. This group, which was observed by the neighbour's baby-sitter, covered all possible escape windows and doors with the exception of the main front door. Before taking up their positions this group shot and killed two sleeping Palestinians. One was Abu Jihad's gardener. (The night was warm and he was sleeping outside.) The other was an old man, Abu Sulaiman, a former bodyguard. (He was asleep in the basement, which was open to the garden.) When all possible exit windows and doors were covered from the outside the second group of four entered Abu Jihad's villa through the main front door.

Upstairs in the bedroom Abu Jihad was alerted to the danger by the sound of his front door being forced open. He crossed the room to grab his pistol. He had put it on the top of the wardrobe, out of Nidal's reach. The sound of Abu Jihad's desperate movements woke Um Jihad. She was out of bed and at his side by the time he got to the open bedroom door. There they came face to face with the Israelis, who had raced up the stairs, across the landing and into the corridor to the main bedroom. The corridor is so narrow that only two of the four Israelis had the space to shoot. Abu Jihad fired one shot. He took a dozen or more before he fell face down. Um Jihad screamed, 'Almighty God! Almighty God!' Then she watched, frozen with shock and grief, as each of the four Israelis stepped forward in turn to fire more shots into Abu Jihad's body. 'It was like they were performing a ceremony, a ritual,' Um Jihad told me later.

But that was not the end of the shooting. One of the Israelis stepped over Abu Jihad's body and sprayed the ceiling-to-floor curtains with two bursts of machine-gun fire. The assumption was, presumably, that a bodyguard could be hiding behind the curtains and that he could raise the alarm and perhaps cause the Israelis to be intercepted before they could escape. (When they entered the villa, the Israelis pulled the main telephone connection out of its socket in the wall. It seems they knew exactly where to find it.) The first burst of machine-gun fire inside the bedroom woke Nidal. He screamed and Um Jihad thought he had been hit and was dying. Bullets did in fact thud into the wall less than two inches from Nidal's cot. The Israeli then turned to leave the bedroom. As he stepped back over Abu Jihad's corpse he fired more shots into it. Um Jihad pleaded: 'Enough. Enough.' To Hanan, who was weeping on the landing, one of the Israelis said: 'Go to your mother.'

According to Um Jihad and Hanan the four Israelis were wearing surgical masks over the lower part of their faces. Only their eyes were visible. Later Um Jihad told me that one of the assassins was in his early twenties. This one had short, curly, blonde hair. Another, a much older man, was probably in his fifties. Um Jihad said this one had white or silver hair and was partly bald.

The four Israelis fled down the stairs. Speed was so important that they did not grab the secret papers stacked on Abu Jihad's desk, papers which would have been of great intelligence value. In his haste one of the departing Israelis dropped the earpiece through which he was taking instructions by radio from those who were directing and co-ordinating the operation. Um Jihad ran to the balcony. She said later that she counted no fewer than twenty Israelis running from all directions for their vehicles.

When the Israelis were gone Um Jihad embraced Hanan and said: 'You were privileged to know your father for some years of your life. Now you must think of the thousands of Palestinian children who never had the joy of being with their fathers.'

It was no secret that Abu Jihad the family man was a soft and easy target. It was obvious, for example, to the many journalists who visited him. Nor was there any mystery about why Abu Jihad refused to be surrounded by bodyguards and guns when he was at home with his wife and children. He believed it was important for him to demonstrate to that vast majority of Palestinians who have no security of any kind that he was sharing the risks of their existence. He also wanted to show by example that it was possible, in spite of everything, for Palestinians to live a normal life. This was the most effective way to give the lie to the old Israeli claim that the Palestinians did not exist. To that extent it could be said that his refusal to accept better protection was a noble but naive gesture of defiance. But there was something else. On one of several occasions when I suggested to Abu Jihad that he *ought* to be better protected, he said he feared that surrounding himself with security men and weapons at home would have the effect of reducing and perhaps destroying his humanity.

The truth is that killing Abu Jihad posed no great problem for the Israelis. The real challenge for them was to make the hit and then escape without leaving behind proof of their identity. Even those Israeli leaders who rarely think twice about showing contempt for world opinion knew they would be in trouble if it could be proved that they had authorized an act of state terrorism. What this meant in operational terms was that the Israelis could not afford to become involved in a shoot-out with Palestinian and Tunisian security forces. The taking of an Israeli – alive or dead – could not be risked.

In the event, Israel did get away with it. Its leaders were able to keep silent, neither confirming nor denying that Abu Jihad's assassination was the work of Israeli agents and forces. The job of briefing reporters about the mission was left to unofficial and unnamed Israeli spokesmen.

But what, if anything, did Israel's leaders expect to gain from killing Arafat's number two? It may be they were hoping that Abu Jihad's death would profoundly damage the morale of the Palestinians and that it would help them to crush the spirit of Palestinian resistance. If so Israel's leaders have learned nothing about the Palestinians in the thirty years since Abu Jihad and Yasser Arafat lit 'the candle in the darkness.'

When I raised with Arafat the subject of Abu Jihad's death some two months after the event, he surprised me by saying, 'It was our fault.' As I listened to the Chairman I became convinced that he was, in fact, blaming himself. He said, for example, that he had told Abu Jihad many times that his home was not secure and that he ought to move to another location. 'Sometimes I shouted at him,' Arafat said. At one point in our conversation I suggested that since the Israelis were so determined to kill Abu Jihad, they would have succeeded even if he had been better protected. Arafat was astonished by my ignorance of such matters. 'You are wrong,' he said, 'and I will tell you a story to prove that you are wrong.'

Arafat's story was about the occasion in April 1973 when Israeli commandos assassinated two Black September leaders in the heart of Beirut. According to the account given to me by Abu Iyad (see pages 361-363), the Israeli attack on Arafat's Fahkani headquarters was a diversion. The main target was the house where the Black September leaders were sleeping. 'It was not so,' Arafat said. 'I was the main target of that Israeli operation. From two big helicopters, they landed nearly two hundred commandos not more than fifty metres from my office. We were eight. Myself and seven bodyguards. In theory we didn't have a chance. We opened fire with automatic weapons. That had two consequences. It confused the Israelis and caused them to delay their assault. It also alerted a unit of Popular Democratic Front fighters and they joined in the battle. And this gave me time to escape.'

The point of the story as Arafat told it was that Abu Jihad would have been able to escape if he had enough bodyguards to engage the Israelis and hold them up, and if he had lived in a house in a less exposed position – a house with a means of escape through or over another building. I am convinced that Arafat believes Abu Jihad would be alive today if he, Arafat, had somehow forced him to live in a more secure location with adequate protection. (If that had been the case my guess is that Israel's leaders would not have authorized the assassination. Abu Jihad was killed because he was a soft and easy target at home with his wife and children.)

In early June Arafat gave the P.L.O.'s estimate of the human cost to the Palestinians of the first six months of the uprising in the occupied territories. According to him 358 Palestinians had been killed, 9,800 had been wounded, and 3,470 more were disabled. The wounded were mostly the victims of Israeli gunfire; the disabled were mostly the victims of Israeli beatings. When the world was expressing outrage at Israel's shoot-to-kill method of dealing with stone-throwing demonstrators, Rabin told his troops to give more emphasis to beating up Palestinians. As we saw on television night after night, many young Israeli soldiers obeyed their political master with enthusiasm. (The P.L.O.'s figure for the number of Palestinian demonstrators killed was higher than the media's estimate by more than one hundred. What explained this discrepancy? According to the P.L.O. the Israelis, when they could, were snatching the bodies of dead demonstrators to bury them quietly – to prevent funerals that would generate more emotional support for the uprising.) Arafat also claimed that about 700 Palestinian women had suffered miscarriages – mainly a consequence, he said, of Israeli 'smoke and gas bombs'. He put the number of Palestinians who had been arrested and detained at 20,000, and he said that 3,700 homes had been demolished by dynamite. In addition, Arafat claimed, olive trees on thousands of acres of land had been destroyed by 'burning, slashing and uprooting'. As he pointed out some of these trees had been growing for over two thousand years. 'Certain Israelis have no respect for anything,' Arafat said. 'They are even against trees.' Shortly before he was

murdered, Abu Jihad instructed Palestinians in the occupied territories to 'fight fire with fire'. So it was that some Palestinians
retaliated by burning Israeli crops.

The question Palestinians inside the occupied territories were
asking was this: had they done enough to make their point that
the status quo could not be maintained? Palestinians everywhere
were asking whether they could now expect the U.S. to be serious
about working with the Soviets to convene an international conference negotiating an end to Israel's occupation of all Arab land
captured in the 1967 war, *and* for the creation of a Palestinian
state on the West Bank and in Gaza – this in exchange for peace
with an Israel behind secure and recognized borders.

The answer to the first question ought to have been yes. For
the first time in twenty years world public opinion had seen for
itself, in television close-ups, why there can be no solution to the
conflict so long as Israel is allowed to occupy the West Bank and
Gaza in defiance of the letter and the spirit of U.N. Resolution
242.

By June it seemed that even Secretary of State Shultz had come
to that conclusion. In Jerusalem he said publicly that Israel's occupation of the West Bank and Gaza was a 'dead-end street'.
Though he did not mention Shamir by name, he obviously had the
Israeli Prime Minister in mind when he added that those who
believed otherwise were 'deluding' themselves. But there was more.
To the Arab leaders he met on his travels Shultz gave assurances
that the U.S. was now determined to see an end to Israel's occupation of all Arab land captured in the 1967 war.

When the substance of what Shultz said to various Arab leaders
was relayed to Arafat and his senior colleagues, they suspected that
the Secretary of State was playing games at the P.L.O.'s expense.
They feared he was offering the Arab regimes an inducement to
abandon their support for the P.L.O. as the only legitimate representative of the Palestinians. At the time the Arab regimes were
considering the stand they would take at the Algiers summit which
was to open on 7 June. (It was called, at the request of the P.L.O.,
to give the Arab regimes an opportunity to express their support
for the uprising in the occupied territories, and to take a position
on Shultz's efforts to advance the peace process by convening an
international conference – which Shamir was blocking.)

Arafat's fear that Shultz was still trying to exclude the P.L.O. from the peace process has a history of its own.

In London, Shultz had a meeting with Hussein and Mrs Thatcher. At this meeting the Secretary of State challenged the King to find the courage to move to the conference table without the P.L.O. Shultz said the uprising had convinced him that there was no alternative to a total Israeli withdrawal from the occupied territories in exchange for total peace. He was ready, he said, to assure the Arabs that the U.S. was now seriously committed to such a policy – but he also had to be realistic. There was no way that he or any future Secretary of State could deliver Israel if the Arabs continued to insist on the P.L.O. being a party to negotiations. It was therefore up to the Arabs in general, and the King in particular, to seize this opportunity. It might be their last. With America's support the Arabs could have what they most wanted – an end to Israeli occupation. The price for America's support was exclusion of the P.L.O. According to my sources the courteous King had to struggle to keep his anger in check. His reply was that there had been times in the past when he could and would have done what Shultz was asking him to do; but the Americans had never given him enough help, and now it was too late. At this point in the conversation Mrs Thatcher took Hussein's side. She looked Shultz in the eyes and said: 'His Majesty is right. You are asking him to commit political suicide.'

Shultz left London knowing that Hussein could not and would not negotiate for the Palestinians unless an Arab summit gave him the mandate to do so. To have a chance of fixing that Arab cover, Shultz needed Moscow's help. He went to work on the Soviets. His objective was to persuade them to drop their insistence that the Palestinians be represented by the P.L.O. at an international conference. The extent of Shultz's success was reflected in the working papers prepared for the Reagan-Gorbachev summit in Moscow. In their paper on the Middle East, the Americans said they did not favour inviting the P.L.O. to an international conference because its presence would 'cause other parties (Shamir's Israel) to stay away'. The Soviets found a neat formula for passing the buck and giving themselves the best of both worlds. Their position paper said that the Arabs should determine who would represent the Palestinians.

By all accounts Shultz was not too unhappy with the Soviet position because it gave him some room for manoeuvre. In effect the Soviets were saying to him: 'We are committed to going along with whatever the Arabs decide at their summit; but if you can persuade them that they have much to gain by excluding the P.L.O. from the negotiating process we will not object.' And that set the stage for a trial of strength between George Shultz and Yasser Arafat – to determine which of the two would have the greater influence on the Arab summit in Algiers.

Shultz decided to make a pre-emptive strike. He asked the Algerians if they would receive him on 6 June – the day before the opening of the Arab summit. (Quite a bold move for a man whom many say is lacking in imagination!) As they were bound to do the Algerians put Shultz on hold and relayed his request to the Arab League's headquarters in Tunis for discussion. The decision – yes or no to a Shultz speech in Algiers, pushing for the P.L.O. to be excluded from the peace process – was for the Arab leaders themselves to make in their various capitals; but the political in-fighting was conducted by their representatives behind closed doors at the Arab League's headquarters.

I was in Tunis at the time, and it was obvious from what I was hearing that the Arab regimes were torn by indecision. On the one hand there was Shultz's assurance that the U.S. was now deter-mined to require Israel to honour U.N. Resolution 242 by with-drawing from all the Arab land it occupied in 1967. Shultz seemed to be serious. So if an Arab-summit decision mandating Hussein and non-P.L.O. Palestinians to negotiate for the Palestinians in place of the P.L.O. would help Shultz deliver, why not? The P.L.O. would be offended to say the least, but Palestinian anger could probably be contained, provided Shultz lost no time in proving that the U.S. really was determined to end Israel's occupation of the West Bank and Gaza. Conclusion: if saying no to P.L.O. par-ticipation in the peace process was the best or the only way to get the Israelis out of the occupied territories, there was perhaps much to be gained by allowing Shultz to make his pitch in Algiers. But, on the other hand, what would happen if the Arab regimes did require the P.L.O. to take a back seat and it then became clear that the Americans either would not or could not deliver Israel? In that event the Palestinians would accuse Arab leaders of betraying their cause . . . again; the charge would stick and the P.L.O. would make common cause with Arab radicals and Islamic fundamentalists everywhere; and sooner or later, probably sooner, Arab leaders would find themselves fighting for their thrones and their presidential palaces. So far as self-interest was concerned, this was the case for reaffirming the Arab commitment to the P.L.O. as the only legitimate representative of the Palestinian people. And if this was to be the outcome of the summit, there was no point in allowing Shultz to have his say in Algiers. To let him come to make a dramatic appeal for the Arabs to move without the P.L.O. and then to tell him to go to hell would be to add injury to insult.

While this dilemma was being discussed by leaders around the Arab world and their representatives in Tunis, there was a great deal of tension in the P.L.O. camp. In confidence some P.L.O. officials were voicing their fears that another Arab betrayal was in the making. Hani Hassan told me the situation was 'critical'. Only Arafat seemed to be relaxed. But even he worried which way the Arabs would go when he learned that President Assad and King Hussein were among those pushing to have Shultz in Algiers on 6 June.

I asked Khalad Hassan what he thought Assad and Hussein were up to. He had absolutely no doubt that Syria did not want the summit to reaffirm the P.L.O.'s position as the only legitimate representative of the Palestinian people. Despite his apparent reconciliation with Arafat after Abu Jihad's burial at a refugee camp in the Syrian capital, Assad still wanted to possess the Palestinian card and to play it for his own ends. His purpose of the moment was to help Shultz marginalize the P.L.O. at the summit. As Khalad and I were talking, Syrian-controlled Palestinian dissidents led by Abu Musa launched an offensive against Arafat's last two strongholds in Beirut – the refugee camps of Chatilla and Burj al-Barajneh. It was reasonable to suppose that this phase of the 'camps war' was timed to distract Arafat's attention from pre-summit politics. With Abu Jihad dead the Syrians probably thought they had an excellent opportunity to make life more difficult than usual for the P.L.O. Chairman. (Arafat suspected that the suggestion for heating up the situation on the ground in the Lebanon came from the Americans – Shultz and his advisers.) About Hussein and his motivation, Khalad said this: 'He is very frightened by the uprising and the possibility that it could be extended to the East Bank of the Jordan, so he keeps on saying that he will not move without the P.L.O.; but he is no doubt hoping, in private, that the summit will give him the mandate to do so.' I mentioned to Khalad that Hani had told me the situation was 'critical' for the P.L.O. and I asked if he agreed with his brother's assessment. 'Oh yes,' Khalad replied with great feeling. 'You can say without fear of contradiction that this is the most important Arab summit in our history.' After all that had happened was it really possible, I asked, that the Arab regimes would be tempted at the summit to say yes to Shultz and no to the P.L.O.? There was, I thought, just a hint of despair in Khalad's voice when he replied. 'You have asked me a question for which I don't have an answer. At this moment I am not even sure that the Arab leaders themselves know what to do for the best to protect their own interests.'

It was then that Arafat made his move. By the time most of his senior leadership colleagues were aware that he had left Tunisia he was in Algeria. When he returned to Tunis a few hours later the Algerians had informed Shultz that he would be welcome in Algiers on 10 June – when the Arab summit was over. Behind the scenes those Arab leaders who were counting on a Shultz inter-vention – King Hussein and President Assad in particular – were furious; but they had to be seen to be part of the Arab consensus. King Fahd of Saudi Arabia had previously let it be known that he would not attend a summit in Algiers unless unity was guaranteed (fixed) in advance. I do not know what Arafat said to the Algerians and, through them, to other Arab leaders. It is possible that he threatened to stay away from the summit if Shultz was allowed to appear and speak in Algiers on 6 June. No Arafat would have meant no Arab summit; and that was not a state of affairs the Arab regimes could live with. A decision to call off the summit at the eleventh hour would have exposed them to dangerous new levels of ridicule and contempt.

The full extent of Arafat's victory (and Shultz's defeat) at the Arab summit was confirmed by its resolutions. They reaffirmed the Arab commitment to an international peace conference 'with the participation of the five permanent members of the Security Council and all the parties to the conflict in the region, including the P.L.O. – the legitimate and sole representative of the Palestinian people – on an equal footing and with the same rights as the other parties.' Also confirmed was the Arab commitment to Palestinian self-determination in the form of a Palestinian state. Arafat got just about everything he wanted, including pledges of hundreds of millions of dollars to keep the uprising going in the occupied territories. It was true that he did not, in fact, get as much money as he had hoped for – he had to settle for an immediate payment of 128 million dollars and a promise of a regular monthly allocation of about 40 million dollars; but he was ready to accept that even the Gulf States were, relatively speaking, facing hard times because of the decline in the price of oil. (Arafat's own estimate was that it could cost the P.L.O. up to three million dollars a day to sustain the campaign of civil disobedience that was to be the second phase of the uprising.)

It is worth noting that the Arab summit resolution on negotiations at an international conference was in one important respect less specific than the statement Arafat had been prepared to make in the P.L.O.'s name back in 1986. At Algiers in 1988, as we have seen above, the Arabs spoke of negotiations involving 'all the parties to the conflict in the region.' By obvious implication 'all' parties includes Israel; but Israel is not mentioned by name. As we saw in the previous chapter Arafat, in return for an American recognition of the P.L.O., was prepared to make a statement about negotiations with all parties 'including the Israeli government'. Here, surely, is more evidence that Arafat would be the first to cross P.L.O. and other Arab red lines – if only the Americans, or better still the Israelis, were prepared to make it worth his while to do so . . . by trading recognition of the Palestinian right to self-determination for P.L.O. recognition of Israel as required by U.N. Resolution 242.

Soon after the Arab summit I spoke with Hani on the telephone. I said, 'I assume you are happy.'

He chuckled and said, 'For once the Israelis have got it right.'

I asked him what he meant.

He said: 'I am looking at an Israeli newspaper; let me read you the headline. It says, "The children of the stones have made Arafat the bride of the summit." '

I said I thought the time was coming, *had* to be coming, when the Americans, if they were serious about peace, would have to accept the P.L.O. as a party to negotiations. I asked Hani if he was optimistic.

He replied, 'I am optimistic provided we survive.'

'You mean if the Israelis don't kill Arafat.'

'If they don't kill both of us.' Arafat's chief adviser went on to say he had been warned by people he had to take seriously that it was no longer safe for him to travel to Western Europe. (The warning that Hani should now regard himself as being on the Mossad's hit-list was probably conveyed to him by Western European intelligence agencies. They, or rather their political masters, have no interest in seeing the peacemakers on the P.L.O. side eliminated. It would not be the first time senior P.L.O. figures had received such warnings from these sources.)

Assad's response to Arafat's political victory at the Algiers summit was swift and predictable. On his return to Damascus the Syrian leader ordered his generals to do whatever was necessary, using Abu Musa and his Palestinian dissidents as their cover, to eliminate the P.L.O.'s military presence at Chatilla and Burj al-Barajneh. For three years previously Syria's main Lebanese ally, the Shi'ite Amal militia, had laid siege to the camps. In those three years the two refugee camps became a living hell for their civilian inhabitants. Those who survived the fighting were reduced to eating rats. When the uprising in the occupied territories started the siege was lifted. Amal's leaders said they were ending the siege as a gesture of solidarity with their Palestinian brothers; but that was an excuse to explain away Amal's failure to break the spirit of resistance in the camps. When the siege was lifted most of the surviving and unarmed refugees left the camps. Within a month of Assad's decision to eliminate the P.L.O.'s military presence in Beirut, the defending forces – Arafat loyalists – had surrendered and were evacuated to Sidon. Throughout the last round of fighting for the ground on which the two camps had stood, most Western correspondents were content as ever to peddle the fiction that the battle was between one Palestinian faction and another. That was a long way from the truth. Though Abu Musa and his Palestinian dissidents gave their name to the offensive, it was massive Syrian firepower – rockets and artillery fired from behind Syrian lines in Syrian-controlled West Beirut – which forced the P.L.O. defenders to surrender . . . in order to live to fight elsewhere another day. It was Abu Musa and his dissidents who claimed the victory, but without Syrian military support and Libyan money they would be nothing. According to Arafat and his senior colleagues Abu Musa knows the Syrians will kill him when he is of no more use to them.

There was, of course, much more to Assad's game plan than revenge. His decision to end the P.L.O.'s military presence in Beirut was part of a strategy to preempt any Palestinian challenge to a secret American-Israeli-Syrian understanding about how the Lebanon was to be stabilized. The U.S. and Israel were determined to maintain the Christians in power – even though the Moslems were the majority. Assad was prepared to go along with this, and to once more do American and Israeli dirty work in the Lebanon, provided the Americans and the Israelis allowed him to keep a few fingers in the Lebanese pie. For its part, Israel was prepared to let Assad do more or less what he wanted in his part of the Lebanon – provided he did not cross the red lines the Israelis drew for him. Assad's hyprocrisy was neatly summed up by a P.L.O. official who said: 'Syria wants us to say "no, no, no" to the Americans all the time while it says "yes, yes, yes." '

The loss of the Chatilla and Burj al-Barajneh was a big blow to the P.L.O. in general and to Arafat in particular; but it could have been much worse. Assad was intending to follow up by smashing the P.L.O. in Arafat's last military stronghold in the Lebanon, the Sidon area. Palestinians everywhere were certain they knew what was coming – Israeli air strikes to soften up the camps and the P.L.O.'s positions and then, after a short but decent interval, a ground offensive by Abu Musa's dissidents supported by massive Syrian firepower. The logic which ran through the thinking of Syrian, Israeli and American policy-makers was not hard to follow. In the other front-line states – Egypt, Jordan and Syria itself – the P.L.O. could not establish a military presence unless there was first a radical change of government policy or, alternatively, a change of regimes. So if at long last the P.L.O. could be finished in the Lebanon, Arafat would be unable to influence the situation on the ground by military means and would, as a consequence, lose a great deal of credibility with many of his own people. Assad would then be better placed than ever to supplant Arafat's P.L.O. with a puppet organization based in Damascus; and those most in favour of excluding the authentic P.L.O. from the peace process (the U.S., Israel, Jordan and Syria) could drive a wedge between the real P.L.O. and the Palestinians in the occupied territories. It might then be possible to persaude the Palestinians in the occupied territories that they had much to gain and nothing to lose by dropping their insistence that only the P.L.O. negotiate for them. To put it another way . . . The hope of policy-makers in the U.S., Israel, Syria and Jordan was that a final offensive against the P.L.O. in the Lebanon would cancel the gains Arafat had made at the Algiers summit. If that was achieved, Shultz could push the Israelis to be serious about negotiating land for peace without provoking the wrath of the Zionist lobby in America – because he would not be asking Israel to deal with the P.L.O. or to recognize the Palestinian right to self-determination.

These were critical days. Everything Arafat and the P.L.O. represented was threatened once more.

But the final offensive against the P.L.O. in the Lebanon did not materialize. While Assad and his Palestinian proxies were making their preparations for it, Arafat and his leadership colleagues sent a quiet but dramatic message to the other Arab leaders. If the attack came the Palestinians in the camps of Sidon and their P.L.O. defenders would fight to the finish. They had no choice. There would be a bloodbath. Were the Arab leaders going to sanction, by their silence, another massacre of the Palestinian people, or were they going to persuade Assad to back away from a final showdown with the P.L.O. in the Lebanon? In response to this P.L.O. message, which was both an S.O.S. and a challenge, the other Arab leaders did put pressure on Syria's President. According to my P.L.O. sources even Libya's Colonel Qadafy played a positive role behind the scenes on this occasion. For many years Qadafy and Assad were, in effect, the real terror masters of the region on the Arab side. Under the terms of their partnership, Libya financed and Syria directed the radical and extremist Palestinian groups which used terrorism as a means of opposing, discrediting and sabotaging Arafat's policy of politics and compromise. Since 1983 Qadafy had been financing Abu Musa and the Fatah dissidents. So it must have come as a shock to them and their Syrian controllers when Qadafy said he would oppose with all the means at his disposal any attempt to liquidate the P.L.O. in Sidon. In the face of Qadafy's pro-Arafat stand and pressure from most other Arab leaders, Assad concluded that it was not the right time for him to be seen to be doing more dirty work for America and Israel. He was in danger of becoming too isolated. His unfinished business with Arafat would have to wait.

On 18 July the Syrian President knew he had made the right decision. That was the day Iran announced its full and unconditional acceptance of Security Council Resolution 598 as the basis for negotiations to end the war with Iraq. (Iran's ailing spiritual leader, Ayatollah Khomeini, said that agreeing to make peace with his hated enemy, Iraq's President Saddam Hussein, was 'like taking poison'.) An end to the Gulf war will put the Arab-Israeli conflict back in its rightful place at the top of the Middle East agenda, and the implications of that for all the parties – the Arabs, Israel and their respective allies and friends – will be profound indeed. But for the short term the man with most to worry about, especially if Saddam Hussein emerges from the Gulf war as the Arab hero who contained the ayatollahs, is Assad himself. The other Arabs in general, and the Iraqis in particular, will never forgive him for supporting Iran's war effort. When you add to that the fact that Saddam Hussein and Assad were rivals and bitter enemies long before Syria became Iran's ally, it is not very difficult to understand why the Syrian leader could yet see all sorts of trouble as his past catches up with him. If he continues to play the wrecking role, the other Arabs, led by Saddam Hussein, could turn against him with more than rhetoric. My guess is that Assad will avoid trouble for himself only if he works within the Arab consensus as it was reflected at the Algiers summit; and that will require, among other things, working with Arafat and not against him. (Assad is also being squeezed by the improvement in U.S.-Soviet relations. All the time the U.S. tried to exclude the Soviets from the peace process, Syria's President was able to win himself extra room for manoeuvre in tight spots by playing one superpower off aginst the other. But as we have seen he was also used by both. For the Americans his main role was to contain the P.L.O. and generally to make life as difficult as possible for Arafat. For the Soviets, and in exchange for arms and diplomatic support, his main role was to sabotage any peace move which promised gains for Washington at Moscow's expense. It follows that an improvement in U.S.-Soviet relations will leave Assad with fewer cards to play. The Soviets will no longer need him as much as he needs them; and if he is unable to do America's dirty work – because he cannot afford to provoke the hostility of his Arab brothers – he will not be of much use to Washington. By October U.S. Assistant Secretary of State Murphy may have come to such a conclusion. He put months of effort into persuading Assad to do whatever was necessary to impose on the Lebanon a president of America's choice in succession to Amin Gemayel. Assad was unable to deliver for his American friend.)

As Arafat thought about Assad's predicament following Iran's decision to seek peace with Iraq, he had reason to hope that the Syrian threat to the P.L.O.'s survival had been contained once and for all. But he was about to be challenged on another and perhaps even more dangerous front.

At the end of July, King Hussein announced that he was cutting Jordan's legal and administrative ties with the Israeli-occupied West Bank. A 1.3 billion dollar development plan for the territory was halted; the Lower House of Parliament, in which West Bank deputies had half the sixty seats, was dissolved; and thousands of civil service posts that were created when the territory was under Jordanian rule – 'occupation', the Palestinians would say – were to be scrapped. (Although Israel administers the West Bank through its military occupation authority, it had been content to allow Jordan to continue the day-to-day running of many public services, including schools, hospitals and religious institutions. The loss of the wages and salaries that went with the jobs to be scrapped was bound to add to the economic hardship of the West Bankers unless or until the P.L.O. could find a way to replace them.)

In the days following Hussein's dramatic and unexpected announcement there was a great deal of speculation on all sides about what it really meant. With the slogan 'Jordan is not Palestine' Hussein himself said he was acting out of deference to the P.L.O. and to allow the eventual creation of an independent Palestinian state. 'We respect the wish of the P.L.O., the sole legitimate representative of the Palestinian people, to secede from us in an independent state.' On that basis it seemed that Jordan was effectively renouncing its claim to the West Bank. If so that was in principle a tremendous gain for the P.L.O.

But politics on both sides of the Arab-Israeli conflict are never, well hardly ever, that straightforward. Hussein's withdrawal obviously implied an assumption that the P.L.O. was ready, willing and able to take up the burden of administering and liberating the Israeli-occupied West Bank. And this implied proviso could be the catch – or so Arafat and his leadership colleagues feared. The P.L.O. was more than ready and willing to take up the challenge of administering the West Bank and negotiating a land-for-peace deal with all parties, including the Israeli government; but was it *able* to do so?

The problem, as ever, was that Israel would not allow the P.L.O. to play any role in the occupied territories or the peace process. (Rabin was quick to announce that Israel would never allow the P.L.O. to fill the vacuum left by Jordan. And representatives of the extreme right in Israel called for the formal annexation of the West Bank.) In this context the question of what Hussein was really up to had a menacing significance for the P.L.O. Many of Arafat's colleagues and supporters feared they were witnessing the opening move in yet another strategy to squeeze the P.L.O. out of business. If Israel's veto on American policy locked the P.L.O. out of the peace process, and if Israeli military opposition kept the P.L.O. from asserting its management and administration on the West Bank, a substantial number of Palestinians on the West Bank could eventually conclude in despair that they were better off, relatively speaking, when they were tied to Jordan, and that it was Hussein and not the P.L.O. who could help improve their lot and end Israel's occupation. Such a development would lead to deep divisions on the Palestinian side – divisions which Jordan, Syria, Israel, America and other powers could exploit to claim that the P.L.O. should no longer be regarded as the only legitimate representative of the Palestinian people, and could therefore be safely excluded from the peace process. In that event the U.S. and the Soviet Union might be tempted to convene an international conference without the P.L.O. The divided Palestinians would then be required to accept the crumbs from Israel's table.

Fears that Hussein was, in effect, setting a trap for the P.L.O. were underlined in many Palestinian minds by two things in particular. In Algiers the King had said that an Arab summit decision which endorsed the P.L.O.'s right to negotiate on its own behalf might mean 'that an international conference will never take place'.

Though Hussein made this observation in the context of a strong attack on the U.S. – which, he said, had no Middle East policy beyond support for Israel – it seemed to many Palestinians that he was putting down a marker for the future. As interpreted by many Palestinians his real message to the summit was the following: 'There is no point in mandating the P.L.O. to negotiate for the Palestinians because Israel and therefore America will never agree to deal with it. However, for the sake of Arab unity, and because I am frightened by the uprising, I am prepared to accept the decisions of this summit. But I am also warning you, my Arab brothers. Those of you who insist that only the P.L.O. can negotiate for the Palestinians are not being realistic in the circumstances in which we Arabs find ourselves. When you discover that I am right I will be ready to lead the negotiations for an end to Israel's occupation – but any accommodation I make with the Palestinians to bring this about will be on my terms.' The second thing that underlined Palestinian fears about Hussein's motivation was that he did not consult the P.L.O. before announcing Jordan's decision to cut its ties with the West Bank. Many Palestinians felt that if the King's real objective was to give the P.L.O. a helping hand, he would have discussed his move in advance with Arafat, in order to give the P.L.O. the time to formulate a strategy for exploiting the new situation.

In my view these Palestinian fears were perfectly understandable. I strongly suspect that when he made his announcement Hussein was indeed hoping that the P.L.O. would not be allowed to deliver and that one day the Palestinians on the West Bank would ask him to pick up the pieces. But I believe Hussein did what he did for one reason and one reason only – to protect the territorial integrity and sovereignty of what is left of his kingdom while ensuring the survival of his Hashemite dynasty. He was, I think, disgusted by America's continuing refusal to require Israel to be serious about peace, and he was frightened that the uprising would spread to the East Bank of the Jordan if a majority of Palestinians continued to regard him as, more or less, an American and Israeli stooge. In short the King was fed up with the way he was being compromised by what passed for American policy in the region. He also knew that there was support in America and Western Europe for the view that the Palestinians, the Israelis, or both should be encouraged to de-stabilize Jordan – to turn Jordan into Palestine and to leave Israel in possession of the West Bank. As Hussein well knows, those diplomats and others who advocate such a policy behind closed doors believe it would spare them and their governments the agony of a showdown with Israel and its powerful lobbies everywhere. Political expediency is alive and well. Once upon a time the Jews were expendable. Then it was the turn of the Palestinian Arabs. Tomorrow the Hashemites . . . ? No says their King. (As I have previously reported it was never a secret that Israel's General Sharon – if he had succeeded in destroying the P.L.O. in Beirut – was intending to follow up by de-stabilizing Jordan, over-throwing the King and telling the Palestinians: 'There's your homeland. Take it and welcome.' At the end of July 1988, one of Hussein's many fears was that a victory for the Likud in Israel's November election would give Sharon the opportunity to try again.)

On the face of it Hussein was telling policy-makers in the U.S. (and Israel) that they no longer had a choice. If they wanted to end the uprising and to move toward peace they would have to accept the P.L.O. as a party to negotiations.

Arafat and the leadership of the Palestine liberation movement responded to Hussein's challenge in mid-November. At a special meeting of the P.N.C. they declared the establishment of an independent state of Palestine in the Israeli-occupied territories of the West Bank and the Gaza Strip; they approved a new policy statement that implicitly but unquestionably recognized the Jewish State inside its borders as they were on the eve of the 1967 war – this implicit but unquestionable recognition was conveyed by the P.N.C.'s acceptance of U.N. Resolutions 242 and 338 as the basis for negotiations at an international conference; and they reaffirmed previous P.L.O. statements renouncing – and denouncing – terrorism. Arafat was also given the greenlight to set up a provisional government when he judged the time to be right.

The unilateral declaration of independence was partly theatre, to give new hope to Palestinians everywhere and especially to those in the occupied territories. In the aftermath of the Israeli election two things were obvious. One was that Mr Shamir would continue in office as Prime Minister. The other was that Shamir, Sharon and other Israeli hardliners were determined to use whatever force was necessary to crush the uprising. The P.N.C. was hoping that the declaration of independence would boost the morale of the Palestinians in the occupied territories, and would inspire them to continue their resistance when the expected Israeli onslaught came. Though Hussein had effectively renounced Jordan's claim to the West Bank and had vowed that he would never again succumb to Israeli and American pressure to represent the Palestinians, the declaration of independence was also seen as a means of preventing the King from changing his mind.

But the main message from the P.N.C. was addressed to President-elect Bush and the man he had already named as his Secretary of State, James A. Baker. By stating their willingness to accept U.N. Resolutions 242 and 338 as the basis for negotiations at an international conference, and by reaffirming the P.L.O.'s previous statements condemning and renouncing terrorism, the majority of those Palestinian leaders and other representatives making up the Palestinian parliament-in-exile were in effect saying the following: 'In advance of negotiations we have now gone to the outer limits of what we can do to signal our willingness to make peace with the Jewish State. We have committed ourselves and our people to negotiations that will give the Jewish State the recognition, the legitimacy and the security it seeks – this in exchange for the establishment of a small Palestinian state on less than twenty-five percent of the land that is rightfully ours. We Palestinians have earned the right to a seat at an international conference and it is not for other parties to determine who our representatives will be. It is now up to the U.S. to do whatever is necessary to require that Israel be serious about peace.' Schultz, the outgoing Secretary of State, responded to the P.N.C.'s signals by refusing to grant Arafat a visa to allow him to address the U.N. General Assembly in New York. Most countries in the world were outraged by this attempt to deny Arafat a hearing. The General Assembly was moved to Geneva to allow the Chairman to speak there.

Arafat and his senior Fatah colleagues told me they were not totally pessimistic about getting a more positive response from a Bush administration. But such optimism as they had in the middle of November 1988 was overshadowed by one great fear . . . that Israeli agents would be authorized to create turmoil on the Palestinian side by assassinating Arafat – when and if there were signs that the U.S. was prepared to accept the P.L.O. as a party to negotiations and was making ready to press Israel to do the same. At the P.N.C. meeting in Algiers this fear was expressed to me by all of Arafat's senior leadership colleagues and by many other Palestinians. If it is the case that Arafat is the only Palestinian leader who can keep the door to compromise open at a time when Israel seems more determined than ever to solve the Palestine problem by force, his assassination would effectively sabotage the prospects for peace on the Arab side. And that, say many Palestinians, is why Mr Shamir and other Israeli leaders might well conclude that it was in their interest to sanction the murder of the P.L.O. Chairman.

# Last Thoughts

Yasser Arafat is without doubt the Houdini of international politics. But is he, when all is said, more than a great survivor? After forty years of confrontation with Israel – twenty of them as the Chairman of the P.L.O. and commander-in-chief of its military forces – he has liberated no territory; he has lost ground in the front-line Arab states, some of it to Israel; and in many respects the plight of the Palestinian refugees is worse than ever. Could it not be said that Arafat the liberation leader has been to date a spectacular failure and a disaster for his people?

The view that Arafat has nothing concrete to show for forty years of struggle is the one favoured by most of those who write editorial columns in, and letters to, mainstream newspapers and journals in North America and Western Europe; but in my judgement such a conclusion is more an echo of the wishful thinking of Zionist propaganda than a product of open-minded consideration of the facts. With the Palestinian struggle for self-determination not yet over, and actually heading for its climax, the point is not that Arafat has *so far* failed to liberate even one square metre of territory. The point is that he has inspired and directed the regeneration of Palestinian nationalism; and because the existence of Palestinian nationalism is now an established fact of history, it can be only a matter of time before a majority of Israelis are prepared to acknowledge the legitimacy of the Palestinian demand for self-determination – provided reason is allowed to prevail in the Jewish State. (The alternative, as I outlined in the preface, is an explo-

sion with catastrophic consequences for the region, Jews everywhere and probably the world.) Some Israelis may see to it that
Arafat himself does not live long enough to witness a Palestinian
state come into being, but they will not be able to deny him his
place in history as that state's principal architect.

Precisely what future historians will make of Arafat must remain
a matter for speculation. If they take full account of the odds
against him, they might well present him as the Palestinian David
who successfully confronted the Israeli Goliath. Would they be
exaggerating to make a point? I think not. As this book has tried
to show, the Palestinians were vitually alone. According to the
norms of international power politics their liberation struggle was
a mission impossible. When Israel had established itself at the expense of the Palestinians, the big powers of the day took the view
that challenging the Zionist *fait accompli*, in order to right the
wrong done to the Palestinians, was not the game they wanted to
play. The best interests of all concerned (including the Arab regimes, but, of course, excluding the Palestinians) were to be served
by closing the Palestine file. In effect Israel was given the greenlight
to keep the file closed. As we have also seen, Israel – the military
superpower of the region – employed two main strategies. Both
relied on the application of brute force to solve a political problem.
From the beginning Israel's policy was to punish the front-line Arab
states for the hit-and-run attacks of Palestinian guerrillas. But Israel's massive reprisals were more than punishments. Their real
purpose was to force the regimes of the front-line Arab states to
themselves do whatever was necessary to prevent a regeneration
of Palestinian nationalism. When this policy failed, largely because
Arafat, Abu Jihad and others constantly outwitted the various Arab
intelligence services, Israel decided to do the job itself. It did not
succeed. By the time Mr Begin came to power, the demon of Palestinian nationalism was alive and well. So it had to be contained
and, if possible, liquidated. And this was the logic which took
Sharon and the full might of what is called the Israel Defence Force
all the way to Beirut in the summer of 1982. For days then weeks
the big powers, West and East, did nothing to stop the Israeli
onslaught. In advance of the Israeli invasion, which they knew was
imminent, Arab leaders (and the Soviets) refused to sell to the
P.L.O. anti-tank and other weapons to slow down the Israelis when

they came. Then, for too long, these same Arab leaders sat back and watched while Sharon attempted a Final Solution to the P.L.O. problem by military means. . . . Given these odds is it not remarkable, even astonishing, that there has been a regeneration of Palestinian nationalism?

Could it have happened without Yasser Arafat? On balance I think not. The Arafat I have come to know, like and admire is both an enigma and a wonder. In my judgement he is not the sort of leader the Palestinians could have invented had he not existed. Without the inspiration and the real leadership Arafat has provided I do not believe the Palestinians would today be in a position to demand at least a measure of justice in the form of a small state of their own. Without Arafat I strongly suspect that the Arab regimes would have captured the Palestinian card, and would then have used their influence to require the Palestinians to accept whatever crumbs the Jewish State and its American ally were prepared to offer them from Israel's table. In this context it can be said that Arafat's greatest contribution to the Palestinian struggle (and also the peace process) was, and is, his insistence on the independence of Palestinian decision-making. And his stubbornness on this matter, even at the price of confrontation with Arab regimes that wanted to possess and play the Palestinian card for their own ends, points up to the wisdom of the man. Arafat knew better than anybody else that the vast majority of his people, including his leadership colleagues, would reject the idea of compromise with Israel if the decision to compromise was not made by the Palestinians themselves. Put another way, Arafat could not have sold the idea of compromise to his people if they had perceived him as anything but a fiercely independent nationalist who was calling for these unthinkable concessions on the basis of what he truly believed was best for the Palestinians. If he had been seen as an agent or puppet of the Arab regimes, insisting on compromise to protect their interests at the expense of the Palestinians, he would not have been listened to and would probably have been assassinated.

Inside the Palestine liberation movement the main criticism of Arafat concerns his style of leadership. He is, many of his colleagues say, more of a dictator than a democrat. If what those who make the charge really mean is that Arafat has frequently made a

mockery of collective decision-making by taking major policy initiatives without consulting them . . . well, they have a point. But
I would argue that the cause of Palestinian nationalism (and peace)
has to date been well served by Arafat's individualism. Probably
the best of many illustrations of the point is what happened in
September 1982, when Arafat enraged his leadership colleagues
and the whole Arab world by making his peace with Egypt's President Mubarak. It was – as we have seen – a masterstroke, keeping
Arafat and the P.L.O. from being shunted to the sidelines of Arab
politics after Arafat's and the P.L.O.'s defeat in, and expulsion
from, the Lebanon. Arafat did not consult his leadership colleagues
in advance of his dramatic visit to Cairo because he feared that
internal divisions about the timing and even the wisdom of a proposed visit would force him to abort, or at least delay, his initiative.
With the future of the P.L.O. in the balance, Arafat was not about
to risk letting the collective leadership play games when he had
the opportunity to turn the tables on his Israeli and Arab opponents. Is there not a case for saying that what some call Arafat's
tendency to dictatorship could also be firm, true and at times really
inspired leadership?

At the highest level of Palestinian decision-making, the charge
that Arafat is more of a dictator than a democrat does not bear
serious examination. When the P.N.C. meets to determine P.L.O.
policy, even Yasser Arafat must accept the majority view. It is true
that he has in the past swayed the P.N.C. by threatening to resign,
but there was never anything to stop P.N.C. members calling his
bluff – except, perhaps, their knowledge that they could not do
without him.

Arafat's style of leadership was not however without great risk
for the Palestinians and their cause. Because it effectively reduced
the P.L.O. (though not the P.N.C.) to a one-man show, Arafat's
individualism required the Palestinians to gamble everything on
his survival. What would have happened if one of the many attempts to kill him had succeeded? There would have been a leadership crisis and, probably, a bloody power struggle – a fight which
could have lasted until the P.L.O. destroyed itself or, at the very
least, lost all credibility. In short the cause of Palestinian nationalism could have suffered a death blow. It was partly to minimize
the risk of such a disaster happening that most of Arafat's senior

colleagues favoured the idea of a collective leadership. They believed it was foolish to invest so much in the survival of one individual. In theory they were probably right. In practise they were wrong. With its necessary mixture of pro-Western, pro-Soviet and fiercely independent personalities, the collective leadership was a mechanism for indecision. And that is why Arafat imposed his will.

In the Introduction I said that the story this book had to tell invited the conclusion that – within the limits of what is politically possible on each side – no leader, Arab or Jew, has done more than Yasser Arafat to prepare the ground for a comprehensive settlement of the Arab-Israeli conflict. The evidence supporting this conclusion appears in two areas.

The first is that Arafat risked everything, both his credibility and his life, to persuade the vast majority of his people and the P.N.C. – the ultimate decision-making body on the Palestinian side – to come to terms with the reality of Israel's existence. As we have seen, the result of much heart-searching on the Palestinian side (and a great deal of prodding by Arafat) was a formula for peace based on Palestinian recognition of the Jewish State inside its more or less pre-1967 borders, *in exchange* for Israel's recognition of the Palestinian right to self-determination, this right to be exercised in a small Palestinian state to be created on the West Bank and in the Gaza Strip after Israel's withdrawal. This approach to peace-making became official P.L.O. policy when it was approved by the P.N.C. in 1979.

That is on the one hand. On the other is the fact that no Israeli leader has had the courage to make a similar effort – to persuade his or her people that, *in exchange* for recognition and peace, they must be prepared to accept the reality of Palestinian nationalism and its legitimate demand for self-determination.

An honest examination of the record shows that for the past ten years in public, and longer in private, Arafat has been signalling his readiness to do serious political business with the Jewish State. From the perspective of late 1988, my overall conclusion is that there is nothing more he can do to advance the peace process without a positive response from Israel. What even Arafat, the miracle worker on the Palestinian side, cannot do, is to give Israel the formal recognition and legitimacy it seeks without something concrete – Israel's recognition of the Palestinian right to self-determination – in return. My own impression is that an easy majority of Jews everywhere would favour negotiations with the P.L.O. if they knew the truth about its leader, what he really represents and, more important, what he is offering them in the name of real peace. And that is why I have dedicated this book to my many Israeli and other Jewish friends.

# Palestinian Leaders and Organizations

The main purpose of the following list of Palestinian leaders and organizations is to help readers identify those who figure prominently in this book. It is by no means a comprehensive list of all P.L.O. leaders and organizations.

LEADERS

**Abu Adeeb:** the P.L.O.'s chief representative in Kuwait, a lifelong friend of the Chairman, and a senior P.L.O. leader.

**Abu Amar/Yasser Arafat:** co-founder with Abu Jihad of the first Fatah cell, formed in 1957. Chairman of the P.L.O. since 1969.

**Abu Daoud:** commander of all Palestinian militias in Jordan until the P.L.O.'s expulsion from that country after the second stage of the civil war in 1971. A senior Fatah member.

**George Habash:** with Wadi Haddad and others a founder member of the Arab Nationalist Movement; leader of the P.F.L.P.

**Hani Hassan:** in the early 1960s the leader of the Union of Palestinian Students in Europe and then the President of the General Union of Palestinian Students. He led his own underground commando group in Germany and joined Fatah in 1963. Today he is Arafat's chief adviser on day-to-day political matters.

**Khalad Hassan/Abu Sa'ed:** a member of Fatah since 1963, Chairman of the Palestine National Congress Foreign Relations Committee and the P.L.O.'s most important roving ambassador and trouble-shooter.

**Abu Iyad:** Arafat's oldest friend, a member of Fatah since 1963, spiritual godfather to the Black September terrorists, and the executive responsible for P.L.O. security and counter-intelligence.

**Ahmad Jabril:** became a member of the Palestinian underground in the early 1960s as an agent for Syrian Military Intelligence, which he has served ever since. He was head of the Palestine Liberation Front (P.L.F.) which merged with the P.F.L.P. in 1967. Jabril broke away from the P.F.L.P. in 1969 to form the P.F.L.P.-G.C. (General Command), a small anti-Arafat faction within the P.L.O.

**Abu Jihad/Khalil Wazir:** co-founder with Arafat of the first Fatah cell, formed in 1957, and today the Chairman's second-in-command.

**Um Jihad/Intissar Wazir:** wife of Abu Jihad and his secret and special assistant for many years. She was Fatah's first Chief of Staff and Co-ordinator of Military Operations for a period in 1965.

**Abu Lutuf:** the P.L.O.'s official Foreign Minister.

**Hammad Abu Sitar:** an independent member of the P.L.O. Executive Committee, responsible for the day-to-day management of Palestinian political affairs in Jordan and the occupied West Bank and Gaza.

**Abu Youseff:** Fatah's first military commander in 1965 and a leader of the Black September Organization. He was assassinated by the Israelis in Beirut in 1973.


ORGANIZATIONS

**Assifa:** the name under which Fatah launched its first military operations in 1964.

**Black September Organization:** an organization within Fatah from 1970 to 1974, named after the month in 1970 when the P.L.O. was crushed in Jordan. It began its operations in November 1971 when it claimed responsibility for assassinating Jordan's Prime Minister and Minister of Defence, Wasfi Tal, in Cairo. Its leaders were Abu Youseff, Kamal Adwan and Abu Hassan Salameh, all three of whom were close associates of Abu Iyad.

**Fatah:** the biggest and most influential of the liberation organizations which make up the P.L.O. From 1957 to 1965 it was a network of secret and underground cells. The original leaders of the underground network were Arafat and Khalil Wazir (Abu Jihad). Fatah became a functioning organization with a Central Committee in 1963, but it did not emerge from the underground until 1965. Fatah took control of the P.L.O. in 1969.

**fedayeen:** Palestinian commandos.

**P.D.F. (Popular Democratic Front):** headed by Nawef Hawatmeh and formed when Hawatmeh and his supporters broke away from the P.F.L.P. in 1969.

**P.F.L.P. (Popular Front for the Liberation of Palestine):** headed by George Habash.

**P.F.L.P.-G.C. (Popular Front for the Liberation of Palestine General**

**Command**): an anti-Arafat faction within the P.L.O. headed by Ahmad Jabril and formed in 1969 when Jabril broke away from the P.F.L.P.

**P.L.F. (Palestine Liberation Front)**: headed by Ahmad Jabril and formed in 1961 as an intelligence-gathering organization for the Syrians. It merged with the P.F.L.P. in 1967.

**P.L.O. (Palestine Liberation Organization)**: formed in 1964 under the Chairmanship of Ahmad Shuqairi, it was originally intended to be no more than a puppet of the Arab regimes. It became a more or less independent Palestinian liberation organization when it was taken over by Arafat and Fatah in 1969. The P.L.O. is made up of a number of organizations – eight main ones. Fatah is by far the biggest and most influential. Others are the P.F.L.P., the P.D.F., and the P.F.L.P.-G.C. Two significant organizations not mentioned by name in this book are the Syrian-backed Saiqa and the Iraqi-sponsored Arab Liberation Front (A.L.F.).

**P.N.C. (Palestine National Congress)**: the ultimate decision-making authority of the Palestinian people; in effect their parliament-in-exile. The P.L.O. is answerable to it.

# Notes

1. *Palestine and International Law: The Legal Aspects of the Arab-Israeli Conflict*, second edition (Longman Group, London 1976), p.10. My later summaries of the legal aspects of the Palestinian problems in recognizing Israel are drawn from *Palestine and International Law*. Henry Cattan is a Palestinian and a jurist of international repute. His book is both authoritative and informative and was widely acclaimed as being so when it was first published in 1973.

2. *ibid.*, p.48.

3. *Diplomacy in the Near and Middle East*, vol. II (Van Nostrand, New York 1956), p.70.

4. *Hansard's Reports*, House of Lords, 21 June 1922, p.121.

5. Letter dated 2 November 1917.

6. *Documents on British Foreign Policy 1919-1939*, 1st series, vol. IV (H.M.S.O., London).

7. Quoted by Colin Legum in the *Observer*, 13 November 1977, in a profile of Begin.

8. Quoted in Larry Collins and Dominique Lapierre, *O Jerusalem* (Weidenfeld and Nicolson, London 1972), p.280.

9. *The Revolt* (Nash Publishing, Los Angeles 1972), pp.164-5.

10. *Ha Sepher Ha Palmach*, vol. 2, p.286.

11. *op. cit.*, p.75.

12. *The Forrestal Diaries* (Viking Press, New York 1951), pp.345-7.

13. Quoted in Collins and Lapierre, *op. cit.*, p.302; and emphasized by Arafat and Abu Jihad in conversations with me.

14. U.N. Document A/648.

15. According to Abu Jihad this well-known quote was recorded in secret minutes of the Arab League meeting at which the truce was discussed and agreed.

16. (George G. Harrap, London 1962), pp.69-70; reprinted by the Institute for Palestine Studies, Beirut, in 1969, Reprint Series No. 2.
17. *Diary of the Sinai Campaign* (Weidenfeld and Nicolson, London 1966), p.9.
18. *ibid.*, p.4.
19. Private conversation between Ben Bella and Arafat, as told to me by Arafat.
20. Private conversations with Arafat and other Fatah leaders.
21. Official report of the summit, recorded in *Malaff watha'iq filastin, al-Juz' al-thani, 1950-1969.*
22. Commentary on Damascus Radio, quoted in Ehud Yaari, *Strike Terror* (Sabra Books, New York 1970), p.85.
23. *ibid.*, p.97.
24. Quoted in Stephen E. Ambrose, *Rise to Globalism: American Foreign Policy 1938-1980*, second revised edition (Penguin Books, London 1980), p.353.
25. Quoted in Randolph S. and Winston S. Churchill, *The Six-Day War* (William Heinemann, London 1967), p.127.
26. *op. cit.*, p.150.
27. U.N. Document S/8052, *Official Records of the Security Council, Twenty-second Year, Supplement for July, August and September 1967.*
28. *The Times*, 23 March 1968, quoted in David Hirst, *The Gun and the Olive Branch* (Faber and Faber, London 1977), p.284.
29. Text of the Palestinian National Charter as published by the P.L.O.'s Research Centre formerly in Beirut, new location at present under discussion.
30. *ibid.*
31. *ibid.*
32. Quoted in Seymour M. Hersh, *Kissinger: The Price of Power* (Faber and Faber, London 1983), p.214.
33. *Financial Times*, 2 July 1977.
34. Henry Kissinger, *Years of Upheaval* (Weidenfeld and Nicolson and Michael Joseph, London 1982), p.212.
35. (André Deutsch, London 1983), pp.49-50.
36. *op. cit.*, pp.465, 466, 467.
37. *ibid.*, p.483.
38. *ibid.*, pp.455, 472, 473.
39. Official document published by the P.L.O. Research Centre.
40. *op. cit.*, p.628.
41. *ibid.*, p.1137.
42. Official text of the statement issued by the Saudi Ministry of

Information quoted in Kissinger, *op. cit.*, p.1131.

43. *op. cit.*, p.1265.

44. Quoted in *Peace-Making in the Middle East*, ed. Lester A. Sobel (Facts on File, New York 1980), p.67.

45. *ibid.*, pp.67, 68.

46. *ibid.*, p.159.

47. *ibid.*, p.165.

48. 'The Israeli War Machine in Lebanon', *Journal of Palestine Studies* (Institute for Palestine Studies and Kuwait University), vol. XII, No.2, winter 1983.

49. *Guardian*, 2 September 1982.

50. Ze'ev Schiff and Ehud Ha'ari, *Israel's Lebanon War* (George Allen and Unwin, London 1985), p.255.

51. *ibid.*, p.246

52. *ibid.*, p.247

53. *Guardian*, 23 December 1983.

54. *Guardian*, 16 November 1984.

55. *Guardian*, 23 November 1984.

56. Verbatim transcript of the White House press conference as published in full in the *Jordan Times* on 20 May 1985.

57. Official White House statement made 29 May 1985.